ELIZABETH

ELIZABETH

The Life and Career of

Elizabeth Taylor

DICK SHEPPARD

Doubleday & Company, Inc.
GARDEN CITY, NEW YORK
1974

Grateful acknowledgment is made to Elizabeth Taylor for permission to quote from her autobiography *Elizabeth Taylor* published by Harper & Row © 1964, 1965 by Elizabeth Taylor.

Library of Congress Cataloging in Publication Data

Sheppard, Dick, 1933–
    Elizabeth: the life and career of Elizabeth Taylor.

    1. Taylor, Elizabeth Rosemond, 1932–   I. Title.
PN2287.T18S5   791.43'028'0924 [B]
ISBN 0-385-07348-8
Library of Congress Catalog Card Number 73-15366

Acknowledgments

This book is a project which took three-and-a-half years from inception to completion. These acknowledgments of help and support are thus numerous but genuine. John Donne said it once for all of us. "No Man Is an Island . . ." The author wishes to express sincere gratitude to the following:

To the resources of the Library of the Academy of Motion Picture Arts and Sciences, and to the assistance, ungrudging and unstinting, rendered by its personnel, most especially Bonnie Rothbart, Mildred Simpson, Verna Ramsey and Midori Martin;

To De Witt Bodeen, Stephanie Sidney, Carol McKeand, Lon McAllister, Roddy McDowall, Richard McInnes, and John Bonomo for critical reading and helpful comment on portions of the manuscript;

To Charles Moehlman, Gunnard Nelson, Sharon Dennison, and Louise Herington for their help in preparation of the manuscript;

To Bill Campbell, Lloyd Harkema, William McCullough, Richard Butcher, Howard Sandum, Pat Golbitz, Lawrence Ashmead, and Michele Tempesta for their crucial parts in making publication a reality;

To Robert Synes, Merwin Mordine, Robert Smith, Jerry Bragg, and Mr. and Mrs. Irving Blau for their invaluable friendship and encouragement.

To Elizabeth Taylor and To John Herington—
Without Either of Whom This Book Would Not
Have Been Possible

CONTENTS

FOREWORD

She has been publicly adored as "the most priceless package in human form today." She was mobbed at her second wedding and lifted bodily above the feverish clutches of her admirers. In Boston frenzied fans once slammed her up against a lobby wall and tore hair from her head for souvenirs. She has been pushed, mauled, shoved, hassled, and trapped inside of numerous cars during various public appearances. Photographers have pursued her posing as priests and washerwomen, scaling walls and jumping out of shrubbery to have at her. One once deliberately struck her in the stomach to get "something unusual."

She has also been publicly vilified as "an intemperate vamp who destroys families and devours husbands." The Vatican condemned her as an erotic vagrant and an unfit mother. Mobs of shrieking harridans have reviled and spat at her around the world. What the mind of man (or woman) could not conceive, fate has often stepped in to supply. In Rome her evening gown went up in flames. In Sardinia her dressing-room trailer rolled off a cliff and plunged 150 feet into the sea—minutes after she'd stepped out of it. In Mexico daggers were thrown at her in a public arena.

Looked at from another angle, her life has been one long head-to-toe course in Anatomy and Physiology, that is, hers. She has broiled a finger, broken a foot, ulcerated an eye, twisted a colon, and locked cartilage in her left knee. A nervous collapse in Denmark, food poisoning in Italy, appendicitis in Hong Kong, and three ruptured spinal discs in the Bahamas are all well-publicized parts of her medical history. Also acute bronchitis, chemical thrombosis, phlebitis, sciatica, double pneumonia, a tracheotomy, three Caesarean sections, and a partial hysterectomy. It hasn't been all downhill. A flu virus once saved her from death in an airplane crash. Death again came away empty in

London. She is today the only known survivor of a particularly virulent strain of staphylococcus pneumonia.

Musing on all of the above to a reporter in Puerta Vallarta some years ago, Richard Burton remarked, "Before I met Elizabeth I was making a hundred-seventy-five-thousand dollars a picture. Now I'm making half a million. It makes you think, doesn't it. That girl has true glamour. If I retired tomorrow, I'd be forgotten in five years, but she would go on forever. She's a legend in her own lifetime."

The legend had its unmistakable beginnings thirty years ago upon the occasion of her first starring role.

Famed critic James Agee had his enthusiasms—Charles Chaplin and John Huston, to name two—but ordinarily he defended them with formidable powers of acute perception and rational analysis. On December 23, 1944, all that went right out the window. Wrote Agee:

> Frankly, I doubt I am qualified to arrive at any sensible assessment of Miss Elizabeth Taylor. Ever since I first saw the child, two or three years ago, in I forget what minor role in what movie, I have been choked with the peculiar sort of adoration I might have felt if we were both in the same grade of primary school. I feel I am obligated to this unpleasant unveiling because it is now my first duty to try to review her, in *National Velvet*, in her first major role.

After this amazing confession, Agee went on to attempt an objective appraisal of her particular gifts, having admitted that his peculiar passion had fogged his vision to the point where objectivity was at least suspect, if not downright impossible. He concluded:

> Since I think it is the most hopeful business of movies to find the perfect people rather than the perfect artists, I think that she and the picture are wonderful, and I hardly know or care whether she can act or not.

Lest anyone put this down as the kind of ecstatic homage any man might pay to beautiful children and horses, let us move on to Hollis Alpert almost a quarter of a century later. The film was *The Taming of the Shrew*, and Alpert evaluated what was achieved by Elizabeth Taylor on that occasion:

> She has held nothing back in attacking the role with blazing fury, and in her final moments, when she is at

also win her first Oscar. She would then go to Rome as the first actress ever to command $1 million per film, would adopt another child, and would again become the focus of what may possibly prove to be the last of those peculiar public morality dramas which the United States has suffered itself to endure—a two-year nightmare which officially ended in March 1964, when she married Richard Burton in Montreal.

For her sake was realized the longest, costliest film ever made. Subsequently she had the unique experience of being sued in Federal Court to enjoin her from continuing to give a typically frank opinion of the way it turned out. The highest fee yet paid to a performer for a single television performance was paid to her. And the costliest single piece of jewelry ever offered at auction (a 69.42-carat white diamond the size of a peach pit) rests in her possession. To the title "World's Most Beautiful Woman" was recently added the title "World's Most Glamorous Grandmother," this one having passed to her from Marlene Dietrich, who was never overly fond of it anyway.

On the professional front: As to the 170 Academy Awards given to date for best performance by an actor or actress in a leading or a supporting role, Elizabeth Taylor stands within the charmed circle of eighteen stars who have won at least two of them.* In addition to five Oscar nominations to date, she holds the awards of the New York Film Critics, the National Board of Review, and numerous trophies and citations from all over the world. And fourteen of her films sit proudly on the roster of all-time box office champions ($4 million plus). Critical opinion has run the full spectrum, from *Time* magazine, which has almost never praised her, to the Hollywood *Reporter*, which has never panned her. The public has reacted to her with a possessive kind of love-hate that, for longevity and intensity, is totally without parallel. Only Elizabeth Taylor, after seven years of distressingly dismal and inferior films, could have been named 1974 Golden Globe winner as World Film Femme Favorite. Her films may fail but popular fascination for Elizabeth is unflagging. Measured strictly in terms of sheer public impact, she is simply the greatest star of all time.

She has risen to this eminence on an astonishing scarcity of truly first-rate films, scripts, or directors. Out of the forty-five films in which she has made feature appearances to date, only six—*A Place in the Sun, Ivanhoe, Giant, Cat on a Hot Tin*

* The others: Ingrid Bergman, Marlon Brando, Walter Brennan (3), Gary Cooper, Bette Davis, Olivia de Havilland, Helen Hayes, Katharine Hepburn (3), Glenda Jackson, Vivien Leigh, Jack Lemmon, Fredric March, Anthony Quinn, Luise Rainer, Spencer Tracy, Peter Ustinov, Shelley Winters.

last the tamed wife—adjusted to her situation, so to speak—she is magnificent. I don't know exactly why I felt proud of her, but I did.

I know why, and so do millions of other people. For the simple fact is that between Agee and Alpert, and right up to the present, in a uniquely personal sense that absolutely defies rational explanation, Elizabeth Taylor has been a part of all our lives. The bare bones of her life and legend are thus not totally unfamiliar.

She was born in London, England, on February 27, 1932. She stands five feet, four and one-half inches, her hair is basic black with numerous gray accessories (she once affectionately tagged all the newcomers "Burton"), her weight fluctuates with circumstances (for example, professional demands), and so does the color of her eyes, which can be varying shades of blue and violet, though they are commonly thought to be exclusively the latter.

She achieved stardom at the age of twelve in *National Velvet* and shortly thereafter had the first proof of it when she managed to upstage V-J Day in Chicago. Shortly after that, under severe provocation, she told Louis B. Mayer and MGM, singularly and collectively, to go to hell. L.B. had been verbally consigned to the flames before (though not often, and rarely to his face) but the temerity of a teenager telling MGM to go to hell in his presence must have been a singular experience.

In 1949, on the occasion of her seventeenth birthday, *Life* published a dazzling full-length color portrait of Elizabeth, and everyone was suddenly and surprisingly aware that the little girl was a little girl no more. In the same year *Time* did a feature story on the flux within the movie industry and put Elizabeth on the cover as the brightest hope for Hollywood's future. As 1950 dawned, two romances of brief duration were behind her and a national magazine commented on "the intense spotlight of publicity which follows everything she does." Later that year, her first husband would publicly grumble, "I didn't marry a girl—I married an institution!" and the pattern of public passion for Elizabeth Taylor was set.

She would marry three more times in the 1950s, would know the joy of three children, the tragedy of young widowhood, would end the decade in a storm of public criticism which was only a prelude for the hurricane which awaited her later in Rome. Before that occurred she would be stricken with an illness which would take her perilously close to death, and would

Roof, Cleopatra, Who's Afraid of Virginia Woolf?—were deemed worthy enough to even be nominated for an Oscar as Best Film of the Year. And none was a winner. In other words, after spending a third of a century to date as a working actress in films, Elizabeth Taylor has yet to appear in a film voted the Academy Award as Best Film of the Year. The situation with regard to scripts is slightly better and slightly worse. Only five of her scripts have been thought worthy of the Award —*Father of the Bride, Place, Giant, Cat,* and *Virginia Woolf*— but *A Place in the Sun* at least came home a winner.

The only indisputably great director she has ever worked with is George Stevens, and the good fortune has been mutual: Stevens won his Oscars for *A Place in the Sun* and *Giant.* Mike Nichols guided her to the biggest triumph of her career to date, but greatness is rarely bestowed on the evidence of five films, all the current adulation of Sam Peckinpah to the contrary notwithstanding. With Vincente Minnelli and Joseph L. Mankiewicz she has been both lucky and unlucky, and she worked with William Dieterle and John Huston when they were, to put it mildly, not at their best. George Cukor and Edmund Goulding were justly renowned for their ability to help feminine stars to significant achievements, but Elizabeth never worked with either. Daniel Mann guided Shirley Booth and Anna Magnani to Oscars, presided over Susan Hayward's impersonation of Lillian Roth, and was director of *Butterfield 8,* for which Elizabeth won her first Oscar—but under circumstances, considering the general ineptitude of everyone and everything else about that film, which reflect more credit on her than on him. And that about says it all. You will search in vain among Elizabeth's films for the names of John Ford, Elia Kazan, William Wyler, David Lean, Alfred Hitchcock, Billy Wilder, Fred Zinnemann, or William Wellman. They are simply not there.

The honor of thus ascending to unrivaled pre-eminence on generally inferior material is not yet all. In its review of *Cleopatra, The New Yorker,* never one to inflate the claims of mere film stars, made the following remarkable observation:

> As for Elizabeth Taylor, she is less an actress by now than a great natural wonder, like Niagara or the Alps, and it was right for the director, Joseph L. Mankiewicz, to deal with her as the thing she has become —the most famous woman of her time, and probably of all time . . .

A large claim, that, but if it be admitted that the world-wide thrust of the various technological media in the twentieth century makes what previously passed for fame seem ludicrous by comparison, then such assorted worthies as Helen of Troy, Cleopatra, Eleanor of Aquitaine, Joan of Arc, Elizabeth I, and Catherine the Great did not enjoy and could not have imagined, in their day, the fantastic degree of universal recognition and adulation that Elizabeth has enjoyed in hers.

Nor had they ever to contend with the intimate scrutiny and the enormous pressures, at times merciless and unceasing, which have been a part of such acclaim. Others have been scorched by smaller blasts of this fiery, double-edged public devotion and have reacted accordingly. Ingrid Bergman and Ava Gardner fled from it; Marilyn Monroe and Judy Garland collapsed under it; Greta Garbo retired so that she could be relatively free of it. Elizabeth Taylor has survived by far the largest measure of it, with honor, and in a manner which is a revealing measure of this remarkable woman. Refusing either to scream *at* the public, or bleed *for* it, she has, from the first, stubbornly, silently, steadfastly, and successfully resisted public encroachment on that part of her domain which she regards as exclusively personal. In an era when personal privacy is under attack as never before, such a battle and such a triumph are not the least of her legend.

Her thirty years of survival in a profession notoriously highpressured, tenuous, and insecure rests, like a well-crafted table, on four solid supports: a sound family foundation and a consequent inner assurance which has never failed her; the mutual love and devotion of those closest to her; a bond with the public which transitory crisis could never sever; and a professional knowledge of the crafts of film acting second to none.

Each of these will be examined in its turn, particularly the last, in a work which makes no pretension to being the "inside story," presuming such a thing were possible about anything so complex as a human being. Elizabeth herself had a brief go at that sort of thing in 1965, and anyone who rushed to the bookstore thinking they were going to "know all" and to get the totality of Elizabeth Taylor compressed between the covers of a book must have been bitterly disappointed. Again, presuming that such a thing were possible, expecting this particular woman to write that kind of book would be like asking her to breathe underwater. Time and again she drew the veil of discretion over matters which she deemed not in the public domain. If you didn't get it there, you aren't going to get it here—or anywhere else, for that matter.

Elizabeth herself has long since become inured to the fact that the average member of her public has his own particular image of her, in which fact or logic play insignificant roles. To many she remains the apotheosis of the eternal temptress—beautiful, capricious, willful, sinful, cruel breaker of hearts, reveling in her jewelry and diamonds and various and assorted luxuries—a major-league Maria Montez, as it were. A generation of American women have turned on to this sort of crapulous nonsense under the hair-dryer. Much of it has been harmless rubbish, and if it occasionally went beyond the bounds, a battery of lawyers has stood waiting in the wings.

Like any self-respecting human being, Elizabeth Taylor has a pronounced aversion to being dragged under a microscope, and then dissected, sorted, analyzed, labeled, and categorized. And she has been uncommonly successful at eluding such procedures.

In the first flowering of their love for each other, Richard Burton observed, "There's a strange mystery about Elizabeth. No matter how open she may seem to be, you can't put your finger on this mystery—it's insoluble." Ten years later he would add, "Elizabeth is a little like litmus paper. Whatever personality you dip her in, she changes color. If she's with someone she likes being with, she's one person. But if she meets someone she dislikes, a veil falls over her face. If she's happy, she's a different creature again."

So this work is not an explanation of this complex, multi-faceted woman; it's a celebration—a personal tribute to a presence that has enriched my life. Above all, it is a repository for the record, so that future generations, who know only the legend, can go to the events that went into its making.

DICK SHEPPARD

Los Angeles

PART I

PRINCESS

1932-1951

Every kid's dream is to be older, to dress up, to make believe. And to live in a world of fantasy. My world of fantasy really happened. Just imagine the thrill of being a kid at MGM in its heyday. It was like going to Disneyland every day.

—Elizabeth Taylor

1

As the Oracle at Delphi might have told it:

All the Goddesses were summoned to Olympus for the birth of a Goddess destined to rule in the twentieth century. All arrived bearing their various gifts of Beauty, Love, Intelligence, Courage, Magnetism, Good Fortune, Artistic Talent, Maternity, Fertility, and so on. But there were some notable absentees. The Goddess of Good Health was laid up in traction and couldn't be moved an inch. The Goddess of Punctuality got there so late the festivities were all over. And the Goddess of Neatness and Order had such a time trying to locate all the various parts of her drag that she never did get there either.

As an Astrologer might have told it:

The Sun was in Pisces, the Moon in Scorpio, with Libra rising on the Eastern Horizon. Pisces generally bestows upon its natives no great wordly ambition, a hatred of confinement and an affinity for travel, a love of the ocean (and a tendency to drift with the tide), the gift of satirical humor and/or biting sarcasm, a sense of cosmic consciousness, devotion to friends and causes, love of home and children, a dread of dependency, a basic respect for conventions of the social order, a tendency to overbalance reason with impulsive emotion, and a curious ability to wallow in luxury and various forms of self-indulgence at one point, and rise to the very heights of self-denial at the next. Also, qualities of illusion, idealism, altruism, and compassion, and sound powers of learning and memory, imagination, interpretation, observation, perception, and judgment. Pisceans generally are thought to be calm, modest, sensitive, and reserved.

Piscean women, specifically, are pictured as totally feminine, subtle, vulnerable, inwardly timid and self-doubting, sentimental, possessive, complex and changeable with circumstances, psychic and commonsensical.

As to the specifics of the Natal Horoscope:

The Sun-Moon combination (Pisces-Scorpio) would tend to reinforce qualities of perception, intuition, imagination, and humor; to give some interest in metaphysical concerns, to indicate a sizable share of nervous tension, and the promise of a varied love life.

Libra Rising would point to a taste and talent for the arts, and to a need for harmony and balance in basic personal relationships and situations.

The Sun in conjunction with Mercury would promise basic sanity and stability and the ability to withstand stress. Also, perseverance and a nature pliant and cooperative until pushed, at which point it could become stubborn and immovable.

The Sun in conjunction with Mars would produce an aggressive assurance that knows no fear; temper; an ability to fight things through to the finish and never cry for mercy, no matter what the pressures.

The Sun in square to Neptune would hint at susceptibility to unreliable persons and influences due to vague and impractical idealism, and the reliance on intuition instead of reason.

Mars in square to Neptune would confer exceptional personal magnetism and authority, especially if it stemmed from basic insights into the world of the spiritual and metaphysical.

Minor aspects of the horoscope pointed to financial extravagance and culinary overindulgence (and a basic optimism about both), fondness for the nice things in life, additional stability and financial good luck, and a tendency to daydream with a mind that might wander too much for its own practical good.

As a Numerologist might have told it:

The child would be born and would live under the double influence of the number *Eight*, both as the Birth Number (the Number of Personality) and the Name Number (Number of Development and Attainment). Eight is the most powerful of all numbers. Around it cluster such qualities as strength, success, authority, courage, energy, magnetism—such adjectives as loyal, blunt, aggressive, dynamic, original, creative—such character traits as self-discipline, intense concentration, tremendous drive and determination (for good or ill), an aversion to the mediocre and a horror of failure, a seeming aloofness stemming from aversion to public displays of emotion, financial shrewdness, a

love of fighting, a tendency to dominate, and a long memory
for personal slights and injuries. Above all, Eight confers un-
paralleled inner stability and basic balance because, divided in
half, it consists of two equal parts (4+4), and the parts halved
again consist of four equal parts (2+2+2+2).

These portents from Antiquity, Astrology, and Numerology
were mere possibilities, but all would become reality, in varying
degrees, in their time and in their season. The only indisputable
fact was that, in a hospital in London, England, on February 27,
1932, a baby girl was born weighing eight and a half pounds.
Her eyes were shut tight for ten days, and she seemed to be
covered with an alarming excess of black fuzzy hair. Eventually
the hair would disappear, and the eyes would open to be framed
by an extraordinary set of double lashes. And she would be
named Elizabeth (for both her maternal and paternal grand-
mothers) Rosemond (for her aunt, Mabel Rosemond Young)
Taylor.

* * *

She was born to Francis and Sara Taylor, Americans resident
in England, which conferred dual citizenship upon her at birth,
a circumstance which would later produce a week's worth of
newspaper flap in 1965. Her mother was born Sara Warmbrodt
in Kansas City, Kansas, and grew up to be a petite, energetic,
and attractive lady whose looks were often compared to those
of Laraine Day. Sara left the Midwest to try for a career on
the stage as Sara Sothern, and made her debut with Edward
Everett Horton's stock company in Los Angeles in the role of
the crippled girl healed by faith in *The Fool*. She played this
part for four years in Los Angeles, New York, and London.
Ultimately she retired to marry Illinois-born Francis Taylor,
whose family had moved to Kansas, where they met each other.

Many years later, when, as Elizabeth archly put it, "I got a
bit famous," the press were pushing hard for angles and discovered that Sara had once been an actress. Enter Plot #4:
Beautiful daughter is forced into a luxurious life of misery and
despair by frustrated mother. The tone of this kind of material
clearly indicated that MGM wasted a pile of money on *I'll Cry
Tomorrow*, paying Susan Hayward and Jo Van Fleet to enact
the saga of mother-driven Lillian Roth. They should have just
put Elizabeth and Sara in front of the cameras and cranked
away.

Sara Taylor refuted such distortions with some heat. "Everywhere we have gone," she wrote in 1949, "people have congratulated me on Elizabeth's success, taking it for granted that, as a former actress, I had always had ambitions for my child. Nothing could be further from the truth. I not only gave up the theater when I married Francis Taylor, *I never looked back*" (her italics).

The man Sara married was the London representative for his uncle, affluent New York art dealer Howard Young. Francis managed the gallery at 35 Old Bond Street, and the family lived a happy and comfortable upper-middle-class existence at Heathwood, their home in the Hampstead section of London, and at the Little Swallows, their country retreat in Kent. It is the wonderful times in Kent, in a more relaxed setting and out in natural surroundings with a multitude of pets, that Elizabeth remembered best when she reflected on her childhood in England and pronounced it "idyllic." Those seven years contained some interesting indications of things to come.

For one thing, before she was out of diapers, Elizabeth put the first notch on an illness-and-accident record that simply boggles the mind. In the time-honored way of babies and "nono's," she crawled toward a fascinating electrical fire in the grate at Heathwood and broiled a finger. In March 1935 a sore throat terminated in abscessed ears which had to be lanced on eight separate occasions, this while her temperature hovered at 103 degrees for three weeks, and her distraught parents ran the gamut from hope to despair. In June, with Elizabeth mercifully recovered, Sara took her and her brother, Howard, to the Regent Park Zoo. There Elizabeth got her first taste of frenzied male adoration—as it happened, from a chimp named Jocko. Jocko posed perfectly peacefully with Howard as a souvenir photo was snapped. But he took one look at Elizabeth, wrapped his long arms around her, and had almost embraced the breath right out of her before keepers beat him off. All this time Elizabeth was neither screaming nor crying. She was merely staring at him in a nonplussed fashion as if to say, "Sweetie, what *is* your problem?"—a technique she would later employ to advantage on other heavy-breathing, self-consciously male admirers.

It was also in 1935 that ballet lessons with Madame Vaccani, ballet mistress to the Royal Family for two generations, led to Elizabeth's participation in a recital at Queen's Hall before Elizabeth, Duchess of York, and her daughters, the Princesses Elizabeth and Margaret Rose. Elizabeth danced, appropriately, as a little angel, and the finale had the entire troupe bowing low on the floor before the royal box, fluttering like butterflies, after which they were to exit together. All went according to plan until a head count in the wings revealed that one of the angels was still out somewhere on her own trip. Elizabeth was taking a series of unscheduled bows, stage center and solo, and all the whispered pleading from backstage could not compete with the thrilling thunder she was hearing from out front. When parents of famed offspring are asked when ambition first made itself known, they can usually remember incidents like this one.

Still at age three, Elizabeth was gifted with her first horse, a pony named Betty. It was like the visit with Jocko all over again. Howard rode Betty around for a while and got on fine with her. Elizabeth got onto her and Betty immediately tossed her into a patch of stinging nettles. A governess then applied some soothing handfuls of dock weed to the child's tingling flesh and the incident would have ended, in a majority of cases, with a hysterical child being taken into the house for a pacifying dish of ice cream. Little Elizabeth stood her ground. She went right back to Betty, walked her around while talking to her, got back on board still talking to her, and rode off.

A year later Elizabeth somehow managed to upend herself in a creek and was in imminent danger of drowning when her brother came to the rescue and pulled her out. He performed the same service several years later when Elizabeth was swept unconscious into a treacherous undertow off Malibu. Admirers of Elizabeth Taylor thus owe Howard a double debt of gratitude so, at this point, he may be brought briefly and reluctantly out from the wings.

Howard Taylor was born in 1929, two years and eight months before Elizabeth, and so resolutely has he insisted on living his own life, with the complete cooperation of his sister, that a diligent search through the mountainous stacks of publicity about Elizabeth cannot reveal even his birthdate. He remained impervious to repeated offers of a film career when it could have been his for the asking, and matters came to a climax when he was finally maneuvered into taking a screen test at the age of seventeen. Howard dutifully showed up for the great day having shaved his head totally bald. "How I admired Howard's disdain for the movies," Elizabeth later commented.

He would be an usher at his sister's first wedding in 1950, would himself marry Mara Regan in 1951, would serve a tour of duty with the Army, and would then go on his own private way—as a skilled oceanologist, and as husband and father. And he would discreetly surface at his sister's side during the various crises in her life, and always publicly silent. In the twenty-five years of Elizabeth's incredible fame, there has been no public comment from Howard, no quotes, not even a solitary sentence. One might say he has never succumbed to the temptation to jump into print with "How I See My Sister" or "Elizabeth Taylor's Brother Speaks Out!" But one cannot succumb to a temptation that was never there. Finally, with the pattern of his own life firmly established, he agreed to a bit part in one of Elizabeth's films. You can see him in the first reel of *Boom!*, throwing his brother-in-law bag and baggage from a speeding motorboat.

Currently Howard and his family live in Hawaii, but it would be a mistake to look for them in any of the posh places on Oahu. They are not there. Howard has always preferred to live his life far from the madding crowd, and he has had the strength of character to do it, enormous material pressures to the contrary notwithstanding. Anyone pondering the Taylor determination to go one's own way, to make one's own mistakes, to choose one's own path and follow it no matter what, can chew over that for a while.

In March 1939, Hitler swallowed what was left of Czechoslovakia. In April, Neville Chamberlain, then British Prime Minister, was publicly expressing his horror at the ideal of children in gas masks going through air raid drill. At that point, Francis decided to send Sara and the children to a safer climate in America until the situation resolved itself. The three travelers arrived on May 1 in Pasadena at the home of Elizabeth's maternal grandparents for what was expected to be a temporary stay in America.

As Sara made the social rounds with seven-year-old Elizabeth that summer, several people she met who were connected with films made identical comments as they gazed at Elizabeth. With *Gone With the Wind* currently in production and the number one topic of conversation, Sara was repeatedly told, "That child is the image of Vivien Leigh. Get her over to Selznick's. They're testing for the part of Scarlett O'Hara's daughter." Much to Elizabeth's disappointment, her mother firmly rejected such a possibility, which was something of a shame. In all the calamitous catalogue of horrendous Hollywood child performances, that of Bonnie Blue Butler in *Gone With the Wind* must take pride of place—if you can call it that. What Elizabeth would have made of the part had Selznick tested and signed her can only be imagined. Sara communicated her decision to Francis in England, who was in complete agreement. With war now imminent, Francis cabled back that he had made his decision to relocate in California and would join the family presently as soon as he could wind up affairs in London.

Meanwhile September came and the children were enrolled in school in Pasadena. The headmaster introduced Elizabeth to her class thus: "Listen to Elizabeth, children. Her English is perfect." With Europe now at war, Elizabeth was also invited into a faculty meeting to give a firsthand report on conditions in England. These marks of adult favoritism were a great way to get off to a fierce start with classmates and they retaliated by mocking her English accent with nonsense sentences like "I cawnt take a bawth on the grawss with the banawnas." Fortunately Elizabeth's tenure in Pasadena was brief. Francis had arrived and set up an art gallery in the old Château Élysée in Hollywood, opening up crates of paintings stamped "Safely convoyed by the British Navy." The reunited family now took up residence in Pacific Palisades.

In her new school Elizabeth experienced an unreciprocated crush on John Derek, beat up other boys who tried to get "mushy," and one memorable day braved the certain taunts of classmates to give voice to what was fast becoming the central dream of her young life. When her teacher asked her what she wanted to be when she grew up, she unhesitatingly replied, "An actress." The resultant ridicule failed to intimidate her. "I don't want to be a movie star," she continued unruffled. "I want to be a serious actress like my mother was." Her classmates were not much moved, and neither were her parents. Despite the occasional comments to the effect that "that child is pretty enough to be in pictures," Francis and Sara Taylor had no intention of overtly abandoning their beloved daughter to the well-known rigors of show business. Francis was probably more opposed to it than his wife, who, after all, had once had a lucky bite from the bug. But they both agreed that a world of numerous possibilities lay before Elizabeth. Acting was just one of them, and her desire for it was just a phase, like earlier dreams of becoming a professional horsewoman or her yearning to be a ballerina. And if it weren't just a phase—well, the family held religious convictions and Elizabeth was left to the ultimate consolation of providence. If it was meant to be, it *would* be.

Among Elizabeth's classmates at Pacific Palisades were children of famous film people like Norma Shearer and Darryl F. Zanuck, and it would be charming to be able to report that little Richard and Darrylin Zanuck went home one night and refused to touch another spoonful of tapioca until their father agreed to give Elizabeth a screen test. But it didn't happen that way at all. As a matter of fact, Elizabeth made it into films on her first contract minus any test at all.

Francis Taylor was the unwitting agent of what happened. Amid the collection of paintings he had managed to bring out of England was a generous selection of the work of famed English portrait painter Augustus Johns. The paintings were now on display in the gallery. A lady named Andrea Berens heard about them. She had once had her portrait painted by Johns and was a great admirer of his work. Additionally, she was also engaged to marry Cheever Cowdin, the chairman of the Board of Directors of Universal Pictures. She called the gallery and made an appointment. On the afternoon of her visit, she was enjoying the paintings when Sara and Elizabeth dropped in to see Francis. Miss Berens was introduced and was so taken by Elizabeth that she told Sara, "Cheever must see this child." Sara invited them to tea the following Sunday. Andrea Berens could enjoy additional Johns portraits at the house, and Cheever Cowdin could meet Elizabeth.

Well-bred children were expected to assume some of the responsibilities of hospitality early on—to make guests welcome, to attend to their needs, to see that their stay in one's home was a pleasant one. At teatime, Elizabeth attended to all of these things charmingly and without any of that self-conscious brattiness which makes adult gorges rise. Mainly she entertained Cheever Cowdin with her doll collection and by the end of the afternoon he was completely captivated. Child stars were becoming a fixture in Hollywood, thanks to the phenomenal success of Shirley Temple, and anyone at Universal had particular reason to be aware of it: Deanna Durbin had recently saved the company from outright bankruptcy. Cowdin thanked his hostesses, told Sara that she must bring Elizabeth out sometime for a test, and departed. At that point, Elizabeth's hopes soared but Sara realized that nothing definite had been said. It might have been no more than a spur-of-the-moment courtesy. So that the issue was right back in the lap of inscrutable providence. But not for long.

A few days later, Elizabeth went for her regular ballet lesson at a studio on La Cienega. At that time she had a naturally beautiful singing voice—loud, clear, with excellent pitch and an impressive range of top notes. She was taking singing lessons, as a matter of fact, from Deanna Durbin's vocal coach, Andre De Segurola. While waiting for class to begin on this particular day, a classmate sat down to play "The Blue Danube" on the piano and Elizabeth trilled along with it. Carmen Considine had just deposited her children at the rehearsal hall and was impressed by this impromptu performance. Mrs. Considine was the wife of producer John W. Considine, Jr., who had come to Metro-Goldwyn-Mayer in the 1930s and who worked with Arthur Freed and Jack Cummings under the overall supervision of Sam Katz in the production of MGM musicals. That evening, Mrs. Considine told her husband, "You really ought to hear this child, John. She sings just like a bird."

Mrs. Considine set up the appointment with Sara, and shortly thereafter Elizabeth entered the gates of mighty Metro in Culver City for the first time. In Considine's office, Sara improvised scales on the piano, Elizabeth sang, and without further ado mother and daughter were whisked down the hall to the biggest office of all, that of studio chief Louis B. Mayer. They happened to catch the boss in transit, so that L.B. had no time to interview Elizabeth or seriously evaluate her possibilities. He merely threw a piercing glance in her direction and then roared at Considine, "Well—what are you waiting for? Sign her up! Sign her up!" and vanished in a cloud of importance.

MGM offered a straight seven years, with yearly options, at $100 per week, and Sara demurred, playing for time. She and Elizabeth were naturally flattered, she told Considine, but they had promised Cheever Cowdin a test at Universal before they signed any contract anywhere. As a ploy to get Elizabeth better terms and more money, it failed. Sara left Culver City, having told Considine that the matter naturally had to be discussed at home with her husband and that they would be in touch. She then contacted Cheever Cowdin and let him know that Metro was ready to sign Elizabeth for seven years at $100 a week to start. This particular ploy was in time-honored show business tradition and this one worked. For it is indisputable that, in an acting career, you alternate from periods when you might just as well be buried six feet underground to periods when you cannot handle all the offers that come your way because, by some perverse logic, the act of being wanted by one employer leads inexorably to a universal demand by all of them. And after a peak period of recognition and acclaim, you suddenly find yourself off in limbo again, and the cycle begins anew. This is the unwritten law of an acting career and those who cannot conform to it come to speedy grief and are advised to seek gentler employment elsewhere. "Feast or famine," it is generally called, and the "feast" part is referred to, in trade parlance, as a condition of being "hot." Sara Taylor set up this particular equation and Cheever Cowdin responded to it.

"You say Metro offered her one hundred a week?" he queried. "Well, we'll pay her two hundred."

At that point everyone was in total ignorance of Elizabeth Taylor's acting talents for the simple reason that they had yet to be put on display anywhere. To have two major studios bidding for you simply on the reported basis of one song improvised while killing time at a ballet class was an impressive achievement which augured well for the future, but not for the immediate future.

Sara and Elizabeth subsequently went out to Universal to meet the casting director, and Elizabeth immediately got a case of what today would be called bad vibrations. The feeling was mutual. In a quote that would haunt him through the years, casting director Dan Kelly later observed to associates, "The kid has nothing. Her eyes are too old. She doesn't have the face of a kid."

After the interview, Elizabeth's intuition clearly told her that she didn't belong there, and her sharp sensory capacity to appraise a situation on a feeling level was even then beginning to make itself known. In this instance, she was right on target. She would work under the aegis of Universal only three times in thirty years, and the first film was so insignificant that, to this day, even Elizabeth herself has forgotten the correct title of it. The other two instances, *Boom!* and *Secret Ceremony*, are eloquent testimony to the power of that early E.S.P. Elizabeth begged her mother to sign with MGM. She had a better feeling about it, she just knew it was right for her. Sara weighed all the factors. Universal offered twice the money and a personal contact with its chairman. True, MGM was a far more impressive studio—"More Stars Than There Are in Heaven" was Metro's proud boast—but for that very reason, it might not be right for Elizabeth. She could easily get lost in the shuffle. Perhaps a smaller studio would be better after all. So, in June 1941, Elizabeth signed with Universal at $200 a week. It was a choice that practically strangled her career at birth.

Two things happened to Elizabeth during the year with Universal. She was put on a rigorous weekly regimen of singing lessons which effectively throttled what vocal talent she had for good and all. And in September she was given three days' work on a little gem then called *Man or Mouse*. According to Universal's publicity department, this was "a hilarious hodge-podge of hokum. It tells what happens in the sleeping little village of Witumpka Falls when one of the local lights, played by Hugh

Herbert, invents a patent prepared pudding which has a veritable treasure of Vitamin Z and is consequently full of Zumph." Wicked rivals try to pooh-pooh his pudding, but Herbert exposes them and is elected mayor, presumably by constituents who have seen the light and are full of Zumph. "Roars Galore! Gyps off the old Block, Stuffing the Ballot Box with Hilarity! An Entertainment Tonic Rich in Vitamin Glee!" So proclaimed the ads.

In what was essentially a three-way contest between veteran comedians Hugh Herbert, Guy Kibbee, and Edgar Kennedy, Elizabeth was not exactly in the center of things. She and Alfalfa Switzer, he of the old "Our Gang" comedies, played Herbert's youngest children. They sang an off-key duet together and, as Elizabeth best remembers it, spent the rest of the time "running around and shooting rubber bands at ladies' bottoms."

The studio retitled the film *There's One Born Every Minute*, and the publicity department obligingly sent out the following: "Movie Newcomer: Elizabeth Taylor, 9-year-old singer and dancer recently signed by Universal Studios, makes her screen debut in *There's One Born Every Minute*." But by the time it went into the theaters for a mercifully brief run in August 1942, the "movie newcomer" had been without a contract for three months. Universal had dutifully paid out $200 a week for a year and then dropped her. Bette Davis recently observed that Universal fired so many future stars that every young actor used to pray he'd be dropped by Universal because it eventually became the Hollywood equivalent of Boston's "stepping in doggie-do." Miss Davis was shown the door at Universal, and Humphrey Bogart, Clark Gable, Rosalind Russell, and Robert Montgomery also joined the parade. And now, at the age of ten, so did Elizabeth Taylor.

At this critical juncture, in the summer of 1942, Sara Taylor wangled an audience with Hedda Hopper. For those unaware of that lady, she was a quasi-actress who can occasionally be seen on the Late Show hamming her way through supporting parts in such films as *Topper, Reap the Wild Wind,* and *Sunset Boulevard.* Shrewdly sensing that total reliance on an acting career would for her be a precarious arrangement indeed, she somehow parlayed her personal contacts, acid tongue, and a certain flair for millinery into a career as Hollywood's number two gossip columnist (number two because she stood always in the broad-beamed shadow of Louella Parsons, of whom more anon). Miss Hopper flavored her daily reports from Hollywood with a generous coating of McKinley Era political sentiments and an annoying predilection for telling other people what they ought to be doing at any given moment. This obnoxiousness was suitably rewarded on several occasions, most notably one fine Valentine's Day when Joan Bennett sent her a live skunk. In 1942 Hedda Hopper was already a power to be reckoned with, which is why Sara brought Elizabeth to see her.

Sara reviewed the meager facts of her daughter's career to date, and then had Elizabeth sing a chorus of "The Blue Danube," doubtless hoping that luck would strike twice. It didn't. Miss Hopper's response was characteristically blunt. "Frankly," she told Sara, "I don't think Elizabeth's future lies in her singing." Beyond that, she ventured no predictions. Possibly she dismissed the pair as just another ambitious mother–talented daughter combination, of which Hollywood has never had a scarcity. It was to be Elizabeth Taylor's first encounter witih Hedda Hopper, but not her last.

Francis Taylor had now relocated his art gallery, from the Château Élysée to impressive new quarters in the Beverly Hills Hotel, and the Taylor family now moved from Pacific Palisades to a spacious Mediterranean-style home with a red-tiled roof on Elm Drive in Beverly Hills. This was to be Elizabeth's home from that day until the day she married. It had a large olive tree in the front yard which was Taylor-made for jungle games indulged in by Elizabeth and Howard and by their nearest neighbor, Anne Westmore (of the Paramount Westmores, to distinguish the tribe of brothers who seemed to be in every makeup department in every studio in town).

Elizabeth's brief taste of a career was presently submerged in all the activity of moving into a new house, of making new acquaintances, of plans for her entry into a new school in the fall. And in the simple daily round of activities as a member of a family which had been close-knit since the first summer after Elizabeth's birth, when Francis, Sara, Howard, the new baby, two servants, and a dog all piled into a rather elegant trailer and traveled gypsy-fashion all over England for two months. The family relationship was always characterized by mutual respect. There is no record of either of Elizabeth's parents ever laying a hand on her. With Howard, being a boy, the situation was slightly different. "I used to get furious when my parents bawled my brother out," Elizabeth once recalled. "And if I'd see Howard getting a spanking, I'd feel like leaping on my father."

With Elizabeth, such extremes were not necessary. Obstreperous and stubborn she could be, and given to occasional imperious temper tantrums. At such times she was put "in coventry," that is, told to leave the room and go off by herself until she could present herself in a more acceptable fashion. Her parents stood always ready to talk anything over in an intelligent manner, but screaming, crying, and other hysterical behavior made such a thing impossible. They could communicate with the nice Elizabeth, the intelligent one; with the other, they would have nothing to do. So because, at these times, she was not struck across the face or thrown around the room, but treated with basic respect, she grew up with a basic respect for herself. Many people spend many fifty-minute hours on many couches painfully trying to acquire this priceless commodity. Elizabeth was lucky. It was a gift from loving, sensible parents in the years when it was of crucial importance.

As befitted a child in her circumstances, Elizabeth was also the recipient of a thorough training in the manners and social graces thought to be the most beneficial to the development of good character, most of the marks of which she retains to this day. She credits Howard for giving her a lifelong abhorrence of the diminutive "Liz," not only because it can be made to sound like one long hiss, but because Howard, in the time-honored tradition of older brothers, frequently embroidered it as "Lizzie the Lizzard" and "Lizzie the Cow."

During Elizabeth's childhood there was no such thing as commercial television, so there was no boob tube in front of which she was plunked for hours on end to keep her out from underfoot. And mutual respect worked both ways. Your parents respected your basic right to be listened to rather than constantly silenced or otherwise treated as a chattel of inferior worth and capacity. In return, you respected them by not clamoring for their individual attentions sixteen hours per day. You were expected to go off at intervals with an activity of your own—reading, drawing, etc.—which fostered at least three things: your independent ability to function by yourself, your ability to entertain yourself, and, concomitantly, not to depend wholly on commercial entertainment and thus deprive yourself of the benefits of developing your own rich resources. Nor was the idea ever allowed to take root that life consisted mainly of being entertained.

To this day, Elizabeth is still a voracious reader. She has never had to depend on endless hours of media entertainment and/or the constant attentions of other people, at parties or wherever, to feel secure. Quite the contrary. When the later circumstances of her life resulted in periods of enforced isolation, she could make the necessary adjustment because the basic resources for it had been developed early.

If there was no television, there were movies and radio, both in their heyday. Both were privileges which were chiefly dependent upon good behavior. The film titles were perused for suitability of subject matter. The films were generally a week-end privilege, when the inflexible hour of bedtime could be relaxed, if need be. Radio offered a veritable cornucopia of riches, the pleasures of which are incapable of being fully communicated to today's children. When you can have both audio and video, they want to know, how could anyone have ever possibly been satisfied with just audio? Strange as it may seem, they were.

A sense of responsibility was encouraged by the performance of suitable tasks around the house—dishes, cleaning chores, etc.— the satisfactory performance of which was rewarded by the doling out of a weekly allowance, which started small and, by an intricate process of collective bargaining, grew larger. You were naturally expected to take suitable care of your own room and possessions and to be neat and tidy about them. In the Taylor household, as in many others, that extended to not sitting on the bed and rumpling the bedspread. This part of the training failed to take with Elizabeth. Years later, while she was married to Michael Wilding, Sara went out to visit her and found mother, babies, and animals plunked happily in the middle of the bed. Thinking of the hassles they had gone through on this particular point, Sara remarked ruefully, "Perhaps I shouldn't have been so strict about it. After all, what *good* did it do?"

As for the rest of it: You came to the dinner table with clean hands, refrained from lunging at food no matter how hungry you were, waited for it to be passed to you, and passed it to others. You ate everything with a fork, which later gave rise to feelings of delicious guilt when such edibles as bacon and chicken were popped directly from your fingers into your mouth. You were on all accounts to refrain from glancing disgustedly or expressing overt disapproval of food you didn't like. In Elizabeth's case that meant rice, cabbage, and cauliflower. All the food on the table was good and wholesome, your parents knew what was good for you, and, besides, there were currently all those starving children in war-torn China who would have given anything for just one bite of it. Should the thought of Oriental suffering fail to move you to at least make an attempt at it, you could wind up without something else you valued, that is, dessert.

Relationships with those outside the family were likewise firmly structured. "Children should be seen and not heard" was then a widely respected national maxim. It fostered a respect for authority and for the greater wisdom of older people. You were to restrain your adolescent yearnings to drink, smoke, wear makeup, and stay up to all hours. These privileges, and others as well, would be yours when you were old enough to handle them. And that time, as your parents never wearied of telling you, would come sooner than you thought.

Meanwhile you were to defer to adults. You rose when they entered a room, and should they be without a seat, you gave them yours. You answered their inquiries courteously, no matter how foolish you might privately think some of them, and you patiently listened to whatever they had to say, even on those occasions when you longed to tell them that they simply didn't know what they were talking about.

In public you behaved yourself. Tantrums, arguments, and other unpleasant displays of emotion were simply not allowed. Good manners were a credit to your parents; bad manners were deeply embarrassing to them, and persistence in such behavior could mean that you were left at home until you thought better of it. The subjects of your conversation were definitely not to include "family business," for example, finances and economics, firsthand reports on who said what to whom, who did what to whom, who thought what about whom, who got punished for what, etc. The family unit was something very special, and talking about it in too intimate a fashion, aside from the trouble it could cause, somehow devalued and cheapened it. The twin senses of public decorum and family privacy were standards which Elizabeth carried proudly into battle in a business which values neither, and the inevitable conflict would form a pattern in her public life which endures to this day.

And so, in this summer of 1942, Elizabeth settled into the comfortable circumstances of an upper-middle-class upbringing on Elm Drive in Beverly Hills, looking forward to a future that apparently was not to include an acting career in films. She had had her shot at that and it was behind her. Soon there would be a new school and a whole new world of relationships to discover and explore.

A new world there would be, and very shortly—that part of it was correct. But the new world would be in Culver City, not in Beverly Hills. Opportunity was about to knock for the second time, and this time it entered with an air of permanence about it. Given Elizabeth's lifelong love of animals, it should come as no great surprise that the agent of her good fortune was to be a dog.

❀ 2 ❀

As Groucho Marx was later to put it, "Ever since the public found out that Lassie was really a male, they've been thinking the worst about Hollywood." Prior to November 1943, the public knew nothing about him-her and couldn't have cared less. By then, a dedicated little group over at MGM had been working for over a year to change that situation.

In the summer of 1942 the low-budget unit supervised by Harry Rapf and Dore Schary went into preproduction on a film version of Eric Knight's novel about a faithful collie dog called *Lassie Come Home*. Already they had produced well-deserved minor vehicles for Fay Bainter (*The War Against Mrs. Hadley*) and Conrad Veidt (a dual role as twin brothers in *Nazi Agent*) and sent Margaret O'Brien on to stardom with *Journey for Margaret* and *Lost Angel*. These modest successes had upped their budget to a point where, for this new one, they were now allowed Technicolor—still an expensive process, still utilized comparatively rarely, and almost never on a "B" picture. Elated at this unusual mark of favor, the unit addressed itself to the task of finding a star for the film.

To this end, Producer Samuel Marx and Director Fred M. Wilcox went in fear and trembling to a mass public dog audition at L.A.'s Gilmore Stadium, got thoroughly barked to death, and came away empty-handed. Professional trainer Rudd Weatherwax was then recruited to bring a station wagon full of collies to Culver City. All the beauties were paraded, examined, and found wanting. Finally, almost as an afterthought, Weatherwax trotted out a one-year-old male named Pal, for whom he had paid ten dollars. The search was over. Shooting began September 1, 1942.

The basic plot of *Lassie Come Home* tells of one dog's unswerving fidelity to her young master, her enforced separation from him, and of the incredible obstacles she surmounts to return to him. In view of the way it all turned out, a partial look at the story synopsis is indicative of how ludicrous it could have been in the wrong hands—a sort of canine *Portia Faces Life*.

"Freed at last, Lassie starts southward. For days she walks, trots, and runs. She swims rivers. She battles her way through snow storms in the mountains, and rain storms along the seacoast. She fights ferocious sheep dogs set on her by sheepherders, who shoot and wound her. On the verge of death on one occasion, she is nursed back to health by a kindly Scottish couple. Then she resumes her unswerving trail to the South."

The "kindly Scottish couple" were played by Dame May Whitty and Ben Webster, then simultaneously celebrating their Golden Wedding Anniversary and her fiftieth year as an actress. It would have been interesting to get Dame May's reaction when she first saw the script. Her part called for her continually and audibly to respond to the dog's psychic vibrations, and ultimately to unlatch her cottage gate and let the dog go, gazing raptly into the distance (actually into a welter of lights and cameramen) and intoning, "She's on her way," with all the mystical grace and fervor of Ethel Barrymore reciting, "That's all there is/There isn't any more."

Edmund Gwenn's assignment was hardly less exacting. As a peddler Lassie saves from a vicious assault by two crooks in the woods, he and the dog were also ultimately to part—but only after a conversation and disagreement about which road to take. Aside from Gwenn and Dame May Whitty, the cast included Donald Crisp and Roddy McDowall, fresh from their triumphs in *How Green Was My Valley* and again playing father and son, with Roddy as Joe Carraclough, Lassie's young master; Elsa Lanchester as his mother; and Nigel Bruce, on one of his occasional sabbaticals from Basil Rathbone and Baker Street, as the rich aristocrat to whom Lassie is sold. Shooting was progressing right on schedule until the sudden vacancy in a key role threatened to bring production to a standstill.

As the Duke of Rudling, Nigel Bruce has a little granddaughter whose part is crucial: she it is who frees Lassie for that long trip South. There are two versions of what MGM's problem was at this point and of how they solved it. In one version, the little girl hired for the role had to be let go because her eyes were too weak to withstand the brightness of the lights. Edgar Selwyn overheard Marx and Wilcox discussing the problem and contacted Sara Taylor.

In the more familiar version, Francis Taylor was out walking the block one evening, tin helmet on head, doing duty as an air-raid warden. In this first year of World War II in America, the West Coast was still jittery about a possible Japanese invasion, and several thousand Japanese-Americans were incarcerated in internment camps as the hapless proof. It was an air-raid warden's duty to see that the hours of blackout in the evening were strictly observed. Francis came upon neighbor Sam Marx doing the same duty, and asked him how his film was coming along.

"It's almost finished, but the girl is too tall for Roddy McDowall," Marx told Francis. "We're going to have to get a smaller child."

Francis acquainted his neighbor with the fact that Elizabeth was small, that she still retained much of her English accent, and that she had been under contract at Universal for a year and done a film there. With a possible production halt staring him in the face, Marx could not afford to refuse a gift like this, however unfruitful it might prove. He told Francis to ask Sara to bring Elizabeth to MGM on the following day for a test. As Marx later told it:

"We had five other girls whom we were considering. We practically had selected one because I didn't expect much from Elizabeth. But the moment she entered there was a complete eclipse of all the others. She was stunning, dazzling. Her voice was charming and she had no self-consciousness whatsoever. We gave her a test, and when we looked at it the next day, we knew we had a find."

The test was a very impromptu affair. Mother and daughter arrived at the studio late in the afternoon, were rushed to the sound stage, and Elizabeth was put before the cameras sans makeup or other preparation. She was given only a couple of minutes to acquaint herself with a few lines. Then she was to pretend to pat a collie dog while Fred Wilcox read Nigel Bruce's lines off-camera. Wilcox later remarked: "We took one look at those eyes and she was in. There's something behind them. I don't know . . ." Here he trailed off, wisely refraining from attempting to articulate that which would remain forever elusive.

Roddy McDowall and Elizabeth Taylor were to meet on this film and form a lifelong friendship, and one of his fondest memories is of the day Elizabeth made her entrance onto the set of *Lassie Come Home* for her first day of shooting. Cameraman Leonard Smith, immersed in the business of setups and light placement, glanced briefly at the newcomer and said, "Honey, would you mind going back to the makeup man to have him remove part of your makeup? You have on too much mascara and eye pencil." There was a small pause followed by a small voice. "It isn't makeup. It's me!" Smith then took a stunned second look, the first of many cameramen who would do so to assure themselves that what they were seeing was actually there. And Elizabeth made ready for her first scene, in which, as the little Priscilla, she comes out to see the new collie purchased by her grandfather.

The opening scenes of the film have firmly established Lassie's beauty and intelligence and her strong affection for Roddy. Every afternoon she trots across town, and shopkeepers affectionately observe her and set their watches, because at four o'clock she is always on hand to greet Roddy when he gets out of school. But this is Depression England, and as the family's only negotiable commodity to ease their poverty, she is sold to the Duke of Rudling. She makes her first escape by digging under the kennel fence. The second time she simply vaults over it to freedom.

Elizabeth is on hand when the dog is returned for the second time, and has a chat with Roddy about how she can help Lassie. In her third scene, she passes on Roddy's tips about grooming to the surly trainer. Next she returns to find Lassie chained and gets the Duke to order the trainer to untie her and give her exercise. The Duke and his granddaughter then go on holiday in Scotland, taking Lassie with them. After a hassle with the trainer in the woods, Lassie breaks free of him. In this scene, it is Elizabeth who opens the gates to the estate, thus allowing Lassie to escape. "She's going south, Grandfather! She's going toward Yorkshire!" It is a thrilling moment as Lassie makes her way out to the Scottish coast and the music rises to a crescendo, underlining the vivid beauty of the crash of spray onto the rocks.

Thereafter, Lassie has her various adventures—with Dame May Whitty, Edmund Gwenn, homicidal sheepherders, et al.—and Elizabeth finally shows up at the Carraclough cottage with her grandfather. Lassie has made it back and Roddy's parents are hiding her. Elizabeth conspires with Nigel Bruce to conceal their knowledge that the bedraggled wreck before them is actually Lassie. The last scenes, wherein Lassie limps through town as shopkeepers once again affectionately observe her, leading up to her reunion with Roddy at school, are enough to squeeze tears out of Scrooge. A final shot has Elizabeth and Roddy bicycling happily together, with Lassie, fully restored to vigorous health, running joyously behind them.

The film is drenched in gorgeous Technicolor, and on this occasion, MGM's typical marshmallow music works just fine. So does everything and everyone else. Lassie is totally remarkable, and her ability to feign injury and then limp because of it is astonishing. Donald Crisp and Elsa Lanchester are important for establishing the proper Yorkshire atmosphere, and they work hard and well. Essentially, the film is a beautiful fairy tale, and all hands worked with serious professionalism to bring it off. It was good experience for Elizabeth because, fifteen months later, she would be making another fairy tale, and this one she would have to carry on her own small shoulders.

The reviews of *Lassie Come Home* were excellent. Samples: "Heartwarming . . . a remarkable picture . . . moving sincerity . . . touching . . . the cast without exception is outstanding . . . Elizabeth Taylor looks like a comer." (Hollywood *Reporter*)

"The most enchanting picture to come out of Hollywood in many a day . . . a magnificent job . . . little Elizabeth Taylor is lovely." (Los Angeles *Herald-Examiner*)

Lassie Come Home would launch two sequels, a career for its remarkable star, and a long-running TV series acquainting a new generation of children with canine intelligence and fidelity. Not bad for a "B" film hatched in the low-budget unit at MGM. Pleased with it and with Elizabeth Taylor, MGM made ready to further utilize her services in two highly touted films of 1944. For the first, *Jane Eyre*, she was loaned to 20th Century-Fox.

Charlotte Brontë's heavy-breathing tale of the tortuous relationship between governess Jane Eyre and her mysterious employer, Edward Rochester, had been done before and would be done again. George C. Scott and Susannah York recently wandered through it to no particular purpose. David O. Selznick then owned the property, and Aldous Huxley and John Houseman had worked for two years on a script. Joan Fontaine was set for the title role, Robert Stevenson was to direct, and William L. Pereira had worked out a production design. Selznick then unaccountably sold the whole package to Fox. The publicity releases subsequently sent out by Harry Brand are an amusing example of how big pictures were sold in the Golden Era.

According to Brand, "Stevenson waited eight impatient years for the opportunity of directing *Jane Eyre*." According to Stevenson, "It is my firm conviction that Welles is the only actor on either side of the Atlantic who could successfully essay the role of Edward Rochester."

Be all that as it may (and never was), Selznick's first choice was Ronald Colman. When Colman proved to be unavailable, Selznick would then have reteamed his *Rebecca* costars, presuming that Laurence Olivier, then in England preparing *Henry*

V, would have preferred to let all that go and return to Hollywood in the middle of World War II. Which, of course, he would not. Orson Welles had played Rochester on five separate occasions on Mercury Theater radio adaptations and the publicity department had him solemnly asserting that "*Jane Eyre* is the most fascinating and challenging piece of dramatic novelwriting that it has been my privilege to read and study."

Miss Fontaine was encouraged to report that "no role has inspired me as has this of Jane Eyre"—doubtless said, if at all, between tightly clenched teeth at the thought of taking second billing in a film which was, after all, entitled *Jane Eyre*. Finally, "Two extremely artful youngsters, Margaret O'Brien, bright star of *Journey for Margaret*, and Peggy Ann Garner, the wistful refugee star of *The Pied Piper*, have assumed key roles." There was also a third "artful youngster," unheralded and unbilled.

Jane Eyre was in production from February through April 1943, and what finally emerged is respectable, but certainly not in the class of other Victorian goodies such as *Wuthering Heights, Great Expectations* or *Oliver Twist*. Part of the problem lies in the basic situation. Unless one is addicted to the sigh-and-suffer school of passionate encounters, unrequited and/or unconsummated love is a drag, both on screen and off.

Elizabeth played Helen Burns, a lovely and generous classmate of the young Jane Eyre (Peggy Ann Garner) at Lowood School. First she brings a crust of bread to Jane, who is "standing punishment" up on a stool. Then they play together out on the heath, after which she has her beautiful curls cut by sadistic headmaster Henry Daniell. Jane and Helen are then forced to work a punishment tour out in the rain, after which Helen dies of pneumonia. Elizabeth played the role with appropriate sweetness but got no billing for it, a circumstance noted by the Hollywood *Reporter:* "The little girl Jane befriends in school wins a credit which is regrettably omitted."

This leads to an amusing occurrence during occasional theatrical revivals of the film, when whispers of "That's Elizabeth Taylor!" sweep the theater upon her first appearance. On television, there is no problem. In the regular ninety-minute channelchow prints—that is, prints which passed through the hands of local TV station butchers—Elizabeth and Peggy Ann Garner have vanished altogether, and the film begins with the adult Jane Eyre leaving Lowood School. Elizabeth recently got personal proof of this when she hunkered down with her daughters to watch *Jane Eyre* on the tube. She wanted the girls to know this classic story and thought it would be a treat for them to see her when she was much younger than they were. On came Joan Fontaine. "I'll be on in a minute," Elizabeth announced. As time passed the atmosphere got a bit strained. Mother Doesn't Lie is a cardinal truism in the household. Still . . . And since she received no billing credit, there was no proof that she was in it at all. "Maybe it's a flashback," Elizabeth declared uncertainly. "That's it—it must be a flashback." And so on, right up to "The End." (They haven't yet managed to cut out Joan Fontaine, but doubtless someone is working on it.)

Elizabeth returned from her brief stint at Fox to be cast in another prestige production, *The White Cliffs of Dover*, this one to be done on the home lot. Anyone reading two press releases on the subject, put out on the same day, could be forgiven any confusion about who Elizabeth Taylor was, how old she was, and exactly how many films she had made and where. They might also be justified in wondering just who was minding the store at MGM on that particular day.

Under the heading *Child Actress Given 'White Cliffs' Role*, we were informed: "Elizabeth Taylor, 11-year-old child player who made her film debut in *Lassie Come Home* at Metro-Goldwyn-Mayer and was given a contract as a result of excellent work in this film, has been given her second assignment by the studio." Subsequently, under the heading *Moppet Thespian Cast in White Cliffs of Dover*, there was an announcement about "9-year-old Elizabeth Taylor" and another error was embroidered thus: "Her movie debut was in a similar role in *Lassie Comes* (sic) *Home*."

The White Cliffs of Dover was in production four months, and proved to be a long (125 minutes) beautifully mounted sermon on the virtues of Anglo-American unity which was called everything from "a gorgeous emotional experience" to "a dull, slow, tedious exhibit." Irene Dunne, however, got glowing reviews. It was the general consensus that she had given the best performance of her career as an American girl who marries a titled Briton on the eve of World War I, loses him in the war, raises their son, comes to love England between the wars, and then loses the son in World War II.

In *White Cliffs*, Roddy McDowall played Miss Dunne's son as a young boy, and Elizabeth's part as Betsy, the neighbor girl, was simply to love Roddy. She simpers coyly at him in one scene, and bids him an emotional goodbye as he supposedly sets off to America in another. There is then a brief glimpse of

Roddy and Elizabeth up on a hill before they are suddenly and magically transformed into Peter Lawford and June Lockhart.

Elizabeth's film career now consisted of four minor roles, and the Metro publicity department could be forgiven for fudging the basic facts of her existence because they had no overwhelming reason to take any undue note of it. Film five lay just over the horizon, however, and after its seven months of arduous production were over, and the result went into the theaters, that situation was changed for good and all. From a vantage point of thirty years, Elizabeth looks back on this particular film, and everything connected with the making of it, with a combination of love and pride that render it unique in her memory to this day.

❦ 3 ❦

National Velvet was a 1935 bestseller by Enid Bagnold which told a charmingly implausible tale of how a butcher's little daughter in a rural English village won a horse called "The Pi" (short for "pirate") in a raffle. Teaming up with a jockey down on his luck, she trains him to run in England's Grand National Steeplechase, and eventually rides him to victory herself.

Pandro S. Berman was then producing at RKO, and he immediately saw it as a vehicle for Katharine Hepburn. Before he could persuade the studio to buy it, Paramount snatched the rights. Casting difficulties prompted Paramount to sell the rights to MGM in 1937, and MGM got as far as thinking out loud about Margaret Sullavan as Velvet and Spencer Tracy as her father. Could Berman have sold Metro on the idea of Hepburn, we might have had a *National Velvet* with Spencer Tracy playing Katharine Hepburn's father. The property was shelved, however, and the beginning of the Tracy-Hepburn partnership put off to a more appropriate occasion five years later.

In 1941, Berman moved to MGM as a producer and was at last united with the property which had never been far from his thoughts. Casting the all-important role of Velvet Brown still bedeviled the best minds at the studio and frustrated any attempt at production. And small wonder. The actress who would play her had to be a child genuinely fond of horses and an expert horsewoman, because many of the shots could not be faked. She should also have an English accent or be able to counterfeit it convincingly. Nor could her other acting talents be merely passable. She must possess the star power necessary to carry the film, because chiefly on her would rest the burden of seeing to it that audiences left the theaters in a state of glowing fulfillment, not snickering at a silly story about a little girl who was around the bend for horses.

An incident during the shooting of *Lassie Come Home* had earlier alerted the studio to Elizabeth's possibilities. During a scene, later deleted from the finished film, Elizabeth was to ride her horse to a specified mark, dismount, and exchange dialogue with Nigel Bruce. Rehearsals went well, but when a take was called, the horse shied from a reflector now casting several thousand watts of light at him, bolted and reared high in the air. To the wonder of all present, Elizabeth clung on to him, patted and soothed him, rode to the appointed mark, and dismounted to get on with the scene. That horse later got some of his own back when he put another notch on Elizabeth's record by stepping on her foot during the last day of shooting. Even then, she continued to the end of the scene. By then, her foot had swollen so badly her boot had to be cut off. Metro executives were impressed. The child had spunk, and she obviously knew a lot about horses. To further her knowledge, she was sent by MGM to a Mrs. Leo Dupee for riding lessons.

Elizabeth knew very well what this was all about. She had read *National Velvet* and so passionate was her identification with Velvet Brown that she was determined from the first that the role would be hers. After all, she had jumped horses without a saddle since she was three, she had lived in England for the first seven years of her life, and had utilized an English accent in her last three films. But it was not to be that easy. She marched resolutely in to see Pandro Berman about the matter and met with initial frustration.

Elizabeth marshaled all her arguments—she was "going on twelve," she loved horses and loved to ride them, she had the English accent. Berman sadly shook his head.

"Sorry, honey, but you're just too short."

To cushion the blow for what was obviously a grievously disappointed little girl, he stood her in the doorway and put a pencil mark on the wall to mark her height.

"No one would ever believe that you could get in through the jockey's weighing room. You look like a child. You need at least three more inches."

"Well, I'll grow," replied Elizabeth.

"Three inches in three months? That's when we start."

"I'll grow," she replied firmly.

Then began a dedicated regimen of stuffing herself daily with hamburgers, eggs, hash browns, and pancakes for breakfast; of steak dinners; of swimming and of other exercising; of riding an hour and a half before school each day to sharpen her already considerable skills on horseback. To the green chintz drapes and the flowered green chintz bedspread on her double bed, and the prints of ballet dancers on her bedroom wall, were now added saddles and bridles of every description. The saddles were draped on the chairs and the bridles hung from the wall lamps. Elizabeth also began a collection of miniature horses—made of china, glass, wood, and metal—which eventually added up to twenty-one separate horses of varying sizes.

"It isn't respectable to keep so many animals in one house," Sara jokingly told her daughter. "We need a ranch." But Elizabeth was pursuing her vision and her dream with unbounded determination. She literally willed it to be, and it was. When the three months were up, she returned to Pandro Berman's office, stood up against the old mark on the wall, and proudly presented him with the three inches. The part was hers, in the first of five films they would work on together. Their relationship would fluctuate through the years, terminating in the nightmare that was the making of *Butterfield 8*, but Berman never underestimated her will to succeed at that on which she had set her heart. He had just been given a vivid personal demonstration. Lest he forget it, he kept that mark on the wall in his office at MGM, and it remained there until he left the studio twenty years later.

National Velvet went into production on February 4, 1944, under the direction of Clarence Brown, for whom Elizabeth had worked briefly in *The White Cliffs of Dover*. Mickey Rooney was engaged for the starring role of Mi Taylor, the jockey who leaves racing after an accident and is tramping the roads of England and comes to the outskirts of Sewels, which is where Velvet first meets him. Donald Crisp and Anne Revere were to play Velvet's parents, Angela Lansbury and Juanita Quigley her sisters Edwina and Malvolia ("Mally"), and six-year-old Jack "Butch" Jenkins her little brother Donald. There was a nice part for Reginald Owen as the irate owner of "The Pi" who raffles him off, and a good bit for Arthur Treacher in the climactic steeplechase scenes. There was no role for Roddy

McDowall in this one, but Roddy's sister Virginia had a bit as one of Velvet's schoolmates.

To play "The Pi" MGM secured the services of a gorgeous gelding named King Charles, a strong-willed grandson of Man o' War, who came to the studio with the reputation of having thrown Sir Anthony Eden three times before Sir Anthony apparently decided that enough was enough. Everyone at Metro gave him a wide, respectful berth—everyone but Elizabeth. Australian jockey Snowy Baker had been hired by MGM to train Elizabeth for the steeplechase scenes as well as to double for her in the most hazardous shots. They worked out together at the Riviera Country Club. It was there Elizabeth first made the acquaintance of the notorious King Charles, and she did it initially by talking gently to him through the opening high up on the wall of his stall, through which his hay was pitched down to him. Ultimately she lowered herself down onto his back, and after a few moments of fright and friskiness, King Charles decided that he had found a friend. This was a singular mark of favor and everyone else was well advised to keep his distance.

"That horse was really a lunatic," Elizabeth recalled. "Just for the hell of it, he once jumped over an automobile." But Elizabeth he followed around the lot like a dog, and she could jump him bareback six feet with no problems at all. Between takes she talked to him and nuzzled him, her tiny head pressed close to his huge one. This all got to be too much for Mickey Rooney, who had dubbed his petite costar "Mona Lizzy" and who was genuinely fond of her.

"Keep away from that horse's head. That horse is a killer. He'll eat you," Rooney would say. "Oh, God, you never can tell kids anything." After which he would stalk away muttering. Sara grew a bit apprehensive and reminded Elizabeth that once she'd been nuzzling King Charles and he had chewed the front of her blouse. Elizabeth answered that with irrefutable logic. "If he'd wanted to, he could have taken my tummy."

If Clarence Brown had any worries about the matter, they were more than offset by the daily rushes, where the off-camera relationship was vividly up there on the screen where it counted. What Brown and other Metro executives worried about was that, with Elizabeth riding and jumping in every spare moment, something would happen to her before they got the film into the can. Accordingly, she was ordered to restrict her riding only to what was necessary for actual scenes in the film. "I was doing forty jumps a day," she proudly told a reporter, "when the studio grounded me."

Clarence Brown was beginning to be asked questions about his little star-to-be. "There's something behind her eyes that you can't quite fathom," he told his questioners. "Something Garbo had." This was no mere persiflage: Brown was Garbo's favorite director and guided her through seven films. Of Elizabeth's talent generally? "I really hate to call her an actress. She's much too natural for that." This was a fact that Mickey Rooney unexpectedly encountered when, in a spirit of generous good fellowship, he tried to help Elizabeth with a heavy emotional scene.

The scene was the one in which Mi and Velvet discover "The Pi" is seriously ill, and Velvet naturally cries at the prospect of what may happen to her beloved horse. (This was also the scene, incidentally, during the preparation for which King Charles took a hunk out of the trainer, who was teaching him to play dead.) As Elizabeth remembered it:

"Mickey put his arm around me and said, 'Honey, you know in this scene you have to cry.' And I said, 'Yes, Mickey, I know.' 'Well,' he said, 'you should think that your father is dying and your mother has to wash clothes for a living, and your little brother is out selling newspapers on the street and he doesn't have shoes and he's cold and shivering, and your little dog was run over.'"

Elizabeth regarded him for a long moment, and then the picture of Francis expiring upstairs, Sara slaving over the neighborhood wash downstairs, and poor Howard running barefoot through Beverly Hills selling newspapers got to her, and she began to giggle. The more she tried to suppress the giggles, the worse they became, until they approximated a mild case of hysterics. Doubtless puzzled at such an unexpected reception of his good intentions, Mickey Rooney carefully kept any further acting tips to himself. When it came time to do the scene, Elizabeth was Velvet, and her magnificent horse was ill and in danger of death, and she wept at the prospect—period.

Through the years Elizabeth has listened to endless conversations about the art of acting. Her personal observations of different systems at work before the camera are unusually extensive. She twice worked with Spencer Tracy, still generally considered to be the finest screen actor the medium has yet produced. On the other end of the scale, four of the foremost exponents of the Stanislavski System, and the particular application of it called The Method, have been her costars: Montgomery Clift, Marlon Brando, James Dean, and Paul Newman. There have been studio-trained costars such as Robert Taylor, Van Johnson, and Rock Hudson, and brilliant mavericks such as Rex Harrison, Peter Ustinov, and Alec Guinness. Her husband, of course, is a superb example of classical training in the British tradition, and he had acquired quite a fund of information about other acting systems as well.

Elizabeth has heard about them all, has seen them all at work with varying degrees of success, and has always carefully refrained from being exclusively identified with any of them. She has never had an acting lesson per se, a suspicious circumstance in a country which continues to expound the preposterous proposition that anything in this world can be shoved between the covers of a textbook and taught in a classroom. After all, the most important part of an actor's job is to communicate a sense of believability about whatever it is he is doing or saying, and Elizabeth has possessed this quality from the first. She has prefaced several interviews on the subject with "Don't ask *me* about acting," and this has often been taken to mean "I don't know enough about it to talk about it," which was not what was meant at all. A better translation would be "I don't talk about it, I do it." When pressed she is wont to remark, "I sweat real sweat and I shake real shakes," and leaves theorizing to others.

Elizabeth's main problem through the years has been one common to every other film actor or actress with an extensive career: bad scripts. To the "feast or famine" rule previously laid down about the nature of a motion picture career may now be added a corollary: during the "feast" part, much of the menu is garbage. One hears the echo of Charles Boyer's comment upon the retirement of Greta Garbo after *Two-Faced Woman:* "She shouldn't have let one bad picture upset her. Most of us have had many bad pictures." Amen.

There are several ways to deal with a bad script. First, one can refuse it outright, but in the Golden Era this usually meant contract suspension and subsequent financial problems, and Elizabeth could not safely avail herself of this option until she married Mike Todd.

Alternatively one can do one's best and hope that critical opinion is to the effect that "poor so-and-so struggled valiantly with inferior material," and one's professional reputation comes through unscathed. There is a catch to this, however. If an actor works too hard at it, he falls into the trap of bringing up the full arsenal of equipment for use with situations and dialogue that are too frail to support it—"swatting flies with sofas," as the French say. The actor thus looks bad and is pronounced guilty of overacting.

Many stars have possessed a peculiar kind of personal magnetism and acute intelligence which projects so strongly that they have been able not only to rise above inferior material but almost to stand apart from it.

Elizabeth's method of survival during the period when, as she put it, she was "walking around like Dracula's ghost in glamorized 'B' movies," was to walk through and take the money. Her intelligence was neither so lacking nor her acting ambitions so fierce that either would permit her to seriously apply herself to obvious drivel. But when the role and the script were right, the power and the talent would be equal to it. Such a role was Velvet Brown and such a script was *National Velvet*. Clarence Brown wrapped *National Velvet* in October 1944, and what he and Pandro Berman had achieved is still such a beautiful children's classic that one would like to chew out whoever at MGM eventually threw it into the grab bag for TV sale, instead of exempting it, like *The Wizard of Oz*, for special annual showings.

It begins deceptively. The fairy-tale Technicolor, the syrupy score, the whole look of it is faintly quaint, not to say patronizing, particularly with regard to a startlingly beefy Angela Lansbury's fierce yen for a local lad. One can almost see the eventual advertising campaign: "See Bumpkins Burn! See Yokels Yearn!" Velvet meets Mi the jockey at the village crossroads and brings him home to dinner, where we first meet the family and learn about them.

Velvet is immediately established as mad about horses, Edwina has her yen for boys, Mally has her canary, little Donald carries his insect collection in a bottle slung from his neck, Mother is unsentimentally sensible, and Father is repeatedly given to taking firm stands and then backing off them, much in the manner of Woodrow Wilson, who, as one wag put it, "began by shaking his fist and ended by shaking his finger." As these people go about their various businesses, and interact with each other, quaintness gives way to such well-structured reality that one occasionally finds oneself thinking of the Brown family and what they are up to days after viewing the film.

Mi is given a job in the family butcher shop, and helps Velvet to achieve her impossible dream: the training of "The Pi" to run in the Grand National. In an exquisite scene, her mother tells Velvet, "I too believe that everyone should have the chance at a breathtaking piece of folly at least once. Your dream has come early. But remember, Velvet, it'll have to last you all the rest of your life." So saying, she gives her daughter the hundred gold sovereigns she had won years ago for swimming the English Channel, and the money goes for "The Pi's" entry fee.

In the final scenes, the jockey previously chosen proves unsuitable, and Velvet elects to masquerade as a boy and ride "The Pi" herself. In some of the most thrilling horse-racing footage ever shot (thirty hazardous jumps over four miles of rugged track), Velvet rides to victory but falls from the saddle just as "The Pi" crosses the line. The doctor in the dispensary discovers her sex and she is disqualified. But she has achieved her dream and Mi's faith in himself has been restored. The film ends as it begins: Mi is once again on the road, and Velvet rides out to him for a last goodbye.

The finest performances in the film are those of Elizabeth Taylor and Anne Revere, and the balance alternates skillfully between Elizabeth's rapturous enthusiasms and Miss Revere's brusque humanity. "You're all lighted up!" Velvet is repeatedly told, and Elizabeth moves through all the twists and turns of her star part with a naturalness and with a radiant incandescence that are unforgettable. Mickey Rooney skillfully portrays a man who pictures himself as a loser, and Donald Crisp, in a part that could have been really foolish, manages to steer clear of total incompetence and buffoonery. MGM gave *National Velvet* a general release in February 1945, amid a cascade of unanimous critical acclaim.

Anne Revere subsequently captured the Oscar as 1945's Best Supporting Actress. Another Oscar went to Robert J. Kern for his editing. The honorary awarding of occasional Juvenile Oscars was initiated in 1934, and the list of recipients ran from Shirley Temple through Deanna Durbin, Mickey Rooney, Judy Garland, and up to the most recent winner, Margaret O'Brien (for *Meet Me in St. Louis*). Certain it is that Elizabeth was considered for the Award, but 1945 also witnessed another superb performance by a juvenile which was given, ironically, by Elizabeth's old acquaintance in *Jane Eyre*. The 1945 Juvenile Oscar went to Peggy Ann Garner for her memorable Francie in *A Tree Grows in Brooklyn*. An Oscar for Elizabeth was still fifteen years away, but stardom was now hers in full measure.

In the spirit of Merry Christmas and Happy New Year, MGM prereleased *National Velvet* to New York's Radio City Music Hall for its 1944–45 holiday attraction. Elizabeth personally had a happy holiday when producer Joe Pasternak stopped by her table in the commissary and asked her what she wanted for Christmas. "A horse, Mr. Pasternak," she replied, and was flabbergasted when he called to tell her to come and pick it up. Which is how Prince Charming—he of the chestnut coat, black mane and tail, three white socks, and a white star on his forehead—made his way into the Taylor ménage.

A further surprise was hers two months later on the occasion of her thirteenth birthday. MGM presented her with King Charles. Elizabeth said, "Jeepers!" four times and burst into grateful tears. After a lifetime of sitting stoically through numerous Hollywood tribal rites, Metro executive Benny Thau called that the most sincere and eloquent speech of acceptance he ever heard. This was in the same month that *National Velvet* went into its general release, and audiences everywhere watched Donald Crisp gaze affectionately at his daughter in the last reel as he delivered his final line to Anne Revere: "That girl's got something." Millions of moviegoers were now in happy agreement with him.

❧ 4 ❧

The studio at which Elizabeth Taylor had now achieved stardom not only boasted of "more stars than there are in the heavens," but also housed a company of professional craftsmen in the various cinema arts which had no equal, and the like of which may never be seen again. The real tragedy of the disappearance of the "star system" and the current unsettled state in which Hollywood finds itself is the dissolution of this silent army of Metro craftsmen, and others like them at other studios, whose skills were honed to a fine edge by years of experience and expertise, and who jointly comprised the greatest single pool of artistic talent on earth. As many as eighteen films were shot at Culver City at one time, and the sound stages, labs, and cutting rooms hummed with the activity.

Careers were multimillion-dollar investments and they were the business of the entire studio and everyone in it. The Story Department searched everywhere for particular properties for particular stars, and a gaggle of scriptwriters packed into offices and cubbyholes in the Writers Building hunched over typewriters pounding out the various screenplays. If you were a star at Metro, cameramen had looked at you from every conceivable angle, Wardrobe studied every line of your body, Makeup knew every pore in your face, and Sound was acquainted with every decibel of your voice. In Publicity, Howard Strickling and his staff devoted themselves to star-building and star-preserving via proper promotion in the press and other communications media, in personal appearances, and in friendly but firm tips about your private life and how it could best conform to the studio's image of you. All involved were totally concentrated on discovering what it was about you that drew customers to the box office. Once the formula was arrived at, you would be merchandised in endless rehashes of tried-and-true plots and situations. What this procedure did to whatever talent you might possess was secondary. Your primary function was to make money for the studio.

"The star system was a golden, studio-protected cocoon," Elizabeth remarked almost twenty years later. "The people in it never smelled real life. Today you have to *act*. Before, you were promoted into a box office draw and *only* then, as a star, were you given even the chance to grow in acting. It was a vicious, self-protective, and unadventurous circle."

Ultimately it would all disintegrate under the hammerblows of antitrust suits, television, foreign competition, domestic economics, and a demand for reality not obtainable exclusively in Hollywood. In the mid-40s, however, the system had grown fat and fabulously wealthy from feeding an entertainment-hungry America during the war years, and it was operating at its peak.

After everyone involved in the making of a film had done his particular job, extensive and expensive advertising campaigns were launched to guarantee that MGM films, which were then booked into the vast theater chains of Loew's, Inc., returned top grosses, thus furthering the careers of their stars. Nor was any feature permitted to leave the studio before the top brass had seen it and pronounced it fit to make the trip and be preceded by the proud roar of Metro's trademark, Leo the Lion. Features found wanting were shelved for a while and then reviewed for appropriate action, or were returned immediately for recutting or for the shooting of additional scenes, or were turned over to other directors to see what they could do with them. Given the conditions of mass production in such an uncertain business, not every film could be a big winner, but the studio worked unceasingly to catch big losers before they escaped. In extreme cases, when salvage was deemed impossible, features were released for a quick playoff in multiple situations where they would hopefully recoup their negative costs. Then their disastrous names would be heard no more—not until they later popped up on TV to haunt their makers. Each star had at least a couple of these clinkers, and in the twenty-one films she made under contract, Elizabeth was to have four of them.

Louis Burt Mayer was the founding father of this enterprise in 1924, and he fed it with the genius of such production giants as Irving Thalberg, David Selznick, and Sidney Franklin; such ace directors as George Cukor, Clarence Brown, Robert Z. Leonard, W. S. "Woody" Van Dyke, and Victor Fleming; such cinematographers as Joseph Ruttenberg, Harold Rosson, and William Daniels; such talents as Cedric Gibbons, Urie McCleary, and Edwin B. Willis in Art Direction and Set Decoration; Adrian, Irene, and Helen Rose in Wardrobe; and Douglas Shearer in the Sound Department. Ultimately, what made the Metro factory more impressive than its rivals was a collection of stars which, like the studio craftsmen, had no equal, and whose like will most certainly never be seen again.

In 1943, the year of Elizabeth's first film for MGM, Mayer and six rows of stars sat for the famous *Life* portrait. In the center of the front row sat L.B., flanked by Katharine Hepburn (triumphantly attired in slacks) and Greer Garson. From left to right were James Stewart, Margaret Sullavan, Lucille Ball, Hedy Lamarr, Irene Dunne, Susan Peters, Ginny Simms, and Lionel Barrymore. Directly behind this phalanx were such luminaries as Red Skelton, Mickey Rooney, William Powell, Spencer Tracy, Walter Pidgeon, Robert Taylor, and Gene Kelly. Spotted throughout the remaining rows were George Murphy, Donna Reed, Van Johnson, Marjorie Main, Esther Williams, Mary Astor, Bert Lahr, June Allyson, Dame May Whitty, Spring Byington, Gladys Cooper, and Desi Arnaz. Missing from the studio that day were Clark Gable, Lana Turner, Ava Gardner, Judy Garland, Robert Young, Ann Sothern, Charles Laughton, Kathryn Grayson, Van Heflin, Lena Horne, Frank Morgan, Margaret O'Brien, Herbert Marshall, Robert Montgomery, Melvyn Douglas, Peter Lawford, and Lew Ayres. Also missing were Jeanette MacDonald and Nelson Eddy, recently departed after nine memorable years at Metro; Norma Shearer and Greta Garbo, both of whom had recently retired; Rosalind Russell and Myrna Loy who had left the studio to freelance; and Joan Crawford, on her way to resurrection at Warner Bros. after eighteen years at MGM. Shortly to arrive on the scene were Fred Astaire, Frank Sinatra, Jane Powell, Angela Lansbury, and Ann Miller.

Elizabeth became a member of this glamorous family when it

was at the zenith of its power and popularity, and she stayed long enough to see all of its members leave it, with ruin and desolation stalking the house, until the master suite was hers alone and the other rooms were empty and echoing. Altogether, her contractual association with Metro-Goldwyn-Mayer was to span seventeen and a half years, from *Lassie Come Home* in September 1942 to the finish of *Butterfield 8* in the spring of 1960.

Like the movie fan she was, and pretty much remains to this day, Elizabeth was thrilled to be in such exciting company, to see them walking to and fro on the lot, to meet them in the commissary at lunch. Proximity to Clark Gable never lessened his charm for her, not a bit, but unfortunately they would work together only as themselves in a cameo scene for something forgettable called *Callaway Went Thataway*. She initially took to carrying her autograph book into the commissary, gathering signatures of the stars, until Katharine Hepburn's ill-concealed impatience at such a request one day decided her against doing it anymore.

Meanwhile, her life at the studio had begun to settle into routine. She arrived at nine in the morning, ready for the three hours of class required by law. The schoolroom was located in Thalberg's former bungalow on the lot which Elizabeth would later refer to sardonically as "MGM University." Her personal tutor-teacher was Mrs. Birdina Anderson. After a morning spent with "Andy," as she was called, there would be lunch at noon in the commissary. Elizabeth next went on to singing and dancing lessons and was home usually around three. This routine prevailed, when she was not before the cameras, from September 1944 until June 1945, when MGM announced her for a property first titled *Hold High the Torch*, then *Blue Sierra*, and then finally *Courage of Lassie*.

Courage was to begin with a three-month location up in the beautiful Lake Chelan country in Washington State starting in late August. Accordingly the Taylor family elected to go to Howard Young's summer place in Wisconsin for a July vacation. It was there that Howard Young listened to his niece's happy recitation of her adventures with her animals, and, noting her growing beauty, reportedly gave her a piece of advice that was to prove prophetic. "As long as you love horses and chipmunks," he told her, "you're safe." The Taylors were passing through Chicago en route to Hollywood when V-J Day was proclaimed, ending World War II. The family went into a nearby church to quietly give thanks, and emerged among joyous throngs on Michigan Boulevard, who suddenly realized that little Velvet Brown was in their midst. V-J Day temporarily took a back seat while Elizabeth signed a clutch of autographs. After which the family proceeded to Los Angeles, and Sara and Elizabeth headed north to Washington and *Courage of Lassie*.

Courage of Lassie could well be subtitled "A Children's Picture Adults Weren't Ashamed to See Made by People Who Knew What They Were Doing." That they *had* to know what they were doing is clear when one examines the plot they had to work with.

The film begins with a lengthy sequence, actually a self-contained forest idyl, which managed to work in most of the animal acts. We see a wild but friendly collie puppy shying from a cougar, trying to befriend a skunk (which sprays him), playing with a fox, and then with a bear by a stream. The bear throws a fish out of the water for himself, and the puppy makes off with it. A coyote, an owl, and an eagle are also prominent in these proceedings. There are no humans at all for the film's first ten minutes, and it is this sequence which caused many reviewers to compare the film to MGM's all-time nature classic, *Sequoia*.

A coyote chases the puppy into the river, where he floats downstream on a makeshift raft, and emerges in the vicinity of Elizabeth, who is sunning herself on a partly submerged log. The puppy steals her pants and boots and she gives chase and spies him playing with a fawn and a raven. He gives her the slip momentarily, only to be heard in the bushes by two neighborhood boys, who mistakenly shoot him.

Elizabeth rushes him back home and, with friendly neighbor Frank Morgan's help, nurses him back to health and names him Bill. The puppy grows up, in the process becoming a crack sheepdog (and also becoming Lassie). By himself on a subsequent run across the road with the sheep, Bill is struck by a truck and immediately taken off to the vet's. A distraught Elizabeth goes out looking for him and almost drowns in a storm.

At the vet's, the unknown dog is taken by a Quartermaster Corps representative and shipped off for training. Sergeant Tom Drake gets him and christens him Duke. There is an interesting sequence of dogs going over an obstacle course. After which we move to the Aleutian Islands, for a wartime sequence of a night patrol under mortar fire. The platoon is surrounded by the enemy, and Bill-Duke-Lassie is sent back through enemy lines with a message for reinforcements. He crawls through swamp grass, goes down a sheer mountainside all the while being sprayed with shrapnel, fords a river, carefully picks his way through a minefield covered with mud, and finally collapses with fatigue and wounds. The message he was bringing has been shot away. Drake gets him back on his feet, and in a display of bald animal guts, Bill leads the rescue team to the trapped unit—and then cracks up with battle fatigue. (Anyone who ever wondered about star billing for a dog is urged to see this particular one going through this incredible sequence.)

Shipped to Seattle for convalescence, Bill escapes from the train taking him to the convalescent center, and we begin another *Lassie Come Home* sequence. The shell-shocked Bill becomes a killer dog, steals a haunch of venison, breaks into sheeppens, and finally makes it back to Elizabeth pursued by three angry ranchers. Elizabeth follows him into a cave to hide him from the hunters. He snaps at her, knocking her unconscious. This act restores him to health, as he suddenly realizes who she is. The hunters then take the "mad dog" to court. As Lassie sits muzzled there, Frank Morgan pleads for him in the name of all veterans, and he is acquitted. The End.

Frank Morgan amassed some luscious credits during a memorable career, which included *Bombshell, The Great Ziegfeld, The Wizard of Oz, The Mortal Storm,* and *The Human Comedy.* But he never did a finer single piece of acting than in the final courtroom sequence. Like his entire work throughout the film, it is simple—no tricks—and all the more effective for it. Elizabeth, playing mostly in a shirt and jeans which failed to hide her ripening figure, neatly complemented Morgan's work. With the exceptions of Richard Burton and Montgomery Clift, she never loved a costar more convincingly than she did Lassie, granting the fact that asking Elizabeth to love an animal is like asking water to run downhill.

In the early scenes, the combination of Elizabeth and Lassie and that cottony MGM music and all the breathtaking scenery gorgeously photographed makes for a lush experience. The melodramatics in the Aleutians are something of a strain, but overall the film is wonderfully produced with a sure touch. MGM sent it out in November 1946, to the general opinion that it was easily the superior of *Lassie Come Home*'s immediate sequel, *Son of Lassie.*

It was while awaiting word on what MGM had next for her to do that Elizabeth had a fierce run-in with Louis B. Mayer. That worthy combined a passion for horses, politics, and certain of his actresses (Jeanette MacDonald and Ginny Simms, to name two), with a gift for manipulation through his own considerable acting talents that was the wonder of all who saw it. "I am your father and whenever you're in trouble and whenever you need me, come to me," Elizabeth remembers him saying. "You are all my children and I am your father." Which puts one in mind of the time Robert Taylor, after lengthy agony over the matter, finally screwed up his courage and went in to ask L.B. for a raise. He got the full treatment. "Well, did you get the raise?" a friend asked him. "No," Taylor rejoined brightly. "But I got a father!"

Mayer had also a ruthless drive, executive wizardry, vindictive traits, and a volatile temper which were the terror of those unequipped to deal with them. He had punched more than one producer on the lot, and one memorable night at the Cocoanut Grove, John Gilbert was making chic cocktail conversation and idly remarked that he was pretty sure his own mother had been a whore. Mayer floored him on the spot.

"He was a man of violent reactions," Bosley Crowther wrote. "His mind was stubborn, his patience was short, and his emotional reflexes were unpredictable to a bewildering and terrifying degree." Elizabeth was about to get a vivid personal demonstration—and to give as good as she got. Nor have the mists of time obscured or otherwise softened her own vivid personal memory of Mayer one whit.

"I thought he was a beast. He was inhuman," she recalled recently. "He used his power over people to such a degree that he became not a man but an instrument of power. He had no scruples and he didn't care who he cut down or who he hurt. He never hurt me because . . . I don't know . . . maybe I was too young."

Particularly stupefying to Elizabeth was Mayer's annual studio birthday party. "There we all were, gathered around him. We all had to pay homage to this man who was obviously slightly crazy." One of the happiest moments of her young life occurred the year Perry Como was the featured sycophant. "He got up and sang, 'Happy Birthday to You/Happy Birthday to You/Happy Birthday, Dear L.B./Happy Birthday, _____ YOU!'" And what happened? "He was blackballed from every studio in Hollywood." Movie buffs who still think that such forgettables as *Doll Face* and *If I'm Lucky* downed Perry Como's budding movie career now know better.

On the particular occasion of Elizabeth's confrontation with L.B., she and Sara had read that Metro had purchased something about a little English cockney girl called *Introduction to Sally* with Elizabeth in mind. So, having finally secured an appointment, they went in to ask "our father" about what Elizabeth would have to do to prepare for it. "His office was like Mussolini's. His desk was way, way at the end. You had to walk what seemed like a mile over this white carpet up to this white oak desk. And it was terrifying."

Sara put the opening question and never got any further. "How dare you come into my office and tell me how to run my business?" Mayer roared at her. "You and your daughter are nothing. Guttersnipes. I took you from the gutter and I can put you back there." A torrent of profanity and obscenity followed at full flow. "He started to foam—literally *foam*—at the mouth." By then Sara was trembling and on the verge of tears. Elizabeth was on her feet without thinking twice.

"Don't you dare speak to my mother like that!" she hurled at him. "You and your studio can both go to hell!" Then she herself fled the office in tears and ran right into the comforting arms of Richard Hanley, then Mayer's private secretary. Later, after she had regained control, she was advised to go back in and tell Mayer she was sorry. She absolutely refused. She was sorry for having lost her own temper but not for what she said. Her instincts plainly told her that no one on earth had the right to abuse another human being in such a fashion. Mayer did it fairly regularly, but Elizabeth vowed then and there that he would never get another chance to do it to her because she would never again go into that office. Nor did she—not as long as he sat there. Nor did she ever see him or speak to him again.

It is interesting to speculate about what might have resulted later had Mayer, with his idea of stars as public possessions, really locked horns with Elizabeth, with her stubborn insistence on an independent private life. The confrontation might have produced a roar of thunder heard all the way from Culver City to Universal, out in the San Fernando Valley. Fortunately both parties were spared such an encounter. Dore Schary came to the studio on July 1, 1948, and Mayer was thereafter locked in a desperate battle for survival which gave him little time to worry about anything else. On August 31, 1951, the man who founded the studio left it for good.

He did not, in this present instance, fire her or suspend her. What he did was loan her out to Warner Bros. Loanouts for something inferior were occasionally used as a form of punishment. They were supposed to make rebels eager to return to the home lot and more amenable when they got back. Sometimes the treatment backfired, for example, when Clark Gable was loaned to Columbia for a little nothing called *It Happened One Night*, or when Bette Davis was sent off to RKO, supposedly to hang herself in *Of Human Bondage*. This present loanout might have been interpreted as punishment, except for the fact that it was for *Life With Father*, and that Mrs. Clarence Day, the author's widow, had specifically requested Elizabeth for the part.

The film was put into the capable hands of ace Warner director Michael Curtiz, a lusty Hungarian who was Oscared for *Casablanca* and who had a remarkable way with various aspects of Americana (*Angels With Dirty Faces, Santa Fe Trail, Yankee Doodle Dandy, Roughly Speaking, Mildred Pierce,* et al.). William Powell was the unanimous choice for Father, but there were extensive tests for Vinnie, and the part was eagerly sought by a bevy of veteran actresses, including Mary Pickford. Irene Dunne was finally signed for it. Elizabeth was to play Mary, the visiting teenager brought to the Day home by Cousin Cora, played by Zasu Pitts. Jimmy Lydon, the screen's "Henry Aldrich," was given the part of Clarence Jr., whose head and heart are set awhirl by the pretty young visitor.

Warners shot the works to re-create the New York of the 1880s: authentic interiors for the house on Madison Avenue, Delmonico's Restaurant, McCreery's Department Store, Father's office, and an Episcopal church. The studio went to great lengths to get everything just right, for example, the Western Union Museum in New York was prevailed upon to lend an old stock-market ticker under a glass dome for Father's office. And when Powell found it impossible to smoke the steady flow of regular cigars required by the script, a New York firm was commissioned to make special denicotinized cigars and fly them to Hollywood.

Life With Father was in production five months, and what finally emerged on the screen is a handsome entertainment which, nevertheless, as an ultra-careful reproduction of a stage play, tends to be slightly ossified around the edges. The sets, costumes, etc. are perfect to a fault, and the performances and situations tend to be a trifle too set. Also, Irene Dunne is and has been many things on the screen, but a really convincing scatter-brain was never one of them. She simply radiates too much good sense. Myrna Loy would probably have been a better all-around choice, particularly for the zany qualities of Vinnie. But with Powell and Loy again costarring, just the mere thought of what the publicity department at Warners would have had to go through to convince the public that *Life With Father* had somehow not become another *Thin Man* sequel was enough to shoot the idea down before it ever got off the ground.

Life With Father may not be the most accurate representation of what life was really like in America in the Gilded Age, but it is an accurate view of what most Americans fondly *thought* life was like—"for the people who mattered," as they would have put it. Its central concerns and some peripheral matter date it somewhat, for example, whether Baptism is indeed essential for entrance into the Kingdom of Heaven, the yawning gulf between an Episcopalian and a Methodist (doubly nonsensical in an ecumenical age), etc.

Max Steiner's musical score is nostalgic and effective, particularly his use of "Sweet Marie," which leads to one of the most quietly affecting scenes in the film. Father has come home early from the office, and he and Vinnie wind up side by side on the sofa doing an *a capella* duet to "Sweet Marie." Curtiz dollies slowly back from them in a lingering, loving longshot, and it points up the difference in eras just as well as anything. Though always noted for our penchant for speed and hustle, Americans then seemed to prize their quiet moments more highly, and they took better advantage of them: for love, for tenderness, for the deep satisfaction of taking a moment and relaxing with it in pure enjoyment.

As Mary, Elizabeth was asked alternately to bubble with girlish enthusiasm and to palpitate with puppy love, and she is delightful in the part. Her comic high spots come in a duet, with her at the piano and Lydon on violin, in which her heart triumphs over her ear, since what she is feeling overwhelms the screechy sounds she is all-too-plainly hearing. Later, out on the balcony, she rapturously surrenders herself to Lydon, only to be unceremoniously dumped off his lap. Already at fourteen, she was extraordinarily well developed physically, and looks elegant in the period costumes, both sweet and shyly seductive.

Before *Life With Father* was released, Warners resolved a curious billing impasse by decreeing that William Powell would be first-billed on half the prints, and Irene Dunne would get first billing on the remainder. In both cases, Elizabeth was third-billed in smaller type. Skowhegan, Maine, where the whole saga had begun in 1939, was granted the honor of having the world premiere, after which the film was nationally released to great critical and popular acclaim.

"*Life With Father* is more than a movie, folks—it's a memory to be cherished," said the New York *Times*. *Variety* pulled out all the stops: "one of the real motion picture masterpieces of all time . . . one of Hollywood's most magnificent accomplishments." There were solid raves for William Powell, and Elizabeth shared in the general triumph.

"Lovely Elizabeth Taylor as the oldest boy's sweetie is charming and clever," announced the L.A. *Times,* and the Hollywood *Reporter* pronounced the film "a triumph . . . with Elizabeth Taylor particularly appealing . . . an example of Hollywood craftsmanship at its very finest." And *Time* made probably the most astute comment when it noted: "*Father* was put on film when the play was already an enormous success. It is filmed like a success; it has the glitter, the good humor, and the rather beefy adroitness of a success. The chances are a hundred to one that it will be a success."

Before she left Warners, Michael Curtiz had publicly stated that "Elizabeth is the most promising dramatic ingenue in years." Warners agreed, and tried to borrow her and buy *Green Mansions* from Metro, which had bought it with Elizabeth in mind as Rima the Bird Girl, and then shelved it. MGM rejected the deal. (*Green Mansions* was finally made, and not well, in 1959, with Audrey Hepburn in the role.)

Back at the home lot, a new property was added to her future agenda: *Young Bess,* a stormy tale of Elizabeth I before she came to the throne. Immediately upcoming was *Cynthia,* in which Elizabeth would star in the title role. So that the career launched by *National Velvet* continued to zoom, and with that part of it she could have no quarrel. What it was doing to her personal life, and how she herself felt about it, however, was a different story altogether.

※ 5 ※

At first it had been all fun and games—working with animals, going on location trips, associating with famous stars, being the adored child of everyone on the lot, then home to race up and down the block on roller skates with Anne Westmore and to play games with their other neighborhood chums until Sara called her in to supper. By 1946, however, the phase of "Howard

Taylor's kid sister who also happens to be in movies" was a thing of the past.

She was now a star, she who had once stood amazed at Margaret O'Brien's ability to gush tears like Niagara on cue, and had secretly envied Margaret her privileged position at studio functions like L.B.'s birthday parties, when Margaret sat up on the dais like a princess and Elizabeth sat below her like a peasant. Elizabeth was now eclipsing Margaret O'Brien and every other child star of the '40s—Roddy, Peggy Ann Garner, Ted Donaldson, Connie Marshall, "Butch" Jenkins, Sharyn Moffat, Claude Jarman, Jr., Natalie Wood, and all the rest. They twinkled brightly but briefly. The glow of Elizabeth's star grew brighter and bigger. She even went that champion child Shirley Temple one better. The public adored its curly-topped Shirley Temple Doll of the '30s, but the awkward adolescent of the '40s struggled along until personal misery and her innate good sense told her it was time to quit. Elizabeth somehow escaped an awkward age, and simply developed from a beautiful child into a beautiful girl, minus any of the physical evidences of pimples, voice change, gangling extremities, personality displacement, and all the rest of it.

There was thus no reason for the studio to retire her briefly before she was brought back to realize her potential like a long-term capital gain. The studio could go right along realizing immediate returns on its investment and Elizabeth would continue making films without a break, in properties carefully chosen for her particular age, until she could make a smooth transition into adult roles. It was a unique situation for a child star and a unique opportunity for the studio. It also foreclosed any possibility of a remotely normal childhood. As George Stevens remarked:

"She had an artificial patriarchy imposed on her—the studio. It took the place of her own retiring father. The studio, like a domineering parent, was alternately stern and adoring. All day long, some official was telling her what to do and what not to do. She spent all of her pre-adolescent and adolescent days inside the walls of Metro-Goldwyn-Mayer. She worked on the set every morning and spent three hours in the MGM classroom every afternoon. She had no time to play, no contact with other children."

Elizabeth drew deeply on her own inner resources to adjust to the situation in various ways. Requests from fan magazines for interviews were beginning to multiply, the result of rising reader interest, and Elizabeth was a usually obedient and charming subject. She balked, however, when one magazine doing a photo layout requested her to pose while drying dishes. "Oh, please don't take that one," she pleaded. "They'll think I like drying dishes and kids everywhere will wonder what's wrong with me." Fan magazine articles with titles like "Baby Bernhardt" and "Let's Visit With Elizabeth" established the fact that the Taylor household now contained four humans plus Monty, an English golden retriever; Spot, a spaniel; Twinkle, a cocker; a black cat named Jeepers Creepers; King Charles, Prince Charming, and Sweetheart (Howard's horse); and, at one time or another, eight chipmunks plus a squirrel which bit Francis six times before it was given away.

One of the chipmunks was named Nibbles, a present from animal trainer Curly Twyfert up on the *Courage of Lassie* location. Nibbles lived in a little house next to Elizabeth's bed, which was actually a small log with knotholes into which Nibbles packed cotton fuzz to make a nest for himself. In the daytime, he usually lived at the end of a long string which dangled from Elizabeth's neck, and he hid either in her pocket or up on her neck behind her hair. The commissary at MGM bent the rules to allow Elizabeth to bring him in with her, which is where Hedda Hopper met him. Nibbles took one look at her and promptly ran up the inside of her coat sleeve. One fast scream later, Miss Hopper was stripping as if her life depended on it. Elizabeth wrote a little book about her prize chipmunk called *Nibbles and Me*, which was published in 1946.

Along with the time spent on publicity work and on writing the book was time spent in the hospital and, later, in a plaster cast and on crutches. This all came about in the MGM commissary when Elizabeth was dawdling over lunch one day in her perennial battle with time, a contest in which she has rarely been a winner. This particular episode cost her dearly. She suddenly realized she was late for her singing lesson and was sprinting for the door when her toe caught in a seam of the linoleum and she fell forward with an agonizing scream. "The bone broke; I heard it break," she cried. It did indeed—in three places.

The book and the accident were exceptions to a placid existence in which she spent much of her time away from the studio reading, cultivating her growing taste in classical music (especially Chopin), and in drawing. She developed sufficient artistic skill to sell one of her watercolors to a greeting card company. She saw a lot of movies and on weekends she and Howard would usually try to get off somewhere to go riding together. At night, when other kids were struggling through homework or calling each other on the phone, Elizabeth would often be in bed with her attentions divided between a script and a favorite radio program. The radio usually got the major share of her attention because Elizabeth has always been a quick study and memorizing scripts has rarely been a problem for her. In the morning, while Sara drove to the studio, Elizabeth sat beside her, studying spelling lists or other homework due that day.

Mother and daughter were now inseparable, for MGM had put her on the payroll as Elizabeth's chaperone and artistic coach. Sara breakfasted with Elizabeth, drove her to the studio, was with her every moment on the set, sitting off to the side where Elizabeth could see her. Reportedly they had worked out a system of signals. When Elizabeth's voice became high and shrill, Sara touched her stomach. If there seemed to be a lack of sufficient feeling, Sara touched her heart. If Elizabeth seemed lackadaisical and unthinking about her lines, Sara touched her head with her finger. Sara ate with Elizabeth in the commissary, accompanied her on shopping expeditions, and was right beside her during interviews, frequently giving the answers for Elizabeth and prefacing them with "Elizabeth thinks" or "Elizabeth says." Fortunately, mother and daughter genuinely liked each other, onerous though such constant parental supervision must have been on occasion. Possibly as a result of her mother's total preoccupation with her daughter's career, Elizabeth's parents separated for four months, reconciling on Washington's Birthday, 1947, when Sara became ill and Francis came to her side. Elizabeth's only public reference to these events was totally in character in at least two particulars: it was so oblique as to be almost opaque, and it was made many years after the fact. "Perhaps for a few years they loved me too much," she recollected carefully. "I was too much a part of their lives. They had no lives of their own, especially my mother."

Elizabeth's co-workers at the time remember "a basically sweet nature," and a placid exterior marked by shyness, obedience, and an excessive sense of decorum. Piscean waters run deep, and Elizabeth kept her resentments carefully submerged from public view. There was the twin frustration of being considered different by kids she had known prior to her stardom, and being considered a freak by those who had met her since. She avoided other film juveniles' parties, which always mysteriously wound up in the fan magazines flimsily disguised as a housewarming, a pool christening, a sewing bee, a cooking session, etc. They were all designed for the sweet sake of publicity, and Elizabeth found them inherently phony.

Particularly galling to her was the manner of her schooling, and it came to symbolize for her, in its particulars, her loneliness and, in general, the artificial and abnormal situation in which she found herself. At home she eagerly absorbed all that Howard had to tell her about his life at Beverly Hills High: of the camaraderie in and out of class, of the pranks and punishments, of extra-curricular activities shared and enjoyed. Nothing of the kind enlivened her daily routine at the Thalberg bungalow.

The few students it contained were all in different grades so they didn't even have homework in common. At first Jane Powell had been there, and she and Elizabeth had munched a peanut butter sandwich or two during recess. Later she tossed a baseball around at recess well enough to have Claude Jarman, Jr., exclaim, "She catches and throws better than any girl I ever saw!" Jolly times at recess were no substitute for a sound education and the total experience that went with it and Elizabeth knew it. Her grades ranged from good (Art) to poor (Arithmetic).

Always an active daydreamer, Elizabeth sought partial refuge in her various fantasies. Samuel Goldwyn had just filmed Thurber's *The Secret Life of Walter Mitty*, in which Danny Kaye was a milquetoast who had several hilarious fantasies in which he starred as the hero. Elizabeth thus had a name—"Walter Mittying"—for what she had been doing ever since she could remember. She was doing it in the bathroom one day when her teacher caught her and lectured her for it before the class. On a subsequent trip to the john, Elizabeth entered the following vital information on the blackboard in small print: "E enters bathroom 10:03." When she returned, she added a second line: "E exits bathroom, 10:06, mission accomplished." She got a lecture for that too.

What really put the capper on the whole situation was the fact that when Elizabeth was filming she was tutored in snatches between takes—ten minutes, fifteen minutes, twenty minutes, anything necessary to get that mandatory daily three hours required by the state. So that she was expected at one point to have all the requirements of a script in mind—camera position, floor marks, dialogue, motivation of the character, etc.—and when "cut" was called, immediately to go right into conjugating verbs or working out algebra equations. After several minutes of this, the scene was set, a rehearsal or take was called, and she was before the cameras again. MGM called this an education, and every fiber of Elizabeth's intelligence told her it was no such thing. Her accumulated frustration eventually erupted in a mother-daughter hassle over the whole situation which, judging from the evidence, must have been a corker.

In the Taylor household, a simple apology usually sufficed to make amends for an ordinary act of rudeness or display of bad manners. There were times, however, when tempers flared, harsh words were exchanged, and the lingering hurt could only be dispelled by a written apology. Sara Taylor kept a few "sorry notes" from such occasions. In this instance, Elizabeth had apparently given full voice to her unhappiness and there had been the suggestion, either overt or implied, that she had been put into her current situation with little or no say-so. Unwilling to go on playing the heavy, Sara Taylor reviewed the facts as she saw them and laid down what amounted to an ultimatum: Elizabeth could go on with the career, or drop it right there and go on to whatever she thought would make her happier. Either way, from now on the decision would be hers. Elizabeth went off to give the matter some serious thought and later that evening pinned a "sorry note" to Sara's pillow. It read in part:

"I realize that my whole life is being in motion pictures. For me to quit would be like cutting away the roots of a tree . . . I've made up my mind *for myself* so I'll take all the hardships and everything else that comes along—because I know (and I'll always realize) that I was the one who chose to stay *in*—and that I'm the one who must take them without grumbling and wanting to quit."

She had reached her decision and, typically, once her word was pledged, would keep it, in future circumstances the "hardships and everything else" of which she could not have possibly imagined. Meanwhile MGM had *Cynthia* ready to go and it went into production in October 1946.

Cynthia was originally a Broadway flop called *The Rich Full Life* by Viña Delmar. One critic dubbed it "Junior Mess" and further commented, "The ending is syrupy, sappy, contrived, fraudulent, and an insult to the intelligence of actors and audience." Metro paid $75,000 down for this turkey, having foresightedly bought 25 per cent of it before it opened and closed. It was to be the occasion of Elizabeth's first screen kiss, and MGM publicity made the most of it. "Her First Kiss" was plastered all over the ads, and some wit had Elizabeth say, "It's only going to be a peck—and not a Gregory." If that didn't turn your tummy, there was always the plot.

For openers, George Murphy and Mary Astor are teenage college sweethearts. They wed, but their dreams of a trip to Europe are drowned in the flood of doctor bills for Elizabeth, their sickly daughter. She is overprotected by her parents and everyone she comes in contact with and is growing up in a state of permanent convalescence. Then a boy (Jimmy Lydon, her old flame from *Life With Father*) asks her to the prom. At this point, one can almost hear the voice of an announcer proclaiming to a throbbing organ accompaniment, "The Picture That Asks the Question: Will a Frail and Lonely Teenager Risk Pneumonia (or Worse!) and Venture Forth in the Cold and Rain to Keep Her First Date at Her First Prom?" She does, gets "Her First Kiss," and is henceforth liberated from a lonely life of Kleenex, overshoes, and jigsaw puzzles. Reviewers were not enthusiastic.

Apparently fearing an imminent attack of sugar diabetes, Bosley Crowther asked, "Do you like candy—gooey candy—such as those nickel (or six-cent) nut-fruit bars? If so, you probably will like *Cynthia*, for *Cynthia*, bless its little bloomers, is a nutty and fruity little tale . . . a synthetic morsel, right out of the Metro candy box."

The New York *Herald-Tribune* reported: "Elizabeth Taylor does a brilliant job with the title role." That was just one of several excellent notices for Elizabeth personally.

What Elizabeth had done was inject a large measure of her own attractively vulnerable femininity into these turgid proceedings, and she had come away with a personal triumph. Especially noteworthy in *Cynthia* is the first solid evidence of a quality that was to become one of Elizabeth's strongest points as a film actress: her extraordinary sense of self-possession and quiet reality, a natural ease before the cameras that was and is exceptional. What transpires around her in *Cynthia* only emphasizes it. S. Z. Sakall is a delight as her music teacher, and Mary Astor struggles gamely with a thankless part as her mother, but the rest of the adults are bona fide drags. The juveniles without exception play an embarrassingly frenzied game of looks-like-and-sounds-like, that is, characters based on stereotypes. Never mind. And no matter that the film is mercilessly stretched out to include George Murphy's totally implausible transformation from mouse to man, or that it includes such gaucheries as—on the night of the big prom—a torrent of rain falling as hadn't been seen since Tyrone Power's forbidden passion for Myrna Loy in India in 1939. When Elizabeth is up there on the screen, there is warmth and interest and reality.

Many moviegoers fell permanently in love with Elizabeth when they saw *Cynthia* (Mike Nichols was one of them), and they remember it warmly to this day. They don't so much remember *it* as they remember her, and the way she affected them and made them believe her and sympathize with her and the rest of the film be hanged. *Cynthia* was thus good practice for similar situations in the future. MGM sent it out in August 1947, the same month in which Warners released *Life With Father*, a double shot which prompted *Life* magazine to announce that "Elizabeth Taylor has suddenly become Hollywood's most accomplished junior actress."

This mark of critical favor was doubtless welcome, but Elizabeth's romantic predicament in *Cynthia* was a lot closer to her own reality than any of the critics would have suspected. Nature had given her a miraculous dispensation from the awkward age. For all the masculine attention she should have been getting as a result of it, however, Elizabeth might just as well have been the dreariest wallflower that ever went steady with a potted palm.

Her first date had the fine hand of publicity written all over it. *The Yearling*, an MGM film, was having a splashy Hollywood premiere, and Marshall Thompson, a young actor then under contract to Metro, called her up and asked her to go with him. They were in good company; their mothers went with them. Elizabeth and Thompson subsequently dated a couple of times minus chaperones, and one night, after a movie and ice cream at Will Wright's, he gave Elizabeth her first kiss in real life just shortly before Jimmy Lydon did it in reel life.

Elizabeth's room at the house on Elm Drive had meanwhile undergone some major changes. Saddles and bridles were banished along with all the green chintz. The carpet was dyed a deep red, and a bedspread, curtains, drapes, and upholstery of white and pink and red came in to match it. Pictures of horses gave way to two watercolors of roses hung on the walls. After a slight hassle, Elizabeth won the right to wear lipstick—in discreet shades and not too much of it. The stage of young womanhood was thus all set for suitors, who disappointingly failed to materialize. The combination of Elizabeth's celebrity and her mother's constant vigilance was just too intimidating.

In Sara Taylor's defense, let it be said that Hollywood, all publicity malarkey to the contrary, is not just "Anywhere U.S.A.," and never has been. There are creatures running loose who wouldn't know what decency was, unless they read it in a contract or a script, presuming they could read at all. True, they are not indigenous to Hollywood; there just seem to be more of them. All the hit-and-runs were not confined to the freeways, and Sara Taylor steered her young daughter through this permissive show business atmosphere with a necessarily sharp eye. At the same time, she worried about Elizabeth's dateless situation and wondered what she could do about it. Howard was no help. In the only public breach of brother-sister solidarity on record, he reportedly told her, "Get your own dates. You got to take chances like other girls. Call up a boy, get turned down, maybe, like any other girl."

Elizabeth spent a good deal of her time Walter Mittying in her newly redecorated room, and one afternoon Francis passed by and saw her lying on the bed gazing raptly at the ceiling. "What does she *do* all afternoon," he asked his wife, "just looking at the ceiling like that?"

"She's growing up," Sara replied. Occasionally when the dream world got too thick to penetrate, Sara would address the following request, "Would you please come down to our workaday world?" Meanwhile Sara Taylor was trying out various stratagems to see if she could find some nice boys for Elizabeth to go out with.

When Elizabeth was fourteen, Sara told Howard to put it around among his friends that there would be an open house at the Taylor beach house in Malibu. Down came a crowd of eager eaters, and a good time was had by all, devouring steaks and hot dogs, and swimming and playing on the beach. Then, as the sun sank slowly in the West, couples began to drift off to interesting activities on the darkened fringes, leaving the junior hostess solo in what light remained. The senior hostess naturally had adult responsibility for all of these straying guests and, with a huge bell ringing loudly in her hand, went along the fringes announcing that the party was over. That was the end of the open-house plan.

The following June, Howard graduated from Beverly Hills High School. Elizabeth had gone to a few dances there with Anne Westmore and other chums, and the pattern was depressingly familiar. She would stand or sit off to the side, endure the usual amount of ogling and gawking at the pretty movie star, and occasionally a few nervy numbers would summon sufficient courage to ask her to dance. As often as not, they were the runts of various litters.

"A boy's personality is what counts," Elizabeth told an interviewer. "Whether he's a 'drip' or not. Of course, it's really unfair to call them 'drips,'" she added hastily, "but . . . well . . .

personality means so very much." She eagerly looked forward to Howard's senior prom but it turned out to be more of the same. Metro publicity encouraged her to report at the time, "I went simply as Howard Taylor's sister. They talked to me about all the other kids in school. Just as if I were one of them. Just as if I knew all of them. And I pretended I did. It was wonderful!" It was not. The occasion rests in Elizabeth's memory stamped "perfectly miserable." These two years of romantic frustration were shortly to come to an end. For an unusually beautiful girl of keen intelligence and deep sensitivity, they were a rough stretch. Later, in that summer of 1947, the Taylor family again went to Howard Young's in Wisconsin. After which Elizabeth reported back to the studio for the start of her only musical, *A Date With Judy*, based on characters in a then-popular radio show.

In this one, Elizabeth, long of face and slim of figure, played Little Miss Moneybags, wealthy best friend of heroine Jane Powell. For love interest, Metro gave her—of all people—Robert Stack, then almost twice her age. Stack began his career nine years previous to this doing the same kind of thing with Deanna Durbin. As a matter of fact, Stack gave Deanna "*Her* First Kiss." Here he was, back at the old stand, playing a soda jerk with lines like "There ought to be more fancy ice cream sundaes in everybody's life."

The film was organized around the general notion that all teenagers were cute vacuous twits, a notion for which the United States was to begin to pay dearly in the '60s. Elizabeth's character thus has no depth, but she gives this teenage sophisticate some amusing airs and graces, and also projects that appealing vulnerability which was fast becoming a hallmark of her screen personality. In a succession of scenes, she vamps Stack in the malt shop, sits beside him on a sofa watching Jane and boy friend Scotty Beckett whoop it up to "Strictly on the Corny Side," has a tantrum with Stack, a nice bit explaining the "terrible" nature of men to Jane, and a family scene where she is ignored by her father, Leon Ames, who is preoccupied with the stock market.

A running scene throughout the film has Jane's father, Wallace Beery, sneaking away from his wife, Selena Royle, to rendezvous with Carmen Miranda for secret rhumba lessons. Ultimately Jane and Elizabeth confront Carmen as a shameless husband-stealing hussy. Which poses the question: Will Beery rhumba well enough to convince Selena that all he was doing with Carmen was the rhumba? In a Joe Pasternak musical produced under the benign aegis of Louis B. Mayer at the MGM of 1948, you better believe it. Selena does. In the nightclub finale, Stack is manfully pitching woo at Elizabeth at a ringside table as Jane happily trills, "It's a Most Unusual Day." It certainly was.

Judy finished shooting in January 1948, and Elizabeth went immediately into *Julia Misbehaves* as the daughter of Greer Garson and Walter Pidgeon. Miss Garson had made a dazzling debut in 1939's *Goodbye, Mr. Chips,* and gone on to amass six Oscar nominations—and one Oscar for *Mrs. Miniver*—in seven years, a feat equaled only by Bette Davis. Then, like every established star at Metro in the postwar years, she fell on hard times.

There was *Adventure,* a turkey with the famed ad line, "Gable's Back and Garson's Got Him," which both stars loathed. Next came *Desire Me,* a catastrophe so total that neither of the directors who worked on it would permit his name to be put on the finished print. Metro then decided, as *Life* put it, "that the combination of Greer and drear was wearing thin." Hence, *Julia Misbehaves.* This was to be a comedy in which Greer is a lady who deserts her husband (Pidgeon) and infant daughter for a career in the London Music Halls. Eighteen years later, the daughter (Elizabeth) is about to be married in posh circumstances in the South of France, and invites the mother she has never seen. Ma arrives and promptly turns everything upside down. This particular plot has done yeoman service through the years, most notably in *The Pleasure of His Company.*

From the opening shot of Greer in a bubble bath, the script called for her to give a flashy leg show and be manhandled by acrobats, be locked out in a drenching rainstorm, get dumped in a lake, and, finally, be thrown flat in the mud. Metro finished Garbo with this kind of treatment in *Two-Faced Woman,* and *Time* then commented that it was "not unlike seeing Sarah Bernhardt swatted with a bladder. It is almost as shocking as seeing your mother drunk." *Julia Misbehaves* was to continue the deterioration of Greer Garson's career "little by little in small pieces," as Bette Davis phrased it in *Winter Meeting,* which was accomplishing the same thing for *her* career over at Warners at precisely the same time.

In *Julia Misbehaves,* Elizabeth had Peter Lawford as her fiancé (she would marry him in her next film as well). She also had a tremendous crush on him off-camera and everybody on the set knew it. At one point, the script called for them to kiss passionately, after which Elizabeth was to say, "Oh, Ritchie, what are we going to do?" They got through the clinch, Elizabeth turned a bright pink, and murmured soulfully, "Oh, Peter, what am I going to do?" As roars of laughter rocked the set, Elizabeth flushed scarlet and silently begged in vain for a magic power that would enable her to vanish instantly.

Julia wrapped in April, and MGM sent out both *A Date With Judy* and *Julia Misbehaves* the following fall. Neither set any box office bonfires nor were the critics much moved. Bosley Crowther found *Julia Misbehaves* "grotesque," regretted "the awkward spectacle of Greer Garson being a card—or, if you'll excuse the expression, sowing another wild oat," and put the whole thing down as "an indiscriminate hodge-podge of chaste and constricted burlesque."

A Date With Judy was called "beguiling" and "light, gay, rollicking entertainment" by the Hollywood trade papers, still floating in postwar euphoria. It was also called "trivial," "silly," and "uninspired," and the L.A. *Times* man found it "all very homey, very comfy, and very Joe Pasternak . . . seemed to me twice as long as *Gone With the Wind*." For Elizabeth the film was a personal triumph. Archer Winsten's review in the New York *Post* could have passed for a public mash note. "Young stars have come and gone," he wrote. "Some have survived youthful fame to rise again to success as adults. But never has there been a case which can quite match that of Elizabeth Taylor, the girl whose high point was reached in *National Velvet*. Now she reappears, billed as a spoiled beauty, no longer a child. And every time one of the characters refers to her beauty, the spectator echoes the thought . . . Obviously the proper way to enjoy *A Date With Judy* is to forget everything but Miss Taylor. The time, the clichés, and the silly chatter pass quickly when you begin to review the roles she could now enact with enchantment."

With reviews such as this, Elizabeth's career had obviously moved to an exciting new level. Events in her personal life matched it nicely. In February 1948 she turned sixteen and put her childhood behind her with a cake and party on the set of *Julia Misbehaves*, and later, with her first formal night out, in a birthday celebration at the Cocoanut Grove. And in July, her dateless dilemma was brought to an end at a meeting which was soon being commented upon in every newspaper, gossip column, and fan magazine in the country.

❁ 6 ❁

For a girl who'd undergone two years of hard times in the romantic department, the next two years more than made up for
it, and at the end of them she would be altar-bound for the first
time. Six men moved in and out of Elizabeth's life during the
next two years. Two of them she would eventually marry, two
were passing fancies, one never got to first base, and one she
would love in a very special way to the day of his death many
years later.

The act of becoming sixteen seemed to be the signal for a
more active social life. To begin with, MGM gifted Elizabeth
with a wardrobe, and her parents gave her a blue Cadillac with a
gold ignition key. This one was a follow-up to the Ford convertible they'd given her two years previously. Elizabeth expressed delight with the Cadillac, but suggested that her parents
use it instead of their Chevy. She would stick with the Ford—
"driving back and forth in it between home and Metro will be
the only *fresh air* I'll get," she said. She paid out thirty-nine
dollars to have it outfitted with twin pipes, and regaled co-
workers with the noise until a Culver City ordinance banned
dual exhausts and she had to have them taken off.

It was about this time that one of the cameramen on the lot
told her, "I thought you'd like to know that the boys voted you
the most beautiful woman they've ever photographed." Elizabeth
could scarcely contain herself until the man was out of earshot.
"Mother!" she gasped. "Did you hear what he said? He called
me a woman." And why not? Her 112 pounds were neatly distributed over a figure which featured a 35-inch bust, 22-inch
waist, and 34-inch hips. She was beginning to favor tight, waist-
cinching belts, along with peasant blouses and full skirts, which
showed it off to maximum advantage. The studio, however, was
still pushing the image of the nature-loving child, and one interview from the summer of 1948 is a bona fide gem. It went as
follows:

PRESS AGENT: "When she was twelve, the studio took some
    shots of her at a ranch. The problem was how to get some
    unbridled half-wild ponies to pose with her. Elizabeth heard

us talking about it, threw back her head and whinnied. The ponies came right over to her."

REPORTER: "What do you mean 'whinnied'?"

PRESS AGENT: "She whinnies just like a horse. Most unearthly sound you ever heard. She also chirps like a squirrel and makes bird noises."

REPORTER (to Elizabeth): "Let's hear you whinny."

PRESS AGENT (hastily): "The studio doesn't want her to whinny any more. It's too rough on her throat."

(At this point, Elizabeth finally got in a word and volunteered the information that Nibbles once lived in her coat pocket. "She answered my questions with patience," remarked the reporter, "but was palpably relieved when the interview was over.")

PRESS AGENT: "She is late for a barbecue."

Fan magazines continued to thrill readers with the news that "if you don't like animals, Elizabeth won't like you." This image of nature's little darling had obviously begun to become a bit of a bore when Elizabeth impatiently told one interviewer, "After all, you can't just love animals all your life." She and her dates, of which there was no longer a scarcity, found plenty of things to do besides going to the zoo. The usual date was a movie, followed by a late snack, either a hamburger or ice cream at Will Wright's. She liked to bowl, to play gin rummy, to go on the roller coaster at P.O.P.—the amusement park in Santa Monica whose current absence is sorely missed. More formal dates usually meant an evening of dining and dancing at the Cocoanut Grove, as often as not in a group, since Elizabeth generally preferred to date that way. She continued to adhere to the rule that prospective dates be first brought home to make the acquaintance of her parents, and vice versa.

In the summer, the swains came to the Taylor beach house in Malibu for a Sunday of touch football, swimming, and barbecue. Sara Taylor once described these carefree days at the beach:

"On Sunday the crowd collects. In fact they start collecting Saturday night. Elizabeth and a girl friend take over Daddy's room, which has twin beds, and he comes in with me. I never know how many there'll be and I don't care. One morning I woke to find five pairs of feet sticking out of a sleeping bag on the porch under my balcony. Howard had two boys in his room, two more were on the big couch in the living room, and another snoozed peacefully in the back seat of our Buick. When there's a gang like that for breakfast, I announce to the boys that they'll have dishes to wash and send the girls upstairs to make beds. By trial and error I've discovered it's best to separate them at their labors. Fewer dishes get broken, and they spend less time flipping tea towels at each other.

"All day long they're in and out of the water, riding those rubber lifeboats. By six-thirty, a buffet supper is on the table, then it's charades and guessing games for the rest of the evening. I've often been asked, 'But don't the youngsters want to get off by themselves and play records and dance?' Apparently not. Maybe it's because we've always done things as a family, never excluded the children from our adult parties, never thrown up a barrier. They enjoy our friends, feel a sense of comradeship with them, call them by their first names. From the way we act, there's no apparent difference in age. And if you could see the hilarity that goes on, you'd agree it would sound pretty pointless to cut in and ask, 'Wouldn't you kids rather be doing something else?' "

It was on such a Sunday in July 1948 that a Metro publicist brought one of the nation's champion athletes, Glenn Davis, down to Malibu to meet the screen's prettiest girl. Any excitement Elizabeth had caused thus far on the nation's movie pages had been more than equaled by Glenn Davis on its sports pages. He and "Doc" Blanchard were the fabled "Touchdown Twins," co-captains of Army's victorious football team. He had also captained West Point's baseball team, and starred on its basketball and track teams as well. Now he was twenty-four, a lieutenant, and in Los Angeles to play a special exhibition game for Army prior to shipping out for a tour of duty in Korea.

Elizabeth was playing touch football (of all things) on the beach, and had just fallen face-first in the sand when she caught sight of him. Flustered, she rose to her feet and introductions were made all around. He then volunteered to play on her side, and by day's end she was attracted to him. Aside from all the obvious reasons, he was unassuming and didn't throw his weight around. For a national hero, he seemed to exhibit a pleasing lack of vanity or obnoxious self-absorption. Elizabeth liked that quality; she always has.

They were to have seven dates that summer, each of them eagerly reported by the press to a rising crescendo of reader interest. With its bloody-but-unbowed addiction to the happy ending, the public had plainly decided that this was the consummation devoutly to be wished. "My God," Elizabeth remembers thinking, "they think it's a big hot romance." She read the press reports almost as if this Great Romance were happening to someone else. Which, in point of fact, it was. It certainly wasn't happening to her. The public, however, was encouraged to think that it was, a fact which was subsequently to have unpleasant repercussions. Her days were fully occupied at Metro that summer, for *Little Women* had begun shooting in June.

This was to be the third version of Louisa May Alcott's enduring classic about the March family and their life during the Civil War in Concord, New Hampshire. Paramount made one version in 1919, and the classic version had come from RKO in 1933, with David Selznick producing and George Cukor directing. In September 1946, after almost a year's preparation, Selznick was readying a color remake to star Jennifer Jones as Jo. Mervyn LeRoy was set to direct and *Gone With the Wind* sets were being taken down to make way for it at the Selznick Studios. Then a long studio strike snagged the plans. By March 1948, Selznick was preparing to embark on the long winter of his discontent, and sold the whole thing off to MGM. Metro cast June Allyson, Elizabeth, Janet Leigh, Margaret O'Brien, Peter Lawford, Mary Astor, Rossano Brazzi, and Lucile Watson in the roles played in 1933 by Katharine Hepburn, Joan Bennett, Frances Dee, Jean Parker, Douglass Montgomery, Spring Byington, Paul Lukas, and Edna Mae Oliver.

From the very first titles, done in sampler frames to tinkly music-box period tunes, the audience is put on notice that this version will be a good deal gooier than 1933's, a point on which there was to be general agreement among the critics. As Amy, Elizabeth wears a blond wig; sleeps with Margaret O'Brien (they are the youngest girls)—and with a clothespin on her nose for the sake of beauty; goes into rhapsodies over popovers, and food in general; stands in front of her class holding a slateboard proclaiming, "I Am Ashamed of Myself" (for drawing a caricature of her teacher instead of doing her addition); flounces around amusingly as a spoiled, vain, selfish little minx; goes to Europe with Lucile Watson, and finally marries Peter Lawford. Elizabeth carries the whole thing off with a nice comic flair, particularly in a scene where she tells off her classmates, in the grand manner, in a speech sprinkled with malapropisms.

Essentially the film is a star vehicle for June Allyson as Jo in a series of family vignettes: the girls take their breakfast to the poor; Jo goes visiting Laurie, the boy next door, and catches fire (literally); the girls go to Laurie's party and overhear malicious gossip; Laurie's grandfather gives Beth a piano; Jo cuts her hair to get money to pay for Marmie's trip to Washington to see Father; Beth contracts scarlet fever while nursing the poor but recovers; Meg marries; Jo rejects Laurie and goes to New York; Beth dies—and so forth. Allyson's tomboy is a bit heavy-handed and leans to the unpleasant side (it doesn't come as gracefully as Hepburn's), but she manages the tears with practiced efficiency, and her maturity is charming and believable.

The film's major liability is Margaret O'Brien as Beth. Someone seems to have mixed up the reels and Beth begins wasting away as a monotonously dreary little girl from reel one onward. There is not a shred of variety or lightness to the character. "My poor Beth" is a constant refrain, helped not one whit by lines such as "It seems I was never intended to live very long" and (to Jo) "I think I will be homesick for you—even in heaven." This was to be Miss O'Brien's last year at Metro, and for the onetime wonder child of the lot, it was a limp exit.

Rossano Brazzi, sexy sensation of postwar Italian films, made his American debut in *Little Women* as—of all things—a dumpy, middle-aged, penniless, German émigré professor. The scene in which Brazzi is required to serenade Miss Allyson with "None But the Lonely Heart" in German, all of this in a heavy Italian accent and with eyes smoldering with Latin passion, is so incredible you really can't believe it's happening even while you're looking at it.

As for the rest: Mary Astor's dialogue sounds as if it should have been embroidered on samplers, but she manages it like the pro she is. Lucile Watson bounces in and out in a chronic state of dyspepsia, and makes her every moment count—as, indeed, when did she never? Janet Leigh, who resembles Frances Dee, does charmingly with the same part. The film is low-voltage overall, but its characters and its charm eventually win you over. Metro released it as its Easter Attraction for 1949 to generally favorable reviews.

"Get out your hankies, kiddies, and prepare for a nice soggy weep," advised Bosley Crowther, and *Time* observed that the story "still jerks tears with easy efficiency." To which the Hollywood *Reporter* added: "Elizabeth Taylor has just the sense of humor to make Amy the lovable snob she is." Oscars eventually went to Cedric Gibbons and Edwin B. Willis for their handsome Art Direction and Set Decoration. The Academy also voted Herbert Britt a Class III Technical Award "for the development and application of formulas and equipment producing artificial snow and ice for dressing motion picture sets." This was a liquid chemical which, sprayed onto the set, solidified like packed snow. It could not convincingly simulate actual snowfall (they're still searching for that), but it packed like actual snowdrifts, left tracks, could be molded into snowballs, and didn't melt. It was used for the first time in *Little Women*.

The film wrapped in September 1948. The night before he shipped out to Korea, Glenn Davis left Elizabeth in possession of his miniature gold football, his All-American sweater, his "A" pin, and a replica of his West Point ring. Later she parried the prying questions of eager reporters.

"You feel funny telling. It's something you like to keep just with a person. Anyway, what do two people in love *usually* talk about—politics?" As to any understanding between them, she quipped, "We're engaged to be engaged." Any pain she was feeling over the separation was at least partially offset by exciting new developments in her career.

Metro had upped her salary to $1,000 a week, and in October, Elizabeth dutifully went to court to get legal approval of it, as required of minors by California's "Coogan Law." MGM released the news that in a single six-month period, the studio had received a total of 1,065 bids from colleges all over the United States who wanted Elizabeth for everything from Prom Queen to Homecoming Mascot. On October 16 she sailed for England on the *Queen Mary* for the start of *Conspirator*, which Metro was already proudly heralding as Elizabeth's first adult love story. Robert Taylor was to be her partner.

Conspirator was in production from November 1948 until February 1949, and all sorts of interesting things happened—not, however, in the film. The idea of Elizabeth in an adult love story was obviously an idea whose time had come. As she herself remembers, "I was sixteen and looked about twenty-four." Unfortunately it collided with MGM's desperate, half-baked attempts to restore Robert Taylor's prior potency at the box office. The result was a disaster.

Taylor had come to stardom opposite Irene Dunne in the first *Magnificent Obsession* and opposite Garbo in *Camille*. He lived down a "pretty-boy" tag, survived the required stint opposite Hedy Lamarr, and became one of MGM's top moneymakers in a string of hits such as *Three Comrades, Waterloo Bridge, Escape, Billy the Kid, Johnny Eager,* and *Bataan*. His marriage to another top favorite, Barbara Stanwyck, was an added plus. After a two-year stint in the Navy, he returned to Metro and the studio handed him *Undercurrent*. In this one, Taylor's attempts to murder wife Katharine Hepburn are foiled by Robert Mitchum. Taylor shuddered when he saw the script, but as one of the most amenable stars who ever worked in Hollywood, he did his best. It bombed. Well, if they didn't want him as a wife-murderer, how about as a *supposed* wife-murderer incarcerated as a psycho? This one was called *High Wall* and the public stayed away en masse. Next came *The Bribe*, with Taylor as a federal agent involved in a lurid melodrama about smuggling in the Caribbean with Ava Gardner, Charles Laughton, Vincent Price, and others. They all sank together. Then came the ultimate brainstorm. Let him play another wife-killer, but not just any old wife-killer. Make him a communist. Asking Robert Taylor to convincingly portray a communist would be like asking Jane Fonda, all other things being equal, to play General Custer. That, plus a sickly script, doomed the enterprise before a single foot of film was shot.

The Los Angeles Board of Education had given its permission for "Andy" to accompany Elizabeth to Elstree Studios, and Elizabeth's chief memories of *Conspirator* are of rushing from the passionate embraces of Robert Taylor to the off-camera demands of grammar, algebra, etc. and back again until, as she put it, "it kind of made your eyes go crossed." At night she usually managed to get off a letter to Glenn Davis. And one day at Elstree, she spied Michael Wilding, a popular British actor twenty years her senior, and conceived a crush on him which would later take them both into matrimony. After that occurred, Wilding recalled one of her lunchtime maneuvers with some amusement.

"Rather than ask the waitress for some salt, she'd walk clear through the commissary to get it from the kitchen, wiggling her hips. Then she'd wiggle her way back."

Elizabeth was unfazed. "That was for your benefit alone, darling," she replied triumphantly, "even if it didn't work at the time."

On the set of *Conspirator*, cast and crew were admiring her unaccustomed projection of adult passions before the camera, and Elizabeth made an attempt to explain it all.

"Usually it isn't at all hard to get a character. It's either one thing or another. Mostly I just read my lines through three times at night and then I go to sleep like a log and don't think about anything. I don't sit down and figure should I do this gesture or should I do that. I know it sounds funny for me to say but it just seems easy, that's all."

Director Victor Saville couldn't quite buy this:

"I'm always puzzling about Elizabeth's ability. Somewhere she has acquired complete repose in her work, and she shows amazing clarity, boldness, and timing. No matter what she says, she must brood about her parts and feel them emotionally. She often moves me when she plays a scene and I'm sure it can't be accidental."

Saville enlarged on this with a professional appraisal as true to-day as the day he first made it:

"She is gently bred. Her people are nice people. She has manners. And she is absolutely a *screen* actress. She doesn't learn the attitude of an emotion and repeat it over and over again, as on a stage, but expresses it sincerely right now. She knows if she feels it, it'll photograph. Also she knows that she hasn't any possible bad angle. So she forgets the camera. The depth of her belief is how good she is."

Robert Taylor paid his own compliment to Elizabeth's ability to get into a role. "They told her to kiss," he noted appreciatively, "and she kissed!"

One gala evening she was thrilled but nervous when she attended the Royal Command Performance of *That Forsyte Woman*, Metro's anemic rendering of part of *The Forsyte Saga*. She'd been sick from food poisoning that day and whispered to Myrna Loy, standing next to her, that she was afraid she'd have an attack of nausea upon presentation. Miss Loy bucked her up by telling her she too felt a little queasy and Elizabeth's introduction to King George, Queen Elizabeth, and the royal newly-weds, Elizabeth and Philip, went off charmingly. Later, at a ball given by Lord Louis Mountbatten, America's Princess Elizabeth had the additional thrill of dancing with Prince Philip. And at the end of *Conspirator*, she enjoyed one of the prime thrills of anyone's life: her first trip to Paris. She had to do some fancy operating to get there.

France was in the throes of a flu epidemic, and the studio vetoed the proposed trip as too hazardous to their valuable star's health. Elizabeth then made the rounds of Elstree with a petition, gathered a few dozen signatures, padded these with a few more ("Lord Byron," "Scarlett O'Hara," etc.), and submitted it to the London studio chief. It read:

> We, the undersigned, agree with Elizabeth Taylor that she *should* be allowed to go to Paris on a shopping spree;
>
> Inasmuch as she has promised:
>
>   1. To be a good girl
>   2. To shun all flu germs
>   3. Not to contract even as much as a runny nose.
>
> Her sole purpose in going to Paris is to acquire a few handmade pink unmentionables, gloves, handkerchiefs, etc.
>
> We feel that this *Most Necessary* trip should *not* be *denied* her.

It wasn't. Sara and Elizabeth flew over one weekend and compromised on their objectives: sightseeing in the morning (for Sara), shopping in the afternoon (for Elizabeth). This was also France's first look at Elizabeth Taylor in the flesh, and the shopping expedition came to grief because the Parisians continually stared unashamedly everywhere she went. Sara Taylor remembers that one wife finally told her husband, "Stop staring at that girl. It's very rude." To which the husband replied with unassailable French logic, "My dear, it is no more rude to stare at that beautiful creature than it is to stare at the Mona Lisa. It is like looking at a picture." Mother and daughter returned to England, and subsequently to America, via the *Queen Elizabeth*, in February 1949. Elizabeth expected to be back in Europe shortly; her next film was to be *Quo Vadis*.

Metro officials were left to grapple with the fruits of three months' labor at Elstree, and unpromising fruits they were. During the Depression Decade of the '30s, when Warners sent out a string of films dealing with issues of social conscience (*I Am a Fugitive From a Chain Gang, Black Fury, The Life of Emile Zola*, et al.), Metro's solitary contribution was the Fritz Lang–Joseph L. Mankiewicz *Fury*, a searing study of lynching and mob violence starring Spencer Tracy and Sylvia Sidney. Metro was criticized for not doing more in this area, and they commonly retorted, "When we want to send a message, we use Western Union." Now they had gotten daring and made a film about communism. In this instance, they should have used Western Union.

Robert Taylor, a handsome guard in His Majesty's Service, meets Elizabeth, a visiting American, at a London ball, sweeps her off her feet and marries her. He is also a Soviet agent, and his failure to inform the Party about his matrimonial plans is branded "a serious breach of discipline." Taylor gets sore. "The Party doesn't leave a man much time for his private life," he remarks plaintively. A brief excursion into the psychological has his aunt remark that he's never really been able to love anybody more than himself. Ergo, he became a communist. Ultimately Elizabeth discovers the awful truth and they have a fight in the bathroom where she hits him with a wet sponge. Next they move to the bedroom for philosophical discussion.

HE: "I'm a loyal supporter of the greatest social experiment in the world."

SHE: "All I know is it's wrong and I hate it!"

From this point on she is a marked woman. Taylor's communist boss slips him the word with all the squinty-eyed malevolence of Ming the Merciless: "As a soldier you must know there are always . . . (pregnant pause of three minutes) . . . casualties in war." Failing to blow Elizabeth to pieces with a shotgun out on a hunting trip, Taylor makes another attempt at home, is trapped, and shoots himself. The End.

The entire film is put together with all the subtlety of an ambulance siren. The script reads like a collection of clumsily assembled highway signs. The music is dreadful. Every time Taylor goes off to a clandestine meeting, the orchestra goes into a nervous breakdown. Elsewhere the score is loud, blatant, hysterical, obvious at all the worst moments. Robert Taylor marches through these proceedings grim, stoic, and unsmiling. After all, who ever heard of a happy communist? Elizabeth's work cannot really be faulted. She is fully adequate to the demands of this bum script, and moves through it looking gorgeous in a succession of Helen Rose creations. She might just as well be moving through a fashion show; she simply has no picture. Metro officials in Culver City took a dismayed look at "Elizabeth Taylor's First Adult Love Story," shoved it back in the can, and sat on it, in a state of nervous uncertainty, for the next thirteen months.

Elizabeth returned to the United States in time to spend her seventeenth birthday at Howard Young's place in Florida, which is where Suitor No. 3 entered her life. He was William D. Pawley, Jr., then twenty-eight, the son of a man who was a former U. S. Ambassador to Brazil. The Pawleys were well-to-do, and Bill was, at that time, a vice-president in his father's bus business. He had been invited to be Elizabeth's escort at the party, and he was instantly smitten. He was in good company. Another gentleman was vainly working the fringes of Elizabeth's love life, but given his peculiar passion for privacy, this particular extracurricular activity was not made known until some years later.

"If you had a date with Howard Hughes," *Motion Picture* magazine brightly informed its readers, "you'd have a date with a man whose fortune is in excess of $145,000,000; a man whose enterprises include controlling interest in TWA, Hughes Productions, Hughes Aircraft Corporation, Hughes Tool Company, and the largest brewery in Texas. You'd also have a date with the man who recently wrote Floyd Odlum a check for $8,825,000 for 929,000 shares of RKO stock. What's more, the check was good!"

And what else? "He is gay, amusing, witty . . . a shy person, partly due to good breeding and partly because he is a little deaf . . . extremely well informed." But: "Many glamour girls who have dated Howard Hughes complain that he doesn't spend any time with them. He is always on the telephone. He races from spot to spot. He's looking over their shoulders with his thoughts a mile away. This is hardly flattering." Nevertheless: "Mr. Hughes's scalp, along with his charms, are today being viewed acquisitively by the biggest female stars in Hollywood."

Correction. One of the "biggest female stars in Hollywood" had been getting close exposure to Mr. Hughes's "scalp" and "charms" and remained singularly unmoved. As to when Hughes first spotted Elizabeth is uncertain, but this novel treatment must have been intriguing to a man who had dated Ginger Rogers, Lana Turner, Ava Gardner, and other filmland beauties.

He had recently enjoyed a singular triumph. In a tangle with a Senate Committee in Washington, Hughes left them all looking like a pack of dolts. One, in particular, was exposed as such a complete dunce that the voters speedily retired him at the very next opportunity. Flushed with this victory, Hughes redoubled his efforts to capture his elusive prize. Two paintings were bought from Francis Taylor, Elizabeth and her parents were invited to several dinners, and one weekend they all went to Reno together. None of it worked. Not only did Elizabeth refuse to view Howard Hughes acquisitively, she finally refused to view him at all. "If Howard's coming, I'm not," was her wary reply to invitations to dinner parties which had been carefully plotted to ensure that the two would meet. She didn't particularly dislike him. She simply could not remotely envision him as a romantic prospect for herself, period. Bill Pawley was another matter.

He and Elizabeth dated during February and March 1949, and then the press rang the alarm in every newspaper coast-to-coast: Glenn Davis was flying in to Miami, on leave from Korea, and he was supposedly bringing a ring. A cascade of flashbulbs popped at the Miami Airport as the two embraced, and flashbulbs went right on popping whenever the couple showed themselves in public.

"Maybe I should have fallen for a bus boy or something," Elizabeth told a reporter. "Then the whole thing wouldn't cause so much attention." As to whether Elizabeth and Glenn Davis might have developed something beyond their initial attraction is a moot point. They were simply never given the chance. They went on to Hollywood, where Elizabeth was kept busy at a steady round of publicity activities.

First she was crowned Princess of the 1949 Diamond Jubilee of the Jewelry Industry Council. The crown was a $22,000 diamond tiara. Elizabeth's natural admiration for beautiful things that sparkle manifested itself in her first question after the crowning. "May I keep it?" she asked prettily. There was a hearty ha-ha all around and they took it back.

Next came the 1949 Academy Award Ceremonies, with Davis standing off to the side as Elizabeth basked in the limelight, responding to the ever-present attentions of reporters and photographers. At this point, the U. S. Army was beginning to make nervous noises about all this publicity, and Davis had had a full taste of dancing attendance on a girl who seemed to be regarded as everyone's public possession, whether she liked it or not. He definitely didn't like it, and returned to Korea carrying his ring and his miniature gold football. The end of this romance saddened newspaper readers all over the country—all but one of them, that is.

On to Los Angeles came Bill Pawley for three weeks of ardent courtship. The evenings usually ended at Will Wright's over ice cream, with more ice cream being brought home to be consumed over the kitchen table in late-night talkathons. There were long automobile rides, long walks, long hours of listening to music together. At the end of it, Bill Pawley returned to Miami the possessor of a big secret.

Meanwhile, in May, *Quo Vadis* finally got off the ground. But only temporarily. John Huston checked in at Metro to write the script he hoped soon to be directing in Rome. Gregory Peck, Elizabeth, and Walter Huston were assigned star parts, with location work to start in July. Then Peck contracted an eye infection, and the whole thing was postponed. Next, the Los Angeles Board of Education was heard from. It had okayed one overseas tutorial trip for Elizabeth on *Conspirator*. Another one to Rome was out. That would set back the date of Elizabeth's graduation, when she could finally get off her little academic merry-go-round, and she not surprisingly opted out of *Quo Vadis*. By the time filming finally began in Rome in 1950, Mervyn LeRoy had replaced John Huston, Robert Taylor and Deborah Kerr were in the leads, Walter Huston had died and Finlay Currie had replaced him as St. Peter.

In May, Elizabeth was named Honorary Queen of the Miss Junior America Pageant for 1949: "An outstanding example of what is expected of a Miss Junior America." Later that month, she had her first formal interview with the redoubtable Louella Parsons.

Fat, foolish, frivolous, and frumpy Miss Parsons could appear, and could be made to appear, but she had several things going for her. One was an engaging modesty about her literary talents, which prompted her to title her autobiography *The Gay Illiter-*

ate. Unlike Hedda Hopper, she rarely allowed her personal value judgments to get in the way of her shrewd sense of whomever or whatever the public favored, whether she personally approved or not. What set her securely above her competition was not only the firm backing of William Randolph Hearst, but also a newsman's strong nose for a story that rarely betrayed her, as Rita Hayworth and Ingrid Bergman could attest, to name two. Woe to you if she had correctly smelled out a story and you lied to her. Then she could be hell-on-wheels.

Elizabeth had gone to her first grownup party at Louella's, a cocktail affair to which little Elizabeth wore a full black velvet skirt and at which she was the darling of all the grownups present. She had entered with Nibbles perched on her shoulder, and when asked if she really liked animals, had replied with her natural candor, "Of course. More than I like people." Now Hollywood's Queen of Gossip and its outstanding young star sat down to business. Miss Parsons' report of this session was stamped with a certain wary admiration which would underscore all of her reports on Elizabeth.

"Elizabeth is a very unusual young girl," she wrote. "She is reserved and unemotional, but at the same time, she has great sweetness, and the same interests of other girls her age. Her face was completely void of expression while we were talking. She is an actress, I thought. She can conceal her real thoughts better than most grownups."

She certainly could. At that moment she was sitting quietly on a piece of news not to be made public until a week later, when the Taylors flew to Miami and Sara made the official announcement. Her daughter was engaged to marry William D. Pawley, Jr. Sara subsequently characterized Bill Pawley as "brilliant, understanding, strong, poised, but also boyish and full of fun," and she expressed the wish that marriage would bring out of her daughter "some hidden domestic talents." *Life* subsequently published a picture of the engaged couple, a tribute to the public's enormous interest in Elizabeth since movie-star romances were rarely the business of national magazines. After which, Elizabeth reported back to Hollywood to prepare for something called *Drink to Me Only* (subsequently titled *The Big Hangover*), and to keep the telephone wires humming to Miami.

Jane Powell was to be married in September, and Elizabeth gave her her first bridal shower. A round of other parties and activities for Jane kept her busy, including an outing to the Mocambo, which was Elizabeth's first trip to a nightclub. Somewhere along the line, Elizabeth's status as the most promising star

in films collided with Bill Pawley's picture of a wife happily retired from movies and living totally within the means of her
adoring husband in Miami. Try as she would, Elizabeth couldn't
quite tune in to that picture. Everything came to a head in September.

Pawley flew West for a showdown, and when it was over, the
engagement was broken. It was decided that he would make the
announcement when he got back to Miami. First he would stay,
as planned, for Jane Powell's wedding. He stayed long enough
to see Elizabeth come up the aisle as a bridesmaid, to watch Elizabeth slip two neatly wrapped peanut-butter sandwiches into one
of Jane's suitcases (mementos of the days at MGM University),
and to watch her, ironically, catch the bridal bouquet at the
wedding reception. Then he departed. The wedding party proceeded on to an evening at the Mocambo, where Elizabeth unaccountably burst into tears. Vic Damone was the headliner, and
he was extra-solicitous that evening, singing a number directly
to her and coming over to sit for a while at her table. The next
day, Bill Pawley made his announcement in Miami and the timing
couldn't have been worse.

Not only was the American public confronted with the spectacle of Elizabeth Taylor and what they regarded as two broken
engagements within six months, but what was this? On the
very night when she should have been properly secluded with a
broken heart, there she was laughing it up with Vic Damone.
This misconception resulted in the first bad press Elizabeth had
ever known.

Magazine articles with titles like "Elizabeth Taylor: Subdeb
or Siren?" plainly intimated that Elizabeth was a fickle woman of
the world heedlessly careening from romance to romance, cal-
lously leaving a wake of broken hearts. Thus was born the legend
of the amoral temptress. The London Sunday *Pictorial* bluntly
observed that Elizabeth's recent behavior "has been as silly as a
schoolboy smoking cigars," and suggested that "somebody should
administer a series of resounding smacks behind the bustle of
her latest Paris creation." It further castigated her as "a living
argument against the employment of children in the studios."

Sara Taylor was plainly distressed. "If I had known it would
turn out like this," she was quoted as saying, "I would not have
let Elizabeth go into pictures. The situation has us both worried
sick." To which Elizabeth reportedly added, "If I were the kind
of person they write me up to be, I'd hate myself."

MGM was no happier. To a film which they were still afraid
to release had now been added a bitter dose of press criticism.

Unknown to Elizabeth, her mother, or the studio, two milestones in her life were just around the corner. Paramount asked to borrow her for *A Place in the Sun*. She would meet Montgomery Clift on that one, and at luncheon in the Paramount commissary, she would also make the acquaintance of Conrad Nicholson Hilton, Jr.

❀ 7 ❀

Nicky Hilton, as the press called him, was the oldest son of hotel magnate Conrad Hilton, and had been working for his father since he was fourteen. A course in hotel management in Switzerland had prepared him for his present position, at age twenty-three, as Hilton vice-president and manager of the posh Bel Air Hotel. He was handsome, wealthy, charming, widely traveled, and already was becoming known as something of a playboy. As a matter of fact, he had been out to the Mocambo looking over the field on that doleful night of Jane Powell's wedding. One look at Elizabeth and the field suddenly lost all its charms. He wangled an introduction through his pal Peter Freeman, son of Paramount executive Y. Frank Freeman, which is how the couple were first brought together over luncheon in the commissary.

Elizabeth returned home from filming that day to find a box of three dozen, beautiful long-stemmed yellow roses. Thus began six months of courtship during which, like most young people in the first flush of romance, they carefully showed each other their best sides. Press and public were overjoyed. They were both so young, so good-looking, so wealthy, so lucky. It was all like something right out of a fairy tale. It was really, as fans noted happily, "too good to be true." Really.

There were dates at sporting events, movies, dining and dancing out on the town, family dinners at the Taylor home in Beverly Hills and at the Hilton manse in Bel Air. For Christmas both families went up to Lake Arrowhead. On Christmas morning Nicky presented Elizabeth with diamond earrings set in clusters of pearls, and in the afternoon he secured her father's permission to ask for her hand in marriage. A month later he was on hand to witness the final absurdity of Elizabeth's academic career.

Elizabeth had already taken her final exams for her senior year

—on a Friday the thirteenth, as it happened—and the crew of her current film had presented her with a necklace of rabbit's feet for luck. She came out with a B+ average. But the Los Angeles school system passed out no diplomas at the Thalberg bungalow. When its students were certified ready for graduation, they were packed off in cap and gown to stand in line and receive a diploma at a school somewhere in the city. Which explains why, on the night of January 26, 1950, Elizabeth, formally attired in cap and gown, sat on the platform at University High School, trying hard to ignore a general buzzing of "Is it really *her?*" and/or "What is *she* doing here?" The principal gave out with one of those fight-the-good-fight exhortations to struggle in the battle of life no matter how hard the way. Elizabeth, whose weekly salary was then in four figures and who was being courted by a millionaire, began to have some wicked Walter Mittys about all of this. Her giggles transmitted themselves to the girl in front of her, and subsequently were passed around until the speech finished in what Elizabeth called "this awful rustle —like mice or chipmunks nibbling away." After which, she received her diploma, threw off the cap and gown, and headed for the Mocambo, where Nicky once again pressed her to marry him.

Metro, meanwhile, was still on the rack. To *Conspirator*, which had now gathered a year's worth of dust in the vaults, had been added *The Big Hangover*, and the studio's woes were doubled. They were loath to let either one of them out. The romance with Nicky Hilton was a hot item, and exhibitors and public clamored for another Elizabeth Taylor film. There hadn't been one for almost a year, and that one, *Little Women*, had really been June Allyson's, not Elizabeth's. The demand intensified from every quarter.

In February, Hallmark placed her on an enlarged Valentine Card and named her "Typical American Sweetheart." Elsa Maxwell saluted her as "The Most Exciting Girl in Hollywood," and wrote: "She may well have before her such a life and such a career as great beauties used to know." "Is Lana Jealous of Liz?" ran one story which proclaimed: "The gossips are saying that the Metro lot is getting too small to hold both Lana Turner and Elizabeth Taylor." This was a publicity throwback to the days when Norma Shearer, Greta Garbo, and Joan Crawford supposedly prowled the lot, each jealous of the other's turf.

Another article, titled "The Luckiest Girl in the World," trumpeted the word that "the big star buildup is complete. The new Elizabeth Taylor, polished, gleaming, mature, is ready for you to take to your hearts. Now it's up to you. Will you make her the Luckiest Girl in the World?" And: "Elizabeth Taylor is on the threshold of a career that may rival the brilliance of Bernhardt's or Garbo's or Bergman's. Elizabeth is eager to step through the door. Only you can say whether it will open for her."

Metro-Goldwyn-Mayer would have done anything to open that door, but not if it meant letting *Conspirator* out with her. They had not put in five years of heavy investment and careful planning to have Elizabeth finally emerge doing the turkey trot. They continued to thrash with the problem until two events in late February came to their rescue in a manner so fortunate they must rank among the most fortuitous coincidences of Elizabeth's or anybody else's career. Metro officials were then viewing the final cut of the film Elizabeth had just finished. Even in its rough form, minus music and final editing, it was plainly a winner. The celebration in the Thalberg Building was still going on when, a week before Elizabeth's eighteenth birthday, word arrived that Sara Taylor had just been pleased to announce that, on May 6, her daughter would be married to Conrad Nicholson Hilton, Jr. MGM joy burst its bounds as officials contemplated the prospective boost to the box office take of the new film. For the picture that Elizabeth had just finished was *Father of the Bride*.

This one not only got Elizabeth's career out of hock; it also put Spencer Tracy back on top. Tracy's postwar plight had not been quite as dismal as that of Robert Taylor, but for a star who sailed into the '40s holding an Oscar in each hand with a growing reputation as the screen's finest actor, the decade was a very mixed bag. It began with a horror called *I Take This Woman* which was Tracy's turn with Hedy Lamarr. This one was so badly botched and was in and out of so many hands that studio wits privately tagged it *I Retake This Woman*. Next he did an ill-advised remake of *Dr. Jekyll and Mr. Hyde*, with the memory of Fredric March's superb Oscar-winning portrayal still fresh in everyone's mind. Tracy came off a poor second. The partnership with Katharine Hepburn was a high spot and produced six films of varying quality. But he had gone to Broadway, flopped badly, and ended the decade with two more clinkers, one of which was stolen right out from under him—the only time *that* happened in his entire career. The film was *Edward, My Son*, and the thief who pulled off the impossible was Deborah Kerr. Most recently he had suffered through a miserable mishmash about rubber smuggling called *Malaya*, which also wasted James Stewart, Sydney Greenstreet, Lionel Barrymore, and John Hodiak as well. Spencer Tracy badly needed a good picture, and he got it.

The ironic postscript to all of this is that, had Paul Douglas not ill-advisedly rejected the part, Tracy would never have been offered it.

Over at Fox, Bette Davis was working on a film whose unique success she later explained as follows: "It was a great script, had a great director, and a cast of professionals all with parts they liked. It was a charmed production from the word go." She was talking about *All About Eve*, but she could easily have been describing *Father of the Bride*, a comedy currently every bit as fresh and delightful as the day it was made. The fun begins with the very first shot of its hero.

"I would like to say a word about weddings," Spencer Tracy wearily remarks, slumped in a chair in the midst of an appalling amount of litter and debris. "I've just been through one." He then returns in his mind to that disastrous day when daughter Elizabeth let he and wife Joan Bennett know that she and boy friend Don Taylor wanted to be married. Prospective in-laws Moroni Olsen and Billie Burke come calling, and the house is thereafter enveloped in a state of hilarious crisis which never lets up. There is a big hassle over whether or not to have a church wedding, another one over how many guests to invite to the reception, and a snotty caterer (brilliantly played by Leo G. Carroll) who apparently won't be satisfied until half the house is torn up and redesigned. Whether fulminating helplessly over the mounting bills, bursting through the seams of an old tuxedo, or trying desperately to keep bride and bridegroom from calling it all off at the last minute, Tracy moves through the film with peerless technique and a comic sense which are absolutely flawless and a joy to behold.

"Less is better" was a film-acting credo Spencer Tracy practiced with rewarding results, and Elizabeth learned a lot from working with him. In one scene, after he has had a comic nightmare, he goes down to the kitchen in the early morning only to find Elizabeth there with her own worries. He reassures her that everything will be okay. "Oh, you are wonderful," she tells him. "Nothing ever fazes you, does it?" The line comes so totally from the heart that it seems to pop right out of the frame and serves not only father and daughter, but actor and actress as well. This film was the proof that Elizabeth deserved sensitive direction, not because she was lost without it, but because she knew how to respond to it and could seize her opportunity. Therein lay all the difference.

She moves through the film in a state of ravishing beauty, looking "like the princess in a fairy tale," as Tracy remarks. Before the wedding he tells her, "You look wonderful, kitten, just wonderful." Father and daughter have beautifully poignant moments before she leaves for her honeymoon, and the film ends where it begins, with Spencer Tracy and Joan Bennett, oblivious to the reception ruins, dancing happily to "their song." It could all have been overdone to death, but it was produced by Pandro Berman and directed by Vincente Minnelli with sensitivity, care, respect for the material, intelligence, and great taste.

Metro now planned shrewdly and well. *Conspirator* could be got out of the way and the sooner the better. With Elizabeth marrying in May, *The Big Hangover* could be sneaked out in that month, hopefully to disappear in the avalanche of wedding publicity. Then, with the wedding still on everyone's mind, Metro would release *Father of the Bride* in June, to take double advantage of the Hilton nuptials and the nation's favorite month for weddings.

First came *Conspirator*. Metro sent it out double-billed with another piece of small change called *Black Hand*, a Mafia-exposé with Gene Kelly which was clearly its superior.

MGM whisked *Conspirator* out and in again—not in time, however, to prevent India from banning it (for political, not artistic, reasons). Nor could Metro's speedy handling of *The Big Hangover* prevent *The New Yorker* from getting in its licks. The following is the complete review:

"In *The Big Hangover* we have another lawyer, this one played by Van Johnson. He has an allergy to alcohol in even the smallest doses, coupled with a desire to do good. He also loves a lady who dabbles in psychoanalysis. The lady is played by Elizabeth Taylor. Miss Taylor is beautiful and cannot act. This puts her one up on Mr. Johnson."

MGM could afford to shrug that one off. Within a month they would be presenting Elizabeth in what now loomed as their prestige film of the year. And as they correctly foresaw, ever since that February announcement, the publicity attendant on Elizabeth's private life easily drowned out any tinny noises emanating from the two turkeys.

The manner of Elizabeth's wedding announcement was the first indication that everything was not to go quite according to plan. By the time Sara Taylor made the formal announcement on February 20, Louella Parsons had scooped her, courtesy of Conrad Hilton, Sr., who leaked the word to the press a day in advance. Pressed by reporters for the details of how she and Nicky met and what they had in common, Elizabeth allowed as how "we both love hamburgers with onions, oversized sweaters, and

Pinza." (Ezio Pinza was even then at MGM watching his *South Pacific* popularity go flushing into the hopper along with two unmentionables costarring Lana Turner and Janet Leigh.)

Other items kept the press busy. It was announced that Helen Rose and Edith Head would split the honors in wardrobe. Miss Rose would design the bridal gown and Miss Head would design Elizabeth's blue silk gabardine going-away suit. The bridal gown, paid for by MGM, was to be of white satin decorated with lilies of the valley in seed pearls. Rumor had it that the neckline might go far enough to get Elizabeth's bosom the major share of attention. That one brought normally mild-mannered Helen Rose out slugging. "It's about as unplunging as anything *could* be," she snorted. "Not half as revealing as Princess Elizabeth's wedding dress." Her trousseau was being designed by exclusive New York couturier Ceil Chapman which necessitated a special trip East and hours of fittings.

On April 15 there was a bland announcement that, though Nicky was a Roman Catholic and the wedding was to be a Catholic ceremony, Elizabeth would remain Protestant. Behind this item was quite a hassle. As the non-Catholic half of the nuptial pair, Elizabeth was expected to swear on oath that she was eager for motherhood and that the offspring would be raised Catholic. She would later look back on herself during this period as "too romantic and too unrealistic," but sheltered, spoiled, and inexperienced as she may have been, she had some firm convictions on certain subjects and this was one of them. Desperately as she might desire motherhood, she believed that sensible people do not bring children into this world until the home which has been prepared for them looks as if it has a fair chance of permanence, all the teachings of Augustine and Aquinas to the contrary notwithstanding. The Church was insistent and Elizabeth began to feel severely pushed. Normally this would have been tantamount to waving a red flag at a bull, and could easily have produced a display of what Pandro Berman once called "her crazy defiance." In this instance it did not. With the wedding less than a month off, Elizabeth took a deep breath and signed the oath.

Wedding presents were now beginning to overflow the house on Elm Drive: an oil painting from Francis, a white mink stole from Sara, one hundred shares of Hilton Hotel stock from her prospective father-in-law plus a three-month all-expenses-paid honeymoon trip to Europe, piles of presents from co-workers and fans, a closetful of suits, coats, evening gowns, etc. from Metro, including several outfits MGM also donated to the bride's mother, the maid of honor, and the bridesmaids.

On the afternoon of May 5, a fleet of MGM limousines began pulling up at the Church of the Good Shepherd in Beverly Hills. There, a crowd estimated at between 2,500 and 3,500 pressed against restraining barriers to ogle and cheer Fred Astaire, Ginger Rogers, Greer Garson, Dick Powell and June Allyson, Phil Harris and Alice Faye, Esther Williams, Ann Miller, Janet Leigh, and other guests as they entered the church. They were helped to their seats by five ushers, including Howard Taylor and Peter Freeman, the cupid who had first introduced the happy couple.

A few things happened which might have given pause to the superstitious. On the day before the wedding, Elizabeth had developed a fever from a cold and was being treated with penicillin. On the nuptial day, she arrived in her own limousine, flanked by her proud parents and preceded by a motorcycle escort through throngs which lined the route from Elm Drive to the church. When she alighted from the car, her gown caught on the door, tearing the veil. Once she was safely inside, the organ suddenly broke down and there was a brief wait for a repair job.

Then, to the strains of the wedding march, Maid of Honor Anne Westmore, resplendent in organdy bouffant, commenced the bridal procession. Behind her came six bridesmaids, including Jane Powell, Mara Regan (Howard's sweetheart), and Barbara (Mrs. Marshall) Thompson. Finally, a solemn Francis Taylor escorted one of the most dazzlingly beautiful brides who ever walked down an aisle in the whole history of matrimony. Her guests gazed at her as she passed them just as if she were, in Spencer Tracy's words, "the princess in a fairy tale." At the altar Nicky waited with Baron Hilton, his brother and Best Man. It was there that Elizabeth finally lost some of her own nervousness when she realized that her bridegroom was inwardly as terrified as she was. With her handkerchief, she mopped at the huge beads of sweat that had popped out on his forehead.

The size of the reception afterward can be measured by the fact that it took literally hours for all the guests to pass through the receiving line. There Elizabeth thanked each of them for their presence and their gifts. She also had two glasses of champagne, one more than she had ever before had on a single occasion. When it came time to go, she managed to have another— this one for courage, as, in the manner of all brides, she left the known and the comfortable for the future, which, for all its undoubted thrills, was also unknown and therefore intimidating.

Initially the honeymooners spent a week up in Carmel. Then they returned to be together with their mothers on Mother's Day. After their final return from Europe, Elizabeth was due to go into *Father's Little Dividend*. George Stevens was still cutting *A Place in the Sun*, but Paramount executives knew enough about it already to know they wanted her for *Carrie*, a planned screen version of Theodore Dreiser's *Sister Carrie*. It would have meant an enviable costarring appearance with Laurence Olivier. It would also have meant cutting short the honeymoon and rushing back from Europe to do it, and Elizabeth regretfully rejected the offer.

On May 16 a huge crowd at the L.A. Airport wished the new-lyweds *bon voyage* as they flew off to Chicago, where Nicky picked up a Cadillac, in which they drove to New York. Then the car was loaded onto the *Queen Mary*, later to be available for sightseeing in Europe. Elizabeth had been disappointed that she and Nicky couldn't get the bridal suite on the *Queen Mary*. The Duke and Duchess of Windsor had already booked it. The Hiltons and Windsors subsequently had tea together on the crossing, which was a charming way to begin a honeymoon.

Promptly in June, MGM released *Father of the Bride* to the delight of critics and the huge audiences who packed the theaters to see it.

MGM read the reviews, happily counted the weekly box office returns, and felt well pleased with the way everything had turned out. The film would go up, along with *King Solomon's Mines*, in MGM's 1950 bid for the Academy Award. For Spencer Tracy it would bring the first Oscar nomination after a drought of twelve years, No. 4 in his eventual record nine Academy Award nominations for an actor. He would lose on this particular one to Jose Ferrer's *Cyrano de Bergerac*, but everyone had been put on notice that the master was back in top form.

Elizabeth, the stresses and strains of past private and professional disappointments behind her, had now been properly launched as an adult both on screen and in real life. Blundering and insensitive though it could be at times, the studio had produced a fine film for her and had knocked itself out to give its favorite daughter the wedding of the year, if not the decade. Unhappily for MGM, it wasn't all taking place under carefully controlled circumstances at Culver City.

Even now the honeymooners in Europe, unknown to anyone at the time, had begun to diverge drastically from the script. "When I married Nick," Elizabeth later said, "I fell off my pink cloud with a thud." The descent was sudden and the thud was heard in divorce court in Santa Monica exactly eight months later.

❀ 8 ❀

As to where it all fell apart, there is no great mystery. It began to strain at the seams in Europe, and went totally to pieces back in America. As to precisely how it fell apart, no one, aside from the actual participants, knows to this day. Everybody put the big mouth of speculation to work on it, from the studio to the columnist to various writers who embellished what wisps of reality they could lay hold of with the kind of soap-opera fantasy that helps sell the sad rags they write for.

At the time, Elizabeth observed, "We were both much too young and immature, and our European honeymoon lasted five months, which is too long. We had no feeling of security or settling down. Until I was married, I had never before spent a night away from my mother." Of her first marriage Elizabeth has written further: "It scarred me and left me with horrible memories."

A firm seal was put on those memories twenty years ago. The other partner to those memories took his share of them to his grave. In February 1969 Nicky Hilton was dead of a heart attack at the age of forty-two. The people with whom she was to seek refuge during her ordeal might have talked, but they were not the kind to be had for money from a smut sheet. Coming from a Christian Science background, Elizabeth was also aware of the positive harm one could allegedly do oneself by dwelling, privately or publicly, on pain and unpleasantness. Some people seem to dote on living in unhappy memories—grooving in the graveyard, as it were. She has never been one of them.

For a marriage so speedily to come to grief, it certainly looked like it had started auspiciously. True, Elizabeth developed a minor infection in her left arm from the smallpox vaccination in New York. But, as soon as the *Queen Mary* docked at Cherbourg, the honeymooners sped on to a lavish suite at the posh Hotel George V in Paris, and a round of fun parties. Somewhat soberly for a new bride, Elizabeth told reporters, "We liked each other, but it was not love at first sight. I was not thinking about love at that time." On to London as the guests of a maharajah at Ascot, where three of Elizabeth's choices rode home winners.

She referred to a "gay time" in Paris where, oddly, she had bought only one dress. Nicky coyly dropped stork hints. Back to Paris and a lavish affair hosted by Elsa Maxwell. Then on to Florence, Verona, Venice, and finally Rome.

Quo Vadis, in which Elizabeth was to have originally starred, was then shooting in the Eternal City, and she persuaded Mervyn LeRoy to let her be costumed and made up and run with the hundreds of Christian martyrs fleeing from the hungry lions in the Colosseum sequence. That attended to, the newlyweds returned to Paris to a great ball at which Elizabeth was resplendent in a Pierre Balmain gown wearing $150,000 worth of diamonds loaned her for the occasion. In September the Hiltons returned to America, he to his duties at the Bel Air, she to report for work on *Father's Little Dividend*.

Elizabeth's return had been preceded by photos taken of her in Europe showing her pale and wan and shockingly thin in the face. Additionally there were rumors being passed around at second and third hand of angry quarrels in the honeymoon suite and tearful scenes in various gambling casinos. Louella Parsons interviewed the couple upon their return, trying in various ways to get Elizabeth to give a rapturous account of her honeymoon. Elizabeth kept firmly steering the conversation back to a little dog Nicky had just given her.

Possibly because she was No. 2, Hedda Hopper, like Avis, needed to try harder. Elizabeth bravely held her own through the following grilling:

HEDDA: "What about all these quarrels?"

ELIZABETH: "Quarrels happen to every young couple. But we didn't have our misunderstandings in public. We don't take marriage that lightly. Every young couple has to make adjustments."

HEDDA: "I heard you quarreled because you didn't approve of his gambling."

ELIZABETH: "Everybody gambles in France."

HEDDA: "I understand he threw poker chips in your face."

ELIZABETH: "False. They don't play poker in France."

HEDDA: "Well, on a gambling ship, then."

ELIZABETH: "False."

The return to familiar surroundings might have been expected to ease the situation. Instead it continued to worsen. Elizabeth had lost twenty pounds in Europe. Now, for a girl who had never smoked cigarettes before, she began chain-smoking them by the pack. The European rumors were being fueled by reports of tiffs at various Hollywood parties.

"Sure we spatted," she snapped irritably at one reporter. "What honeymooners don't?" To Louella Parsons she complained, "Other young people can quarrel and make up, but before we have time to kiss and make up after a quarrel, it's in the newspaper." Louella, of course, printed that. The public had been alerted to the situation, it was hot news, and nothing could be off-the-record.

As the quarrels grew uglier and the bitterness continued to erode the frail thread of physical passion, Elizabeth began unwillingly to confront the unthinkable: divorce. She and her young husband seemed to have so very little in common, and they had begun to argue about everything. "Elizabeth is a very ordinary woman, really," Sandy Dennis was to observe years later. By which she meant that happy times in the privacy of her home, with husband and children and with a few friends she likes and trusts, have always had a high priority with Elizabeth. This is at odds with the screen image of the dazzling beauty who moves through luxurious surroundings in the smart set stunningly gowned, flawlessly photographed, conquering all men with her infinite desirability. How much of the image Nicky Hilton confused with the reality is open to question.

"I didn't marry a girl," he reportedly muttered. "I married an institution." He had also married a girl who by her own admission was "a virgin not only physically but mentally." Not only did she not share in the excitement of his jet-set interests, she was plainly uncomfortable in such surroundings, and betrayed an ignorance of ordinary household matters that was lamentable. "She doesn't know how to go to the grocery store and, if someone doesn't bring food to her room, she'd starve to death," Shelley Winters once remarked. "All her life people have done things for her and have told her what to do." She had been sheltered from the mundane all her life, and was accustomed to having those things done for her. To wait for this child-bride to slowly develop into a capable wife required a patience, given the circumstances of his own upbringing, which Nicky Hilton simply did not possess. Even then he had a notoriously short emotional fuse. When his second wife subsequently sued for divorce, she charged him with "repeated acts and threats of physical violence." The violence, both overt and latent, which Elizabeth both saw and sensed in him doubtless terrified her.

Her initial reaction was a natural one. She went home to the soothing ministrations of Sara and Francis Taylor. And stayed one day. The maturity now being forced upon her brought home the bitter truth of Thomas Wolfe's *You Can't Go Home Again*, which everyone must learn, sooner or later. A retreat into adolescence was no solution. When *Father's Little Dividend* wrapped on November 1, Elizabeth went off to Palm Springs alone to wrestle with her problem. Her husband had gone to Las Vegas but joined her in Palm Springs for a brief reconciliation. They planned a trip to New York which aborted when the plane almost crashed in an emergency landing right after takeoff. After the final quarrel, Elizabeth moved in with her stand-in, Margery Dillon, in order to come to, what she called, "the first grown-up decision I ever made absolutely alone."

Ordinarily Elizabeth can stand off an army when she is convinced of the essential rectitude of her own course of action, "when she is secure in her own mind," as Producer Sam Marx phrased it. In this instance she was overwhelmed by a sense of total failure. There had never been a divorce in her family. If it had to be, this would be the first. There was the numbing sense of having disappointed everyone—her parents, the studio, the public, her bridegroom, and especially herself. And always there had been someone right at hand to help, to lean on, to advise her. Now—by her own stubborn insistence—there was no one.

Sensing the finality inherent in her conduct, Nicky Hilton began an ardent attempt at reconciliation. But as soon as he discovered her current refuge, and bombarded it with yellow roses and unanswered phone calls, Elizabeth dragged herself off to a new one. She was now at the thin edge of a nervous breakdown and an incipient ulcer had begun to nag at her. Friends such as Anne Westmore, Helen Rose, Jane Powell, and the Marshall Thompsons closed ranks around her. When she would show up, haggard and spent, at their door, they took her in, fed her what little she would eat, made her as comfortable as they could, and asked no questions.

By early December the rift was in the newspapers, and a Metro spokesman made a clumsy attempt to handle the situation. He announced, "Elizabeth Taylor went home to mother after a big fight," which, of course, she painfully and deliberately had not. Furthermore: "This isn't the first time they have separated. They always fight about the same thing—his gambling and playing around and ignoring her as a wife. They both have a temper. They've been fighting but they were trying to work it out." Elizabeth's pronounced aversion to publicists poking into her private life must have increased by leaps and bounds, given the inaccuracy and the presumption of inside knowledge which was likewise faulty.

Ultimately she came to stay at the home of her agent, Jules Goldstone, and his wife. It was there she decided that her decision to seek a divorce was irrevocable, and summoned her husband to inform him. They were closeted together in the den for over an hour, when the shouting and the abuse prompted Goldstone to open the door to the den, and also the front door, and to order Hilton from the house.

On December 14, MGM issued the formal statement on her behalf. "I am sorry that Nick and I are unable to adjust our differences," it announced, "and that we have come to a final parting of the ways. We both regret this decision, but after personal discussion we realize there is no possibility of a reconciliation."

Under these doleful circumstances, Metro felt the best thing she could do was keep steadily at work as a form of therapy. It assigned her to play a character named Anastacia Macaboy in something really god-awful called *Love Is Better Than Ever*. Her costar was to be Larry Parks, who had created quite a stir in two films playing Al Jolson. The studio subsequently issued a release stating that Elizabeth was indeed suffering from "incipient ulcers and colitis." Now she was put on a strictly bland diet of strained vegetables, baby foods, and the like. She required a nurse in daily attendance on the set. Her nerves were frazzled and extra care was needed to photograph her in such a thin, exhausted state. Before shooting was finished she would be in Cedars of Lebanon for a few days with flu. The combination of all this plus the rubbish she worked in daily before the cameras might have been enough to knock her totally flat, had it not been for the sympathetic shoulder of the director, Stanley Donen, then twenty-seven, and recently separated himself.

There had been no dearth of admirers willing to pay court since the public announcement of the impending divorce. Prominent among the would-be suitors was, once again, Howard Hughes. That Hughes continued to be deeply smitten is beyond question, considering the extraordinary manner in which he laid himself wide open to the kind of publicity he professes to detest. On one occasion he summoned Sheilah Graham from a sick bed to tell her that he had bona fide proof that one of the men paying court to Elizabeth was a card-carrying communist. Subsequently, on the eve of Elizabeth's marriage to Michael Wilding, Hughes went to Louella Parsons, then in Palm Springs, and persuaded her, against her better judgment, to phone Elizabeth. "Do you think you'll really be happy?" Louella began delicately. Correctly suspecting what was behind all that, Elizabeth gave Louella short shrift for her efforts. Hughes must have realized that Sheilah and Louella would eventually print these incidents, which indeed they did.

She rejected the new overtures from Hughes and the other callers until one night she roused herself enough to go out on a date and found herself smack in the middle of an ugly situation right out of *Mildred Pierce*. It is the scene in which a leering Jack Carson is making an end run around the furniture in a vain attempt to seduce Joan Crawford, and his lines read: "You gotta be educated, Mildred. You've just joined the biggest army in the world—the one that never gets mentioned on the Fourth of July. A grass widow." Elizabeth suffered through one of these sordid wrestling matches and decided that one was enough.

Thereafter she came to rely more and more on the protective attentions of Stanley Donen. This was only his third film, and on his first, *On the Town*, he had shared co-director credit with Gene Kelly. Next was the Fred Astaire-Jane Powell *Royal Wedding*. Upcoming was the brilliant *Singin' in the Rain*. At this point, given this dreary piece of junk, he was conscious of his responsibility to his own career, to the studio, and to Elizabeth both as a person and an actress. He did his best with the material, and provided Elizabeth with every support he could lend her. On days when she just couldn't seem to get through it, Donen dismissed the rest of the cast and crew and gave her his friendly ear and sympathetic counsel. Gradually a romantic attachment slowly blossomed, and between them they finally succeeded in getting *Love Is Better Than Ever* into the can in late January. Metro looked at it and realized they had another horror on their hands. They were still worrying about it when Parks fell under the gun of the House Un-American Activities Committee. The film was then given *Conspirator* treatment: thirteen months in solitary confinement in the vaults, and then quickly out on double bills. Critical reaction was predictable.

"Almost as thrilling as getting a haircut," opined one critic.

"Elizabeth Taylor, ineptly striving for comic form, reveals a photogenic figure," reported *Time*, "but Parks falls flat on his farce." Elizabeth's personal notices were not all bad. Even though it flayed the picture as a "lifeless romantic comedy" and a "listless, indifferent film" the Hollywood *Reporter* observed that "Elizabeth Taylor is as good as the naïve little miss as the part allows." And *Cue* noted: "Quite surprisingly, Elizabeth Taylor indicates a nice talent for underplayed comedy in the role of the dancing school mistress who braves the danger of the big city and bags herself a husband."

Meanwhile, in real life, Elizabeth went into divorce court in Santa Monica, on January 29, 1951, to shed a husband. She had filed a page-and-a-half complaint in the previous month charging "extreme mental cruelty" and had asked for no alimony. Now she took the witness stand and the proceedings went as follows:

LAWYER: "Will you tell the court briefly what your husband's conduct was?"

PLAINTIFF (in a low voice): "He was indifferent to me and used abusive language and . . ." (her voice faded to an inaudible whisper).

COURT REPORTER (stationed two feet away): "I can't hear a word."

JUDGE: "Keep your voice up. Just pretend my reporter is a little hard of hearing."

A ripple of laughter spread through the courtroom, reaching everywhere but to the witness stand. There the plaintiff briefly covered her face with her gloved hands. When she removed them, the tears were streaming down her face. There was a pause. Then:

LAWYER: "May I be permitted to ask some leading questions?"

The judge consented, suggesting that the lawyer put the testimony into the record in his own words and his client could then confirm it. The judge admitted it was slightly unusual, but necessary, in view of the plaintiff's inability to raise her voice. It was then established that, upon the return from the European honeymoon, Hilton had burst into her room and cursed her in front of Sara and of Barbara Thompson. The latter then took the stand to corroborate that bit of testimony and to add that, since the marriage, Elizabeth was not "her gay and usual self," and that she had "lost a tremendous amount of weight during the marriage."

For Elizabeth, the temptation to go into other, less savory details of the relationship must have been enormous. She was painfully aware of what it looked like on the surface—the girl who had broken two engagements and had flunked out in her first marriage before it was a year old. The temptation toward public justification warred with Elizabeth's firmly rooted sense of family privacy, and in that battle, discretion has always been the victor. The divorce was granted without further resort to ugly details.

With the hearing over, Elizabeth consented to return to the witness stand to pose for more pictures but once again broke into tears. She was then taken into the judge's chambers for fifteen minutes, to have a cigarette and to regain her composure. Then she returned, working her way to the elevator through a crush of photographers pleading for "just one more," and a throng of spectators who had come to gawk. Finally, mercifully, it was over.

"When sorrows come, they come not single spies, but in battalions," observes King Claudius in *Hamlet*. Which is Shakespeare's poetic rendering of "it never rains but what it pours." It was now pouring on Elizabeth because a week later, by an unfortunate coincidence of bad timing, the Harvard *Lampoon* announced its annual awards for 1950—and Elizabeth had won four of them. "Won" was hardly the word.

The *Lampoon* named her (1) "one of the two most objectionable movie children" (the other was not specified), (2) the actress who gave "one of the two worst performances of the year" (in *Conspirator*, which was also named one of the "Ten Worst Films of the Year"), (3) "the most objectionable ingenue," and (4) a Special Trophy for "so gallantly persisting in her career despite a total inability to act." The Special Trophy was called the Roscoe ("Oscar, spelled sideways"), and it was established in 1951 with Elizabeth as its first recipient, "to be presented annually to the actor or actress who in the previous year has most shown those qualities of perseverance, leadership, and personal integrity which have helped make Hollywood what it is today." *Samson and Delilah* was also named one of the "Ten Worst Films of 1950" and it was also 1950's biggest moneymaker. Sniffed the De Mille organization: "I guess money is of no interest to Harvard men—so long as their dads keep sending it."

Less than a month later, Elizabeth was in Boston for a Red Cross rally and was at Logan Airport, en route to New York, when fifteen *Lampoon* members and a brass band marched out to meet her carrying a huge bronze bust. It was, they declared, "the Fabian Fall Award, in memory of that well-known and much-respected man." It was graciously being given to Elizabeth as "the actress who has shown the greatest improvement as a result of the previous receipt of the Roscoe." That had been less than a month ago. Somewhat nonplussed at this speedy and unexpected turn of events, Elizabeth could only say, "Thank you—it's very sweet of you boys to be here," and then lug the thing onto the plane with her.

No sooner was she airborne than Harvard University belatedly discovered that the august bust of Fabian Fall, former editor of the Harvard *Crimson*, had mysteriously disappeared from its ancient pedestal. With the police about to be alerted, the *Lampoon* confessed all. Harvard then cried theft and threatened to sue for its return. Elizabeth apparently dumped it out in New York, because she later arrived in Los Angeles without it, and proved she could take a joke. "That big thing?" she laughed. "It was just a gag. Boys will be boys."

Elizabeth was now sharing a five-room apartment on Wilshire Boulevard with Peggy Rutledge, her new personal secretary, who had once served in that capacity to Dolores (Mrs. Bob) Hope. She had effectively, as she phrased it, "kicked herself out of the nest," and there was to be no return to it. This was particularly true since Sara Taylor looked askance at her deepening involvement with Stanley Donen, and the matter led to an estrangement between mother and daughter. One mutually wounding blowoff occurred when Elizabeth brought Donen out to the house in Beverly Hills. Mother and daughter faced off on the threshold, and after a torrent of recriminations and tears, the front door slammed and Donen drove a severely shaken Elizabeth back to her apartment in town.

MGM was no happier with this new romantic turn of events. They had nothing against Stanley Donen. They thought him a fine fellow and one of their most promising young directors. But he was not for Elizabeth. She they had come to regard as some sort of love-victim who had to be counseled, guided, and—if need be—protected against herself for her own good. Elizabeth, however, had just about had it with this kind of well-intentioned direction—whether from her mother, her studio, the columnists, or anyone else. She had played the obedient daughter, gone into something of which everyone had approved and thought was a marvelous idea, and had landed herself in a fierce mess. Henceforth she would steer her own ship. She would go where she chose, date whom she chose, and, ultimately, marry whom she chose. And well-intentioned advisers would be well advised to keep their mouths out of her private affairs.

Metro began to get the vibrations from this declaration of independence and decided to play for time. Elizabeth was still physically weak, still on her special bland diet, still not fully recovered from the draining effects of her divorce. It ill behooved the studio to force a showdown at a time like this. Eventually she would reconcile with her mother, then the malleable, agreeable little girl who looked to her mother for personal guidance and to her studio for professional guidance would once again return. The studio thus awaited the reappear-

ance of a girl whom they had yet to perceive was long gone—
and would never return.

In that spring of 1951, Elizabeth did a day's work in a cameo
part on *Callaway Went Thataway*, a tepid satire aimed mainly at
Bill "Hopalong Cassidy" Boyd and his restoration to fame via
television. Dorothy McGuire and Fred MacMurray are a couple
of hustling agents who latch onto former movie cowpoke
"Smoky" Callaway (Howard Keel). In one sequence, they all
enter Hollywood's Mocambo nightclub where Smoky recognizes
no one but cheerfully whacks everyone on the back in good,
down-home fashion, anyway. Elizabeth rises from her table,
greets him with "Hello, Smoky," and Fred MacMurray barely
restrains him from smacking her on the back. Clark Gable is
not so lucky. He is smacked on the back and gets to be called
"Sam."

In April, MGM released *Father's Little Dividend*, to excellent
reviews which moved *Time* to observe that "unlike most sequels,
it should also repeat the original's success." The new film introduced Spencer Tracy to the joys and pains of grandfatherhood,
and not only was Elizabeth out of the title, but her footage had
shrunk from the amount allocated her in *Father of the Bride*.
Possibly because the original so closely followed real life, and
the real-life script for the sequel went up in smoke in Santa
Monica in January, *Father's Little Dividend* failed to live up
to heady box office expectations. Tracy got his usual raves,
however, and Elizabeth was not slighted either.

The Hollywood *Reporter* called the film "a rollicking sequel
of situation comedy," and noted that "Elizabeth Taylor, always
strikingly beautiful, has more poise and acting ability as the
expectant mother than she has shown previously." In the New
York *Times*, Bosley Crowther credited her with creating "a
real American type, slightly prettified and idealized, we'll grant
you, but never sugared or overdone."

On April 5, MGM gave *Father's Little Dividend* a splashy
benefit premiere at the Egyptian Theater in Hollywood on behalf of the John Tracy Clinic and in honor of Spencer Tracy,
whose fifty-first birthday it was. George Murphy was emcee,
Louise Tracy spoke about the work of the clinic, and then the
whole audience sang "Happy Birthday" to Spence, present in one
of his rare appearances at a premiere. Elizabeth also attended
and entered proudly, and defiantly, on the arm of Stanley Donen.
On April 10, Jeanne Donen filed for divorce.

Metro now moved to put a crimp, hopefully permanent, in
the budding romance. With no picture on her schedule, Elizabeth

had been giving much of her time to work in children's hospitals, to entertaining wounded veterans, visiting troopships returning from Korea, and in recording programs for Armed Forces Radio. Now MGM announced her for the upcoming version of *Ivanhoe*, to begin filming on location in England in July.

Elizabeth received the script and her heart sank. There were two leading women, and neither was really central to the main action, which concerned the restoration to the English throne of Richard the Lion-Hearted after his ill-starred participation in the Crusades. Additionally, since both women could not win the hero, Elizabeth was to be the loser. She was still following doctor's orders, still involved with Stanley Donen, and she was of half a mind to refuse *Ivanhoe* and take a suspension. But she was now on her own, and suspension meant going off salary. That she could not afford to do. So, with ill-concealed resentment, she flew to New York via American Airlines on June 18, and boarded the *Liberté* to cross the Atlantic and be in England for the July start-date on *Ivanhoe*.

What was really unfortunate was that her brother Howard, whom she had seen in New York prior to sailing, suddenly received his Army induction notice. Consequently, he and fiancée Mara Regan moved their wedding date up to June 23 so that they'd be married before he entered the service. Her beloved brother was finally getting married and Elizabeth couldn't even be there. The best she could do was cable her love and best wishes from across the sea.

Small wonder, then, that she arrived in London depressed and out of sorts, and with a full complement of strained foods, without Stanley Donen, and facing the making of a film in which she had absolutely no interest. *Ivanhoe* director Richard Thorpe recalled, "Then and later, I expected her to break down any minute." Even as at a former point in her life which was low, both personally and professionally, a man and a film now came to her rescue.

The man was Michael Wilding, who called her on the morning she arrived. "I honestly thought she might be lonely," Wilding later recalled. Elizabeth told him that she had a traveling companion with her named Peggy Rutledge. Fine, replied Wilding. How about the three of them going to dinner that evening? Which they did, and continued to do five nights thereafter. After which Peggy Rutledge made her own dining arrangements.

As for the film, in August, eighteen months after shooting was finished on it, Paramount finally released *A Place in the Sun*. Out of the sprawling pages of Theodore Dreiser's *An American*

Tragedy, George Stevens had wrought one of the enduring masterpieces of the screen. And the day when anyone could sensibly view Elizabeth Taylor as nothing but a vacuous Technicolor trifle was over for good and all.

❧ 9 ❧

It all began in New York State in 1906. In that year Chester Gillette was convicted of murdering Grace Brown, his pregnant factory-worker sweetheart, and then tossing her body into Big Moose Lake up in the Adirondacks. The State contended that he did it because Grace complicated his plans to marry a rich girl. Chester Gillette was sent to the electric chair.

Working from these lurid bare bones, author Theodore Dreiser subsequently wrote for ten years, structuring a massive indictment of materialism in American society. He called it *An American Tragedy*, and his editors sliced 100,000 words out of the manuscript before they finally published it, in 1925, in two volumes. It was promptly banned in Boston, thus following in the footsteps of the author's own *Sister Carrie*, which had been declared off limits in Beantown in 1900.

The prosecutor at the trial minced few words. "The most disgusting, the most filthy, the most vicious, the most devilish language that a human being could think of" was what awaited anyone who was unfortunate enough to lift the cover of *An American Tragedy*. Furthermore: "Perhaps where the gentleman published this book it is considered not obscene, indecent, and impure for a woman to start disrobing before a man, but it happens to be out in Roxbury, where I come from." Which, to people familiar with Roxbury, must have occasioned an earthquake of mirth.

Theodore Dreiser was a stormy petrel who roared through life on his own truculent brand of high octane, and for all he cared, Beantown could go and fart itself to death. Already, serious claims were being put forward for *An American Tragedy* as the great American novel. A play version was adapted by Patrick Kearney, starring Miriam Hopkins as Sondra, the part Elizabeth would eventually play. It settled down to a gross of $30,000 per week, had 216 performances on Broadway, and subsequently went out on a successful road tour. Paramount paid Dreiser $135,000 for the screen rights, but only after Walter Wanger and Jesse Lasky had been embarrassed witnesses to a nasty altercation over money in the dining room of New York's elegant Ritz Hotel, at the climax of which Dreiser threw hot coffee in his partner's face and stalked off in a rage.

Paramount's subsequent 1931 film version eliminated the sociological indictment and presented the hero as a product of parental neglect and his own criminal tendencies. Fulminating about the depiction of his hero as "a sex-starved drugstore cowboy," the infuriated Dreiser sued unsuccessfully to prevent the film's release. If the courts wouldn't kill it, the public proved far less merciful and gave it a short, unhappy life. This dismal legal and financial background indicated that George Stevens had his work cut out for him trying to persuade Paramount that a remake was in order.

First off, he changed the title from *An American Tragedy* to *A Place in the Sun* because, as Stevens observed, "It is the story of an inarticulate boy frustratedly fighting society and the economic system, attempting without success to find a place of respect for himself." Hence the change to this particular title, and also because it was positive, vs. the original title, which was negative. Negativism, futility, fashionable ennui, and the like were, and are, anathema to George Stevens.

Lest Paramount worry about "radical theories," Stevens covered that flank by observing: "The greatness of *An American Tragedy* lies in the fact it is all things to all people. But that is also a pitfall. Some have tried to make the story a vehicle for personal messages or theories. Any narrow interpretation is false to Dreiser. In the main this might have been the love story of any Johnny or Mary in America, remarkable in simplicity and youthfulness. We'll try to tell it easily and honestly, without dramatic contrivances. One of the book's great charms lies in the fact Dreiser did not marshal his arguments to prove any personal philosophy. He was factual, a man of great compassion, a tremendous realist . . . He made his central character, Clyde Griffiths, one of the most fascinating and controversial figures in literature. You can spend weeks debating Clyde's guilt or innocence, his legal immorality over his spiritual immorality." This was a reference to the key scene on the lake, and the question of murder. The boat upsets and the girl drowns. The boy premeditated murder but the girl upset the boat. Still, the boy did nothing to save her. Or did he?

Along with a title change, Stevens decreed a change of character names, to put a further distance between the remake and the original. Clyde Griffiths became George Eastman, Sondra Finchley became Angela Vickers, and Roberta Alden became Alice Tripp. Stevens also updated the story from the '20s because the theme is contemporary and because he didn't want any "theater" getting between the film and the audience, in the sense that period settings and costumes might be "quaint" and "amusing." They generally were in Hollywood re-creations of the '20s, not least for the inevitable anachronisms (for example, bosoms, hair styles, et al.). Finally, the original setting of a collar factory was changed to a textile plant, where bathing suits are modeled, the better to emphasize the hero's temptations.

Ultimately, the key factor in making this depressing story of frustrated love and of death in the electric chair palatable to the public was correct choices for the three principals. On their shoulders would rest the responsibility of generating maximum empathy so that audiences would come through the emotional wringer to a genuine catharsis, the desired end of all tragedy. One wrong choice could throw the whole thing off and Stevens knew it. He handpicked two of the leads, but the third picked him.

His choice of Elizabeth to play Angela raised eyebrows all over Hollywood. The idea of Elizabeth Taylor as, in any way, a serious actress fit to consort with the likes of George Stevens was definitely not an idea whose time had come. But Stevens knew what he was doing. "The part calls for not so much a real girl," he remarked, "as the girl on the candy-box cover, the beautiful girl in the yellow Cadillac convertible that every American boy, some time or other, thinks he can marry." Stevens simply obtained the best facsimile available. He had never seen her work—maybe a hunk of *National Velvet* somewhere along the line, but he wasn't sure of that. She did, he thought, have the essential quality he was after.

For George, Stevens got Montgomery Clift, then twenty-nine and in the first flush of fame emanating from his good looks, the genuine electricity he generated onscreen, and a growing reputation as one of the finest young actors in America. Clift had come up through the demanding route of the New York theater as almost a living, successful projection of the various acting theories of the Moscow Art Theater's Konstantin Stanilavski. He had made his Broadway debut in 1935, at the age of fourteen, and had enjoyed long-run triumphs in *There Shall Be No Night* (with the Lunts) and *The Skin of Our Teeth* (with the Marches and Tallulah Bankhead). He came to Hollywood wearing his artistic integrity like a hair shirt, and he treasured a piece of advice given him by Elia Kazan.

"If a person turns down lucrative offers for parts he's not right for, and concentrates strictly on improving professionally and taking parts he can perform with integrity, success will come of its own accord." Clift turned down many movie parts before he made a successful double debut in 1948: in *The Search* (which brought him the first of four Oscar nominations) and in *Red River*, the classic Howard Hawks western starring John Wayne. Having now played a G.I. and a cowboy, Clift sought to further extend himself and went into *The Heiress*, a piece of period Americana under the direction of William Wyler.

It was *The Heiress* which first brought Clift and Elizabeth together. Paramount gave it a big premiere at the Cathay Circle, and since Mr. Clift and Miss Taylor were to play lovers in an upcoming Paramount film, the studio commanded him to escort her to it. During the film Elizabeth's attentions were split between the excellent drama transpiring on the screen and the moans and groans of her date, who seemed to be expiring in his seat. Always hypercritical of his own work, Clift slumped further and further out of sight, muttering, "Oh, God, it's awful." About his own work he was substantially correct. Obviously uncomfortable in an ambiguous, badly written part, he had been aced by Olivia de Havilland and Ralph Richardson, working at the peak of their considerable powers.

Thereafter Clift became warier than ever and ultimately was known as one of the most finicky judges of scripts Hollywood ever saw. Some roles he seemed born to play, for example, Raskolnikov in *Crime and Punishment*, and never did. Other roles which would have fit him superbly had already been done by others, for example, Larry Darrell in *The Razor's Edge*, which Tyrone Power had crippled three years previously. When he turned down *Sunset Boulevard*, people shook their heads in wonder. As William Holden shot to full stardom in this rejected part, Clift, for reasons of his own, was off in Germany doing a minor Cold War goodie called *The Big Lift*. *A Place in the Sun* was to be the fulfillment of his earlier promise, and it would introduce Elizabeth to someone who enriched her personal and professional life enormously.

The lady who would play Alice, the factory girl, went after the part as if her professional life depended on it. Shirley Schrift, an East St. Louis Leo, came roaring onto the theater scene determined to become an actress. She changed her name to Shelley Winters and served her time up in the Catskills and in acting

workshops all over New York City. Then she heard that the great
Max Reinhardt was auditioning singers for an operetta. In the
midst of various coloraturas shaking the chandeliers with high C's
and other stupendous displays, Shelley came out doing her old
Borscht Circuit number called "Chi Chi Castenango," which apparently featured everything but Carmen Miranda's wedgies.
This astonishing display of *chutzpah* sent the great one into hysterics. When he stopped laughing, Reinhardt gave her a job. Next
came Hollywood, and a long hard pull in twenty-two films
which certainly were varied. There were bits in gems like *She's a
Soldier, Too*, two Rita Hayworth musicals, a stint as harem background in *A Thousand and One Nights*. When Clift made his star
debut in *Red River*, Shelley was briefly on hand as a dance hall
girl. Ronald Colman strangled her in *A Double Life*, and she
was subsequently run over in *The Great Gatsby*. Liberace had
once been on hand as Shelley cavorted in an opus called *South
Sea Sinner*, wearing an outfit the bodice of which was plastered
all over with question marks. At about this point, the direction
of her whole career had become one big question mark.

Then she heard that George Stevens was to do a remake of *An
American Tragedy*. She grabbed hold of Norman Mailer at a
cocktail party and begged him to write a letter to Stevens on her
behalf. Stevens couldn't believe what he read. Shelley Winters—
blond sex tigress and exotic little flower of Universal? He consented to meet her, reluctantly and briefly, in the lobby of the
Hollywood Athletic Club. She was late, and while waiting impatiently, his attention was drawn to a plain, mousy-haired frump
huddled over in a corner. As he stared at her, he began to think
his eyes were playing tricks on him. What Shelley had done was
to borrow her sister's clothes and make herself as plain and un-
attractive as she thought the character of Alice would be. Finally, Stevens walked over to her, and after the two had talked,
he asked her the crucial question: "Would you *really* allow yourself to be photographed like that?" At that point, after six dizzy
years in Hollywood, the real Shelley Winters stood up. "Mr.
Stevens, you can photograph me any way you want to so long as
I get that part." She got it.

In October 1949 Stevens took his cast and crew to Northern
California for two weeks of location work. Elizabeth wrapped
her last scene in *The Big Hangover* at five o'clock one evening,
and was on the train for the Lake Tahoe location at eight-thirty.
There she found herself in her most challenging and demanding
role since *National Velvet*. She would subsequently call it "my
first real chance to prove myself," and of the part, she wrote: "It

was tricky because the girl is so rich and spoiled that it would have been easy to play her as absolutely vacuous. But I think she was a girl who could care a great deal."

The company worked for two weeks at Tahoe, Echo Lake, and Cascade Lake and then returned to the Paramount lot in Hollywood. By then Elizabeth was working under a variety of pressures, not least of which were the relentless demands of her director for nuance and subtlety in characterization that went well beyond anything she had previously attempted. Elizabeth was now in her ninth year as an actress and with thirteen films behind her, she had the fundamentals pretty well nailed down. She knew how to position herself for various actions before the camera, how to move, how to hit floor marks and be seemingly unaware of them, which eye of her costar to concentrate on in a close two-shot, some of the things not to do (for example, not to get so thoroughly involved in a kiss that, when two mouths part, a rope of spit hangs between them), and so forth. She had developed the patience demanded when she had to sit around an entire morning made up and in full costume waiting for a set to be lit, and with her energy conserved, go before the cameras in the afternoon still fresh and ready. She learned to stay calm and unruffled, to mind her own business, and keep her temper and her peace while various people were losing theirs.

What she was now learning was how much more of herself there was to give, and it was both exciting and frustrating, for Stevens was a superb, if exacting, teacher. His constant demands for endless retakes induced feelings of inadequacy and insecurity she had never known in her professional life. Additionally, she had come into *Place* straight from *The Big Hangover*, and her weekends were being consumed with fittings for *Father of the Bride*, which she was to start immediately after her work at Paramount. The tensions all of this produced were reflected in brief, intermittent flashes of what Stevens called her "distemper."

A concurrent pressure was an attraction Elizabeth felt for Montgomery Clift from the moment she met him, compounded about equally of his looks and his reputation. These were as nothing compared to what happened when they went before the camera together. Clift worked with a concentration and an intensity Elizabeth had never seen before. And he gave of himself in a scene to a degree which affected her physically, like a series of electric charges. Soon she began to respond in kind, and the chemistry all of this produced would eventually illumine the screen like successive surges of heat lightning.

Clift's method of working was not without its cost.

"I'll tell you the big difficulty," he was to say years later. "Your body doesn't know you're just acting. It sweats and makes adrenalin just as though your emotions were *real*."

Off camera he was withdrawn and preoccupied with investigating every nuance of his character, even applying for, and receiving, permission to spend a night in the Death House at San Quentin, to key himself for the right mood and feeling for the film's climax. Such total dedication to his craft wrung him out physically and emotionally, and his unconcealed contempt for filmdom's peripheral frills did not sit well with Hollywood's elite. Later there would be bad-mouthings about a "narcissus complex" and a "death wish," chiefly by people who had expectations and demands which Clift either would not or could not satisfy. Then they vilified him, much in the manner of castigating an apple for not being an orange.

Montgomery Clift was undoubtedly an education for Elizabeth in accepting a person on his own terms and for his own values. Her own life-style demanded matrimony; his compelled him to remain free, uncommitted, solitary. A demand for the impossible would bring the loss of a person she respected and admired. Wisely she accepted a loving friend, and kept him to the day of his death fifteen years later. When she talked with him about the various facets of Angela, Clift reportedly told her, "Whatever you do, Elizabeth, begin at the beginning, and let the character unfold itself within you. Keep *thinking* this girl—and soon she will grow to full stature before the camera."

A year later, Elizabeth was asked for the "secret of her success." She replied, "Getting the breaks. I've been awfully lucky." She reflected a moment and then added, "Good fortune can put you there but you stay there through hard work. I don't necessarily mean lessons in acting but work to acquire understanding of your tools and yourself. When you play a part it's like a course in psychology. You have to know emotion. You can't pretend—that's phony. You have to *be*."

The genesis of this kind of thinking can be traced to Elizabeth's association with Montgomery Clift, George Stevens, and *A Place in the Sun*. Eventually Stevens wrapped the picture and retired to his cutting room with over 400,000 feet of film. What finally emerged remains a masterpiece in every foot and frame. Not least among the abundant riches is the economy of the film, which is simply stunning. The whole thing moves forward with inexorable precision, yet there is not the slightest suggestion of overplanning, rigidity, or arbitrary impositions that would falsify it. The story ebbs and flows and is true to its own rhythms. And every single shot makes a point and moves it forward.

We open with a shot of George, in nondescript clothes, hitch-hiking out on the highway. He regards a billboard featuring a pretty girl in a bathing suit. His look mingles envy and desire with the furtive air of someone whose status has denied him the good things in life but who nevertheless hungers for them. The most important things about George—his circumstances and his desires—are thus immediately presented to foreshadow the hero's problem, which will be the main line of the action. The billboard features bathing suits made by the Eastman Company, owned and operated by wealthy relatives whom George is on his way to see. He has come from Chicago and his mother, who runs a mission there.

At the factory, his uncle's secretary shoots him a look of cool appraisal which is a polite put-down. While he waits for her to contact his uncle, he wanders into the boardroom and sits dwarfed in its immensity, staring at a check for $10,000 on the desk. His uncle invites him to the house where he is diffident, in-articulate, ill-at-ease in such surroundings. Elizabeth then comes whirling in as Angela, on her way to a big evening somewhere, bubbling like your average garden-variety deb. Here Stevens resists a cliché, a process he will repeat several times throughout the film. Ordinarily, when two performers were fated to have a grand passion in a film, four eyeballs would immediately lock in some kind of instant rigor mortis. A loud surge of Tchaikov-sky on the sound track was also thought to be helpful. In this instance, George is indeed staring a hole right through Angela, but she doesn't even notice him.

George is given a mundane job at the factory by his cousin and the social bind he finds himself in is a cruel one. The family has decided to ignore him socially, and as an Eastman, he is for-bidden to fraternize with female employees. We get a shot of George—lonely, resentful, hungry for love—listening off-scene to party noises. A quick montage of calendar pages only empha-sizes his torment. Eventually he defies the rules and begins dating a flirtatious co-worker, Alice Tripp. Stevens gives George's sex-ual torment another twist by showing George and Alice sitting uncomfortably in the balcony of the local movie, where the noises which accompany onscreen kissing are appropriately crude and vigorous, and where all the other couples are entangled in steamy embraces like so much wet wash in the laundromat. Like the sexual pressure, the pressure from The System is unabating. When George subsequently takes Alice out in the car for a little action, a cop comes along to hassle him and tell him to go home. Which then sets up the clever seduction of Alice back in her tacky rented room.

George continues to date Alice, but his ambitions for wealth and position only intensify and begin to focus on Angela, who shows up at the factory sitting in her convertible, waiting for someone, again unaware of George. Eventually George is invited to a party at the Eastman house, on the night of his birthday, as it happens. He is in the billiards room, lining up shots at the table, when the door opens and Angela enters. So far we have seen Elizabeth twice—looking beautiful, superficial, and slightly unreal. With this scene she announces unmistakably that ten years of apprenticeship are over.

"Hello," she greets George. After watching him at the pool table for a moment, she observes guardedly, "I see you had a misspent youth." She then moves from social banter to greater intimacy. "Why all alone? . . . Being exclusive? . . . Being dramatic? . . . Being blue?" One is struck by the skillful way she orchestrates just this small bit to intimate to George that she knows something about all of these moods, thus establishing immediate rapport with him. Audiences of 1951 were, with this scene, introduced to an actress they had never really seen before. From this point on in the film, Elizabeth is so rapturously beautiful, so obviously well fitted for the part, and so at ease in it, that viewing her work is pure pleasure.

Much later in the evening, George returns to Alice, who has been waiting to give him a pathetic little birthday party for two. And also to present him with the doleful news that she is pregnant. "George . . . we're in trouble . . . real trouble . . . I think." Stevens shoots her confession from her back as she sits at the table, stolid and stiff like some dumb animal ready for the slaughter. Amid her envious whinings about "all those pretty girls you read about in the papers," the contrast between what most men want (Elizabeth as Angela) and what most men get (Shelley as Alice) is excruciating.

Alice now begins to urgently play her pregnancy for what it is: the only trump she will ever have in her whole life. Against the background of her strident demands that George marry her, he continues to see Angela, which leads them to the famous balcony scene and the full confession of their love for each other. "Oh, Angela, if I could only tell you how much I love you," George murmurs hoarsely. "If I could only tell you all." And Angela surrenders herself in response, "Tell mama . . . tell mama all." Stevens' use of huge, screen-filling closeups to project the intensity of young erotic passion is electrifying. Aside from being shrewd insurance against the noncommercial aspects of the film, they are intrinsic to the relationship. George and Angela are in the grip of devouring passion, and the intimacy of their attraction overwhelms them. Everything they are feeling surges into their faces every time they look at one another.

Throughout the film the choice of shots is continuously interesting. Time and again, the camera angles go well beyond faces and bodies posed to get at the emotions and varying textures of a scene. After a doctor refuses Alice's pathetic request for an abortion, she meets George outside in the car and now demands that he stop stalling and marry her. This is shot in semidarkness, and the lighting and choice of cuts give off a harsh, bleak, disjointed effect and present the scene for exactly what it is: a bad dream which, for the hero, is only too agonizingly real.

The audience has been well prepared for the climax on the lake. We have heard a radio announcer giving grim statistics about holiday fatalities, including drownings, and at another point, George and Angela are resting on the beach by the lake, and she mentions a recent drowning in which one of the bodies was never found. The scene ends with yet another bit of preparation. Stevens has been using lap dissolves to maintain unbroken audience attention, and here he fades from George looking out at the lake to a shot of a pregnant Alice wandering disconsolately to her mailbox. She is thus superimposed into the water in which she will eventually drown.

The scene on the lake is a superb synthesis of all the creative elements. In acting: the sharp reality which Clift and Shelley Winters bring to the scene; in script: the juxtaposition of Alice's banal hopes and plans with the torment on George's face, which shows all too plainly what he is contemplating as he rows the boat out into deeper water; in cinematography, as bright sunlight gives way to the darkening shadows of dusk; on the sound track, the insistent thrust of Franz Waxman's score counterpointed by the eerie sounds of the loons and other night noises; in direction, Stevens' impeccable sense of timing and, with his editor, the choice of cuts to pace the scene properly to its climax.

After the drowning, Stevens plays on the collective psychology of the audience like a virtuoso. The net keeps closing in on George but we know it and he doesn't. The amount of tension thus generated takes up any slack or fall-off from the climax, as "Will he kill her?" gives way to "Will they find her?" Again, the cliché way to answer that question is to have everyone sitting around, and the radio just happens to be tuned to the news, and the accident report just happens to be broadcast, and everyone miraculously shuts up at the particular moment to hear it. Stevens' method is to have a radio out on the float on the lake. The group (including George) who were there are now all in a speeding motorboat which keeps circling the float. Every time it passes the radio we get the news in fragments, but we hear all we need to and, of course, they don't.

"Will they find her?" now gives way to "Will they pin it on George?" A cut to the district attorney—excellently played by Raymond Burr as a big, brooding, bloodhound—informs us that George is wanted for questioning. Stevens continues the tension without letup. George and Angela are out riding in her convertible, and a cop overtakes them to give Angela a ticket for speeding. While he's giving her a lecture, we hear the wanted message on his police radio. But they don't. Later, as George naps with Angela out in the open car, dusk falls and the air is rent with ominous sounds of police sirens. But no police appear. All of this is peripheral to meaningful central action between the principals, and the result is to rivet audience attention 100 per cent.

Ultimately George is apprehended, charged, tried, convicted, and sentenced to death. Angela comes to the Death House to see George for a brief farewell, and the film reaches its emotional high point. The last shot is of George marching stoically to the electric chair. Thus ends one of the most penetrating, finely crafted examinations of the American Dream ever committed to celluloid.

Paramount gave *A Place in the Sun* a splashy world premiere in August 1951 at the Fine Arts Theater in Beverly Hills, with Dorothy Lamour as mistress of ceremonies amid a fantastic outpouring of celebrities and fans. Thereafter critics vied with each other in a battle of superlatives.

Without exception the quality of Elizabeth's work struck the critics with stunning surprise.

"The real surprise of *A Place in the Sun* is the lyric performance of Elizabeth Taylor as Angela, the pampered rich girl who loves the boy and stays with him in his trouble. Always beautiful, Miss Taylor here reveals an understanding of passion and suffering that is electrifying." (*Look*)

Other samples:

"For Miss Taylor, at least, the histrionics are of a quality so far beyond anything she has done previously that Stevens' skilled hands on the reins must be credited with a minor miracle." (*Variety*)

"What Miss Taylor brings to the pictures as a young actress is sheer magic." (L.A. *Times*)

Even critics who were no fans of Elizabeth Taylor came forth with praise of sorts. Reported Al Hine in *Holiday:*

"Stevens has placed Elizabeth Taylor in a part where all the uncomfortable, preening mannerisms that have brought a touch of nausea to her recent screen portrayals are valid. The conceit, artificiality, and awkwardness which mar her playing in most ingenue roles are not only acceptable but essential to her rendition of Miss Rich Bitch of 1951."

Finally, at a private screening, Charles Chaplin reportedly doffed his derby to George Stevens and called *A Place in the Sun,* simply, "the best film ever to come out of Hollywood."

Shelley Winters attended that screening and came out of it with distinctly mixed emotions. On the one hand, she had just witnessed the best work she had ever done in her life, and she knew it. But at what cost! She had trusted Stevens, had played the character of Alice the way he saw it, with no compromises, and now she was angered to the point where she could not trust herself to speak to him. Angered and horrified. Aside from the fact that all of her glamour had been utterly stripped away, up there on the screen were large hunks of insecurity, hostility, envy, and the fear of being unloved which had roots all the way back to the days of a little girl named Shirley Schrift who was born in East St. Louis. Stevens had coaxed it out of her to bring Alice to life, and Shelley felt naked and exposed. She had never brought such a measure of her own honesty and reality to her work, and she flinched at the sight of it—partially because she had yet to come to terms with herself.

One of the most difficult things in life is to find out precisely what it is, as dictated by circumstances and temperament that one is meant to do. Then, having accepted it—because that can be a whole other struggle, since old dreams die hard—to do it to the best of one's ability. Shelley had grown up idolizing the glamorous images of Norma Shearer, Greta Garbo, Jean Harlow, Joan Crawford, and other romantic ladies of the screen. She vowed she would be one of them. So she had come on to Hollywood to take her place with Lana and Ava and Rita. And there had been pounds of makeup, and different hair styles, and beautiful gowns, and a clutch of forgettable films in which she flirted seductively with romantic leading men. And the awful truth began to dawn on her that she was not going to be Rita or Lana or Ava. Or even Elizabeth Taylor. What she was going to be was Shelley Winters, once she could summon the courage to play from her own guts without the fear of rejection. So that Stevens presided over both a death and a birth—the death of an old dream, and the birth of an actress, and the death was painful and so was the birth. But it was the first step along the long road to her many triumphs and enduring popularity, and eight years later, Stevens would come back to guide her to the first of her two Oscars.

As for the Oscars of 1951: Academy voters were faced with an embarrassment of riches. *A Place in the Sun* had garnered the palm of the National Board of Review as the year's best film, but the New York Film Critics Circle had voted their award to *A Streetcar Named Desire*. Had either of them come along a year later, it would have won the Oscar hands down. But here they were in unfortunate competition with each other. The same thing had happened in the previous year when *All About Eve* faced off against *Sunset Boulevard*. At least then the voters had chosen between them and picked *Eve*. In 1951 the voters copped out and voted in *An American in Paris*, which, for all its genuine riches in music and ballet, remains one of the most artificial-looking, oppressively overdressed musicals ever made.

Montgomery Clift's George Eastman likewise collided with Marlon Brando's Stanley Kowalski, and the voters took the opportunity to honor Humphrey Bogart. His *African Queen* partner, Katharine Hepburn, entered the competition along with Shelley Winters, and both of them lost to one of the classic performances of the screen: that of Vivien Leigh in *A Streetcar Named Desire*.

A Place in the Sun thus lost out in three of the major categories for which it was nominated, but not in the fourth. An Oscar went to George Stevens as Best Director, and additional Oscars went to Michael Wilson and Harry Brown for their screenplay, William C. Mellor for Cinematography, Edith Head for her costumes, Franz Waxman for his score, and William Hornbeck for his editing. So even though it lost the big one to *An American in Paris*, both films ended that evening in a tie at six Oscars apiece. The only person who was shut out of all these festivities and nominations—and she was somewhat conspicuous by her absence—was Elizabeth.

Curiously enough this was the first of two films with Stevens on which identical things would happen. The film, Stevens, and her costars would be nominated and she wouldn't. In the final balloting, only Stevens would win. In the second instance, *Giant*, Rock Hudson, James Dean, and Stevens were all nominated and it was Stevens who went home a winner with his second Oscar. For Elizabeth, Oscars and full recognition were yet to come. For the present, her claim to be considered seriously as an actress was successful and sufficient. *National Velvet* brought her to stardom; *A Place in the Sun* secured it.

Now—finally out from under the sheltering protection of her family, and with the experience of an unhappy marriage behind her, Elizabeth stood at the threshold of her adult life. At this point, the lines of Walt Whitman which once served Bette Davis so well in that long-ago classic seemed particularly fitting:

"Untold want by life and land ne'er granted;
Now voyager, sail thou forth to seek and find."

PART II

QUEEN
1951-1961

Name me one actress who survived all that crap at MGM. Maybe Lana Turner. Certainly Liz Taylor. But they all hate acting as much as I do. All except for Elizabeth. She used to come up to me on the set and say, "If only I could learn to be good," and, by God, she made it.

—Ava Gardner

She has always had a very strong mind of her own.

—Sara Taylor

When the curtain fell on *The Lion in Winter*—that stormy saga of Henry II and his venomous family—audiences left the theater with feelings of foreboding for dear England which were amply justified historically. Old Blighty was to suffer the successive reigns of Henry's two surviving male heirs, each of them of opposite temperament, but both equally ruinous to the fortunes of the kingdom.

Richard, surnamed the Lion-Heart, spent the better part of his ten-year reign abroad chasing various rainbows and, if recent evidence be accepted, making love to his lute-player and other gentlemen who took his eye. The governance of England then rested in the hands of the ambitious and unscrupulous, led by his brother and heir, Prince John. When John finally succeeded to the throne, far from holding England of little consequence, he loved it and everything in it so dearly that his barons were to ultimately force him at Runnymede to set written limits to the royal greed.

One of Richard's overseas adventures was the disastrous First Crusade to reclaim the Holy Land from the Turks. After squandering a ton of blood and treasure on this enterprise, Richard was returning to England when, with the connivance of John, he was seized by Leopold of Austria, imprisoned, and held for ransom. John then proclaimed himself Sole Regent in England, the prelude to his ultimate usurpation of the throne. All of this is familiar background to the Robin Hood legend. It is also the point at which Sir Walter Scott's most popular potboiler, *Ivanhoe,* begins.

The Saxon knight, Sir Wilfred of Ivanhoe, has returned to England to raise the ransom and free Richard. He comes home prudently disguised, since Saxons still sweat rebelliously under the yoke of their Norman overlords and, as a matter of fact, Cedric, his proud Saxon father, has disinherited him for serving the Norman king. Ivanhoe reveals himself only to his beloved, the Saxon princess Rowena, and to Isaac, a wealthy Jew whom he rescues from robbery and possible murder. In gratitude, Isaac's beautiful daughter Rebecca gives Ivanhoe the wherewithal to outfit himself as "The Black Knight" and to enter the lists in the great tournament at Ashby. There in the presence of the infuriated Prince John, Ivanhoe proceeds to humiliate the flower of Norman knighthood in successive combats. Badly wounded, he is brought to Isaac's home and nursed back to health by Rebecca, who conceives a hopeless passion for him. Subsequently, Cedric, Rowena, Isaac, and Rebecca are tricked and taken captive to Torquilstone Castle by DeBois-Guilbert, a ruthless Norman who has conceived his own hopeless passion— for Rebecca. Ivanhoe, with the aid of Robin Hood and the men of Sherwood, successfully storms the castle and takes it. Rebecca, however, is carried off by Guilbert to court, there to stand trial as a witch. Prince John decrees Trial by Combat. Guilbert is chosen to fight for the crown; Rebecca chooses Ivanhoe as her champion. As she stands bound to the stake at which she may burn, the two knights engage in a bloodcurdling duel to the death with axe, mace-and-chain, and other grisly medieval mementos. Ivanhoe triumphs, and in the moment of his victory, King Richard, who has earlier arrived in England, now rides in with his warriors and reveals himself, to the mortification of John, who bends his knee before him. The liberated Rebecca casts a sad farewell glance at Ivanhoe and Rowena, and then departs the scene with her father.

Ivanhoe had been filmed twice, both times in 1913, but repeated attempts by various studios to do a sound version always aborted. When MGM finally secured the rights, the studio spared nothing to make the production superior in every department. For example, after vainly canvassing Britain for a castle which would serve, Metro decided to build its own Torquilstone Castle. It was begun in 1949, finished in 1950, and allowed to weather one year before the cameras turned. This gave Robert Taylor, always the first and only choice as the hero, time to get *Quo Vadis* and *Westward the Women* out of the way.

Taylor had suffered further indignities since playing Elizabeth's homicidal hubby in *Conspirator*. There was a penny-ante western called *Ambush*. Then MGM decreed a 360-degree turn from villainy to nobility and put him in a bummer called *Devil's Doorway* as, of all things, an American Indian. *Westward the Women* was simple-minded silliness in which wagonmaster Taylor escorted a gaggle of mail-order brides safely through the perils of the Wild West to eager husbands in California. Gregory Peck's inability to do *Quo Vadis* fortunately rescued Robert Taylor and placed him in his perfect cinematic element, that is, as the blunt, taciturn, handsome embodiment of abstractions of masculine integrity and courage. *Quo Vadis* and *Ivanhoe* together rejuvenated Taylor's career, so that when he finally left MGM in 1958, he had been under continuous contract for twenty-four years—still the record for any star at any studio. In *Ivanhoe*, in the opening sequence, Taylor strummed his lute outside of Richard's prison in Austria, and sang for the second (and final) time onscreen. (Previously he had ripped off a chorus of "I've Gotta Feelin' You're Foolin'" in *Broadway Melody of 1936*.)

Impeccable casting was the order of the day all along the line —Elizabeth as Rebecca, Joan Fontaine as Rowena, George Sanders as DeBois-Guilbert, Emlyn Williams as Wamba (Ivanhoe's comic squire), Finlay Currie as Cedric, Felix Aylmer as Isaac, Guy Rolfe as Prince John, plus the considerable talents of Robert Douglas, Basil Sydney, Sebastian Cabot, and Megs Jenkins in other roles. Having cast and set it with great care, MGM spared nothing to make *Ivanhoe* the biggest film, in terms of size and cost, to be made in Britain up to that time, far ahead of such expensive forerunners as *Henry V*, *Hamlet*, *Christopher Columbus*, and *The Red Shoes*. A sample call sheet, for a day's shooting on the Ashby Tournament sequence, called for the presence of all the principal actors plus 12 trumpeters, 15 Norman and 15 Saxon squires, 25 special foresters, 135 ordinary foresters, 160 members of a rough Saxon crowd, 120 mixed Normans (whatever that meant), 60 horses, a truckload of arrows, and 6 cows.

Nor was the production expertise confined merely to laying on a ton of men and money. At one point, a host of principals and extras sat down to a feast of mutton, fish, and venison, with roast potatoes. One of the players, a medieval expert, remarked that he was sure potatoes hadn't been brought to England in the twelfth century. A quick call to the British Museum proved him right. Everything then ground to a halt until the potatoes could be removed and roast apples substituted. What that little interruption cost in terms of salaries of cast and crew alone can only be imagined, but producer Pandro Berman and director

Richard Thorpe were determined to do all possible to make *Ivanhoe* a worthy companion to the handful of first-rate films which have brought Medieval England to accurate, surging life on the screen. In that they succeeded admirably.

From the opening titles, set against F. A. Young's vivid cinematography and reinforced by one of Miklos Rozsa's best scores (both Young and Rozsa were subsequently Oscar-nominated), *Ivanhoe* moves at a pace and sets a consistent tone that is brisk, forthright, vigorous, and unsubtle. The lavish pomp and pageantry are especially noteworthy in the film's three great set pieces: the Tournament at Ashby, the Siege and Capture of Torquilstone Castle, and the Trial by Combat of Rebecca.

As Rebecca, Elizabeth's first scenes are wordless. We see her as she appears at a window, and subsequently as she glances through a beaded curtain. Thereafter her beauty is spellbinding and she utilizes all of her powerful screen presence to project, quietly, the ill-starred child of persecution. Her key scene, wherein she averts rape with passivity, is a splendid example of why the casting was so crucial.

At the mercy of the lecherous Guilbert, Rebecca rushes to the edge of a parapet and threatens to throw herself off should Guilbert take one more step toward her. The resourceful Guilbert then informs her that Ivanhoe is even now a prisoner within the castle. If he is to be saved, Rebecca must submit herself. As Guilbert eagerly reaches for his prize, Rebecca folds into his arms and goes totally limp. Whereupon George Sanders as Guilbert steps back from her and gets off the following mouthful:

"Rebecca, you mistake the nature of our bargain. I want you alive, not dead. When next I come to you, meet me with desire on your lips and fire in your breast, or no man's life is saved this day!" (Exit glowering.)

To keep that whole scene from high camp, as well as to deliver dialogue like that, required actors of intelligence who not only knew what they were doing but how to go about it. *Ivanhoe* contains a full complement of them. The scene works, as does everything else in the film.

MGM wrapped *Ivanhoe* in September 1951 and released it the following June, giving it the same promotional push they gave *Quo Vadis*, with handsome results: $1,743,500 in its first seven engagements. After setting records across the country, it became the first MGM film ever to open simultaneously at two first-run houses in Los Angeles. The accompanying reviews were exuberant and enthusiastic. *Ivanhoe* subsequently entered the Oscar lists as a nominee for Best Film of 1952, along with *High*

Noon, Moulin Rouge, The Quiet Man, and *The Greatest Show on Earth* (the winner).

Nevertheless, *Ivanhoe* is not one of her films which ranks high in Elizabeth's esteem. At the time she made it she complained:

"My neck is killing me. Every morning at six o'clock they tape me into a wig that weighs two pounds. It's full of pins that stick into me all day long. By night I really have a neck-ache—and a headache." Her daily routine meant leaving her Savoy Hotel suite at five-fifteen for the forty-five-minute drive to Elstree Studios. Into Makeup at six for the session with the hairdresser, and then into Wardrobe for another long session. "We wear long dresses of wool jersey and heavy capes," she explained, "and it sometimes seems to take an hour to lace up a dress." She was on the set at nine and home by six. "Evenings I stay home and improve my mind by reading mystery stories," she quipped. Double ha-ha.

Elizabeth has since dismissed *Ivanhoe* as essentially "just a big Medieval Western," and has also termed it a piece of "cachou," which, if Webster be trusted, is an oral deodorant in pill form. Like it or not, she would have no film remotely comparable to it for four long years. But *Ivanhoe* was in no sense of the word *her* film, and at the time she made it, her main attentions and romantic hopes were indeed centered on an Englishman. But he did not live in the twelfth century and his name was not Ivanhoe. It was Michael Wilding.

The six-foot-one, blue-eyed Wilding was born July 23, 1912, a descendant of the Archbishop of Canterbury who crowned Queen Victoria. Also of John of Gaunt but, as Wilding was wont to add in his own charming way, "on the wrong side of the blanket, I'm sorry to say." He had gone through Christ College excelling in swimming and high-jumping and, after a few years of varied stage experience, made his entry into films in 1933 on the Continent in something called *Pastorale*, in which he was a telephone operator and only the back of his head was seen. Back to England and the stage and then his British film debut in a little item from 1939 called *There Ain't No Justice*. Thirteen nondescript films led up to Alexander Korda's sumptuous 1947 production of Oscar Wilde's *An Ideal Husband*, dressed by Cecil Beaton, in which Wilding was, as usual, an aristocrat. "I've played enough Earls to fill the House of Lords," he once cracked. Next came two of Hitchcock's worst: *Under Capricorn* and *Stage Fright*. But it was a string of appearances opposite Anna Neagle (in *Piccadilly Incident, The Courtneys of Curzon Street, Spring in Park Lane, Maytime in Mayfair*) which had brought him to his current eminence as Britain's Most Popular Film Actor. So firmly established was he as a skilled light comedian that he was often referred to as "England's Cary Grant" (which sounds odd until you reflect that it was America which turned Archie Leach into Cary Grant). Later, during the Hollywood experience, which not only damaged his career but almost obliterated his desire to act, Wilding remarked, "Thank God for those old British movies on television. Else the American public would think me a dreary ass." His highly polished screen image plus the well-known fact of his long-time companionship with Marlene Dietrich had stamped him in the public mind as the very essence of sophistication.

Privately Michael Wilding was a charming, genial, witty, easy-going man. On a studio biography form he had recently written in the blank after "Ambition": "To be rich and not have to work too hard." As to the satisfactions he derived from acting: "I am never so happy as when I know an audience is laughing, having a good time." But even Michael Wilding's *bonhomie* had its limits. As, for example, in 1963, when Hedda Hopper, in *The Whole Truth and Nothing But,* charged that he suffered a certain amount of confusion as to his sexual identity and that his long-standing friendship with a fellow British actor was more than platonic. Wilding slammed her with a $3 million libel suit and a demand for a public apology, charging the statements exposed him to "hatred, contempt, ridicule, humiliation, and obloquy," and were made "in a reckless, wanton, and malicious manner with utter disregard to his rights and feelings." Had Miss Hopper bothered to check her facts, she could easily have learned that, like any good-looking young actor coming up in the theater, Wilding had been the object of a number of urgent propositions and had rejected them all—courteously when possible, firmly when pressed. This fact was common knowledge to his friends in the theater. Now, thrashing around on the losing end of a lawsuit, she paid legmen to go out and bring back the information she should have known in the first place. She escaped the public apology but that's all. She and her publisher paid out in six figures to settle the suit, and the offending passages were excised.

At the time Michael Wilding first met Elizabeth, when she was making *Conspirator,* she was always overweight a pound or two, and all of it makeup. "When I first met her," Wilding remembered, "I wondered why a girl so beautiful felt she needed all that makeup." About which Elizabeth explained: "I had a mad crush on Mike and it was an adolescent attempt to add years to my appearance. Between the ages of sixteen and eighteen I did everything I could to look older." Now she was approaching twenty, and they resumed their acquaintance, dating discreetly and quietly at the theater, supper clubs, or on simple outings in and around London.

For Elizabeth, colitis and ulcers and illness were a thing of the past. "At the sight of him I decided to forget my baby food," she said. "I ate everything I liked, and in a month I was cured of all my ailments." Wilding was still worrying about their twenty-year age difference, but the girl he later called "a seething mass of feminine wiles" was doing everything she could to minimize it. One tactic she allegedly employed could have backfired. He mentioned that he'd never seen any of her films, and she ordered one run off for him. And the one she chose was *National Velvet*.

"I finally proposed to him," she related unabashedly. "He was everything I admired in a man and I thought him remarkable. We already said we loved each other earlier. But he said I was too young; I'd change my mind. When I objected, he said we should wait." On their last night together in London, they partied till dawn and Elizabeth sent a wire to Sara telling her that she couldn't wait to get home to see her. The breach between mother and daughter was healed.

On October 7 Wilding took Elizabeth out to the airport for her flight to New York. She kissed him and headed for the plane. A moment later he ran after her and was kissing *her*, and the enormity of what he was feeling he could no longer hide even from himself.

In New York, Elizabeth ensconced herself in a lavish suite at the Plaza, as a complimentary guest of the management—or so she understood when she signed in. "Movietime U.S.A." was then in full swing, an industry-wide public relations effort in which groups of stars went on personal appearances all over the country pressing the flesh in their homey role of "just folks." The grand climax to all of this occurred in Hollywood when one of filmdom's most erudite producers surprised his actress-wife and her agent in the back seat of a car and shot the agent in the groin "for trying to break up my home."

Metro asked Elizabeth to go to Washington, D.C., for her appearance, and she took Peggy Rutledge with her. For Elizabeth it was a return to the capital, since she had been there in 1946 to help open the March of Dimes campaign that year. She had gone to the White House, met Mrs. Truman, and was standing behind her for the picture-taking when she froze in horror. Out of habit she had kicked off her shoes, and one of them had somehow got out of reach. The next nervous moments were spent trying to retrieve the shoe without the First Lady catching on to what was afoot (or off-the-foot, as the case may be). If the people who manufacture shoes and stockings had had to rely exclusively on Elizabeth Taylor, they'd have gone bankrupt. She consistently loathed both items from adolescence onward, and her favorite position, both at home and at the homes of friends, was to plunk herself delightedly down in supreme comfort, barefooted and cross-legged, on the floor. One great candid shot shows Elizabeth greeting Vincente Minnelli and Stanley Donen in the lobby of the posh Beverly Hills Hotel, and her size sevens are as naked as the day they came into the world.

It was also in Washington that Elizabeth finally got a chance to see *A Place in the Sun*. An exhausted Peggy Rutledge went with her and snoozed all the way through it. "Elizabeth didn't try to wake me up," Miss Rutledge remembered, "but she was good and mad afterwards."

Back to New York and the daily phone conversation with Michael Wilding, still in England. Sara and Francis Taylor came East, and Elizabeth was with them for the celebration of their twenty-fifth wedding anniversary. There was a nasty episode when a twenty-nine-year-old jobless elevator operator sent bomb threats through the mail, and then began calling Elizabeth at the Plaza, impersonating an FBI agent. Authorities insisted that she hold him on the phone so that they'd have time to trace the call and nab him—which she did, through what seemed like an eternity of obscenity and insanity. It turned out that he'd been sent to a mental hospital for three months seven years previously for doing the same kind of thing to Kathryn Grayson. This time they sent him to Bellevue.

Elizabeth had had a prior experience with this kind of lunacy. In November 1949, three letters arrived, all postmarked from Brooklyn. "They were obscene, demanded money, and threatened Elizabeth's safety," Sara Taylor informed the press. "I did not see them. Mr. Taylor turned them over to the FBI." Three months of police protection paid off when the culprit was apprehended climbing over a back wall onto the grounds of the Taylor home in Beverly Hills. He was tried, jailed for six months, and deported to his native England. The unnerving postscript to that episode was written in the summer of 1951.

Elizabeth and Peggy Rutledge had flown to the South of France for a short holiday from *Ivanhoe*, and on the plane she had the eeriest feeling that she was being watched. At her hotel, a dapper, rather elegant little man seemed to attach himself to her wherever she went—in the bar, in the dining room, in the casino, on the beach—whenever she looked up, there he was—watching and waiting. Finally he handed one of her friends a note for her, which read: "Dear Miss Taylor, Quite clearly you do not remember me. I am the man you had thrown in jail for six months and deported from the United States of America. I think you owe me something and I intend to collect."

"What are we going to do?" Elizabeth queried her friends. "What does he mean?"

"Well, I don't know," one of them answered. "It just sounds like he's trying to frighten you."

"Well, you want to know something?" she rejoined. "He *has* frightened me." And that was the end of the holiday in France.

In the fall of 1951 the press speculated that Nicky Hilton would marry Betsy von Furstenberg when his divorce was final. An MGM spokesman then pictured Elizabeth as "emotionally upset" at that news. According to Elizabeth, MGM was definitely in error. A reporter then asked her about her "heart interest" and the following exchange took place:

ELIZABETH: "My heart is just fine and it has quite a few interests."

REPORTER: "Can you be specific about that?"

ELIZABETH (sweetly): "I could be but I'd rather not."

Hilton flew from Houston to New York to meet Elizabeth at the Plaza and tie up loose ends of the property settlement. In her suite they sat four and a half feet apart on an eight-foot sofa. Photographers asked them to "close it up." Hilton asked if she'd mind. "Well, not too close. After all!" She later told columnist Earl Wilson she found that "terribly embarrassing," and for the last time publicly she asked plaintively, "Why can't I have a normal life?" About Nicky Hilton, she commented, "I bear him no animosity."

The press had now taken to covering her comings and goings with descriptions of "luscious Liz," "lissome Liz," and "lovely and luscious Liz." This public obsession with her beauty, to the exclusion of everything else, prompted one critic to remark in the mid-'50s, "It has been enough to see her serenely aristocratic face above her voluptuous body." That kind of thing used to drive Vivien Leigh, who was bedeviled by the same problem, right up the wall.

"It's very, very irritating," Miss Leigh once complained, "because people think that if you look fairly reasonable, you can't possibly act, and as I only care about acting, I think beauty can be a great handicap, if you really want to look like the part you're playing—which isn't necessarily like you."

Many times Sara Taylor heard Elizabeth burst out with, "Oh! I'll be so glad when people stop writing about how 'beautiful' I am and start writing, instead—I hope—of how well I can act." She brushed aside one interviewer's compliments by observing, "It's more important what a person is than how they look. A box of candy can look wonderful but suppose there are worms in it?" Her own construction never struck her as perfection, anyway. "I always wanted to be taller. Tall girls are so graceful, so willowy. I am only five-foot-four—and only when I'm standing *very* straight. How could I hope to look willowy?" Once she spied Marlene Dietrich walking by. "Such beautiful legs," she exclaimed. "Mine are terrible—much too short."

Any ideas of becoming a blonde were terminated when she had to be one in *Little Women*. "I don't like myself as a blonde," she said at the time. "I think it gives me a white, faded, peculiar look. But we wouldn't dare change Amy to a brunette. Too many people have read the book and know exactly the color of her hair. They would resent a change." When Makeup wanted to bleach her eyebrows to match the wig, she rebelled. "How would I look at night going around with coal-black hair and blond eyebrows?" (They covered the eyebrows with makeup.) A brief flirtation with the idea of being a redhead ended abruptly when she tried a red wig on in Makeup one day and everyone shrieked in unison, herself included. She resigned herself to the twin frustrations of staying as Nature made her and having the public think that that was all there was. When director Richard Brooks later waxed enthusiastic about the quality of the work she was doing in *The Last Time I Saw Paris*, Elizabeth shrugged fatalistically. "What's the use of my being a good actress? They'll just say that, as usual, Elizabeth Taylor looked beautiful."

Along with the public infatuation with her looks, a quote kept persistently surfacing in the press and it was rendered in two versions. "I had the emotions of a child in the body of a woman" was the more familiar, though Dorothy Kilgallen quoted it as "I had a child's mind in a woman's body" and called it "the only profound remark ever attributed to her." Possibly because it *was* one of a kind, and because its exact origins are unknown, the idea grew that it really came out of a press agent's mouth, and a columnist subsequently said so. After a lifetime of being quoted out of context and having all manner of inanities attributed to her, Elizabeth was nettled. She had indeed said it and her comment about the disbelieving columnist was succinct. "You want to meet whoever said that and give him a knuckle sandwich."

In November 1951, MGM was beckoning to Elizabeth to come to Hollywood for a week's worth of retakes on *Ivanhoe*, and she made ready to leave the Plaza. Whereupon the management rendered a bill for $2,500. Elizabeth promptly went into shock, and when she came out of it, she was outraged. She had not understood that only her first week was complimentary, but misunderstanding or no, the management remained adamant. Elizabeth then called Montgomery Clift to let off some steam, and over to the Plaza came Clift and Roddy McDowall. Amid the busy hanging of pictures upside down on the walls and the unscrewing of bathroom fixtures, the three conspirators dipped liberally into a pitcher of martinis and soon were busy dueling with each other utilizing a clutch of double chrysanthemums, the petals of which obligingly fell all over the place. Just before they left, Clift made a clean sweep of all the bathroom towels and took them home with him. Elizabeth later called the Plaza, and was properly contrite about it all. The incident was disturbing in that it was symptomatic of the crazy, rootless, impulsive life she seemed to be living. Her determination to marry Michael Wilding only intensified.

As luck would have it, Wilding came to California in December to promote *Lady With a Lamp*, his fifth costarring stint with Anna Neagle, who played Florence Nightingale in it. He and Elizabeth made a foursome with Stewart Granger and Jean Simmons (then married to each other). Matters were where they had been left in October: Wilding was still hesitant about the age difference, though he had, in the interim, secured a divorce from his wife, actress Kay Young. They had wed in 1937, but had lived apart since 1945. Then one evening Wilding gazed at Elizabeth and murmured, "Darling, you should wear sapphires to match your eyes." It was the opening she had been waiting for. The next morning she summoned him to the jewelers, and asked him to help her choose between several sapphire rings she was considering. With the choice made, Elizabeth asked him to slip it onto the third finger of her left hand. The matter was settled.

Amid a flurry of rumors that the pair would elope to Las Vegas or Acapulco, and against the drone of a gratuitous Greek chorus of counselors who advised against it—"he's too old, too British, too sophisticated"—Elizabeth moved confidently and joyously into her second marriage. In her private life she would bear two sons. Professionally she would suffer a succession of glossy mediocrities on film. And out of the crucible of motherhood, money worries, career frustration, and personality growth would come a woman far surer of herself and far more astute about her career and the management of it than had once seemed possible.

❀ 11 ❀

On February 1, 1952, Elizabeth made the simultaneous announcements of the official end of her marriage to Nicky Hilton and of her plans to wed Michael Wilding. Queried as to why she wasn't waiting, she quipped, "It's Leap Year so I leapt!" Then, more seriously, "I just want to be with Michael, to be his wife. He enjoys sitting home, smoking his pipe, reading, painting. And that's what I intend doing—all except smoking a pipe!" To which Wilding added, "Elizabeth is affectionate and kind. People forget she has been through a very trying year. She wants to be married to someone who will love and protect her and that someone—by some Heaven-sent luck—turns out to be me. I won't let her down."

En route to London, Elizabeth happily joked with reporters, and allowed as how Wilding was indeed twice her age "but a mere child at heart." Meeting her at London Airport, Wilding was introduced to one of his bride's traits with which he would become thoroughly familiar. It first came to public knowledge on New Year's Day, 1948, at the Rose Bowl, when the University of Southern California played Michigan. The U.S.C. quarterback had sent Elizabeth two complimentary tickets and Jerome Courtland was her escort. As they walked into the stadium, Courtland said, "Let me have the tickets." A pause. A scream. "Oh, no! I left them at home." A quick call to the house and Francis Taylor saved the day by hopping into the car and bringing them over.

Keeping track of things has never been Elizabeth's strong suit. This is not to be confused with not being aware of things. When the yacht *Kalizma* was undergoing extensive refurbishing, the decorators were removing various hangings and other bric-a-brac. Was it going to be thrown out? "We never throw anything out," one of the decorators replied. Then, with a nervous glance over his shoulder, "*She* never forgets anything." Keeping track of it all is another matter. "She's not an organized housekeeper and she doesn't know where anything is," was how Richard Hanley put it years later. In this present instance, she had forgotten to bring her divorce papers, without which the wedding could not proceed. The crisis was passed when photos of the papers were radioed from New York.

On the eve of the nuptials, the happy couple and a few friends feasted on lobster, chicken, and wine at a dinner party in her hotel suite behind locked doors barred by Wilding's firm orders to "admit no one on any pretext." Then, in a ten-minute ceremony in the registry of London's Caxton Hall, on February 21, Elizabeth became Mrs. Michael Wilding. Anna Neagle and her producer-husband, Herbert Wilcox, were the witnesses, and Helen Rose designed the bridal outfit: a gray wool suit with rolled collar and cuffs of white organdy.

Outside a mob of three thousand had gathered, and when the newlyweds appeared, things became slightly hysterical. Elizabeth's hat was ripped from her head and a policeman finally lifted her bodily above the crowd and got her to the limousine for the ride to the reception at Claridge's. "I was thrilled," she related, "but I'm glad I'm still alive." Photographers asked the Wildings to kiss but Elizabeth demurred. "I'm too shy." Years later she would file six simultaneous lawsuits against a gaggle of fan ragazines for, among other things, depicting her as "an experienced and shameless courtesan who engages in acts of lovemaking and displays passion in public without restraint or modesty." The entire range of everything from public petting and smooching through true confession and breast-beating on up to nudity and all the way into smut and pornography always was, and still is, foreign and offensive to her. She did confess that she wanted a family—"just as many as possible." After which the newlyweds went on to a smaller reception at Wilding's apartment, and finally came home exhausted to their honeymoon suite at the Berkeley Hotel. "For our wedding supper we ordered pea soup, bacon and eggs, and champagne—the waiter almost dropped dead," Elizabeth remembered. Four years later they had the same meal on their anniversary at Romanoff's. "It startled the waiter there too."

There was just time for a brief eight-day honeymoon at a hotel high in the French Alps, where Elizabeth incidentally celebrated her twentieth birthday. After which Wilding came home to work on his sixth film with Anna Neagle (*Derby Day*) and

Elizabeth set up housekeeping in Wilding's flat on a little street off Berkeley Square. The unwrapping of wedding presents and writing of thank-yous was mercifully brief. In contrast to the plethora of wedding gifts which she received at her first wedding, there were just three this time: a pair of diamond earrings, a crystal martini-shaker, and the Oxford English Dictionary. Thereafter the Wildings settled contentedly into a quiet home life of getting better acquainted with each other. A bit of excitement enlivened their routine one evening in April, when the flat below theirs caught fire, and they refused to evacuate the building, calmly sitting and sipping their after-dinner coffee until the firemen down below put it out.

In London just prior to the wedding, Elizabeth had been quoted as saying, "I've never put my career first. A career is not all that important anyway." Subsequently she recalled, "When I married Mike, I had no acting ambition at all—I didn't even want to be an actress. All I wanted at first was to be Mike's wife and have a baby right away." MGM was well aware of what she was thinking and feeling about this particular issue, and the thought of it sent a collective shudder through the whole corporate structure. For Elizabeth's contract was about to expire.

It had been signed in court on December 27, 1945, and Nibbles was a witness. He had kept bobbing in and out of her pocket. The judge reportedly didn't mind; chipmunks didn't come to court every day. The contract called for an initial salary of $750 per week (which eventually went to $1,500) with six-month options, and a minimum of 15 per cent of the salary was ordered put into savings bonds. Now the contract was coming to its end, and Elizabeth made no moves toward its renewal. The Hollywood sun had begun to set on the era of the long-term studio contracts, and the sound of the tax lawyers and accountants, along with the seductive whispers of capital-gains advantages, were beginning to be heard in the land. Many stars were now profitably freelancing. At Universal, James Stewart would take a percentage of the gross on *Thunder Bay*, thus blazing a new trail. Burt Lancaster was about to set up his own production company.

In 1949 Elizabeth's face had decorated the cover of *Time* in a feature story about aging stars and Hollywood's worries about the problem. "One studio that is less desperate than most is Metro-Goldwyn-Mayer," announced *Time*. "That is partly because MGM has already turned up a jewel of great price, a true star sapphire. She is Elizabeth Taylor. At 17, 5 ft., 4½ in., 112 lbs., Elizabeth Taylor is a great beauty." Then, lest they be caught unqualifiedly endorsing anything in Tinseltown, *Time* added tartly: "In Hollywood, which has long since proved its theory that even a flea can be taught to act a little, Elizabeth Taylor is a sure star of the future." Now it looked as if that star might not be shining at MGM.

To meet the various threats from advisers who counseled Elizabeth to go her independent way, the studio campaigned strenuously and well. Every tie of friendship and long association was stressed. A new seven-year contract was offered with salary inducements which made the old one look like an insult. For her first film MGM dusted off their old 1931 hit, *A Free Soul*, and retitled it *The Girl Who Had Everything*. Elizabeth would thus have the title role. Also top billing, a status she would relinquish in feature roles only three times in the future: on *Beau Brummel, Raintree County*, and *The Comedians*. Shrewdly sensing that the way to this particular woman might be through her husband, Michael Wilding was offered a three-year contract with MGM as well.

What finally tipped the scales was the fact that, in late spring, Elizabeth learned that she was going to have a child and became, in her own words, "absolutely idiotic with pride." Whereupon the Wildings signed the contracts.

"I re-signed because I got cornball sentimental about Benny Thau and all the other nice people at the studio and because Michael and I would be working there and we could have lunch together," Elizabeth explained. "But, mainly, it was because I was pregnant. We needed money to get a home of our own—a nest in which to hatch the egg."

In June, Metro summoned Elizabeth to begin work on *The Girl Who Had Everything*, and she left Wilding behind to wind up affairs in London. Then studio officials told her that there would be a delay of a month or so to get the script into proper shape. Elizabeth joyfully hit them with the news that she was pregnant. The studio joined in the chorus of congratulations, carefully concealing whatever else they were thinking. By executive decree, the film was ordered before the cameras in two weeks after what Elizabeth was told would be "a fast polishing job." In this case they must have polished with Sani-Flush.

The original, *A Free Soul*, was a melodramatic concoction about an alcoholic lawyer (Lionel Barrymore) and his strong-willed daughter (Norma Shearer). The lawyer brings a gangster named Ace Wilfong (Clark Gable) to a dinner party, and the daughter promptly drops her society boy friend (Leslie Howard) to see how the other half lives. Eventually the gangster turns menacing and the jilted boy friend shoots him. In a wow finish at the murder trial, the lawyer-father publicly confesses that this whole doleful turn of events was all his fault, and promptly expires in the courtroom. This pulsating package of purple passions is memorable today because (1) Lionel Barrymore used that courtroom scene to get himself an Oscar as Best Actor and (2) Clark Gable slugged Norma Shearer and instantly rose to the full stardom which had been eluding him since his debut as an extra in 1924. Thereafter the manhandling of women was a Gable specialty.

Supporting Elizabeth in the remake were William Powell as her lawyer-father, Fernando Lamas as the gangster, and Gig Young as the society boy friend. In her first scene as Jean Latimer, Elizabeth is presented as voracious, spoiled, predatory, undisciplined, and reckless. She calls her father "Steve" and quotes the Latimer Coat of Arms: "I shall make my own mistakes." Then, as the film develops at a pace that would shame a snail, what we actually have is a decorous, well-bred young lady whose every closeup is a portrait in beautiful Helen Rose gowns. The wardrobe is great for Elizabeth: girlish,with full skirts, puff sleeves, modest and smart, tastefully expensive—and almost totally wrong for the kind of girl the script keeps assuring us she is. It has no slink and no daring. A Free Soul she ain't. Even Queen Norma—who, when the mood was upon her, could summon up the grandest assortment of ladylike airs, graces, vapors, and what not to be found this side of Kay Francis—got more wanton excitement out of this vehicle than Elizabeth ever comes close to.

She gets absolutely no help from the script, her director, or her fellow actors. "I'll try anything once" is both a sample and an accurate measure of the dialogue she is given. At another point, Lamas asks her, "How many men have told you you're the most beautiful girl they've ever seen?" When it isn't too busy with snappy one-liners like these, the script borrows assiduously, for example, James Whitmore is brought in as a crony of gangster Lamas à la Van Heflin in *Johnny Eager* (minus the booze). There is a nod to the televised proceedings of the Kefauver Crime Commission, then a national sensation. Also a takeoff on Edward R. Murrow's *Person to Person*. None of it works. At the very end, some shock therapy is tried. Lamas socks Powell, Elizabeth slaps Lamas, and Lamas hits her back. Twice. By then it is too late; the patient is stone-dead.

William Powell wobbles along the surface of the role minus any real verve or belief. Fernando Lamas is frozen of face and, at this point, still struggling with the complexities of the English language. Gig Young just fades away in a totally thankless role. As for Elizabeth, she goes through these proceedings in a trance, running a placid gamut from A to A Minor and, in the end, reacts to her plight with all the virtuous outrage of a nice Girl Scout suddenly aware that someone naughty has been slipping pot into her brownies. In her big scene, wherein she explodes after Powell has taken her away to part her from Lamas, director Richard Thorpe shoots her standing stock-still in the doorway in a medium shot. There were at least six different, and better, ways to go with that scene, for example, the kind of thing that John Cromwell and Bette Davis worked out for *Of Human Bondage* where Miss Davis is vainly trying to persuade Leslie Howard to have sex with her. The varying thrusts of her body and the other physical tensions she packed into the scene give off the musky aroma of a woman who is literally ready to jump right out of her skin. Granted that Miss Davis was playing a slut, and Elizabeth was not, when it comes right down to the nitty-gritty, sexual frustration is sexual frustration. The nitty-gritty, however, was rarely allowed to sully the sound stages at MGM in 1952.

Looking back at her work during the period 1952–56, Elizabeth has written: "The films I did then have sort of blanked out in my mind, because they were so distasteful to me." This was about the worst. It was wrapped in August and then cut to the bone. MGM finally released it in April 1953, at which time it was fired upon from all sides and quickly sank from sight. "Elizabeth Taylor as *The Girl Who Had Everything* has everything but good sense and a decent script," grumped the L.A. *Citizen-News*. "Over-talky drama of little interest," muttered the Hollywood *Reporter*. "Makes a long 69 minutes."

Promptly upon the completion of her work in this bomb, MGM presented its "jewel of great price" with a suspension. She would be off salary until such time after the birth of her child as she could return to work in the next gem they came up with for her. Metro was well within its contractual rights, but the action staggered Elizabeth, and she ultimately came to look upon it as a betrayal. She had listened to the honeyed words and pleadings, had ignored the tempting offers to go out on her own, had signed on the line for another seven years chiefly to insure ample comfort and security for her new family. Now the means to supply it had been cut off. "Cornball sentiment" was banished at a stroke, to be replaced by references to "kindhearted old MGM"—and she rarely smiled when she said it. Some years later Fox sweated out ten anxious months before

Elizabeth was satisfied clause-for-clause and finally signed the *Cleopatra* contracts. Spyros Skouras charged that off to personal antagonism to himself, but it had roots that went far deeper than mere spite. The roots were planted right here, and subsequent events would make them flourish and multiply like the green bay tree.

Michael Wilding had meanwhile come on from England, and the night he arrived, Elizabeth gave him just time to shower and eat and they both went prowling all over Beverly Hills looking at houses with "For Sale" signs on them. While she was filming, Wilding kept house-hunting, more than slightly pained at the knowledge that what they wanted fell in the $60,000–$100,000 price range. At some point they both found time to get over to I. Magnin's and buy two, huge expensive teddy bears in anticipation of the blessed event. Eventually they selected a two-bedroom house on an acre and three quarters of ground on top of a mountain. The price was $75,000 and an additional $50,000 was to go into it for rejuvenation and redecoration. Anent the salary suspension and the bills that were beginning to pile up, an acquaintance reportedly asked Elizabeth, "Do you realize this baby is costing you $150,000?" Her response was immediate and unhesitating: "I wouldn't care if it cost a million!"

As usual she was wrestling with her own anxieties in private, and one bitter memory from this period rankles to this day.

"I remember a time when I went down on my knees to an executive at MGM who shall remain nameless. I was married to Michael Wilding and was pregnant and they put me on suspension. We had bought a house and we desperately needed $10,000—or else we would lose it. I begged him to loan me $10,000. It seemed the end of my world.

"He said, 'You didn't plan things very well, did you?' I said, 'I'm truly sorry I'm making a baby instead of making a picture, but all I'm asking is a loan.' He pulled out a wallet choked with hundreds and thousands. He held it before me to humiliate me. He dressed me up and down and made me realize I was nothing to him but one of the cattle. I got the money only on the condition that I would make an exhausting tour—pregnant, mind you—to promote a picture. I vowed then and there that I would never have to ask anybody for anything again."

Immediately after she finished *The Girl Who Had Everything*, Elizabeth jumped delightedly into maternity outfits. "You would have thought I was the only woman who had ever conceived and carried a child," she wrote. Not even the suspension was allowed to rain on this particular parade; for her, it was an experience totally without parallel. Of the entire miracle of conception, pregnancy, and maternity, she has further written: "You feel an affinity with all the vast things in the world since time began. And you feel so small. Procreation is like the tide, it's like the planets, it's like everything inexplicable. And yet it's so utterly personal. And the baby is so tiny, so vulnerable, everything is so tentative. Because you're such a crucial part of such a miracle, I think every mother when she's carrying a child must feel tremendously important. I know I've never felt so important in my life. I've never felt so beautiful."

While their home was undergoing renovation, Elizabeth and Wilding and the usual complement of animals (that is, a small zoo) moved into the Taylor manse in Beverly Hills. Sara and Francis fled east to Howard Young's, eventually returning to have Thanksgiving dinner with their daughter and son-in-law in the new house. To pay for that expensive refurbishing, Elizabeth came down to the Los Angeles Hall of Records in November and finally picked up $47,000 worth of bonds which could have been hers for the taking in June of 1950, since she was then eighteen and married. The bonds represented 15 per cent of her childhood earnings, along with an additional 10 per cent ordered put in some form of savings and likewise put in bonds. Why did she take so long to pick them up? "I have been just too busy to come down and get them," she remarked with charming nonchalance.

To supplement the bonds, the Wildings further borrowed a huge amount from Metro, payment to be deducted from Wilding's salary until Elizabeth was off suspension, then from their joint salaries. This probably looked like a shrewd move in the front office. Not only were both Wildings under contract to the studio, they were both now in hock to it as well. If any of the management thought that this state of affairs made either less averse to eating the run-of-the-mill swill that Metro-Goldwyn-Mayer was dishing up in the early '50s, they were in for a couple of rude surprises.

On the proven theory that you should always ride a good thing right into the ground, Metro was planning another Robert Taylor-Elizabeth Taylor-Pandro Berman-Richard Thorpe parlay. Accordingly the publicity department issued the following hopeful announcement: "Lovely Elizabeth Taylor, who was one of two women in love with the same man in Ivanhoe, will have two men battling for her love alone in the forthcoming All the Brothers Were Valiant. And they will be two of the screen's top he-men—Robert Taylor, whom she played opposite in *Ivanhoe*, and Stewart Granger." That's what *they* thought.

Elizabeth calmly awaited the script. It turned out to be a gory farrago set in the 1880s about two brothers in the whaling business in love with the same woman, and featuring a cruise to the South Pacific, a storm on the high seas, an enraged whale, multiple murders over a fortune in pearls, a native girl, a climactic mutiny, murder of the bad brother (Granger), and reconciliation of the good brother (Taylor) with his bride, who now realizes she truly loves him. Elizabeth scooped this mess back into its envelope and returned it to the studio with firm instructions to pass it on to somebody else.

At the same time, Michael Wilding was holding up his end of the family feistiness. Lana Turner and Fernando Lamas were currently, as they say, "an item," which hadn't hurt the grosses on *The Merry Widow* a bit. The story department happily threw together some odds and ends for a return engagement and called it *Latin Lovers*. By the time the cameras were ready to roll, however, Miss Turner and Mr. Lamas had gone, as they say, "phfttt," and Ricardo Montalban was drafted. So was Michael Wilding, for the part of a British playboy, but he refused to serve. The role was then given to that well-known Englishman, John Lund.

It was later estimated that, between them, the Wildings ran up a record amount of suspension time for any married acting couple in the entire history of motion pictures. At this point in her life, Elizabeth couldn't have cared less. She was indulging her every food whim, informing anyone within earshot whenever the baby kicked, and just generally vegetating in a blissful daze. She did get out for a few games of polo with friends, including director Jean Negulesco, until her stomach got so large she sometimes couldn't see the ball and she was playing so lackadaisically that Negulesco looked as if he wanted to hit her over the head with his mallet—at which point she stopped. Negulesco also painted her eight months pregnant, in a full purple smock, and laughingly titled it, "There's Never Too Much of Liz." But there was. She had blissfully ignored the warnings of her obstetrician and zoomed from the ideal 112 to a scale-shaking 150. It would make for a more difficult Caesarean delivery and a slower recovery, and she would not make that mistake again. On the second pregnancy, she gained about twelve pounds and had it off shortly thereafter.

Michael Howard Wilding came into the world somewhat earlier than expected weighing seven pounds and three ounces.

He was born, via Caesarean section, at 11:47 P.M. on January 6, 1953, in Santa Monica Hospital. Unlike an earlier quack who had frightened her by telling her she could never conceive without getting expensive thrice-weekly shots in his office for a year, the doctor at Santa Monica told Elizabeth what proved ultimately to be the truth: only two more babies safely. After which the proud parents took home their "Baby Wilding" (as he was first identified by a strap on his little wrist). Thereafter he would be fondly tagged, variously, "Mikie," "Sport," "Britches," and "Jughead."

When she was ready to go back to work, MGM again offered her *All the Brothers Were Valiant* and Elizabeth again disdained it. When that dud finally made it into the theaters in November (with Ann Blyth stuck in the role), *Time* noted acidly: "Since this movie has been made so often, it is curious that Hollywood cannot at least make it well." Elizabeth's reward for trusting her own intelligence was renewed suspension. It would have taken another *Place in the Sun* to even begin to compete with all the wonder and the ups and downs of learning to care for her new baby. "When he cries," she confessed at one point, "I cry."

One enticing film prospect unfortunately came to nothing. Director Frank Capra vainly sought Elizabeth and Cary Grant to play the parts of the visiting princess who plays hooky and the journalist who goes along with her in *Roman Holiday*. The studio vetoed it on grounds of budget and by the time it got made, William Wyler was in the director's chair, Gregory Peck was playing the newsman, and the part of the princess had slipped further through the hands of Jean Simmons and into those of newcomer Audrey Hepburn, who won her Academy Award for it. The new suspension stretched out to six weeks, and the impasse was finally broken, not by either of the parties concerned, but by a desperation call from Paramount. Vivien Leigh had suffered a nervous breakdown and Elizabeth was being sought as her replacement in *Elephant Walk*.

Douglas Fairbanks, Jr., had bought this property in 1951, intending to produce it independently if he could borrow Deborah Kerr from MGM. When that plan fell through, he sold it to Paramount, which set Irving Asher to produce it and William Dieterle to direct it. Asher went to London where Laurence Olivier finally turned down the male lead, pleading the press of his duties as actor-manager of the St. James's Theater. Vivien Leigh (then Lady Olivier) agreed to do the picture, and Peter Finch was signed to make his American film debut as the male lead. Dana Andrews was subsequently signed for the other leading role, and a month's location work was to begin in Ceylon in February 1953. It was there that the fierce pace she had set for herself finally caught up with Vivien Leigh.

In 1939 Miss Leigh was already a great beauty, but only a minor film actress, when *Gone With the Wind* brought her an Oscar and sent her soaring into the upper reaches of stardom, where she would remain until her early death in 1967. Her unique blend of beauty, femininity, charm, intelligence, steely purpose, and nervous energy would grace only eight more films after her triumphant creation of Scarlett O'Hara. For it was to be the irony of her professional life that she scorned the medium that she was born for in order to pursue a goal which, for her, would remain forever elusive: true greatness on the stage. But Vivien Leigh was never one to back off the challenges.

After fresh triumphs in *Waterloo Bridge* and *That Hamilton Woman*, she returned to England to resume the learning of her craft on the London stage, and not all the clamor of her legions of fans nor the various legal maneuvers of David O. Selznick could budge her. As if in retaliation to her attitude, her remaining films, *A Streetcar Named Desire* excepted, were not happy occasions. She miscarried during the exhausting, ruinously expensive filming of *Caesar and Cleopatra* in the African desert and for many years thereafter could not bring herself to look at that film. *Anna Karenina* carried the double curse of torpid direction and Kieron Moore, and only Ralph Richardson emerged with honor. *The Deep Blue Sea* she damaged by playing against the role. What there was to steal of *The Roman Spring of Mrs. Stone* was made off with by Lotte Lenya. In her final film, *Ship of Fools*, her footage was so shredded that, top billing notwithstanding, she wound up in support of Simone Signoret.

Always petite and physically delicate, she had been felled briefly by tuberculosis in the mid-'40s. After which she went through a grueling nine months on the London stage as Blanche Dubois in *A Streetcar Named Desire*. As of May 1950 she revealed: "I feel physically exhausted. The play has sapped all my energy. Doctors have watched me constantly since we started and they have now advised me to give up acting for the time being." But Vivien Leigh was not one to submit quietly to the limitations of her body (she had her nightly sleeping ration down to four hours, which, curiously enough, was also Mike Todd's) and if anything were to get her down, it had literally to knock her flat. On to Hollywood for the film version of *Streetcar* and a second Oscar. From that back to England for the 1951 Festival of Britain, in which she made stage history by alternating the roles of Shaw's and Shakespeare's Cleopatra, a grueling feat she repeated in New York in 1952 at the Ziegfeld. All the strain had told more than she knew.

In Ceylon she was sometimes unable to sleep at all, staying up until dawn haunting ancient ruins and watching native dances. Producer Asher gently noted that all of this was taking a toll on her appearance, and unwittingly struck a very sensitive nerve. "I am no longer young," she retorted. "I shouldn't look like an ingenue." The seventy-two-hour flight from Ceylon to Hollywood was—for a person afraid of flying—"the equivalent of being scared to death." So said her personal physician. Back at Paramount for the filming of interiors, she began to address Peter Finch as "Larry." Her nervousness expressed itself in compulsive housework and the desire to keep up a mad round of parties and never to be left alone for a moment. She began to suffer hallucinations. On March 12 she collapsed on the set in hysterics and her physician ordered her to bed. At that point, David Niven called Olivier, then on holiday in Italy. Olivier flew posthaste to Hollywood on March 14, and Paramount announced that Vivien Leigh was suffering an acute nervous breakdown and could not continue. At that point, over a million dollars had already gone into the footage shot in Ceylon, and the studio desperately sought to salvage at least that part of it in which there were only long-shots of the principals. Which meant getting an actress of the approximate size and coloring of Vivien Leigh. Elizabeth, Jean Simmons, and Claire Bloom were announced as replacement possibilities.

On March 19, Vivien Leigh, sedated into unconsciousness, strapped onto a stretcher, and accompanied by a distraught Olivier, was flown to New York on the first lap home to England. The same day Elizabeth was signed as her replacement. In July, rested and recovered, Vivien Leigh observed, "You mustn't blame the elephants. It was the heat of those overpowering afternoons. The flight back to Hollywood was the last straw. I hope Elizabeth Taylor is very good in the part."

It was a part with roots in the hoariest traditions of the cinema: the bride who is brought into alien, hostile surroundings and then ultimately triumphs over them. Variations on it had been rung by Irene Dunne in *Cimarron* and *The White Cliffs of Dover*, Joan Fontaine in *Rebecca*, Ginger Rogers in *Kitty Foyle*, Gene Tierney in *Dragonwyck*, Claudette Colbert in *The Egg and I*, Ingrid Bergman in *Under Capricorn*, Grace Kelly in *High Noon*, Jane Powell in *Seven Brides for Seven Brothers*, Greer Garson in *Sunrise at Campobello*, Julie Andrews in

Hawaii, and so on *ad infinitum.* As a matter of fact, Elizabeth would be doing it all over again shortly, but the location would be Texas, not Ceylon, and the film would be *Giant.* In *Elephant Walk,* Elizabeth had her hands full to overflowing. The script pitted the new bride against, successively, her father-in-law's ghost, a neglectful husband, his cronies, a recalcitrant major-domo, an ardent "other man," a cholera epidemic, rampaging elephants, and a fiery holocaust.

The film opens with a nice surprise in a London bookstore. We are led to believe that Elizabeth, the clerk, does not know customer Peter Finch. Actually he is her tea-planter fiancé, ready to marry her after short acquaintance and take her to Ceylon. At the airport in Colombo, and on the ride into the plantation, the long-shots incidentally are of Vivien Leigh. At the estate Elizabeth meets the manager, Dana Andrews, who is given what was becoming the obligatory line in all of Elizabeth's films. In this case it is "Pardon me for staring but it's a new experience to see someone like you around here." The lushly romantic musical score is loaded with peril motifs to reinforce the strangeness of the terrain to Elizabeth, the menace of a trumpeting bull elephant, the problem of a father-dominated husband, et al. Thereafter Elizabeth contends with her various problems and, at the end, she and Finch stand on a hillside surveying the flaming ruins of their mansion ready to begin life together anew on a better basis.

Elephant Walk wrapped in late May 1953, at a cost close to $3 million and with a net effect that proved grievously disappointing. The opulence of the production compared to the anemia of the script is as if all the fine china, crystal, and best silver were laid on for a lavish banquet and the main dish turned out to be ground round. The film is truly an eye-popper to behold. The settings, both interiors and exteriors, are stunning and are superbly photographed. The costumes, particularly one off-the-shoulder Grecian affair which Edith Head got up for Elizabeth, are dazzling. Sadly the script and treatment are too routine and pedestrian to match the splendid visuals. The film maintains a voltage throughout that is resolutely low, and there are missed opportunities all over the place. When Finch churlishly orders Elizabeth to stay out of household affairs, the scene could have been taken up into a full-throttled conflict of wills, thus pumping some needed juice into these stately proceedings. Again, when Dana Andrews takes Elizabeth out to some Ceylonese ruins and attempts to make love to her, the script squanders another chance to come to interesting life.

Peter Finch is believable but his effectiveness is reduced by the banality of the script. Dana Andrews has little more to do than stand around and pant after Elizabeth. As the disapproving servant, Abraham Sofaer is a mere echo of Judith Anderson as Mrs. Danvers. As for Elizabeth, *Time* commented, not unkindly: "Elizabeth Taylor, though very beautiful, is too young and inexperienced an actress to fill a role designed for Vivien Leigh." True enough, but with Vivien Leigh in the role, *Elephant Walk* would have *had* to be a different film, in the way the age difference would have affected the relationships.

With the completion of her work in *Elephant Walk*, Elizabeth looked eagerly forward to a good, long uninterrupted reunion with her new baby but fate decreed otherwise. Of Elizabeth, Michael Wilding once observed, "She is incapable of worry. I have never known anyone like her." Subsequently he isolated the quality he respected above all others in his wife. "To me, I think the most important thing about Elizabeth is that she is very brave. Brave about actual physical things, afraid of no person and no animal, nor of any illness that may affect her person. And apart from physical dangers, illnesses, and such, she is undismayed by life." Which went with a similar observation made by one of her directors in 1948. "I have never seen Elizabeth, in any circumstances, exhibit any evidence that she has nerves. She is afraid of neither man nor beast."

All of these statements were now to be put to the test.

❦ 12 ❦

It happened during post-production work on *Elephant Walk*. Elizabeth, Peter Finch, and Dana Andrews were posing for publicity stills. They were sitting in a jeep with a huge wind machine blowing full blast at them. This was apparently Paramount's method of putting the excitement into the advertising which they'd neglected to put into the film. With her hair streaming in the wind, Elizabeth suddenly felt something strike her right eyeball. Every time she blinked, it felt as if she'd scratched it. As she subsequently wrote:

"Later, when the eye got goopy and stuff was coming out, I went to a doctor who probed around and said, 'My dear, you have a foreign object in your eye.' And I said, 'Anybody I know?' Another doctor put my head in a little vise and operated to get out my foreign object. It had shot deep into the eyeball and had rusted. They can't knock you out because you have to keep your eye open and stare at a certain spot on the wall. They have a needle with a tiny knife at the end and you can hear them cutting your eye. It sounds rather like eating watermelon on a minor scale."

After he had bandaged the eye, the doctor cautioned her to be very careful with it since she wouldn't want the fluid to leave the eye. And what would happen in that event? The doctor then pictured a socket containing something dried and shriveled and looking alarmingly like a raisin. Elizabeth left the office determined to hang on to her fluid. Little Michael knew nothing about this, of course, and a few days later his mother was playing with him and he popped her right in the eye. Along with the pain came seepage from under the bandage. "Oh, my God!" exclaimed the doctor when he removed the bandage. An ulcer now covered the eye and surgery was ordered. First she was injected with typhoid fever, strangely enough to lower the chance of infection. Then came the operation and bandaging of both eyes. In two weeks the bandages would come off and Elizabeth would learn whether or not she had lost the eye.

Lying in the hospital Elizabeth had plenty of time to take stock of her situation. Her interest in her career was fast vanishing, given the type of pictures she was getting. She later recalled, "There came a time when you'd do anything to get through. I used to hate turning up at the studio in the morning. That went on for years." The situation was doubly galling after her triumph in *A Place in the Sun*. She had returned from the loanout at Paramount anticipating great things, only to find herself stuck as a glamorous clotheshorse in a dismal parade of inferior films. But Elizabeth was not the first star to have scored on a loanout only to come home to business as usual.

Bette Davis hounded Jack Warner for months so she could go to RKO and be a sensation in *Of Human Bondage*. The scripts she got when she returned to Burbank so sickened and enraged her that she finally fled to England where she and Warner faced off in a courtroom. After her triumph as Melanie in *Gone With the Wind* had brought her a first Oscar nomination, Olivia de Havilland returned to Warners to be stuck in her sixth Errol Flynn epic—as the second female lead yet. Two years later she escaped to Paramount, won another Oscar nomination (for *Hold Back the Dawn*), and came back to her eighth (and final) Errol

Flynn epic. Ultimately Miss de Havilland also went to court. Deborah Kerr was almost smothered with gentility at MGM before Columbia's *From Here to Eternity* proved that she knew you could do other things on a beach besides collect seashells. And so on; the list is a long one.

The studio discovered you, molded you, and slotted you for commercial purposes. And there you stayed in the image they made of you. You were to get your beauty sleep, do a requisite number of poses for the camera, take the money, smile all the way to the bank, and keep your mouth shut. The most famous rebels against this system nested at Warner Bros., where it seemed, at one time or another, Jack Warner was in violent conflict with everyone from Bette Davis to Bugs Bunny. During a steady diet of prison flicks, John Garfield reportedly cornered Warner one day and startled him with a two-word plea, "Parole me!"

MGM apparently valued Elizabeth Taylor chiefly as a beautiful woman to be dressed, lit, and photographed to maximum advantage. The scripts were of secondary importance. Hash would thus continue to be served on gold plate. The problem for Elizabeth was that her intelligence would not permit her to cop out. She knew she was incapable of summoning her best efforts for inferior material, so that the level of her work could rise no higher than the level of the scripts. That knowledge had begun to grate on her. Lying in the hospital bed, she reflected that, if she were to lose the eye, she would say goodbye to the career with few real regrets.

She also occupied herself in the hospital learning to fend for herself in the total darkness, almost as if it were a part she was playing, which of course she knew very well it wasn't. She kept the blues at bay, however, by figuring out exactly where everything was within reach—Kleenex, water glass, radio, perfumes, etc. When Wilding came to visit, she was proudly demonstrating her expertise when she hit a perfume bottle, which fell off the table and smashed on the floor. And she wept. Suddenly it wasn't a game anymore. Eventually the bandages came off and luck was with her: the eye was saved. Metro gave her just enough time to convalesce before the June start-date on her next winner. This one was called *Rhapsody*.

It began as a 1908 novel called *Maurice Guest* by Australian writer Henry Handel Richardson (a woman) and was a brilliant and perceptive study of a young music student and of the unhappy love that leads to his suicide. Hal Wallis bought it in 1948 and sold it to Paramount in 1951. Ruth and Augustus Goetz did a script and Charles Vidor was set to direct. In 1952, MGM acquired the script and Vidor's services and assigned Fay and Michael Kanin to do a new script. What finally emerged from all this was a name change from Maurice to James, a locale change from Germany to Switzerland, a change of focus from James to his girl, and an ending change: suicide is out. After a brief bout with the bottle, *amor vincit omnia*. In other words, schmaltz.

Spoiled rich girl Elizabeth has conceived a crush on a talented violinist (Vittorio Gassman) to the annoyance of her cynical father, Louis Calhern, who pours out a cascade of pithy one-liners as if he thought he were doing Noel Coward (and undoubtedly wished that he were). "You have an almost neurotic need to be needed," he tells her, and adds, "Let's leave need to the needy." Elizabeth just won't listen. "Accept it, my dear," Calhern intones. "There are some people who are simply not possessable." But Elizabeth shows self-awareness. When Calhern asks her, "Have I ever stopped you from doing anything?" she retorts bitterly, "No—unfortunately!"

She pursues Gassman to Zürich where she is obviously out of place among students of serious music, for example, she begins the day in her Swiss chalet with champagne and orange juice. This kind of frivolity is frowned upon by Gassman's music teacher, played by, of all people, Michael Chekhov, who had obviously come a far piece from Stanislavki and the Moscow Art Theater. (Though not so far as Maria Ouspenskaya, who once wound up in the middle of the jungle in *Tarzan and the Amazons*.) Chekhov righteously warns, "There can be no great art without discipline. And no discipline without sacrifice." Even the dumbest clod in the back of the balcony knows what a speech like that means: he and she will never make we. Nor do they. Gassman leaves her and Elizabeth takes pills. She is rescued by pianist John Ericson, whom she marries on the rebound. He then takes to drink but is eventually assured that she truly loves *him* and the happy pair go cresting into the future on a flood of Rachmaninoff. The End.

All of this *sturm und drang* would have taxed even Loretta Young on her old thirty-minute TV show. Metro padded it out to five minutes short of a numbing two hours. It does contain some luscious location photography of Paris, Zürich, St. Moritz, Rome, and the French Riviera smoothly integrated into the proceedings. It also contains one of those scenes dear to the hearts of connoisseurs of high camp from the Golden Era. In a cafe scene, for want of anything better to do, Vittorio Gassman decides to play a full concert version of Liszt's *Hungarian Rhap-*

sody since all the music students just happen to be there with all of their instruments—violins, cello, harp, even a piano. Essentially the film is romantic bilge, trading on music-drenched memories of Crawford & Garfield in *Humoresque*, Bergman & Howard in *Intermezzo*, Mason & Todd in *The Seventh Veil*, Johnson & Howard in *Brief Encounter*, et al. But not even the generous supporting talents of Tchaikovsky and Rachmaninoff, though heard in top form, can save this script.

Again, speaking of her early-'50s films, Elizabeth wrote: "A lot of them I haven't seen, but I must have been appalling in them." Never. In thirty-three years as a film actress, Elizabeth has never gone below the level of bare competence. Her own natural gifts, her intelligence, her professional pride, and who she is and the hundred different things she represents to widely varying film audiences all over the world have all made such a thing impossible. Adequate and uninspired she could be, also uninvolved and uncomfortable when moving at times like a beautiful zombic through various pieces of *dreck*. There would be times when she would overreach to meet demands which were of questionable dramatic validity to begin with, for example, in the scene with Rex Harrison at the tomb of Alexander the Great in *Cleopatra*. (Which gets us into the lamentable lack of proper post-production work on *Cleo*, about which much more anon.) But "appalling" is a description reserved for handsome dummies whose ignorance of the technical demands of the craft combined with the stupefying emptiness they projected as people provided experiences which were deeply embarrassing. Hollywood has had its full quota of these but Elizabeth Taylor was never one of them.

For future purposes, *Look*'s 1954 comment on Elizabeth's artistic predicament was the most prescient of all:

"The producers of MGM's *Rhapsody* and Paramount's *Elephant Walk* have placed Elizabeth Taylor, the star of both films, in the incredible position of being rejected by a total of four men she chooses to love. Elizabeth puts up a game fight, though. She wins their reluctant hearts by means of sheer grit rather than through her natural charms—a most unsatisfying arrangement for any girl. These woeful tales, however, have a curious power in the hands of Miss Taylor—an indication of her growing talents as an adult and honest actress, who can make an audience believe just about anything."

That kind of comment was not lost on Elizabeth. Almost miraculously her career continued to survive and even flourish. Movie audiences were apparently being kept happy on the diet of stew meat, kidneys, and other less desirables which her financial condition forced her to accept. What might happen on the day when she could command nothing but the choice cuts? Aware of her growing power, she bided her time with what patience she could muster. And she would need it, for one more dud lay just over the horizon.

Elizabeth finished her work on *Rhapsody* in early August at the same time Michael Wilding wrapped his last scene in *Torch Song*. They then decided to take a European vacation, which Wilding called "the last part of our honeymoon," to complete those earlier eight short days in the French Alps. If Elizabeth had any doubts about her growing power over and fascination for the moviegoing public, events in Copenhagen dispelled them. The Wildings were besieged by mobs of teenage fans everywhere they went, and at one point Elizabeth made seven separate appearances on her hotel balcony before the throngs were finally persuaded to disperse. The couple then fled to Fredensborg, twenty miles north of Copenhagen, where Elizabeth suffered a nervous collapse, apparently complicated by back trouble and flu. A flurry of items then popped up in the U.S. press about heart trouble which Wilding called "greatly exaggerated." Elizabeth recovered, and the Wildings continued their spin around the Continent, including a stay in Madrid where Elizabeth took in her first bullfight and made a quick exit minutes after it began, having had enough of that. By October they were in England for the second purpose of the trip, which was to introduce Wilding's parents to their grandchild. There was also a formal christening for Michael Howard Charles and little Michael reacted, not surprisingly, by making a grab for the vicar's spectacles, then patting his nose, then bursting into frustrated tears.

In October, MGM had Elizabeth's next film, *Beau Brummel*, ready to go, on location in England. She would thus remain where she was, but Michael Wilding could not afford to. The British tax bite on celebrity salaries was a fierce one. It was Noel Coward's verbal attack on it, delivered from on board a ship which had temporarily stopped at Southampton, which reportedly was responsible, more than any other single factor, for keeping him away from his eventual knighthood for over a decade. As a British subject, were Wilding to stay in the country for an extended period of time, he would have to pay the tax. Accordingly he went to Paris, and Elizabeth flew over on the weekends to join him. There they discovered little out-of-the-way restaurants and street cafes, browsed in art galleries, and just generally prowled around taking in the sights and sounds of the City of Light. Aside from the welcome reunions with her husband, these weekend respites must have been doubly welcome to Elizabeth, given what was going on before the cameras in England.

Originally Eleanor Parker had been announced for *Beau Brummel*. It was to be a rematch with Stewart Granger, with whom she had created some lively onscreen combustion in *Scaramouche* the previous year. MGM decided instead to send Miss Parker over to Paramount to fight man-eating ants (and Charlton Heston) in *The Naked Jungle*, and then shipped her to Egypt, along with Robert Taylor, to poke among the pyramids in *Valley of the Kings*. Elizabeth then inherited the role. Eleanor Parker was well out of *Beau Brummel*, a film which wound up pleasing almost nobody.

Historically, Beau Brummel (1778–1840) was the witty son of the private secretary to Lord North, the British Prime Minister who had a large, fumbling hand in the loss of Britain's American colonies. Beau was the first gentleman publicly known to wash daily, and it was further rumored that he then regularly took three hours to dress. He caused men to stop powdering their hair, and set the style for long trousers and also for starched collars and cravats. He was an intimate of George, Prince of Wales (later George IV), and also nurtured a chivalrous devotion to the married Duchess of York. Gaming debts which would have put him in debtors' prison caused him to flee across the Channel, where, after twenty-five years in exile, he died destitute and insane in the Asylum of Bon Sauveur in Caen.

That master of hoary old melodrama, Clyde Fitch, got a play out of all that and it proved to be what was undoubtedly the legendary American actor Richard Mansfield's greatest star vehicle. He got four separate long runs out of it on Broadway, unfailingly generating tremendous audience sympathy in the final scenes when Beau goes mad. Warners filmed a two-hour version of the play in 1924 starring John Barrymore and Mary Astor, and one critic reported breathlessly: "Incidentally, when John Barrymore and Mary Astor confront each other in the closer closeups [sic], the spectator has the opportunity to behold the two most perfect profiles in the Anglo-Saxon world."

For the new version, MGM opened the purse strings with a vengeance, to obtain what the *Saturday Review* later termed "the most elegant clutter of treasures any auction hound ever sighed for." One of the several fancy location spots was at Ockwells Manor (built in 1440) near Windsor Castle. There Elizabeth got to nap in a bed slept in by Elizabeth I, and during the Hunt Breakfast Scene, to dine at a polished mahogany table once the property of Oliver Cromwell. The sets, costumes, and Eastman Color cinematography were of such surpassing excellence that Bosley Crowther, in his New York *Times* review, would eventually salute *Beau Brummel* as "one of the loveliest films ever made. That can be said without a quaver. Its display of Regency costumes, of palace interiors, and English houses in the fading days of George III, fox-hunting rides and gaming tables and parades of red-coated hussars are as brilliant, tasteful, and felicitous as any this reviewer has seen. Too bad that the drama is not as impressive and rewarding as the picture's sensational decor." Yea and amen.

Richard Addinsell's titles sound just like Miklos Rozsa (and so does much of the rest of the score). They precede a film which is in almost total thematic disarray. *Beau Brummel* is a film it is almost impossible to see even while you're looking at it. The mind wanders because the picture is literally all over the place. Politics, fashion, history, romance, royal intrigue, etc. flash on and off and overlap to no particular purpose. As Lady Patricia, Elizabeth first appears in a blond wig, which makes her look totally artificial—like something that should be sitting on a china-shop shelf. Just when one despairs that nothing was learned from *Little Women*, it appears that apparently someone was indeed watching the rushes. She turns up at the prince's gala in her own black hair looking her own gorgeous self. Thereafter, for no reason anyone ever alludes to, she never does go back into the blond wig, for which much thanks to somebody.

Granger meets her at a banquet and boldly strips off her diamond earrings with the remark that one should never try to embellish perfection. Elizabeth's part thereafter calls for her to slap Beau for impertinence, then dally with him, then refuse him on grounds of financial insecurity, then be rejected when she offers to share his disgrace in exile. Her diction is too loose and sloppy for the patrician aristocrat she is supposed to be, and her ultimate projection is the stolid inertia of an actress who is not only not sure of what she is supposed to be doing in this mish-mash but has long since given up trying to figure it out. Elizabeth later wrote: "I never saw *Beau Brummel* until after Richard and I were married. It was on television and Richard turned it on. I had to change stations after about five minutes—I mean *I* was so embarrassing in it."

At no time is she the center of attention and eventually, almost unbelievable to report, neither is Stewart Granger. *Variety* later called Elizabeth "a victim of motivation obscurity" and that applies in spades to Granger as Beau. The script is never sure whether Beau is a patriot or opportunist, and the character swings wildly between heel and hero and never quite enough of either. Not surprisingly Granger thus generates neither sympathy nor empathy. Into this void of artistic chaos, of sumptuous *mis en scène* with nothing much transpiring in front of it, strides Peter Ustinov as the Prince of Wales, pulling off one of the niftiest heists in cinema history.

MGM released *Beau Brummel* in October 1954, at which time both film critics and historians fell on it.

The most lethal critical barrage occurred in London. *Beau Brummel* was chosen for the 1954 Royal Command Performance. Royal Film Galas had begun in 1946, and MGM had now had the honor of presenting three selections. But *That Forsyte Woman* (Greer Garson in ersatz Galsworthy) and *Because You're Mine* (Mario Lanza in the Army) hadn't started any critical stampedes, and the critics were apparently waiting to carve up the next one. Amid vitriolic remarks about the choices of films for royalty—" 'safe' now equals 'boring' and 'suitable' is synonymous with 'stupid' "—the British critics unanimously flayed the film ("Beau Bloomer," "Bore Brummel," "looks like a musical comedy with the tricks and the tunes left out," and so forth). Whatever it was, Elizabeth returned to America in February 1954, glad to have it behind her. She did not know it at the time but her turkey trot had finally come to an end.

In April, MGM put *The Last Time I Saw Paris* before the cameras, and Elizabeth went into her fourth film in a year's time. This one was taken from F. Scott Fitzgerald's short story, "Babylon Revisited," which producer Lester Cowan bought from him for $3,000, originally intending to co-produce it with Mary Pickford on the Goldwyn lot. In 1951 Cowan sold it to Paramount, which had the Epsteins (Julius J. and Philip G.) do a script, tentatively planning it for Gregory Peck and William Wyler to follow their collaboration on *Roman Holiday*. MGM purposely bought it in 1953 as a vehicle for Elizabeth and they bought well. With this one she moved up to a new plateau, and her days of routine assignment to B-bombs were over.

The original story dealt with a reformed drunk, a writer, who tries to reclaim his daughter from the custody of an unforgiving sister-in-law, determined to make him go on paying for the manner of her sister's death (while drunk, and after an argument, he locked his wife out in the bitter cold and rain, and the resultant pneumonia killed her). The film script included a long flashback detailing how the couple (Elizabeth and Van Johnson) met, married, lived it up, and came to grief. The time was also updated from post-World War I to post-World War II. There were to be two weeks of location filming in Paris and Cannes, and the remainder of the film was to be shot in the studio at Culver City.

What finally emerged was the kind of heady emotional experience which dismays the serious critics and enraptures the general public. *The Enchanted Cottage, Leave Her to Heaven, Love Letters, Tomorrow Is Forever, Back Street,* and *The Fountainhead*—to name half a dozen—all fall into that category. The reviews on *The Last Time I Saw Paris* ranged over the entire spectrum. Those who liked it were in no doubt as to what they liked best about it.

Variety called it "an engrossing romantic drama that tells a good story with fine performances and an overall honesty of dramatic purpose. Performancewise, Miss Taylor's work as the heroine should be a milestone for her. It is her best work to date and shows a thorough grasp of the character, which she makes warm and real, not just beautiful." Even *Time* was moved to extend a hand to Elizabeth, though typically, it was the left hand. "With better than her usual lines to speak, Actress Taylor sometimes manages to speak them as if she knew what they meant."

Of her own work on this one, Elizabeth later remarked, "Rather curiously, a not-so-good picture, *The Last Time I Saw Paris*, first convinced me I wanted to be an actress, instead of yawning my way through parts. That girl was offbeat, with mercurial flashes of instability—more than just glib dialogue." Because the subordinate talents in filmmaking (that is, subordinate to the actor, director, writer, and cameraman) are so little understood and so seldom appreciated by the general public, the following critical note is worth quoting in its entirety:

"Dropping into the neighborhood theater to enjoy *The Last Time I Saw Paris* for the third time, I was struck by the strong dramatic values provided by the costumes which Helen Rose designed for Elizabeth Taylor. And by the hair styles of Sidney Guilaroff. Up until this picture, Miss Taylor has been just about the loveliest thing seen in a fan magazine. The trouble was that when you went to see her in the theater, she still looked like she was in a fan magazine. Her appearance was so perfect that, before every take, you could almost see the makeup men running off the set with their powderpuffs.

"In *Paris* Mr. Guilaroff and Miss Rose make her look like a woman instead of a clotheshorse. And with no loss of glamour.

The long black hair bob looked attractively mussed when she was shown getting out of bed or receiving visitors in the hospital. The plain well-fitted black coat and sweater, in the opening sequence, for once let the girl dominate the wardrobe. During a bedroom argument, an eggshell slip, caught up slightly on the hip, proved that she could look utterly desirable while on the verge of sloppiness. A purple coat with a deep careless cowl, in the playground scene, gave the feeling of a woman who could look smart while thinking of something else. The white brocade in the big quarrel scene emphasized her having physical perfection when she was losing everything else. And the pathetic bravery of the scarlet gown which she wore in the rain, when her drunken husband refused to answer the door, had the climactic overtone of a chord of music."

Given this mixed bag of a film, Helen Rose naturally received no nomination for her work. For her continuous and significant contribution to the public image of the screen's most beautiful woman, Helen Rose never did receive *any* nomination. Miss Rose was to go twice into the winner's circle for Oscars, but it was Lana Turner (*The Bad and the Beautiful*) and Susan Hayward (*I'll Cry Tomorrow*) who brought her there, not Elizabeth.

Some films wear well with time but *The Last Time I Saw Paris* is emphatically not one of them. Today the script sounds flat, the pacing is torpid and sluggish, and eventually it becomes impossible to believe any of it. Also, almost everything is filmed in medium shots which become severely monotonous. On his sixth film, Richard Brooks had yet seemingly to learn what to do with a camera. The supporting characterizations don't help. In the previous year Donna Reed had cracked her goody-girl image, played a hooker in *From Here to Eternity*, and won an Oscar for it. Now here she was playing a bitch (the unforgiving sister-in-law), which was artistically admirable except that she's just not a very interesting bitch. As the little daughter, Sandy Descher is the gorge-grabbing quintessence of the Hollywood Child. Also *Paris* is the kind of film in which nobody ages, though Elizabeth does get her hair cut. Some of the exteriors put one in mind of Walt Disney's Matterhorn, which towers in all of its papier-mâché glory next to the Santa Ana Freeway. Elizabeth has her moments, particularly in a scene by the river with Van Johnson, and he has flickers in the scene wherein he begs for the child. But it is all done in a context which is relentlessly phony to look at and listen to.

At the time, the notion that Elizabeth Taylor could carry a film of some substance was a novel one, and *The Last Time I*

Saw Paris served a worthy purpose. The promise of *A Place in the Sun* had finally been redeemed.

Immediately after wrapping her work in *Paris* in June, Elizabeth went home for a long, well-deserved rest. After four films in a row she had earned it and, as a matter of fact, it was a necessity. She was once again pregnant. This time she played it very shrewdly and kept it a secret for four months. At one dinner party she became ill, and a series of covert glances were exchanged around the table as the more enterprising made ready to call Louella and/or Hedda at the first opportunity. Elizabeth saved that situation by turning to Wilding and announcing firmly, "I *knew* I shouldn't have eaten that shrimp last night!" The conversation then turned to a general discussion of how finny friends from the deep could turn on you once they got onto your dinner plate.

This time Elizabeth followed doctor's orders, kept the weight down, and didn't go into maternity clothes until the fifth month. Previously, when the call came for *Elephant Walk*, she'd had to get off fifteen pounds in three weeks. There was rigorous dieting—"I have coffee for breakfast, eggs for lunch, and steak for dinner—with pink grapefruit coming out my ears," was how she once described one favored method. Also deep massage, steam baths, diet pills, and the whole number. "It was dreadfully difficult," she said at the time, and vowed not to have to go through it again. Instead of reaching for the snacks, three daily showers were one way she employed to cope with occasional discomfort.

She agreed to give the studio an additional year on her contract, in lieu of another suspension, which would have been disastrous. This time, instead of buying expensive, impractical teddy bears first, the Wildings went to an ordinary department store and ordered a few dozen diapers. And Elizabeth once again reveled in the maternal role.

"I'm sick all the time and couldn't care less," she told one interviewer. "It's a wonderful feeling to be sick and like it. You like it because you know what it's for. I love all my symptoms." She enlarged on this in a firm attack on the fears of some of her glamorous associates. "I simply cannot understand the attitude of some actresses who dread pregnancy because they will be what they call 'ugly.' It's true you can't look like a Powers model! It's equally true that for some women there are those early days characterized by a bit of daily 'tossing' and later months of disquieting sensations around your middle. Discomforts are to be expected but worth the rewards! The day you come home from the hospital with your new baby, for me, is reward beyond compare. I've read that in Victorian days ladies-in-waiting took their airings after dark so their bulging figures wouldn't cause them, or the public, embarrassment. We've come a long way since those days."

So Elizabeth waited in happy confinement for the birth of her second child, and the happiness was made all the sweeter when MGM released *The Last Time I Saw Paris* in November, and she could read some of the best critical notices she had ever received. They merely confirmed her in her determination to dig her heels in and refuse to suffer another career setback calmly. She would need every ounce of intelligence and perseverance she possessed in order to steer safely through the miasma of fear, panic, and desperation that was now beginning to descend over Culver City. For the mighty empire which Louis B. Mayer, Irving Thalberg, Nicholas Schenck, Marcus Loew, and so many others had jointly wrought had now begun, finally and unmistakably, to topple into pieces.

13

All of those memorable fringe benefits had gone first: Lena Horne, Xavier Cugat, José Iturbi, Virginia O'Brien, Lauritz Melchior, Jimmy Durante, et al. It couldn't be helped. In 1946 the industry had towered triumphantly at an all-time peak of receipts: $1.7 billion based on 82.4 million average weekly admissions. Things then went rapidly downhill in a seven-year slide. By 1953 the receipts had been cut to a flat $1 billion and the average weekly admissions had shrunk almost in half.

MGM had managed to field *The Yearling* for an Oscar in 1946, but they would have nothing in 1947, or again in 1948. Films like *Cass Timberlane, The Green Years, Green Dolphin Street, Homecoming,* and *State of the Union* made some money but they were no masterpieces. Musical fluff like *Ziegfeld Follies of 1946, Till the Clouds Roll By, The Harvey Girls, A Date With Judy,* and *Two Sisters From Boston* also showed a profit but did nothing to revive the sagging prestige of the studio which had once proudly ruled the roost in Hollywood. And divertissements like *Adventure, Undercurrent, Desire Me, Easy to Wed,* and *The Hucksters* did nothing for anybody.

The misuse of star talent was appalling. The struggles of Spencer Tracy, Greer Garson, and Robert Taylor have already been discussed. Clark Gable watched his prewar prestige relentlessly squandered in a series of ordinary vehicles that—setting *It Happened One Night, Mutiny on the Bounty,* and *Gone With the Wind* to the side—couldn't even begin to compare with *Test Pilot, Too Hot to Handle,* or *Boom Town.* As for Katharine Hepburn: the Tracy-Hepburn partnership had so far enlivened five films—mostly to the good. Metro had also put her in among the strangest collection of Chinese ever to people the screen (*Dragon Seed*), squandered her in witless melodrama (*Undercurrent*), then placed her in a bomb about Clara and Robert Schumann (*Song of Love*)—all to the bad. Once before Katharine Hepburn had been publicly labeled "Boxoffice Poison" (in 1938) and, having fought her way back to the top, was not about to sit calmly by and watch history repeat itself. She waited impatiently for her contract to expire, at which point she might leave Culver City with some remnants of her prestige intact (she hoped).

Plainly Leo the Lion was suffering a bad case of the blahs, and Dore Schary was brought in as production chief in 1948 to cure them. In the first three years of his tenure, Schary cut costs 27 per cent across the boards. Producers went down from 30 to 13, directors from 35 to 13, writers from 110 to 35. Metro had once averaged 13.7 writers per script in the great days. There were special talents for boffo gags, wow finishes, transition scenes, etc. All of that was history. By 1955 the average was 1.7. What all this drastic surgery did to the contract list was regrettable but necessary under the circumstances.

The fine character talents of Marjorie Main, Selena Royle, Spring Byington, Leon Ames, Mary Astor, Reginald Owen, Edward Arnold were lopped from the rolls. Such stellar lights on the second string as John Hodiak, Angela Lansbury, Keenan Wynn, Marshall Thompson, Arlene Dahl, Gloria de Haven, Marilyn Maxwell, and Audrey Totter headed for the exit. Nor did the collection of crown jewels escape the purge. Margaret O'Brien and Mickey Rooney were cut loose in 1949. Shortly thereafter Frank Sinatra left to fend for himself. So did Van Heflin, George Murphy, and Ann Sothern. Wallace Beery came into this world on April Fools' Day in 1889 and coincidentally went out of it on the same day in 1949. Death would also take Lionel Barrymore, Louis Calhern, Frank Morgan, and Lewis Stone.

Metro showed a ruthless new firmness in dealing with even the mightiest. Displays of temperament which had once been allowable were now no longer affordable. When Robert Walker couldn't get it together to the studio's satisfaction, MGM let him go. Judy Garland went successively and briefly in and out of *The Barkleys of Broadway, Annie Get Your Gun,* and *Royal Wedding,* and then was out of MGM permanently, leaving Ava Gardner the role of Julie in *Showboat.* By July 1952, four thousand employees total were contracted to turn out twenty-nine films per year, on a lot that had once known eighteen going all at one time. Additionally, Schary launched an economy drive and ordered all executives earning $1,000 a week or more to take pay cuts of 25 to 50 per cent for one year.

Possibly as a result of all this retrenchment, MGM revived. But only briefly. The studio got back into the Oscar sweep stakes with *Battleground* (1949), and stayed in it for five years thereafter, with *King Solomon's Mines* and *Father of the Bride* (1950), *Quo Vadis* and *An American in Paris* (1951), *Ivanhoe* (1952), *Julius Caesar* (1953), and *Seven Brides for Seven Brothers* (1954)—though perhaps significantly, only *An American in Paris* was a winner, for reasons still not clear to this day. Films like *Asphalt Jungle, The Red Badge of Courage, Singin' in the Rain, The Bad and the Beautiful, Scaramouche,* and *Adam's Rib* and *Pat and Mike* (Katharine Hepburn's final two) also added to the studio's prestige and/or profits. But that was only one side of the coin.

Conspirator, The Big Hangover, Love Is Better Than Ever, and *The Girl Who Had Everything* were on the other side. Also *The Next Voice You Hear,* in which James Whitmore and the future Mrs. Ronald Reagan sat around listening to the voice of God on the radio. Also *Across the Wide Missouri,* which lingers in the mind only because Clark Gable's marriage to Sylvia Ashley came to predictable grief up on location. Also *Plymouth Adventure,* which may have been the worst thing to happen to the Pilgrims since they were swallowed up by Massachusetts Bay Colony. By 1953–54, the boomlet had collapsed.

"When MGM seemed for a time to be dying," Elizabeth wrote, "the death rattle was truly horrendous." The time was at hand. MGM would have nothing up for the Oscar in 1955, 1956, or 1957. Finally *Gigi* and *Ben-Hur* would rush in at decade's end to save the studio from total artistic and financial collapse. Only to have it get right back into the suicide sweepstakes with the ruinous remake of *Mutiny on the Bounty*. All of that was in the future.

In Phase II of the dismantling of the MGM empire, Peter Lawford, Janet Leigh, Ricardo Montalban, Jean Hagen, and Nina Foch were set free. The day of the long-term, seven-year contracts was done. They were replaced by single deals for a specific film, or multiple-picture deals for a limited number, or by one-picture-a-year non-exclusive contracts. Lana Turner, Gene Kelly, Stewart Granger, and Eleanor Parker were still tenuously tied to MGM by the latter.

Katharine Hepburn had left in 1952. In 1953 Fred Astaire, Kathryn Grayson, Red Skelton, Deborah Kerr, and Ethel Barrymore followed her. On the firing line that year was Mario Lanza. The studio had fought with him for four fiery years, and decided that enough was enough. On his fifth film, *The Student Prince,* he was sacked, leaving his sound-track recordings to issue strangely forth from out of the mouth of Edmund Purdom. June Allyson left in 1954 to be followed shortly by Van Johnson. Gable and Garson (He Who Came Back and She Who Got Him) both left in March 1954. "They're not making my kind of picture anymore," Miss Garson reportedly remarked. No indeed.

There was no ceremony of any kind on the day that Gable wrapped his last shot on *Betrayed,* a title which perfectly fitted "The King's" grim mood that day. "It was a ruthless business," Elizabeth recollected. It was indeed. Gable—who had been the brightest star in the crown in the '30s; Gable—who was responsible for the most colossal deal ever negotiated (his loanout for *Gone With the Wind*), not one penny of the enormous profits from which ever accrued to him; Gable—who had suffered silently through nine years of dreary postwar junk which all turned a profit, so powerful was his hold on the public; for Gable, on this final day, there would be nothing. He left the studio having bitterly vowed never again to set foot in Culver City. Nor did he.

Walter Pidgeon, Jane Powell, Howard Keel, and Ann Miller left in 1955. Esther Williams swam off, leaving the Metro tank desolate and forlorn. The most regrettable departure, both as regards to circumstances and the talent involved, was that of Spencer Tracy. The studio had assigned him to an ordinary oater called *Tribute to a Bad Man,* and having long since soured on what Gloria Swanson in *Sunset Boulevard* called "the masterminds in the front office," Tracy reacted predictably, that is, at his cantankerous worst. The studio fired him off the picture up on location. After which Spencer Tracy and MGM speedily terminated his contract "by mutual consent."

By late 1955 the star roster was down to Robert Taylor, Ava Gardner, Cyd Charisse, Leslie Caron, Debbie Reynolds, Grace Kelly, and Elizabeth. The twenty-nine films turned out in 1952 had shrunk further, to twenty-seven in 1954 and 1955. Metro had appropriated Tracy's acting credo of "Less Is Better" and applied it to feature film production, which seemed to make sense. TV had already killed the "B" picture or programmer; people were getting that kind of quality at home for free. Besides, Hollywood had showed a greater aggregate profit on the 257 films made in 1954 than on the 354 made in 1953. Ergo, fewer films—but bigger and better. As a plan of action, "Less Is Better" might have had its points, but it certainly couldn't be applied to most of what Metro was turning out and of that Elizabeth had firsthand knowledge. She watched the swirl of rolling heads around her—not only those of actors, producers, directors, and executives, but also of clerks, messengers, secretaries, crew, guards, et al. She watched the upheavals of a leviathan desperately striving to retool itself for circumstances and conditions for which it was not equipped. And she knew that when she came back to the studio, it would be a brand-new ballgame.

At home little Michael, now age two, was crawling around pulling every light plug he could lay his tiny hands on, dialing on the telephone (and occasionally getting a number he could then have his own conversation with), and thoughtfully investigating the contents of every closet and every bureau drawer. He was doing all this in a new home, for the two-bedroom, top-of-the-mountain home had become inadequate for the expanding family. The Wildings again went house-prowling and eventually wound up neck-deep in debt with a $150,000 home high up in the Hollywood Canyon country which Elizabeth called "the most beautiful house I've ever seen." They had not intended to buy anything so expensive, but from the moment they saw it, they couldn't stay away from it. Sara Taylor eventually told her daughter that the architect, an old family friend, always designed with a particular person in mind and that Elizabeth had been his inspiration for this one. That did it. The place was perfection for a person who has always been happiest out of doors —a stunning meld of nature and human habitation that even Frank Lloyd Wright might have envied.

The basic materials were fieldstone, off-white brick, and weathered driftwood the color of oak. In the spacious living room, there was floor-to-ceiling plate glass on the pool side. On the other side the view presented a dazzling panorama of the city beneath and the ocean in the distance. Another wall in the living room was of bark, on which ferns, mosses, and other foliage were hung and which also boasted a small waterfall. The bar was made all of stone, and a whole tree stood in a massive floor planter. There was also a huge fireplace with no chimney—the smoke went obligingly out through pipes in the wall to re-emerge through the barbecue pit outside. At night dramatic lighting silhouetted the rock formations, Hawaiian tree ferns, and other tropical blooms on the pool side. In the first house, Elizabeth had had a whole lot of periwinkle-blue material left over from something, and she put large swatches of it together with a green chair and two huge purple chairs in the living room. A bedroom done all in pink completed this colorful ensemble. "I was pregnant when I decorated that one," she later explained. In the new house she decorated with subtle beiges and off-whites, with just a few bold splashes of accent, so that the natural colors of the surroundings would be pre-eminent.

Into this demiparadise came Christopher Edward Wilding, born via Caesarean section at 9 P.M. on his mother's birthday, February 27, 1955, and weighing 5 pounds and 12 ounces. Previously, with sibling rivalry on her mind, Elizabeth had talked to little Michael about the new baby that was coming and placed a big doll in the bassinet near his bed. He played with the doll until its place was taken by Christopher, who was tagged "Criffy" by his delighted brother.

The Wilding manse now housed two parents and two infants plus Honey, a golden retriever; Fricka (or Freaka), a wirehaired foundling adopted after she had been advertised in a London newspaper; Gigi, a poodle; Mugwumps, daughter of Gigi; four cats—two Siamese and two Maltese; the venerable gelding King Charles; plus a duck, whose favorite perch got to be Elizabeth's shoulder. For a while he had perched on the crib while Michael was a baby, but he would shriek loudly every time Elizabeth left the room and finally figured out that her shoulder afforded him the opportunity to travel in and out with her. This happy collection of humans and animals coexisted in a serene atmosphere which was the last word in unruffled comfort.

One interviewer noted Elizabeth's "remarkable lack of vanity," which complemented an observation of Michael Wilding's: "Acting-wise, Elizabeth is also unselfish—completely. She's always throwing a line, a scene, a closeup to somebody else. She has a natural generosity of spirit, an astonishing lack of ego. The star complex is simply not in her." The interviewer also called her "probably the most casual housekeeper in America," and noted that "her dressing table looks like a cosmetic counter during a fire sale." Additionally: "Most of the Wildings' sheets are ripped, and the grass-cloth wallpaper near the 7-foot-6-inch bed she shares with Michael is shredded by cat claws. Their guests, while eating from a glass-and-teakwood table and drinking vintage wines, find themselves using such mismatched utensils as long-handled iced-tea spoons to pry out grapefruit sections."

All of that might have produced severe palpitations in Emily Post, but Elizabeth never ran a household with her eye on the things in it. Her chief concerns were for the life in it. This could sometimes produce a minor crisis or two.

"Elizabeth has very little of the housewife in her," Wilding further remarked. "She's vague about household things. Forgets to order dinner. The dinner hour strikes. 'Oh, migosh,' she groans. 'We haven't anything to eat.' She never learned to cook and I have no reason to believe she's going to learn now. Exception: She does do bacon and eggs and she thinks they are the best in the world. But she never remembers to warm the plates—result, cold eggs!" This was not the whole truth. Fudge had once been in her repertoire. Also popcorn. Also one special dish: sliced tomatoes and capers fixed in fresh bacon grease. And that was about it.

"She hangs her things up on the floor," Wilding continued. "Any floor. She can make a room look more like a typhoon hit it than a typhoon would. Any room. It's kind of a disease with her." Which went with Sara Taylor's observation that her room always looked "as though it had been stirred, vigorously, with a giant tablespoon." Then there was the matter of time. "She was *born* without a sense of time!" Wilding burst out in frustration. "Her intentions are pure gold. She always starts in time, then idles, does her nails, puts on a long-playing record on the record player, dreams while you—and I—wait." An interviewer asked Elizabeth about that. "What do I do for so long? Well, I tint my fingernails, then my toenails. I cut my hair. I pluck my eyebrows. I brush and rebrush my hair. Also I do all my Walter Mittying when I'm making up. I sit with lipstick in hand reliving a scene that took place last week, wishing I'd said this instead of that." Here too there was an exception and it had to do with the children. "Their meals, their bath hour, their playtime, and their bedtime are on the tick," Wilding noted. "The only thing she does on time."

By 1961 things hadn't changed much. Elizabeth took her own inventory of all of the above and typically it was succinct and right to the point. "I'm lazy. I'm unpunctual. I'm sloppy. Food is one of my major vices. I like anything fattening. I also like to eat before I go to bed." To which Richard Hanley added, "She's never upset by trivial things. She's always calm and she never allows herself to be in a rush. The most even-tempered girl in the world." And she was married to a man who had the same internal makeup as she.

"Mike is always relaxed," Elizabeth observed. "He is as lazy as I am." To which she later added, "We're both lazy and un-ambitious though needing money. I've never regretted being an actress. It's an easy way to make a living. Michael's an actor by profession, but actually the most unactorish person I've ever known. Basically, he's unsophisticated, regardless of his reputa-tion to the contrary."

With regard to "needing money," one of the character traits she neglected to put into her inventory was extravagance, but in her husband she had met her match. They delighted in giving each other presents. It was later estimated, during their marriage, that she had given him three automobiles, and they were not your garden-variety Ralph Williams veterans either. He, in turn, had given her an automobile plus thirty-odd necklaces, bracelets, and earrings set with diamonds, sapphires, and emeralds. About all that, Elizabeth remarked, "We're broke but we don't care." Then, with that inimitable financial *savoir-faire* which is the despair of the social-conscious, "We get great pleasure out of spending money—so why not enjoy it?"

The financial squeeze, however, kept them close to the hearth. Neither was about to be found running around a tennis court, etc.; the strenuous athletic scene was not for them. Nor big par-ties when they could avoid them. They relaxed at home listening to records, watching TV, and entertaining married friends like Deborah Kerr and Tony Bartley, Jane Powell and Pat Nearney, Stewart Granger and Jean Simmons. Another acquaintance of the Wildings was Richard Burton, a Welsh actor who had initially come over to do three films at Fox, and was now back doing two more.

Aside from their marriage to Englishmen who were them-selves longtime friends, Elizabeth and Jean Simmons also had a role in common. At the time Metro had originally bought *Young Bess* for Elizabeth in 1948, the studio had done some tests and her vocal limitations had become apparent. When se-verely pushed, her voice went into a register which tended to be shrill and thin. MGM then shelved the property. It went to Jean Simmons in 1953, who gave a performance which helped her to win the Best Actress Award from the National Board of Review that year.

The canasta craze, into which Elizabeth had once willingly been swept, was now long gone. Poker took its place at occasional parties at the Wildings. They both also loved to paint and to browse in art galleries. Wilding once commented: "I'd much rather be a good artist than a good actor." Over and above all of the varied social activity was Elizabeth's continual delight in her children. In conversations about the Role of Woman, Wilding frequently heard her remark, "Husband, home, and children are purpose enough in any woman's life—*if she does them well*," and the italics were hers. Nor, as the boys grew older, had she any patience with far-out, progressive child-rearing theories. Casual she might be about which spoon got laid out with the grapefruit, but the care of her children was another matter. Total permissiveness she thought harmful hooey and never made any bones about it. When push came to shove, and misbehavior got into the picture, Elizabeth's method was two warnings— "one calm, one firm. Then they know if they don't obey, their little behinds will be warmed for them. After that process, they very seldom do it again."

Eventually, in the spring of 1955, Elizabeth reluctantly faced up to the necessity of going back to work. The studio had nothing definite in mind. A planned remake of *Kings Row* to star Elizabeth, Montgomery Clift, and Frank Sinatra never got beyond the talking stage. Someone thought Daphne du Maurier's *Mary Anne* might make a good vehicle. Then Elizabeth got wind of a development at Warners concerning another Metro star, Grace Kelly, and she knew exactly what she wanted to do. MGM couldn't see it her way, and Elizabeth promptly went in and raised a little hell in the Thalberg Building. Amid all the uncertainties still roiling the waters at MGM, the new firmness and resolution Elizabeth now exhibited might have been refreshing were it not so unsettling. Henceforth she would rely primarily on her own sharpened instincts. She would—she informed the studio—do this film or nothing. The studio acceded. It was to be the first of two roles Elizabeth would inherit due to Her Serene Highness' inability to do either.

Her Serene Highness, the Princess Grace of Monaco, nee Grace Kelly of Philadelphia, had gone from socially prominent circumstances into minor television and stage work, into a bit part in *Fourteen Hours*, into a better part as Gary Cooper's Quaker bride in *High Noon*, and eventually into a contract with MGM. The studio first utilized her in their remake of *Red Dust* called *Mogambo*. In this entertaining jungle epic, director John Ford helped her to a Best Supporting Actress Nomination. Then, as an illustration of the kind of executive deep-think going on in Culver City, she was farmed out to make millions for other studios in first-rate films they should have been making with her at Metro. There was *Dial M for Murder* at Warners, then over to Paramount for *Rear Window*. Again, at Paramount, the pregnancy of Jennifer Jones and her consequent inability to do the role put Grace Kelly into *The Country Girl*, for which she won her Oscar. All three of these films won Miss Kelly additional Best Actress Awards from the New York Film Critics Circle and the National Board of Review. Director Alfred Hitchcock was no lover of actors. "The chief requisite for an actor," he once remarked, "is to do nothing well." Furthermore, "Walt Disney had the only really satisfactory way of dealing with actors. If he didn't like his actors he tore them up." Grace Kelly and her talent, however, so enchanted Hitchcock that she shares only with Ingrid the Adored the distinction of being used by Alfred Hitchcock in three films. Belatedly MGM realized what a treasure they apparently possessed and dragged her home to do a dud called *Green Fire* about emerald-mining in Colombia.

Grace Kelly was nobody's fool. She was good and she knew it, and she could get a lot better—but not in junk like that. Hoping to recapture some *Ivanhoe* magic, the studio offered her Sir Walter Scott's *Quentin Durward*. She refused it. "On every other page, it reads, 'She clutches her jewel box and flees.' I just thought I'd be so bored," Miss Kelly remarked at the time. Next they offered *Tribute to a Bad Man*, Tracy's waterloo, and she rejected that one too. Of course she wanted to work with Spencer Tracy; what actor in his right mind didn't? But not in that script. Out to Paramount for two more A-1 films away from MGM: *The Bridges at Toko-Ri* and *To Catch a Thief*. When Warners put in a call for her services for *Giant*, MGM had had it. They drew a firm line. No more loanouts. She would come home to do Ferenc Molnar's *The Swan* and a musical version of *The Philadelphia Story*. To make things all the sweeter, Metro bought *Cat on a Hot Tin Roof* expressly for Grace Kelly, with ace "woman's director" George Cukor set to direct it, once they had licked the major problem in the script, that is, the hero's latent homosexuality. All of which left the lead in *Giant* wide open. It was the role Elizabeth went after in firm fashion and obtained. It was to be an experience she later recollected as almost a constant state of perpetual warfare.

Edna Ferber's novel *Giant* handed Texans their greatest col-

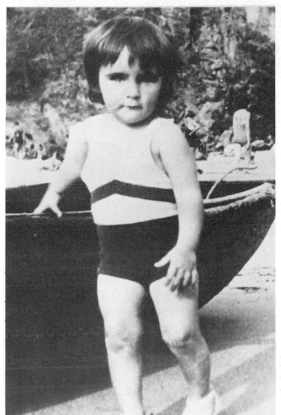

Elizabeth at age two (RAY STUART
COLLECTION, COURTESY OF SARA
TAYLOR)

At MGM School, 1943 (Darryl Hickman is on her left) (MGM)

Elizabeth at Universal, 1941. "E.T.-1": her first publicity photo (UNIVERSAL)

Elizabeth in 1945 (RAY STUART COLLECTION)

Young teenager Elizabeth has her cat while brother Howard holds Jeepers Creepers and at his feet sits Spot (or is it Twinkle?) (RAY STUART COLLECTION, COURTESY OF SARA TAYLOR)

Mr. and Mrs. Nicky Hilton
(RAY STUART COLLECTION)

Mr. and Mrs. Michael Wilding with two-month-old Michael Jr. (MGM)

1956 Academy Awards . . . the Michael Todds backstage (ACADEMY OF MOTION PICTURE ARTS AND SCIENCES)

The Eddie Fishers relax on the Costa Brava during *Suddenly Last Summer* filming (COLUMBIA)

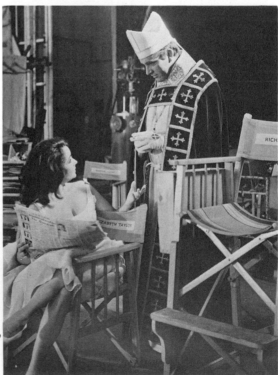

Set-sitting with Richard Burton as *Becket*, 1964 (PARAMOUNT)

Lassie Come Home (with Donald Crisp, Nigel Bruce, Lassie, and Elsa Lanchester), 1943 (MGM)

The White Cliffs of Dover (with Roddy McDowall), 1944 (MGM)

National Velvet (with Mickey Rooney and Anne Revere), 1945 (MGM)

With Lassie, in *Courage of Lassie*, 1946 (MGM)

Cynthia (with George Murphy and Mary Astor), 1947 (MGM)

Life With Father (with William Powell and Zasu Pitts), 1947 (WARNER BROTHERS)

A Date With Judy (with Scotty Beckett), 1948 (MGM)

With Peter Lawford in *Little Women*, 1949 (MGM)

Conspirator (with Robert Taylor), 1950 (MGM)

With Spencer Tracy in *Father of the Bride*, 1950 (MGM)

A Place in the Sun (with Montgomery Clift), 1951 (PARAMOUNT)

On location at Lake Tahoe with Montgomery Clift and Shelley Winters for *A Place in the Sun*, 1951 (PARAMOUNT)

Ivanhoe (with Robert Taylor), 1952 (MGM)

Elephant Walk (with Dana Andrews), 1954 (PARAMOUNT)

With Vittorio Gassman in *Rhapsody*, 1954 (MGM)

Beau Brummel (with Stewart Granger), 1954 (MGM)

The Last Time I Saw Paris (with Van Johnson and Sandy Descher), 1954 (MGM)

lective shock since the forces of Santa Anna gobbled up the Alamo. She had set out to write an epic which would portray Texans in all their lusty, egomaniacal, provincial, commercially shrewd, infuriating, ingratiating, prejudiced, hard-working, patriotic glory. Whether she had succeeded was debatable, but that she had made a goodly portion of them mad as hell was indisputable. George Stevens, Henry Ginsberg, and Miss Ferber formed a corporation to film *Giant*, checked in at Warners in October 1953 for preproduction work, and the flak was still falling. About which Miss Ferber commented, "I think they're kind of getting worn down now, like you do after a good big fight. They're wiping the sweat from their collective brows and admitting, 'Well, maybe some of us are like that, at that.'"

The action of *Giant* spanned approximately three decades, from about 1923 to 1953, and as Leslie Benedict, Elizabeth would be playing an age range from eighteen to fifty. The role thus offered her her greatest scope and challenge to date, and it provided her with a reunion with George Stevens. Since *A Place in the Sun*, Stevens had done the magnificent *Shane* and a modest film about Alcoholics Anonymous called *Something to Live For*, which came and went so fast even Andrew Sarris has forgotten it. To play Bick Benedict, the Texan who wins Leslie in a whirlwind courtship in Maryland and brings her back home to Texas, Stevens signed Rock Hudson, an action which raised the same collection of eyebrows in Hollywood which went up when Stevens originally signed Elizabeth for *A Place in the Sun* and for the same reason. What in hell was Taza, Son of Cochise, doing in a Stevens film? The third lead, Jett Rink, the volatile nouveau riche, went to James Dean. It was also his third film. And it was to be his last.

From October 1953 to the actual start of production in June 1955 was a long period, but by now it was axiomatic in Hollywood that George Stevens took his time. He was famous for calling production halts on the set and mulling a problem till he had worked it out to his satisfaction. At such times the creative process was accompanied only by the repeated noises of Stevens sucking on his pipe, which resounded on the hushed set. All of this got to be too much for Carole Lombard, an impatient, nononsense type, when she worked for him in *Vigil in the Night*. Legend has it that she phoned her agent, Myron Selznick, in the middle of the night. "Myron," announced Miss Lombard purposefully, "I've finally figured out what that sonovabitch Stevens is thinking when he's sucking on that goddamn pipe." "What's that?" responded Selznick groggily. "Not a goddamn thing!" she shot back and hung up.

For Wardrobe, Elizabeth had forty-one costumes, ranging from girlish chiffon, organdy, and dotted swiss in bright colors to matronly brocades, wools, and velvets in rich tones of green, brown, and gold. This last group was designed to help her, at age twenty-three, as she played the mother of Carroll Baker, twenty-four and Dennis Hopper, nineteen. For emotional scenes, Stevens used the old silent-film technique of playing music on the set to key actors for the proper moods. But the sounds of beautiful music were not the only sounds heard on the *Giant* set.

For one thing, James Dean and Stevens locked horns in a conflict of wills that smoldered from one end of shooting to the other, erupting in violent arguments about how a scene should be played, how a line should be read, character motivation, et al. At one point, Dean went on a three-day strike and didn't show up at all. Nor did he help matters by referring to his director as "Fatso" (among other endearments), but Elizabeth noticed that, even while Stevens was bringing all of his expertise to bear on the preservation of his authority, he could sometimes look at Dean, personal antagonisms notwithstanding, with the eyes of a man who respected talent. And that Dean was talented was beyond dispute.

He had been born in Fairmount, Indiana, in 1931, and by 1949 was in Los Angeles studying with James Whitmore's acting group. He then headed for New York and the Actors Studio. Minor TV roles led him to the crucial part of the Arab boy in *The Immoralist* on Broadway. Dean got himself bounced out of the play in the first week, after which Elia Kazan brought him to Hollywood for *East of Eden*. The *sine qua non* of screen stardom has frequently been defined as the ability to convey the existence of a whole secret self, hidden but potentially interesting. Elizabeth always possessed this quality, and James Dean had it in spades. *East of Eden* brought him instant stardom, and he consolidated it with *Rebel Without a Cause*, one of the earliest films to deal with the serious trouble brewing between the generations in America.

The film was ahead of its time but then so was Dean. He was usually lumped with Montgomery Clift and Marlon Brando, but whereas Clift and Brando were usually labeled nonconformist, huge areas of James Dean seemed bafflingly eccentric. "You're an odd one, aren't you?" Elizabeth tells him in *Giant*. He was indeed. His abiding distrust of and contempt for the Establishment and its values would have been explicable, even fashionable, in the mid-1960s, but it was not so in 1955. Also, with regard to his particular problems with George Stevens, as Jett Rink, Dean was playing the part of the Rebel Outsider versus the Establishment Insider of Rock Hudson. Since he worked from the Stanislavski System, which calls for the construction and utilization of personal reality to aid in characterization, how much of that rebellious spirit lingered between takes is an imponderable. At any rate, and for whatever combination of reasons, George Stevens never did tune in to James Dean's particular wavelength, and very few others got onto it either.

One lady reporter made the long trip to the Texas location for an interview, was constantly rebuffed, and finally confronted him out of desperation. "Mr. Dean, I've come all the way from New York to see you," she announced hopefully. "Madam," he replied, "I've come all the way from New York to make a picture." Period. End of interview. Nor did Jane Withers, playing the role of the neighbor girl who loves Rock Hudson, have any better luck with friendly overtures. The cast ate dinner together nightly in the town hotel dining room, and Jane endured the sight of Dean in the same sport shirt for three weeks running and then made her move.

JANE: "Look, I'm getting tired of that shirt, aren't you?"
DEAN: "No, I like this shirt."
JANE: "Then would you let me wash it for you?"
DEAN: "No, I like the shirt the way it is." The End.

One of the handful of people who did get close to James Dean was Elizabeth. This association set off a silly bunch of romantic rumors to accompany another set, equally foolish, which were wafting around at the same time concerning Elizabeth and Rock Hudson. Her attraction for Dean is illustrative of one of Elizabeth's major strengths as a human being, made all the more remarkable for the fact that how she developed it, given the circumstances of her life, is something of a mystery.

If you were to become a friend or acquaintance of Elizabeth's, you would find yourself in the presence of someone who would not festoon you with garlands of value judgments, snippets of conventional morality, or any of the other bits and pieces of gamesmanship which carefully insulate most human beings from the reality of most other human beings. She once paid her friend Roddy McDowall a high compliment by calling him one who seeks for the good in people and makes everyone feel of individual worth and importance. On her part, Elizabeth accepts people for what they are *as* they are.

All of the world's great religions and ethical value systems seem to have one thing in common: You shall not willingly inflict hurt or harm on another human being, that is, with malice aforethought. To that she subscribes. Other than that, she values people too highly to be flipping through the pages of a rulebook to learn whether she ought to be accepting them or not. People come into her atmosphere armed with all the usual conventional protection, and then come to realize that they don't need it. They can discard it. They are truly free to be themselves.

When she was ten, Elizabeth was gifted with a little gold pin from her music teacher. It was a musical note—B natural—and on it was inscribed one word: Always. She treasured that pin for years. As a staunch believer in the maxim, she has tried to extend the privilege to others. For those who have been severely threatened—whether by mother, society, the economic system, sexual repression, and all the other odious factors which operate to cripple human growth and potential—this kind of acceptance is like manna in the wilderness, and a wide range of people have opened up to Elizabeth and revealed sides and aspects of themselves they have revealed to few others.

By rights she might have become one of the really impossible prigs of all time. People generally start out in life hewing closely to a set of idealistic and unrealistic assumptions about human nature they heard parroted by their parents or read in a book or saw posted on some church wall. Then the realities of the economic picture and the struggle for professional advancement and personal recognition induce necessary qualities of understanding, sympathy, and compassion. But Elizabeth has never known a day of real material want in her whole life. Nor had she ever to fight her way into a successful career, a circumstance which makes her almost unique among performers. How natural it would have been for her to look down from self-satisfied heights, disdainful and uncomprehending, at the struggles and misfortunes of others. As an adult she never has.

The mantle of acceptance is not total. Like most intelligent people, she does not suffer fools gladly, particularly professional incompetents, and phonies and hypocrites she cannot abide. Also, if you're the kind who would tiptoe nervously into her presence projecting a kind of exaggerated deference toward some Great Thing, you are likewise advised to go elsewhere. Other than that, you're home free. Elizabeth's friends and intimates have always known and valued this in her. James Dean did. Elizabeth also gifted Dean with a Siamese cat, one of a long procession of animals she has found homes for. It was a singular mark of favor.

Elizabeth wouldn't be caught dead giving an animal to anyone she neither liked nor trusted.

Gossip had it that Michael Wilding's visit to his wife and children on the Texas location was to spike the various romantic rumors about Elizabeth and her costars. Actually it was primarily for moral support, for the making of *Giant* was rugged. Stevens was again the implacable perfectionist. One short scene, in which Elizabeth steps briefly into the mud and oil oozes up into her footsteps after Dean has helped her out of the mud, took hours to shoot. Each time her dress was dry-cleaned on the spot, her legs wiped free of stains and splashes, and they went right back to it until Stevens was satisfied. He was also, as usual, shooting from every possible angle for protection. The one scene where Jett refuses Bick's offer for his little bit of land runs four minutes and forty-five seconds onscreen. It was filmed three times in master shots, and then Stevens moved in for multiple closeups. Elizabeth well knew that working for such a taskmaster would be fatiguing. That was to be expected. What was a total surprise was the fact that she was hardly getting along with Stevens any better than James Dean.

One gigantic set-to was staged over one of the costumes, during the course of which Stevens castigated her for putting glamour before characterization. He knew better, but was probably using it as a technique to beat her down. It failed. She battled him to a draw on that one. On another occasion he chewed her out in such vigorous fashion before the cast and crew that he reduced her to tears. Immediately after which she, not unappropriately, had to go into a heavy emotional scene. Afterward the suspicion lingered that the old fox had staged the whole thing just to set her up for it. Then there was the matter of her illnesses.

In 1953 there had been the eye surgery and the nervous collapse in Copenhagen, and in 1954 an injury to her right knee had put her leg in a cast and delayed the start on *The Last Time I Saw Paris* for two weeks. These were isolated incidents, but now the illnesses began to stack up and to become a marked and unwelcome feature of her public image.

Director Richard Brooks later remarked, "If she opens a beer can, she cuts herself; if there is a chair in the middle of the set, she falls over it while talking over her shoulder to someone." Minor illnesses on *Giant* and *Cat on a Hot Tin Roof* reportedly added an aggregate total of $75,000 to those budgets. On *Raintree County* an overly tight corset brought on what was called a "hyperventilation syndrome" and the insurance company paid out $45,000 to Metro for that.

On *Giant* she was stricken in the back with recurrent bouts of sciatica, a neurological disease the freaky nature of which subjects its victims to alternate periods of pain which can really be excruciating and then periods when it disappears so totally you could almost wonder if it had ever been there. Almost. This fluctuating now-it's-here-now-it-isn't illness naturally played havoc with the production schedule, but it was certainly nothing that anyone in his right mind would wish on himself. Probably the simplest way to run afoul of Elizabeth is to accuse her of flagrant dishonesty, and she bitterly resented the heavy implications she sensed from certain members of the production staff that she was merely utilizing the sciatica to goof off. She had gone to St. John's Hospital, Santa Monica, in August, for what was termed "a moderate, superficial infection of her right leg." The cause had been attributed to the wearing of a too-tight jodhpur on *Giant*. Much of September she spent on crutches with the sciatica, and she was also laid low with flu. She had recovered from both and was watching rushes at Warners on September 30 when the phone rang in the projection booth and what had become an unusually onerous session of filmmaking now became tragic as well.

James Dean customarily drove his Porsche at frightening speeds, and Warners had banned him from driving it during the making of *Giant*. Dean had finished his last scene a day or so prior to the other principals, and the ban was lifted. He got into the Porsche and headed up Highway 99 for what became a rendezvous with death. That was the news that came through in the late evening, and Elizabeth plunged immediately into a frenzy of phoning various sources frantically hoping that the accident report was false. It wasn't.

Stevens insisted that she return to studio next day for filming of her final scene, and Elizabeth was appalled. Not all her pleas and the unspoken assertions that he was callous and uncaring could budge him. The next morning, weeping and disheveled after a sleepless night, she reported to Warners for the scene. Stevens had a film to wrap. Elizabeth had a friend to mourn. Meaningful communication between the two points of view was nil, but somehow they made it through the day. Not surprisingly Stevens was not satisfied with the scene and asked her to report again the next day. But on that day, Elizabeth was rushed to UCLA Medical Center suffering abdominal pains later diagnosed as emanating from a twisted colon. She was hospitalized for two weeks, after which she again returned to Warners, and the scene, and the film, were wrapped.

Finally the toughest film she had ever done was behind her. She had fought her way into it and seemed to have fought her way all through the making of it. She was left with the rueful consolation that at least Stevens picked on people his own professional size, unlike a director she had recently lectured on twelve separate occasions for taking his Napoleonic complex out on the crew. She could also take heart from the fact that *Giant* contained, thanks to her own professional growth and the exasperating but brilliant guidance of George Stevens, the most finished performance she had yet given on the screen.

❀ 14 ❀

George Stevens took a year to put *Giant* together to his ultimate satisfaction. Warners fretted about the story (not thought sufficiently interesting for the foreign market) and the length. At three hours and eighteen minutes, it was twenty-eight minutes short of *Gone With the Wind*. Stevens stubbornly refused to change it or cut it. "I'd rather have it all in one big one," he told Warner executives, "than two smaller pictures." When *Giant* was finally released in October 1956 the box office vindicated him. The film did sensational business everywhere. At a final cost of $5,400,000, its projected eventual world gross was $25,000,000 on the first run alone. It went up for ten Academy Awards: for Picture, Direction, James Dean, Rock Hudson, Mercedes McCambridge (as Hudson's possessive sister), Screenplay, Art Direction and Set Decoration, Music, Costuming, and Editing. As aforestated, Stevens was the sole winner, and deservedly so. That he managed to sustain high interest in such thematically diffuse material for the film's long running time was enormous tribute to his talents.

Warners reissued *Giant* in 1970 with the observation that "its elements are even more timely and vital today than they were when the picture was first made. Even before its time it opened a window on the rebellion of youth, racial intolerance, and a lustful materialism. We think this is a film that is definitely for today."

Giant's major problem is that all the windows frequently seem to be open at once, generating crosscurrents no one of which is developed with a depth and purpose that would lift the film from the status of colorful epic into the company of great films. There are at least six pictures here: a battle of differing cultures (Elizabeth vs. Hudson), prejudice against Mexican-Americans (a steady thread culminating in Dennis Hopper's marriage to a *chicano*), Women's Lib and the treatment of women as vacuous but pretty sexual objects, the class warfare (Dean vs. Hudson), changes in America and Texas over the three-decade span, and a full-scale domestic marital drama of growth and adjustment, with Dean's muted, unrequited love for Elizabeth in the background. The film may go in too many directions for its own ultimate good, but Stevens keeps it all moving with a cinematic sense second to none.

The opening shot of Hudson gaping through a train window at fox-hunters galloping alongside, including a dazzling glimpse of Elizabeth on horseback, pits the train against the horse, and says everything about the differing cultures before the actors get a chance to open their mouths. Other memorable moments are the gloriously romantic shot of Elizabeth and Hudson standing at the fence after their twenty-four-hour courtship, Elizabeth's first glimpse of that hideous house rising up on a sun-baked prairie in the middle of nowhere, and her hilarious dead-faint after a long, mercilessly sunny outdoor barbecue culminates in the serving of calves' brains. The vivid imagery of Dean pacing off the bit of land that has been left to him, and his unrestrained jubilation when his well finally comes in, likewise lingers in the mind. So does the entire sequence when Hudson returns to Maryland to reclaim his estranged wife at her sister's wedding. Also the scene where Dean invites Elizabeth in to have tea in his little shack, and we get the superb bit in which Elizabeth complacently assures Dean that "Money isn't everything," and he rejoins evenly, "Not when you got it."

For interesting variety, as well as for psychological toning, Elizabeth's separation speech to Hudson at their fireside is shot with her face entirely in shadow. Again, after the couple have reconciled and they are in bed talking about their children, Hudson is reading a newspaper and the angle completely blocks Elizabeth. All we hear is her voice, a refreshing change from glamour shots full-face and in closeup. This is also a long prelude to the real scene, which has been deftly constructed, in which the parents find themselves at comic cross purposes over the objectives of their children. Both scenes are illustrative of Stevens' contempt for unsupported cinematic idiosyncracy and shock for shock's sake. His choices, when he finally makes them, always combine variety with the dramatic purpose of the scene.

At one point Elizabeth contributes welcome fire to an otherwise all-male discussion of politics, when she pops off about the roles of women vis-à-vis men. This was a consideration then beginning to surface insistently in her private life. Overall, however, the script could have given Elizabeth more substance. She does her best in the role as written, but at no time do her several crises have the necessary urgency for total emotional involvement. Also, after Dean has given her the obligatory line ("You're probably the best-looking woman we've seen in these parts"), he confines his passion to a newspaper clipping of her bridal picture pasted on his wall. Which brings us back to the *Jane Eyre* syndrome, and there, somewhat regrettably for purposes of plot voltage, the script leaves it.

Both men are more interesting because they have further to go and consequently more to play. *Giant* contains what is still the most sustained, successful characterization Rock Hudson has yet attempted on the screen, a judgment which, at this distance of almost twenty years, he is reportedly tired of hearing. The judgment reflects not on his talent but on some of the lamentable uses to which it has subsequently been put. As for James Dean: his final scenes as the aging Jett are inept, and some of his mannerisms verge so constantly on the cute that one sometimes wants to cry out—as director Joseph Anthony reportedly barked at one "busy" actress—"Don't just *do* something; STAND THERE!" But you never stop watching him and, had fate not decreed otherwise, it is safe to say that audiences would still be watching him.

In September 1956, Elizabeth finally played her part in the long-running Hollywood version of Immortality: her handprints, footprints, and signature went into wet cement, along with those of Rock Hudson and George Stevens, in the forecourt of Grauman's Chinese Theater. In October *Giant* opened at Grauman's and elsewhere to generally affirmative reviews.

By the time the reviews were being read, principal photography was finished on *Raintree County* and Elizabeth had that one behind her as well. She and Michael Wilding had not lived officially as man and wife for three months. And she was immersed in the hectic whirl of a courtship which would take her shortly into her third marriage. All in all, it had been some year, going back to the previous October when *Confidential*, in the fun spirit of Halloween tricks and treats, handed the Wildings a little memento.

Confidential, an odiferous rag which did things for "innuendo" that Webster wot not of, was then at peak circulation. Its unofficial motto was *honi soit qui mal y pense*—and the more the better. "Everyone in Hollywood reads it," Humphrey Bogart reportedly cracked, "and then blames the maid for bringing it into the house." The public had tired of the umpteenth rehash of how Lana Turner was discovered sipping a soda at Schwab's. Now they wanted to know every juicy detail of what happened afterward. *Confidential* rushed in with willing eagerness to supply this vociferous demand for dirt. Unfortunately, in most instances, the promised pecks turned out to be scanty specks. Undaunted, the magazine's staff labored monthly with bellows, alchemy, and what not to puff small grains of sand into full-blown dust storms. This particular one was called "When Liz Taylor's Away, Mike Will Play."

As nearly as could be made out in the swirl of purple prose, while Elizabeth was on location in Texas, Wilding and a buddy had brought a couple of strippers home, and one of the cuties had done her act around the pool. The spiciest thing that happened, apparently, was that she removed her bra. After which she wandered into the bedroom and Wilding ordered her out of it. Hardly enough in any of that to give even Elisha Cook, Jr., in *Phantom Lady* a case of the sweats. Still—with father-figure Ike benignly presiding over the United States, and the sternly Calvinistic Dulles who sitteth (or satteth) at his right hand, that was pretty naughty for 1955.

Despite what Bogart thought, *Confidential* was not required reading at the Wilding home. It wasn't even optional. As Elizabeth remembered, "By the time the magazine came out, I was back home in Hollywood. Neither Michael nor I knew about the article until it had been on the newsstands for three days. Then a columnist telephoned poor Michael at home to know how I'd acted about it. Horrified, Michael rushed out and bought the magazine. Then he telephoned me on the set. He was absolutely aghast, and his voice was so pale gray that I couldn't help giggling." A *Giant* executive offered to fix her up with bachelor digs on the automatic assumption that it was Splitsville. Elizabeth gave him one of her long looks. "You mean you want me to leave my home, my husband, and my children?" And went off shaking her head. "Whether it's true or not," she later added, "you can't let an article like that break up your marriage."

The marriage nevertheless was beginning to come apart with a finality of which Elizabeth was only too disturbingly aware. Fortunately for the general sanity of the human race, and contrary to what actors who love to chew scenery may prefer to think, most marriages—particularly those between two people who truly love each other, and not just each other's bodies, money, or what not —do not come apart at the end of a gun or to the horrendous sounds of smashing crockery or rending flesh. They erode. Slowly. They begin on a high tide of passion with all the individual difference indigenous to human beings well submerged. Then comes the period of adjustment as the tide goes in and out and the differences are revealed. They will never disappear, but if the fit is fundamental, the tide will wash over them in the manner of water wearing away the sharp edges of a stone. They are smoothed, adjusted; they can be lived with. If the two people begin to grow in different directions from each other, however, the tide recedes farther and farther, the differences become more sharply revealed until, at length, the tide—and the magic—are gone permanently. At that point, strive as desperately as one may, all the king's horses and all the king's men . . . etc.

By her own admission in an unusually frank (for her) interview in mid-1956, Elizabeth revealed that the marriage was in danger. "We don't pick and quarrel but we do fight—it's garbage to say we don't," she admitted. "Until a year ago, we didn't; we always counted ten. But I think it's healthy to blow your lid now and then. What infuriates me about Michael is that he can be so underplaying. My temper is Irish and when I blow, I blow. But while I am shouting in an Irish temper, there he is, blasé and unruffled. Finally I yell at him, 'Oh, you—you—you—*Englishman.*'" This was somewhat toned down for the delicate sensibilities of 1956 magazine readers. The final shot, as often as not, was phrased, "You're such a goddamn Englishman!"

The new belligerence in the marital relationship was matched by a new firmness in Elizabeth's social performance. Of her old behavior at parties, she recalled, "I used to watch, observe, overhear conversations, and make my own comments to myself, some cynical. I was never bored but neither did I mix." Richard Burton remembered that period well. "I first met Elizabeth when she was nineteen. I thought she was the most beautiful and sullen creature I had ever met: difficult, unreachable, unmanageable, unobtainable, impenetrable, and—again—difficult."

He had met her at Sunday brunch at the Stewart Grangers'. She was off to herself by the pool, reading, and coolly ignoring the one-man show with which Burton was patently attempting to impress her and everyone else. She later revealed that she thought he was rather full of himself. Subsequently she threw a few four-letter words in his direction, at the use of which she was even then no slouch. It was a little technique she had developed. Mona Lisa speaking in the Vulgate was always sure to get a rise out of somebody. Its effect on Burton was to bring him to a state of almost cold-sober. After which she ignored him and he went home in defeat to an eager audience who wanted to know all about *her*. "Dark. Dark. She's dark," he muttered. "She probably shaves!"

"When I married Michael, I couldn't detach myself from his apron strings; I'd follow him from group to group like a puppy dog," Elizabeth continued. This routine of wifely abasement came to a screeching halt one night at the Charles Vidors'. Elizabeth came out of the powder room, ran into Humphrey Bogart, and asked the automatic question, "Where's Michael?" At which point Bogey chewed her out on the spot. "Let me talk to you, kid. It's damned stupid for you to keep following your husband around. You should be asserting yourself. Be something in your own right. Stop being a shadow." For a person naturally shy and reserved among large groups, it was hard advice to take. She took it, however, and soon found herself at the center of interesting conversational circles at parties. She had broken through the shell and was being treated not simply as an extraordinary beauty but as a person of knowledge and intelligence. This new evaluation of her worth was obviously at odds with Metro's idea of her. It also made the routine at home untenable.

Two years later, in her own typically oblique way, Elizabeth would comment, "I don't want to go into the past but it's nice to be married to someone who thinks I have a brain. That also contributes to making me feel like a woman." By 1956 Elizabeth had begun to question Wilding's once-unchallenged opinions, and his rejoinder was usually a reminder that he was twenty years her senior, with all the superior wisdom and maturity which that implied. Elizabeth wasn't buying it anymore. "If you tell me black is red, I won't believe you, regardless of your age," she reportedly once retorted. "But if you can give me a good story, I will. I'm not your daughter. I'm your wife."

That which Michael Wilding had feared prior to the marriage had now become bleak reality. The twenty-year chasm was becoming unbridgeable. "The happiest years of my marriage were when you were so dependent on me," he told her. "I hate it now. Now I follow you around. Now I'm left in a corner." To the interviewer he added, "I'll admit I've developed a complex about Elizabeth. I thought I'd influence this trembling little creature; I thought I'd guide her along life's stony path. Not at all. Lately, I'm simply told to shut up. Marriage is a loving work. But it's a work."

Both partners were still working at it. Wilding had come down to visit on the *Giant* location, and for her part, Elizabeth accompanied him to Morocco in the winter of 1956 for several weeks of unrelenting heat and generally dismal living conditions on location for *Zarak*, a sex-and-sand opus costarring Victor Mature and Anita Ekberg. All of the movie people were staying at the same hotel. This gave *Confidential* a chance for an encore, and the magazine intimated that Elizabeth and Mature were generating enough offscreen voltage to light up a full-scale revival of *The Desert Song*. Typically, once you hacked your way through to the two sentences' worth of fact, it developed that on some days, Wilding had a camera call, Mature did not, and he somewhat peculiarly—according to *Confidential*—preferred to spend his free time back at the hotel rather than wander around alone somewhere out in the dunes. When the Wildings returned to Hollywood, Elizabeth had just enough time to get squared away before *Raintree County* began shooting in April.

In 1944 MGM had launched a semi-annual prize novel contest, the better to corral suitable original material for filming. The top prize was $150,000. *Green Dolphin Street* had been a previous winner, and in July 1947 the big money went to Ross Lockridge, Jr., a thirty-three-year-old English instructor from Bloomington, Indiana, for his 1,060-page blockbuster, *Raintree County*. He wrote for six years and was down to a hundred dollars when the award was announced. MGM assigned Carey Wilson to produce it with Robert Walker or Richard Hart to do John Shawnessy. Van Heflin and Gene Kelly were also mentioned for the part. For Susannah, the femme lead, it would be either Lana Turner or Ava Gardner. Janet Leigh was set for Nell, the second woman in the hero's life. In January 1948 *Raintree County* was the Book-of-the-Month Club selection; by May, it topped the bestseller list. Its author never lived to witness this new triumph; he had killed himself in March. In July, Dore Schary launched the first phase of the economy drive at Metro and shelved the property. In January 1955 he ordered it reactivated, and almost a year was spent on the script. The original fifty-two-year time span, 1839–92, was reduced to 1859–65. Scores of flashbacks were eliminated. What resulted from this attempt at clarity and compression was, paradoxically, a script that was wordy, shallow, overextended, and pretentious. As Montgomery Clift later bitterly commented, "The actors and director, Edward Dmytryk, tried to lift its lousy script from the soap-opera level. But we couldn't raise it more than a couple of inches, which was far from getting it to the realm of merit." The great Northern screen epic of the Civil War, a fitting counterpart to *Gone With the Wind,* was never to be realized.

MGM nonetheless proceeded to take lavish aim at that objective. The film's initial budget was set at $5,300,000 and Metro proudly touted *Raintree County* as "the highest budgeted domestic film in MGM history." Additionally, the film was to have the honor of being the first to be shot in the new MGM Camera 65 "Window of the World" Process. Some 216 tons of props, set decorations, camera equipment, and other gear were ordered shipped to Danville, Kentucky, for the estimated two-and-half-month location jaunt. All hotel space and some private homes were rented to accommodate the cast and crew of 134. Money poured out unstintingly. The Battle of Atlanta sequence alone, which would engage the principals and eight hundred extras, cost $200,000. Additional money would be needed, and the budget would run to a whopping $6 million total, due primarily to the horrible accident which befell Montgomery Clift.

Since *A Place in the Sun,* Clift and Alfred Hitchcock had failed to communicate up in Quebec on *I Confess,* which its director later ruefully observed "should never have been made." A promising collaboration between Clift, Jennifer Jones, Vittorio de Sica, and David Selznick on *Terminal Station,* shot in Rome, turned into the chopped calamity shown (very briefly) in the United States as *Indiscretion of an American Wife.* Far outweighing these setbacks was *From Here to Eternity,* in which Clift, as Private Robert E. Lee Prewitt, gave one of the great performances of the screen. To his everlasting credit, director Fred Zinnemann, holding his first Oscar at a moment of great personal triumph, told the assembled reporters and photographers, "I couldn't have done it without Monty."

Clift entered *Raintree County* at the peak of his prestige. He had rented a house a few minutes away from the Wilding house high up in the canyon. He and Elizabeth had taken to getting together in the evenings and checking out the problems in the script and investigating various areas of characterization. On the particular evening of May 13, Elizabeth and Michael Wilding were host to Clift, and to Rock Hudson and Kevin McCarthy as well. Things broke up well before midnight, and what next happened is best related by Elizabeth, who has never forgotten a single ghastly moment of it:

"Monty left. He was tired, but had only taken two drinks. Suddenly Kevin came lurching, white-faced, into the living room. He was saying something incoherent and finally one got the words: 'My God, oh God, Monty's dead.' We finally made out that Monty's car had crashed into a telephone pole about a block and a half down the hill.

"We all ran down. My only thought was to get into that car and Monty would be alive. The doors were jammed shut, but we could see that Monty's head looked like it had been mashed right into the steering wheel and the windshield was all broken, the dashboard was all smashed. He was bleeding from the head so much that it looked like his face had been halved.

"Finally somebody got one of the doors open and we all kind of backed away from the car and lifted him away from the steering wheel. I found that he was breathing and moaning. All my revulsion about blood absolutely left me. I held his head and he started coming to. You could hardly see his face. It was like pulp. He was suffering terribly from shock, but he was absolutely lucid. There was a tooth hanging on his lip by a few shreds of flesh, and he asked me to pull it off because it was cutting his tongue.

"We had to wait forty-five minutes for the ambulance. It got lost. The ambulance came and we got him out of the car and, oh God, it was horrible. He was squirting blood all over his face. He never once complained. I rode in the ambulance, and by the time we reached the hospital his head was so swollen that it was almost as wide as his shoulders. His eyes by then had disappeared. His cheeks were level with his nose. The whole thing was like a giant red soccer ball . . . His jaw had been broken in four places, his nose in two places, and he was badly cut around the eyes. And his upper lip—it was like a spoon had gouged a great big hunk out of his mouth and teeth."

Eventually plastic surgery and nature brought Clift's face back to a reconstruction of his former semblance, but the accident cost Metro a six-week production halt. As if this near-tragedy weren't trouble enough, Clift later fell asleep in his hotel after taking sleeping pills and badly burned two fingers. Subsequently he broke a toe. It was a miracle he survived the making of the film at all.

During the production hiatus Elizabeth got off some considered conclusions about her own professional progress to date. "I'll never be afraid of suspension again," she announced firmly. "Never again will I play a part in which I don't believe." She would go back on that resolve just once and not of her own volition. Metro rammed *Butterfield 8* down her throat and she swallowed it so that she could terminate the contract and be free to do *Cleopatra*. As for her budding talent, "Some day I think I will be an actress. I'm now learning and developing. I'm trying. I've always been an instinctive actress as opposed to an instructed one. I have no technique. I just try to *become* the other person. Some people act by charts—or by the Stanislavski Method. I can only do it by forgetting myself completely, even moving or picking things up by impulse."

How had the fires of ambition been stoked in a woman who seemingly had been content to do without them for so long?

"The reason I suddenly became interested in acting the past two years," she explained, "is that I finally got tired of all the garbage. In fifteen years I've only made four pictures I really loved: *National Velvet, A Place in the Sun, The Last Time I Saw Paris,* and *Giant.* I also love the picture I'm making now, *Raintree County.* But how would you like to act year after year in pictures with no story content? I've made up my mind that I'll do only films I'm enthusiastic about. I've been good so few times—but I would like to be good."

She eagerly looked forward to the end of her contract when she could go out on her own in films of her choice and at her own price.

"With luck," Michael Wilding noted, "she can earn a million dollars in seven years and be independent the rest of her life."

"With luck," Elizabeth added crisply, "I can also act only in pictures that interest me. I will never have to do garbage again."

At this point Michael Wilding had reportedly turned down the role of Henry Higgins in the national company of *My Fair Lady.* He was content to be at home, to read and to paint. Seemingly he had lost all interest in an acting career, and small wonder.

Torch Song, his first chore under the MGM contract, paired him with Joan Crawford. In this one, Wilding worked skillfully to portray a blind pianist, but the film hewed strictly to Crawford formula, that is, tears and torment featuring the brassy dame with the heart of foam rubber, the kind of thing which forced Miss Crawford to leave Metro ten years previously. Next MGM loaned Wilding to Fox for *The Egyptian,* the film which caused Marlon Brando to flee to a psychiatrist. Literally. The role of the physician-hero was then taken by Edmund Purdom, who was simultaneously involved with slave girl Jean Simmons, who expired bearing his child during a rebellion, and Babylonian harlot Bella Darvi, who rotted away from a naughty social disease movies didn't talk about in 1954. Into these colorful surroundings wandered Wilding as Pharaoh, pushing the idea of One God— and getting few takers. All of this blended about as well as three films shooting on the same sound stage at the same time. Next there was *The Glass Slipper,* in which Wilding was Prince

Charming to Leslie Caron's Cinderella, and *The Scarlet Coat*, minor twaddle about Benedict Arnold. *Zarak* was the kind of thing Jon Hall and Maria Montez used to do at Universal—cheaper and better. Such a collection of gems might have taken the steam out of Sammy Glick.

Whether it was Wilding's career woes, or the joint financial pinch, or Elizabeth's new maturity as woman or actress, or whatever, the marriage had entered into that numb, lifeless state where the partners were careful not to say anything of real substance to each other because there was really nothing more to say. They were too fond of each other to engage in useless recriminations. Nor was either about to turn their home into an arena where they contended for the loyalty of their children. A sense of sadness and regret weighed heavily on both of them. At one party Elizabeth let slip some of her unhappiness, and when the tears fell despite her best efforts to hold them back, she quickly left the room to compose herself. The final step was inevitable. It confronted her first thing in the morning, and last thing at night, and, like it or not, it had to be taken.

Hedda Hopper visited the house for an interview in May and reported, "She seemed moody and quiet to me—her mind removed from the things at hand and so different from the sparkling, gay Liz I'm accustomed to." Miss Hopper put it down to her preoccupation with the *Raintree* script. Elizabeth, however, was still carefully sitting on her own secrets. The official separation announcement hit the newspapers July 19. "Much careful thought has been given to the step we are taking," it read. "It is being done so that we will have an opportunity to thoroughly work out our personal situation. We are in complete accord in making this amicable decision."

At this point Elizabeth might have been reflecting that trying to get it all together in life was like trying to nail all the tent flaps down in a high wind. Her professional future had never looked so promising, and the bottom had just fallen out of her personal life. Even if, by some miracle, you got them both working in high at the same time, a dozen pitfalls always lurked in the inscrutable future: illness, other personal misfortune, financial reverses, deaths or mishaps to friends and loved ones, impersonal decisions reached in Washington or Moscow or Peking or wherever—all calculated to mock the delusion that man controls his own destiny. She had little time to brood about any of this, however, for a number of fascinating personalities now entered her life.

One was a high-school dropout from Minneapolis originally

named Avrom Goldbogen, who ran a legal lottery, two bookie joints, and served as a gag writer for comics before hitting it big at the 1933 Chicago World's Fair as the producer of a "Flame Dance." A diaphanously clad damsel ran into a tower of flame, lost what little she was wearing, and fled into the wings to appreciative wolf whistles. Her triumphant manager sat beneath the stage carefully controlling the gas jet.

Then there was a con artist—a cigar-chomping vulgarian—who promoted such attractions as Pete the Personality Penguin, a flop personal appearance tour for radio's "Lone Ranger," and a Christmas novelty called Kute Kris Kringles. He had two 1937 turkeys on Broadway called *Call Me Ziggy* and *The Man From Cairo* before success came at the 1939 New York World's Fair, where he proudly boasted four separate successful attractions on the midway.

Then there was an erudite fellow, a Shakespearean expert and art lover, who was self-taught by voracious readings in the classics, history, philosophy, and encyclopedias. This one had to his credit two successful associations with Cole Porter (*Something for the Boys* and *Mexican Hayride*), plus a revival of Molière's *The Would-Be Gentleman, Catherine Was Great* with Mae West, a musical about Boss Tweed (*Up in Central Park*), and the longest-running *Hamlet* Broadway had ever seen, with Maurice Evans (a record subsequently broken by Richard Burton).

Then there was a compulsive gambler who had his own $2-million-a-year contracting business when he was eighteen, went bankrupt when he was nineteen, came out to Hollywood and built a second fortune soundproofing sound stages, went bust again in the Great Depression, played gim rummy as if money were going out of style, bought and lost the Del Mar Racetrack, invested in the Cinerama Process, was dealt out of it, went to American Optical and started his own screen process, and dealt himself out of that too.

Another unfortunate had a first wife who died under peculiar circumstances on the operating table after a freak accident, and the press did everything they could to hang the rap of wife-killer on him. After which he went bankrupt and was hounded by creditors determined to imprison him. And his second wife, Joan Blondell, divorced him after a stormy, seven-year relationship.

One producer was a genuine eccentric. He seemed to go unvaryingly for the challenges, like jazzing up Gilbert and Sullivan for *The Hot Mikado*, making burlesque respectable with Gypsy

Rose Lee in *Star and Garter*, doing a successful musical satire on the first Lady President of the United States called *As the Girls Go*, getting the King of Siam to do the score for *Peep Show*, and producing a Johann Strauss operetta outdoors at Jones Beach.

Then there was the undercover agent who helped the FBI to put the lid on Gerald L. K. Smith and his sick circle of Jew-baiters, and got badly stomped in the process. He twice tried to enlist during World War II, made it to Europe on his own, was almost killed in a private plane, and got through Russian lines to become the first American to enter beaten Berlin.

Finally a man who had earlier dropped $40,000 in an abortive attempt to produce *Around the World in 80 Days* on the stage had struggled through the making of a movie of it, often one jump ahead of his creditors. In this summer of 1956, he was in Hollywood putting it together.

All of these personalities were named Michael Todd.

❀ 15 ❀

Of a unique individual, it is often said, "They broke the mold when they made him." With Mike Todd, there was no mold, and if there was, no one ever found it. Again, rugged individualists are said to march to the beat of a different drummer. No one ever succeeded in getting Mike Todd's particular score down on paper, either, and it wasn't for lack of trying. Every major newspaper and magazine had profiled him, and Art Cohn finally undertook the impossible task of full biographical treatment in *The Nine Lives of Michael Todd*. As the plethora of facts and anecdotes mounts, and opinions pile up from Todd-lovers and Todd-haters and all the in-betweens, one has the eeriest feeling that one is not reading the book alone. Someone is sitting beside you and his name is Michael Todd. He regards you with a shrewdly penetrating glance and a bemused smile as if to say, "Not bad, huh?" The important thing is that he is outside of the book.

Todd worked from a core of incredible complexity, and he simply defied pinning down—in life, in the pages of a book, or wherever. Damon Runyon saluted him as "the greatest natural gambler I've ever known." A man who shed his yesterdays like so many dead skins, he moved zestfully through an incredible life of monumental insecurity. "Poverty is a state of mind," Todd fervently believed. "When you start thinking with your wallet, you're always wondering what you *can't* do instead of what you can do, and you're never going to get off your back." Todd hustled his back through a whirlwind of activity with an immunity to fear coupled with absolute self-confidence that were breath-taking to behold. This long-running high-wire act would have made basket cases out of any 999 out of a thousand other people. For Todd, it was as natural as breathing. He thrived on it, and whenever things threatened to become too stable and predictable, Todd could be relied on to shake up the immediate circumstances with his contagious air of excitement and dedication to the thrilling, the daring, the unpredictable.

"When you know what you can do, do something else" was a maxim of which he was the foremost living exponent. A cursory examination of all the opinions passed on Michael Todd yields the following: fearless, moral, prudish, shy, exciting, extroverted, domineering, compulsive, intelligent, shrewd, gregarious, honest, tense, driven, loud, egotistical, demanding, generous, blunt, psychopathic, dangerous, brazen, uncompromising, undisciplined, tender, sensitive, intuitive, explosive, brassy, charming, scrupulous, indefatigable, irresistible, irrepressible, and incorrigible.

Mike Todd could be any of these, or any combination of them, at any given moment. The immediate purpose was generally the self-promotion of Mike Todd, and as a promotional genius, Todd had few peers in the entire history of show business. "You made me what I am today," he had jauntily written on a photo for his press agent, "but I still like you." His most familiar public face was that of gaudy, cigar-chomping, grammar-fracturing, diamond-in-the-rough. If business competitors bought this Bumpkin-From-Second-Avenue stereotype, so much the worse for them. It was a mistake they never made twice.

The stereotype was all Elizabeth had in her mind the day someone pointed him out to her in the MGM commissary. As a group, producers were never her favorite breed of *Homo sapiens;* several unpleasant exercises in noncommunication had pretty well turned her off. When she saw Mike Todd, however, she thought, "Oh! He's really quite good looking—for a producer." For his part, Todd was equally wary of involvement with actresses. "To live with an actress, you got to be able to worry about her hair," he once cracked. "And when their bosoms start to drop, they get panicky and run to head-shrinkers."

Elizabeth next saw Mike Todd at Romanoff's where, with Dietrich on his arm, he stopped by her table for a brief hello. Next, through the agency of a mutual friend who was an assistant director on *Around the World in 80 Days*, the Wildings spent the weekend of June 30 cruising on Todd's rented yacht off Southern California. His steady companion was then Evelyn Keyes, very much in evidence, and Elizabeth's net impression of the weekend was inexplicable hostility from Mike Todd. She couldn't understand it because he really didn't know her at all. Was it his natural scorn for actresses? Had he picked up on snippets from her public image which displeased him? Or was it perhaps the defensive reaction of a man who felt the unmistakable stirrings of a violent attraction to another man's wife?

Subsequently the Wildings were invited to a lavish party given at Todd's house for the Edward R. Murrows, to a barbecue there, and to the studio to see *Around the World in 80 Days*. None of that was the remotest preparation for what next happened, but there had been a couple of clues along the way. At the Murrow party, where Elizabeth's overwhelming feelings of despair and unhappiness had caused her momentarily to leave the room, Todd's reaction had shown that she was very much on his mind and that he was well aware of her current situation. At another affair, they had been sitting back to back, scant inches between them, on an open divan, and an overpowering tingling sensation discomfited Elizabeth to the point where she eventually got up and moved. (Todd later confirmed the fact that the tingle had been mutual.)

On July 20, one day after the Wilding separation announcement had hit the newspapers, Todd called Elizabeth and told her he had to see her right away. She met him in Benny Thau's office in the Thalberg Building. Without a word, he took her by the arm, dragged her imperiously down a corridor, thrust her into an elevator, hustled her out again, marched her down another corridor, located an empty office, took her in there, plunked herself and himself down in adjacent chairs, and launched into a long, well-reasoned, urgent, and incredible proposal of marriage.

"I see that you have decided to shed that guy," Todd told her. "Now understand one thing and hear me good, kid. Don't start looking around for somebody to latch on to. You are going to marry only one guy, see, and his name is me!" There followed a confident explanation of why such an arrangement was not only desirable but inevitable. Todd remembered that Elizabeth gave him a cold stare, then a smile meant to be disdainful. He was also sure that, at the same time, a hopeful light brightened her eyes.

Elizabeth's inner reaction to this unexpected onslaught was at least twofold. It was the most audaciously crazy thing she had ever heard. The man was an obvious loony and ought to be certified. Somewhere in the midst of the nonstop torrent, she got an image of herself as a mongoose being petrified by a large cobra. Too, she was just coming out of a marriage where the age difference had proven to be an insurmountable handicap. Mike Todd's birthdate was set (with no little controversy among his own family) at June 22, 1909. That put at least twenty-three years between them. He had taken his first wife five years before she was even born, and his son, Michael Todd, Jr., was over two years her senior. All of these reasons were sufficient cause for her to terminate this nonsense forthwith and assert her independence against such an outrageous attempt at domination. She had never given him the slightest encouragement for such a thing. Who, after all, did he think he was fooling around with?

What stayed her was the overwhelming, countervailing sense that what he was saying was the literal truth. It *was* desirable. It *was* inevitable. And the sense of it rendered her powerless. It was the From-the-moment-I-saw-you-I-knew-there-could-be-none-other-for-me syndrome familiar from a hundred romantic encounters in literature and films. Elizabeth had just done this very number with Rock Hudson in *Giant*. Now, in a deserted office in the Thalberg Building at MGM, the reality of it hit her with frightening force and paralyzed her will to deny it. They kissed perfunctorily, Elizabeth promised to think about the matter, and she headed out of Culver City in a daze. She had been criticized in the past for being impatient, impulsive, for jumping into things without weighing the consequences. One thing she knew. She must get off by herself somewhere where she could sort all of this out in a sane and sensible manner. Fortunately, her personal and professional needs meshed at this point. Montgomery Clift had recovered, and Elizabeth went almost immediately to Danville, Kentucky, for the location shooting on *Raintree County*.

There, masses of flowers greeted her daily on the set, courtesy of Mike Todd. He called nightly from California. "At first we talked only a few minutes," Elizabeth recalled. "Soon we were talking for hours." Todd then came East and on three weekends sent a chartered plane to bring her to New York. Once they met in Chicago just for lunch. This whirlwind courtship, complete to phone conversations that occasionally went on until five in the morning, might have been expected to leave Elizabeth little energy for her work before the cameras. Not so. The combination of the best part she had yet had, plus the stimulation of love and renewed self-confidence, resulted in one of the authentic gems among her collection of film performances.

Overall, *Raintree County* is a jumpy, abrupt affair and a failure on motion picture terms: a succession of expository scenes told but not really *felt* via the senses. It opens with a high-school graduation in pre-Civil War Indiana, and we meet John (Montgomery Clift), a dreamy type who spouts some piffle about a symbol of wish fulfillment called "The Raintree" ("It opens all locks, it heals all wounds," etc.). Thereafter Clift moves through everything with a lack of conviction or interest in any of the proceedings that, coming from an actor of his proven gifts, is appalling. He is loved by a goody-two-shoes named Nell, played by Eva Marie Saint on a monotonous note of petulant jealousy.

At a subsequent celebration, Clift is maneuvered into a foot race against local hot-shot "Flash" Perkins (Lee Marvin). It is here that Elizabeth makes her brief, wordless entrance. Looking radiantly beautiful, she discreetly vamps Clift and then exits into a photographer's studio. There she reveals herself as an amiable, predatory Southern belle. She emerges from the studio to crown Clift the winner in the race, and to vamp him some more. Thereafter you can forget about Clift, Miss Saint, the Raintree, and everyone and everything else in this swollen botch of a film. Elizabeth is the strongest, most clearly delineated character in it, and she commands her role, and the film, with presence and authority from first to last.

After she and Clift have become lovers, she lies about pregnancy and traps him into marriage. During their honeymoon scene on a riverboat, she lays out her dolls and the music hints eerily at her coming madness as she maunders about Abolitionism and how "one drop of Nigra blood" can ruin a person. Ultimately the roots of her insanity are exposed via skillful monologues from Elizabeth and bits and pieces from other characters. Her mother had gone insane after her birth. The father subsequently took her Negro governess, Henrietta, as his mistress. Elizabeth apparently wished that Henrietta had been her true mother, but couldn't live with the idea because Henrietta was black. Her conflicting loyalties compelled her to send an anonymous note to her mother about her father and Henrietta. Whereupon the insane woman fired the house, and burned herself, the father, and Henrietta to death. From that time, Elizabeth has carried the load of guilt which will eventually destroy her.

She and Clift have a son, and Elizabeth plays on her fear of Negro blood immediately after childbirth with a fixation that "another one was put away—a dark one." The Civil War breaks out, Elizabeth's sanity cracks altogether, and she flees South with the child, leaving a note in which she refers to anonymous "forces" that are after her. Clift then joins the army to find her, and reclaims her from an asylum after the war, locating his son as well. Back in Indiana, Elizabeth feels that she will never be anything but an onerous burden to Clift. Her growing awareness of the sacrifice she feels compelled to make is affectingly done, as is her final goodbye to her son. After which she flees into a swamp and drowns herself. Fadeout on a glowing shot of Clift, Eva Marie Saint, child, and raintree.

To give *Raintree County* its full due, there is a gloriously romantic musical score by Johnny Green, and the highest level of technical excellence in the camera work of Robert Surtees, the costumes of Walter Plunkett, and in the art direction and set decoration—a level of excellence which, now that it has almost vanished, we realize we once shamefully took for granted. Nigel Patrick contributes a stylish characterization, and Lee Marvin moved that much further ahead on the road to his eventual full stardom in the '60s. In those moments when *Raintree County* really comes to life, however, the prime mover is Elizabeth Taylor.

The role is an actress' dream: even when off the screen she is talked about, her character probed, her behavior and motivations analyzed, etc. This dream could have been a nightmare in the wrong hands. Elizabeth, however, is never off target, and delivers a skillful, moving, sensitive portrayal of a doomed Southern belle. It was the closest she was ever to come to playing a prototype of Scarlett O'Hara, and she was fully equal to the challenge. Too bad the film didn't match her. As she herself noted, "I had an interesting part as the schizophrenic bride, but the picture was bad."

Monumental was Metro's disappointment when they finally released *Raintree County* in October 1957. They had launched it with a world premiere in Louisville, Kentucky: an expensive, two-day hoopla with planeloads of stars converging from Hollywood and New York. All the best p.r. work in the world, however, could not alter what went up on the screen.

"Begins in tedium and ends, 168 leaden minutes later, in apathy," pronounced *Time*, and *Newsweek* dismissed the film as an "opulent emotional circus." The *Saturday Review* added: "The story seems ponderous and slow-moving for too much of its

length and is certainly not helped by a lot of symbolical gob-
bledygook about a tree called the raintree."

The verdict from the trade papers was no more helpful, and
Metro's last hope, the local press, went glimmering in reviews
like the following from the L.A. *Times:* "It is something less
than the masterpiece that might have been anticipated in view of
all the advance exploitation . . . Too much of it seems to rely on
very flimsy substance . . . it just doesn't get anywhere . . .
amazingly diffuse."

Montgomery Clift subsequently commented, "Another unfortunate thing about that movie is that the audience spends too
much time trying to figure out which scenes were *after* my
accident. And can you imagine charging sixteen dollars for four
people to see *Raintree County?* That's what some friends of mine
on the West Coast had to pay because it was being road-shown
on a two-a-day basis. I mean, isn't that absolutely ridiculous?"

Yes, it was, agreed an alarming number of theater exhibitors.
MGM had anticipated lucrative long runs on hard ticket at a few
select locations. The disappointing critical reception fueled exhibitor resistance to this scheme, and Metro reluctantly abandoned the plan. A month after *Raintree County* opened, MGM
announced continuous performances at reduced prices and with
a print cut from three hours five minutes to two hours forty-
eight minutes. And the prints were in CinemaScope, not in
Camera 65 "Window of the World." The film's domestic gross
of $6 million presumably paid its cost, with what came in from
overseas plus the TV sale sending it into the black. For what
was lavished *on* it and what was expected *from* it, *Raintree
County* remains one of the most grievous disappointments MGM
ever had.

For Elizabeth the film was, and is, a personal triumph, the
third great one of her career. This one was doubly sweet in that,
unlike her work in *National Velvet* and *A Place in the Sun,* it
was not achieved in a setting of general excellence. This one she
pulled off by herself, and in the process, finally licked her old
bugaboo. Previously she had sunk right along with inferior material. This time she triumphed.

"Elizabeth Taylor dominates the picture with her finest performance," proclaimed the Hollywood *Reporter.* "It shows that
this legendary beauty can be a really good actress if she desires.
For the first time she seems an adult woman." *Cue* noted that
"Miss Taylor is far superior to the rest of the players," and
Redbook stated flatly: "Elizabeth Taylor gives the best performance of her life. There is a large cast with some interesting

performances but Miss Taylor's beauty and acting outshine everything in this monumental picture."

Back in the summer of 1956, during the making of *Raintree County*, Elizabeth and Mike Todd were getting fully acquainted through the good offices of Alexander Graham Bell. He called her every day but one, and on that day, she worried that something serious might have happened to him. The next day he called and remarked impishly, "I hope you missed me yesterday." She had. Elizabeth managed to get two weeks off from shooting, and Todd sent a chartered plane to bring her to New York. She was first off the plane and raced down the ramp and into his waiting arms. "There was no more discussion. That was it. We were getting married." Discussion would have been superfluous.

In WPA-"make-work" marriages or relationships, the considerations go something like this: "She has all those fatherless children and I could give them a good home," or "We both have pretty much the same interests and we could maybe make a nice life together," or "He's kind and generous and maybe in time I could learn to love him," or "I'm thirty-five and he may be my last chance—I better take it," and so forth. Elizabeth would have a subsequent experience with this sort of thing, but this one was decidedly not it.

"What we've got is so great and so right it scares me," Todd told Art Cohn. "I'm afraid I'm dreaming and all of a sudden I'm going to wake up. We've got the right chemistry. She digs me." He, for his part, worshiped and adored her. It was nothing that could be, or needed to be, articulated. It was simply and wondrously there, a fact of their lives. Later, when their celebrated fights had rung a few rafters, large segments of the public waited for the divorce announcement. That the fundamentals in the relationship were firm, and that the fights were a form of extracurricular fun, was something that the public didn't seem to understand. But, then, how could they? And whose business was it, anyway?

For the Labor Day weekend, Todd chartered a plane and he and Elizabeth flew to Atlantic City, where he presented her with an official engagement ring: a plain gold band set with garnets. After which Elizabeth returned to Hollywood for the final studio shooting of *Raintree County*. She enlivened the long waits between camera setups with one of her exercises in deadpan humor. The annual World Series madness was then current, and Elizabeth sidled innocently over to a bunch of grips who were huddled excitedly around a radio. "What are y'all listening to?"

she inquired. A ballgame, they told her. "Oh. A ballgame. Well . . . what kind of ball are they playing?" Baseball, she was told. "Oh. Baseball." Here a wild flutter of the double eye-lashes. "Well . . . Is that anything like football?" And so on. "Drives 'em crazy," she later told a visiting reporter.

On October 4 the news that Elizabeth had definitely decided to seek a divorce from Michael Wilding hit the newspapers and was greeted with much clucking in the columns, the substance of which came down to "there she goes again." The following item from Hedda Hopper was typical: "I hope and pray that after her divorce she will take some time to consider her next move" (which translated out as "and then do what I think is best for her"). "But knowing her as well as I do, I doubt if she will." Miss Hopper may have been irked at her failure to recognize what was right under her nose the previous May. Her proprietary tone can be explained by the fact that Sara had brought little Elizabeth to sing for her when she was nobody. And, after all, as she never tired of rehashing (and finally, and incredibly, put into a book): Hadn't she once personally saved Elizabeth, age twelve, from the fate worse than death? (At the hands of Mickey Rooney, yet!)

On the night of October 17, Mike Todd and Elizabeth were together in New York City for one of the most important nights in both their lives: the world premiere of *Around the World in 80 Days*. On that night, Todd personally sat at the sound controls, and Elizabeth sat next to him, helping him with them. He had made the film with an indefatigable devotion and a refusal to fold up in the face of numerous calamities which are still a wonder to contemplate even at this distance.

Eventually Mike Todd would proudly wear the Triple Crown of Film Awards: an Oscar, plus the Award of the New York Film Critics Circle, and the laurel wreath of the National Board of Review, all saluting *Around the World in 80 Days* as Best Film of 1956. Considering who he was, and what he had done, and what he had had to do to *get* it done, his remains a singular achievement. Since Elizabeth now owns 40 per cent of the film, it would become one of the finest gifts among the many he would give her, material and otherwise.

At the celebration after the premiere, Todd and Elizabeth formally announced their engagement and Elizabeth exhibited a new diamond ring. Press estimates of its cost ran anywhere from $92,000 to $100,000. "The diamond is one inch across and five-eighths of an inch deep," enthused one scribe, "and nothing like it has been seen since the Maharajahs went out of business." Prior to this, Mike Todd had derived no little amusement from taking Elizabeth around to various of his New York friends and introducing her as Miss Lizzie Schwarzkopf (Blackhead). One of them peered at her at length and then announced, "You know, you look a lot like Elizabeth Taylor but you're heavier." Todd slapped her playfully on the fanny. "See, I told you you're getting fat," he chortled. After the engagement announcement, that was a thing of the past, and the new clucking heard in the columns was a disapproving refrain of "Off with the old/On with the new."

The end of a marriage or a relationship has been compared, in psychic terms, to a death, particularly as concerns the survivors. First there is a period of intense heartache and grief, followed by a period of mourning in which the hurt becomes less acute and a gradual adjustment is made to the new reality. Ultimately the pain passes, one accepts, and puts away the past so that new things can happen. The marriage Elizabeth was leaving had been long dead and the mourning for it was over as well. The public saw only a divorce announcement followed immediately by plans for remarriage. With regard to her personal life, Elizabeth saw not the slightest need to explain anything to anybody. She never has.

For all his public flamboyance, Mike Todd could also be remarkably circumspect about certain things. After praising his future wife for her "compulsive honesty," he touched briefly on the matter of her past romances. "They have been surprisingly few. I know because she told me about them—even the ones I didn't want to hear about. It was, after all, none of my business." He was still no big booster of actresses. "Anyone who marries an actress marries a problem. Mostly it's worth it. Actresses, let us not forget, are darned attractive people. Anyway, in the case of Elizabeth, my son approves," he cracked, "so I have some mature judgment to guide me. They tell me Elizabeth is spoiled, hot-tempered, difficult. She is also deeply loyal and devoted. I can do no better than to quote my friend, Nick Schenck, on the subject. He said, 'So she's spoiled. What man wouldn't want to indulge a girl like her?'"

Elizabeth had been having her own thoughts about her future. "The blending of a career with marriage does not seem to work out satisfactorily," she remarked. "So retirement from maximum activity is the most desirable thing." This, in October 1956, was her first public comment on the subject of retirement, an idea with which she has had a long-running flirtation ever since. The

age difference between future bride and groom was much remarked upon and about that Elizabeth commented, "He is so
young and full of energy that he makes me feel old." Todd took
the sniping in good-natured stride. At a big society bash out on
Long Island, his friend, ex-champ Gene Tunney, noticed
Todd's very black hair and decided to needle him.

TUNNEY: "I see you use the same hair oil I do."

TODD: "Yeah—I use shoe polish and dye mine. And don't
bother telling her I wear a toupee because she's seen it!"

Which was a lie but Elizabeth loved it.

On November 14 Elizabeth filed for her divorce in Santa
Monica, charging "extreme mental cruelty," asking for custody
of the boys, $250-per-month child support, and no alimony. A
day later, Todd and Elizabeth flew to Miami for a vacation
and she told the press, "I may never work again."

During the Florida vacation, they found time to sail over to
the Bahamas to visit Lord Beaverbrook. Coming back on the
yacht, Elizabeth was descending a steep stairway while conversing with Todd, who was behind her. Without warning, the boat
gave a violent lurch, her feet went out from under her, her
body flew out from the staircase, and she landed with a sickening
crunch flat on her lower spine. Thus began the involvement
with recurrent illness that would sound a regrettable obbligato
to most of their married life together. The pain was excruciating
but Elizabeth minimized it. It was not her first experience with a
bad back. "I'll see a chiropractor and have him pop the bone
back in," she reassured the anxious Todd. "No, you won't," he
announced firmly. "You'll go to Harkness and see a proper bone
man."

They flew to New York where Elizabeth checked in to the
Harkness Pavillion of Columbia-Presbyterian Medical Center for
tests. X rays revealed a mass of crushed spinal discs and in a few
days all feeling in her right leg was gone. On December 8,
Elizabeth underwent a five-hour operation to sort it all out. They
cut three spinal discs away altogether, replacing them with a
reconstruction taken from her hip, her pelvis, and from a bone
bank. Then, because she was paralyzed from all the surgery
attendant upon surrounding nerves and muscles, and because it
was essential that the new construction calcify properly and not
sag one way or the other, she was repositioned at set intervals
by being rotated on her sheet. One edge would be pulled up
and eventually she would flip over. Because her doctors were
loath to give her the heavy dosage of drugs which would

effectively kill the pain, this part of it was sheer agony. "I felt rather like a pig on a spit," she wrote. "You hear this dreadful coward someplace in the hospital screaming and you think, 'God, I wish they'd stop.' Then you realize that it's yourself and then you burn up with pain and black out."

Mike Todd did everything he could for her during this ordeal. Catered food was ordered from the now-defunct Colony Restaurant, a favorite New York eatery of Elizabeth's. Her hospital room was painted "a sort of pale vomit green," as she put it. Todd promptly went out and got a Renoir, a Pissarro, a Monet, and a Frans Hals to hang on the walls. "And if I had any class," he cracked, "I'd have sent her a fifth painting—for the ceiling." On January 5, he was in London, having just bought the most expensive British automobile he could lay hands on. He had phoned her the news in the hospital, and then told the press about it.

TODD: "She seemed quite pleased. She should be! This is quite a car. It's going to have a bar—and a place where you can cook up a meal."

REPORTER: "Will Elizabeth really be happy with it?"

TODD: "There's no such thing as a happy actress. But I think I know a girl who's going to be a happy housewife."

REPORTER: "Cooking on an automobile stove?"

TODD: "Well, not exactly. I've bought a yacht, too."

The car was a silver-cloud Rolls-Royce, and Todd had the bar outfitted with separate trays stamped "Liz" and "His." After Elizabeth left Harkness, and she was still in a brace and in some discomfort, Todd put a phone in the car as well. Ultimately, two baby shoes would dangle from the rear-view mirror and would mean more to a proud father than the car and everything in it.

On January 21, Elizabeth checked out of Harkness after six weeks' convalescence. Her Santa Monica divorce action, scheduled for a prior hearing, had been postponed to February due to the illness. She and Todd then flew to Acapulco, where they were joined by Michael Wilding. The Santa Monica suit was dropped and the three interested parties then worked together to expedite a Mexican divorce. Amid various items about the supposed difficulty of obtaining the divorce, and the news that Mike Todd was gifting Elizabeth with two Chicago theaters as a wedding present, the press took snide note of the fact that husband-that-was and husband-to-be were apparently getting along fine together. "I won't let her down," Wilding had said at the time of their marriage. He was true to his word. For her part, the woman pictured by many as a creature of whim and caprice, who supposedly didn't know her own mind from one moment to the next, was in the process of dissolving an unsatisfactory marriage in a dignified and mature manner. No one reported that. It wasn't what they wanted to see.

With the granting of the divorce on January 30, Francis and Sara Taylor, and Elizabeth's brother Howard, and his wife Mara boarded the plane that would take them to Acapulco and the wedding. At the Los Angeles Airport, Francis Taylor made his solitary foray into the public prints. "I wish for my daughter the same thing that every father wishes—that she will find happiness," he told the assembled reporters. "I hope that this time her dreams will come true."

The wedding was held February 2 at the seaside villa of Fernando Hernández, an intimate of former Mexican President Miguel Alemán. The premises were guarded by troops of the Mexican Army. Inside, kerosene torches lit up the beautiful terraced gardens, and a grandstand was erected on which were festooned sixty bushels of orchids and gladioli. Each guest wore Tarascan Indian sport shirts provided by Todd and monogrammed ET and MT. Helen Rose again did the honors for Elizabeth. She designed a simple, cocktail-length, hydrangea-blue dress which set off Elizabeth's deep tan and black hair. With the dress, Elizabeth wore a sheer chiffon kerchief over her hair, and also a pair of blue garters she had recently bought in Mexico for her "something new" and "something blue." A matching ring-bracelet-and-earrings set of diamonds completed her ensemble. Plans for a Jewish ceremony had to be canceled because no rabbi could be found in time. The Mayor of Acapulco performed the simple civil ceremony. Michael Todd, Jr., Cantinflas, and singer Eddie Fisher were Todd's Best Men; Fisher's wife, actress Debbie Reynolds, and Mara Taylor were Elizabeth's attendants.

Eddie Stauffer catered the elaborate cocktail party and champagne buffet that followed. One table groaned with tacos, tamales, enchiladas, and fresh fish caught off Acapulco. The other table offered turkey, smoked ham, and caviar. Towering over everything was the huge wedding cake, topped by two figures: a *charro* (horseman) and *China poblana* (the legendary Chinese lady who came to Mexico bringing good luck). After the party, Todd carried Elizabeth, still recuperating from her operation, up to the upstairs balcony. She sat in a lawn chair, set up so that she could watch the dazzling fireworks display (a gift from Cantinflas) and the dancing down below which followed it. Finally, the nuptial pair retired to a honeymoon cottage on the estate.

The Michael Todds would have little more than a year together. Into it they managed to pack more excitement, joy, and sheer exuberance than many people know in a lifetime.

❀ 16 ❀

Joseph L. Mankiewicz, who later directed Elizabeth in *Suddenly Last Summer* and *Cleopatra*, once commented, "More than anyone realizes, Mike Todd was responsible for the intellectual and emotional awakening of this girl. For all his flamboyance, he was a man of an infinite variety of interests. Through him, Elizabeth became the step-grandmother of three children. She also traveled widely, meeting world statesmen and artists, swindlers and scientists, bankers and racket chiefs. Before that, she had been a sort of a Sleeping Beauty in an isolated castle. Mike took her through the cobwebs to the outer world, in which there is something more than movie producers and wardrobe women. Before Todd, the people she knew outside the motion picture industry could probably be counted on the fingers of one hand."

The Todds' peripatetic life-style saw them journeying all over the globe, chiefly and appropriately to publicize *Around the World in 80 Days*. The press followed them everywhere, for Todd was, as usual, marvelous copy, and the subject of his public dissertations was invariably the wife he idolized. "When I caught up with this little dame," he exulted, "I found all the happiness there is in this world." On rare occasions he would try to rein it in. Regarding persistent requests for a marriage story, he replied flatly, "Absolutely not. Just about every newspaper and magazine from Moscow to Tokyo has been after me for a marriage story, but I won't do it. I don't want our marriage reduced to the what-they-eat-for-breakfast and who-leaves-the-cap-off-the-toothpaste level. I think you can understand that." Then, as often as not, he would drop snippets like the following: "You know, I don't like cats. But Liz does, so we have two cats. *And* several dogs. *And* a duck, *and* whatever else has turned up in the animal line since I left this morning. Liz is probably the only gal who ever flew to New York holding a duck on her lap."

He could deny her nothing. On her twenty-fifth birthday, shortly after their marriage, he gifted her with a Renoir, a diamond bracelet, and a mink coat. On their sixth-month anniversary Todd asked a furrier to bring her two mink coats, one a diamond mink, the other a diadem mink. "Take your choice," he announced generously. Elizabeth gave them her expert scrutiny, and after long moments of weighing the merits of each, finally made her choice. "I'll take them both." She got them. The presents were not always that grand. Sometimes he'd surprise her with a lipstick or some trinket from a dime store.

For her part, Elizabeth was beginning to luxuriate fully in marriage to a man who not only expressed his continuous devotion with material things but in the way he treated her as a human being. Long years before Women's Lib began pushing hard on the notion for public consumption, Elizabeth had entered a union that was a true partnership. "Mike and I talk over almost everything he does," she revealed, and subsequently recalled, "He listened while I talked. He made me feel that what I had to say was worth while." Of another of her husband's facets, "His energy is contagious. We spent an evening in New York recently with my uncle, Howard Young. He's eighty years old and during the evening we figured by the time Mike is Uncle Howard's age I'll be sixty and much too old for him. It was very depressing. Life with Mike is never dull. It's fun, more fun than I've ever had. Of course it takes a while to get accustomed to my husband. He talks in shorthand and you have to fill in the things he leaves out."

As the marriage grew and prospered, Elizabeth's career drive, never the strongest component in her makeup, steadily weakened in direct ratio to her growing interest in the attractive idea of semi-retirement. Her role as Mrs. Michael Todd was offering her a wonder and a fulfillment with which nothing that took place on a sound stage could compare. She thought seriously of conversion to Judaism, but Todd cautioned her not to be hasty about it. "Be slow, be deliberate, be careful," he told her. "Don't do it on account of me. In ten years, then do it." She had already worked out a little motto for them, a free rendering of the words of the most famous Jewish convert in the Bible, Ruth the Moabitess: "Wither thou goest, I will go too, Buster!" And she lived it.

Their Mexican honeymoon had been interrupted when back pain struck her on a flight from Acapulco to Mexico City. Todd brought her to Harkness, and after an overnight stay she was released. He leased Marion Davies' home in Palm Springs for a continuation of their honeymoon, and after picking up his Showman-of-the-Year Award from the L.A. Press Club, off they went to Palm Springs. In March they attended a banquet at the Ambassador Hotel, Elizabeth's back acted up again, and she returned to Harkness for another checkup. Then it was back to Hollywood for three days of additional shooting on *Raintree County* and for a most important announcement on March 20. Elizabeth was once again expecting a child. At month's end the Todds attended the Academy Awards ceremonies.

Giant went up with its ten nominations that evening, against *Around the World in 80 Days*, which went up in eight categories (it won in five of them). There was no doubt as to where Elizabeth's loyalties lay. Emcee Jack Lemmon introduced her as "the most beautiful thing Mike Todd left out of *Around the World in 80 Days*." Viewers then saw Mrs. Michael Todd, radiant in a diamond tiara, gratefully accept the posthumous Oscar to Victor Young for his score. At the evening's climax, the nominees for Best Film were read out: *Around the World in 80 Days, Friendly Persuasion, Giant, The King and I,* and *The Ten Commandments.* The winning producer bolted from his seat, tore halfway down the aisle, suddenly realized what was truly important to him, dashed back, kissed his wife, then headed for the stage and the prize that made it such a big night for both of them. Backstage, he clutched his Oscar and bearhugged Elizabeth with his free arm, repeatedly kissing her while photographers pleaded with him to turn toward the cameras for a full-face shot. "Nuts to them," he announced between kisses. "I want the whole world to know how much I love this dame."

In April the Todds, with Michael and Christopher, sailed to Europe via the *Queen Elizabeth*. Todd rented the Villa Fiorentina at Saint-Jean-Cap-Ferrat on the Riviera. It was a luxurious estate boasting a villa with Italian marble floors and acres of wooded forest. The Todds gave one huge bash while the Cannes Film Festival was at its height. Otherwise they lived quietly in seclusion, the quiet broken only by the different openings of *Around the World in 80 Days.* In Paris, Elizabeth was stunning in yellow tulle plus the one new jewel which Todd added to her collection at each opening. Also in Paris, Aly Khan was auctioning off some of his paintings and Todd bought $71,428 worth: a Degas, a Utrillo, and a Carzo. "They'll think I'm crazy when they hear about this in Hollywood," he muttered. "Paying that much for pictures that don't even move."

On to London and their Mayfair Hotel, where the Todds had an ear-splitting set-to, a vivid throwback to the halcyon days of Humphrey Bogart and Mayo Methot. "Sure, we had a hell of a fight," Todd informed one startled reporter. "This gal's been looking for trouble all her life. Trouble is, everybody was too nice to fight back. Not me. When she flies into a tantrum, I fly into a bigger one. She's been on a milk-toast diet all her life with men; but me, I'm red meat!" To which he added, "We fight because we love it—and because it's so damn much fun to make up again."

All of which was prelude to what occurred at the London Airport June 21. As Elizabeth remembered that one, her husband was juggling three transatlantic phone calls simultaneously. They got to the airport too late for the plane to Nice, and the following occurred:

ELIZABETH (exasperated): "It's your fault. *Now* what shall we do?"

TODD (tauntingly): "For a change it was *my* fault that we were late here."

ELIZABETH (enraged): "I'm getting fed up with that line. I am always blamed for the delays. I could hate you for saying that!"

TODD (to secretary): "Charter a plane to take us to Nice with a two-hour stop at Paris."

ELIZABETH (angrily): "I don't want to go to Paris. Paris bores me!" (Secretary returns with word that plane has been chartered. Elizabeth sits stonily silent, methodically flipping the pages of a book.)

TODD (to secretary): "Tell them to order only a one-hour stop at Paris."

(Secretary returns; mission accomplished.)

ELIZABETH (quietly furious): "I will *not* go to Paris!" (Pause.)

TODD (to secretary): "We fly straight to Nice."

All of the above was punctuated freely with vigorous Italian body language and staged before an openmouthed gaggle of passengers, air hostesses, tourists, reporters, and photographers. One of the latter snapped a widely reproduced photo which Elizabeth called "the world's only talking still picture." The only caption remotely necessary would have been one in braille. The chartered plane cost $1,500, and the Todds stepped out of it in Nice and into a crowd of reporters all waiting expectantly for the big scoop. "Everything is all right between us," Todd told them, doubtless hating to spoil their day. "We made up."

Fireworks went off again in London in July, and not just at the

American Embassy. Todd had planned a gala charity premiere for *80 Days* at the Astoria Theater July 2, to be followed by a huge party at the Battersea Amusement Park, which he had taken over for the evening. He also had a pregnant wife still not fully recovered from surgery whom he was vainly trying to persuade to curtail her activity. The operation had wiped out all of her holiday fun in the previous Christmas and New Year's. Now she had a gorgeous ruby-red chiffon Dior, with a new necklace of rubies and diamonds which her husband had given her to mark the London opening. And she wasn't about to miss one marvelous moment of it.

A glittering assemblage awaited them at the theater, topped by the Duchess of Kent and her daughter, Princess Alexandra, and Todd lost no time making his point. After what seemed an interminable wait for some late-arriving bluebloods, Todd lost his temper. "Hell, she's having a baby this fall," he exploded to other notables in the reception line. "What would you do if *your* wife was having a baby? Gangway!" At which point Elizabeth's husband rushed her to her seat. The audience greeted the film with tumultuous acclaim. "It's one of the greatest things I ever saw," the Duchess of Kent noted obligingly as Todd led her to her car. The remaining guests (estimated at from 2,000 to 2,500) headed for the chartered double-decker buses which would haul them to the Thames, where a fleet of motorboats waited to take them to the Park.

All the stars, debutantes, diplomats, members of the British Cabinet and nobility got right into the spirit of things. At one point Todd paused to watch the Duchess of Argyll board a bus. "Ain't that a beautiful sight?" he marveled. "Imagine! A duchess on a bus." Rain had begun to fall, and even though Todd had prepared for the possibility, the arrangements went awry. "Raincoats. Raincoats. Where the hell are they?" he barked. "I bought two thousand today for just such an occasion." The raincoats were down by the Thames, and guests got them as they boarded the boats. "I thought I'd heard everything," Todd remarked, "but one guy—the descendant of a former prime minister, too—well he came and complained that his free coat didn't fit."

On board the boats champagne began to flow from the bars. "I flew the stuff over from Paris and, brother, I hate to see the bill. I got a telegram from my son in New York today. He told me the picture is doing fine over there. He wrote, 'Dad, we're making almost as much money as you're spending.'" To which the host added expansively, "If you have money, you gotta spread a little sunshine with it, even in this rain." The press tried to pin him down as to the cost of the blowout (estimated as high as $126,000) but Todd waved them away. "Hell, I'm an artist—not a bookkeeper!"

At Battersea Park there were sixteen separate orchestras, chefs from seven nations presiding over hundreds of pounds of fish and chips and other goodies, and seven bars dispensing champagne, hard liquor, beer, and soft drinks. Todd even provided buckets of newly minted coins for guests to feed into the slot machines. During the course of the night's revels, Laurence Olivier, Vivien Leigh, and Aly Khan happily rode the carousel, the Douglas Fairbanks, Jrs., careened around in a dodgem, U. S. Ambassador Jock Whitney went ankle-deep into a mud puddle, and Sir Hartley Shawcross did a snappy rhumba. Eddie Fisher was mistaken for a waiter as he rushed a trayload of champagne to his table.

At some point a drunken guest staggered into the table where Elizabeth was sitting and it struck her in the stomach. She screamed in pain and fear. Todd seized the sot by the shoulders and marched him right to the water's edge while onlookers held their breaths. He let him off easy. "My wife is pregnant," he finally rasped. "Will you please be a gentleman?" Elizabeth assured him she was all right and then speculated about her approaching baby. "If it's a boy he's got to be just like Mike, and I don't think the world is ready for another Mike."

By dawn five hundred guests were still hard at it and Todd exclaimed, "Wow! I forgot the aspirin and headache powders. Every guest should have been furnished some." As to the reason for it all, he had earlier coyly observed, "You never know. Something about the party and the picture might sneak into the papers." It did indeed. "Wild and wonderful and brash and noisy. London has never seen anything like it" (*Daily Herald*). "Mike Todd pulled his greatest ever stroke of ballyhoo by turning the center of London into a fantastic Victorian carnival" (*Daily Mirror*). "Mad, marvellous, gaudy, supercolossal, stupendous" (*Daily Sketch*).

Back at his hotel the host had had it. "I surrender. I'm tired and my feet hurt. Liz and I are heading for the country to lose ourselves. This is going to be a party for two—not two thousand." The press noted that Todd had been sporadically edgy during the evening. At one point Elizabeth and Michael Wilding were engaged in a lengthy tête-à-tête and Todd strode over and snapped curtly, "Break it up!"

An enterprising reporter rang him up to ask about this.

REPORTER: "There's a report you and Elizabeth had a spat last night. Is that true?"

TODD: "Sure we had a fight. A real good one. Better than the fight we had at the airport a week ago that they made pictures of. You see, I love my wife and I wanted to protect her. Her back is not in good shape. I didn't want her to walk up and down stairs and bow to a lot of dukes and duchesses at the opening. You see, she's a little pregnant and I have to look out for her. Any husband would understand how I feel."

REPORTER: "Who won?"

Voice of ELIZABETH: "Hang up. We're going to the country."

TODD (to Elizabeth): "I can't hang up. I'm talking to the press. They want to know how the party went." (to reporter) "You see, we're still fighting. We fight in public and we fight at home. The kids notice it. Why, the kids say, 'Mommy and Pop fight. Isn't that cute?' But I'm worried about Elizabeth. I don't want her to overdo and she doesn't like that."

The phone rang again with yet another inquiring reporter.

TODD: "Do we scrap? Of course we scrap. We scrapped last night, we scrap every night—and we're going to keep on scrapping till the day we die. They didn't give us three months when we were married. Well, this marriage is going to last! I wish every married couple could have fights like we do. It's great. You fight and make up and are more in love." Pause. "I've got to hang up now or my wife will tear my hair out!"

At which point Elizabeth got him off the phone, out of the hotel, and off to the country for some rest. Back in London on July 4, they were preparing to sail for New York and threw a farewell party in their hotel suite. While Todd was regaling all and sundry with praise of his wife's beauty and virtues, Elizabeth came out of the bedroom looking distraught and it went like this:

ELIZABETH: "Something terrible has happened. I've lost my traveling bag with our passports!"

(Todd dispatches four people to look for it. No luck.)

TODD: "Call the American Embassy!"

SECRETARY: "It's the Fourth of July. They're closed."

TODD: "Call the American Consul in Southampton!"

(An amused observer to these proceedings is Michael Wilding, who is standing in the middle of the room with a broad smile on his face.)

TODD: "Look at him. He's laughing!"

WILDING (breaking up): "Yes, I *am* laughing. It all sounds so familiar."

(Elizabeth wrings her hands in a gesture of despair.)

TODD: "Come on. We gotta hurry if we're gonna make the boat train. (In Southampton the U. S. Consul issues temporary passports and off they sail on the *Liberté* as scheduled.)

In mid-ocean things got not-so-funny. At the time she learned she was pregnant, Elizabeth's doctors feared that a growing fetus would do irreparable harm to her new spinal construction. They counseled abortion. She refused absolutely to even consider it. They then attached elastic gussets to the back brace she still wore so there would be sufficient room in front for the child yet adequate support for the spine. Crossing the Atlantic, Elizabeth went into premature labor, made all the more nerve-wracking by her frightening conviction that the ship's doctor knew nothing whatever about Caesarean section. "I got the feeling he thought babies came out your nose," she wrote. Eventually they anesthetized her and that stopped the labor.

Upon their arrival in New York July 10 the Todds obligingly went a few rounds for the press. "I'm going to keep my mouth shut," Todd announced, to which Elizabeth riposted, "Oh, no, don't do that. It would be out of character." She allowed as how she had "bought a few hats abroad." Todd mumbled, "Yeah—about fifty." And what about all those fights? "Neither of us is inhibited," Elizabeth observed. "We speak freely to each other. Also we happen to love each other. We have more fun fighting than most people do making love." To which Todd added, "We're not 'Hollywood Happy,' either. This is the real thing."

Elizabeth checked into Harkness for observation and consultation on the approaching birth. The brace had forced the baby to grow up under her ribs, which in turn repositioned her heart and subjected her to a racing pulse and fainting spells. Todd took off for a whirlwind thirty hours in Minneapolis where he was given the honors due a famous native son and, of course, presided at the Twin Cities' opening of *Around the World in 80 Days*. Toward month's end Elizabeth was deemed sufficiently fit to join Todd at the twenty-three-room Westport estate he had rented for the summer. On July 28 she was rushed back to Harkness, again in premature labor.

"She's in terrible pain," Todd told the press. "But unless it's a sheer outstanding emergency, they don't want to take the baby for two and a half weeks. The baby is due about October 15 and if she can hold out for two and a half weeks, it'll be seven months and that could do it. I'm spending all my time at her bedside. She's crying all the time. She had a bad night last night. The night before they gave her an anesthetic or something and she slept pretty well." On July 30 a news item read: "Liz Taylor Better; Scolds Mike." On August 2 she was released from Harkness and on August 4 collapsed at the dinner table in Westport. With sirens screaming at full pitch, a motored escort of Connecticut State Police rushed her back to the hospital. This time the doctors would wait no longer. "Please don't take her," Elizabeth pleaded in vain. "She's not cooked yet."

On August 6 Elizabeth was wheeled into the operating room. A team of eight attended her: an obstetrician, a pediatrician, a diagnostician, two neurologists, a resuscitationist, and two other doctors. Elizabeth Frances Todd made her debut via Caesarean section at 12:03 P.M. weighing four pounds, fourteen ounces. She did not breathe for fourteen and a half minutes. Dr. Virginia Apgar, the resuscitationist, worked over her during that time, and at the end of it, Liza lived. Her jubilant father told the press, "Liz and I are very grateful we got what we wanted most, but really the hard way. It was a miracle, thanks to the extraordinary medical genius of the lineup assembled by Dr. Dana Atchley, that this has come off."

Liza spent her first two months in an oxygen tent, and her parents made their next public appearance at the L.A. County Museum on September 28, where Todd presented paintings by Frans Hals, Pissarro, Renoir, and Monet on indefinite loan. Asked about how Mike Todd and art ever got together, Todd obligingly played the mug. "My governess got me started," he announced daintily. "Of course I only collected hot postage stamps at first. It's a great hobby. You never know when you might turn up broke and have to hock a painting." Reporters then asked about Liza. "She told us she didn't want to come along. She looks just like Liz. How's she gonna get along with a handicap like that?" To which Elizabeth retorted smartly, "She's got her father's personality. How about *that* for a handicap?"

October 17 was fast approaching: the first anniversary of the world premiere of *Around the World in 80 Days*. Todd racked his brains for something grand enough which would be worthy of such a momentous occasion, and at length hit on it. He would rent Madison Square Garden for the evening and stage a public birthday party the like of which the world had never seen. And the world ultimately got exactly what was promised.

Why Madison Square Garden? "Liz and I have never fought in the Garden," he repeatedly quipped, to which Elizabeth began to reply, "Mike, dear, you've already used that line." Vincent

Korda, then working on the production design for Todd's next film, *Don Quixote*, was flown over from London to decorate the vast arena. He trimmed it in blue and pink, and, at the far end of the arena floor, erected a 24-foot Oscar made of russet-toned baby chrysanthemums. In the center was the huge cake, 14 feet high, 30 feet in diameter, and weighing almost a ton. Swans Down had obligingly donated $15,000 worth of cake mix, 2,000 eggs, 68 gallons of water, etc. It was baked, carted into the Garden in sections, assembled, and given a pale blue icing. Out of the cake popped one huge lighted candle, and high above it floated a replica of the *80 Days* balloon. On the near end of the arena floor sat the grand prize among what were to be 14,000 free gifts: a Cessna airplane (complete with free flying lessons). Around it were clustered some of the other gifts from a list which included 4 automobiles, 6 Vespa motor scooters, hi-fi's, 100 cameras, 4 mink stoles and other furs, 250 bottles of vodka, 10,000 imported cigars, 100 pairs of ivory chopsticks, 6 ladies' revolvers (in pastel colors), 75 Swedish telephones, 50 elephant bells from India, 100 cases of Scotch chocolate biscuits, 6 Olivetti typewriters, 1,000 Decca albums, 40 Siamese cats, Austrian toy bears, a Japanese rickshaw, a mammoth jar of German mustard, toy kangaroos from Australia, and so forth.

All of the merchandise was donated, and there were offerings of 15,000 hot dogs, 15,000 buns, 200 gallons of vichyssoise, a ton of baked beans, 10,000 egg rolls from the Chinese Merchants Association, pizza pies, 15,000 doughnuts, ice cream from the Borden Company, etc. CBS obligingly paid $300,000 to pre-empt *Playhouse 90* and thus put the party on national TV for ninety minutes. TWA flew members of the press in from the West Coast and from London, and Quantas did likewise from Australia, both gratis to Todd. His basic expense was $5,000 rental for the premises, plus the cost of decorating and miscellaneous expenses, including payment to a camera crew who would be grinding away during the proceedings on a color short called *How to Throw a Party*, which would later be released commercially.

On the great day, 18,000 invitations had gone out for what was billed as "An Intimate Little Party for a Few Chums." The invitations specified strictly black-tie. The Madison Square Garden marquee announced: "A Little Party." All was in readiness, though the *80 Days* balloon was showing a distressing tendency to release bubbles which floated straight down. "Stop it!" screamed Todd. "I don't want soap on my cake!" It was stopped, the gates opened, and the party began. Emcee George Jessel much later remarked wearily, "Such an evening will not happen again. Nobody could stand it." Shakespeare couldn't have put it better, except that he did—*Macbeth*, Act II, Scene 3: "Confusion now hath made his masterpiece."

To begin with, the circus parade which had come triumphantly up Eighth Avenue couldn't get through the crush at the front doors in time, and finally straggled in looking like a defeated army. *Life* called this portion of the entertainment "a colossal hodgepodge of bagpipers, folk dancers, Philadelphia Mummers, Russian wolfhounds, oxen, Siamese cats, elephants, clowns, and fire engines." As an added treat, a plainly petrified Sir Cedric Hardwicke began to slide off his elephant. Thousands watched spellbound as the man who had played African missionary David Livingstone struggled for survival in a situation 3,000 miles removed from that nice safe sound stage. Sir Cedric clung gamely on and even managed a jaunty wave of the hand before the great beast carried him off.

Entertainments competed with each other in great colorful chaos. At one point Dancing Fountains were to be applauded, while at the same time, famed clown Emmett Kelly was doing his thing in one spotlight, and Arthur Fiedler was leading the Symphony of the Air in a memorial tribute to Toscanini in another. Senator Hubert Humphrey, from Todd's home state, got up to intone, "This entire occasion symbolizes good neighborliness . . . International understanding is apparent here tonight." At that point, the waiters had begun to hustle the free domestic Renault champagne at $2, $3, and $5 a bottle and on up to $10 for a magnum. Not to be outdone by chiseling waiters, the ushers began hawking the free souvenir programs for $1.

As hostess, Elizabeth was resplendent in a ruby-red velvet gown designed by Helen Rose, and a diamond tiara, with the necklace and earrings of rubies and diamonds, and she looked every inch a queen. Her principal task in these colorful proceedings was to cut the cake, which she did after mounting a special, red-carpeted stairway built up to the top of the mammoth pastry, delicately tasting the icing on her fingers. "I don't know if this is the best party I've ever been to," Elizabeth remarked warily. "It isn't over yet."

People sitting in the balcony were really frying-mad, because there was no passage from the balcony to the main floor. You had to leave the Garden and come back in, and once you got out, there was no certainty they'd let you back in. That they were stuck where they couldn't parade their compulsory black-tie finery was bad enough. But all the food was circulating on fifty jeeps down in the arena, and people sitting on the main floor were getting it all.

At length, a doughnut lady on one of the jeeps took pity on the starving multitude and began throwing doughnuts into the balcony. Several of the guests, after being liberally sprinkled with flying powdered sugar, threw them right back at her. In this melee of flying doughnuts, one august dowager reportedly got smacked in the eye. The hot-dog wagon went by and some idiot began throwing franks and buns (but at least he spared the mustard). A mink-clad matron was seen holding out paper cups to a passing man, pleading, "Please, please—just a little champagne—twenty waiters have passed me by already."

In the midst of the shambles all about him, Todd took to the microphones. "I hoped things would run smoother than they did," he announced philosophically, "but some nights are better than others." The distribution of the gifts was simply impossible under the circumstances. When word of that got around, two enraged guests took possession of the Cessna and threatened to fly it right out through the Garden roof. One fellow boldly looted the prize pile of a hi-fi set and made off with it. He had better luck than another, who was caught rolling out a washing machine. At the end, crowds had broken open huge cartons of toys, Duke Ellington's music rent the air, and pandemonium predominated.

Todd left word that the gifts would later be mailed to guests via a system of winning numbers, and the numbers would be selected by "Liz, who is honest." Whether every guest finally got a gift is as much a mystery as the final disposition of *How to Throw a Party*. Either it became the Todds' favorite home movie or it was taken out and sunk in the deepest part of the Atlantic, if indeed it even went to the labs for printing. After they had secured a bottle of real, unwatered champagne, the Todds went home and passed a somewhat hysterical next few hours regaling each other with the memories of all the strange sights they had seen that night.

Todd took some ferocious static from the press over this fiasco, so much so that journalistic overkill began to set in. After all, some reasoned, everything had been free. Transportation had even been paid to and from New York in many instances. What were they all so sore about? So it turned out to be a bust. It hadn't cost them anything. Some 18,000 came eagerly forward that night, many of them rushing in like pigs to the trough. In an industry which has always groaned under the notorious weight of freeloaders, Mike Todd's "Little Party" remains a rather delightful memory of one fine night when the takers got took.

Undaunted Todd planned a round-the-world trip, which began with a noisy, enthusiastic welcome at the Honolulu Airport November 1. From November 5 to 9, the Todds were in Sydney, Australia, where they got a bad press. They were criticized for standing up reporters, being ninety minutes late for a news conference, and then announcing they were too tired to hold it. Todd was additionally criticized for kissing his wife in the middle of an official luncheon while seated next to the Prime Minister of New South Wales. He was unrepentant. "I would be a phony if, when the urge came, I did not kiss my wife. A lot more people should kiss their wives in public." Elizabeth good-humoredly modeled for the press in a plain sugar sack. Fans had picked up an interview remark that she "didn't have a thing to wear" to a certain dinner and sent it to her.

By November 15 the Todds were in Hong Kong, where Elizabeth was stricken by an attack of appendicitis. It passed, but Todd announced that, after they spent two days in Japan, they would return to the States so that she could have the appendix out. They finally made it back November 25, and were seated in the back seat of a black Cadillac limousine at the L.A. International Airport when reporters and photographers surrounded the car. There then ensued a freewheeling public performance, a marvelous example of what kept the Todds constantly on the front pages.

TODD (emerging from car): "Come on, Liz, get out! The boys want some pictures."

ELIZABETH (emerging from car in tight black silk Chinese dress slit halfway up the thigh at the sides): "Hi there!"

TODD: "Look at that dress! She's gonna start a whole new epidemic! It's liable to bring sex back. We bought twenty-five of 'em."

ELIZABETH: "In Hong Kong."

REPORTERS: "Give her a kiss, Mike."

TODD: "No kissing. We don't want to shock the natives."

ELIZABETH: "Absolutely not!"

TODD: "No kissing in public anymore. In Australia—Sydney— I gave her a little peck and you'd have thought the whole economy was gonna collapse. Kissing's trouble."

ELIZABETH (crawling back into car): "That's trouble?"

TODD: "Liz doesn't talk much. See? She gets hoarse listening to me talk. Come on out—they want some more pictures."

ELIZABETH: "Michael, come on!"

TODD: "See? That's the way she talks. That's what caused all the trouble in Australia. She says, 'Come on, flannel-mouth, get in here.' The country will never be the same."
(Elizabeth re-emerges from the car displaying a wealth of nylon-sheathed leg.)

REPORTER (regarding her diamond ring with awe): "What's that?"

ELIZABETH (in a tone of mock shock): "What's *that?* It's THE RING!"

TODD: "What's that, he says!"

REPORTER: "You going to give any more big parties, Mike? Like that one in Madison Square Garden?"

TODD: "No more parties with more than eight people."

ELIZABETH (crawling back into car): "Party! That's a dirty word."

TODD: "Come on, honey. They want some pictures."

ELIZABETH (re-emerging from car showing great expanse of satiny leg): "I'm getting old just getting in and out of this car."

REPORTER: "What line did you fly in from Hong Kong?"

TODD: "I am not going to tell you. They charged me $1200 for excess baggage."

ELIZABETH (sweetly): "That was for Mr. Todd's coats."

TODD: "It was nothing of the kind."

REPORTER: "Where you going now?"

TODD: "Palm Springs. We're going to be homebodies for a few days. See the kids. Then Liz has to have an operation."

ELIZABETH: "My appendix. It's subsided since Hong Kong. But I'm going to have it out." (Crawls back into car.)

TODD: "Then we're going to pick up the trip again. Purely a vacation. No business. Just for us."

(Michael Todd, Jr., drives up in a convertible.)

TODD: "Come on, out, honey. Here's Mike."

ELIZABETH (re-emerging from limousine): "I'm getting old just getting in and out of this car."

(The Todds leave the limousine, get into the convertible, and drive off in the direction of Palm Springs. Curtain.)

Elizabeth checked into Cedars of Lebanon December 17, had the appendix out, and stayed in a week. Todd went in with her and took a connecting suite. "This will be her last time to the hospital," he told newsmen as they left together. "We're going to take off for Europe first thing in January. But no more hospitals."

On January 17 the Todds arrived in London en route to Moscow. "I thought it might be good to show off Liz to the Russians," Todd announced. "She's the best secret weapon we've got. It may undermine their whole structure." He planned to confer with Russian filmmakers and government officials on a possible co-production of *War and Peace* and also a possible distribution of *Around the World in 80 Days* in Russia. By January 21, Todd got the bad news that Minister of Culture N. A. Mikhailov was absent from Moscow and that his deputy was ill. The trip seemed to be off. But . . . "I am finding it difficult to convince Liz there is no point in going to Moscow now that no one is available there." As a matter of fact, he found it impossible. Such technicalities were not about to get in the way of Elizabeth's firsthand look at Russia. "We will be leaving for Paris tomorrow on the first leg," Todd subsequently announced. In Paris famed hair stylist Alexandre was suddenly handed a message which was to begin an association that endures to this day. "Please reserve appointment for Elizabeth Taylor," it read. "Set aside whole day. Mike Todd." The Todds emerged from the elevator at noon. "Do whatever you like," Todd announced. "Telephone me when it's over. She has the right not to say anything." He kissed her and vanished. Alexandre then went to work and cut Elizabeth's long tresses to a short, wind-blown bob. "I'm ruined," Todd kidded her upon first sight of it. "Who is this woman?"

Arriving in Moscow, Todd cracked to Western reporters at the airport, "This is the only time and place Mike Todd is not Mister Elizabeth Taylor." The Todds spent a week in Moscow, and the public highlight was their appearance at the Indian Embassy on the occasion of the tenth anniversary of India's independence. Elizabeth made quite a splash in a cocktail suit of glistening black broadtail fur with diamond buttons. A diamond pendant hung at her throat and, of course, there was "the ring." Diplomatic guests gladly forsook the teetotaling Indians' tangerine juice and caviar to swarm around her and make her the center of attention. Nikita Khrushchev later attended and made off with some of the spotlight but the two did not meet.

The Todds attended *Swan Lake* at the Bolshoi, and Elizabeth's chief memories of the stay were of the people she met and observed—at the circus, where they responded to a strange mix of the truly amazing and the completely cliché with free, childlike enthusiasm—in the streets, where they admired her jewels and furs, totally unself-conscious and without a trace of envy or hostility. "These people can't be our enemies," she remembered thinking. "It's the people running the governments we should be afraid of." Amen. Todd later quipped, "The Russian people were impressed with the fact that a juvenile delinquent could grow up in America and get a better job than the President—Elizabeth Taylor's husband!"

From Moscow, it was on to Prague, Athens, Belgrade, Nice, Madrid, then home to New York and, subsequently, to Hollywood. The traveling part of the honeymoon was over as both prepared to take up film work. "I have the picture of the year, the bride of the year, and the baby of the year," Todd had publicly rejoiced. "What man could want more?" He also had certain fears.

According to Elizabeth, "He was afraid someone might find out he was really a softie."

According to Mike Todd, "I carry a constant fear that something will happen to me. I am so happy and I have so much that according to the law of averages I am afraid I will have to lose something to compensate."

Thus he gave voice to mankind's deep fear that the gods and the forces which rule the universe raise a man to a pinnacle only to hurl him from it—that great good fortune precedes calamity —a belief rooted in the earliest plays of the Ancient Greeks. The woman referred to almost automatically by many as "The Girl Who Has Everything" was about to lose a very large part of it.

❀ 17 ❀

Preproduction on Mike Todd's next film *Don Quixote*, was already under way. Vincent Korda was in England working on the production design, Picasso had even done a thematic drawing for it, and Art Cohn, concluding his work on Todd's biography, was set to do the script. Famed French comedian Fernandel was penciled in to play the hero, and Cantinflas and Elizabeth would eventually play Sancho Panza and Dulcinea.

As usual Todd had plenty of other irons in the fire. One was a joint deal with Frank Lloyd Wright, Pat Weaver, and Henry Kaiser to build aluminum-dome, multipurpose theaters for worldwide use. "I saw your Imperial Hotel in Tokyo just last week," Todd told Wright. "It's still standing." The famed architect changed the subject to the one topic which could even momentarily throw Todd off-balance. "You look younger," Wright told him. "Marriage agrees with you." Todd shyly ducked his head.

There were future plans for capturing La Scala opera performances in the magnificence of Todd-AO. And there were still additional openings of *Around the World in 80 Days* to oversee, and receipts to count on the film it was confidently estimated would be the first to break the $100 million mark world-wide. "My God, did you see the business in Honolulu? It's unbelievable!" Todd exclaimed, scanning a recent report. "We're a hit. Look at that total—$29,600,000." A production associate good-humoredly asked, "How much of it have you spent?" Todd replied, "I've spent $29,599,999 and I'm still going strong. It's gonna be tough to spend the rest of it."

His wife was perfectly willing to help. Once, on the eve of flying from New York to Chicago, she decided on a last-minute shopping expedition, and it went like this:

ELIZABETH: "Give me money."

TODD: "I *gave* you scads of money."

ELIZABETH (watching him pull some from a huge roll): Don't be so stingy. They're only *twenties.*"

TODD (aghast): "Those are *hundreds!*" (They kissed). "All right, Mom. 'Bye. We're ready to go. Be sure to get back before dark. We don't want to take off in the dark."

The airplane they were flying on was one of the things Todd had spent for, the better to hustle him back and forth among his varied interests. It was a twin-engine Lockheed Lodestar which Todd christened *The Lucky Liz.* He had bought it from a Texas oil man. "The oil man had gin-rummy tables, and I took them out. We have a nice double-bed in their place," Todd revealed. "Liz does everything for herself in this plane. She even opens her own champagne. That's what I call the pioneering spirit."

Tease her though he might in public, Todd continued to show unfeigned devotion in their private life. For one thing, he gave up cigars, roughly the equivalent of Durante without a nose or Veronica Lake in short hair. For another, a longtime friend noticed a dwindling number of telephones in Todd's quarters and asked him about it. "Liz made me do it. She hates telephones, especially in the living room," he confessed wistfully. "So far I've been able to keep one in the plane." The full import of this revelation can only be appreciated by Todd associates' firm belief —and nothing could have persuaded them otherwise—that Mike Todd came out of the womb and into this world with a phone in each hand.

By March 1958 the Todds were back in Hollywood, having rented a twelve-room villa on Schuyler Road in Coldwater Canyon. Their return had been preceded by a bit of news which was sweet music indeed to Elizabeth. Academy Award nominations were announced in February, and up for Best Actress were former winner Anna Magnani (for *Wild Is the Wind*), veteran nominee Deborah Kerr (for *Heaven Knows, Mr. Allison*), and three newcomers to the lists: Joanne Woodward (for *The Three Faces of Eve*), Lana Turner (for *Peyton Place*), and Elizabeth (for *Raintree County*). Since Miss Kerr already held the New York Film Critics Circle Award, and Miss Woodward the Award of the National Board of Review, Elizabeth would be going up as a longshot. Longshots had won before, however, and at least it was an honor to have finally made the list. She notified the Academy that she would be happy to be there in person and present the Awards for Short Subjects and Documentaries at the Oscar Ceremonies March 26.

Elizabeth had now not been before the cameras for over a year, though she had been considered for Nellie Forbush in *South Pacific*, along with Doris Day, Jane Powell, Janet Blair, and numerous others.

"I tried to get them to use Elizabeth Taylor," director Joshua Logan remembered, "because at the time she was freckle-faced and young and very ambitious. But she went up and sang for Dick Rodgers, and she was so scared, she croaked. I took her downstairs afterwards, and she broke into song when she saw Mike Todd—quite good, loud song—but she was just too nervous."

That one went to Mitzi Gaynor. The role which had finally brought Elizabeth back to Hollywood was the second she owed to Grace Kelly. Miss Kelly had dutifully returned to Metro for *The Swan*, an elaborate soufflé apparently concocted chiefly of biscuit dough which featured Alec Guinness in a classic demonstration of an actor walking through for the money. Biscuit dough was also an ingredient in Miss Kelly's next for Metro, *High Society*, the *Philadelphia Story* musical remake and a lumpy affair which looked slightly sad then and looks positively tragic today. *Cat on a Hot Tin Roof* was next but, even though Dore Schary had personally done a treatment approved by the Motion Picture Producers Association (and its censor arm, the Johnston office), George Cukor backed away from it. How to film a drama revolving around the suspicion of homosexuality stumped him. Schary then handed it to Richard Brooks, who (with James Poe) wrote a film script which toned down latent homosexuality to what everyone was assured was a "delicate implication." In an era where "X" marks the spot at every three movie-houses out of five, this may all sound too quaint to be believed, but that's the way it was.

For the stage, Tennessee Williams wrote two third acts at the behest of director Elia Kazan, a happenstance which was a source of much *angst* in their relationship. Now, with Williams' permission, Brooks wrote a third version of the third act, the cellar scene, in which is resolved what has now become the hero's chief problem: moral weakness resulting from prolonged adolescence and failure to assume adult responsibilities. Or, as Big Daddy was to put it in the film, "I've got the guts to die, boy. Have you got the guts to live?" *Cat on a Hot Tin Roof* was finally ready for the cameras, but Grace Kelly had not waited around for it. In April 1956 she traded the sound stage at Metro for the palace in Monaco. The script was then offered to Elizabeth.

She accepted it, with one condition she laid down in a conference in the Thalberg Building. Her present contract had three more years to run, but she had decided to terminate it. Even now some of her old dogs had been let out of the MGM kennel to TV and were to be seen yelping on the Late Show. There were to be no more of those. "I'm thinking of retiring the commodity known as Elizabeth Taylor, Movie Star," she earlier told an interviewer. "It would be wonderful if you could just treat acting as a job. But you can't and that's what I don't like about it. It makes too many demands. I will make three more films: *Cat* for MGM, *Don Quixote* for my husband, and perhaps one more film for him sometime in the future"—possibly Pearl Buck's *Imperial Woman*, which Todd thought would make a good vehicle for her. As to any unhappiness such a course would cause movie audiences: "I've had people say I owe it to my public to stay in movies. I think that's nonsense. I owe the public exactly what they see on screen and nothing more. I think my fans will be glad to have me do whatever makes me happiest."

Metro put a year's worth of retirement remarks together with Elizabeth's new financial security and braced for the worst. Mike Todd spoke for both of them: "*Cat on a Hot Tin Roof* will be her last film for MGM or she won't do it." If it had been 1938 or even 1948—but this was 1958, and not only was the prize filly threatening to leave the stable, but all the adjacent stalls were all but empty. The studio desperately tried the old treatment. "We'll put her on suspension," they told Todd. "Fine," he rejoined. "In that case she'll just retire right now." Plainly it was to be *Cat* or nothing. MGM acquiesced but shrewdly (as things turned out) saw to it that nothing was put in writing.

Cat on a Hot Tin Roof began shooting on March 12. Todd

rented office space on the Metro lot so that he could be near Elizabeth, and at night they watched the daily rushes of *Cat* together in the projection room. As high as he was on her Oscar chances for *Raintree*, he was even more enthusiastic about the level of this new work. "If you don't win this year," he told her, "you'll win next year for *Cat*."

The second week's shooting began and the Todds lunched with Mickey Rooney, comic Joey Forman, and Art Cohn, who was dividing his time between the *Don Quixote* script and putting the final touches on *The Nine Lives of Michael Todd*. "It's all finished except for the ending," he reportedly told friends. "I haven't got a good ending." Coming up on Saturday was a Friars Testimonial Dinner at the Waldorf-Astoria in New York at which Todd was to be the guest of honor. Reservations had been taken for thirteen hundred. Elizabeth had arranged her shooting time so that she would be free to go with him on Friday night. Then the plans began to go awry.

On Wednesday she was stricken with a virus which took her off the film and confined her to bed. By Friday her temperature had climbed to 102. Elizabeth was sure she was well enough to go with him, but Todd adamantly insisted that she was not. This time he had his way, backed up by their doctor, Rex Kennamer. The weather was rotten and getting worse. It was no time for her to run such a risk. He would only be away a couple of days— four at most, if he came back by way of Chicago and stayed for the Sugar Ray Robinson-Carmen Basilio fight on Tuesday.

Mike Todd spent Friday afternoon playing with Michael and Christopher in the huge sunken bathtub, and Elizabeth contentedly watched their mirrored reflection from her bed. He had not had much luck inducing others to make the flight. Kirk Douglas, Joe E. Lewis, and Kurt Frings (Elizabeth's agent) had all turned him down. So had director Joseph L. Mankiewicz, whom Todd was trying to interest in *Don Quixote*. "C'mon—it's a good safe plane," Todd told him. "I wouldn't let it crash. I'm taking along a picture of Elizabeth and I wouldn't let anything happen to her. Besides I've got three million bucks' worth of insurance. You'd be covered." Mankiewicz declined, as did AP reporter James Bacon, who'd originally said yes.

"The weather scared me," Jim Bacon remembered. "It was the worst night I ever remember in Southern California—thunder, lightning, and torrential rain. Takeoff was scheduled for around 10 P.M. Mike called me around nine to report that the trip was on, weather or not. I told him I wasn't going. 'You bastard,' said Mike characteristically. 'You're not going because Elizabeth is not going.'" Finally, Art Cohn agreed to make the trip. They'd have time to work the *Don Quixote* script en route to New York.

When it was time to go, Todd kissed his wife goodbye and then kept returning to her. He did it a half dozen times. They were terribly superstitious about being parted. Only twice before had he gone to *80 Days* openings without her, and then only because she had been hospitalized. Downstairs he told the butler, "All right, now. Make sure and look after everyone for me." He then picked up a fried-chicken box lunch and left the house.

At the airport in Burbank, Todd called Elizabeth and promised to call her from Tulsa when the plane set down for refueling. He would also be calling her from Kansas City, where there were plans to pick up Jack Benny after his benefit performance there and take him along to the Waldorf. Todd and Art Cohn then entered the plane along with pilot Bill Verner and co-pilot Tom Barclay and shortly thereafter *The Lucky Liz* was airborne.

Back at the house in Coldwater Canyon, in the early hours of March 22, Elizabeth remained wide-awake with feelings of foreboding she could not shake. The weather outside was continuing to do its worst; perhaps that was it. As the hours passed—two, three, four—there was no phone call. "Well, he knows I need the rest and doesn't want to waken me," she reassured herself. Subsequently she asked her maid to give her feverish body an alcohol rub. Finally, at 6 A.M., she picked up the phone and dialed Todd's private secretary, Dick Hanley.

"It's so strange that Mike hasn't let me hear from him," she told him. "It's the first time since we were married that he hasn't sent word to me some way. Do you think anything could have happened? It was such a miserable night." At which point she rang off.

Across town at about the same time another phone rang. "Hello," Jim Bacon answered groggily. "Thank God! It's you!" responded the AP man in Albuquerque on the other end. "There's a plane down near here with your name on the passenger manifest." Bacon then called Hanley, who gasped, "Oh, my God," and then rang up Rex Kennamer. They all made plans to get out to Schuyler Road immediately, praying all the while that no news would have reached Elizabeth before they could get there to be with her when she first heard it.

At the house, Hanley and Dr. Kennamer came through the bedroom door and there ensued a moment, almost too fleeting to measure, in which nothing was spoken and everything was said. "No!" Elizabeth screamed, throwing her hands up to her ears, jumping out of bed and rushing past them. If she couldn't hear it, she didn't have to know it. "The minute we walked through that bedroom door, Elizabeth knew why we were there," Dr. Kennamer remembered. To which Dick Hanley added, "Her first impulse was to run away from the news. Although she had been in bed since Wednesday with a fever of a hundred and two, she jumped out of bed in her bare feet and darted through every room in the house, trying to get outside. She screamed so loud that even the neighbors heard her, and went completely hysterical. As she dashed for the front door and the open street, Dr. Kennamer grabbed her and we took her up to bed. She submitted to the sedatives that eventually quieted her."

Quieted her, but could not put her totally out. That consolation was denied her in the horror which had suddenly engulfed her and which she initially refused to confront. "No, no, no—it just can't be," she wept. "He'll phone me soon—he always does when he's out of town. Every time I hear the phone ring I think it might be Mike." Debbie Reynolds arrived to express condolences and to take the boys over to stay at her home. Francis and Sara Taylor cut short their Miami vacation to fly back immediately. MGM executives Eddie Mannix and Benny Thau came to call. So did Helen Rose, Kurt and Ketti Frings, Peggy Rutledge, and Michael Wilding. Even Garbo was rumored to have visited during the ordeal.

As the wires of sympathy flowed in and the callers made their way to her bedside, Elizabeth began to accept the awful fact. Dr. Kennamer encouraged her to talk out some of the heavy burden of grief. "Mike and I had so much planned," she said sorrowfully. "Little things we just talked about last night. Things we would do when I finished the picture." Repeatedly she returned to the mischance of her illness which had separated them, and reproached herself. "If only I had been with him. Without him now, I feel like half a pair of scissors. That's what he always used to tell me when he was away from me. I knew I shouldn't have let him go. He could have waited another day. I don't think he really wanted to go." And over and over again, she asked the question which would remain forever unanswerable—"Why?"

The late Saturday editions and Sunday papers spread the grim story out in black headlines all over the world. Shortly after 2 A.M. pilot Verner had radioed that the wings were icing, requesting permission, which was granted, to seek a higher altitude. Sometime after that the plane crashed at seven thousand feet in the Zuni Mountains of New Mexico. There was a suspicion that only one engine was working at the time. The wreckage was scattered over about two hundred square yards of what the

Indians called "malpais" (badlands). Workers at the crash site identified the remains by means of dental charts. One thing that was recovered was Todd's gold wedding band. It was brought back to Elizabeth, who held it in a tightly clenched hand as she passed between consciousness and unconsciousness.

Wires kept coming in from all over the country, including one from the White House which read: "The President and I extend our deepest sympathy" (signed) "Mrs. Dwight Eisenhower." Also wires from seventeen foreign nations. Joan Blondell, then appearing on Broadway in *The Rope Dancers*, expressed public condolences to the widow of her ex-husband, and then canceled her TV appearance on *The Ed Sullivan Show* that Sunday. MGM was the eventual recipient of thirty-five hundred wires and letters of sympathy, many of them bearing checks made out to Children's Hospital, in lieu of flowers, as Elizabeth had requested. Tributes were published from major filmmakers all over the world, including the following from two men who partook of the same rugged, individualistic spirit as the fallen comrade they eulogized:

"Michael Todd was a great showman, one of the greatest of our times," proclaimed David O. Selznick. "His courage and magnificent gambling spirit did much to revitalize the motion picture industry. The sympathy of the entire world will be extended to his wife and family in their great loss." To which Samuel Goldwyn added, "Hollywood has three things that have saved the film business in times of crisis—sound, the big screen, and Mike Todd." Goldwyn also visited the house and told Elizabeth of all the many tributes being paid to Todd in the papers. When she asked to see them, he went out to his car and brought them back up to her. "I am comforted with the thought she is going to come out of this all right," he told reporters upon leaving. "She has a great future ahead of her for she is the dominating actress in our business."

The funeral was set for the following Tuesday at Jewish Waldheim Cemetery in Zurich, Illinois, outside Chicago. Michael Todd, Jr., had wanted the body cremated in Albuquerque, whence it was taken from the crash site, but Elizabeth balked at the idea. She and his father had discussed cremation, she told him, and Mike Todd did not want it. So the way was prepared for what became a truly hideous example of life imitating art, in this case the classic Hollywood story, *A Star Is Born*, and, specifically, the funeral sequence. Neither Janet Gaynor nor Judy Garland on film, however, experienced a fraction of what awaited Elizabeth in Chicago. Only constant sedation was keeping her calm, but she refused all suggestions that she remain in Los Angeles. They would have had to put her under physical restraint to keep her from paying her husband her final respects.

On Monday the Los Angeles City Council adjourned its meeting in Mike Todd's memory. Howard Hughes had thoughtfully put a TWA airliner at her private disposal, and Elizabeth was helped up the ramp at L.A. International Airport by Metro press agent and old friend Bill Lyon. Inside she joined her brother Howard, Dr. Kennamer, Helen Rose, Eddie Fisher, and Dick Hanley, who were accompanying her on the sad journey to Chicago. An hour after they were airborne, Helen Rose helped her to her berth and Rex Kennamer went to talk with her. He then took her to a rear seat, covered her with a blanket, and she slept bolt-upright for what little time she slept at all. "I just couldn't sleep in that berth alone," she explained painfully. "Mike and I always took a berth when we flew."

The scene at Chicago Airport was a foretaste of things to come. A screaming throng was waiting. Michael Todd, Jr., met her and they got into a limousine. Three hundred then broke through police lines and the car barely got away before it was surrounded. The funeral party took up fifteen rooms on the fifth floor of the Drake Hotel. A heavy guard was stationed there, in addition to which eight detectives were assigned by the Chicago Police Department to guard Elizabeth personally. On the morning of the twenty-fifth, Elizabeth, wearing a black broadtail fur suit with black velvet cloche, heavy veil, black leather gloves, and carrying a mink wrap, entered the six-car funeral cortege, which was to be escorted by two police cars out to Waldheim.

Heavily sedated though she was, Elizabeth remembered it all in bits and fragments. Two girls were hanging out a factory window and one screamed as the car went by, "Oh, dig that crazy widow's veil!" The family had set the actual time of the ceremony up two hours from the announced time, but to no avail. The throngs had begun to gather at 6 A.M. and now there were thousands in the cemetery. Mobs had double-parked all along the route, making free access to or from the gravesite all but impossible. People perched on tombstones and mausoleums, and freely trampled graves in their desire to get closer. Women giggled, babies cried, teenagers playing hooky from school ogled Eddie Fisher with undisguised glee. Two helicopters hovered noisily overhead taking pictures. Elizabeth also remembers Coca-Cola bottles strewn all over the place and empty potato-chip bags flying in the March wind.

Earlier a band of twelve gypsies showed up with violins and

tambourines, and volunteered to play music. The family declined the offer. Ropes surrounded a 150-by-150-foot area in which a large tent stretched over the open grave. A burlap carpet covered with the petals of a thousand roses surrounded the grave, and a fifty-yard carpet was laid from the roadside into the tent. With the crowds screaming in her ears and lunging at her, Elizabeth stepped out of the car supported by her brother Howard and Rex Kennamer. "Oh, God! Oh, God!" she gasped as they half-carried her across the carpet and into the tent. She screamed when she first beheld the casket, twice cried out "No!" during the service, and at the end placed her hand gently on the bronze casket and whispered simply, "I love you, Mike." All of the foregoing was translated by the press into a headline which sold papers all over the world: LIZ HURLS SELF OVER COFFIN, SCREAMS "NO!"—a non-event hotly denied by those who were there.

As the rest of the mourners entered the tent, an unseemly family quarrel rent the air and threatened to stop the service. Todd's brothers, David and Frank, and his sister, Shirley, all lived in Chicago. Another brother, Carl, was a cab driver in Long Beach, California, and had apparently been estranged from the family. Long ago he and his wife Esther had once done extra work in crowd scenes for *National Velvet* starring a twelve-year-old child named Elizabeth Taylor. Today she was his brother's widow. He had come to the Coldwater Canyon house upon news of his brother's death and been denied entry. Now, as everyone entered the tent, Carl screamed, "Get that Hanley out of here. He wouldn't let me in the house." Dick Hanley attempted to explain, and Carl turned to his brother. "Frank, please take that man away from me. He wants to talk to me but he's only a liar and a dirty hypocrite. I don't want him to come near me." David, with whom he had earlier quarreled, attempted to reason with him. Carl retorted, "Throw me out. I dare you to throw me out. I will not be here while Hanley is here. I know I am only poor Carl." Frank then took over and calmed his brother.

Family harmony was no sooner restored than a disagreement over where the photographers were to stand erupted, and there was a short-lived attempt to push them physically out of the tent. After some shoving, order was restored, and the ceremony could finally proceed. The Kaddish, the Jewish Memorial Prayer, was read by Rabbi Abraham Rose and the responses made by Michael Todd, Jr., and by David, the family's only Orthodox Jew. Due to the fact that the funeral fell within the two weeks preceding Passover, there was no eulogy. Michael Todd, Jr., stated simply, "I have something important to say—and it is most important. He was not only my father but the greatest human being in all the world. That is all I have to say." After which the mourners left Elizabeth alone in the tent, in deference to her wishes, as she said her last goodbye to her husband, leaving him behind in Waldheim—with fiery, free-thinking Emma Goldman —with the four anarchists lynched by the State of Illinois for the Haymarket Square bombing—and with Chaim Goldbogen, the gentle rabbi and father whose memory Mike Todd venerated all his days on earth.

Outside the police had lost control. The entire thirty-three-minute ceremony had been conducted against a steady chant of "Liz! Liz! Come on out, Liz!" Now when Elizabeth stepped out of the tent, the mob rushed at her like a great tidal wave. Howard got to her side and, while her veil was being torn apart for souvenirs, managed to get her safely into the car, which was immediately engulfed and rocked from side to side. A mammoth traffic jam had everything tied up for miles. "Please, for God's sake," Elizabeth was heard to cry out at one point, "get the car moving." Somehow they made it to the airport. There two columns of police struggled unsuccessfully to hold back screaming reporters and photographers. After a shoving, punching hassle with photographers, the funeral party finally made it safely onto the plane.

"People just don't behave like that," Elizabeth wrote in retrospect. "But they do." And did.

The night after her return, Howard and his wife, and Bill Lyon, kept her company as she watched the Academy Awards on television. The Award to the Todd-AO Process early in the ceremonies was a sad reminder of the man who would have been there to joyfully accept it, a proud wife at his side. Jennifer Jones had agreed to substitute for Elizabeth as a presenter, and should she win as Best Actress, Miss Jones would accept for her. The winner, however, was Joanne Woodward. Later, at the Academy Awards Ball, where the newly-wed Newmans were celebrating the triumph, Joanne Woodward was handed a huge box of white orchids, with a card which read: "I am so happy for you. Elizabeth Taylor Todd and Mike, too."

On April 1, Rex Kennamer announced, "Going back to work will be the best medicine in the world for Elizabeth. Both her health and her outlook are much improved now." She told a friend, "If I could only cry, but when I start, I get an icy feeling and my mind says, 'You must control yourself. You have a job to do.'" A job for herself, for her children, and, above all, for Mike Todd, who was so sure with what little he'd seen of it, that her work in *Cat on a Hot Tin Roof* would be her greatest triumph to date. On April 14, Elizabeth returned to work on the film.

"Starting like a robot, I put myself into the world of Maggie the Cat," Elizabeth said years later. "—seeing, feeling, touching. It was marvelous therapy." On the day she returned, her dressing room was full of roses from her costars and violets (her favorite flower) from the crew. She was eight pounds thinner, having taken no solid food for the previous three weeks. "She was so weak from lack of food," noted producer Lawrence Weingarten, "that she couldn't lift a suitcase off a bed in the first scene she played." To which he added, "She was remarkable. She was working on a string for the first two weeks after her return, but you can't see a flaw in her performance."

Director Richard Brooks was aware that he had a woman in deep psychic trauma and decided to ease her into the work by shooting Big Daddy's Birthday Party sequence, in which she had comparatively little to do. Ordinarily prop food is covered with fly spray so it won't wilt under the hot lights during successive takes. In this instance, Burl Ives kindly conspired with Brooks to have fresh ham, sourdough bread, and fresh vegetables ready at each take, and Elizabeth ate ravenously. Initially she was given to stammering, and the script's large concerns with Big Daddy's cancer, and with death generally, sometimes cracked her. There were lines like her own "I know what it's like to lose someone you love," and Judith Anderson's "I guess things never turn out the way you dream they are going to turn out." Always she would pull herself together and go back to it. The film wrapped on May 16. Commercially it is still the most successful of the fourteen Tennessee Williams' works filmed to date. Artistically, it yields pride of place only to *A Streetcar Named Desire* as the most successful cinematic realization of the blend of sublime poetry, sexual malaise, and well-structured, full-throated theater that make up the unique world of Tennessee Williams.

Cat on a Hot Tin Roof begins slowly as the basic situation is laid out. "Big Daddy" Pollitt (Burl Ives) is the lusty, crusty absolute lord of a Deep South estate which he ringingly proclaims to be "twenty-eight thousand acres of the richest land this side of the Valley Nile." He is also dying of cancer, a fact Big Mama (Judith Anderson), the wife he apparently abhors, refuses to recognize. The inheritance will pass to one or both of his two sons,

Gooper (Jack Carson) and Brick (Paul Newman), and there seems initially little to choose between them. The plodding, earnest Gooper is a successful lawyer but with a large swatch of self-pity constantly on display. He has always felt odd man out in the family. His scheming, shrewish wife Mae (Madeleine Sherwood) is the unpleasant realization of what Lady Macbeth might have been like had she been born on Tobacco Road. Gooper and Mae have brought forth a litter of five obnoxious brats aptly named "the no-neck monsters"—and a sixth is on the way. In the struggle for the inheritance, Gooper and Mae have been playing fertility like a card that just can't be beaten. Brick and his wife, Margaret (Elizabeth), on the other hand, have seemingly produced nothing but corrosive mutual hostility. Brick's development was apparently fixated in his status as crack high-school athlete, and he went out and broke his leg one night under the delusion that time and he were stuck in the same rut. When we first meet him, he is morose, uncommunicative, drinking heavily, and hobbling around on a crutch, a handy excuse for the nonperformance of his marital duties. Maggie, at this point, is climbing the walls out of sheer sexual starvation.

Not the most promising lot and certainly none you'd care to spend an evening with by choice. Gradually the masks slip away, motives are probed and characters laid bare in moments of dynamic revelation. Like the play before it, the film builds slowly, then roars into high and stays there with scenes of tremendous power. Big Daddy has been hounding Brick like Javert dogging Jean Valjean, trying to get at what exactly it is that is destroying his favorite son. In a pivotal scene, Maggie risks her husband's everlasting enmity to reveal what it is, and the truth of Elizabeth's work in this scene is not only the strongest thing she does in the film but the highwater mark of her seventeen years in films up to that time. It is *her* scene, and the camera comes in close and goes right with her as she hurls it all out in great blazing fragments. As the Hollywood *Reporter* noted: "Instead of the usual trite intercuts of listening characters, the camera pans and dollies with Miss Taylor in most of her superbly delivered great speeches. These had to be recorded in one take, an accomplishment that reflects great credit on the actress, the photographer, and the director."

Elizabeth moves through the film looking ravishingly beautiful —soft, imperious, coiled internally like a fine steel spring— single-mindedly pursuing reconciliation with her husband— proudly holding her own among the flawless cast as sizzling ex-

aminations of the nature of truth and the nature of love go
crackling around among the characters, and then come flying off
the screen in a shower of hot sparks to electrify the audience.
Tennessee Williams later commented, "I love Elizabeth. I think
she is—can be—a great actress. I loved her in *Cat on a Hot Tin
Roof*. I think she was the best in the film." And "Big Daddy"
Burl Ives, who'd known his share of Maggies in New York and
on tour, observed, "She's the best of the bunch." MGM released
the film in September to near-unanimous raves.

Elizabeth had emerged from the valley of the shadow to fully
justify Mike Todd's faith that she could make this her greatest
triumph to date. Her recent professional progress could be
charted on a steadily ascending line, each performance better
than its predecessor: *Last Time I Saw Paris*, *Giant*, *Raintree
County*, and now *Cat*. She was a cinch to get her second Oscar
nomination in a row. She should have been basking in the plaudits
and fully enjoying that exhilarating feeling of having given a top
performance in one of the top films of the year. Instead, she was
being guarded around the clock and had become, by force of
circumstances, almost totally inaccessible.

In September 1958, the month in which Metro released *Cat
on a Hot Tin Roof*, a real-life melodrama came along and totally
eclipsed it and put just about everything else in the shade as well.
Speaking of the essential nature of melodrama in his superb sur-
vey of the Silent Era, *The Parade's Gone By*, Kevin Brownlow
observed, "The purveyors of entertainment find melodrama an
invaluable asset. It requires not the slightest effort on the part of
the audience. They are not required to think; they merely watch.
They will not miss any subtlety because there will not *be* any
subtlety. The values are simple, the threat is clear, and the resolu-
tions action-filled and straightforward. There is seldom any
characterization in pure melodrama, never any complex motivation. Life is reduced to the infantile level of an adventure strip."

A simply super serving of all the above was now concocted for
the entertainment of the general public. It played with tornado-
like fury on the front pages for a solid week. There would be
subsequent revivals over the next few months until the curtain
finally came down on it in Las Vegas the following May. In the
fan ragazines it seemed to run forever. It had a cast of three:
Wicked Woman, played by Elizabeth; Callous Cad, played by
Eddie Fisher; and Injured Innocent, played by Debbie Reynolds.

🎑 18 🎑

September 1958 actually saw the simultaneous beginnings of two earth-shaking occurrences which would ultimately become inextricably intertwined. In that month, Producer Walter Wanger moved to Twentieth Century-Fox on his new contract. With him he brought a book, *The Life and Times of Cleopatra*, for the film rights to which he had paid $15,000. After consultation with Fox President Spyros Skouras, Wanger announced that it would be his first film under the Fox contract. It would also be his last, for Fox or anyone else. That prosaic announcement was the herald of five tumultuous years, a small beginning to what ultimately became a nightmare of epic proportions. It proceeded by fits and starts and its climax was far in the future. September's other storm was about to burst full-blown. Before the curtain rises on "The Seven Days That Shook the World," some program notes are in order on the other players.

Edwin Jack Fisher was born to Jewish parents in South Philadelphia in 1928. With Mike Todd's precise distinction between "being broke" and "being poor" in mind, poor he may never have been, given the love of his parents plus four sisters and two brothers. Broke the family was, and often. In Depression America, they moved around quite a bit in Philadelphia, were frequently on welfare, and at one point, "Sonny Boy" (as his parents called him after the Jolson film they saw just prior to his birth) was out on the streets helping his father peddle fruit for a living. One thing he possessed from birth was a naturally beautiful singing voice. His parents took enormous pride in it, never-failingly encouraging him to show it off to visiting friends and relatives. Once when little Eddie refused to perform, he reportedly was sent to his room until he thought better of it. Early on it was impressed on him that the voice would be his eventual ticket out of the ghetto and racking poverty, the sure way to the love of his parents and the countless others who would hear it, his passport to a world of fame, glamour, power, and wealth. Not surprisingly he pursued this vision with single-minded determination and to the exclusion of just about everything else in his life.

At the age of seven, he entered and won an amateur contest, the first of many. At age twelve, he was singing on a local radio show. His mother conscientiously kept his shoes mended so that he could walk the three miles to the studio. When the station found out about this, they magnanimously agreed to a salary: two trolley tokens per program. Upon graduation from high school, there were several lean years in New York City. Of bunking on the floors in friends' apartments—of a monotonous succession of meals featuring a ton of spaghetti and nothing else—of some days that were not only meatless but just plain eatless—of a brief name-change out of sheer desperation which failed to produce the hoped-for break. Still he hung on. Finally Milton Blackstone signed on as his personal manager for 50 per cent of him, an arrangement which prevailed until it was terminated in the 1960s.

He began to get some brief band spots, with Buddy Morrow and Charlie Ventura, and an appearance as intermission singer at New York's Paramount Theater at $75 a week. There was also a short stint at the Copa. His big break came on Labor Day, 1949, at Grossinger's, the resort hotel in the Catskills. Singing for a charity benefit, he was heard from backstage by no less a person than Eddie Cantor. Cantor was so impressed he came on-stage and, in front of the audience, invited Eddie Fisher to accompany him on what became a successful cross-country tour. A subsequent appearance at Bill Miller's Riviera led to movie, radio, recording, and TV offers. At the age of twenty-one, after a lifetime of dogged dedication, the golden door had finally opened for Eddie Fisher.

A year before this, Debbie Reynolds made her film debut with two days' extra work on the Bette Davis-Robert Montgomery comedy, *June Bride* ("If you blinked, you missed me"). It was all pretty much of a lark at that point anyway, though she had had to move a small mountain of opposition to get even the extra work. By then, going after things with high resolve and getting them with hard work was second nature to her.

She had been born April Fools' Day, 1932, in El Paso, Texas, was christened Mary Frances and was called Frannie by her parents and older brother, Bill. The family moved to Burbank when she was eight, and subsequently the diminutive (5' 1½"), green-eyed, golden-brown-haired Frannie Reynolds was well known to classmates at Burbank High. She poured all her youthful energy and enthusiasm into excelling in high-school athletics, played both French horn and bass viol with the Burbank Youth

Symphony Orchestra, and managed to bring home an astonishing total of forty-seven merit badges for her work with the Girl Scouts.

In 1948 her attention was drawn to the annual "Miss Burbank" Contest. "There was that beautiful blouse being offered as a prize," she remembered. "I wanted that blouse." She went after it and got it. On the night she was crowned "Miss Burbank of 1948," Warner talent scout Sol Baino was in the audience. Subsequently he offered her a year's contract with Warner Bros. and unwittingly handed her a large problem.

The Reynolds family were members of the Church of the Nazarene, a strict fundamentalist sect. Not only were church members forbidden to act, they were forbidden to even *see* a movie. Movies were evil and an occasion of sin, church members told her. When it was learned that she was actually seriously considering the contract, they began to pray for her. Eventually her parents went over to the Warner lot for a firsthand look, and having been pleasantly surprised at the workmanlike atmosphere, left the decision up to her. She took the contract. A year's worth of movie work might make for interesting reminiscences some day, though one thing about it she disliked right off the bat.

"Warners decided against Mary Frances and named me Debbie," she recalled. "I not only hated it, I didn't answer to it for at least two years." After *June Bride*, there was a long spell of nothing. "I helped the secretaries file, helped the teacher straighten up the classroom, helped the gardeners garden, and went crazy." Occasionally friendly crew members allowed her to go high up on the catwalks where she watched other films being shot. She liked it up there because her one mortal fear was of a face-to-face encounter with Jack Warner, at which point she was sure he would demand to know what on earth she was doing on the lot, and fire her then and there. Eventually they wrote a bit part in for her as June Haver's sister in *The Daughter of Rosie O'Grady*, and that did it. The year was up and Warners dropped her. Just like Elizabeth at Universal, she'd had her fling at movies and could now put it behind her. Also, as with Elizabeth, opportunity would knock twice, but whereas Elizabeth waited four months, Debbie only had to wait a week.

Sol Baino was again her benefactor. He took her over to MGM and landed her the part of "Boop-a-Doop Girl" Helen Kane in a specialty number for the Fred Astaire musical *Three Little Words*. That led to a Metro stock-contract-with-options and the part of Jane Powell's sister in the charming period musical *Two Weeks With Love*. In this one Debbie and screen-swain Carleton Carpenter dueted on "Abba Dabba Honeymoon," which was taken from the sound track, released as a single, and promptly became a million-record seller. Suddenly Debbie was launched on a personal appearance tour, she was being paid $2,500 per week, and ambition had finally struck with a vengeance. Up to then she had fancied herself as neither singer, dancer, nor actress. With the new success, she determined to learn the craft that apparently was to be hers and immersed herself in a grueling daily regimen of lessons in voice, diction, dramatics, and dancing.

Next came the wondrous and terrifying news that Gene Kelly had personally selected her to costar with himself and Donald O'Connor in *Singin' in the Rain*. She had two months to learn to match the nimble expertise they had been developing for many years. To the daily six-hour grind were now added nightly sessions at the American Society of Dancing. Gene Kelly, Carol Haney, and Ernie Flatt all worked with her at the studio. On some days she could be seen hurling her dance shoes up to the ceiling and into the walls out of sheer exhaustion and frustration, unleashing a vigorous string of Anglo-Saxonisms learned at her salty grandfather's knee. One day she flung her tap shoes at a huge mirror, cracked it, and let out a violent string of curses at it for good measure. The stunned faces of witnesses to this outburst persuaded her to take a walk and have a long talk with herself. Surely there was a better way to achieve a goal than this kind of nonsense. She returned to work, redoubled her efforts under better control, and 1952's *Singin' in the Rain* brought her to well-deserved stardom.

At this point Eddie Fisher was midway through a two-year stint for the Army, most of it spent making appearances for Special Services. During furloughs he continued to cut the records that eventually totaled eighteen straight hits. Increasingly he was hailed as "the only singer who can follow in Al Jolson's footsteps." Upon his discharge in 1953, he was hired as the headliner at New York's Paramount at $7,500 per week—exactly a hundred times more than he'd been paid for his first stint there. During his performances the screams of "Eddddiieeeeeee!" recalled the salad days of Sinatra on the same stage. "When he begins to sing," noted one dazed reviewer, "the din from the young audience is a combination of the trumpeting of an elephant herd and the squeal chorus of shoats at the evening feeding hour."

He now moved with a constant entourage headed by Milt Blackstone and was the focus of violent attentions from shrieking teenagers whenever he showed himself in public. His following was not confined merely to bobbysoxers. Eddie Fisher's ringing baritone voice had won the public endorsement of Presidents Truman and Eisenhower, as well as that of Queen Elizabeth, Prince Philip and Princess Margaret. He was on top of the heap, and only one thing was missing. Occasional girls there had been but never love. When had there really been time for it?

If Eddie Fisher's career was now in full bloom, Debbie's was not. After the triumph in *Singin' in the Rain*, Metro utilized her for a guest bit in *Skirts Ahoy*, and then rushed her through three minor 1953 musicals made back-to-back: *I Love Melvin*, *The Affairs of Dobie Gillis*, and *Give the Girl a Break*. The title of that last one was ironic because as months of continued inactivity began to pile up, it didn't look like it was going to happen. Debbie ultimately suspected that Dore Schary wasn't very high on her talent, and that she was in imminent danger of being dropped permanently. When Dick Powell over at RKO asked to borrow her for *Susan Slept Here*, Debbie leaped for the loanout that, as she later put it, "saved my life." It was on this film that something mortifying happened to her which was eloquent testimony to Debbie Reynolds' sheltered life vis-à-vis men.

"This was actually my first big romantic role," she recalled. "There was a scene where I was to reach up, put my arms around Dick's neck, and kiss him. I shut my eyes, missed his mouth, and hit his nose. The director yelled 'Cut!' the crew was hysterical, the makeup man rubbed the lipstick off Dick and I almost died of embarrassment. Dick just said, 'Keep your eyes open until you're kissed, Debbie.' "

Little did anyone on that set realize how inexperienced she truly was. As a teenager she'd worn no lipstick or makeup of any kind, felt awkward and ill at ease with boys. One day she'd been hiding behind the sofa when brother Bill and some pals were grandly bragging about which girls they knew "put out." Debbie vowed then and there she was one girl who wasn't ever going to be passed from mouth to mouth in *that* fashion. She and five girl friends formed the N. N. (for "No Necking") Club. To the occasional boy who summoned up nerve enough to ask for a date, she would respond accusingly, "You really want to see the movie or you just want to neck?"—this in an aggressive tone practically guaranteed to take the steam out of any prospective swain. So it happened that in June 1954, on the set of *Athena,* producer Joe Pasternak introduced the girl who knew nothing of love to the boy who'd never had time for it.

On their third date at Eddie's Cocoanut Grove opening, flash-bulbs illuminated the couple in a steady glare, and seemingly everyone in America moved right into the act. Rarely have two people been so publicly shotgunned into marriage. They were crowned "the cutest couple in show business" in what became virtually a command performance. "It's a rarity—a vision of innocent love," sighed a columnist rapturously. "Both have the clean-featured handsomeness of the illustrations for a *Good Housekeeping* short story. Neither has ever been divorced. Neither has ever made a public statement tainted by intellectual sophistication." After five months of incessant public inquiry and romantic speculation, Eddie and Debbie became engaged at a party given by Fisher's mentor, Eddie Cantor. Their plan to thus take some of the heat off with a long engagement misfired totally. What they had done was to jump right from the frying pan into the fire. The intensifying public interest was now focused on a single query about the forthcoming marriage: "When?"

For his part, Eddie Fisher wasn't at all sure he was ready to settle down to marriage. Worse still, his record sales dropped immediately after the engagement. "Look, kid, you forgot what we told you," an adviser noted grimly. "You were to tell the press that you honor marriage. You are anxious to get married but you haven't found the right girl. Your engagement is a million-dollar mistake."

For her part, Debbie Reynolds had fallen in love but she wanted to know a lot more about her prospective groom before she committed herself to matrimony. Between her film work and his singing engagements here and in Europe, she wasn't really getting the chance. June 1955 came and went without wedding bells and the fan magazines had a fit. Wicked adult advisers were standing in the path of true love; Debbie was crying her eyes out; Eddie was beside himself with frustrated passion. Against this background of clamorous public demand, and personal fears and doubts, Eddie Fisher and Debbie Reynolds were finally married at Grossinger's on September 26, 1955.

What was fed to the public from then on was unalloyed bliss. Upon news of Debbie's first pregnancy, RKO obligingly dusted off the old Ginger Rogers-David Niven hit, *Bachelor Mother,* put Debbie and Eddie in the leads, and called it *Bundle of Joy.*

It was a modest success but produced no demands for Fisher's meager acting talents. That was okay because he now had a weekly NBC-TV show sponsored by Coca-Cola. On October 21, 1956, Debbie gave birth to their first child, Carrie Frances. On the surface it all looked like young love's dream, but privately, by 1957, serious problems had set in.

"I knew Debbie was unhappy," her close friend Marge Champion would later reveal, "and she was miserable for a long time after her marriage." For one thing, she and her husband moved to different rhythms. Her whole career had been one long struggle for survival in a brutal business. After supporting Jane Powell in two more mediocre Metro musicals, *Athena* and *Hit the Deck*, she'd landed a plum role opposite Frank Sinatra in the romantic comedy, *The Tender Trap*, and then topped that with such a solid dramatic job in *The Catered Affair*, she picked off the National Board's Best Supporting Actress Award for 1956. From that it was over to Universal for something icky called *Tammy and the Bachelor*, out of which Debbie managed to wrest yet another triumph: "Tammy," her second million-record seller. She was peppy, positive, disciplined, and indefatigable. Her husband was far more easygoing, less ambitious, less driven than she. When he could pick up $500,000 for a day's recording work, why wouldn't he be? The frictions thus provided by their differing personalities were compounded by differing values as well.

Eddie Fisher thrived on the glamour and excitement of night life, the thrill of being a high-roller at the Vegas crap tables. After one heavy session with the dice, Debbie reportedly told him, "Eddie, you lost enough last night to put our children through college!" The life-styles of Frank Sinatra and Dean Martin and Mike Todd dazzled him. Todd he idolized in every particular and the affection was mutual: Mike Todd often referred to Eddie as "my boy," and the Todds and the Fishers frequently made a foursome. A little bit of all that went a long way with Debbie. Glamorous public appearances and late hours on the nightclub circuit held little appeal for her, and when she was actively working on a film, they were an impossibility. "It really wasn't our kind of life," she reportedly told a pal. "Mike and Liz were too fast company for us." Correction—for *her*.

By mid-1957 Eddie Fisher had concluded that they were simply the wrong people for each other, told her he was fed up and wanted out. Then Debbie learned that she was once again pregnant, which made any separation out of the question.

Their son, Todd Emmanuel, was born February 24, 1958, one month before the man for whom he was named was killed. As aforestated, Debbie took Michael and Christopher to her home while Eddie accompanied Elizabeth to Chicago for the funeral. Mike Todd's death was a terrible shock to Eddie Fisher and it moved him that much further along the road to greater maturity. He acceded to Debbie's request that they place their problems in the lap of a marriage counselor. What came out of these proceedings was Debbie's sincere belief that, finally, her marriage was on the firmest footing it had ever been. Love, however, is almost never a fifty-fifty proposition, and her husband continued to nurse his own private doubts, his hand partially stayed by a legitimate fear of what a split-up might do to their careers. He also had unhappy memories of the time he had rushed home on an Army furlough and engaged in a long, exhausting, ultimately vain attempt to keep his own parents from going to pieces after thirty years together. The very idea of divorce was abhorrent. Yet as he also noted, "I realized what it meant for people to go on living together in misery. They grind each other, and their children, to shreds."

Of all of this the public knew nothing. Aside from the fact that it was really none of anyone's legitimate business, it was to the definite interest of the parties concerned, their agents and managers, plus Metro-Goldwyn-Mayer, NBC, RCA-Victor Records, and the Coca-Cola Company, that it not *become* anyone's business. The potential nevertheless existed for a crisis which would not indefinitely be postponed.

Elizabeth meanwhile was gamely going about the business of picking up the pieces of her life, trying to reassemble them in a manner which would get her through the worst period immediately after Mike Todd's death. After the terrible early hours of March 22, a friend had commented: "Elizabeth is going to be all right now. She finally realizes that Mike is dead." Yes and no. For weeks she would not allow the sheets on their bed to be touched, the pajamas he last wore were folded under her pillow, his clothes still hung in the closets, nothing was rearranged in the house. Many nights she was tormented by a recurring nightmare in which she too was a passenger on that plane, and as it crashed in flames, she would waken screaming. The burned, scarred wedding band brought back from New Mexico now rested on her hand. "I'll wear it always," she told a friend. "They'll have to cut off my finger before they get it off my hand."

First off Elizabeth filed a $5 million damage suit charging three aircraft corporations with negligence in the death of Mike Todd.*

She spent long hours with Michael Todd, Jr., talking about the man they had both loved and planning for the future of the Todd Company. Todd's estate had been split between them and they were now business partners. They mutually agreed that *Don Quixote* should be postponed indefinitely. In the 1940s Mike Todd had been intrigued by a newspaper account of a New York City bus driver who one day liberated the bus (and its passengers) and took off for Florida. He paid Ben Hecht and Paul Jarrico $20,000 to develop a script called *Busman's Holiday*, and then shelved the project. Now Todd's widow and his son announced plans to film it, with Elizabeth to star as a beauty contest winner who gets taken for the ride. The plan foundered on the inability to produce a decent script.

MGM meanwhile reminded Elizabeth that, according to them, she was still under contract until 1960. According to her, that had been disposed of at the conference in the Thalberg Building. According to them, there was no written record of any such proceeding. At which point—out of a mixture of grief, anger, and a sense of betrayal—she told them, "In that case I'll just quit now." Privately she was not so sure. Once more she was alone. Was she going to retire at the age of twenty-six? And then what would she, or could she, do? Acting had been her whole life; it was all she knew. They hassled it back and forth, and she finally agreed to finish *Cat* and to give them one more film within the contract period.

Cat wrapped in May, and slowly over the summer months Elizabeth emerged from the shell of sorrow in which she had enclosed herself. First she went down to La Jolla to stay with Howard and Mara and her nieces and nephews. Film magnate Arthur Loew, Jr., had always been deeply devoted to her and his sister Jane invited her for a stay at their ranch in Tucson. She came back from the ranch to move from the house on Schuyler Road into a cottage at the Beverly Hills Hotel. Her children were being cared for at Loew's house, and columnists and friends were busy playing matchmaker. One night the following occurred:

LOEW (dramatic stage whisper to a parlor full of guests): "Will you tell them . . . or shall I?"

(A sudden and complete silence.)

---

* The suit was settled five years later with an award of $40,000. Legal fees took approximately a third of it. The remaining $27,092.55 was legally earmarked "for the sole use and benefit of Elizabeth Frances Todd."

ELIZABETH (blushing furiously): "*You* tell them."

LOEW: "Dinner is served."

Then it was on to Palm Springs for additional rest, to New York for a visit with Montgomery Clift, and back for her first public appearance at Eddie Fisher's Vegas opening, after which Elizabeth, Eddie, and Debbie posed happy and smiling together for the cameras. Finally she decided to lease a house in Tucson and put down some roots. The address of the prospective house leaked out and Tucson police were utterly unable to contain the throngs of the curious. Elizabeth explained in vain that she required audiences for her films but not for the times she wanted to swim in the pool at her own home, and then gave it up. Ultimately she thought she might go overseas for a while, to Antibes for a start.

In New York the Federal authorities told her that her passport was a joint one for "Mr. and Mrs. Michael Todd" and that she'd have to have a new one. Eddie Fisher was in New York on TV business, and Elizabeth seized the opportunity, while waiting for the passport, to get together and talk about the man who was still foremost in her thoughts.

Elizabeth and Eddie went out together a few times, once to the Blue Angel in the company of Eva Marie Saint. Flashbulbs popped and accompanying items in the columns noted that Eddie Fisher and the Widow Todd had been seen out together and nobody thought too much about it. Then they went off to a carefree weekend at Grossinger's, accompanied by Milt Blackstone and the usual entourage. When they returned to Manhattan, and were seen dining and dancing at the Harwyn Club, a great many more flashbulbs went off and the buzzing began in earnest. There was no further mention of any European trip on Elizabeth's agenda. Back in Los Angeles, it was learned that Debbie Reynolds had gone out to the airport early one morning and had returned solo. Her husband had apparently decided to spend an additional week in New York. The press put all of this together and the fat, as they say, promptly went into the fire.

On September 9 there was a small headline: "Eddie Fisher Romance With Liz Taylor Denied." Debbie Reynolds had decided to say something before things got out of hand. "I've never heard of such a thing! I am so shocked that such stories would be printed that I won't even dignify them with any comment. Eddie and Liz are very good friends. What's wrong with a friend taking a friend out in the evening?" In New York, Elizabeth was quoted as saying, "You know that I'm a friend of Eddie's. Everybody knows that. I can't help what people say."

By September 10 the headline was larger and strictly page one: DEBBIE AND EDDIE FEUD; LIZ RETURNS. Eddie had preceded her. He was now closeted at home with his wife, surrounded by an acre's worth of reporters and photographers, and Debbie was hearing firsthand that which she had desperately refused to believe. "What's the matter with you, anyway?" she was heard to cry out at one point. Back at the airport in New York, Elizabeth was having breakfast when she was surrounded by reporters all clamoring for a comment on what had now become Topic A.

ELIZABETH: "I'm not interested in that kind of garbage."

REPORTER: "Then why are you going back to California?"

ELIZABETH (tersely): "Because I've got three children there!"

Arriving in L.A. that afternoon, she strode down the ramp and declared flatly, "I have nothing to say but hello. Too many quotes from me have been coming out of New York. I don't even know what all the reports are. I haven't seen any of the newspapers." After which she entered a limousine in which Kurt Frings was waiting for her, and it was promptly surrounded. A barrage of questions went unanswered. Finally a reporter begged, "Miss Taylor, won't you please say something?" To which Elizabeth responded smiling sweetly, "Hello." After which the limousine sped to the Beverly Hills, the door flew open, Elizabeth dashed out, sprinted through the lobby, and was seen no more.

September 11's headline read: EDDIE AND DEBBIE TELL SEPARA-TION. After a few fruitless attempts to get Elizabeth on the phone in an attempt to straighten it all out, Debbie Reynolds had finally thrown in the towel. "A separation exists between Eddie and Debbie," read the official Metro press release. "No further action is being taken at this time." Eddie moved in with comic Joey Forman, an old childhood buddy from Philadelphia. Debbie initially fled with the children to Marge and Gower Champion's to get some peace and think things out.

She returned to a house now being guarded by a cordon of MGM press agents, who were obligingly passing out hamburgers and ice cream to the weary reporters. "I am still in love with my husband. I hope this separation will iron out the difficulties and we can get together and be happy," Debbie told them. "I am deeply shocked over what has happened. We were never happier than we have been in the last year. While Eddie was in New York he called me every day." Elizabeth was "a friend, never a good friend," she noted carefully. "Eddie is a great guy.

Do not blame him for what has happened," she concluded. Seemingly the finger should be pointed in another direction and it already was. On the same front page was a big bonus for readers under the by-line of Hedda Hopper.

At this point Elizabeth was virtually a prisoner at the home of Kurt Frings (whence she had fled from the Beverly Hills), and she was smoldering at the plain fact that she and Eddie had been placed at what she felt was the bad end of a bum rap. Hedda Hopper she had come to regard as almost a foster mother. Hedda had auditioned her as a child, had known Nibbles, had been an invited guest in her home almost as part of the family, had seen her through good days and bad. Whereas Debbie Reynolds couldn't get through to her on the phone, Hedda Hopper did. Elizabeth felt she had to talk to somebody, and unburdened herself freely and frankly. What resulted was one of the most damning interviews ever printed.

LIZ TAYLOR'S OWN STORY OF EDDIE'S MARITAL RIFT proclaimed the headline. "She Maintains Fisher Never Has Loved Debbie, Says She Had Divine Time in New York."

"I've known Elizabeth Taylor since she was nine years old—always liked her, always defended her," began Miss Hopper. "But I can't take this present episode with Eddie Fisher. I've just talked with Liz to ask her what this is all about. Her reply was unprintable."

After that promising beginning, Miss Hopper persevered, and the salient excerpts of the conversation went as follows—according to her:

ELIZABETH: "You know I don't go about breaking up marriages. Besides you can't break up a happy marriage. Debbie's and Eddie's never has been. I like him very much. I've felt happier and more like a human being for the past two weeks than I have since Mike's death."

HEDDA: "What do you suppose Mike would say to this?"

ELIZABETH: "He and Eddie loved each other."

HEDDA: "You're wrong. Mike loved Eddie. In my opinion, Eddie never loved anybody but himself."

ELIZABETH: "Well, Mike is dead and I'm alive."

HEDDA: "Well, you can't hurt Debbie like this without hurting yourself more because she loves him."

ELIZABETH: "He's not in love with her and never has been. Only a year ago they were about to get a divorce but stopped it when they found out she was going to have another baby."

HEDDA: "Let me tell you, my girl, this is going to hurt you

much more than it will hurt Debbie Reynolds. People love her more than they love you or Eddie Fisher."

ELIZABETH: "What am I supposed to do? Ask him to go back to her and try? He can't. And if he did, they'd destroy each other. I'm not taking anything away from Debbie Reynolds because she never really had it."

At that point Miss Hopper told Elizabeth she was plain out of her mind, rang off, and went immediately to the typewriter.

All of this struck the public with stunning force. The union of America's Sweethearts, which they had commanded and about which they had noted nothing but sweet harmony, had suddenly, from their point of view, gone to pieces. There was now no doubt as to who had caused this catastrophe. Elizabeth's public image underwent instant devaluation. The deal with celebrities seems to be: We will give you power, wealth, and fame and you will be what we will you to be. And God help you if you fail to conform to our image of you. Or, as Elizabeth was to put it years later and after an experience ten times worse than this: "The public puts you up on that pedestal, then they wait like vultures to tear you down." Elizabeth's public image as Grieving Widow vanished at a stroke, an experience Jacqueline Kennedy Onassis would later come to know well. And before she came to know it, it was Mrs. Kennedy, ironically enough, who warned William Manchester in the heated hassle over *The Death of a President*, "Anyone who is against me will look like a rat unless I run off with Eddie Fisher."

Never thereafter did Elizabeth deny the interview or anything in it. What saddened her was that someone she regarded as a close personal friend could have caught her at a moment of intense pressure and then betrayed her confidence. What angered her was the fact that she had been quoted out of complete context and there had been significant omissions.

"I wouldn't hurt Debbie that way," she subsequently told another interviewer. "I don't think I'm a cruel person." The "Mike's dead and I'm alive" quote really rocked her—as indeed it did the general public.

"That hurt me terribly. What I really said was, 'Oh, God, you know how much I loved Mike. I loved him more than my life. But Mike is dead and I'm alive and the one person who would want me to try to be happy is Mike." Retractions and corrections rarely measure up, in public attention, to originals. In a feature story with pictures, *Life* vainly noted: "It didn't seem to matter much that home-loving Debbie and fun-loving Eddie had been squabbling for a year. And so last week Hollywood was caught with its make-believe down." By then such reality was not in demand. The damage had been done.

On September 12 the third party got into the headlines: EDDIE FISHER TALKS, SAYS HE'S SICK MAN. He was reportedly bedded with infectious mononucleosis and was suffering pains in his sinuses, but he put out the following statement:

"Debbie and I tried very hard to make our marriage work. We have been having problems for some time. Debbie especially has done everything possible to make our marriage succeed. I alone accept full responsibility for its failure. Our marriage would have come to an end even if I had never known Elizabeth Taylor. The breakup was inevitable."

Snorted Debbie's lawyer in response, "There is nothing magnanimous about Eddie assuming the blame for this tragedy. That's exactly where the responsibility rests. So far as I personally am concerned, his attempt to relieve Miss Taylor from any responsibility falls on completely deaf ears. I'm not going to spare anyone if it is necessary to protect the rights of Debbie and her two fine children."

On September 13 it was again Debbie's turn and the headline read: DEBBIE WILL SEEK DIVORCE FROM EDDIE. "It seems unbelievable to say that you can live happily with a man and not know that he doesn't love you," she exclaimed. "That, as God is my witness, is the truth. We had marital difficulties in the beginning as most couples do, but for the past year and a half I have truly believed that we had found our happiness. I know I had. I now realize when you are deeply in love how blind one can be. Obviously I was. I will endeavor to use all my strength to survive and understand, for the benefit of my two children."

After the searing experience with Hedda Hopper, Elizabeth redoubled her determination to stay out of these public volleys of statement and counterstatement and remained in strict seclusion while the battle raged around her. By now the "Eddie-Debbie-Liz Biz" had seemingly become national priority No. 1 and could be found on the editorial pages as well.

THREE CHEERS FOR LOVE! began one L.A. editorial, a sardonic salute to the fact that such trivia as Lebanon, Quemoy and Matsu, and the matter of Sherman Adams and the vicuna coats— all current crises—had been nosed right out of the headlines. A *New Yorker* cartoon showed an enraged wife holding a rolling pin at 4 A.M. while her drunken husband staggered in the open doorway, having thought up a new excuse to tie one on: "I got to worrying about Debbie and Eddie."

The next three days' headlines are self-explanatory: September

14, DEBBIE & EDDIE CANCEL JOINT CHARITY APPEARANCE; September 15, EDDIE, DEBBIE PREPARE TO RETURN TO WORK; September 16, FISCAL PROBLEMS SNARL DEBBIE'S DIVORCE PLANS. Finally the story left the headlines, though by no means vanished away altogether. It was merely the end of Act I, and the curtain came down on a properly artistic note. On September 26 the Fishers would have been married three years and Debbie had commissioned a portrait of herself to surprise Eddie with from a Miami Beach artist. Now, complained the painter, she didn't want it and what was he going to do with it? "Paintings, I am sure, are the last thing on Debbie's mind right now," a friend commented tersely.

After a suitable intermission for things to quiet down a bit, the curtain rose on Act II as Debbie returned to work September 29 on *The Mating Game*. She made one minor request to Metro for a script change. Her sister in the film was to have been called Liz. The studio changed it to Susie. Eddie went back to work on his TV show muttering, "I'm the heavy in this situation but I'm going to take it." The first public evidence of this occurred when Steve Allen announced Eddie Fisher's upcoming appearance on Allen's TV show, and the audience booed loudly. Eddie canceled, pleading rehearsal commitments for his own show.

October produced the kind of rank hypocrisy which Elizabeth will never truly comprehend, not if she lives to be 105 and sits crowned with all the fabled wisdom of Solomon. The Theater Owners of America publicly announced that they had canceled plans to name Elizabeth "Star of the Year" for *Cat on a Hot Tin Roof*. "The movie industry is at the mercy of public opinion and to award Miss Taylor the honor at a time like this was out of the question," they clucked virtuously. "Her name was pigeonholed and Miss _____ was chosen for her stature and conduct in the industry."

First of all, Miss _____, at that point, had recently sued her husband for a divorce, and he had countersued in a move to get custody of their children, charging that a screenwriter "stole my wife's affections," and specifically, in Vienna. Furthermore, while the name of Elizabeth Taylor was popularly decreed to be a scandal and a shame, eager audiences jammed the theaters, pushing the grosses on *Cat* up to just short of $10 million, making it financially the fourth most successful of her forty-five features to date. That, in turn, finally vaulted Elizabeth into the select company of the Top Ten Moneymaking Stars. In 1958 she was No. 2 (right behind Glenn Ford). In supermarkets and drugstores, her picture was being featured on fan ragazine covers wall-to-wall, and business was never better, about which Walter Wanger later noted contemptuously, "The same publications which chastise her in print put her picture on the cover to sell copies—a blatant form of hypocrisy."

By November the sheer volume of the trash being printed— all about how a temptress knifed her best friend and stole her husband, thus destroying an idyllic love—had begun to nauseate Debbie Reynolds. She finally agreed to see an eminent freelance writer. He approached her in fear and trembling, determined to avoid any mention of "the issue" and was nonplussed when she plunged right in.

"First of all, *Miss* Taylor and I were never friends. Eddie and Mike Todd were friends and we went a lot of places together, the four of us, but she and I were *never* close friends. *Miss* Taylor had—has—*few* female friends. It's not true that Eddie and I were dreamy together. When he wasn't working, I used to get home from the studio in the afternoon and find the front room full of his friends, in their *undershirts*, all eating pastrami sandwiches, playing cards, and listening to records."

This exasperated attempt at putting things into better perspective was of no help to Elizabeth. The public script was set and there were to be no rewrites. She had rented Linda Christian's Bel Air villa, which was now being guarded around the clock. She and Eddie either stayed there or went occasionally to the MCA projection room to see a film. "Until Debbie filed for divorce we didn't dare go out in public," she later remarked. "Friends, at least people I thought were friends, didn't seem to want to have anything to do with us." Once they borrowed a car and drove up Hollywood Boulevard incognito. "It was wonderful seeing people, being just a person too." Such times were rare as the storm continued to rage, fueled by continuous spurts of venom, like the following from Hedda Hopper:

"Too bad Eddie Fisher isn't free so he and Liz could marry immediately; would serve them both right," she hissed. "We'd give that union just about six months. You can't build a marriage on sex alone." Furthermore: "I understand after all this delay Liz denied she ever gave me that revealing interview. She waited a long time to say it. She said many more things that I couldn't and would not print." Which is truly vintage Hopper: no matter how venomous your entree, you can always improve it by basting generously with innuendo.

Later in her book, *The Whole Truth and Nothing But*—the very same over which Michael Wilding took her to the cleaners for six figures—Miss Hopper claimed that she and Elizabeth made up. In this same amazing chapter, Elizabeth is successively put down as a lousy mother, a widow whose grief was a fraud, a schemer whose New York meeting with Eddie Fisher was prearranged, and, ultimately, as an impossible creature with delusions of imperial grandeur. The crowning touch comes when Elizabeth supposedly told Miss Hopper that she had loved her more than her own mother "because you were kinder to me." Toward the end of *All About Eve*, scheming actress Anne Baxter sends a note to playwright's wife Celeste Holm begging her to meet with her. "Well!" announces Miss Holm incredulously. "This beats all world's records for running, jumping, or standing gall." Not quite.

Elizabeth was prepared to cope with the above, and any number of other attacks like it, indefinitely if need be. Aside from the fact that she had been pushed into a corner by misrepresentation and distortion, her private life was her own affair, and all of her pride and stubborn defiance rushed up to defend the position. "Stubbornness, pride—they're not particularly attractive attributes," she would later say, "but they are necessary to keep you alive." A day after the Hopper attack, however, something occurred which could really have cracked her. Fifteen-month-old Liza was rushed to UCLA Medical Center with double pneumonia and her condition was pronounced serious.

"She was completely unconscious and sort of blue-gray," her distraught mother later wrote. "They punctured her lumbars and had great big pipes going into her little chest. There were great big needles going into her veins, and her little arms were strapped onto boards taped to the bed." After three anxious days the hospital announced that her general condition was better, and Elizabeth's worst fear was put to rest. "If she had died, that really would have been the end," she wrote. "I don't think I could have borne that."

There was enough to bear as it was and it all seemed to be coming at once. The Tucson realtor who'd rented her the house sued her for $3,000 for backing out of the deal (she later settled it for $2,500). Then a lady in Vienna sued Elizabeth for $1 million, claiming that the title song from *Around the World in 80 Days* was a direct steal from her father's operetta. She got nowhere, unlike a Riverside, California, songwriter who claimed *he'd* first written it in 1922, submitted it to Todd in 1955, and received no credit. This one was settled out of court, to the end which Mike Todd had specified: that 100 per cent rights to the song be purchased by the Todd Company for Elizabeth, to be, as he put it, "a permanent little nest egg."

On December 4 Debbie Reynolds went to court and sued for a divorce. "This divorce is a disgrace," rumbled the judge, "if Fisher's publicity is only one-tenth truthful." That night Elizabeth and Eddie went out to Romanoff's in the company of Michael Todd, Jr., the party making its way past tables full of erstwhile friends who either nodded curtly or suddenly became fascinated with their menus. The filing of the divorce might have been expected to produce some sort of truce. A truce was six months away. Full reconciliation would not come until Elizabeth had gone right to the very gates of death itself.

19

On January 6, 1959, NBC personally wished Eddie Fisher a Happy New Year: his TV show was to be dropped as of March. The press simultaneously came up with a little gift for Elizabeth: a page one report that she was about to enter the Menninger Clinic for treatment. That tore it. They wanted to smoke her out and they succeeded. "This is a cruel and terrible thing to do," she announced heatedly. "It is frightening to see a black headline insinuating that I'm mentally disturbed. I'm going out with Eddie Fisher to Chasen's Restaurant where everybody can see me." Out they went, and met the press for good measure. This little item also produced one of Rex Kennamer's rare public statements. "I can take an oath that the thought of entering Menninger's never even occurred to Miss Taylor. That such a story should be put out is beyond my comprehension."

By now Elizabeth's future course of action was set in her mind. She would marry Eddie Fisher and the sooner the better. "I think it's better for us to get married as soon as possible than to have all those headlines every time we go out to dinner together," she told Louella Parsons. "We wouldn't really be news if we were married." A friend read about the plans for a marriage which Elizabeth would later label "clearly a mistake" and reportedly attempted to dissuade her.

"Eddie is just like your first two husbands. Weak. He's charming and attractive but he has all the maturity of a child. You'll be too strong for him." To which Elizabeth retorted firmly, "I love him and I intend to marry him." The friend dropped it. He knew better than to push further into an area which Elizabeth regarded as strictly private territory, particularly now that she had made up her mind.

She was living a strange existence, making all the proper overt responses to people around her, but secretly withdrawing for long periods into a private place where she and Mike Todd still lived together. "We both loved Mike," she continued to stress, and it was a powerful bond. With Mike Todd she had known a passion she was convinced could come only once in a lifetime. Eddie knew this. Their mutual status as pariahs and outcasts was another tie between them. "I'm not sure that Eddie and I were—well, not exactly thrown together," she later observed, "but the world-wide blowup certainly was a tremendous bond." Also she was a young widow, now twenty-seven, with need for a husband, and with three small children, who had need for a father. Elizabeth had never been psychologically capable of long-term affairs or prolonged sexual liaisons outside the bonds of matrimony. For her, such things were out of the question. Eddie adored her, and she felt she loved him well enough to make him happy. Out of this complex of reasons she reached her decision.

On February 19, Debbie Reynolds received her interlocutory decree and a million-dollar property settlement. "I'm not bitter about them—not the least bit," she told the press. "I wish them every happiness together just as I want my own life to be happy. The book is closed and locked. It's not forgotten because that would be hard to do. But a year from now, when the divorce is final, I'll throw away both the book and the key."

A week later Academy Award nominations were announced and Elizabeth had again made the list of nominees for Best Actress. "I think that all the publicity surrounding my private life will hurt my chances to win an Oscar," she remarked forthrightly. But there was more to it than that. 1958 was unusually rich in top performances by actresses. Ingrid Bergman (*The Inn of the Sixth Happiness*), Kim Stanley (*The Goddess*), Joanne Woodward (*The Long Hot Summer*), Shirley Booth (*Hot Spell* or *The Matchmaker*), and Leslie Caron (*Gigi*) would have made a perfectly respectable slate of nominees, except that none was nominated, not even Miss Bergman, who got the Best Actress Award from the National Board that year. The actual list of nominees included Deborah Kerr (*Separate Tables*) and Susan Hayward (*I Want to Live!*), each up for the fifth time; Rosalind Russell, up for the fourth time, for her classic *Auntie Mame;* newcomer Shirley MacLaine for a brilliant job in *Some Came*

Running; and Elizabeth for *Cat on a Hot Tin Roof.* Miss Hayward was the eventual winner.

It was also at this time that producer Sam Spiegel offered Elizabeth the film version of Tennessee Williams' *Suddenly Last Summer,* to be filmed abroad in the following summer. Elizabeth read the script—a heady brew of incest, homosexuality, and cannibalism—and then talked it over with her associates. Their opposition was unanimous. Those who didn't find it sickening *per se* doubted that it would ever get past the censors. And even if it did, it would never make a dime. And why, at a time when her personal stock with the public apparently was at rock bottom, was she even considering doing a bomb that might kill her professionally? Elizabeth heard all this and chose to rely on the career instincts which had yet to fail her. She thought the work artistically valuable, and her part offered her marvelous scope and a chance for further growth. Tennessee Williams had recently been lucky for her; perhaps he would be again. After years of dreaming about the day she would be free to pick her own films, her hour had finally struck. Did they expect her to play it safe with another of those masterfully produced, expertly photographed, gorgeously dressed exercises in emptiness? She signed the contract.

A year had now passed since Mike Todd's burial. David Goldbogen's earlier plan for a nine-foot, two-ton marble Oscar to mark his brother's grave was vetoed by Michael Todd, Jr., and by the displeasure of the Motion Picture Academy. On March 2 Elizabeth went to Chicago, accompanied by Rex Kennamer and Dick Hanley, to dedicate a simple grave marker. Later in the month she presented herself at Temple Israel, Hollywood.

"Entreat me not to leave thee, and to return from following thee; for whither thou goest, I will go; and where thou lodgest, I will lodge; thy people shall be my people, and thy God my God." With those beautiful words of Ruth, Elizabeth became a Jew, taking for her name Elisheba (the Hebrew equivalent of Elizabeth) Rachel (the "beautiful and well-favored" wife of Jacob). Her parents, Christian Scientists both, were her witnesses. "It has nothing to do with any future marriage plans," she commented. "This is something I've wanted to do for a long time." She had been studying the tenets of Judaism ever since Mike Todd's death. "She was a good pupil," said her teacher, Rabbi Max Nussbaum. "She has a good understanding of Jewish life and has read extensively in Jewish history. She is very intelligent." To which Elizabeth later added, "I felt terribly sorry for the suffering of the Jews during the war. I was attracted to their heritage. I guess I identified with them as underdogs."

There was an immediate reaction from the Arab world. Not only had she publicly converted to the faith of the hated enemy, she had also, at a Friars Dinner honoring George Jessel, pledged to buy $100,000 in Israeli bonds. Egypt slapped an immediate ban on all Elizabeth Taylor films, and Jordan soon followed suit. As of December 2 the Arab League was able to announce a complete boycott of all Elizabeth Taylor films in all Arab countries in Africa and the Middle East. To the legions of fan ragazine readers noshing righteously on the monthly garbage had now apparently been added all of the Arabs in the world as well.*

Earlier Elizabeth had leased the Hidden Well Ranch in Paradise Valley, Las Vegas, about five minutes' drive from the Tropicana, where Eddie Fisher was scheduled to open a six-week stand April 1. At the same time Debbie Reynolds publicly rejected Eddie's plea for a quickie Nevada divorce. "I've already granted him a divorce," she remarked. "I don't approve of divorce, especially the Nevada kind. It would be embarrassing to my children to one day find that their father had two wives at the same time." Nevertheless events now moved swiftly to a climax.

On opening night at the Tropicana, Elizabeth attended with Francis and Sara Taylor, with Howard and Mara Taylor, and with Burl Ives. At the party afterward she exhibited a bracelet of fifty diamonds as her engagement present and announced her hope to be married within six weeks. The ensuing press conference allowed Elizabeth to give her own candid appraisal of the last seven stormy months.

"Eddie and I are proud of our feelings toward each other and we have never tried to hide them," she told assembled reporters. "We have been accused of being indiscreet, and rightly so, but we haven't tried to cover up anything. We have been honest in what we have done. And we have ourselves to live with. We respect public opinion but you can't live by it. If we lived by it, Eddie and I would have been terribly unhappy through all this turmoil. But I can shamelessly say that we have been terribly happy. I am literally rising above it." (About which Max Lerner later commented in the New York *Post*, "Where so many people have become desensitized in our world, I welcome this forthright celebration of the life of the senses.")

* *Cleopatra* put a temporary end to this nonsense in March 1968. Nasser saw it at a private screening and approved openings in Cairo and Alexandria "because it is good propaganda for Egypt."

"We intend to travel and see as much of the world as we can," Eddie remarked. "And we would like to travel as man and wife," Elizabeth added. How would that be possible if Debbie would not consent to a Nevada divorce? "Debbie was very much hurt at first to find out that Eddie and I were in love," Elizabeth noted. "I think the hurt has now left and that she will consent to Eddie getting a divorce here. What has she got to gain by opposing it?"

A day later Debbie Reynolds arrived at L.A. International Airport after four weeks' location work abroad on *It Started With a Kiss*. She was notified that a huge crush of reporters and photographers was waiting for her. "What are y'all here for?" she cracked as she came through the plane door. Then, after walking down the ramp, "You always know before me." A deep breath. "Now what?" They filled her in. "You mean to tell me they held a press conference in Las Vegas? Fantastic!" Then: "I find it very difficult to be always informed, and to be asked a very personal question, which means a great deal to my life, over the telephone or secondhand. I hate divorces, especially quick divorces. And I feel a year is really a very short time to wait. But the position I've been put in leaves me only this alternative."

Having thus signified her assent to the Nevada proceedings, she than rang down the curtain on her part in the drama. "I don't believe I've ever stood in the way of their happiness and I never would. This has caught me a little by surprise. However, this will be my last statement on the subject. I feel that every question that could be asked has been asked and has been answered. I wish Elizabeth and Eddie happiness. However, I feel that any questions concerning them should be asked of them. I am no longer a part of their lives, nor they of mine."

A week later another gaggle of reporters waylaid her and learned that Debbie Reynolds meant what she said. "I'm sure everyone is as exhausted by this topic as I am," she told them, thus publicly and permanently putting the most difficult time of her life firmly behind her.

Elizabeth was ecstatic when she learned there'd be no impediment to a Nevada divorce. "I couldn't have planned it to work out any better. I am so happy I almost passed out with the news." How did she know Debbie would consent? "Just chalk it up to a woman's intuition." She also announced her plans to retire in the near future. "My personal life has always been more important to me than anything else. I want to devote my free time to being a wife and mother." She mentioned the commitment to do *Suddenly Last Summer* and tentative agreements with the Mirisch Bros. for *Two for the Seesaw* and *Irma La Douce*. There was no mention of the film she still owed Metro.

In mid-April Elizabeth returned to Los Angeles with an infected throat and checked into Cedars of Lebanon for a tonsillectomy. Simultaneously Eddie Fisher was bedded with a virus and laryngitis. By May 11 both had fully recovered for the prenuptial champagne party at the Tropicana.

On May 12 a cordon of police stood guard at the Temple Beth Sholom in Las Vegas. Earlier in the day Eddie had received his divorce. At the Temple the appointed hour came and went. The throngs were so great, Elizabeth's limousine couldn't make it into the parking lot. Eventually she entered the Temple wearing a moss-green chiffon, cocktail-length dress designed by Jean Louis, and carrying a bouquet of yellow and green orchids. Her mother had also lent her a white lace handkerchief for her "something borrowed." Michael Todd, Jr., was Eddie's Best Man and Elizabeth's sister-in-law Mara was her Matron of Honor. The private ceremonies were performed under a canopy of carnations, orchids, and gardenias. Only invited guests were admitted to the Temple proper. Reporters and photographers went to an adjacent gym to hear the ceremonies piped in via loudspeaker.

Holy matrimony notwithstanding, the rock-throwers were still in there pitching, like columnist Robert C. Ruark who delivered a lengthy morality lecture, including the following: "This monument to busting up other people's homes, this solid statue to the ignoring of the ordinary tenets of widowhood and girls' marriages—especially when great female friendships were involved—seemed a little gamey for a Temple." At that point the newlyweds were totally oblivious to this kind of perpetual running commentary on their private lives. They flew to L.A. and immediately from there to New York.

"It's my wedding day and I feel wonderful," Elizabeth announced upon arrival. "We didn't sleep a wink. We spent the whole night in the lounge." Added Eddie, "It's a heck of a way to spend a wedding night, but we are anxious to be off to Europe." Photographers asked them to embrace and Elizabeth ran true to public form. "We're saving that for ourselves." After which they spent a night at the Waldorf and then flew to Spain. On May 16 the rented 200-ton Swiss yacht *Olnico* set sail from Barcelona for a long, leisurely Mediterranean honeymoon cruise. The master suite, right down to the nuptial bed therein, was said to be an exact replica of Christopher Columbus' cabin on the *Santa Maria*.

The newlyweds returned to Spain in June so that Elizabeth

could play a bit part as a corpse in Michael Todd, Jr.'s *Scent of Mystery* (later retitled *Holiday in Spain*). Then, after some location shooting for *Suddenly Last Summer* on the Costa Brava, it was on to London and Shepperton Studios, where the major part of the film would be shot. A press conference was scheduled and the British reporters went right to work with their famed acidity. Hollywood stars to the British press were, in Shakespeare's pithy phrase from *Lear*, "as flies to wanton boys."

QUESTION: "What is your greatest ambition?"

ELIZABETH: "To be a good wife and mother."

COMMENT: "But you said the same thing eighteen months ago with Mr. Todd."

Elizabeth walked out in a towering fury and that was the end of that. Thereafter the set was closed to the press—which couldn't have made Katharine Hepburn exactly unhappy. What finally set Miss Hepburn off was what she regarded as the inexcusably miserable treatment accorded Montgomery Clift by the director and producer. Ultimately she spat twice, literally and publicly, to show her unmitigated contempt for such behavior. For their part, Mankiewicz and Spiegel were struggling to get a performance out of an actor whose ability to function fully was now sadly a sometime thing. The private demons which would hound him to his early death had already made frightening inroads. These kinds of problems this particular production really didn't need. All hands involved were challenged to the utmost in transferring to film one of the most terrifying nightmare visions of the world as devouring organism ever seen on the screen. The works of Tennessee Williams are a familiar battleground for the fierce struggle between the poetic and the primitive. In this instance Blanche Dubois was not to be let off merely with rape and a strait jacket. She was (in the person of the poet, Sebastian) to be literally gobbled up.

The plot is simple but horrifying (some might amend that to read "simply horrifying"). Somewhere in an unnamed state in Williams' beloved (?) South, Lions View State Asylum is falling apart for lack of funds. Wealthy eccentric Mrs. Venable (Katharine Hepburn) is perfectly willing to help—for a small consideration. Her niece Catherine (Elizabeth) has been adjudged insane and committed to another asylum. The poor girl's torment could so easily be mercifully terminated by a lobotomy. Might not Lions View chief surgeon Doctor Cukrowicz (Montgomery Clift) perform the operation in return for the necessary funding?

The doctor questions Catherine and learns that her psyche was first derailed when she was seduced and deflowered by a married roué after a Mardi Gras ball. What has thrown her completely off the track is revealed in the film's riveting climax, which also clarifies the intriguing ad line: "Suddenly Last Summer . . . Cathy Knew She Was Being Used for Something Evil." For years her cousin Sebastian and his mother, Mrs. Venable, had traveled around the world to all the fashionable watering spots. The beautiful Mrs. Venable was a decoy to lure the kind of handsome young men with whom Sebastian wished to have sexual liaisons. Alas, the ravages of time have demagnetized Mrs. Venable's sensual charms, and Catherine is then pressed into service.

One day she is performing her job admirably, in a tight white bathing suit which leaves nothing to the imagination, when disaster strikes. A gang of adolescent urchins turns on Sebastian, pursues him up a hill, surrounds him, tears him limb from limb, and then devours him, while Catherine looks on in horror. It is this memory which Mrs. Venable is determined to have literally cut out of the girl's head. In the end, Mrs. Venable withdraws into her private world where no such thing could possibly have happened—Lions View will presumably have to look elsewhere for funds—but Catherine has been enabled to articulate this repressed horror and is thereby saved.

Malignant and repulsive *Suddenly Last Summer* may well be. It is also undeniably fascinating because the central vision is brilliantly realized. The basic music score Malcolm Arnold had been writing for years—a sort of perpetual-neurosis-and-hysteria —is perfect in this setting. So is the production design of Oliver Messel, never more so than in the first of the film's set pieces: Mrs. Venable's interview with the doctor outside in her strange, overgrown garden. The atmosphere is properly humid, oppressive, menacing for the film's view that the world and nature are brutal, cruel, and devouring. "All poets, whatever age they may seem to others," Miss Hepburn observes, "die young." Attention is then focused on the garden's centerpiece: a Venus's-flytrap, one of nature's own killers. After which Miss Hepburn launches into a brilliant monologue about the birth of sea turtles in the Galápagos Islands, vividly picturing their pathetic crawl back to the sea as rapacious birds rend them to shreds. Homosexuality and the Oral Symbolism are constant undertones leading up to the final act of cannibalism. "The way he talked about people . . . as if they were items on a menu," Elizabeth remarks at one point. "Fed up with the dark ones . . . famished for the light ones."

In acting, the honors split right down the middle between

Elizabeth and Katharine Hepburn. Albert Dekker plays the head of Lions View as if he'd never eaten anything but corn pone in his whole life. As Elizabeth's greedy bird-brained mother, Mercedes McCambridge has everything going for her but some badly needed subtlety. As for Montgomery Clift, he looks almost immobilized with a peculiar facial stasis, and his accent is distractingly Mittel-European. This is the kind of actor's choice that always looks, intellectually, like a winner; after all, the man's name is Cukrowicz. In reality it's wrong because it calls undue attention to itself. Ultimately Clift fades into the background as strictly an "I Am a Camera" neuter.

As for Elizabeth's work in *Suddenly Last Summer*, director Mankiewicz observed, "She is close to being the greatest actress in the world and so far she has done it mostly by instinct. She is still a primitive, sort of the Grandma Moses school of acting." Tennessee Williams had thought her wrong for the part but was nevertheless moved to remark, "If nothing else, it demonstrated her ability to rise above miscasting." Of her own work on this one, Elizabeth has always been justifiably proud.

"It was the greatest, the most emotionally draining, the most emotionally stimulating experience of my life," she said at the time. "I have enormous admiration for Tennessee Williams' high theatricality, his rhetoric and images." Her prize memory is of the long climactic monologue in which she shares the screen, in voice-over and most of the time in split-screen or overlap, with the re-enactment in mime of the death of Sebastian (whose face is never seen).

"The final scene, with its twelve pages of monologue, was shot in two days," she related. "They just let the camera roll on and on until it was out of film. I also had to repeat certain sections for different camera angles. You have to work yourself up to an emotional pitch for something like this. I ended the scene down on the floor screaming—and I couldn't stop crying even after it was finished."

"*Suddenly Last Summer* was in every way a gratifying experience for both of us," Mankiewicz recalled. "The last-act 'aria' of the girl was as long and difficult a speech, I venture, as any ever attempted on the screen." He did four or five takes and wasn't getting it. He called a break. Elizabeth went behind one of the sets, slumped onto the floor, and gave vent to her bitter disappointment by breaking into racking sobs.

"Elizabeth had quite simply been brought to her knees by her own demands upon herself. Her talent is primitive in its best meaning; she hadn't the technique for rationing herself; her emotional commitment was total each time." Mankiewicz then squatted beside her and cannily suggested that they wrap for the day and begin fresh in the morning. Elizabeth's reaction to this unspoken challenge to her ability was exactly what Mankiewicz expected. She pulled herself together, rose to her feet, and vowed firmly, "No. Now!" The next take was the print. "You'll rarely come across a more honestly realized performance by an actress."

When *Suddenly Last Summer* finally went out in December 1959, the critical pros and cons were varied and vehement.

"A preposterous and monotonous potpourri of incest, homosexuality, psychiatry and, so help me, cannibalism," snarled *The New Yorker*.

"Drama of Soaring, Poetic Power," headlined the *Film Daily*. "Wonderfully Cast and Directed. Forceful, Literate, and Adult."

"The most bizarre motion picture ever made by a major American company," gasped *Variety*. "Its viewing is like lifting the roof on a corner of Hell."

"Indeed," queried the stunned *Motion Picture Herald*, "can we describe this as popular entertainment?"

"A wholly admirable rendering into film of a work that is at once fascinating and nauseating, brilliant and immoral," proclaimed the *Saturday Review*. "Elizabeth Taylor works with an intensity beyond belief; hers is unquestionably one of the finest performances of this or any year."

"Malignant masterpiece," hailed the L.A. *Examiner*. "Elizabeth Taylor plays with a beauty and passion which make her, in my opinion, the commanding young actress of the screen . . . she tears the heart out of you."

While all of these various critics were having at each other, the makers of the film were under attack. Mexico banned the film for all patrons under twenty-one, and the Spanish Government beefed to Sam Spiegel that the film showed "starving youths devouring a man." They were naturally sensitive to intimations of hunger in the Falangist Paradise. They weren't happy about the homosexual overtones, either. Spiegel announced he wasn't afraid of Franco but henceforth ordered that all the publicity regarding the shooting refer only to England. "This is a highly moral motion picture," he proclaimed, "bringing out the theme that one cannot abuse other human beings without paying for it with either one's life or sanity." Sure it was shocking but the shocks made the point. "Why, it's a theme the masses can identify with."

Columbia was at pains to inform everyone that all references to cannibalism were *out*, but the abbreviated cable title for *Suddenly Last Summer* between the home office and overseas branches was "Devour." Said Joseph L. Mankiewicz, "I never thought about homosexuality or cannibalism when I was directing it—only its basic humanity." Meanwhile Motion Picture Producers Association chief Eric Johnston had gone to Washington to testify on pornography and obscenity in U.S. films before a House Subcommittee particularly interested in how *Suddenly Last Summer* ever got a Code Seal of Approval.

"You can read homosexuality into it or you can read incest," he told them primly, "if you wish—if your mind goes along those channels." There was an appropriate pause for nervous mutual glances among the Congressmen in the Lord-is-it-I manner of the Last Supper. "But I don't think there is anything like that in the picture. It is a story of deep motherly affection, an abnormality of deep mother love."

Finally John Wayne came out with six-guns blazing. "I deplore the garbage that is now being splashed on our screens," declared Big Duke. "The trash and filth now going onto American screens will lead to a crippling censorship, unless motion pictures quit telling dirty stories to our kids." He allowed as how *Suddenly Last Summer* was one of the films he was referring to. Had he seen it? No—and he wasn't about to, either.

All of the controversy notwithstanding, Elizabeth was elated with her personal notices and by the fact that, with the grosses on the film (which eventually totaled $6,375 million domestic), her professional judgment had once again been vindicated. The following February she got the additional good news that, for the third year in a row, she was again going up for an Academy Award. The third time could have been a charm, as they say, but it wasn't. Katharine Hepburn went up right along with her for one of those distressing exhibitions of what the trade calls "killing each other off."

Eleven times in the Academy's forty-six-year history to date, more than one performer from the same film has gone up in competition for a top acting Award, and only twice has it resulted in victory. Once, really, since the first time was an anomaly. In 1944, Bing Crosby did indeed beat fellow nominee Barry Fitzgerald for *Going My Way*. But Fitzgerald was also nominated that year for a Best Supporting Oscar—which he won—making him the only performer in Academy history to be nominated in two categories for the same role. In 1961 Maximilian Schell beat fellow nominee Spencer Tracy for *Judgement at Nuremberg*. Otherwise, Clark Gable, Charles Laughton, and

Franchot Tone all slaughtered each other over *Mutiny on the Bounty;* Bette Davis and Anne Baxter came to grief with *All About Eve;* likewise Burt Lancaster and Montgomery Clift with *From Here to Eternity;* James Dean and Rock Hudson with *Giant;* Tony Curtis and Sidney Poitier with *The Defiant Ones;* Richard Burton and Peter O'Toole with *Becket;* Dustin Hoffman and Jon Voight with *Midnight Cowboy;* and Lawrence Olivier and Michael Caine in *Sleuth.**

The reasons for this are not hard to find. Choosing annually among five excellent but widely disparate performances for "the best" is a trifle absurd. To take one example: How really can you view Gloria Swanson's Norma Desmond (*Sunset Boulevard*), Bette Davis' Margo Channing (*All About Eve*), and Judy Holliday's Billie Dawn (*Born Yesterday*)—three of the classic creations of the screen—and then name one of them "the best"? That's what voters had to do in 1950. Americans like to crown their heroes and heroines in singular fashion, and people with an eye on the box office wouldn't have it otherwise. Bogart's wisecracking solution was to "let each of the five nominees play *Hamlet*—and may the best man win." If taken seriously, that would give any nominee with Shakespearean experience an unfair edge.

Given this demand for *a* champion among champions, a *primus inter pares* as it were, voters grasp gratefully for anything that will narrow the field. Is *she* unpopular? To hell with her. Does *he* already have one? That's enough. Are two performers up from the same film? The field is narrowed to three. In this specific 1959 instance, Elizabeth and Katharine Hepburn stalemated each other, Doris Day twinkled for a brief moment of histrionic acclaim (for *Pillow Talk*), and Simone Signoret (*Room at the Top*) then nosed out Audrey Hepburn (*The Nun's Story*), who already had an Oscar. For Elizabeth, three nominations three years running was a prestigious achievement, and her next role might give her the best shot yet at the Award. It was to be *Cleopatra*—or so she thought.

Since his announcement in September 1958, Walter Wanger had not been idle. His biggest stumbling block was Fox President Spyros Skouras, who had no initial faith in *Cleopatra*'s prospects as a moneymaker. Skouras dropped a moth-eaten script of the 1917 Theda Bara silent version into Wanger's lap with instruc-

* In the supporting categories, sixty-one performers to date have collided on twenty-nine occasions, and only Hattie McDaniel, Teresa Wright, Celeste Holm, Helen Hayes, Cloris Leachman, Ben Johnson, and Tatum O'Neal have beaten the jinx.

tions to give it an update. Like a bad dream, that idea fortunately vanished away and the studio began talking about a $2
million remake of the 1934 De Mille version, which had starred
Claudette Colbert, with Joan Collins or Dana Wynter in the part.
Wanger had bigger things in mind. He visualized a modest spectacular with intellectual muscle—a penetrating examination of
history's most fabled enchantress and what made her tick—and
the only star in Wanger's mind who could really bring it off,
both in terms of box office and talent, was Elizabeth Taylor.

To that end, he left her a copy of *The Life and Times of
Cleopatra* when he ran into her as she sat having a drink with
Arthur Loew, Jr., at the Polo Lounge of the Beverly Hills in
November. Thereafter he would contact her from time to
time, trying to fan the fires of her enthusiasm. He got no help
from Skouras, who found Elizabeth too bluntly honest (a quality
he came seldom in contact with) and too much of a risk in too
many ways. She was certainly not amenable to control like a
20th Century-Fox contract player. She didn't seem to give a
damn what the world thought or said about her, and she got
away with it. People stoned her with one hand and threw money
at her with the other, pushing the grosses up on her films and
making her top box office and thus twice as unmanageable.
"She'll be too much trouble," Skouras told Wanger. A Fox
flunky loyally echoed the chief. "Who needs a Liz Taylor? Any
hundred-dollar-a-week girl can play Cleopatra."

Skouras was very high on Susan Hayward for the role. Her
name went into the steady swirl of publicity releases, along with
those of Brigitte Bardot, Marilyn Monroe, Jennifer Jones, Kim
Novak, Audrey Hepburn, Sophia Loren, Gina Lollobrigida, and
Suzy Parker. The studio actually planned to test Suzy Parker,
but when push finally came to shove, Miss Parker burst into
tears and had to reveal her closely guarded secret. She was
pregnant. That was the end of that plan.

Wanger thought Laurence Olivier and Richard Burton would
be ideal for Caesar and Antony, but Fox thought better box
office would be Cary Grant and Burt Lancaster. Other choices
for Caesar: John Gielgud, Yul Brynner, Curt Jurgens. For
Antony: Kirk Douglas, Marlon Brando, Stephen Boyd, Anthony
Franciosa, Jason Robards, Richard Basehart.

In July a first-draft script was ready and Kurt Frings sub-
mitted it to two of his clients: Elizabeth and Audrey Hepburn.
Both indicated interest. Then Paramount refused to release
Audrey Hepburn for it and that took her out of the running.
Elizabeth's problem was that by now she wanted to play the

role but she thought the script was atrocious. On September 1 the phone rang in London. It was Walter Wanger calling about *Cleopatra*. Eddie Fisher relayed the message. Elizabeth figured she'd take herself off the hook by asking for the impossible. "Tell him I'll do it for a million dollars against 10 per cent of the gross." Wanger said he'd convey her terms to the studio. The idea that they would actually even consider such a fantastic deal got her more interested than ever.

Back in Hollywood in mid-September Elizabeth relayed her basic demands to Fox: $1 million, script changes, and a foreign location for shooting. Publicity items now appeared heralding the news that Elizabeth was on the verge of signing the most lucrative deal ever given a performer in film history. At which point MGM was heard from. Had she forgotten that she still owed them a film? Time was running out. They'd bought a property specifically for Elizabeth called *Ada*, a seamy saga about a hooker who became a lady governor. (Ironically Skouras' candidate for Cleo, Susan Hayward, eventually came over from Fox to Metro to do it.) If that didn't sound too tempting—and it didn't—MGM had another one in mind. Elizabeth's worst suspicions that Metro was somehow choosing parts to fit her tarnished public image were fully realized when she got a look at the script.

If "You're only as good as your last picture" were the literal truth, Elizabeth's career would have been stone-dead as of November 1960, the release date. The film was *Butterfield 8*.

❀ 20 ❀

Elizabeth fired the opening salvo in "The Battle of *Butterfield 8*" with all stops out.

"It's a terribly mean thing they've done to me," she told a UPI interviewer. "Sol C. Siegel, head of MGM production, insists I appear in a picture called *Butterfield 8*. I refused for two reasons. First, it's the most pornographic script I've ever read, and secondly I don't think the studio is treating me fairly." This was a reference to the fact that, via the terms of her contract, Metro had first call on her services and fully intended to exercise it. "They have the power to keep me off the screen for the next two years unless I agree to do *Butterfield* and it looks as if that's what they're going to do. I've been with the studio seventeen years. During that time I never was asked to play such a horrible role as the one in *Butterfield*. The leading lady is almost a prostitute. When I pointed this out to Mr. Siegel, he said he would clean up the script. But she's still a sick nymphomaniac. The whole thing is so unpalatable I wouldn't do it for anything— under any conditions."

Author John O'Hara had based *Butterfield 8* on the sad story of Starr Faithful, a beautiful hooker found murdered in Long Beach in 1931. O'Hara was already slightly paranoid at the sight of Nobels and Pulitzers constantly passing him by and going to such as Hemingway and Faulkner, and he wasn't about to take any lip from a mere film actress.

"Her basic mistake was in giving the remarkable opinion that the heroine of my novel was 'practically a prostitute,' " he later fired back. "Bear in mind she was eager to play Cleopatra, not Joan of Arc. Bear in mind, too, the fact that the then Mrs. Eddie Fisher had already been Mrs. Todd, Mrs. Hilton, and Mrs. Wilding, though not yet thirty years old and had long since changed her public image from that of the little girl who loved a horse in *National Velvet*."

O'Hara said that Elizabeth's real beef was not with the character but with the fact that she had to play Gloria (the heroine) for $150,000 when she hankered to get started on *Cleo* for $1 million. He was partially correct, but not even $1 million for *Butterfield* would have made this particular woman want to play that particular character. Nor need O'Hara have taken such umbrage: the final result was to bear as much resemblance to his novel as *Rhapsody in Blue* to the life of George Gershwin or *Night and Day* to the life of Cole Porter.

Elizabeth thrashed with the hateful problem, and her lawyers and agent thrashed right along with her, but to no avail. Once she and Mike Todd had put Metro on the short end—now the tables were turned. At Fox, after much pulling and hauling, Wanger, backed up by Production Chief Buddy Adler, had finally won the reluctant Skouras over to his point of view: Elizabeth for *Cleopatra*. And Metro had her over the proverbial barrel: no *Butterfield*, no *Cleo*. Reportedly Elizabeth finally confronted Sol Siegel in that office in the Thalberg Building which she had long ago fled as a child, vowing never to return. "Is this the way to end a seventeen-year relationship?" she asked. To which Siegel responded, "Fortunately or unfortunately, Miss Taylor, sentiment went out of this business long ago."

After a week's suspension, she capitulated, and then handed

MGM a long list of demands, to many of which they agreed. The film was to be shot in New York. She must have Helen Rose for her wardrobe, Sidney Guilaroff for her hair, other favored crew members. Eddie Fisher would have to cancel overseas engagements to be with her; therefore he must be given a role in the film. There must be further revision on a script she still found stupefying.

With this unpleasantness attended to, Elizabeth went over to Fox on October 19 and formally agreed to do the film which would make her the first feminine star ever to command $1 million for a single film. Buddy Adler disposed of a year's worth of publicity items by hailing Elizabeth as "our first and really only serious choice." Rouben Mamoulian was subsequently signed to direct *Cleopatra*. The Russian-born Mamoulian had staged the original theatrical productions of *Porgy and Bess*, *Oklahoma!* and *Carousel*, and was renowned for presenting film femmes in some of their highpoints: Helen Morgan in *Applause*, Jeanette MacDonald in *Love Me Tonight*, Dietrich in *Song of Songs*, Garbo in *Queen Christina*, Miriam Hopkins in *Dr. Jekyll and Mr. Hyde* and *Becky Sharp*, Rita Hayworth in *Blood and Sand*—on which he also presided over a breath-taking use of color for dramatic effect. He certainly seemed like the right man.

At this point two studio researchers had already begun to compile research on life in both ancient Egypt and Rome, a two-year project which would produce fifteen fat, bound-and-indexed volumes. There were still locations to scout, and a script which was nowhere near the shooting stage. Elizabeth felt that the opening scenes were inept, but her overall concern was that there be artistically valid development of the character all the way from immature child-woman to tragic adult queen. Vivien Leigh had played the child, and Claudette Colbert the adult, but no one had ever taken on the task on film of playing this incredible woman practically all the way from the cradle to the grave. If she were to bring it off, Elizabeth needed the widest arc possible, and a mediocre script would doom the project from the outset. Getting all of these items attended to would give her more than enough time to get *Butterfield* out of the way before the cameras turned on *Cleo*.

On the personal front, she and Eddie had attended the Khrushchev luncheon at Fox (at which Skouras and Mayor Norris Poulson of Los Angeles became the delight of all Right-thinking Yahoos for publicly baiting the guest of honor). Then it was off to Las Vegas, where Eddie Fisher opened a stand at the

Desert Inn. It was here that the public got its first look at the manner in which Elizabeth was helping her husband, a sight which would become familiar on numerous such occasions. She would enter at the last moment, the object of the stares of all present as she made her way to a seat at a ringside table. Eddie Fisher would run his numbers to the end and then announce, "I feel so lucky that she's here tonight. I think you know how I feel. I'd like to present—Mrs. Eddie Fisher." To cheers and whistles, a radiant Elizabeth would stand and wave to the audience, blow Eddie a kiss, and sit down again. Which was the cue for him to cap the evening with his second rendition of "That Face," the lyrics sung directly to his wife—"Those eyes, those lips, that fabulous smile."

New York got a look at this act in November when Eddie opened at the Empire Room of the Waldorf-Astoria. For this one, Elizabeth not only invited seventy guests to the opening, at a reported cost of $1,500, but she also paid the bill for one table's worth of recalcitrant ringsiders, who had seen the early show and refused to vacate the table, planning to sit right through the next show as well. After which, exactly a year after Liza had suffered through it, her mother went into Harkness with a severe case of double pneumonia. Rex Kennamer flew up from Alabama, where he was spending the Thanksgiving holiday with his family, to attend her. While Elizabeth recuperated in the hospital in New York, her lawyers were busy working for her in London.

It had now been over a year since the original "Eddie-Debbie-Liz" uproar, and over six months since Elizabeth had become Mrs. Eddie Fisher. Surely there were plenty of other things over which people could gnash their teeth but, if so, large segments of the public preferred not to find them. Matters of the heart are not ordinarily to be found in the catalogue of serious crimes, all popular phraseology to the contrary notwithstanding, for example, "stole my heart," "cradle robber," "love thief," et al. In this particular case, the court of public opinion had settled into perpetual session and the jury was apparently prepared to sit forever.

"We wouldn't really be news if we were married," Elizabeth had optimistically told Louella Parsons. She was now getting an indelible lesson in just how uniquely incredible her impact on the public really was—and she wasn't liking it. She remembered that the Ingrid Bergman-Roberto Rossellini stink had been ugly enough at its height, but once they were wed, they were let go their own way in comparative peace. Not so Elizabeth. Her conduct had inexplicably hit people like one of those rending family disputes which results in an open wound that refuses to heal.

Perhaps Mike Todd's greatest gift to Elizabeth had been an enormous growth in her confidence in her own resources as person and actress. She was no longer the shy girl who could be easily intimidated by so-called experts and authorities, many of whom she had personally discovered to be frauds. The trust in herself had correspondingly increased the innate self-respect she had always possessed. The malice and spite in all of the rubbish being printed about her private life, which showed no signs of abating, had now to be dealt with. "If you don't fight, you're compromising yourself, and I can't live that way," she announced. "It's like living without honor. I'd rather fight for what I believe in." Henceforth she would no longer be the unprotesting target.

The first evidence of this firm attitude was to be seen in London in December. There the High Court awarded Elizabeth damages and costs against *Weekend*, a British publication, over a front-page story headlined: FRANKEST INTERVIEW EVER! LIZ TAYLOR "I DIDN'T STEAL EDDIE." The "interview" was a total fiction. What this course of action meant was the expense of additional legal counsel and subsequent hassles in the courts. If it resulted in greater care over how the name of Elizabeth Taylor was bandied about in print, then the money, and the hassles would be worth it.

In January 1960 *Butterfield 8* began shooting in New York City. Elizabeth originally went into it almost determined to stink it up which, given the still-abysmal nature of the script, would have been no problem at all. For director the studio had given her Daniel Mann, who had guided Shirley Booth (*Come Back, Little Sheba*) and Anna Magnani (*The Rose Tattoo*) to Oscars, and had helped Susan Hayward to her triumph as Lillian Roth in *I'll Cry Tomorrow*. On camera was the brilliant Joseph Ruttenberg, winner of four Oscars for his work on *The Great Waltz*, *Mrs. Miniver*, *Somebody Up There Likes Me*, and *Gigi*, and additional nominations for *Waterloo Bridge*, *Dr. Jekyll and Mr. Hyde*, *Madame Curie*, *Gaslight*, and *Julius Caesar*. *Butterfield 8* was to bring him his tenth Academy Award nomination.

Metro had certainly selected well, but Elizabeth's loathing of the position into which she had been forced initially blinded her to that fact. Reportedly she told costar Laurence Harvey, "This is going to be a rough one, but don't take it personally." Producer Pandro Berman had worked with her on four happier occasions: *National Velvet, Father of the Bride, Father's Little*

more. I have no problems anymore. I'm in love." Then there is a tearful scene with mother. "Mama, face it. I was the slut of all time!" Her mother slaps her. "If only you'd done that before—every time I came home all soaked through with gin." She apparently started on the road to ruin when a lecherous friend of mother's came to call. "He stayed in that house one week and taught me more about evil than any thirteen-year-old should know." (Dramatic pause so that everyone in the audience can visualize all the nasties perpetrated on thirteen-year-old Gloria.) "Mama—maybe you can look at me now without wishing I'd never been born." But all is surely not lost. "Maybe it's too late for marriage—but it's not too late for love." And then the real prize: "You know that motto, *sic transit gloria?* Well, I'm the Gloria, and, in my case, that *sic* is real sick! I'm not sure about the *transit.* I think it has something to do with my car."

Whenever Gloria gives it a rest, other characters bravely shoulder the load.

DUNNOCK (innocently) to Field: "Don't joke about Gloria's work. It's very important to her. Gloria is one of the few girls of her kind in this city."

FIELD (dumbfounded) to Dunnock: "I pass!"

DUNNOCK to Field: "If only she had a father who was wise enough and strong enough to keep her on the right path."
(Mildred and Betty spend all their scenes discussing Gloria.)

OLIVER to Fisher: "Is she or is she not the biggest tramp in this city?" (Susan and Eddie spend all their scenes fighting over Gloria.)

At one point everybody shuts up so that Harvey and Elizabeth (gorgeous in a basic-black cocktail dress with plunging neckline) can go to a local bar and have a pain contest. He twists her wrist and she plunks a spiked-heel into his shoe and twists it. Then it's back to the basic theme with variations, that is, characters talking about Gloria *to* Gloria.

SUSAN (noticing just the slip under the mink coat): "What happened to your dress?"

ELIZABETH: "Well, a funny thing happened. One minute it was there—the next minute it wasn't."

SUSAN: "Much like your virtue, I presume."

Laurence Harvey has his own opinions of his beloved. "You're a joke—a dirty joke—from one end of this town to the other!" he shouts at her. Later, throwing the mink coat at her: "You want me to give this back to my wife—after something like *you* has touched it?"

Enough. When Metro let *Butterfield 8* out of the can in November, the critics quite properly stomped on it.

Time pronounced it "a slick and libidinous lingerie meller . . . script reads as though it had been copied off a washroom wall . . . Motel proprietor to hero, who betrays a certain anxiety to get to bed with heroine: 'Yeah, yeah. Man's gotta get his rest—an' he's gotta get it regular. Ha-ha!' Ha-ha."

Newsweek neatly summed it up. Of *Butterfield 8:* "The number you have dialed is not a working number."

Several of the actors were taken to task but the casting was downright peculiar to begin with. Betty Field is good for a few laughs, but after that, drop your voice. Laurence Harvey was asked to play a lusty ex-Marine. Dina Merrill, who can lacerate with finishing-school bitchery like few actresses in the business, here plays a nice, dull, faithful *Hausfrau.* The intelligent Mildred Dunnock is stuck as a tearful twit who refuses to believe facts about her daughter plastered all over every subway wall in New York City. Susan Oliver's genuine magnetism is wasted on the dreary nag she plays here. Eddie Fisher—stiff, clumsy, sluggish—is simply not an actor. The one performer who escaped, not only unscathed but with new laurels, was Elizabeth.

"Miss Taylor justifies the $1,000,000 she is now asking per movie," thought *Look.* Her intriguing study of an amoral girl transcends a weak script and gives the movie importance." *Variety* likewise isolated the film's sole redeeming feature. "The picture's major asset, dramatically as well as financially, is Miss Taylor, who makes what is becoming her annual bid for an Oscar. While the intensity and range of feeling that marked several of her more recent endeavors is slightly reduced in this effort, it is nonetheless a torrid, stinging portrayal with one or two brilliantly executed passages within. *Butterfield* is a picture thoroughly dominated by Miss Taylor."

With this one Elizabeth gave double-proof, if any were still needed, that her stardom was fully earned. Using Bogart's yardstick of pulling your weight at the box office as a measure: *Butterfield 8* ran up an astonishing gross of $8¼ million, strictly a tribute to Elizabeth's star power. There was certainly no other reason to go into a theater to see it. This new triumph paved the way for a greater one. In 1961, Elizabeth was the top moneymaking star and reigned supreme at the box office, the only time to date she has occupied the top position. With *Butterfield 8* she had taken a weak vehicle and transformed it with her talent, authority, and presence. Helen Hayes had done likewise with *The Sin of Madelon Claudet,* ditto Bette Davis with

Dangerous, and Olivia de Havilland with *To Each His Own*—
and all had won Oscars. If anyone had told Elizabeth at the time
that she would eventually join their ranks, she would have told
them that they were—in a pet phrase—"out of their tiny Chinese
minds." Her own forthright opinion (frequently unprintable) of
this turkey has never varied a hair.

"I couldn't stand it," she commented a year later. "I thought
it was a very bad script from a good book. For one thing I
thought it should be more faithful to the sort of jazz-age period
of the book. Instead, the period you saw in the movie could be
anywhere from 1920 to 1980. In the book the heroine died
dramatically under the paddlewheels of the Albany Night Boat.
But one of the executives at MGM liked the idea of motels better
than a night boat. I've never seen *Butterfield 8.* I did see a very
rough print—with scenes missing, no music"—on which occasion
she reportedly kicked her slippers at the screen. "I have no desire
to see it. They put a gun to my head to make it because I had
this one final picture to do under my old contract. Now I'm
free." Subsequently she told another interviewer, "*Butterfield 8*
stinks. I hate the girl I play. I had them rewrite the whole thing,
but it still stinks."

Adding insult to injury was the cold farewell Hollywood's
greatest studio paid one of its greatest stars. "After I had ended
my eighteen years of servitude at MGM, wouldn't you expect a
phone call, or a telegram, or one wilted rose? I got nothing," she
later recollected. "Some of the stars say that at least the man at
the studio gate says goodbye to you. But even this didn't happen.
They didn't even congratulate me on my Academy Award for
Butterfield 8." Had it ever been otherwise? Garbo and Shearer
were allowed to slink away with nothing but the unfortunate
odor of turkey—and not from any farewell banquet. Crawford
and Garson fled before they were dropped. Garland they fired,
and Gable and Tracy likewise went with bitterness and enmity.
As Sol Siegel had told her, "Fortunately or unfortunately, Miss
Taylor, sentiment went out of this business long ago." But at
least she was free to do *Cleopatra.*

Over at Fox things were in a state of ominous confusion. The
script was still not ready, and a hassle over locations was still unresolved. The first plan was to shoot all the interiors in Hollywood and exteriors in Egypt and Italy. From Elizabeth's point of
view, all of it had to be filmed abroad so that she could get a
tax break on her M.C.L. (Michael+Christopher+Liza) Films,
S.A. (Swiss) setup. Someone then mentioned Turkey, and a
group went over and found the proposed location remote and

inaccessible. Then the idea of a Fox-Italian co-production floated for a while. Rouben Mamoulian went over and spent six weeks firming up proposed Italian locations. As Mamoulian remembered, "Then Skouras said, 'No, let's go in London,' and started building sets on nine acres at Pinewood." Egypt in England? Mamoulian thought it was insane and said so. "I'm the President of 20th Century-Fox," Skouras retorted. "I'll decide where we'll spend $6 million. Go ahead and shoot." Fox had chosen England to get benefits from the British Government Eady Plan, which offered generous subsidies to foreign companies shooting in England. At last they knew where they wanted to film *Cleopatra*, even if they still had nothing worth filming. The money, however, had already begun to flow. Some $500,000 had been paid out by Fox to take a rival production of *Cleopatra* (by Italian filmmaker Lionel Santi) off the market.

Elizabeth had been tuned in to all of this and she was getting bad vibrations. She had specified that Sidney Guilaroff be on *Cleo* to do her hair, and when the British unions would have none of it, she was ready to pull out of the deal. She had agreed to do the film in the previous October but had yet to sign a contract. The hairpull with British labor was resolved when it was decreed that Guilaroff could prepare Elizabeth privately in the early mornings but he was not to set foot in Pinewood. In July, Elizabeth finally signed the contract. Highlights: $125,000 for sixteen weeks' work; $50,000 for every week thereafter; $3,000 per week living expenses; round-trip transportation for Elizabeth and her children to London or wherever; one all-expenses-paid, round-trip for Kurt Frings per location; a 16-mm print of the film.

Before she left the United States, Elizabeth attended the Chicago premiere of the Todd Company's *Scent of Mystery*, passing through a ferocious gauntlet of harpies shrieking "homewrecker," "husband-stealer," "why did you steal Debbie's husband," and so forth. She showed no visible emotion for she had by then worked out her own method for coping with this kind of situation. "Faced with crowds," she wrote, "I want to run pell-mell through all those people with their little cameras and the flashbulbs they shoot off two feet from your eyes. But you make yourself walk and you find a point to focus your eyes on and keep going toward it."

In August she and Eddie Fisher took a leisurely cruise on a chartered yacht among the Greek Islands in the Aegean. She had seen them before, and now wanted to share their beauty with Eddie. They eventually debarked at Naples and flew to

London, where Elizabeth firmly refused any and all interviews, still smarting over the *Suddenly Last Summer* treatment. "I must say she has a lot of courage," Walter Wanger observed. "There are very few actresses with nerve enough to stand up to the British press." This was one of them, and it would cost her, in terms of renewed malice—and, as it happened, it also cost them, in terms of money.

Elizabeth had thought of renting the lavish Fox Warren Estate in Surrey, but two kidnap threats against the children decided her against it. They were not the first. At the time of her marriage in Las Vegas, a similar kidnap plot had been hatched by several interested parties and then dropped. When it finally came to light, the Vegas authorities made no arrests and pressed no charges. This hit Elizabeth where she has always been most vulnerable, and she demanded angrily, "How can the public be sure that their children are safe while these kind of people are still at large? If they would hatch a plot like this once, what is to keep them from doing it a year from now, or even tomorrow?" In this present instance Elizabeth and Eddie opted for the penthouse suite in the Dorchester Hotel in London.

By the end of September, eight and a half acres of Ancient Alexandria had risen at Pinewood Studios. John De Cuir had spent two years designing them and overseeing their construction at a cost of $600,000. There were various palaces and temples requiring 80,000 cubic feet of lumber, 750,000 feet of tubular steel, and 7 tons of nails and screws. Several ponds and pools were filled with water and blue paint. Oliver Messel had designed forty dresses and headdresses for Elizabeth at a salary of 10,000 pounds (approximately $24,000) plus cost of 17,000 pounds ($40,800) to have them made. Eighteen major actors had been signed, including Peter Finch as Julius Caesar and Stephen Boyd as Mark Antony. All was in readiness, though the only action on the set had been provided by a 350-pound lion who somehow got loose and scared hell out of everyone for an hour before it was cornered and caged.

The first day's shooting was announced for September 30. By then Elizabeth had been attacked by a virus and fever which was to keep her temperature hovering around 100 degrees for a month and make it impossible for her to work. It was decided to go ahead and shoot necessary exterior scenes requiring no dialogue. On that first day the temperature was 45 degrees and there were two minutes twenty seconds of sunshine. That was five seconds better than the total on October 3: two minutes fifteen seconds. Subsequently heavy fog swirled into Pinewood and five hundred extras got lost in it. As the days passed, with Elizabeth still unable to work, Skouras, who periodically flew in to London, favored shutting down the production and letting the insurance company take the loss.

"The insurance company panicked," Mamoulian recalled. "They said shoot some scenes while waiting around. We tried— in rain, sleet, cold, and mud, and with seven hundred extras. Whenever a word was spoken, you could see the vapor from their mouths. It was the North Pole, not Egypt."

By the end of October everyone was unhappy. Fox had sustained losses of over $2 million on the stalled production. Skouras didn't like that, and he didn't like the brief rushes he had seen of Peter Finch as Caesar. Mamoulian was frustrated at the impossible attempt to turn wintry England into tropical Egypt, and the script was still not right. Elizabeth likewise thought the script terrible, and she was increasingly irked at press insinuations that she was to blame for all the problems. The London *Daily Mail* finally asserted point-blank that the sole reason for all the delay was because Elizabeth was "too plump"—a libel for which she later nailed them in court and won "a substantial sum" and "sincere apologies." Elizabeth also missed her husband, who had gone to Los Angeles on business.

Eddie Fisher had now not taken a singing engagement for over a year, not since the Waldorf, and had settled into a status comparable to that of a queen's consort—a mistake which ultimately weighed heavily on their relationship. "I hate to leave Elizabeth," he told a friend, "but I miss my work and around here there is nothing for me to do." To which the friend added, "It hasn't interfered with his devotion to Elizabeth. He is fighting it the best way he knows how, but it is very difficult for him. The only way he can pursue his own career is to leave Elizabeth and go back to the United States, but she gets despondent when he is not around and, in fact, while he was in America last week, she didn't leave her hotel for a minute. They ran up a fantastic bill, phoning each other two and three times a day."

Eddie was back at month's end when general unhappiness turned into genuine alarm. Lord Evans, personal physician to Queen Elizabeth, was summoned for consultation. Elizabeth's virus had all the symptoms of flu, yet stubbornly refused to go away. On October 31, Lord Evans ordered her into London Clinic for tests and observation. On November 2 there was a tentative diagnosis of Malta fever, an infection from goat's milk. By November 10 the villain had reportedly been found: an abscessed tooth, which was extracted. Elizabeth returned to the Dorchester, her fever finally gone. Fox executives were still experiencing their first real joy in three months when the events of November 14 wiped it out.

LIZ AGAIN HIT BY MYSTERY MALADY screamed the headlines. She had been carried out of the Dorchester on a stretcher, weeping and moaning and clutching her head, and rushed back to the London Clinic suffering what was termed "a terrible headache causing unbelievable pain." Amid unconfirmed rumors of meningitis or a hidden tumor, Rex Kennamer flew in from the States to join Lord Evans, again in attendance. The diagnosis this time was meningism, an irritation of the spinal cord or brain which simulates the symptoms of meningitis. One doctor declared that it might be another tooth infection—"She has a very bad set of teeth"—which compelled Eddie Fisher to publicly deny that a full-mouth extraction was imminent. Whatever it finally was, the treatment worked. "I've never been so glad to be alive," Elizabeth announced November 21. "There were moments when I thought I would never see another day. It makes the world seem a doubly wonderful place."

By then the troubled first phase of *Cleopatra* had been over for three days. Everything had been filmed that could be filmed, up to that point, without Elizabeth. On November 18 Walter Wanger went to Pinewood and announced to cast and crew that production was shutting down, to resume (hopefully) on January 3. The Fishers took advantage of the hiatus to attend to something they had been planning for some time. Associates counseled that it was probably a losing proposition but they felt they had no choice. At this point, they felt compelled to do something.

Originally fan magazines generally featured glamorous puff pieces about the reigning favorites—Gloria Swanson, Mary Pickford, Valentino, et al. Then—even as with biography and portrait painting—they entered a more realistic era of "warts and all." Of warts there never was a deficiency—the Fatty Arbuckle Scandal, the Paul Bern Suicide, the Thelma Todd Mystery, the Errol Flynn Rape Trial, the Sad Deaths of Lupe Velez and Carole Landis, to name just a few—and the press draped the public clothesline with all the dirty laundry the traffic would bear. These were the vivid exceptions to the general run of positive pieces about stars in their homes, at parties, on the set—all designed to bolster their public images as people audiences wanted to spend money to see on the screen. Many bits and pieces of spice and nastiness were frequently sat on for the good of the community. And if a great deal of fiction was still going out about stars' private lives, it was generally harmless. Of fan magazines in this period, Elizabeth remarked in 1949, "I know they're full of baloney. They make up things about everybody, even me. Say I was out holding hands with people I've never even met. But I still read every one I can scrape up."

In the late 1950s the old studio system began to disintegrate, and with it went the control and the sense of community. "This town has to keep its skirts clean!" the Hedda Hopper character played by Ilka Chase had righteously intoned in Clifford Odets' Hollywood drama, *The Big Knife*. With *Confidential* leading the way, off came the skirts and the underclothes as well, as the magazines became ragazines and plunged gleefully into an era of "warts alone." From the long-ago view of Hollywood as a place "where never is heard a discouraging word," the pendulum swung all the way over to an equally phony picture of Hollywood brimful of adultery, lechery, treachery, bitchery, deceit, heartbreak, and anything else to bolster the elevating notion that, given half a chance, human beings can really be 100 per cent rotten. The particular gimmick was (and is) a scandalous teaser blurb on the cover, which led to a story every bit as full of baloney as what Elizabeth had been reading in 1949. By 1960, however, the smell of harmless baloney had been replaced by the stench of unprocessed raw sewage, and people were doing a lot more than just holding hands.

The only remotely amusing note in this new situation was struck the day little Liza's governess reportedly took her out for an airing, and as they passed the typical newsstand decked out like an Elizabeth Taylor Festival, the child cried out, "Oh, look! There are all of Mommy's magazines." Her confusion was perfectly understandable. Along with all the cover pictures were blurbs like the following: "Is Liz Breaking Her Marriage Vows?", "Stephen Boyd Has Split Up Eddie and Liz!", "Liz-Eddie-Debbie: Are They Planning to Live Together?", "Trouble Between Liz and Eddie: Eddie Flees to Debbie!" This kind of mindless garbage could be suffered in silence and for the most part was. Never from the very beginning of his career had Eddie Fisher been able to comfortably articulate his private thoughts and feelings, but he made a rare exception in a talk he and Elizabeth had with columnist Art Buchwald in Paris.

"It hasn't been all smooth sailing. We had the typical problems of any young newlyweds," he noted sarcastically, "like getting seven thousand letters a week threatening us, like receiving voodoo dolls and communications from different chapters of the

Ku Klux Klan. Worse than that, Hedda Hopper said she wasn't going to write about us anymore." Then he added: "Debbie and I were unhappy from the start. We were cast as America's Sweethearts in the minds of a great many people and nobody wanted to believe otherwise."

"I've never been America's Sweetheart," Elizabeth interjected tartly, "so I never had Eddie's problem." Furthermore: "The papers reported me pregnant. It's not true. When I denied it, they said I had a miscarriage. And when *that* was denied, there was a rumor that I had a child secretly in a clinic in Yorkshire."

"That hardest part of this thing," Eddie continued, "is to show we're sincere and not what everyone tried to make it. I'm just a guy whose marriage was at an end. I knew it, Debbie knew it, our friends knew it. The fan magazines didn't know it and Debbie's studio wouldn't admit it. So I was happily married as far as the public was concerned, long after I was unhappily married. The point we haven't been able to get over is that I fell in love with Elizabeth and she fell in love with me after my marriage was on the rocks. That doesn't make her a homebreaker. One of the things that has hurt most is that Elizabeth has been accused of being unfaithful to Mike Todd. They say she didn't have the right to fall in love again or so soon after his death. Who puts a time period on when a young woman falls in love or whether she has a right to or not? Who is to say? Apparently everybody thinks they should be the ones to decide. I know we don't have a right to privacy, being in the public eye, and we can't stop people from thinking what they want to think, but it isn't fair."

Unfairness ultimately turned into something else, as blurbs like "Eddie Named Father of Liz' Child" (concerning the adoption of Liza) and "Will Liz' Children Be Taken Away From Her?" began to appear. In June 1960 an item entitled "Are Liz' Kids Ruining Her Marriage?" in *Movie Life* brought forth a stern letter of warning from Eddie Fisher.

"The story used quotes that were never uttered, described situations which never existed, and mentioned events which never occurred. When children are attacked, either directly or by innuendo, it is time for action. You and your publication, in particular, have overstepped the bounds of decency by making use of innocent children in a totally false story concerning them. Further publication of such an offensive nature will be met with every recourse at law or equity."

Privately, in the summer of 1960, the Fishers pleaded with publishers in vain to keep the children out of it. "The pressures on Elizabeth are enormous," Walter Wanger noted. "She is made of far sterner stuff than most of us. I am amazed by her stamina." If the high price of her particular fame demanded that she be continually slammed in print for a period of time, so be it. She didn't like it but she could take it. Public abuse of her children she would neither take nor tolerate. On December 1 she and Eddie Fisher filed seven separate suits asking both punitive and compensatory damages totaling $7.5 million.

Given the entrenched and honorable American principle of Freedom of the Press, which effectively shields even the raunchiest segments, Elizabeth was not overly optimistic about the eventual outcome. Nevertheless, if these rags were determined to strike at her where she was most vulnerable, in her children, she would retaliate and hit them where *they* were most vulnerable—in their wallets.

With this attended to, she and Eddie went on vacation to Paris and Palm Springs and then returned for the resumption of *Cleopatra*. The omens were not favorable. On December 28, Elizabeth dutifully reported in the early morning to Makeup and Wardrobe preparatory to a series of tests. Thereafter she sat idle until midafternoon. Someone had forgotten to turn on the heat and the sound stage was freezing. Given what Elizabeth had just recovered from, this ineptitude smacked of sabotage.

In early January, Mamoulian finally got something with Elizabeth in it onto film. He did six takes of the carpet scene, in which Cleopatra comes into the presence of Caesar rolled up in a rug. Elizabeth did it in the nude, after being convinced that the scene was historically accurate, and after being assured that she would have the utmost privacy (screens surrounding the set, no crew up on the rafters). Mamoulian also shot the first dinner scene between Elizabeth and Peter Finch. After which they both protested to Mamoulian that the next scene was simply unplayable, and production again ground to a halt.

By then the studio had drafted Nunnally Johnson (for $140,-000) to see what he could do with the script. A feeler was also sent out to Paddy Chayefsky. On January 18, Rouben Mamoulian had finally had it. After a total expenditure to date by Fox of $7 million, and with sixteen months on the film and exactly twelve minutes of usable footage to show for it, he quit. A few days later, Elizabeth pleaded publicly for her release. The script had undergone two massive revisions and was still a mess.

At this point, ordinary prudence should have dictated to all concerned that they simply give it up. In the Fox executive offices, however, the counsels of prudence had been superseded by the dictates of desperation. People can always come up with a multitude of plausible reasons for throwing good money after bad, for getting sucked deeper and deeper into a situation impossible on its face, for example, the United States and Viet Nam. In the case of 20th Century-Fox, and Spyros Skouras specifically, there was the best of reasons: survival.

By far the largest factor in the series of storms which ultimately wrecked *Cleopatra* had nothing whatever to do with *Cleopatra*.

❧ 21 ❧

The sad story could be seen in the 20th Century-Fox Accounting Department, where the books floated in a sea of red ink: production losses of some $70 million in the five years prior to *Cleopatra*. Long gone were the palmy days when consistent high grosses from the Alice Faye and Betty Grable musicals enabled Darryl F. Zanuck to gamble on such prestigious achievements as *The Grapes of Wrath, The Ox-Bow Incident, Wilson, Gentleman's Agreement,* and *The Snake Pit.* Long gone was Zanuck himself, now based in Europe and involved in a series of artistic and financial duds which only added to Fox's problems. Gone also was the day when it was Fox which had primarily revitalized an ailing industry with the wide-screen revolution, and counted grosses of $17.5 million on *The Robe,* CinemaScope's pioneer, and $7.3 million on *How to Marry a Millionaire,* its immediate successor. To understand how Fox got into the predicament which would ultimately cause the studio to operate out of ever-deepening panic, a quick rundown of the studio's poor competitive performance within the industry might prove helpful.

In the period 1955–61, 20th Century-Fox had only three real winners: *Peyton Place* ($11.5),* *The King and I* ($8.5), and *The Seven Year Itch* ($6). The biggest grosser in 1958, *South Pacific* ($17.5), was a Fox release, but the producers, Magna Corp. (Rodgers and Hammerstein, Edward Small, Joseph Schenck, et al.) took the lion's share of that loot. In this same

---

* All figures given are in the millions, and are domestic (U.S. and Canada) grosses only.

period, MGM had *Ben-Hur* ($40.6), *Cat on a Hot Tin Roof* ($9.7), *Guys and Dolls* ($8), *King of Kings* ($8), *Gigi* ($7.7), *High Society* ($6.5), *North by Northwest* ($6.3), *Raintree County* ($6), and *I'll Cry Tomorrow* ($6). Warners had *Giant* ($14), *Sayonara* ($10.5), *Auntie Mame* ($9.3), *Mister Roberts* ($8.5), *Battle Cry* ($8.1), *No Time for Sergeants* ($7.4), and *The Sea Chase* ($6). Paramount had *The Ten Commandments* ($40), *Psycho* ($11.2), *The World of Suzie Wong* ($7.5), *War and Peace* ($6.2), and *Strategic Air Command* ($6). United Artists had *West Side Story* ($28.1), *Around the World in 80 Days* ($23), *The Apartment* ($9.3), *Some Like It Hot* ($8.3), *The Alamo* ($8), *Trapeze* ($7.5), *Not as a Stranger* ($7.1), and *The Vikings* ($6). Walt Disney had *Swiss Family Robinson* ($14.5), *The Shaggy Dog* ($11.6), *The Parent Trap* ($11.3), *The Absent-Minded Professor* ($11.1), *Ole Yeller* ($8.2), *Sleeping Beauty* ($8.2), and *Lady and the Tramp* ($8). Universal had *Spartacus* ($14.6), *Operation Petticoat* ($9.5), *Pillow Talk* ($7.5), *Imitation of Life* ($6.5), and *To Hell and Back* ($6). Columbia had *The Bridge on the River Kwai* ($17.2), *The Guns of Navarone* ($13), *Picnic* ($6.3), and *Suddenly Last Summer* ($6.3). Even Cinerama had two bigger than anything Fox had: *Seven Wonders of the World* ($12.5) and *Cinerama Holiday* ($12). Obviously big money was still being made, but not by 20th Century-Fox.

To simplify further: If you were to compile an overall list of the period's top grossers, you would have thirteen films—*Ben-Hur*, *The Ten Commandments*, *West Side Story*, *Around the World in 80 Days*, *South Pacific*, *Bridge on the River Kwai*, *Spartacus*, *Swiss Family Robinson*, *Giant*, *Guns of Navarone*, *Seven Wonders of the World*, *Cinerama Holiday*, and *The Shaggy Dog*—before *Peyton Place* finally got onto the list as No. 14. In the period 1960–61, a sad situation became disastrous as a series of terrible turkeys all came home to roost in one fowl swoop: ill-advised remakes of *State Fair* and *The Cabinet of Dr. Caligari*, ersatz Hemingway (*Adventures of a Young Man*), ersatz Fitzgerald (*Tender Is the Night*), Cold War crud (*Satan Never Sleeps*), dreary historicals (*Francis of Assisi*, *Sodom and Gomorrah*, *The 300 Spartans*), other assorted duds (*Lisa*, *Madison Avenue*).

Not since *All About Eve* in 1950 had the studio seen a Best Film Oscar. In the period 1955–61, they had fielded an Oscar nominee in every year but one: *Love Is a Many-Splendored Thing* (1955), *The King and I* (1956), *Peyton Place* (1957), *The Diary of Anne Frank* (1959), *Sons and Lovers* (1960), and *The Hustler* (1961). But none of them won, and if ever Fox needed a winner to restore its shattered artistic and financial prestige, the time was at hand. And they needed it tomorrow.

All of which explains why, with *Cleopatra* having ground to a halt for the second time—with losses estimated at $7 million to date and overhead piling up at $45,000 per day—there was now no thought of abandoning it. The harassed Skouras, dreading the confrontations with hostile bankers and his increasingly unhappy Board of Directors, had finally caught some of Walter Wanger's messianic fervor for *Cleo*. A deathbed conversion it might be, but it was nonetheless real. "What do you care how much *Cleopatra* costs?" Elizabeth would later bluntly tell him. "Fox pictures have been lousy. At least this one will be great—though expensive." He prayed she was right. The Greek worrybeads he perpetually carried had taken to clicking like the castanets in the studio's old Carmen Miranda musicals. He moved hopefully forward on two fronts.

Lloyds of London had publicly called for Elizabeth's replacement by Marilyn Monroe, Kim Novak, Shirley MacLaine, or Rosanna Podesta. "No Liz, no Cleo!" Walter Wanger ringingly retorted, and Skouras backed him up. Furthermore he took Lloyds to court to pry $3 million out of them to help cover the fall production losses. The film had been insured for $7 million, spread among several companies, and Lloyds had the largest chunk. The greatest payoff prior to this had been $1,219,172, laid out by the San Francisco Insurance Co. to United Artists in the death of Tyrone Power during the making of *Solomon and Sheba*. Lloyds offered to top that with $1.25 million but Skouras was adamant. The suit was eventually settled at $2 million to Fox.

Meanwhile Skouras sent an S.O.S. to Joseph L. Mankiewicz, then in the Bahamas as a house guest of the Hume Cronyns, partly vacationing and partly scripting on what he hoped to do next: the screen version of Lawrence Durrell's *Justine*. Would he fly up to New York for a day and meet with Skouras and agent Charles Feldman at the Colony?

Over lunch, Skouras made his pitch: as a personal favor, would Mankiewicz please step in and rescue *Cleopatra?* He estimated it would take about fifteen weeks. Mankiewicz mentioned his binding commitments to Figaro Films, and Skouras proffered $3 million from the dwindling coffers of 20th Century-Fox to buy out his contract. With that attended to, Joe Mankiewicz flew to London to take over what he would later call "the toughest three pictures I ever made."

As Mankiewicz later told it: "I arrived in England in February 1961, where I found the script unreadable and unshootable. I looked at the twelve minutes of film already shot and could not see how they could be used. As for the sets—they were a disaster." There were too garish for his taste. The last thing he wanted was an updated C. B. De Mille epic full of ornate cat symbolism. During this change in command, Elizabeth's original costars were completely in the dark as to what next to expect.

"I really don't know what's going on with the picture; I'm trying like hell to find out," complained Stephen Boyd. "The only word I've gotten from anybody was a cable that came the other day from the production department which said 'Don't cut your hair.' That's all it said. I met Elizabeth Taylor once before I left London. Rouben Mamoulian, Peter Finch, and I met her in her suite at the Dorchester to read over the script. And then she got sick. I also shot a couple of scenes while I was there. But trying to work at night in the fog and the rain was a little rough. I don't think we got much footage."

As Peter Finch looked back on it all:

"I did Caesar's arrival in Alexandria—and I took a bath. In this scene I was in a chopped-off barrel, what they call a 'field-bath,' and they were supposed to cut from me to Elizabeth Taylor in *her* bath. You know, the Egyptians were really hot on baths. But, of course, they never got a shot of Elizabeth because she was ill at the time." Then followed her arrival in the rug and their dinner scene. "After that, nothing happened. We just sat around the studio twiddling our thumbs and around four o'clock we'd all wind up in the bar. A very sad business." Regarding the press treatment of Elizabeth: "They kept saying her continued absence from the film was temperament or because she was too fat. Ridiculous! She was as sick as anybody could possibly be. They really kicked this girl around. They were a bit cruel to her." Finally: "After *Cleopatra* closed down, a fellow came to me and asked me if I'd like to play Pontius Pilate. I told him, 'I never want to see another toga as long as I live!'"

Mankiewicz had meanwhile begun to articulate his particular approach to *Cleopatra*, putting a careful distance between this version and previous treatments, for example, Bernard Shaw's. "Shaw's life is full of letters to naïve young girls, instructing them in the ways of the world. He wrote *Caesar and Cleopatra* as if he'd come upon Cleopatra himself in that pile of rocks. The play is a Shavian dream of intellectual omnipotence, but it has nothing to do with Caesar or Cleopatra." To which Wanger added: "Our extensive research has shown that Cleopatra was neither the strumpet pictured by Shakespeare nor the silly teenager envisioned by Shaw."

In Mankiewicz's view, Cleopatra's tragedy stemmed from the clash between her ambition to rule the world and the fires of her emotions. The conflict was symbolized by the nature of her two great loves. "In Caesar—in her growing awareness of his power—she saw the means to her end. She never dominated him as she did Antony. Theirs was a relationship based on mutual need." After his assassination, she went after his successor with the same ends in mind, but politics gave way to passion. "The hook she threw to catch Antony caught her too. Passionately—for the first and only time—Cleopatra fell in love." As for the character of Antony: "He stood always in Caesar's footsteps—right up to and into Cleopatra's bed. He is a masculine façade, threatened by Caesar, the all-powerful father figure. His love for Cleopatra was, in the beginning, as guilt-ridden and frightening as that of a son in love with his father's mistress."

All concerned were excited by these new concepts, particularly since the old ones were finally to be flushed, for example, a view of Cleopatra as a virgin who could be deflowered only by a god. Sidney Buchman and Lawrence Durrell were engaged to translate Mankiewicz's story outline into dialogue. One thing the studio would not give Mankiewicz was time. His basic job was to "save the picture" and "use Liz." Interiors were to resume shooting in London on April 4, to be followed by exteriors in Egypt. Mankiewicz remonstrated to no avail. He couldn't possibly have a shooting script ready by then, and wouldn't it be far cheaper in the long run to keep Elizabeth on salary until the sets were finished and the script was ready? The studio turned a deaf ear. "This film was done in opposition to every basic rule of the professional filmmaker," he would later growl. As it happened, he got his time via a happenstance which, comparatively speaking, faded all of *Cleopatra*'s prior woes into insignificance.

Elizabeth and Eddie Fisher had utilized the new hiatus on *Cleo* to fly over to Munich February 13 for some merriment at the annual Pre-Lenten Carnival. At a party on the night of February 16, Eddie doubled up with stomach pains and was flown posthaste to London and operated on for appendicitis at the London Clinic. In the haste to get back, and the ensuing anxiety, Elizabeth contracted Asian flu. Which is why she spent her twenty-ninth birthday on the twenty-seventh in bed, but had a party for the children anyway. She got an additional gift that day when Academy Award nominations were announced

and, doubtless to her surprise, *Butterfield 8* had put her in
contention for the fourth year in a row. Professionally it
wouldn't hurt but she had absolutely no illusions about the outcome. Her competitors were Greer Garson in *Sunrise at Campobello*, Deborah Kerr in *The Sundowners*, Shirley MacLaine in
The Apartment, and Melina Mercouri in *Never on Sunday*—
sterling performances all, and all given in vehicles far worthier
than hers. An additional bonus came her way on March 3 when
the Foreign Press named her Best Actress for *Butterfield 8*. By
then she was in no condition to enjoy anything.

Her flu had steadily worsened, and early on the morning of
March 4, the private nurse on duty, alarmed at her gasping for
breath and the deepening blue in her face and the spreading
black under her fingernails, rang the Dorchester desk with an
emergency request for a doctor. The quick-thinking operator
at the desk rang a nearby suite where a party was in progress.
Down the hall came a doctor on the run—as it happened, J. Middleton Price, one of London's foremost anesthesiologists. He
instantly realized that lung congestion was choking off Elizabeth's oxygen supply and that she was slowly suffocating to
death. He shook her by the heels to loosen the congestion. He
struck her in the chest to achieve the same result. He thrust his
fist down her throat to gag her back to consciousness. Nothing
worked. He then gouged at her eyes to see if pain could bring
her back. It did, but only momentarily. She opened her eyes
and then went right out again. Privately he figured she had
about fifteen minutes maximum to live in this condition. He
then took a thin, plastic tube from his bag, worked it into her
mouth, down her throat, and into her windpipe. He attached
the other end of it to an oxygen tank and fed her pure oxygen.
After ten minutes she regained consciousness. The tube had to
come out, but a tracheotomy was absolutely necessary to ensure
an adequate flow of air to the lungs. That meant a hospital. There
was always the risk that the renewed congestion might kill her
en route, but the chance had to be taken. "I have no doubt that
our decision to move her for the operation saved her life," Dr.
Price later said.

Afternoon editions all over the world blared out the news: LIZ
TAYLOR GRAVELY ILL; QUEEN'S DOCTOR CALLED. Lord Evans was
again in attendance, along with Rex Kennamer, who had again
flown in from America. The diagnosis was acute staphylococcus
pneumonia, and her temperature was at 103 and rising. She was
in a coma, and the physicians at the hospital privately thought
she had about an hour to live as she was wheeled into the operat-

ing room for the tracheotomy. "The prognosis is not good," a grave Dick Hanley told the crush of reporters massed outside the London Clinic.

"I did come to on the operating table," Elizabeth later wrote. "I couldn't even whisper. Now you can't imagine how terrifying that is. That's when I thought maybe I was dead. My whole body was paralyzed. But I guess my eyelids were moving, my mouth was trying to move. I don't know how long nobody noticed—I screamed inside—like one of those awful horror stories you read of somebody waking up in a coffin. Finally one of the nurses saw that my eyes were open and there must have been a look of such terror in my eyes, because she bent over and told me that I was in the London Clinic and that I was going to be all right. And I knew I was going to die. I gestured that I wanted to write something, because the feeling of being unable to communicate was more frightening than anything. And I wrote, 'Am I still dying?' The writing looked like that of a 190-year-old creature—it took up a whole page. Then I went into another coma."

The day's worth of headlines in Los Angeles alone had the increasingly apprehensive public on the rack: LIZ RALLIES (*Mirror-News*); LIZ SINKS (*Herald Express*); NO BETTER, NO WORSE (*Citizen-News*). There was one ironic note in all of this. After years of sardonically referring to MGM's Thalberg Building as "The Iron Lung" ("you know, the executives tell you just how to breathe"), Elizabeth finally got one of her very own. It was a Barnet Ventilator, rushed to the London Clinic from sixty-five miles away, and put into service immediately after the operation. A tube was inserted in her windpipe through the tracheotomy incision, and the other end hooked into the ventilator, which forced air in and out of her lungs and reinforced her own inadequate breathing.

The headline on March 6 was ominous: LIZ TAYLOR TAKES TURN FOR WORSE. The pneumonia was now complicated by anemia. A tube went into her left leg for periodic blood transfusions. She was being drip-fed through an incision in her ankle, and a heavy dose of antibiotics went in every four hours. At the point where she again stopped breathing for a time, doctors took Eddie Fisher aside and told him it was hopeless. Though weakened by his recent appendectomy, Eddie nevertheless remained constantly at her bedside. When she was occasionally conscious, he could hear her talk only if he held a stethoscope to her lips. Since talking was agonizing, she wrote notes, with messages like, "Can I die any more because I feel like I can."

By March 7, six physicians were in attendance and their mutual prognosis was "improved." A weary Dick Hanley told reporters, "I am more hopeful now." The tenor of Elizabeth's notes had changed from thoughts about death to "How am I getting along?" and "How are the children?" Her chief anxiety was that the boys not learn from the newspapers and that they not be upset.

LIZ IMPROVED, STILL NOT OUT OF DANGER proclaimed a headline on March 8. She had come out of a coma to whisper, "I want my mother." Sara was in the room (both parents had been with her as often as they were permitted) but Elizabeth did not recognize her. A third tube had now been attached, through her chest, to drain the lungs. Her bed was tilted to keep her in a semi-sitting position, and she was frequently turned from side to side, to keep the lungs emptying. At day's end, with her temperature receding to normal, Elizabeth opened her eyes and asked Eddie, "What happened to me?" Curiously enough, even with this first sign of definite progress in London, a death rumor swept the United States and the news media were deluged with thousands of phone calls.

By March 9 crowds were massing so thickly around the London Clinic that a police van was summoned to clear the way. Mail was pouring in from all over the world and was sorted in huge laundry baskets. (Sample: "6000 of us here at the Boeing Plant are praying for you. We know you'll pull through.") The Soviet Embassy made an official offer from the Russian Government to fly in drugs and other medical equipment necessary, one of several such offers from around the world. Elizabeth's chest, leg, and ankle tubes were now removed, and the windpipe tube came out for short periods so that she could talk. Instead of the ankle tube, she was being fed through a gastric tube inserted in her nose. The crisis had been passed. "If progress is maintained, she will shortly be out of danger," her physicians announced. A day later they amplified that statement.

"She has made a very rare recovery. Much of it can be attributed to the special drugs, but of course she herself, with her remarkable will to live, was the biggest factor in overcoming the illness. She put up a wonderful fight." They later added, "She is a woman of great courage. We had to sedate her occasionally because the essential thing is complete and absolute rest, and Miss Taylor often struggled more than was good for her." Elizabeth remembered five separate occasions when she knew she was going out—when she could feel the oxygen leaving her system with no more coming in—and she screamed inside with pain and the desperate desire to stay alive.

On March 12 she tried her first solid food—a piece of orange—and couldn't manage it. Thereafter she was put on a diet of soups and broths. The next day the tracheotomy tube was removed permanently. March 15 witnessed the most wonderful happening of all, next to the fact of her survival. Two small sons and a baby daughter were brought to the hospital and came into the waiting arms of the joyful mother who had come perilously close to being parted from them forever.

On the same day, there was the flat announcement that, no matter what happened, Elizabeth would *not* be making *Cleopatra* in England. For Fox there was both good news and bad. For the third time, *Cleopatra* was back at the post and what couldn't be covered by insurance was total loss. The doleful order went out to scrap $600,000 worth of sets, a demolition job expected to take fifteen weeks. Actors and crew were paid off and all energies turned toward making ready for the prospective new start in Rome in September. The good news was that not only had their star survived, but she had become the focus of a world-wide wave of sympathetic attention. Without question she now reigned supreme as the world's most important film star. Also *Cleopatra* had been getting the kind of publicity money couldn't buy—and a usable foot of it had yet to be shot.

On March 27, attended by her husband, her parents, and Dr. Kennamer, Elizabeth made ready to leave London Clinic for the flight back to America. She sat in a green leather wheelchair wearing a sable coat and with a white scarf covering her throat. Thick bandages covered her infected left leg, where all the antibiotics had caused a chemical thrombosis. Outside the Clinic a flying wedge of twelve policemen got the party through five hundred photographers and admirers. At that, Elizabeth was almost knocked out of her chair. At London Airport a score of policemen patrolled the throngs and barricades were erected right up to the ramp. "I don't understand it," an airport official remarked in amazement at the clamorous reception. "This never happens even for the Queen." Elizabeth was lifted bodily in a canvas blanket up into the plane, and her mother gave reporters the last word. Said Sara Taylor, "I'm glad my daughter's going home."

After an overnight stay in New York, it was on to Los Angeles. "It's good to be home again," Elizabeth told waiting reporters, and then divulged that her destination was Palm Springs. "I want to lie in the sun and get lots of rest and get my health back. I won't do anything for at least several months. I have to do what my doctors tell me." On April 12 the children came in from London via New York, so that they were to be with their mother for the upcoming Academy Awards. Elizabeth was about to undergo an experience later described by fellow nominee (and fellow winner) Peter Ustinov.

"You really prepare yourself to lose. You wonder how you should behave. As graciously as possible. And then all of a sudden you hear your name. Then you're not sure you've heard right. You linger for a moment, because nothing could be worse than to get up suddenly, realize you've made a mistake, and have to sit down again." (Rosalind Russell bravely covered this embarrassment when it once happened to her, by staying on her feet and leading the applause for surprise-winner Loretta Young.)

On the night of April 18, Elizabeth and Eddie went to Santa Monica Civic Auditorium, where Oscars were then bestowed. The first time she'd undergone this particular torture test, she'd been sitting in her own living room and watched Joanne Woodward win. The next two times she and Eddie had braved the coldness and the unspoken hostility to attend, only to see Susan Hayward and Simone Signoret capture the prize. Tonight would be far, far different. Even though a straw poll of the previous weekend had correctly named Elizabeth and Burt Lancaster the top winners, Elizabeth still didn't believe it would happen. She had come chiefly, as a matter of fact, prepared to accept for Shirley MacLaine, then filming on location.

Outside of Santa Monica Civic a clamorous reception awaited her. "I came from Riverside just to see you, honey," a woman called out from the crowd. "We all love you there—not just a fan club, but everybody." Which went with a sample fan letter published that morning by Louella Parsons. "I used to hate her. This morning, in church, I prayed that she be spared for her husband and children, for her parents, for all us fans whose uneventful lives have been enriched by her beauty and talent. And I also said a little prayer for her future happiness. I hope she wins the Oscar for *Butterfield 8*."

"It's amazing how the public switches moods," a columnist noted. "Not too long ago there was almost universal condemnation of Elizabeth Taylor and Eddie Fisher." Not so amazing when you consider that, in this particular civilization, what has been aptly termed the Greatest Story Ever Told has been ingested right along with mother's milk for the better part of two thousand years—an annual drama of triumph (Palm Sunday), then suffering and torment (Crucifixion), then renewed triumph (Resurrection). Elizabeth had run the full cycle, and shortly would be going through it again. "I've been through it all," she would later observe. "I'm Mother Courage. I'll be dragging my sable coat behind me into old age." Furthermore, the line was notoriously razor-thin between hate and love, and one could change to the other in the twinkling of an eye. And had.

Inside the Santa Monica Civic, as the list of nominees for Best Actress was read, Elizabeth turned to Eddie and whispered, "I know I'm not going to get it." At the reading of her name as winner, Elizabeth's hands flew up to her face and she gasped, "I don't believe it!" Whereupon Eddie Fisher assisted his wife, her left leg still heavily bandaged, on the slow walk down the aisle and up to the podium amid a thunderous ovation which shook the hall for minutes and no one who heard it will ever forget it. She who had been reviled, despised, maligned, rejected was once again Undoubted Queen. Among the legions of loyal subjects applauding vociferously in that auditorium were several erstwhile friends who had been permanently unavailable when she called—or whose agendas had been unbelievably crowded when she wanted to see them—or who had cut her publicly, face-to-face and in print. Rejoicing right along with them were several millions of TV watchers, their rocks miraculously transformed into roses.

At the Academy Awards Ball afterward, Elizabeth called that trek to the podium "the most walking I've done since I left the London Clinic," and then uttered her only positive public words about *Butterfield 8:* "I worked very hard on it." Shirley MacLaine later reportedly muttered, "I was beaten by a tracheotomy." Elizabeth agreed with her. "I knew my performance had not deserved it," she wrote. "It was a sympathy award." After four nominations it was nice to have, however, and there was no thought of giving it back. "I waited for that Oscar for a long time." Miss MacLaine inherited *Two for the Seesaw* and *Irma La Douce* as a result of Elizabeth's inability to do either, so that was some compensation.

That last summer prior to the resumption of *Cleopatra* was an oasis of peace and contentment, a freedom from problems and hassles the like of which Elizabeth had not known for three years, and she luxuriated in it. "I'm not thinking about anything," she told one interviewer. "I'm at peace with the world." Of the fair-weather friends who had made themselves so scarce when the big storm blew up, she remarked, "I understood how they felt. They were afraid to get in the middle. Public opinion was very strong and it was not popular to be on our side. They were not directly unfriendly—they just backed away." Nevertheless, "To back away is just hypocritical and I don't consider these kind of people friends."

Professionally she was at the very top. Privately she would waken in the mornings and invariably yell for the children. Later, as often as not, the four of them would settle on the floor for a session of drawing together. Or they'd get restless and go into a wild rough-and-tumble all over the place. Or they'd all take out after the five Yorkshire terriers, two cats, and a St. Bernard who also inhabited the house.

"She blossoms in the company of children and animals," Eddie Fisher noted, possibly because she felt at her most free, because Elizabeth Taylor, Public Property, could be most completely forgotten. Irene Sharaff made the same observation when she saluted "a quality of femininity that, at its best, is intuition keen, direct, sympathetic, and absolutely real. Evident at diverse moments, it is, of course, very difficult to put into words. It is there, though, when she is playing with children and animals."

With Eddie she could often be found at the beach. Both were sun worshipers. Both loved to laze on the beach or to take long walks on it, or to swim, water-ski or go deep-sea diving. Much of the time Elizabeth spent in the favored pastime of reading—bestsellers, historicals, plays, and the scripts and film treatments that came to her in a never-ending flow from hopeful producers. Socially she divided her time between glamorous full-dress appearances at restaurants and clubs, or at dinner parties at the homes of close friends. These contrasted with easy times at home in un-madeup, barefoot comfort when the chief item on the dinner menu might be chili or pizza.

The quality in his wife which Eddie Fisher prized most highly was a new-found interest and absorption in the world around her which sparked a continuous excitement. "Being married to her is like having a rainbow in my living room," he rhapsodized joyously. "She is, above all, alive. She is curious, imaginative, quick-witted. Everything interests her. 'Why did that happen?' 'Why did he say that?' 'Why do people feel that way?'" The brush with death had raised her sensory capabilities to a level previously unknown. "I once thought acting was a hobby and a chore. It was chic to be bored," she told an interviewer. "Now I think it's a waste of time to be bored. It's a *sin* to be bored."

Along with the new vitality came a new freedom in talking about herself. "I am an impetuous person," she observed. "I very rarely count to ten. It's something I'm trying to change—to control my temper." Again: "My toughest role is trying to grow up." Her interviews of this period give the picture of a consummate professional. She had learned to deal with her day dreaming, her unpunctuality, her genuine loathing of formal portrait sittings and of costume fittings. Once having committed herself, she met her professional obligations with the proficiency and dispatch developed from a lifetime of experience. When she got there, she was ready to go and knew exactly what was expected, whether posing or giving an interview. An interview would be direct, unhesitating, with no minced words, no weighed words, or whatever. This same direct approach was always to be seen before the cameras.

"She does turn it on with a no-nonsense air when those cameras go," reported the *Cleopatra* flacks, otherwise no great admirers of Elizabeth Taylor. "She has an amazing quickness for feeling her way deeply into a role, and into the meaning of each scene," Joe Mankiewicz observed. "There is no groping or stumbling, none of the unpreparedness of the trumped-up star." To which he also added, "Elizabeth's personal life is almost completely guided by emotional motivation. She's also at her best when she plays something with emotional rather than cerebral approach."

Therein lay the rub. People who dealt with her professionally could become mightily exasperated, and p.r. people in particular could go right up the wall, at the amount of time she would frequently require to make a firm commitment. Many charged it off to arrogance or temperament. But as a person who operated almost exclusively on a feeling, intuitive level, she required (and requires) plenty of room and time to sort things out and to examine professional propositions from all angles—to let them lie and come back to them with fresh approaches—and she would not (and will not) be crowded. Because once she had made a commitment, her word was her bond, and she despised to break it.

How had she successfully resisted the enormous pressures which would have allowed the public Elizabeth Taylor to overwhelm her?

"It's up to you, yourself, to guard your own privacy, whoever you are. You can't always be attainable to people or you have no life of your own. Most of the time people are good-natured and friendly—and they understand this about me. They mean well." She had become a past mistress of the art of serene withdrawal amid a mass of confusion.

"She can be the center of attention in a crowd and remain unperturbed," Eddie Fisher commented. "There are so many times when people cluster around and she must withdraw inside her own thoughts, behind the privacy of those violet eyes, to go on with whatever she is doing. On a movie set, for example, she can have the hairdresser, the makeup man, and the wardrobe woman fussing with her all at once, and perhaps the director and the producer standing by, and other actors and actresses coming up to chat, and she seemingly will be listening to everybody, bestowing a smile here and a nod there, and yet I will know that she is really concentrating on her lines. Even when she is not working, there are always people tugging at her for attention, pleading for autographs, asking her for pictures, or telling her a story. Sometimes strangers reach out to touch her, as if to reassure themselves she is real."

As for himself, Eddie Fisher had good-naturedly resigned himself to some of the public fringe benefits of being husband to Elizabeth Taylor:

"Sooner or later, everyone asks me about my wife. Not only interviewers seeking some new tidbit, but strangers who stop me on the street in the most casual way. Questions about her are tossed at me wherever I go, in every context and in every situation. Everyone I meet—some indirectly, some shyly, some brazenly, some so offhandedly that I barely catch the drift—inquires about Elizabeth. They ask about her health. They send their love. They insist that I relay the most complicated messages. They offer detailed critiques of one of her pictures, or business tips, or technical medical advice. They have a daughter or a niece or a girl friend who looks like her. However we meet, whatever else they say to me, some reference is made to her. I wait for it. It has become a gambit of almost every conversation I have. If someone doesn't ask about her, I wonder what he has against me."

Together the Fishers gave three parties for the visiting Moiseyev Dance Company, and their guests' informal invitation to visit Russia became official when the U. S. State Department invited the Fishers to represent the United States at the upcoming Moscow Film Festival. Before they made the trip, Elizabeth accepted an invitation to appear at a banquet at the Beverly Hilton as guest of honor at a combined Cedars of Lebanon–Mt. Sinai fund-raising affair for a new multimillion-dollar medical center. She was asked to appear in her role as "a symbol of the miracle of modern medicine." Joe Mankiewicz helped her polish the remarks she would deliver to the assembled guests. On the night of July 9, Elizabeth took her place on the dais, directly next to Robert F. Kennedy, then Attorney General of the United States. Here is part of what she had to say:

"Dying, as I remember it, is many things—but most of all, it is wanting to live. Throughout many critical hours in the operating theater, it was as if every nerve, every muscle, as if my whole physical being were being strained to the last ounce of my strength, to the last gasp of my breath.

"Gradually and inevitably that last ounce was drawn, and there was no more breath. I remember I had focused desperately on the hospital light hanging directly above me. It had become something I needed almost fanatically, to continue to see, the vision of life itself. Slowly it faded and dimmed, like a well-done theatrical effect, to blackness. I have never known, nor do I think there can be, a greater loneliness.

"Then it happened.

"First there was an awareness of hands—how many, I could not tell. Pushing, pulling, pressing, lifting; large, rough hands and smaller, gentler ones, insistently manipulating my body as if to force it to respond.

"Then the voices from a great distance at first, but ever so slowly growing louder. Like the hands, some were gentle, some harsh; some pleaded with me; some shouted, cajoled, and commanded. They said I was to bring myself to cough . . . to move . . . to breathe . . . to look . . . to *live*.

"At that moment, my life was nothing more than those hands and those voices. But I was no longer alone.

"I coughed, I moved, I breathed, and I looked. The hanging lamp—the most beautiful light my world has ever known—began faintly to glow again."

The hushed audience who heard this testimony later came forward to pledge over seven million dollars toward the new medical center—a record amount for a Los Angeles charity function.

On July 11, Elizabeth was at the airport in New York, en route to Moscow, and was trapped by a friendly mob inside of her car for some seven minutes before the police finally got through and freed her. In Moscow, surprisingly, there was more of the same. She stepped outside of the Sovietskaya Hotel only to be engulfed by a hundred fervent Russian admirers, and speedily beat a retreat back into the lobby. Friendly Russian policemen then delivered a short lecture to the crowd, and when she re-emerged, she was allowed to go her way. "Four years ago I could walk down a street here and nobody recognized me," she remarked ruefully. "It was very quiet." On the prior trip with Mike Todd, Russians had frequently asked her interpreter, "What is she? A ballerina?" There were no queries like that on this trip. The first Elizabeth Taylor film had been shown in Moscow in

1960 (*Rhapsody*, of all things), and fans now trailed her everywhere.

A day after her arrival, a splendid reception was held at the Kremlin for the foreign representatives to the Moscow Film Festival. "Where is the American Delegation?" demanded an obviously nettled Minister of Culture Yekaterina Furtseva. Refusing to wait, she read the official speech of welcome to those assembled. Elizabeth then made a grand entrance an hour late and walked right into a fashion disaster. She was wearing a white lace cocktail dress from Dior, with a boat neckline and a wide, bell-shaped skirt. There stood Gina Lollobrigida in the identical dress. What's more, both women sported the same hairdo. Elizabeth was unperturbed. "I don't think Gina was amused but I was. Mine is the original." So it was. An Allentown, Pennsylvania, department store owner subsequently filed suit against Dior for selling Elizabeth a dress to which he thought he had purchased exclusive rights. The House of Dior then explained stiffly that Elizabeth's was indeed the original, Gina's was a copy by an unknown Italian designer, and that it is rare for a Paris house ever to sell exclusive rights to a model to one firm.

Fashion matters aside, Elizabeth attended the various screenings, left Russia publicly ruminating on the possibility of a return to do a remake of *Anna Karenina*, and subsequently entered Cedars of Lebanon for plastic surgery on her tracheotomy scar (which was removed but eventually reappeared. "There was a fifty-fifty chance that it would—and it did."). On the *Cleopatra* front, the summer of 1961 was mainly taken up with slotting the other principal actors prior to the resumption of shooting in September. After Trevor Howard proved unavailable, Rex Harrison was signed to play Julius Caesar.

"I took the part purely because Joe Mankiewicz was doing the film," he later commented. "I never saw a script beforehand or anything. I'd worked with Joe before and knew his tremendous talent and almost brutal refusal to be sidetracked from what he wants to achieve. There's only one other person I'd take on professional trust like that—Carol Reed."

The actor both Wanger and Mankiewicz very much wanted for Antony—Richard Burton—would have preferred to see a script, even a partial script, before he committed himself. And if he finally did, it would be over the adamant opposition of Spyros Skouras. "You can't understand a word he says," Skouras repeatedly asserted. (Skouras must have mixed Burton up with Eric Portman, presuming that Spyros Skouras ever heard of Eric Portman.) Skouras also had sour memories of the past five years, when a career brilliant with promise had unaccountably hit the skids. Prior to that, Richard Burton's climb to fame and prestige had been an almost-unbroken succession of triumphs.

He was born Richard Jenkins, Jr., on November 10, 1925, in Pontrhydyfen, South Wales—twelfth of thirteen children born to the rugged, sparse life of a Welsh mining family. As Elizabeth later wrote: "Richard got his education through the scholarships he won by intuition and drive and ambition and lust for learning and a great love for words. Without those he would be down in the mines. He never would have made it." His mother died when he was two and he was subsequently raised by a beloved elder sister, Cecilia. Along with the drive and ambition and the love of the cadences of Shakespeare and the Bible, he brought also from his childhood facial pockmarks from a bout with chicken pox.

At grammar school, teachers Meredith Jones and Philip Burton worked with him, forcing him to speak English, drilling him in Shakespearean soliloquies, enforcing intellectual discipline. Of his childhood and of the man whose name he would take for his own, Burton later commented succinctly, "I was chubby and short, spoke only Welsh, and had pockmarks on my face. Mr. Burton took me and made something from nothing."

Burton recently reminisced further about the two fathers in his early life.

"My real father gave me his love for beer. He was a man of extraordinary eloquence, tremendous passion, great violence. I was greatly in awe of him. He could pick you up with one hand by the seat of your pants. My adopted father is the exact opposite. A pedant, a scholar, meticulous in his speech, not given readily to passion. I'm still frightened of him. He still corrects my grammar."

Philip Burton's initial reaction to Burton's earliest expression of his acting ambitions was indeed meticulous and right to the point.

"It's impossible. You're too short and your voice is too high-pitched."

Burton privately reflected that two of his childhood idols, James Cagney and Edward G. Robinson, "were too short to cut cabbage"—so height didn't seem insurmountable. And the voice? "To get my voice deeper I went and shouted on Welsh mountaintops to the perfect audience . . . sheep. No response of any kind."

Finally convinced, Philip Burton reputedly advised him with regard to the acting career, "Stay quiet, speak clearly, and reduce everything to absolute simplicity."

The next surrogate father was author-playwright-actor-director Emlyn Williams, who cast him for a small part in a provincial production of Williams' *The Druid's Rest*. Thereafter he went to Oxford on scholarship for a year, and then saw service with the RAF from 1945 to 1947. In 1948 he made *The Last Days of Dolwyn*, the first of four unremarkable films on an initial contract with Alexander Korda of a hundred pounds a week.

The memorable thing about *Dolwyn* was that, on it, he met fledgling actress Sybil Williams, who became his wife in February 1949. Subsequently they had two daughters, Kate and Jessica. Of Sybil, Burton's sister Cecilia once commented, "She is the most amazing girl. From the very beginning it never mattered to her what Richard did, or wanted to do—she would always say all right. Rich would leave for somewhere in the morning and say he'd be home for lunch. Perhaps he wouldn't come home till late that evening. And Sybil would never chide him, the way almost any other wife would do. She understood him from the beginning. She loved him. I couldn't have been happier when they married. Or chosen a better girl for him." And one of Burton's cousins saluted Sybil as "a girl in a million."

Sybil's husband concentrated his professional energies in the theater, in appearances in both the London and New York productions of *The Lady's Not for Burning* (with Gielgud), other Christopher Fry plays (*Boy With a Cart* and *A Phoenix Too Frequent*), as Prince Hal in the 1951 Stratford production of *Henry IV*, in London in *Montserrat*, and on Broadway in Anouilh's *Legend of Lovers* (which Burton called "A Streetcar Named McGuire," in sardonic tribute to costar Dorothy McGuire).

Along with the great influences of Philip Burton and Emlyn Williams, another was now added.

"The third and perhaps most profound was Sir John Gielgud, with whom I worked for many years," Burton commented recently. "His influence on me was so profound that I had a devil of a job getting rid of his particular way of speaking verse. To this day I still do gestures which are strictly Sir John Gielgud's."

He was doing a full assortment of them during the Stratford *Henry IV*, including what he deemed a particularly dramatic way of extending his hand. Fellow actor Alan Badel repeatedly taunted him about it. "You're doing a John Gielgud again." Burton denied it. So the next time he stuck his hand out, Badel plunked a huge roll of sausage into it. That cured him of *that* one.

It was also during the Stratford *Henry* that Burton underwent an experience so mortifying it remains in a class by itself to this day. It is intimately bound up with Burton's oft-proclaimed role as "professional Welshman."

Most Americans refer to what lies northwest of the European continent as either "England" or "Ireland" and let it go at that. Those sensible to the national feelings of others (a minority) are indeed aware that there is an entity entitled The United Kingdom of Great Britain and Northern Ireland, and that its constituent parts are England, Scotland, and Northern Ireland. A tinier minority is also aware that there is a fourth constituency and its name is Wales. If this tiny minority has in any way been enlarged during the last twenty years, no man living has done greater service for the cause than Richard Burton.

Even as England has its patron saint, George—he of the dragon, and Scotland has St. Andrew—he of the X-shaped cross, and Ireland has St. Patrick—he of the snakes, so Wales has its patron saint. His name is David, he of the fiery Welsh spirit, brother to the great rebel Llewellyn, and captured, hanged, drawn and quartered during the English conquest of 1282. St. David's Day is celebrated on March 1, and so many producers, directors, and what-have-you have been reduced to quivering wrecks in the impossible task of attempting to get a certain blissfully bombed actor to function professionally that Burton now has a standard clause in all of his contracts. Come earth-quake, fire, flood, imminent corporate catastrophe or visits by royalty to the set—he will *not* work on St. David's Day. Alas, in 1951 it was not so.

In this particular *Henry*, Burton was Prince Hal to the Hotspur of Michael Redgrave and the Falstaff of Anthony Quayle. As Hal, Burton's costume was chain-mail-and-armor. "It took thirty minutes to get into it and a good ten minutes to get out of it." Promptly on this particular St. David's Day, "I be-gan drinking one minute after midnight—and drank steadily all day. Boilermakers. By the time I got to the show that night, I was reasonably painless, shall we say." So painless that he neglected to relieve himself before becoming inextricably encased in all that metallic drag of Prince Hal.

"Toward the end of the play, which lasted three and a quarter hours, it began to get to me. If you can imagine Shakespeare spoken by a man with his legs tightly closed, speaking immortal speeches with the veins standing out on his forehead, and all the while just hoping and praying for that curtain to come down." Hal and Hotspur meet and fight toward the end of the play. "It was arranged in this production that Michael was descending a flight of stairs on one side of the stage while I was ascending another on the other side. At the moment of meeting, I used to do what I thought was a slow dramatic turn. That night—as I turned—Noah's Ark could have floated."

"I stared at Michael for an agonized ten seconds, but fortunately chain mail is gray so it didn't show. Too much. I then went after Michael with such ferocity that my sword snapped in half. So all I had were two little daggers. I didn't know what to do—I was absolutely bereft of imagination. So I picked him up on my shoulder (he weighed at least forty pounds more than I did) and in my frantic shame I threw him across the stage. He, of course, had no idea what was happening."

Afterward Burton went round to Redgrave to apologize and explain. Sir Michael was unperturbed. "Oh, was that it? Oh. I *thought* you were sweating rather more than usual."

Such an incident was the vivid exception in a steadily improving spate of high-caliber work which prompted one critic to hail him as "one of the half-dozen great actors in the English-speaking world." "Congratulations!" promptly wired Laurence Olivier brightly. "Who are the other five?" This rising acclaim induced 20th Century-Fox to offer him a contract for three films at $50,000 per. No sooner had he signed it than Metro offered him Mark Antony in the upcoming *Julius Caesar*, which he had regretfully to refuse. Otherwise he would have played Antony for Joe Mankiewicz ten years earlier.

In Hollywood, Fox first put him into *My Cousin Rachel*, a baffling is-or-is-not-this-woman-a-wicked-poisoner melodrama from the pen of Daphne du Maurier in which, one critic noted, "he was chiefly notable for kissing Olivia de Havilland for a gross of ten minutes." He did better than that, picking up various awards from *Look, Photoplay*, the Foreign Press, and the first of six Oscar nominations to date. Next came the news that it would not be Gregory Peck or Tyrone Power or Laurence Olivier or anyone else for Marcellus in *The Robe*; it would be Richard Burton. After years of aborted attempts, Lloyd C. Douglas' Biblical bestseller was finally to be brought to the screen, and it was to be a new screen called CinemaScope. At that point the publicity mills began churning out the items about the latest comet over Hollywood.

"Britain's Brando" and "The Poor Man's Olivier" were frequent press tags for Burton. *Life* hailed him as "the most promising young classical actor alive today," the *Saturday Evening Post* crowned him the "Angriest Star in Hollywood," and everyone chimed right in with something. Raved *Robe* director Henry

Koster, "His is one of the few talents that can vibrate and glow. He can thrill an audience." A female critic saluted his "combination of sex and poetry," and *Robe* costar Jean Simmons found him "an enviable cross between Groucho Marx and John Barrymore." Louella Parsons called him "one of the most delightful and unaffected actors ever to come to our town," and Hedda Hopper picked him as one of the "New Stars of 1953."* In tribute to his marked success with the distaff side of the population, *Robe* producer Frank Ross called him "a born male coquette."

Socially he roared through Hollywood like a whirling dervish, apparently the *sine qua non* of a successful party. He was charming and irrepressible. At one party, he squeezed Garbo's knee (with permission). At another, he and Humphrey Bogart got into a hassle over the latter's acting ability (a touchy subject) and Bogart rushed out of the room, grabbed his Oscar, rushed back in, and plunked it on the table to settle the argument. "Burton wants to try everything, do everything, all at the same time," observed one Hollywood hostess. "I wonder what won't bore him ten years from now." Said another, "It is hard for him to open a door, pour a drink or blow his nose without making a small dramatic scene of it. The world is literally a first act for Burton." He laughingly told one interviewer, "I'd rather be a fifth Marx Brother than play *Hamlet*." To another he asserted ringingly, "By heaven, I'm going to be the greatest actor, or what's the point of acting?" He was—in Katharine Hepburn's pithy New England phrase—"full of beans."

Personally Burton thought the character of Marcellus something of an ass, but his performance in *The Robe* brought him another Oscar nomination. That, coupled with excellent work in *The Desert Rats*, prompted Zanuck to offer him a $1 million contract—ten films in ten years at $100,000 per. By then Richard Burton was fed up with film froufrou and ready to get back to serious work. He rejected the offer, returned to England and the Old Vic, at $140 per week, for the sterling 1954 season of *Hamlet, King John, Coriolanus,* and *The Tempest*. From this pinnacle of achievement, nothing went right thereafter for six long years.

He returned to Hollywood in 1955 to play Edwin Booth in *Prince of Players*, roundly slammed as "the first flop in Cinema-

* The others were Joanne Gilbert, Rosemary Clooney, Roberta Haynes, Jeffrey Hunter, Robert Wagner, Mari Blanchard, Suzan Ball, Keith Andes, Zsa Zsa Gabor, Nanette Fabray, Barbara Rush, Vic Damone, Phyllis Kirk, Robert Horton, and George Winslow. *Sic transit gloria mundi.*

Scope," and to suffer as the Hindu physician in Fox's turgid *Rains Came* remake called *The Rains of Ranchipur*. Nineteen fifty-six's *Alexander the Great* was a literate spectacle with excellent work by Burton in the title role, Fredric March and Danielle Darrieux as Alexander's royal parents, and Claire Bloom as his bride. The public disdained it. Critics didn't much like him in *Othello* at the Vic that year, and he flopped on Broadway, along with Helen Hayes and Susan Strasberg, in *Time Remembered*. Thereafter Burton rummaged at the bottom of the cinema barrel in four bombs: *Sea Wife, Bitter Victory, The Bramble Bush, Ice Palace. Bramble Bush* producer Milton Sperling reportedly stated, "Richard was doing my picture for money, quite deliberately, and he let me know it." As, indeed, why else would he have done it? Or any of the rest of that rubbish?

That he had not totally lost his grip, and that he could still project his talent with power and precision, was amply proven in 1959 with the film version of *Look Back in Anger*, which contains to this day some of the best work he has yet done on the screen. As Osborne's Jimmy Porter, Burton brought a superior intelligence and compassion to the role, over and above all the shouting and invective, which had been sorely lacking in various stage versions. Mary Ure, Claire Bloom, and Edith Evans all helped him to make it first-class, but—again—the public didn't want it. When he finally left Hollywood after *Ice Palace*, the days of puffy publicity pieces, amusing social notes, and all the rest of it were long gone. The only film work he got was as English narrator of the Czech-made *Midsummer Night's Dream*. As far as Hollywood was concerned, his was a star that had blazed brightly but briefly, and it was good riddance. "He's poison!" David Selznick was told when he vainly sought him for *Tender Is the Night*.

Then, in one of those turnabouts that an actor can ponder until it drives him up the wall and to no avail, the long drought miraculously ended. Churchill had personally selected Richard Burton to be his voice as narrator of the *Finest Hour* TV series hit, and Burton got his proper share of the acclaim. Alan Jay Lerner and Frederick Loewe engaged him to play King Arthur in *Camelot* on Broadway. Critics ran up one side of it and down the other and unanimously concluded that two things were far better than the play. The sumptuous settings and costumes were among the most eye-popping Broadway had ever seen, and Richard Burton was giving far and away the best performance to be seen in New York that year.

The renewed prominence brought him a deluge of offers.

H. G. Clouzot wanted to costar him with Simone Signoret. There
was an offer to appear with Audrey Hepburn in *In the Cool of
the Day*, with John Huston directing. (Peter Finch and Jane
Fonda later did it, with Robert Stevens directing.) Burton and
director Robert Siodmak formed Ancona Films for independent
production of *The Beach of Falesa*, adapted by Dylan Thomas
from Robert Louis Stevenson, plus five other properties (one of
which, *Woman of Straw*, came to the screen with Sean Connery
in Burton's proposed role). A plan misfired to get Burton time
off from *Camelot* to do *The Power and the Glory* on TV with
Olivier, but there were tentative plans for 1964, when a Welsh
National Theater in Cardiff would open with *Othello*, with
Olivier as Othello and Burton as Iago. Finally, there was *Cleopatra*.

Wanger and Mankiewicz ultimately wore down the obdurate
Skouras, and Burton signed on as Mark Antony—not, however,
before a reported faceoff in which Skouras rasped, "No one will
be able to understand you," and Burton shot back, "Like I can't
you?" Fox paid $50,000 to get him out of *Camelot*, and thereafter
he was to be paid $250,000 for three months, plus allowance for
overtime. "I think I have as many costume changes as Elizabeth,"
he quipped when he signed the contract. "I hope she doesn't
mind."

Elizabeth was looking forward to resumption of the revised
Cleopatra. "I hate most historical-period films, with their wooden-
figure characters and their awful dialogue," she remarked. "If
we can capture, in a realistic and human way, the three characters of Cleopatra, Mark Antony, and Julius Caesar—then we'll
have an interesting picture.

A few years later Richard Burton would write a short story
about a childhood Christmas in Wales and about the sister who
raised him.

"When my mother died, she, my sister, had become my
mother and more mother to me than any mother could ever have
been. I was immensely proud of her. She was innocent and
guileless and infinitely protectable. She was naïve to the point of
saintliness and wept a lot at the misery of others. She felt all
tragedies except her own. I knew that I had a bounden duty to
protect her above all other creatures. It wasn't until thirty years
later, when I saw her in another woman, that I realized I had
been searching for her all my life."

His search was about to end.

"I really believe that whole lives can have turning points,"

Elizabeth would also write. "When I came to, that last time (in the London Clinic), it was like being given sight, hearing, touch, sense of color. Like I was, I don't know, twenty-nine years old, but had just come out of my own womb. I knew that I wanted more in my life than what I had." Which fit neatly with an observation of Walter Wanger's: "As for Elizabeth: When the day comes that she knows what she really wants from life, she will—I am sure—get it."

She knew that she wanted more than she had. Ultimately she would learn what it was, and ultimately she would get it. Like all things of inestimable worth, she would have to pay fully for it. The pains of early divorce, of young widowhood, of scandal, of physical agony were mere preparation for the fierce fires— and the great joy—which awaited her.

In September 1961, *Cleopatra* resumed shooting in Rome.

PART III

SUPERSTAR
Cleopatra and Le Scandale

1961-1964

If you can keep your head when all about you
Are losing theirs and blaming it on you . . .
                                    —*Rudyard Kipling*

O, Whither hast thou led me, Egypt?
                                    —*William Shakespeare*

Good Lord, the reputations we had! I mean, I was a
bestial wife stealer, and Elizabeth was a scheming
home breaker. You'd think we were out to destroy
Western civilization or something.
                                    —*Richard Burton*

"Of course most of the literature on love is complete nonsense," Richard Burton once remarked. "Those enormous, writhing love affairs that topple kingdoms and transform lives hardly ever happen." One was about to happen to him and it would shake him to his foundations. "A man who comes through that ordeal of fire in Rome must emerge a different or a better man," was his subsequent verdict. Would he do it all over again? "I sometimes wonder if I *could* go through it all again. I would have to—every pain, agony, and torment of every moment. There was no choice then and there would be no choice now."

Elizabeth agrees.

"Yes, I'd do it all over again, with no provisions made beforehand as to what would happen to me. You can't make provisions in life." As for *Cleopatra*, "It was a little like damnation to everybody. Everything was such a nightmare that it is difficult even to know where to start."

June 30, 1961, would be as good a place as any. On that date Fox made another in the long chain of decisions which led to disaster. In the spring, Spyros Skouras had hit the roof when informed by Elizabeth's doctors that a June start-date was a complete impossibility. Subsequently it was decided to shoot all of her necessary interior scenes in Italy in September, all of her exterior scenes in Egypt in October, and to return her for rest in California, there to be joined by the remainder of the cast and crew for shooting of scenes in duplicate interiors on the Fox lot in the winter. That would enable Skouras to have the film ready for what he was now certain would be a life-or-death confrontation with management in the spring. On June 30 the Board of Directors killed that plan. The space not taken up by television on the Fox lot was needed for George Stevens' upcoming production of *The Greatest Story Ever Told*. All of *Cleopatra* must go in Italy, starting in September. Ironically, in September the Board killed *Greatest Story* (sending Stevens over to United Artists to make it), and in the following January most of the TV was axed as well. They were thus to have overhead on an almost-empty studio in Hollywood and the burgeoning costs at Cinecittà as well. This sorry situation would not hit them in full till the spring of 1962, when everything seemed to explode at once.

On September 1, Elizabeth and Eddie arrived in Rome and took up residence in the Villa Pappa, a beautiful fourteen-room mansion set in the middle of a small park and complete with gardens, tennis court, and swimming pool. It adjoined the Moroccan Embassy on the old Via Appia, and was a few minutes' drive from Cinecittà. It would be the $3,000-per-month home to Elizabeth, Eddie, Michael Jr., Christopher, Liza, Miss Warme (the children's nanny), Bill Jones (a former actor in charge of wardrobe), plus seven animals: a St. Bernard (Eddie's), a collie, three small terriers, and two Siamese cats. An initial guest was Dr. Rex Kennamer, who accompanied Elizabeth to Rome for six weeks (at $25,000 plus expenses). The household staff consisted of a butler, three manservants, four maids, a chef, a kitchen boy, a laundry woman, and a woman who came in part-time four days a week to press the clothes. Additionally there were Lucky, Elizabeth's chauffeur who drove her in the Cadillac, and Carlo, Eddie's chauffeur who looked after Eddie's green Rolls-Royce (a present from Elizabeth). Two other cars stood ready for the servants to use on shopping trips to Rome.

All of this prompted *Life* to announce that "the beautiful lady of tumult" had ensconced herself in a "splendid villa on the Appian Way." Elizabeth has other memories of it. "God, that was a filthy house!" she wrote. "Finally I decided I'd better go to the pantry myself and duel with the rats. One day the sewer erupted and the whole kitchen was floating in sewage." Nevertheless it had a large living room, smaller salon, and dining room for party purposes; was certainly roomy enough for the children and animals; and seemed to afford a necessary measure of privacy (at first). Elizabeth ordered a nylon cover put over the pool when it was not in use to prevent the terriers from falling into it. And she had the carpet in the master bedroom torn up and replaced with three-inch sheepskin shag, on the sound theory that ordinary carpet was murder on bare feet and on the knees when you wanted to roughhouse with your children and/or animals.

Over at Cinecittà everything was being done to assure that the health and happiness of the star took top priority. Her script was specially bound in Moroccan leather. Her chair on the set was of California redwood and Russian leather, specially handcrafted in Rome as a gift from Joe Mankiewicz. For a dressing room, she had a five-room building all to herself. It was nicknamed the "Casa Taylor" and Elizabeth was slightly nonplussed at first sight of it. "It's a little bit much, isn't it?"

Cesare Danova, who played Apollodorus, eventually found all the extravagant attention slightly nauseating. "Somebody was always running over to her to ask, 'How are you darling?' 'Are you all right darling?' 'Can I get you anything darling?' It was a bit sickening." He admitted that Fox's concern was partially justified, in view of all that had gone before, but nonetheless sickening. "If Elizabeth coughs, Fox gets pneumonia," was one description of the situation. Had the fortunes of *Cleopatra* rested solely on the care of Elizabeth, all might have been well. But they constantly bumped up against, and eventually foundered on, the one reef impossible to negotiate: the attempt to do a film of this magnitude with inadequate preparation. And things began to go awry even before the cameras turned.

Italy is the happy home of something called *la mano morta*, in which a lifeless hand falls innocently in the area of a breast or a thigh. If no resistance is offered, the hand undergoes instant resurrection, and its object experiences something else. The ladies playing Cleopatra's slaves and handmaidens complained that they were encountering too many happy hands and on September 12 went on strike against the skimpiness of their costumes. An anti-pinch patrol (at $65 per man per day) settled that. Then, under the headline AMERICAN RACISM FOR CLEOPATRA, Italy's Communist Party newspaper *L'Unità* charged that *Cleo* had been turned into an "Italian Little Rock" because white and black dancers were arriving in separate buses and were supposedly segregated on the set. A letter jointly signed by all the dancers denied it.

Then came the first in what is undoubtedly the greatest collection of lawsuits ever filed in connection with one film in all motion picture history. Lionel Santi's film company sued claiming "notable damages" because their services were not being utilized as allegedly promised when Fox bought up Santi's *Cleopatra* in 1959. A Rome real estate agency slapped an $1,800 suit on Elizabeth, claiming it was the commission she owed them for obtaining her the villa. An Italian circus owner delivered un-trained elephants for use in the Entrance into Rome scene, and during rehearsals they ran wild and he and they were ordered off the set. He sued for $100,000 for slander. That managed to stop Spyros Skouras in mid-scream during the monthly budget harangue. "How," he wondered aloud, "do you slander an elephant?"

Elsewhere on the production front things were in a state of frustration and chaos. The set design for *Cleopatra* eventually called for forty-seven interiors and thirty-two exteriors. By late September, exactly one was ready. A mysterious act of stupidity or sabotage left several thousand costumes ripped in the seams, in addition to which all of Rex Harrison's wardrobe had to be refitted and remade. Original plans called for an exact reconstruction of the Roman Forum on twelve acres at Cinecittà. Then it was found that the original was cluttered with too many buildings for purposes of easy access by the Todd-AO cameras. So a replica was designed based on ten of the original buildings plus others which met technical requirements and they somehow wound up with a Forum larger than the original. "It's too hard to fill," grumbled Mankiewicz. Nor was it to be anywhere near completion when needed, necessitating the shooting of the most spectacular scene in screen history—Cleopatra's entry into Rome —in two hunks six months apart, at a total cost of $250,000. Adding to the headaches was the other major set—twenty acres of Alexandrian palaces which went up on Prince Borghese's private beach at Anzio (at a rental of $150,000). The beach turned out to be still mined from all of that unpleasantness during World War II, and was also immediately adjacent to the NATO firing range.

About all this Elizabeth commented, "It's almost like a bowl of rice that never empties. I see the same things happening all over again. I hear about the same problems and see the same mistakes being made, and yet it's a year later. I thought at first I was on the wrong reel of film that had somehow got all mixed up."

Already Walter Wanger was on a regimen in which nurses gave him blood tests, protein tests, checked his cholesterol, and adjusted his schedule of various medications. Mankiewicz likewise took medications with his meals and again at night before he began to write. He had embarked on a year-long ordeal that would see him through a bad cold, strep throat, nervous exhaustion, and ultimate public humiliation, all of which could have physically or mentally destroyed a man of insufficient stamina. Nor could a lesser talent have even begun to cope with all of the pressure. They were initially on a six-day week in Italy, and Mankiewicz would spend his days shooting, and his nights and Sundays in a frenzied round of writing to keep the production moving. He went out to dinner on an average of once a month, and never on Sundays. Ultimately he took to wearing white gloves, while writing, to preserve what were left of his cuticles. On the set one day, Elizabeth spied him gnawing away. "Joe, don't bite your fingernails," she admonished him. "I'm not," Mankiewicz replied. "I'm biting my knuckles. I finished the fingernails months ago." But Skouras had decreed that *Cleopatra* must start in September, and on September 25, ready or not, it rolled.

Elizabeth was on set fifteen minutes early, pleasantly surprising everybody, doing her best to get the resumption of *Cleopatra* off on the right foot. The right foot, however, knew not what the left foot was doing, as it became clear later in the afternoon. A party of thirteen V.I.P.'s—eleven U. S. Congressmen, a Clerk of the House, and a Massachusetts Judge—were to be seen wandering uncertainly around Cinecittà holding "Press Release #1." It read: "On their tour of the Forum set the group was accompanied by Miss Taylor, who left the shooting set for the specific purpose of greeting them." Enter Walter Wanger. "Miss Taylor is on the set and cannot leave. We are three hours behind with filming. She sends her apologies." Enter Eddie Fisher, breathing fire. "My wife knew nothing about this. She was not even told there would be visitors or that she was to be here to meet them." Exit ten V.I.P.'s, one snorting about "pretty stupid public relations," to which another added, "That's surely an understatement. I don't know what her trouble is. Maybe she thinks she really won that Oscar that was given to her out of sympathy." The three Congressmen who elected to wait four hours finally got together with Elizabeth in the "Casa Taylor," where one of them sidled up to her and sniggered, "I Came, I Saw, I Conquered." Which possibly made some long-suffering Latin teacher back in P.S. 84 happy, but not the U.S. press. Snapped one editorial: "Congressmen, like movie stars, have a public image. Those in Rome behaved like stagestruck schoolboys." A verdict on the first day's shooting might thus be a standard line from all Hollywood spectacles since time immemorial. "The omens are not favorable, my queen."

Moronic politicians and inadequate preparation aside, what really hurt in the fall of 1971 was the foul weather. In Italy the good weather traditionally comes between April and September. Fox gambled and lost. Big. It rained steadily for the first eight days of October and just when beautiful weather threatened to become permanent, the end of the month was rained out as well. In November wind and rain combined for a veritable tempest, apparently the first recorded tempest in the history of Rome, which was scant consolation to anybody. On one of these days Mankiewicz managed to pack ten thousand into that oversized forum, and a wind promptly arose and took off every unanchored object in sight. The day's shooting was canceled—at a cost of $75,000. Wanger estimated the daily overhead at $67,000, most of which was sheer loss on days of no shooting. There were plenty of those during the fall and Elizabeth was responsible for none of them.

Now visibly alarmed at what looked like history grimly repeating itself, Skouras mused aloud about slicing the film in half, settling for *Caesar and Cleopatra* now, and doing *Antony and Cleopatra* sometime in the distant future, that is, never. Having rejected several good offers to come to Rome and be on hand for bits and pieces until his principal work began in January, Richard Burton did not take kindly to that suggestion. "I will sue you until you are puce," he informed Skouras. End of suggestion.

The chief man in Elizabeth's professional life during the fall was Rex Harrison, and he steered determinedly through successive blasts of wind, rain, scandal, front-office hysterics, changes of script, and a nasty faceoff with the Italian Government with single-minded dedication to his work. Harrison later reflected that Henry Higgins had certainly been his most rewarding part from a career standpoint, but Julius Caesar was far and away his most enjoyable challenge. So much so that he still harbors an ambition to do Shaw's *Caesar and Cleopatra*. Along with his dedication to the part came a sense of personal and professional protection second to none.

Yes, he understood that the film was called *Cleopatra* and that it had been conceived as a star vehicle for Miss Elizabeth Taylor, a lady for whom he had a great deal of respect. "Elizabeth is an extremely good screen artist," he commented. "She has an innate talent for it. She has great beauty and a quality of stillness which is very wonderful on the screen. She's immensely relaxed—has a natural gift for it." Having done copious research on Caesar, Harrison's respect for Elizabeth did not extend to a willingness to see historical veracity go down the tubes for the sake of still another puffy Hollywood marshmallow about an ancient sex siren. Wanger and Mankiewicz were generally in accord with his view.

Wanger he checked out over luncheon. With Mankiewicz there was one area of dissent. "I differed with him on only one aspect. I could never quite believe that Caesar, with all the political and military problems that were on his mind at the time, was so absolutely obsessed with Cleopatra. It seems against his character. So I resisted as much as possible the pressure to play it that way."

Harrison had not only to keep a razor eye on what was happening before the cameras but behind them as well. When the various demands of Italian technicians got too heavy, he would disperse them with imperious blurts of "Stupido," "Idioto," etc. Fox's idea of little economies called for more stringent measures, and Harrison was certainly equal to the occasion.

In December the production manager changed Harrison's dressing-room trailer, stopped the rental on his Cadillac and the payment to his chauffeur for good measure. Harrison promptly arrived on the set in the morning and refused to go into costume until a production meeting was held. "I treat my servants better than I am about to treat you," he informed the startled production manager. Then he laced him out in lavender—the pungent Olde Englishe variety—"the worst lacing I ever heard," Wanger noted. According to Elizabeth, a more printable part of the tirade went as follows: "I want my Cadillac and I want it now! And I do not appear on the set until my Cadillac is back! And what's more, I understand that Elizabeth Taylor's chauffeur is being paid far more than my chauffeur. I insist that my chauffeur get the same pay as Elizabeth Taylor's chauffeur. Why the hell should Elizabeth Taylor's chauffeur get more than my chauffeur just because she has a bigger chest!"

Matters were adjusted to Mr. Harrison's satisfaction, and when he eventually arrived in costume on set, he got an ovation. Already deepening resentment of the incessant front-office pressures had divided the production into "them" and "us." Mankiewicz recollected, "All of us were occupied in the making of a serious film. There were no arguments and no tensions among us there on the set." Off the set in that fall of 1961 Elizabeth was slowly undergoing a change which would eventually erupt into full-blown metamorphosis.

At the villa her life initially assumed a set routine of 6 A.M. awakening, then a bath and breakfast, then off to Cinecittà and into Wardrobe and Makeup—a two-hour-plus session in the latter, since Elizabeth had devised her own elaborate eye makeup for Cleopatra—"more accentuated, more colorful, more fantasy-like, to give a catlike look." It chiefly involved the careful application of spangles and gold paint to her upper eyelashes. After the day's shooting, it was home to visit with the children, to bathe, to eat, and to go promptly to bed at nine. The servants called this "The Nine O'Clock Retreat," and it was kept on all but a rare social occasion.

In September she had gone out to receive an award called the Silver Mask from the Italian film industry for her work in *Suddenly Last Summer*. Two thousand adoring Italians mobbed the theater to the point where Elizabeth was thrust into the first vacant car on the street until her own could be driven up to get her safely out of there. In October she attended a party at the Grand Hotel thrown by Kirk Douglas in honor of the one-year anniversary of *Spartacus*. There, while doing a Rhumba with Joe Mankiewicz, she ignited some loose matches on the floor and the ostrich-feathered fringe of her gown began to blaze. A quick-thinking musician jumped from the bandstand and beat out the flames with his bare hands. These occasions were the vivid exceptions to a regimen strictly enforced by her husband.

At this point, if Elizabeth's career were acting, Eddie Fisher's career could be said to be exclusively Elizabeth—literally and financially, since he had foregone a Waldorf engagement to go on the Fox payroll at $1,500 per week. This was Fox's additional insurance that their star could go the distance without any further mishap. Eddie counted the cigarettes she smoked, measured the wine she drank, watched her diet, saw that her food was served hot, took the children out to play, and invariably went to bed at nine to make sure she was up at six. He hovered and fussed over her from one end of the day to the other, and was effusively affectionate in public. "I'm married to a woman who has to be loved and cared for," he would explain.

One part of Elizabeth understood all of this and why it was necessary and was grateful for it. The other part not unnaturally chafed at all the rules and regulations. "But Elizabeth," Eddie admonished her on one occasion, "you know that you have to be careful about your health and that you have to go to bed early." When the butler so far forgot himself as to put a telephone call through to the master bedroom after "The Nine O'Clock Retreat," Eddie instructed him solemnly, "Remember that there isn't anything more important than the sleep and rest of Elizabeth Taylor." The erstwhile playboy, lover of night life and casino glamour, had transformed himself into a nursemaid: doting, devoted, and dull. And in the process had assumed, by force of circumstances, a bad part as old as Hollywood itself: Husband to the Star.

One of the circumstances lay in the nature of Elizabeth's basic emotional needs, which have never changed. For her, love has always meant marriage, and marriage has always meant a total partnership, all-encompassing, both in work and play. Never for her a marriage where the partners were pursuing physically separating careers, with enforced separations, tenuously tied together with what time could be snatched on evenings and weekends. Whether she and Nicky Hilton—one of them in a movie studio, the other in a hotel—could have progressed much further than the point at which their personal differences severed them is a moot point. For the first three years of their marriage, she and Michael Wilding were jointly yoked into the same harness at Metro. With Mike Todd, she immersed herself in his promotional activities for *Around the World in 80 Days,* and was preparing to star for him in *Don Quixote.* She had a professional partnership in mind when she compelled Metro to hire Eddie for *Butterfield 8.* The idea sank in a barrage of negative critical reaction, of which the following is a fair sample:

"The Eddie Fisher case seems to get more hopeless. Its essential fault is in the singer's one, lonely performing dimension. He can't act, can't speak lines very well, is clumsy and seems sluggish. Outside of that he's perfect."

Clearly there was to be no joint acting career for them. His recording career had sagged badly since the initial uproar over his marriage. The NBC contract, canceled in 1959, paid him $100,000 annually for ten years whether he worked or not. Income tax and $40,000-per-year child support to Debbie for the children took the best part of that, and the rest was chewed up in the expenses of his position. So initially Elizabeth lent her physical presence to the s.r.o. engagements at the Tropicana and the Waldorf, but there was never any doubt as to who the chief box office draw was on those occasions. Nor could or would Elizabeth indefinitely continue to prop her husband professionally. "You like a strong man?" an interviewer recently asked her. Her reply was unhesitating. "Definitely. I couldn't live with a weak man." What happened on the last occasion she sat as ringside attraction must really have jolted her.

It was at Eddie's opening at the Cocoanut Grove in the previous July—expected to be a triumphant occasion after Hollywood had publicly trashed the couple and then Elizabeth's near-fatal illness and an Oscar had wiped the slate clean. The $10,000 raised was going to Eddie Cantor's favorite charity, Sunrise Camp for Children in the Catskills. The star-studded audience included John Wayne, Lucille Ball, Henry Fonda, Merle Oberon, Kirk

Douglas, Natalie Wood and Robert Wagner, Laurence Harvey, and Edward G. Robinson. Even before Eddie appeared, a jarring note was struck when friends massed so thickly around the still-convalescing Elizabeth that Rex Kennamer had to take her outside so that she could breathe. Then Eddie came on, and after three songs punctuated by nervousness, flat notes, and a snafu in the p.a. system, the proceedings went as follows:

DEAN MARTIN (loudly): "Come on, Eddie."

EDDIE (weakly): "How about letting me finish the song?"

DEAN MARTIN: "Hell, you ain't finished any of the others yet."

EDDIE (smiling feebly): "You're telling me."

DEAN MARTIN: "You sang the songs *you* wanted to sing. Now sing the ones *we* want to hear."

JERRY LEWIS (carefully seated at an adjoining table with his back to Martin and now jumping to his feet): "And now if an outsider can say a word . . ." (appreciative applause)

GEORGE JESSEL: "I may make a speech myself." (no applause)

DEAN MARTIN (referring to "That Face"): "And that's some face there. I don't know why you're working, boy. If *my* wife had that face, I'd be home with her." (Jeanne Martin must have loved that one.)

After his last song, Eddie walked over to the Clan table in a pathetic attempt to salvage his evening. "Well, I'm waiting. We are honored, ladies and gentlemen, to have with us tonight the Desert Mafia. It was good of them to come. They had to break an important engagement to make it. They were supposed to invade Cuba." The attempt flopped as, nothing daunted, Clan members Frank Sinatra, Dean Martin, Joey Bishop, and Sammy Davis, Jr., spilled onto the stage for a boozy bag of off-color jokes, inside stories and songs. Davis clamored insistently for "Peter Pentagon" to join them, but Peter Lawford (then brother-in-law of the President) remained right where he was. At one point Sinatra was offstage for some moments and when he returned, Dean Martin inquired solicitously, "Have to go to the toilet, pal?" The audience cheered lustily when they finally got off but the evening was a shambles. "It became a real Hollywood evening, if you know what I mean," Wanger wrote to Mankiewicz.

So here it was the fall of 1961 and if circumstances had placed him in a poor role, Eddie Fisher was doing his best in it. As for Elizabeth, she had a husband and a studio totally dedicated to her comfort and well-being. Her incredible public impact was attested to by the mobs which surrounded her at every public appearance. And by the mounting requests for stories and photo layouts from Fox's Publicity Department, driven frantic by Skouras' fear that the *Cleopatra* publicity would be insufficient to help compensate for the film's ever-mounting costs. One constant request for a Sheilah Graham interview was steadily refused by Elizabeth "in a vocabulary that allows no confusion as to meaning," as Wanger delicately phrased it. Finally, hordes of paparazzi pursued Elizabeth with a zeal and fervor comparable to what Don Murray exhibited trying to corral Marilyn Monroe in *Bus Stop*.

The paparazzi, Roman freelance photographers, first came to world attention in Fellini's *La Dolce Vita*. Richard Burton once volunteered a definition of "paparazzi" as "a combination of parrot and cockroach" but the ordinary English translation is "household scum." They delighted in unhappiness and scandal, had a rat's god-given scent for trouble, and could be counted on to do their worst to manufacture some where none existed. Upon being told of Elizabeth's imminent arrival in Rome, then-paparazzi-leader Ivan Kroscenko exulted, "We can hardly wait." He added this remarkable prediction: "You'll see photographs of her—intimate ones—with some handsome actor, fascinating director, or patrician playboy. We're already lining things up."

If Fox thought that this voracious band of rodents could be deterred by ordinary security precautions, they soon learned better. One of the more enterprising came in drag as a washer-woman, and at the point where he-she laid aside the mop and pail to begin snapping his-her photos was quickly hustled away. Fox then ordered the guards on the gates increased tenfold, and no less than twelve men stood guard on each gate at Cinecittà. It was further decreed that all personnel on the *Cleopatra* set, cast members excepted, would wear silver-dollar-size badges: blue for production, yellow for construction, red for visitors. Nevertheless, with thousands passing in and out daily, airtight security was impossible. Every so often a camera would be discovered in a suspiciously ornate hairdo or an outsize tie. Before it was all over, the paparazzi—not content with telephoto shots taken from the trees adjacent to Elizabeth's villa—were coming over the walls on ladders. At which point Elizabeth and the servants took up rakes and brooms and the children manned water hoses to drive them off. The climax to all of this frenzied pursuit occurred the day one of the paparazzi trotted up to Elizabeth and punched her right in the stomach with the hope that something unusual might fetch a higher price. "I wasn't there," Richard Burton once noted grimly, "or I would have long ago walked death's row."

The announcement by *Motion Picture Herald* on December 29 that Elizabeth was the Top Box Office Star of 1961 (thus outranking Rock Hudson, Doris Day, John Wayne, and Cary Grant) placed her at the very summit of her professional achievement. Now she had it all: an Oscar, box office supremacy, the title role expressly conceived for her in what would doubtless be the most expensive film ever made, the adoring husband, the solicitous studio, the feverish attentions of the world press, the love and adoration of millions. All. And all was not enough.

"I try not to live a lie," Elizabeth once said. "Being honest is all a part of being what one is." Now, with a gradual reawakening of her sharp sense of her own reality which made further avoidance impossible, she realized that she had enmeshed herself in a lie. And that its days were numbered.

She had tenaciously clung to the memory of Mike Todd, as loath to part with it as she had been loath to part with him physically on that terrible night which had separated them forever. "You've got to go on living," well-meaning friends had told her. So she had forced herself to do the expected, acceptable things for surface existence, and meanwhile built a shrine with a far more comforting reality to her than the incredible pain of his absence. Eddie helped her to tend that shrine. Wherever they lived, Mike Todd's presence was in the many photos of him throughout the house—in their conversations in which happy memories were repeatedly relived—in the scarred wedding band which Elizabeth pinned to her undergarments when a film role made it impossible for her to wear it in its permanent place on her hand.

"After Mike died I used to sleep fourteen, fifteen hours a day," she wrote, "I think mainly to avoid what waking hours would bring." Self-pity and despair had imprisoned her in the beautiful dream that was her life with Mike Todd. Katharine Hepburn, a person Elizabeth admires enormously, shrewdly sensed this curious unreality when they made *Suddenly Last Summer* together. The actress and fellow professional she gave high marks but there was something missing. "There seemed to be no personal level at all," Miss Hepburn told Garson Kanin. Unpleasant reality threatened from time to time but Elizabeth shrank from the alternatives. The idea of divorce was still abhorrent to her. Her first had put her through enough pain, and the comparative ease of the second had done nothing to change her basic feeling about it. A third divorce was out of the question. She had struck her bargain with life and she would keep to it.

Her first major questioning of the arrangement occurred after she had survived what seemed like certain death with the pneumonia in London. The human certainty that things happen for a reason has survived every rational argument that there is not a shred of scientific proof for it. Even as when people are taken by death—even as Elizabeth had repeatedly cried out "Why? Why?" at the death of Mike Todd—so when people are spared—the same question—"Why? Why me? What for? What has life still in store for me?" The story of mankind is replete with examples in which such experiences have triggered major personal upheavals. At the very least, the reflective person feels impelled to re-examination and possible redirection. While she underwent such a process, Elizabeth remained imprisoned in her dream. The situation was dormant but the stage was set. The man who finally beckoned her to awake from her dream and come forth from that prison was Richard Burton.

Burton came to his present eminence as Elizabeth's costar with a reputation for romantic conquest of previous costars that was already legendary. "I used to knock around a bit in the old days," he is wont to remark. Yes, indeed. Fredric March, who played his father in *Alexander the Great* and who was not ordinarily given to public comment on such matters, couldn't help but note admiringly, "Burton has a terrific way with women. I don't think he has missed more than half a dozen." Elizabeth was well aware of this, and waited expectantly for the opening ploy the first day they met on the set. What occurred was totally unexpected. Burton merely dusted off the world's oldest chestnut. "Has anybody ever told you that you're a very pretty girl?" he murmured into her disbelieving ear. "You've got to be kidding!" she wanted to tell him, but instead contented herself with going back to the dressing room to spread the news that Cleopatra had finally received the tribute from Wales—and it wasn't much.

Elizabeth approached working with Burton with a trepidation proceeding from deep-seated inferiority feelings movie people traditionally exhibited toward stage-trained actors—a situation which obtained until television finally gave the movies something to feel superior to. She was convinced that he would condescendingly offer help where none was wanted or needed. It was quite the other way around. On their first day of work, Burton arrived so hung over she had to steady his shaking hands so that he could get a cup of coffee into him. Then, when they moved into the shot, he promptly blew a line. That disarmed her completely.

Burton, Sybil, and the children were sharing a villa with

Roddy McDowall, who was playing Octavius Caesar. More and more Burton appeared in the company of Elizabeth and Eddie— at the Kirk Douglas *Spartacus* party, at dinner parties in the Villa Pappa, on infrequent outings in Rome. As Eddie nervously noted the lateness of the hour, Burton would dip into his inexhaustible fund of stories—"He knows more stories than Scheherazade," Stanley Baker once cracked. Elizabeth would plead to stay out "just a little longer," Burton would switch her empty wine glass for his full one when Eddie wasn't looking, and keep the charm flowing in his role as Elizabeth's fellow conspirator in the successful attempt to beat "The Nine O'Clock Retreat." Elizabeth loved him for that.

"You must realize I met her twenty years ago and fell madly in love with her," Burton joked recently. "I'm afraid at first it was lust, but then I got to know her and it was love. When we finally did get together, it was a terrible thing. She didn't listen to my stories. She didn't laugh at the right time. She just looked at me through those strange eyes. I had to marry her to teach her."

Elizabeth was listening and laughing too much to suit Eddie Fisher on one particular night at the villa. She had given a small dinner party and the guests were Richard Burton, Robert Wagner, Kurt Frings, and p.r. man Bob Abrams. At one in the morning everyone was in the salon where Burton was amusing Elizabeth with some good stories and she was plainly enjoying them. Eddie, on the defensive, went to the piano and began playing and singing loudly. Elizabeth was embarrassed and annoyed by such obvious rudeness. "Shut up!" she snapped. "We can't talk." Whereupon Eddie slammed the piano top down and stalked into the next room. Suddenly a stereo playing Eddie Fisher records blasted through the walls and rent the air. Elizabeth stuck her fingers into her ears and her face assumed a look of pure rage. Kurt Frings then rose and announced diplomatically, "All right, Elizabeth, we'll go now."

It was an isolated incident. Usually there was unspoken tension —"that awful, heavy, humid, before-the-storm atmosphere," Elizabeth once called it. All of it was symptomatic of what was beginning to happen. As her attraction for Burton grew apace, Elizabeth's need to retreat into a dream world shrank accordingly. At last the present was providing her with a vibrant excitement that could compete with her fantasy. Her gradual withdrawal from the past was helped by gentle reminders from Burton about how much of Mike Todd still surrounded her. But as the central bond between Elizabeth and Eddie thus crumbled and faded, her marriage became increasingly untenable.

Production personnel showed no undue surprise on the day Elizabeth forfeited her day off to come and watch Burton work. Nor were any eyebrows raised on days they worked together in scenes with Rex Harrison, and they were to be seen huddled together in genial, animated conversation off-camera while they waited between setups. After all, they were playing Antony and Cleopatra, two of the immortal lovers of history. Friendly vibrations were essential to the ultimate success of the film. In January they finally played their first scene alone together, and on that day Wanger happily noted in his diary:

"There comes a time during the making of a movie when the actors become the characters they play. This merger of real personality into the personality of the role has to take place if a performance is to be truly effective. That happened today. The cameras turned and the current was literally turned on. It was quiet and you could almost feel the electricity between Elizabeth Taylor and Burton."

Four days later Joe Mankiewicz gave Wanger some electrifying news:

"I have been sitting on a volcano all alone for too long and I want to give you some facts you ought to know. Elizabeth and Burton are not just playing Antony and Cleopatra!"

❀   23   ❀

The first faint flickerings of rumor about what Richard Burton ever afterward referred to as *le scandale* were not deemed worthy of denial. There were just two newsworthy items in the first month of 1962. Elizabeth finally accepted her David di Donatello Award (the Italian Oscar) for *Suddenly Last Summer*, voted to her the previous July. The next day she publicly announced the adoption of a child: a baby girl named Maria. Three Caesarean sections had run the odds of another safe birth dangerously high. Determined to have another child, Elizabeth had decided on an adoption and worked tirelessly for several months to bring it about. Finally, through the joint efforts of Maria Schell and Kurt Frings, a prospective baby was located in

Germany. The authorities were reluctant to allow Elizabeth to have her. She had crippling birth defects and only a "perfect baby" would do for Elizabeth Taylor. Three days of loving attention—holding, feeding, bathing, and changing the baby—had already wrought a change in the solemn infant. Elizabeth assured them that love and everything humanly possible would do the rest, and on December 21, Maria had come into the Villa Pappa under conditions of absolute secrecy. She would shortly return to a Munich clinic for the first of several operations on her crippled hip.

In the first days of February an affair between the *Cleopatra* costars was the topic of open gossip in Rome. On American TV, a *Perry Como Show* skit featured Antony and Cleopatra, with a slave named Eddie getting in Antony's way. So far none of the participants had publicly confirmed or denied anything. "I knew it was going to be very hard and not very pleasant, falling for Elizabeth," Richard Burton recalled years later. "I remember thinking the moment I'd realized what had happened, 'Oh, my God, what a mess!'" Behind the scenes, in a long talk with Walter Wanger, Burton pondered quitting the film. He didn't want to do anything that would hurt Elizabeth, nor did he want anything to hurt his marriage. Over at her villa, Elizabeth revealed to Wanger that she was in a state of utter confusion. Her emotional ups-and-downs had been marked in February, the result of conflicting loves for the two men in her life. And the prospect of once again entering the fiery furnace of scandal and public scorn. "My heart feels as though it is hemorrhaging," she told him. On February 18 the lid blew off, and stayed off, as mounting public fascination transformed *le scandale* into the greatest single news event of 1962 throughout the world.

FOOD POISONS LIZ IN ROME! screamed the headlines. Elizabeth had been rushed to Salvador Mundi Hospital and the reasons given were as varied as the sources. "Bad oysters," said Dr. Richard Pennington. "Miss Taylor's illness is a minor one which had to be faced in a rather dramatic way because of her past history. No doctor would ever like to take the slightest risk with a patient who was so close to going to a better world so recently." A press agent reported the culprit as "a bad bowl of chili" while Wanger said it was "bad beef." Perplexed newspaper readers could also take their pick of boiled beans, a throat hemorrhage, paralysis, nervous breakdown and a possible Seconal overdose. Her blood pressure was reported to have fallen to eighty and there were conflicting reports as to whether a stomach pump had been used.

Coincidentally the three people most concerned with the burgeoning speculation were all out of town. Sybil had gone to New York to be with an ailing Philip Burton, Eddie was variously reported doing a TV show in Lisbon or looking over property in Switzerland, and Burton had gone to Paris to work on *The Longest Day*. With the guessing games rising to fever pitch, what next happened compounded the damage.

LIZ TAYLOR LEADING MAN DENIES ROMANCE, announced the next day's headline. "Dick Burton Says Just Friend, Eddie Fisher Silent." Burton's press agent had issued an Open Letter to the Press under Burton's name.

"For the past several days, uncontrolled rumors have been growing about Elizabeth and myself. Statements attributed to me have been distorted out of proportion and a series of coincidences has lent plausibility to a situation which has become dangerous to Elizabeth.

"Mr. Fisher, who has business interests of his own, merely went out of town to attend to them for a few days. My foster father, Philip Burton, has been quite ill in New York, and my wife Sybil flew there to be with him for a time since my schedule does not permit me to be there. He is very dear to both of us.

"Elizabeth and I have been close friends for over twelve years. I have known her since she was a child star and would certainly never do anything to hurt her personally or professionally.

"In answer to these rumors, my normal inclination would be simply to say no comment. But I feel that in this case things should be explained to protect Elizabeth."

Burton flew in from Paris in a rage and angrily repudiated the statement. "It was a terribly worded statement. Horrendous. I never authorized it. I was very angry." He further characterized all romance rumors as "bloody nonsense" and sacked his press agent, who went away muttering about having expected to be made a scapegoat. Eddie had also flown back to Rome immediately upon the news of Elizabeth's illness, and was kept cooling his heels in the waiting room of Salvador Mundi for seven hours. He then spent an hour closeted with Elizabeth and emerged grim and unsmiling. "I've got nothing to say," he snapped curtly to the army of waiting reporters as he left the hospital.

By February 27 Elizabeth had sufficiently recovered from her illness—whatever it was—to attend a festive thirtieth birthday party hosted by Eddie in the Borgia Room of the Hostaria del Orso. Her husband gifted her with a diamond ring and an antique mirror. On that day Elizabeth also received a bouquet from an anonymous admirer which became a well-remembered present on every February 27 thereafter. She was pretty sure she knew who sent it, but each year Burton was called on anew to swear that he had indeed been the sender. At the party, the guest of honor Twisted gaily with her husband, and on the surface all appeared to be sweet harmony. Once on the trail, however, the columnists were not to be put off and the strident tone of their material plainly implied that two spoiled people, heedless of their obligations to their spouses and their children, had eagerly rushed into each other's arms and to hell with the consequences. Nothing could have been further from the truth.

"Didn't it shake you to realize you had actually fallen in love with Elizabeth Taylor?" an interviewer once queried Richard Burton. "Yes. God, yes. Before Elizabeth I had no idea what *total* love was. I was thrown by it very badly. I was in a terrible state of shock." Elizabeth's matched it. "We really fought and hurt each other terribly to keep it from happening." A blond showgirl acquaintance of Burton's was still very much in evidence, and one day he arrived with her at the studio at seven and didn't show up on the set till ten. The following occurred:

ELIZABETH (obviously distressed): "You kept us all waiting."

BURTON (nastily): "It's about time somebody kept *you* waiting. It's a real switch."

REX HARRISON (after a discreet cough): "Let's rehearse, everyone."

Wound each other though they might, and recite all the reasons to each other why it simply could not be, it *was*. What they could or would do about it was something else. There was one further denial on the occasion when Louella Parsons finally broke a self-imposed silence on the matter. ROW OVER ACTOR ENDS LIZ, EDDIE MARRIAGE, read the headline over her bylined piece on March 9. "It is difficult to appraise how the world will react to another scandal involving Elizabeth," wrote Louella, still carefully hedging her bets where Elizabeth was concerned.

Skouras flew into Rome the next day trailing a raspy stream of comments to pursuing newsmen ("Silly. I don't know anything about it. It is absolutely ridiculous. It's completely false."). Next he sailed into Walter Wanger for insisting on Burton as Antony, and then conceived the bright idea of sending letters to his naughty stars telling them to behave themselves. Burton got his and went up a wall. Upon news of that, Elizabeth went right through the ceiling, and let it be known that the day she got hers, Fox would be minus one Cleopatra. Skouras very prudently decided not to send it, one of the few sensible decisons he had made in three years.

"Liz, Eddie Silent on Breakup," read an item in the next day's news, to be succeeded by LIZ AND EDDIE SPLIT? THEY ISSUE DENIAL. Eddie had got on the transatlantic phone to Louella to deny the story, calling the romance rumors "a lot of junk. The only romance between them I know about is between Mark Antony and Cleopatra—and that's a pretty good one. Elizabeth and I are still very much in love. We couldn't be happier than we are at this minute. We just have to live our lives and not let gossip interfere with the way we feel about one another. As long as Elizabeth and I believe in one another there never will be any truth to the stories." To which Elizabeth added, "Ridiculous. Nothing but rumor." *Life* commented tartly, "Agents for all principals scrambled to reheat their denials. The earth, meanwhile, managed to stay on its axis."

By March 21 things had come to some sort of boil as Eddie suddenly flew to New York "on business" and Sybil and the children returned to London. "Everyone believes that Elizabeth kicked Eddie Fisher out," Burton later told Sheilah Graham. "But it was quite the other way around. Elizabeth and I were doing a very difficult scene in *Cleopatra* when she received a note that Eddie had taken off twenty-five minutes before for America. She turned ashen. Imagine doing that to her in the middle of a scene."

Eddie did a guest stint on *What's My Line?* and then went into hiding in New York amid rumors that, crushed by his marital breakup, he had suffered a nervous breakdown and was confined in a private psychiatric ward. Milt Blackstone denied it, claiming that Eddie was indeed "in a hospital" but only for "rest and relaxation." Elizabeth had inquiries made and learned that he was at Gracie Square Hospital, reportedly bedded with flu. On March 30, Eddie called a press conference at the Hotel Pierre. He appeared chipper and smiling, scoffing at rift rumors and breakdown reports. Of Richard Burton: "He is a friend of mine. We're not close friends—I haven't known him long. He is an amusing, pleasant, charming guy and a very fine actor." Would Elizabeth make a similar statement denying the rift rumors? "I think she will—yes." That was his final, fatal error.

"The quality in Elizabeth that appealed, and still appeals, to me is her total blazing honesty," Richard Burton has said. "She cannot tell a lie." Like it or not, every man who has ever loved her has known it. Eddie knew it, but desperate circumstances had warped his judgment to the point where he somehow believed he could, first of all, publicly back her into a corner, and then make her lie her way out of it. He went off to place the call to Rome. When Elizabeth answered it, he explained about the press conference and asked her for the statement.

"Well, Eddie," she told him, "I can't do that because there is some truth in the story. I just can't do that." He was stunned. "Wait a minute—what do you mean you won't do that?" She repeated herself. "I can't say that because it's not true. There is a foundation to the story." He was dumbfounded. "Thanks a lot!" he hurled at her and hung up, returning to tell the newsmen that she had refused the statement. "You know you can ask a woman to do something but she doesn't always do it," he explained lamely. It was the final curtain. LIZ TURNS DOWN EDDIE'S OCEAN PHONE LOVE PLEA, read the doleful headline.

"April is the cruelest month," said T. S. Eliot. In April, all hell broke loose—and thunderous damnation from what passes for heaven's representative on earth as well. There was one exception. In a poll of American college men, Elizabeth was chosen "the most attractive woman in public life," putting her ahead of runners-up Jacqueline Kennedy, Grace Kelly, Kim Novak, and Gina Lollobrigida. Otherwise April turned into an unrelieved torrent of public criticism and continuous hysteria in the world press.

The day after Eddie's abortive transatlantic telephone call, Elizabeth and Burton decided to turn the tables on the paparazzi by publicly dating on the Via Veneto, grimly impervious to the cascade of popping flashbulbs all around them. Headlines on this, with accompanying pictures, read, LIZ, BURTON GO ARM-IN-ARM ON ALL NIGHT ROMAN DATE and LIZ AND BURTON FROLIC IN ROME; KISS, DANCE. "The spouse-collecting actress frolicked until two o'clock this morning," hissed one report, "openly dating as her marriage to Eddie Fisher went on the rocks." The contrast between such gay abandon in Rome and Eddie's sad plight in New York was noted by all. The onetime Callous Cad now had a new public role, Sorrowing Soul, devitalized and discarded by the imperious whims of a merciless temptress.

Far more ominous was the tenor of the following type of criticism: "The sympathy of the entire film industry can scarcely help going to Spyros Skouras and the 20th gang who have so patiently put up with Liz's antics and mishaps for so long." In these lights Elizabeth was not simply a fickle woman who had changed men. Suddenly she alone was responsible for all the problems of Cleopatra. This developing public campaign to scapegoat Elizabeth with total responsibility for this financial fiasco, and thus exonerate the ineptitude of 20th Century-Fox, would lead straight to a nasty fifty-million-dollar lawsuit.

As the barometer continued to plummet in the press, Richard Burton conspired to keep the newspapers and magazines away from Elizabeth. The same policy prevailed on the set. "Surrounded by an aura of screaming journalism," Mankiewicz recalled, "we were all occupied, very seriously, in making a very serious picture. The technicians worked under extreme difficulties within the cocoon of the sound stages. It was a tremendous strain, but we tried to leave the panic outside." Other friends pitched in to help when the going got too rough. On one outing Burton's chauffeur fended off paparazzi with a broom. On another evening "Elizabeth" left the villa in her limousine sporting a white, cossack-style hat. The paparazzi gave chase, caught up with the car a mile away, and discovered that the passenger was a male decoy. One day Elizabeth telephoned Mike Nichols, then in Rome. "I'm going crazy. The paparazzi won't leave me alone. Help!" Nichols took her to Tivoli, where they strolled among the fountains of the Villa d'Este in peace.

CBS now made a tempting offer to do a documentary on the making of *Cleopatra* but Elizabeth demurred. She also repeatedly refused Publicity's requests to say something about Eddie's illness in New York. By now she was a seasoned traveler in the eyes of various hurricanes. Like all storms, however huge and however long it raged, it would ride itself out. Her natural antipathy to ventilating private matters in public aside, she knew that talking into one of these things could only make it worse. Privately she had now decided, no matter what the future held, that her marriage to Eddie Fisher was finished. With little faith in media of any kind, she entrusted the transmission of the message to Kurt Frings, who characterized it only as "a personal message—a private matter" to a horde of eager newsmen upon his departure from Rome for New York. Columnist Earl Wilson quoted Elizabeth as saying, "My marriage to Eddie Fisher is dead and done," and Attorney Louis Nizer's office issued the press release. "Elizabeth and Eddie Fisher announce that they have mutually agreed to part. Divorce proceedings will be instituted soon." The owner of the Flamingo Hotel in Las Vegas promptly grabbed a headline by announcing that Eddie would soon be there divorcing Elizabeth. Only to be one-upped by the Thunderbird owner, who revealed (on no evidence whatever) that Elizabeth would be at *his* hotel divorcing Eddie.

Characteristically, Elizabeth took only one public action to protect an area in which she felt at all vulnerable. She sent a telegram to the adoption agency in Munich which read: "You may rest assured that I love little Maria-Petra and will take care of the child my whole life." Burton cabled to Sybil in Welsh—supposedly for privacy, but of course it was immediately translated to satisfy panting public curiosity. It read: "Love to all. Everything fine." At some point Laurence Olivier sent a cable to his old friend: "Make up your mind, dear heart. Do you wish to be a household word or a great actor?" Burton's reply was perfectly in character: "Both!" After being pestered unmercifully for comment, Mankiewicz reportedly told Rome's *Il Messaggero*: "She can be in love with whom she wishes, and lose her head over whoever she wishes. I even give her permission to flirt with Mao Tse-tung."

That was merely artful flimflam, according to Rome's *Telesera*, which had the real scoop. Elizabeth was "in love" with Mankiewicz, who was "crazy about her." Burton represented only "a useful idiot"—a decoy in the affair. This searing revelation forced Mankiewicz to come clean. "The real truth is that I am in love with Burton and Miss Taylor is the coverup for us." Predictably at a dinner party that night Walter Wanger was cornered by a scandalized guest. "Isn't it shameful that Burton and Mankiewicz are carrying on and using poor Elizabeth Taylor as a cover!" Fiddlesticks! snorted *ABC*, another paper. The whole thing had nothing to do with love at all. The *real* truth was that Grace Kelly had announced that she might make a new movie (Hitchcock's *Marnie*). This was a threat to Elizabeth's position as "first world star." What's a girl to do! Get a divorce to protect her box office and keep the publicity away from Grace! Unfortunately the Niagara of remaining comment was not nearly so frivolous.

The Vatican Radio fulminated about "caprices of adult children" and "this insult to the nobility of the hearth." Rome's *Il Tempo* slammed Elizabeth as "an intemperate vamp who destroys families and devours husbands." From API-UPI: DOES LIZ NEED A SPANKING? Echoed by the British Press: LIZ WANTS HER BOTTOM SMACKED. ONE OF THE FOUR HUSBANDS SHOULD HAVE DONE IT. In Turin: "Love is a wonderful thing but Taylor is decidedly exaggerating." In Milan: "TOO MUCH LIZ. Let's try not to publish a line on anything concerning the infernal Elizabeth for twenty-four hours."

Elizabeth would have been delighted. If anything really bugged her throughout this long-running public soap opera, it was the assertion that "we don't give a damn what they do, but why do they have to wash all this dirty laundry in public!" As if she personally were hanging it all out on the line and as if she needed publicity and as if she needed *this* kind!

On and on it rolled. From Ed Sullivan: "You can only trust that youngsters will not be persuaded that the sanctity of marriage has been invalidated by the appalling example of Mrs. Taylor-Fisher and married-man Burton." From some Hearst columnist named Suzy: "There must be some kind of self-destructive devil driving this beautiful woman who, with the whole world in her hands, flouts conventions, jeopardizes her career, wrecks other people's lives, and flings herself headlong into folly."

Once again, as with the Eddie-Debbie-Liz Biz, Elizabeth's private life wound up on the editorial pages. A typical cartoon, captioned "Oh, Dear, This Is Terrible News!" showed a kitchen floor littered with discarded newspapers bearing the headlines BERLIN A POWDER KEG, CRISIS IN ARGENTINA, DEADLOCK IN GENEVA, UNEMPLOYED ON RISE. Oblivious to them all was a frantic housewife holding a paper with the headline LIZ AND EDDIE TO SPLIT! That was just too much for Art Buchwald. Elizabeth Taylor was driving nuclear testing, disarmament, Berlin, Viet Nam, and Russo-Chinese differences right off the front pages. Ergo, there should be a world-wide referendum on Elizabeth Taylor's future course "since Elizabeth Taylor's problem has become the world's problem. Those who abstained from voting would be considered to have shirked their responsibility and would have no moral right after that to interfere in the personal life of Elizabeth Taylor—no matter how interested they might be."

Photoplay thought this was a dandy idea and hit the stands with twelve pages of the usual mush, which was fetchingly described as "the most complete and in-depth analysis of Elizabeth Taylor—her exotic life, her tumultuous loves." There followed a two-page spread starkly bannered by the admonition to VOTE TODAY! thus giving all true believers that Uncle-Sam-Wants-You feeling and stopping them in their tracks. "Before you do, before you make your voice heard in our nation-wide poll, we strongly urge you to consider all the aspects of what Liz has or has not done." (Small pause for the wind to whistle through the aviaries which served as brains for the average reader.) "Yours is a great responsibility"—Uncle Sam again—"so think very carefully before you answer the important question: Can *you* forgive Liz Taylor?"

The pressure now began to get to everyone involved in varying degrees. Roddy McDowall moved out of the Burton villa and into town. After repeated takes on a short Forum scene in which he was on horseback, Burton blew his top. "Don't you know what bloody torture it is riding through this crowd?" he shouted at Mankiewicz. "Liz Taylor? I adore her," Sybil Burton was quoted as saying. "She's an old friend of mine." After which she was reported in hiding in London and under sedation. Prior to this she had met her husband in Paris. "Are you going to marry Miss Taylor?" a crush of photographers and newsmen asked him at the airport. "I'm already married," he responded. Any chance of a divorce? "Absolutely none," replied Sybil. Still Burton could not completely suppress his feelings. When asked about Elizabeth: "She's just beautiful, more beautiful than ever. You should have seen her yesterday, shooting a scene in *Cleopatra* wearing a sort of flimsy nightgown. She looked like she was ten years old." After which Sybil returned to London and Burton to Rome. How he and Elizabeth managed to fox the ubiquitous paparazzi is a mystery but fox them they did, as Elizabeth revealed recently: "Richard and I had some of our happiest times in Italy in a really crummy one-room apartment on the beach. We would go down there to be together even though we had a huge Roman villa with a cook and servants. We'd spend weeks there. I'd barbecue and there was a crummy old shower and the sheets were always damp. We loved it—absolutely adored it."

Eddie Fisher started on the comeback trail by recording a series of songs for his own company. Arriving at Los Angeles Airport, he looked pale and drawn. To the usual barrage of questions which would be coming at him for the next two years, he commented, "Well, let's just say the situation in Rome became unbearable for me." He had begun a nonstop series of appearances which began at the Grove, and then took him to Las Vegas, Lake Tahoe, Chicago, Grossinger's, the Latin Quarter in Philadelphia, and on to a five-week engagement at the Winter Garden in New York. By then he had begun to date Ann-Margret. His onstage partner was Juliet Prowse, among whose acts was a little item called "I'm Cleo, the Nympho of the Nile." Eddie vainly pleaded with her to drop it. Sample lyric: "There was not a man she couldn't get/That was Cleo's problem on and off the set." Then there was a Joan of Arc number, complete with bumps and grinds. Sample lyric: "I can give you the kind of action you got from *Butterfield 8*." The critics retched in unison: "Amazingly tasteless. Unforgivably vulgar and dull." When an eager photographer asked Eddie to pose with Juliet in her Cleo costume, Eddie Fisher's usual public equanimity vanished completely. "Are you out of your mind?" he snapped at him.

On April 10 *Life* magazine came out with *its* contribution to *le scandale*—a feature piece which began, "Here begins a grim fairy tale: Richard I, Prince Eddie, and Princess Elizabeth in a disenchanted wood." There followed a heavy-handed recapitulation of Elizabeth's life told in pseudo-Olde Englishe, ending with "Oh, it is all very mixed up, almost as mixed up as the princess herself." These periodic exercises in wit, generally as light and airy as pasta, were par for the course in the rabbit warrens of Henry Luce. Even now Mankiewicz was certain that somewhere in the labyrinth someone was already stocking up on puns to crucify his film, which would naturally be called *Cleopatterer*.

Particularly obnoxious in the current oafish exercise was the attack on Elizabeth's maternal role. "In Elizabeth Taylor's headlong rush from one love to the next, the existence of children in her own home or in any other has produced no noticeable sobering effect. Even when this scandal was brewing, Elizabeth paraded her own brood around the movie set." Even had those who knew far better wished to reply, they would have had no time. This was just the appetizer. The entree arrived two days later. It was an Open Letter in the Vatican City weekly, *L'Osservatore della Dominica*. The writer prudently if not courageously chose anonymity under the signature "XY":

"Dear Madam: When some time ago, you said that your marriage (your fourth) would last for your whole life, there were some who shook their heads in a rather skeptical way. We, always willing to believe the best, kept our heads steadily on our shoulders and did not say a word. Then, when you reached the point of adopting a baby girl, as if to make more stable this marriage which had no natural children, for a moment we really believed that things had changed. But children—whether they are natural or adopted—count little for illustrious ladies like you when there is nothing for them to hold together. It appears that you had the bad taste to state: 'My marriage is dead and extradead!' And what of the 'whole life' you had declared it would last three years ago? Does your whole life mean only three years? And if your marriage is dead, then we must say, according to the Roman usage, it was killed dead. The trouble is, my dear lady, you are killing too many.

"Even considering the marriage that ended by a natural solution, there are still three husbands thus buried with no other motive than that which killed the previous love. But if we start taking such measurings on this sort of competition between the first, the second, and the hundredth love, where will we end? Where will you finish? In erotic vagrancy?

"And your poor children: those who are your true children and the one who was taken from an honest institution. At least, if nature does not allow you to have any more, you should avoid asking around to transform them into half-orphans, orphans of live fathers, and of mothers who marry a second, a third, and a fourth time.

"But don't these institutions think before handing children to somebody? Don't they request moral references? Was it not better to entrust this girl to an honest bricklayer and to a modest housewife rather than to you, my dear lady, and to your fourth ex-husband? The housewife and the bricklayer would have worked harder and would have seriously made sacrifices for their child. You, instead, have other things to do."

So there it was, and it was no good rationalizing, as Walter Wanger did, that since it was presumably a letter from a reader, it was not an "official pronouncement." Everything which issued from the sacred precincts was automatically assumed to carry official approval. For all practical purposes, Elizabeth had been branded by the Vatican before the world as an erotic vagrant and an unfit mother, and headlines around the globe blazoned it forth. This double broadside struck deep into two highly sensitive areas: Elizabeth's love for her children, and a heavy sense of shame and regret over her marital record that no amount of reasoning had ever been able to eradicate. "Can I sue the Vatican?" she cried heatedly, and angrily announced that she would write a reply. On the surface she was determined to carry on in her usual publicly impenetrable manner, but she would have had to be made of stone to bring this one off, and the job was beyond her. At a club on the Via Veneto that night, she Twisted defiantly with Richard Burton, and then went into a Cha-Cha with Mike Nichols. At which point one of her shoulder straps popped, she fixed it, and went right on dancing. Later, frustrated by the swarms of paparazzi, she burst into tears and fled the scene.

"Talk about bum raps!" Joe Mankiewicz once angrily exclaimed. "Elizabeth Taylor is one of the least promiscuous, one of the least profligate beautiful women I have ever known. Perhaps if she had been more calculating and conniving—techniques more palatable to the morality mores she's reputed to have outraged—she'd have saved a great deal of wear and tear on herself. But she took it. Head on. It's the only way she knew; hardly that of a schemer. Elizabeth is a good and generous and honest human being. I'm her friend."

As fate would have it, her friend had written for Elizabeth the greatest scene of spectacle ever put upon the screen—the thrilling highpoint in Part I of *Cleopatra*—the triumphant entry of

Egypt's Queen into Rome. The day after the Vatican blast, amid bomb threats and with thousands of extras presumed to be faithful sons and daughters of the Church, the final portion of that scene had now to be filmed.

The core of Mankiewicz's approach to Cleopatra was that she nourished a burning vision of One World, which had been the dream of Alexander the Great. Her liaison with Julius Caesar had produced his only son, Caesarion. Could she persuade the Romans to accept her son as Caesar's heir, the empires of Rome and Egypt would be joined in him and Alexander's dream fulfilled. To that end Cleopatra planned to enter Rome with her son in fantastic procession as incarnations of the Goddess Isis and of her son, Horus the Sun God. For this scene (as well as her final scene) Irene Sharaff designed for Elizabeth a $6,500 gown made of cloth of 24-carat gold. Prior to Cleopatra's arrival, there would come a series of dazzling shows, then a golden pyramid, then finally a huge sphinx bearing the Queen-Goddess herself. The call sheet for this mammoth undertaking read as follows:

Fifty archers, shooting arrows which unravel veils the color of sunrise, foretelling the approach of Isis and Horus; 26 snake dancers to symbolize the Sacred Snake of Egypt; 38 girls with gilded wings and headdresses to symbolize the Sacred Vulture; 36 trumpeters on 36 white horses; 8 charioteers driving 16 black horses; 8 bowmen on the chariots; a 20-piece Egyptian band; 28 pole dancers (female and fair); 1 old hag; 1 beautiful girl; 3 oxenmen with 6 white oxen; 16 dwarfs on 16 zebras; 7 acrobats (male); 4 acrobats (2 male, 2 female) on 2 elephants; 4 girls with gifts on 2 elephants; 4 mahouts; 12 green-smoke dancers (male and dark); 12 yellow-smoke dancers; 18 dancers (male and dark, four of them with drums); 12 dancers (female and dark); 10 red witch dancers (male and dark); 8 pole vaulters (male and fair); 16 gold fan bearers (male and fair); 7 gold tree porters (male and fair); 30 elite honor guard on 30 sorrel horses; 12 slaves for the pyramid; 8 marble men (dark) to carry Cleopatra; 300 slaves for the sphinx. As part of the Roman Forum crowd: 3,000 men, 1,500 women, 20 children, 6 Egyptian dignitaries, 6 Egyptian slaves, 30 Roman Senators' wives, 20 Roman Court ladies, 150 Roman Senators, 24 lictors (officers bearing the fasces, the Roman symbol of authority), 350 Praetorians, and 12 Roman Trumpeters.

"I was told I could do what I wanted, get anything I wanted, and spare no expense," choreographer Hermes Pan related. "Cleopatra *had* to overcome the prejudice of the Romans with an entrance which would outdo anything they'd ever seen, to entertain and awe them with the might and wealth of Egypt. All elements had to keep moving, both on the ground and in the air."

To that end, chariots would crisscross in and out of the procession shooting forth the flying streamers; the girls on the elephants would toss golden coins to the throngs; Watusi dancers would move in clouds of the green and yellow smoke, the air glittering with tons of golden confetti, as they approached Caesar's throne; the pole vaulters dressed as bird men would vault over the Watusi and seem to fly right into the audience; the golden pyramid bearing the gilded girls would open at the top as it approached Caesar and 2,000 doves would fly out. (Pan remembered that the doves were shut up in the pyramid so long waiting for the take that they went to sleep in the dim interior, and a man had to be stationed in there with a gun and blank cartridges to get them started.) Finally, the massive sphinx, with the incarnations of Isis and Horus between its paws, drawn by 300 slaves and attended by the 8 men (Black Nubians painted like marble so as to be frieze-like) would come through the huge archway and up to Caesar's throne. As finally realized on the screen, the scene is the apotheosis of film as fantasy factory. It has never been equaled nor is it ever likely to be.

On the day her part in it was to be finished, a tense Elizabeth, the Vatican denunciation still pounding at her senses, rode onto the lot with Burton beside her in the limousine. The trip was punctuated by jeers and menacing noises from groups of pedestrians. "I have never seen Elizabeth, in any circumstances, exhibit any evidence that she has nerves," that director had said in 1948. He should have seen her this day. She was expected to calmly sit three stories high in the air on the sphinx, a perfect target for an infinite variety of possibilities—for the plan of any garden-variety cuckoo, now so thoughtfully reinforced in his lunacy by the sweet charity and compassion of organized religion. "I don't think I can do it," she told Burton. "It's all right, baby," he reassured her. "I'll be here and the police are here." Once into the heavy gold costume and into the headdress of Isis (15 pounds and 2½ feet high), she still had doubts. "Being pulled through that mob," she told Mankiewicz, "alone up there—who knows—they'll jeer me and they'll throw rocks at me."

Eventually she summoned the personal courage which has yet to fail her and climbed up on the sphinx. "Action!" shouted Mankiewicz. On through the archway came the sphinx, Elizabeth mounted on it, sitting stiff and immovable like grim death.

The script called for the extras to run screaming toward it, proclaiming "Cleopatra! Cleopatra!" As the huge apparatus approached Caesar's throne, Elizabeth saw the throngs start to break and come toward her. "Oh, my God, here it comes, Bessie," she thought. Suddenly she realized that the thousands had departed completely from the script. Instead of "Cleopatra!" they were screaming "Leez! Leez! Bacci (kisses)! Bacci!" Amid a cascade of cheering and kisses, Elizabeth's composure finally broke and she wept openly. Nor would the cheering be stilled after Mankiewicz had stopped the cameras. Finally a microphone was handed up to her, and the crowd quieted to hear Elizabeth utilize a large part of her Italian vocabulary right from the heart of a profoundly grateful human being. "Thank you very much," she told them. If ever Elizabeth needed a proof that her bond with the public could survive anything the world could throw at her, she got it that day. Not surprisingly she looks back on it as one of the great moments in her life.

She needed all the reassurance she could get as April's storm raged unabated, whipped to new heights by what occurred on the Easter weekend of the twenty-first. Elizabeth and Richard Burton had fled to the island resort of Porto Santo Stefano in the Tyrrhenian Sea to mull over their situation. Naturally the paparazzi followed, and the pair were observed through telephoto lenses sitting on a ledge high above the sea, eating oranges, and talking as they watched the waves below. What happened off camera must have been hectic because Elizabeth returned to Rome alone. The next thing anyone knew she was back at Salvador Mundi for treatment. Suicide rumors were rampant, and *Il Messaggero* declared: "After a violent argument with Richard Burton, Liz Taylor may have tried to kill herself with barbiturates." Police called at the villa, as by law they must, to check out the report. The explanation was that on the return trip from the north, Elizabeth's chauffeur had braked the car unexpectedly and she had sustained severe facial injuries, which were to put her out of work till May 7. At the hospital, the physician who treated Elizabeth, Dr. Bilotta, was aghast at the suicide rumors. "Look, these are all lies. You can write it: that the doctor said they are all invented stories and that newsmen are crazy if they think all these things." It was scant help.

As an added April tidbit, University of Rome freshmen, being hazed by upperclassmen, were instructed to kidnap a film star. Naturally they chose Elizabeth. Police were summoned to disperse a hundred of them outside the villa. Nor should it come as a surprise that, at month's end, a Rome newspaper bluntly demanded that Elizabeth Taylor be declared *persona non grata* by the Italian Government and thrown out of Italy. It had been that kind of month.

❀   24   ❀

At the beginning of May a troubled Sybil Burton returned to Rome. "I'm not going to live my life to please the press," she had earlier made clear, and told waiting newsmen, "I don't read newspapers nor does my husband. I am happy and so there are no problems." The gutter press she had always ignored, but the Porto Santo Stefano weekend had made it into the London *Times*. The London *Times* came into her home and, as generations of believing Britons had confidently pronounced, if one read it in the *Times* . . . She loved and understood the gifted, complex, and driven man she had married—had seen the whole spectrum from devotion, generosity, boyish high spirits all the way down to fierce temper, moments of cruelty, moods of black despair—had known it all. Along the way she had also ridden out her husband's many temporary romantic involvements with a public sang-froid that was the envy and the wonder of those whose egos could not conceive of such a thing.

Sybil Burton, however, was not the simple, unprotesting doormat she was often pictured. At a New Year's Eve party during their first stay in Hollywood, when midnight struck, Burton embraced the beautiful actress with whom he was dancing, and with whom he was rumored to be having an affair, and kissed her in full view of all the guests. Sybil moved quietly across the floor, slapped her husband across the face, and with the same quiet dignity walked to the door and left the house. Clearly he had overstepped the bounds of their agreement, whatever that agreement was, and whatever it was was none of anyone's business. Unhappily now, in Rome, in 1962, it had become the world's business.

"I will say this to you," she later told a reporter who had pursued her via phone to the Alps, where she was spending her Christmas holiday. "Richard and I have been married fourteen years. In that time we have achieved a perfect understanding between ourselves. It is a relationship which has developed over a long period of time and it is rather binding. Can you understand that?"

On this Richard Burton was of one mind with his wife. "Show a Welshman one thousand exits, one of which is marked self-destruction, and he will go right through that door," someone had said. Burton had no present intention of going through that door, secretly pleased as he was at the new star status which prior attempts to conquer Hollywood had denied him, and nervously aware as he now was that the deepening involvement with Elizabeth had passed well beyond anything of a similar nature in his life. I WON'T MARRY LIZ! read the headline on the front-page interview he gave to Sheilah Graham. The following exchange was part of it:

BURTON: "Do you think that all of this rubbish will hurt Elizabeth?"

SHEILAH: "Very much. What do you think?"

BURTON: "It will be a nine-day wonder, and by the time the picture is released, everyone will have forgotten, unless something new happens, like me announcing I am divorcing my wife to marry Elizabeth. But darling, there's no chance of that."

SHEILAH: "You seem to be having a very fascinating life right now."

BURTON: "It's so fascinating I sometimes want to put a gun to my head."

Skouras flew back into Rome happy that at last *someone* had talked to Sheilah, but grumbling somewhat peculiarly that the whole mess would never have happened if someone had been able to tell Elizabeth how to act properly toward Sheilah in the first place. "We are still looking everywhere for that someone who will tell Elizabeth what to do," he was told. "Do you have any idea who it may be?" Silence. After which he went to view the *Cleopatra* footage and was timed snoozing loudly a total of ten times. He had recently been guest of honor at a testimonial dinner and sat stoically through Groucho Marx's crack that "Mr. Skouras faces the future with courage, determination, and terror." Now he returned to New York to the dreaded stockholders meeting to spread the sad word that Fox had lost $22.5 million in the last fiscal year, thereafter to be hectored and badgered unmercifully. Gloria Parker of Brooklyn got up to suggest that since Elizabeth was making so much money on *Cleopatra*, she ought to be on the Board of Directors. Mrs. Irene Martin disagreed vehemently. "It's sheer lunacy to pay a million dollars to any star," was her opinion, after which the two ladies locked horns "and order was restored with difficulty," according to the New York *Times*. As a sop Skouras declared that *Cleopatra* was "almost finished," a remark which had ruinous implications for the future.

In Rome, Elizabeth was being shadowed by three plainclothesmen as death threats and messages from various loonies threatened to get out of hand. While she moved into the final phase of her work on *Cleopatra*, the insatiable public appetite for any news from Rome was being fed by two versions of "What the Butler Saw." Two successive butlers at the Villa Pappa had sold their stories to the press, and slim pickings they were, for example, one butler counted ninety-seven pairs of slacks in the closet and the other counted three hundred dresses. Nevertheless, in the superheated atmosphere which now prevailed, anything was bound to sell.

"My name is Fred Oates. I am Italian," strangely began one of these sagas. Fred was not overly fond of Elizabeth. She color-coordinated all her cigarette holders and special boxes of matches with her clothing and/or the dinner tablecloth and table accessories. This drove Fred bananas. Unkindest cut of all was what occurred when he delivered her morning breakfast tray. Elizabeth's pet Yorkie, Teresa, slept curled up in a little ball on the sheepskin shag right next to Elizabeth's side of the bed. In depositing the tray on the nighttable, Fred frequently stepped on Teresa, who yelped, thus awakening Elizabeth, who would give Fred a look of "supreme annoyance." She *could* have brained him with a lamp, for openers, and if she'd known about his literary proclivities, she might have thought seriously about it. And just think what Teresa could have told him.

The other butler's story was equally entertaining and illustrative of how anything could be twisted to make Elizabeth look bad. In 1962 that was very much the name of the game. First off, he reported that she had a weakness for nice nighties, and that she roamed the house in totally unself-conscious fashion in sheer blue, gray, and black numbers. After all, it was her house. Then one morning he brought her breakfast and found her down on the floor playing with the two Siamese cats. According to the butler, the following occurred:

ELIZABETH: "Am I a nice cat?"
BUTLER: "You are a marvelous cat, Madame."
ELIZABETH: "Yes—and look, I have nails just like a cat."
BUTLER: "Madame, you have eyes like a cat, too."

Obviously there is a problem in English translation here. Elizabeth's first line, in the context of the activity, should read "Am I a good cat," or better, "Do I make a good cat?" But out came the picture of the shameless sex siren, wantonly cavorting on the sheepskin in a see-through nightie, obviously more than a little cuckoo, commanding her abject slave to humor her. If Hedy Lamarr and Victor Mature are still looking for something to follow *Samson and Delilah*, there it is.

A further tidbit took note, supposedly, of Elizabeth's monumental vanity. She bathed twice daily in candlelight, a huge mirror placed strategically on the bathtub wall (the only wall, as it happened, where it would fit). The public received this news with the heavy implication that she had carefully trained herself never to drop the soap lest her gaze be distracted, even for a moment, from the rapturous vision before her. Overlooked was the butler's comment that "I think she did it, besides the fact that it was very fashionable, because the lights often went off in the villa" that "splendid villa on the Appian Way," as *Life* had described it.

Butlers were not the only ones doing the talking in May. In April it had been the Vatican. Now the U. S. Congress got into the act. Congresswoman Iris Blitch (sic), Democrat of Georgia, charged that Elizabeth had "lowered the prestige of American women abroad and damaged good will in foreign countries, particularly in Italy. It is my hope that the Attorney General in the name of American Womanhood will take the measures necessary to determine whether or not Miss Taylor and Mr. Burton are ineligible for re-entry into the United States on the grounds of undesirability." Mrs. Blitch saw it all as a big publicity stunt, a view that must have hurtled Skouras' blood pressure up into the stratosphere. "The real truth of the matter is that the producers of *Cleopatra* in their overzealous quest for box office exploitation have been derelict in their duty not only to the people, but to God and country as well." Gurgled Congressman Joseph P. Addabbo (Democrat of New York), "I would almost guess that Antony and Cleopatra were angels compared to what is going on between Elizabeth Taylor and Richard Burton in Rome."

All of this ceaseless public uproar now had its effect on the area of her life Elizabeth had always relied on most heavily: her family and their joint sense of solidarity in crisis. Sara and Francis Taylor had come to Rome earlier in the month at Elizabeth's urgent request. Always their support had been the single most invaluable prop in her stubborn determination to follow whichever course she had charted for herself. Now, in the hash-ing out of the current situation, family solidarity fractured, a bitter quarrel ensued, and the emotional fallout was severe. Dick Hanley phoned the studio to tell them that Elizabeth was in no condition to be photographed or to work. When next she returned to work, it seemed like everything was conspiring against her.

The scene was a physical fight between Antony and Cleopatra, and called for Burton to give Elizabeth a severe clout and send her flying through the air to land on a specified mark flat on her back—the back which had been a bummer all her life and which contained three painfully reconstructed spinal discs. Both stars approached the scene with severe apprehension and were enormously relieved to get it in one take dead-on. Next day they were informed that yesterday's rushes had been spoiled in transit back to the States for printing, and that everything would have to be done over, including the fight scene. There followed what Elizabeth still remembers as a horrifying, seemingly endless series of retakes, apparently Mankiewicz's insurance against any further spoilage.

At month's end Wanger and Mankiewicz committed a huge blunder. The schedule called for Cleopatra's Death Scene and they filmed it. "Elizabeth Taylor was bitten on the breast by the asp today," read a news item, which was wrong on two counts. It was a harmless Sardinian garden snake and she took it in the hand. They had wanted to use a real asp but found it impossible to remove its venom. On the historical point: "Nobody knows for sure where the asp bit Cleopatra," Mankiewicz explained. "Even if we did know, you certainly don't think we were going to let any asp near Elizabeth."

Historical niceties aside, the blunder, from the creative point of view, lay in the fact that Fox had now been given the one scene without which the film could not do—Cleopatra's Death. Now at last they could wind up this cursed, blasted thing which had exposed them to world derision and was dragging them all down to financial destruction—and the sooner the better. While Skouras lay ill in a hospital with a prostate condition, three Fox executives arrived in Rome June 1 spewing ultimatums in all directions. Walter Wanger was immediately fired as producer. Elizabeth's work must be finished within the week. The entire film must be wrapped by June 30.

The consternation produced by this latest frenzy prompted Mankiewicz to cable Fox a very genuine offer to immediately resign. Never from the first had he possessed the luxury of a finished shooting script or anything like it. Consequently he had been forced into shooting long, from every angle to cover numerous possibilities, as protection against the day when he would finally hibernate and edit all the massive footage down into something the public would be willing to pay money—big money—to see on the screen. At this point 83 hours of *Cleopatra* in Todd-AO was being stored in Technicolor's Hollywood plant (it would eventually stretch out to a staggering 96 hours printed on 120 solid miles of film). Several vital bridge scenes and pieces of connective tissue had yet to be filmed, and two expensive chunks were also coming up: the sailing of Cleopatra's barge to Tarsus and the Battle of Pharsalia.

At Pharsalia in Greece Julius Caesar had defeated his rival, Pompey, who fled to Egypt with the victor in pursuit. Thus it happened that Caesar met Cleopatra. Not surprisingly, the prelude to their story, Pharsalia, was to be the opening scene of the film. The news that it was to be scrapped infuriated and appalled Rex Harrison. Being discovered haggling over the price of figs and lemons in the marketplace of Alexandria was definitely not his idea of how the audience should first see Julius Caesar. He made a written offer to Wanger to pay for the filming of the Battle of Pharsalia himself, if necessary. The magnitude of this gesture can only be appreciated by the fact that in a career now in its fiftieth year, Rex Harrison has been called a great many things—for example, "impossible but adorable" by his current wife, "Sexy Rexy" by the press—but "spendthrift" was never one of them. Harrison's sacrifice proved unnecessary as sanity somewhat reasserted itself. The deadlines were extended, Mankiewicz's offer was declined, Wanger continued producing minus salary or nominal authority, and at month's end, in the Bay of Naples, was filmed *Cleopatra*'s other great set piece—a dazzling companion to the entry into Rome.

Since their original liaison Antony and Cleopatra had become bitterly divided by the former's marriage for reasons of state. Now, for reasons of political strategy, it was essential that Egypt's Queen and Rome's Co-Ruler meet and reconcile. She would not go to Rome nor he to Alexandria. The meeting place chosen was Tarsus, twelve miles up the river Cydnus from the Mediterranean, birthplace of Paul, the world's greatest Christian Apostle, and now part of Turkey, then commercial gateway to Asia Minor. Cleopatra's arrival was a scene of splendor immortalized by poets throughout the ages.

According to Plutarch: "She came sailing up the river Cydnus in a barge with a gilded stern and outspread sails of purple, while oars of silver beat time to the music of flutes and fifes and harps. She herself lay under a canopy of cloth of gold, dressed as Venus."

According to Shakespeare: "The barge she sat in, like a burnish'd throne, burn'd on the water: the poop was beaten gold; purple the sails, and so perfumed that the winds were love-sick with them; the oars were silver, which to the tune of flutes kept stroke and made the water which they beat to follow faster, as amorous of their strokes. For her own person, it beggar'd all description: she did lie in her pavilion, cloth-of-gold of tissue, o'er-picturing that Venus where we see the fancy outwork nature."

The scene in *Cleopatra* cost $500,000 and looks every bit of it plus. The film barge is 250 feet long, with 100-foot masts, and the deck is completely lined in gold. Some 75 swimmers in the water are diving for coins thrown out by 35 of Cleopatra's handmaidens, stationed on the prow. Forty other handmaidens are scattering rose petals on the water. In among them all are some ersatz handmaidens: strong but slim Italian men, costumed and coifed as handmaidens by Irene Sharaff. They were used to steer the barge, a job which proved too unwieldy for the girls.

Over and above the money spent and the superb technicals was the rare accomplishment brought off by Wanger and Mankiewicz. In the awe-struck faces of peasants who behold this vision as they work both sides of the river . . . in the sensuous, insistent throb of the music . . . in the glory and splendor of the barge and its queen . . . fact, fantasy, and legend all swirl into a perfect re-creation of a historical moment on film, leaving the viewer to render the ultimate compliment: "If it wasn't exactly like this, it should have been."

Elizabeth stood behind the sheer veiling of the pavilion, sweltering in the costume originally designed for what was to have been earlier shooting in the spring. She uttered nary a word of complaint. It was to be her last day on the film she now publicly referred to as an "occupational disease." *Cleopatra*'s last day in Italy occurred in July. Two hundred and fifteen days of shooting ended with the scene in which Antony receives the cheers of his troops for their victory over the forces of Brutus and Cassius at the Battle of Philippi.

Elizabeth sat glumly off camera, thwarted in her plans to accompany Burton to Egypt for the final two weeks of exterior shooting. Her contributions to Israeli causes and her publicly proclaimed delight at being "the first Jewish Queen of Egypt" proved too much for whoever was handing out the visas. So Burton went to Egypt, Elizabeth to her home in Gstaad, and there began for both of them a period of torment so severe that neither of them will willingly discuss it to this day. "It was a period of intense agony for both of us," Burton once noted, "and a great deal of soul-searching before we made the complete break." A recent interviewer led Burton into it with the unpleasant implication that he was ready to settle down for a good wallow. Richard Burton's reaction was courteous but definite. "Well, it's very personal, and I'd rather not discuss it any further, if you don't mind." Thus confronted with the very real prospect of conversing with an empty chair, the host speedily changed the subject.

The end of *Cleopatra* notwithstanding, public fascination with *le scandale* continued at fever pitch. Down on the Naples location, Elizabeth, Burton, and a load of celebrities had gone yachting for the day. During luncheon Elizabeth observed that she was sure that someone was taking pictures. Burton retorted that she was becoming slightly paranoid on the subject. Elizabeth insisted and the curtains were thrown back separating the lunching area from the cook's galley. There stood a still cameraman and a newsreel cameraman grinding away. On the same location the couple were spotted by paparazzi via telescopic lenses on the top of the cabin of a white motorboat. What emerged from this were fuzzy photos of two people clad in bathing suits doing what appeared to be some very light smooching. "I never saw anything like it," panted one cameraman. "Even Latins aren't that ardent!" Which was crap, impure and simple, but newspaper readers were demanding a daily diet of it.

Musing painfully on the above, and dozens of examples like it, Elizabeth knew that they would have to break it off. She had absolutely no assurance that such an action would finally plug the volcanic emissions that had been erupting steadily now for six months. But anything was better than the betwixt-and-between state which now prevailed. "Nobody could look anybody else in the eye and children were being badly affected," Burton characterized it. Elizabeth was confronted with a fact implacable and seemingly unbudgeable. Her lover had a wife who loved him and whom he still loved and whom Elizabeth liked and respected. They had simply met at the wrong time for each other. She communicated her decision to Burton in a long letter and then immersed herself in a hectic round of activities with her children which fooled neither them nor her.

Two months later Burton called her from his place across Lake Geneva. Could they get together for lunch? Elizabeth's parents, then staying at their own place in Gstaad, drove her to the rendezvous. There was little of the storybook element about it. They had everything to tell and nothing really needed to be said. The pauses were awkward and, on the way to lunch, the car broke down and they sat for some thirty minutes as traffic whizzed obliviously by them in both directions.

Occasional dating resumed out of which Elizabeth formulated what she called "the most alone, mature, and unpopular decision of my life." It was a move which heretofore would have been inconceivable but she had once again in her life blessedly laid hold of something absolutely true and absolutely real. This time she would put no conditions on it. For once in a life in which she had been pampered, catered to, cajoled, flattered, worshiped, and adored, she would take something on *its* terms, not hers, and she would be glad of it.

"I didn't even want to marry Richard, you know," she revealed recently. "I said to him, 'If you want me to be your mistress'—now there's an old-fashioned word—'then I will. But no more marriages.'" She sensed the feeling of some that such total availability would be fatal strategy. In a game it might have been but this was no game to her. By some stroke of "chance and chemistry," as Frank Loesser had put it, she and her lover had become absolutely essential to each other's existence. Games and subterfuge would have no part of it. If some pain were to be part of the package, then that's the way it would have to be. For a person who up to this point in her life had been trapped in the standard human error that total happiness encompasses only things pleasant, it would be a revelation. And a large step forward to her full maturity.

What reunited the pair professionally was a script, variously titled *International Hotel* and *Very Important Persons*, which Burton had been offered by Metro and which he asked Elizabeth to read. It was a talky casserole by Terence Rattigan about a clutch of jet-setters whose lives are jointly affected when their plane is grounded by fog at London Airport. "It may not be the best picture in the world," Elizabeth observed, "but it will make a fortune." Burton scoffed and lived to regret it; the film eventually did $15 million world-wide. It was his first lesson in Elizabeth's uncanny professional ability to pick moneymaking scripts. Sophia Loren had been all but signed for the role of the wife. "Tell her to stay in Rome," she told him. "I'll do it." Metro agreed, nothing loath to follow in the wide publicity swath cut by Cleopatra's barge. Before they began work on it, they had to report to Paris for additional work on *Cleopatra*, of which there seemed to be no end.

Elsewhere along the *Cleopatra* front things were in their usual stormy state. Spyros Skouras had toppled from the Fox Presidency to be succeeded by Darryl F. Zanuck. Mankiewicz met him in Paris in October with a rough cut of *Cleo*. Zanuck viewed it, told Mankiewicz he was exercising a producer's prerogative of final cut, fired him, and put out the following statement:

"In exchange for top compensation and a considerable expense account, Mr. Joseph Mankiewicz has for two years spent his time, talent, and $35,000,000 of Twentieth Century-Fox's shareholders' money to direct and complete the first cut of the film *Cleopatra*. He has earned a well-deserved rest." Furthermore: "I would rather go to another job than leave picture-making totally in the hands of an artist." Finally: "I don't expect sympathy and I'm not going to get it. I'm the boss."

Mankiewicz still holds the unique, prestigious honor of having won four Oscars two years running—as writer-director of *A Letter to Three Wives* and *All About Eve*. He was not without his champions.

"No self-respecting picture maker would ever want to work for your company," Billy Wilder publicly scolded Zanuck. He scored "the brutal and callous dismissal of people even though they hold perfectly legal contracts. The sooner the bulldozers raze your studio, the better it will be for the industry."

Elizabeth was no less incensed. "Miss Taylor was reached by phone and minced no words," reported the New York *Times*. No indeed. "What has happened to Mr. Mankiewicz is disgraceful, degrading, particularly humiliating," she stormed. "I am terribly upset. Mr. Mankiewicz has put two years of his life into *Cleopatra* and the film is his and Mr. Wanger's. Mr. Mankiewicz took *Cleopatra* over when it was nothing—when it was rubbish—and he made something out of it. He certainly should have been given the chance to cut it. It is appalling."

Publicly Mankiewicz was philosophical: "I've been a cotton picker too long not to know that Old Marse can do with the cotton exactly what he wants. I made the first cut, but after that, it's the studio's property. They could cut it up into banjo picks if they want." Of the entire experience: "It's like coming out of a deep freeze after two solid years. This is the toughest three pictures I ever made." Of Skouras' original optimistic estimate when Mankiewicz first took over the film: "It turned into a long fifteen weeks. The next one I do will involve one man in a telephone booth and will run for approximately five minutes."

Mankiewicz and Zanuck eventually effected a rapprochement

to shoot additional battle sequences (including Pharsalia) in southeastern Spain, and bits and pieces with the stars, ironically at Pinewood in England, where the whole sorry enterprise had begun. The very last of *Cleo* went into the can on March 2, 1963, after eight straight days of shooting, Saturday to Saturday, at a cost of $224,000. There were interior continuity and bridge scenes—a terrace, a garden, inside Antony's tent in the desert. Elizabeth thus passed her thirty-first birthday watching Burton at work.

While studio presidents, producers, and directors were rising and falling, a continual public guessing game was in progress as to just exactly how much *Cleopatra* had cost and why. The most oft-quoted figure was $39 million, exclusive of expenses of distribution (mainly advertising and cost of the prints). Estimates ran from the Hollywood *Reporter*'s figure of $31,000,000 ($44 million with distribution added in) to the *Wall Street Journal*'s $40 million ($62 million including distribution). Significantly Zanuck told the Fox stockholders meeting in May 1963 that if *Cleopatra* earned $62 million world-wide, Elizabeth's take would be $7,125,000. So $62 million must have been the estimated break-even point, that is, the total cost. Now where did the basic $40 million go?

To begin with, the initial aborted shooting in London had already sunk $6 million. At a cost of another $6 million, 6,100 tons of cement, 26,000 gallons of paint, 6 miles of canvas, 2,500 square yards of metal screening, and 50 miles of plywood were lavished on the stupendous sets which sprawled over 20 acres of Alexandrian palaces and 12 acres of Roman public buildings. Elizabeth's basic deal was $1 million outright, plus $50,000 per week overtime for 12 weeks, plus $3,000 per week living allowance, plus her eventual percentage of the gross. Minus the percentage, her front money added up to roughly $1,500,000. Irene Sharaff designed 65 costumes for Elizabeth which cost $130,000, in addition to which Elizabeth also wore 30 wigs and 125 separate pieces of jewelry. The remaining 26,000 costumes for the film cost $475,000. There was a $60,000 charge for beds. The combined estimated cost of Cleopatra's entry and the barge scene was $750,000. So much for some of the big numbers.

Other items in the budget ran from the trivial to the bizarre to the downright incredible. Three Sardinian garden snakes (a principal and two stand-ins) were on the payroll for $3.40. There was a headdress porter to attend to Cleopatra's crowns at $18 per day. The anti-pinch patrol collected $65 per day per man.

The bill for chopped fish to lure seagulls in the Tarsus scene was $1,100.

Then there was the time a cat somehow got into a heavy love scene and the crew spent 45 minutes chasing it around until it went up a wall and disappeared. At which point two low-flying bats got into the act. "There were cats everywhere, even on the rafters," moaned the harassed production manager. One selected the underside of one of Cleopatra's 32 beds as her maternity ward and workmen took the set apart trying to get to the source of the noise. Estimated production costs—for cats: $12,000; for bats, $5,000.

The proceedings were not without Alice-in-Wonderland aspects. "There was an item in the budget for three million dollars for helicopters," Richard Burton recalled. "They were on call for the total of eleven months. But they were never used—possibly because no one could figure out how to get them into the first century B.C." To which Elizabeth added, "They would actually misplace fifteen hundred spears!" The big push to save paper cups caused her to shake her head in wonder. "The bill for bottled water for the American technicians and actors for eleven months was eighty thousand dollars," she related. "This would have meant that each one of us would have had to drink approximately two and a half gallons of water per day. Three weeks before the end of shooting, when thirty-five million dollars had already been spent, there was a unit meeting during the course of which a production manager said, 'Now that we're coming to the end of the picture, I want all of you to cut down on paper cups.'" Fox's fit of the frantics was partially justified by their belief that they were not dealing with the most economy-minded of directors. At some point, Mankiewicz reportedly wanted to go to Egypt for a confrontation scene in which two armies would look at each other. He figured it would cost about $100,000. Grumbled a Fox executive, "It would cost you that just to assemble the cast and serve coffee."

There was also a goodly amount of padding and sheer waste. "They could have saved a few million dollars if they hadn't hired dozens of people who stood around doing nothing," Cesare Danova reported. Anent the inflated bill for bottled water, and multiple examples like it, one of the company managers noted disgustedly, "The Italian technicians robbed us blind." The Italian unions promptly beefed to the Italian Government, demanding that all of 20th Century-Fox activity in Italy be halted because of "the scorn devoid of any element of correctness towards the host country" and because of the importation of one hundred U.S. technicians, which was termed a "clamorous offense to our prestige." In a follow-up in October, an Italian court issued an order to seize *Cleopatra* whenever it returned to Italy for showing because Italian technicians were "illegally laid off" and were claiming five months' loss of wages. All of the above takes little account of the one single item which was the chief villain in this recital: overtime.

"The film cost at least twenty million dollars more than it should have cost," Skouras later ruefully confessed. "I was the President then. I take the blame." Overtime was far and away the largest part of the excess. Robert Stephens, a few years away from his star partnership with wife Maggie Smith, had been spotted by Mankiewicz in the lead in *Epitaph for George Dillon.* Mankiewicz wrote the part of Germanicus for him. Stephens expected six weeks and got seven months. "If Mankiewicz didn't like you, he'd write you out," he related. "He liked me so I ran right through the picture." Stephens was under contract to Fox so he got nothing extra. "The rest made a fortune in overtime." Similarly John Hoyt (Cassius) thought he was getting eleven weeks and likewise got seven months "and during all that time I worked a total of only fourteen days."

Richard Burton's contract called for $250,000 for three months, plus allowance for overtime. By the time he began his principal work he was already practically on overtime. He later estimated he had tripled his salary, which would have brought him to $750,000. Rex Harrison came to work for $10,000 per week plus expenses. Eleven months of that put him in the neighborhood of $500,000. Add to these the salaries for producer, director, other cast members, crew, and thousands of extras—every single one of them inflated way out of proportion by overtime—and most of the mystery of the $40 million vanishes. When it came to pinning down who or what had caused the overtime, push came to shove, first in various newspaper accounts, finally in the law courts.

First off, wind and rain had made hash of much of the fall shooting. Joe Mankiewicz was bedded with the strep throat and a bad cold, Roddy McDowall was down with a boil which had to be lanced, Rex Harrison suffered through a siege of food poisoning, and Richard Burton gave another vivid demonstration of what St. David's Day means to a Welshman (he offered to pay for the delay in shooting). One day was lost when whoever was responsible forgot to heat the sound stage. Bad weather hit again in the spring and one day the NATO firing of weapons at Torre Astura made it impossible to use the Alexandria set. Of course there was practically no contingency schedule—no selection of alternate scenes which could definitely be filmed in emergencies. With the script being written one fast jump ahead of the actors, how could there have been? These various production problems counted for nothing in the public mind. *Le scandale* had made all of the fortunes and follies of *Cleopatra* synonymous with Elizabeth Taylor. What germ of truth there was in this belief was magnified by the fact that all of her problems hit her during the last half of shooting.

She had missed no days of shooting in the fall, despite the onset of phlebitis, a painful inflammation of the veins in her legs. One day she had had to be carried on and off the set in a chair, but she was there. In 1962 she was out five days due to phlebitis, dentistry, and a dislocated thumb (from the scene in which Cleopatra reacts to the news of Antony's marriage by stabbing everything in sight). The post-San Stefano accident, which was to be the nub of the lawsuit against her, put her out from April 20 to May 7. The escalation of *le scandale* probably accounted for another ten days.

"Elizabeth Taylor cost the company money," Cesare Danova asserted. "It's hard to say how much. Many times she would be on the set at 7 A.M. and work straight through the day, but there were other times when she wouldn't show up at all. And sometimes she would take long, long lunch hours, depending on what mood she was in." Elizabeth refuted the tardiness charges. "In eleven months of shooting in Rome, I was late only eleven hours in all. That averages about an hour a month. Any woman is entitled to that."

Another cast member attested to Elizabeth's high popularity with the Italian extras. "They would report early in the morning and go on the payroll. Then about midmorning Miss Taylor would call in and say that she was unable to make it. This news was greeted with enthusiasm by the Italians, who knew they would get another day's pay." Reports like this only confirmed the public belief that the whims of a spoiled star alone had pushed the *Cleopatra* cost up to that insane figure of $40 million.

"She had emotional upsets and she is not the most disciplined of actresses," Joe Mankiewicz observed, "but she did not cost us *that* much money." To which *Newsweek* added for the few prepared to hear it: "To blame Elizabeth Taylor for the cost of *Cleopatra* is like blaming the French Revolution on a shortage of cake."

Breasting successive waves of *le scandale* and public wrangling over the budget was Rex Harrison, struggling to reassert some perspective. "*Cleopatra* is a fantastic undertaking," he told the press. "People might think because it cost all that money and got so much publicity that it must be a supercolossal joke. But it's not, you know. It's a very serious attempt at throwing a new light on one of the greatest stories in history." To reporters who had nerve enough to ask him about *le scandale*, Harrison had a standard retort: "That all happened *after* I was assassinated." Period. Much later he quipped slyly, "My costars were giving each other black eyes so there were long stops in the filming. Otherwise it went swimmingly."

Harrison's eagle eye on the proceedings was still operating when a Fox spokesman unveiled the sales campaign for *Cleopatra*, including the famous ad, with a reclining Elizabeth showing a lot of cleavage and Richard Burton peering discreetly down at it from over her left shoulder. The body in the ad was not Elizabeth's. It belonged to a photographer's model named Lois Bennett who was paid $35 for one hour's work.

"Understated, underscored rather than overgimmicked," proudly proclaimed the spokesman. "You will note the complete absence of both orgies and grapes in the painting. We are selling from strength. We are selling without shouting." Rex Harrison also noted the complete absence of Rex Harrison, and the fact that they were selling without *him*. "I have the greatest respect for my costars, *but* . . ." he exclaimed as he filed suit against Fox asking for equal billing with Burton and unspecified damages. Fox then painted him in behind Elizabeth's right shoulder, staring not at her cleavage but at the back of her head. "I understand that they had to put him in," Elizabeth said before she saw the new ad. "I suppose he sort of floats above us, like a Chagall figure. I really think that Walter Wanger and Joe Mankiewicz should be included to float above *him*. Somewhere there should be Freud looking down at us all."

According to Publimetrix, which keeps track of such things, *Cleopatra* was "the most publicized picture of all time by a wide margin." In the spring of 1963 Fox Publicity kept the activities and press releases steadily flowing to build public interest to a crescendo prior to the New York World Premiere on June 12. Fifty-five of Elizabeth's *Cleopatra* costumes were brought over on the *Cristoforo Colombo* for a fashion show at Pier 84, after which they were sent out on tour. Fox reluctantly abandoned a plan to bring Cleopatra's barge to the current New York World's Fair when they realized that crating, shipping, restoration, and repair would have cost over $2 million. The barge would merely have been an additional pitch to go with the gigantic 30×32-foot animated sign which towered over Times Square—the largest sign ever erected there—flashing silhouetted scenes from *Cleopatra* day and night.

True to the stormy saga of *Cleopatra* from its beginnings, the Johnston Office and the Legion of Decency publicly fell out over the film. The Hollywood guardian of the Production Code granted a Seal of Approval, and a very rare personal commendation from chief censor Geoffrey Shurlock went along with it. "*Cleopatra* is an enormously successful venture and it is easily the peer of any great presentation in the history of the screen." Rubbish! retorted the Legion, granting a "B" Rating (morally objectionable in part for all) to this "pretentious historical spectacle which is seriously offensive to decency because of its continual emphasis upon immodest costumes throughout its four-hour running time. Boldly suggestive posturing, dancing, and situations compound the offense." Along with this anathema went a very rare crack at the Production Code Office for "regrettably compromising its responsibilities."

This was merely further grist for Fox's Publicity mill. Already before a single public showing, *Cleopatra* had become the eighth highest grossing film of all time due to Fox's stiff demands of advance guarantees v. 70 per cent of the gross (the studio's share of the engagements). The Pantages Theater in Hollywood put up a record $1 million alone to secure the rental. A total of $15 million was counted in the Fox till, a fact which went far to mollify stockholders at the annual May Meeting, where the air was rent with accusations and ugly recriminations.

On June 12 occurred what Dorothy Kilgallen awarded "the prize for the wildest, most supercolossal premiere ever held in New York." It was a benefit for the Will Rogers Memorial Hospital Fund and the tickets were $100 each (tickets thereafter were scaled to a $5.50 top). All traffic was halted from Forty-eighth to Fifty-fourth Street on Broadway, and ten thousand fans standing twenty-five deep were controlled by over a hundred policemen, both mounted and on foot, those on horseback riding into the crowd to quell periodic disturbances. From the street to the doors of the Rivoli stretched two red carpets, over which trod Zanuck, Wanger, Mankiewicz, Harrison, McDowall, Irene Sharaff, Alex North (all representing the film), plus Senator Jacob Javits, Leonard Bernstein, Henry Fonda, Anne Bancroft, Mary Martin, and a dazzling array of other celebrities.

A week later the Los Angeles Benefit Premiere for the Music

Center Building Fund (the first of nine separate benefit show-ings) was held at the Pantages, where seventy Los Angeles po-lice and twenty-one studio cops struggled with a crowd of five thousand, pressing forward for glimpses of another shimmering turnout of stars and celebrities. Tickets for the benefit were $250, and many of the seats were sold, resold, and sold again. One anonymous Music Center benefactor reportedly paid $100,000 for his seat. At intermission Rosalind Russell came proudly onto the stage to report that the event had raised a grand total of $1,094,403.06—the largest amount ever raised by a benefit pre-miere in the history of the industry. It went into what is now the Ahmanson Theater of the Music Center.

So, after two and a half years which had seen the highest sal-ary, heavy fog over Pinewood, Malta fever, meningism, change of directors, near-fatal pneumonia, cats, bats, rambunctious ele-phants, rubbernecking politicians, vile weather, food poisoning, other physical and emotional upheavals, the constant fury of *le scandale*, Vatican venom, Congressional criticism, shameful squandering of paper cups, "what the butler saw," palpitating paparazzi, sizzling stockholders, the downfall of Spyros Skouras, inadequate preparation, ruinous overtime, budgetary insanity, front-office frenzy—all of which brought forth the longest and most expensive film ever made, the most publicity, the biggest sign, the two most stupendous premieres—in other words, after a phantasmagoria which was, is, and is destined forever to be blessedly unique—after all this, what finally went up on the screen?

❦ 25 ❦

What finally went up on the screen was four hours and three minutes of an intimate epic spectacular which completely pleased nobody. It was neither the great masterpiece nor the dismal fi-asco devoutly hoped for by those who wished it either well or ill. Like Shakespeare's Brutus, the elements were so mixed in it that no two critics could be found who could agree over practi-cally anything about it.

It was called everything from "a work of cinema art" to "a stunning, entertaining, brilliant panorama" to "a veritable Cecil

B. De Millennium" to "one more overlong, gaudy, and ultimately tedious super-screen spectacle" to "a ponderous, vast artistic nullity, groaning under the weight of its uninspired millions." Some marveled that so fine a film could have been achieved under such abominable circumstances. Others wondered how Fox managed on a mere $40 million. "It looks as if it had cost twice that much" (*The New Yorker*).

As to the performances, overall Rex Harrison received the greatest positive critical unanimity, Roddy McDowall next, and then Richard Burton, negative reaction to whom was invariably coupled with the disclaimer that he did the best he could under the circumstances. No such clemency was vouchsafed Elizabeth. Almost without exception, her notices were mixed at best, and the worst produced the most scathing criticism of her career.

"Overweight, overbosomed, overpaid, and undertalented, she set the acting profession back a decade," spat talkathon maestro David Susskind. "Seldom can such a mountain of a film have given birth to such a mouse of a performance," declared the London *Times*. A mere balanced assessment came from *Newsweek*: "Miss Taylor is not the worst actress in the world. She can do an acceptable love scene, and she has a modest gift for delivering witty dialogue. But she is no Judith Anderson, and even if she were, she would also have to be Eleanor Roosevelt for this script. Cleopatra does not just fall in love and meet her doom. She has a thing for world peace and world government." Therein lay the rub.

Mankiewicz had handed Elizabeth one of the most exacting roles ever written for the screen. His Cleopatra is a rich composite of voluptuous beauty, royal ruler, idealist, lover, politician, and military strategist. She is by turns tempestuous, shrewd, ruthless, arrogant, intelligent, conniving, dignified, vulnerable, and passionate. Elizabeth was expected to achieve this character and command a film for which the sets and costumes are so lavish they constantly threaten to crowd the actors right out of the frame. All of this was to be brought off under conditions of extreme professional ineptitude and personal crisis. Not surprisingly, Elizabeth responded to the demands and under these circumstances with a performance which fluctuates wildly from one end of the film to the other. Her problems begin with her first scene.

Desperately needing Caesar's help, Cleopatra has smuggled herself into his presence rolled up in a rug. Elizabeth rolls out of it awkwardly like a chunky hunk of petrified laundry. She is too hefty by half to convincingly bring off a child-queen, and her diction in the opening scenes badly wants crisper definition. The voice and the weight run up and down the scale for four hours. Her weight is at optimum for the Tarsus banquet scene, and a white gown and stylish hairdo put her at her very best. Later, at the Battle of Actium, she is fat in an unbecoming yellow number. Thereafter her weight retreats to more pleasing proportions. Vocally, she is shrill in the scene with Caesar before the tomb of Alexander the Great, and again nasal and hollow in her first scene with the depressed Antony after Actium. Yet the scene with Agrippa, in which she refuses him the head of Antony, is just right in every particular, as is her scene with Antony before Alexander's tomb. Probably her finest single scene is the one wherein she receives the news of Antony's marriage to Octavia— a quiet scene that throbs and aches with passion betrayed, and in which all of the values are exquisitely realized. After which she goes on a rampage and Mankiewicz leaves her shrieking "Antony!" in decibels more suited to a fish market.

After reading various reviews in which her voice was characterized as "screechy" and "twangy," Elizabeth called Walter Wanger and offered to redub some of the dialogue. It had been realized during shooting that a certain amount of post-production dubbing would be necessary. Fox, at this point, was not willing to spend an extra nickel on *Cleopatra*, only one indication of corporate determination to get the damned thing out and have done with it. Worse was to come.

Way back in October 1959, Elizabeth had worried that the character of Cleopatra would lack sufficient range and growth throughout the film. Ultimately, as written, directed, performed, and edited, this was the fatal flaw which undid her performance. She is playing coolly calculating ambition from frame one. When she comes out of the rug she is far too mature, assured, stolid, blunt, unfeminine. Her early scenes grievously lack some attractive juvenality, a light touch of vivacity, flirting, some pleasing wiliness. All is played too much on one line on a spoiled, petulant, defensive note. Not only is there no suggestion of Shakespeare's "infinite variety," there is hardly any variety at all. At no time is she ever truly vulnerable. Have the armies of brother-husband Ptolemy driven her from her half of the throne, out of Alexandria and into the desert to god-knows what destiny? So what! When Caesar decides in her favor, and dispatches Ptolemy and Herodotus to the certain death of the desert, and delivers Pothinus up to the tender mercies of Apollodorus, there is no surprise, no relief, no triumph, no joy—only arrogant matter-of-factness. Doubtless there were good reasons—historic, histrionic, or otherwise—for such a narrow conception. But all must yield to the final test of any creative choice: Does it play? The answer is that over the long span of four hours it does not.

Elizabeth's failure to command the first part of her vehicle only highlights the considerable triumph of Rex Harrison. For Harrison and Mankiewicz had taken Julius Caesar well beyond either the stick-figure egotist of Shakespeare or the cartoonish schoolmaster of Shaw. Whether counseling his generals, fighting battles, bullying Roman Senators, lovemaking Cleopatra, suffering the spasms of epilepsy, ruminating on life and death, or tutoring his son, Rex Harrison is the most definitive, well-rounded, and interesting Julius Caesar the world has seen since the original passed off spurting blood in 44 B.C. He is by turns wily, subtle, amusing, and commanding, and gives *Cleopatra* its sole unquestioned claim to genuine distinction. For this performance Harrison won the National Board of Review Award as Best Actor of 1963, and nominations for an Academy Award and the New York Film Critics Award as well.

The third member of the star trio fared the worst. At least in Part II, Elizabeth passes well beyond early superficiality, indifference, monotony, into scenes of marvelous self-assurance and greater depth and awareness as the adult queen. The entire death sequence in particular is beautifully done, with Elizabeth quiet, regal, impressive. Richard Burton as Antony comes on in well-managed fits and starts, but the performance was so shredded in the cutting room that it is impossible to care about him. On that point Elizabeth, Wanger, and Mankiewicz agreed totally.

Mankiewicz had edited all the footage down to eight-plus hours, and then cut another three, pleading for a two-film concept of *Caesar and Cleopatra* and *Antony and Cleopatra*, each to run about two hours twenty minutes. Zanuck was adamant about getting it down to one film in four hours, and much of the further cutting came out of Burton's character. "This was the unkindest cut of all," says Shakespeare's Antony, and Mankiewicz's Antony could not have agreed more. What it did was leave Burton nowhere to go but down, and his several scenes of whining, snorting self-pity are an embarrassment, a self-indulgence he would never permit himself today, nor—more to the point—permit any producer, director, or editor to leave him with.

As for the rest: *Cleopatra* remains the most sumptuous, most literate spectacle ever made. The generally high level of the script commands constant admiration, particularly given the hectic circumstances under which it was written. The film was obviously made with a serious purpose; it is never camp. Alas, the overall pace is too stately, the basic material too unyielding, the story perhaps too well known to galvanize the proceedings into the kind of vibrant life that it needs. The second half, particularly, is a long journey down to an overly familiar tragedy and badly lacks forward momentum. Still, it has its great scenes, its great moments, its dazzling visual beauty, and, even with its flaws, comes close to being one of the greatest films ever made.

If only there had been better preparation and more time, if only the production had not been enveloped in such turmoil, if only Fox could have gone the whole way with even more money and proper post-production work . . . *if only* . . .

Cleopatra won nine Oscar nominations for 1963: for the Film, Harrison's performance, Sound, Editing, Music Scoring, Cinematography, Costumes, Art Direction and Set Decoration, and Special Visual Effects. It won Awards in the last four categories, the film losing to *Tom Jones* and Harrison to Sidney Poitier (*Lilies of the Field*).

Elizabeth was initially not sure she would ever see *Cleopatra*. "I was too deeply involved in it in every possible way. It cost so much, and I don't mean just money. If I go look at it now, it may just seem like a piece of cellophane to me, rather than the real thing I know is there." Ultimately Fox maneuvered her into hostessing a London screening for visiting members of the Bolshoi Ballet, and would to heaven it had been just a piece of cellophane. She sat numbly in her seat, dismally aware of all the characterization that had been sacrificed to the spectacle, cringing at the sound-track deficiencies she had vainly offered to correct, heartsick at what had been done to Burton's performance. Speeding back to the Dorchester Hotel, she raced into the downstairs lavatory and threw up.

"I don't want to say much about it," she said rather understandably a year later. "The whole episode was such a botch-up. The concept and the ideas of the second production start were so *good*, too. I was finally forced to see it in London, knowing full well, after what I'd heard, that I'd be sick to my stomach. They had cut out the heart, the essence, the motivations, the very core, and tacked on all those battle scenes. It should have been about three large people, but it lacked reality and passion. I found it vulgar. Yet I suppose I should still be grateful about having made the picture for obvious reasons."

What next happened so sickened and dismayed Joseph L. Mankiewicz that, to this day, he will very rarely mention *Cleopatra* by name. "The most absurdly traumatic experience of my professional life" is one way he refers to it; "the most humiliating experience of my career" is another. "This picture was conceived in a state of emergency, shot in confusion, and wound up in blind panic," he muttered when initially relieved of his chores. Then came the tenuous peace with Zanuck so that something, however compromised and flawed, could get up on the screen and help keep 20th Century-Fox afloat. The sorriest part of it all, to Mankiewicz, was that he lost out on the film version of Durrell's *Justine*, on which he had set his heart, the script of which he had left unfinished when he came to the rescue of *Cleopatra*. He, Wanger, Elizabeth, and Burton had tentatively agreed upon a deal for *Justine* in May, but in the fireworks that marked the completion of *Cleo*, that deal went into the trash. (Fox subsequently passed *Justine* through the hands of two different directors and into instant flopdom.) Now came the absolute last straw. Exhibitors had been bitching about *Cleopatra*'s length, even as they had over the Judy Garland *A Star Is Born*. To please them then, the Garland film was butchered with such ruthless efficiency that no copy of the 181-minute original print is known to be in existence anywhere on earth. Similarly, a month after *Cleopatra* opened, twenty-two minutes mysteriously disappeared.

"Might properly be retitled 'The Amputee,'" commented *Newsweek* after a baffled look at it. Gone were the reasons for Caesar's assassination and a preliminary scene establishing the Egyptian practice of augury and divination by fire. Consequently the audience was totally unprepared for the way the assassination of Caesar was filmed. What in hell was Elizabeth Taylor doing staring into a fire? "All one can be sure of now," *Newsweek* noted, "is that some Italian bigwig is being done in by his chums in a large marble building, possibly a bank." Furthermore: "Those patrons who invest their dollar in a souvenir program can save considerable sums of money by not going to their analysts. There is nothing wrong with the memory of anyone who is puzzled by the fifteen handsome illustrations on a two-page spread and cannot remember five of the scenes. They simply don't exist on the screen." The commendable stink that went up over this forced Fox to restore the complete print.

A year later a far worse print was on display, this one cut by an hour. That enraged the New York *Times*' Bosley Crowther, then the most powerful film critic in America. To Fox's everlasting joy, Crowther had originally hailed *Cleopatra* as "a surpassing entertainment, one of the great epic films of our day," a judgment he twice defended in subsequent feature pieces when the flak began to hit him from all sides. He went back to see it and was dumbfounded:

"I have been shocked at the mutilation that has been committed upon this film in the cutting that has been done to it at various times since its opening. I saw it recently in a three-hour version and was appalled to see that among the many scenes eliminated was the key scene between Cleopatra and Caesar at the tomb of Alexander, wherein the Queen of Egypt transmitted her one-world dream to the Consul of Rome. With this out of the picture, the whole motivation is removed."

That hackwork, which circulated on subsequent reissues, amply deserved Mankiewicz's term "brutalization." Not only was the key scene out but the famous nude scene (Cleopatra's back massage by her handmaidens) consisted of a fleeting fifteen seconds' worth of Elizabeth's lower right thigh. When Antony flees the Battle of Actium, we see him safely aboard Cleopatra's flagship and suddenly he is wandering dazedly in the streets of Alexandria. Several pieces of connective tissue were snipped and the scenes no longer faded gracefully, allowing for gradual transitions of time, place, and mood. They ended with a jerk, propelling the viewer instantly into something else, thus vitiating what little dramatic life the film had painstakingly been struggling to generate. This sort of shabby scissoring went on all over the world.

In Manila the entire nude scene disappeared along with seven other scenes adjudged "too sexy." Madrid got three hours twelve minutes minus all close-in bosom shots and other bits and pieces of flesh. Malta inherited the print from Ireland, in which certain love scenes were out and the entrance into Rome went by in a fast four minutes. The public was said to be not much impressed.

The sorry saga of *Cleopatra* eventually moved out of the theaters and onto television and into the law courts. Fox closed a deal with ABC-TV for two prime-time showings of *Cleo*, thus allowing Zanuck to announce that the film had finally turned the corner, that is, broken even. It also upheld Elizabeth's proud claim that no film in which she has appeared has ever lost money. The welter of lawsuits began with Wanger suing Skouras, Zanuck, and Fox for $2,660,000 for breach of contract, and Skouras countersuing on the same grounds. Skouras dropped his suit and Wanger took a $100,000 cash settlement. The profit split on *Cleopatra* was 55 per cent to Fox, 35 per cent to Elizabeth's MCL Films (the vehicle for her share of the gross) and 10 per cent to Walwa Films (Walter Wanger's shares which he sold to Seven Arts in April 1963). When Elizabeth publicly complained that an unfair share of the initial grosses was going into Fox's pocket to meet its overhead, Fox retorted that "Miss Taylor failed to appear for work on at least forty working days in Italy, which cost the company between $150,000 and $175,000 a day." Furthermore she had been paid over $2 million to date "and that may be all she will receive." Elizabeth promptly sued in Federal Court for her proper cut. Fox answered a month later.

LIZ, BURTON SUED BY FOX: $50 MILLION blared the headlines. This whopping breach-of-contract suit came in three parts. The first part, for $20 million against Elizabeth, charged that she breached her contract "by failure to abide by and observe customary rules, directives, regulations, and orders during production; by not reporting for work; by not reporting for work on time; by reporting for work in a condition which did not permit her to perform her services; by suffering herself by her own acts and fault to become disabled, incapacitated, or unphotographable and unable to perform her services; by conspiring with others and inducing others to break their agreements; by suffering herself to be held up to scorn, ridicule, and unfavorable publicity as a result of her conduct and deportment, during and after production and while film was being distributed, so as to become offensive to good taste and morals and to depreciate the commercial value of the film."

The second part was for $5 million against Richard Burton and leveled approximately the same charges. The third part, $25 million against both, featured more of the same and specifically scored "their conduct with each other although each was, to the public knowledge at these times, married to another." Additionally, Elizabeth was charged with "scandalous and irresponsible conduct" which hurt the distribution of *Cleopatra*, that is, she continued to say exactly what she thought of it—in public. The suit sought to "enjoin her from continuing to impugn the quality of the film."

From Elizabeth and Burton: "An absolutely ludicrous move on Fox's part and we'll let them do the talking." Did this mean, the press wanted to know, that Fox could get back its $62 million only via the courts? Of course not, replied a Fox executive vice president. *Cleopatra* would make a profit of $11 million, lawsuit or no. Upon word of that, Art Buchwald hooted in print:

"As one of the many combat correspondents who covered the sinking of *Cleopatra* from beginning to end, we were certainly interested in the figure 20th came up with. All of us in Rome knew the Elizabeth Taylor-Richard Burton romance was a hot one, but we never figured it was worth $50 million. We also owe the executives at 20th Century-Fox an apology. During the filming of the picture, one of the top men said to us, 'This picture, in spite of everything, will make $100 million.' We scoffed at the time but what we didn't know was that Fox planned to get back $50 million of it by suing the stars."

Three months later four large San Francisco theater chains sued Elizabeth, Burton, and Fox jointly for $6 million. The stars' conduct allegedly hurt *Cleopatra* and turned it into an "inferior attraction." Fox was charged with withholding "crucial information," for example, the fact that the script was written day-to-day. In effect, Fox sold a pig-in-a-poke since they refused to show the film prior to rental. After the ruinous roadshow engagement in the Bay City, Fox countersued to protect its 70 per cent share in the regular runs for which no advance money was put up. One year after *this*, Portland Paramount Corporation up in Oregon filed a $44,653 suit against Elizabeth and Fox. The amount represented anticipated revenue alledgedly lost "because of Miss Taylor's notorious and scandalous conduct," because of her public statements "that the movie was of inferior quality," and because Fox "failed to curb Miss Taylor's activities." There seemed literally to be no end to it all.

"I was involved with *Cleopatra* five years, on and off," Elizabeth noted in her memoir. Considering that Walter Wanger first dropped the idea on her in November 1958, and that items about tag ends of various lawsuits were still spluttering in the press as late as 1968, ten years would be more accurate. It had become far more than an "occupational disease"; it had become a career all by itself. Elizabeth's most active involvement with it ended in July 1962. The following December she went into *The V.I.P.'s*, released in September 1963, for which she got her second set of poor notices in a row.

Essentially the film is good hoke, whick looks better today than it did in the superheated 1963 atmosphere of *le scandale* when more was expected from it. Also, anything remotely well-put-together is bound to look good today. "No one is cleverer than Terence Rattigan at composing attractive dramatic nonsense," noted *The New Yorker*, "and in *The V.I.P.'s*, the artful dodger is very nearly at his best."

The action revolves around the various problems of a clutch of fog-bound jet-setters at London's International Airport. There is a love triangle consisting of zillionaire husband (Burton), wife (Elizabeth), and gigolo (Louis Jourdan); the down-and-out Duchess of Brighton (Margaret Rutherford); tax-harried producer Max Buda (Orson Welles) and his starlet playmate, Gloria Gritti (Elsa Martinelli); and threatened tycoon Les Mangrum

(Rod Taylor) and his faithful secretary, Miss Mead (Maggie Smith).

Two items of solid value emerged from this supercommercial soufflé. The superb scene in which Maggie Smith gets a check out of Burton to save her boss put Miss Smith solidly on the road to full film stardom. As the Duchess, Margaret Rutherford moves with vim and vigor through marvelous scenes rummaging in her bag for her vaccination certificate, having a brandy, looking for a hotel room, her every move smartly backed with a sprightly little Regency sendup by Miklos Rozsa on the sound track. She received both the Oscar and the National Board of Review Award as Best Supporting Actress of 1963. Her notices were naturally the best, but all the players generally got better reviews than Elizabeth.

V.I.P.'s director Anthony Asquith paid full respects to Elizabeth's professional abilities, merely one in a long line of directors who apparently feel compelled to counter the fictional "Liz" of the headlines. If they have never worked with her, they come to her with a spoiled, shallow, frivolous, and demanding stereotype in their heads. Invariably they are pleasantly surprised to learn that they are working with as skillful and knowledgeable a film professional as can be found. Asquith was no exception.

"Miss Taylor is a serious actress. There is nothing frivolous about her work. Whenever she walked onto the set, she knew exactly the point of the scene. She gets into the mood immediately when she steps in front of the cameras—astonishingly good at starting cold. And I have seldom known her to fluff a line." He praised her "natural, instinctive acting talent," "an extraordinary sense of rhythm . . . the timing of her pauses, her movements, even her facial expressions are instinctively right. She is a 'natural' actress in the full sense of the word. She gives complete reality. There is another thing. Like a fine musician, she thinks in relation to the complete score. She is aware of the other roles. Never, during the filming of *The V.I.P.'s* did Miss Taylor intrude when a scene belonged to someone else. And, finally, she is a director's joy; an actress who needs only a minimum of rehearsals. Some actresses get better and better with each take. With Elizabeth Taylor, by the third take there's the feeling that it's all there as you desired it."

Pleasant as that was to hear, the potential in Elizabeth's part—that of a woman at the crossroads, loved by two men and uncertain of which direction to take—goes unrealized in the passive, ponderous manner in which it is written, directed, and played. "Maybe Miss Taylor needs a sabbatical but there is a feeling of

ordinariness about her thesping these days which is disconcert-
ing," complained *Variety*. Even her staunchest supporter, the
Hollywood *Reporter*, felt let down. "Miss Taylor needs something stronger than this to display her talents, and so does Burton." London's *Daily Mirror* commented on the $1 million-per-
film she was now demanding (and getting) and scoffed: "If this
king's ransom was being paid for her acting ability, then in this
film at any rate, she has got away with monetary murder."

Elizabeth could have told them that she fully realized that neither the picture nor the part was any milestone in the cinema
arts. It served its principal purpose. It reunited her with her man,
even if while they were making it at the beginning of 1963,
things seemed to be going as dispiritedly off the set as on. Burton
traveled to Wales to see a soccer game, and en route back to London at the train station was surrounded and stomped by six teddy
boys, one of whom thrust his boot in Burton's eye. "Luckily it
wasn't a winklepicker," he said in reference to a shoe with an exaggerated pointed toe. Two days later, Elizabeth dislocated her
left knee and had to have the locked cartilage surgically manipu-
lated: same London Clinic, same anesthesiologist (J. M. Price),
same exit in a wheelchair with the same left leg swathed in bandages. These items were secondary to the main business of *le scandale*, whose continued confusion apparently only added to its
fascination.

"LIZ TAYLOR, COSTAR DICK BURTON TO WED. Actor's Wife Clears
Way for Divorce," announced Louella Parsons' scoop on January
17. "I can now tell you that Liz will marry Burton," Louella proclaimed authoritatively. WON'T FREE BURTON FOR LIZ, SAYS SYBIL
retorted the next day's headline. "Fisher Ready to Step Aside If
Divorce Asked." From Sybil: "I am not giving Richard a divorce.
The entire matter is ridiculous." From Eddie: "I'm not going to
stand in anybody's way. I will always wish Elizabeth happiness.
Whatever is the right thing for me to do will be done." Burton
publicly remembered that remark at year's end when things
had turned ugly. At this point he denied the marriage story
through a studio spokesman and Elizabeth, as usual, said nothing.

Richard Burton was still agonizing his way to a final decision,
still trying not to hurt anybody, still very much on the fence. As
an example, on February 9, Sybil flew in from Switzerland for
their fourteenth wedding anniversary and he took her to dinner
and then to a performance of *King Lear* at the Aldwych. At
month's end, as aforestated, Burton and Elizabeth were together
for her thirty-first birthday as the last of *Cleo* went into the can.
Years later Burton sorted it all out in retrospect:

"I loved Sybil, my first wife, but in a different way. My love for Elizabeth is more complete, more . . . more necessary, I suppose. I wasn't terribly conscious of it and I didn't rationalize it, but I would say my love for Sybil was much more the love of a man for his daughter. I felt very protective towards her. She was very giggly and bright and sweet and innocent and selfless. I still love her, of course, but whether the feeling is reciprocated, I don't know."

By April, with several adults and children still suspended in a miserable limbo, Burton felt impelled to seek a formal separation and Sybil agreed.

"It wasn't a decision I reached hastily," she announced. "I've had a long time to think about it. And, in fact, I have discussed it with Richard. You might say that we came to a mutual understanding regarding matters. We have worked out arrangements on financial matters, and about visitation with the children. Of course, I retain their physical custody. There are no plans for a divorce. Rich and I have neither considered nor discussed divorce. Yet we have agreed a separation is properly warranted at this time in view of the highly irregular pattern that our marriage has achieved."

After which she flew into New York with her daughters to be with Philip Burton over Easter. The usual crush of reporters surrounded her at the airport, and she deftly parried their questions until one of them stopped her absolutely cold. "Are you going to date Eddie Fisher while you're in America, Mrs. Burton?" Up to that point, Sybil Burton believed she had heard just about everything. Her lawyer, Aaron Frosch, cannily notified reporters that she would be staying with Philip Burton, whereupon all the scribes went up and camped on West Sixty-seventh Street. Sybil then went to her hotel for some peace and quiet. For Richard Burton, the worst time now began.

"I went through great pain when I temporarily lost my children," he recollected. "I didn't see either of them for two years after Sybil and I separated; it was a nightmare time. How Elizabeth put up with me during that period I don't know. I couldn't think of anything else. My dreams were shot with pictures of Kate."

The first definite marriage announcement was made in June and was given to Burton's newspaper pal Fergus Cashin. "I want to marry Elizabeth and I will marry her. No ifs. No buts. She wants to marry me. I want to marry her." "I'm so happy Richard has told you," Elizabeth added. "She says it's true," Dick Hanley confirmed, "but she doesn't want to say any more than that."

Burton then headed into the summer shooting of *Becket*, and Elizabeth signed to make her television debut in London. "We just called her up cold and asked her," claimed the producers. "She said nobody had ever asked her before." She was paid $250,000—then the highest fee ever paid a performer to do a single show in the history of television. She also signed with Columbia to do *The Sandpiper* for $1 million (against 10 per cent of the gross), in the expectation of working with William Wyler, who was postponing *The Sound of Music* to do it with her. Burt Lancaster was sought for the male lead. Additionally Elizabeth appeared with Laurence Olivier and Jean Simmons in a benefit performance for British Theatrical Charities. They had a small script problem. "Sir Laurence's lines are funnier than mine," Elizabeth beefed to the producer. "I think you should do something about it." He did.

Most of the summer of 1963 was taken up with set-sitting, watching Burton as *Becket*. At one point, to liven things up, Elizabeth, unknown to the stars, donned a blond wig and slipped into the scene in which Peter O'Toole as Henry II enters a Saxon hut and finds a sleeping peasant girl. Everyone cracked up at the discovery that she was Elizabeth, but the take was not printed—it was just a gag. Burton retaliated in kind by giving Kenneth Tynan a freewheeling appraisal of Elizabeth, including the following: "She's a pretty girl, of course, and she has wonderful eyes; but she has a double chin, and an overdeveloped chest, and she's rather short in the leg."

The TV show, *Elizabeth Taylor in London*, telecast by CBS-TV in America on October 6, consisted of Elizabeth's own reminiscences of the city plus selections from Wordsworth, Shakespeare, Keats, Pitt, Churchill, Queen Elizabeth I, Queen Victoria, and Elizabeth Barrett Browning. She delivered them in various famed London locales, "fusing the world's most distracting foreground (Elizabeth Taylor) with its most illustrious background (London)," as *Variety* put it. While filming Elizabeth encountered a problem new to her. "All my life I've been trained not to look into a camera," she told photographer Otto Heller. "Now I've got to forget the training of a lifetime. Mr. Heller, do you think you can photograph me?" To which Heller replied with the answer every cinematographer has given when asked that particular question by this particular woman. "*Anybody* can photograph you." The results garnered high praise.

"One of the happiest combinations of the year," raved the Los Angeles *Times*. "A sensitive, poetic, warm, delightful hour, beautifully made in color and a tremendous pleasure to see. Miss

Giant (with Rock Hudson and Mercedes McCambridge), 1956 (WARNER BROTHERS)

Giant (with Rock Hudson and James Dean), 1956 (WARNER BROTHERS)

Raintree County (with Montgomery Clift), 1957 (MGM)

Cat on a Hot Tin Roof, 1958 (MGM)

With Paul Newman in *Cat on a Hot Tin Roof*, 1958 (MGM)

Suddenly Last Summer (with Katharine Hepburn), 1959 (COLUMBIA)

Butterfield 8 (with Mildred Dunnock), 1960 (MGM)

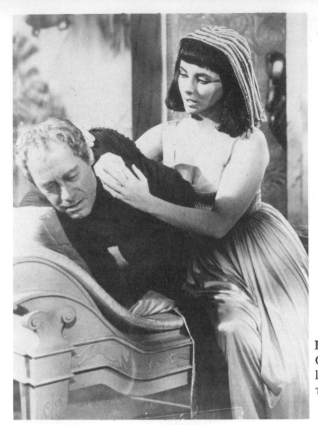

Helping Rex Harrison as Julius Caesar through the spasms of epilepsy in *Cleopatra*, 1963 (20TH CENTURY-FOX)

With Roddy McDowall in *Cleopatra*, 1963 (20TH CENTURY-FOX)

Richard and Elizabeth as the royal lovers, *Cleopatra*, 1963 (20TH CENTURY-FOX)

The V.I.P.'s (with Richard Burton and Louis Jourdan), 1963 (MGM)

With Richard Burton in *The Sandpiper*, 1965 (MGM)

With Richard Burton and George Segal in *Who's Afraid of Virginia Woolf?* 1966 (WARNER BROTHERS)

With Richard Burton in *Who's Afraid of Virginia Woolf?* 1966 (WARNER BROTHERS)

Who's Afraid of Virginia Woolf? 1966 (WARNER BROTHERS)

The Taming of the Shrew, 1967 (COLUMBIA)

The Taming of the Shrew, 1967 (COLUMBIA)

Relaxing between takes with Marlon Brando on the set of *Reflections in a Golden Eye*, 1967 (WARNER BROTHERS)

The Comedians (with Peter Ustinov), 1967 (MGM)

Boom! (with Joanna Shimkus, Fernando Piazza, Richard Burton, and Michael Dunn), 1968 (UNIVERSAL)

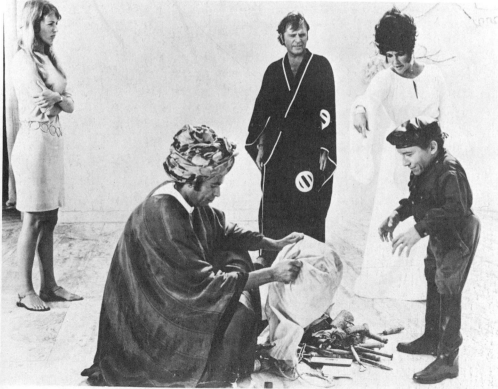

Richard Burton visits Mia Farrow and Elizabeth on the *Secret Ceremony* set, 1968
(UNIVERSAL)

The Only Game in Town (with Warren Beatty), 1970 (20TH CENTURY-FOX)

X, Y & Zee (with Susannah York and Michael Caine), 1972 (COLUMBIA)

Hammersmith Is Out (with Beau Bridges), 1972 (CINERAMA RELEASING)

Ash Wednesday, 1973 (PARAMOUNT)

Taylor gave perhaps the finest performance of her erratic career, reciting with ease the eloquent script provided by Lou Solomon and S. J. Perelman. It has been reported that Miss Taylor was coached in her reading of classic lines by her friend Richard Burton, who can swing a mean Shakespearean passage. If so, Burton did her and the audience a great favor—she read the great passages flawlessly. Miss Taylor said her viewpoint of the city was purely subjective. It was a delight to share it with her." *Variety* saluted Elizabeth's serious work on a much-criticized area when it noted that "Miss Taylor looked good (it is difficult for her to look otherwise) but what impressed one even more was the rich quality of her voice—ordinarily an attribute overlooked because of her visual beauty but emphasized in this case owing to her narrative role."

Elizabeth read those reviews in Mexico, whence she had gone to be with Burton for *The Night of the Iguana* filming, thus continuing, as *Time* observed, "a saga of togetherness rarely matched by two people who are married to other persons." Unknown to anyone at the time, *le scandale* had moved into its last act and it was to be an appropriately fiery finale. The press began to show a marked tendency, that is, more than the usual, to invent snappy quotes to compensate for the principals' distressing failure to follow the public script.

"I have decided not to marry Richard Burton," began one of these phonies. "Just because I have been seeing Dick doesn't mean I'm going to marry him." Anyone aware that Richard Burton is as delighted to be called "Dick" as Elizabeth is to be called "Liz" would have read no further. The masturbatory frenzies of the fan rags could be totally discounted. Knowledgeable people knew that they had to be strictly in-house hackwork since Elizabeth had not talked directly to one in almost a decade (nor has she since). The regular press recognized Elizabeth as the champion in this battle of her silence versus their ability to get her to talk publicly. She had bested them before, gone on to greater popularity, and now needed them less than ever. They knew better than to try anything with her since her legal counsels were not on the payroll for nothing. Burton, though about 75 per cent more publicly expansive than Elizabeth, could become explosive and downright dangerous when questioned too closely about personal business. Eddie Fisher they eventually goaded into a public performance. Sybil Burton, however, was the biggest problem. "I'm not going to live my life to please the press," she had said and she meant it. This pleasant, well-mannered, but determined lady obstinately refused to shriek on cue in public as the wronged woman. It was on her that the cruelest press tricks were practiced.

"I would never allow the father of my children to become the fifth husband of Elizabeth Taylor," Sheilah Graham quoted her as saying, a statement best taken with the whole salt shaker. Similar bits and pieces of fiction led up to the worst, which came out of a front-page fabrication in the now-defunct New York *World Telegram and Sun.* "My children and I have him tied hand and foot like so much lend-lease. I'm not going to cut the leash. And when I get him back he'll be $2 million richer." Only with her children being tortured in front of her could this woman have conceivably said such a thing in public. Sybil immediately demanded a retraction and filed a million-dollar libel suit. "I do not wish to dignify that untruthful story with a reply," she commented. The bogus story had served its immediate purpose, however. It sold a day's worth of newspapers.

Elizabeth and Burton encountered their own press problems when they flew from England to Mexico via Canada. Deplaning at Montreal, they were engulfed in a mob scene that left them shaking with fury. It began as reporters thrust a barrage of microphones into their faces with the question "Do you plan to get a divorce in Mexico?" To which Elizabeth replied, "I wouldn't tell you if I knew." Burton added, "Who knows? I don't." Then, according to Elizabeth, "They asked Mr. Burton about his sleeping habits and wanted to know if he was going to sleep with Ava Gardner and other members of the *Iguana* cast. They asked him if he always had the habit of sleeping with his leading ladies. We don't think we have to stand for that kind of talk. We are very happy together." What really sickened her was that Liza, held under Burton's protective arm in the dangerous crush, was being exposed to this mindless filth.

"The press in Montreal is the rudest and dirtiest-minded in the world," Burton later exploded. "The British press can be gentlemen, the French press is not too bad, and the Italians terrible, but not as bad as they are in Montreal." The pair were then separated by the hordes and Elizabeth was left to fend off more questions about Burton's boudoir plans, all the while trying to make her way back to him and her daughter. Eventually they reunited in the car which took them to Toronto for their flight to Mexico. There a reporter quoted Elizabeth as saying, "I'm even learning to cook and I'm doing an awful lot of knitting. I'm going to be with Richard when he comes to Toronto in January or February to rehearse *Hamlet.* Perhaps we'll be married by then. But you have to remember that we're involved with a number of other people."

Arriving in Mexico City a furious Richard Burton claimed, "I made no such statement!" and punched a photographer in the nose amid a screaming, pushing horde of a thousand, mostly teenage fans. The couple were shoved and stepped on and Elizabeth lost her shoes and her purse (later retrieved) escaping to the safety of the Immigration Room. Burton held Liza over the heads of the crowd and got her safely to the car. A press conference was scheduled at the Reforma Hotel from which Elizabeth and Burton understandably absented themselves. *Iguana* director John Huston fielded questions with his tongue stuck so far into his cheek it could have poked right though his face. Sample exchange:

REPORTER: "Is it true that Sue Lyon is trying to steal Richard Burton away from Elizabeth Taylor?"

HUSTON: "I don't think so. No."

REPORTER: "Who's that with her—a boy friend, too?"

HUSTON: "No, she came with her teacher."

REPORTER: "Like Miss Taylor?"

HUSTON: "Like Miss Taylor. Miss Taylor hasn't anything to do with the picture. She's merely along. She is Mr. Burton's teacher. She's his teacher. And Miss Lyon has a teacher, too."

Mr. Burton and his "teacher" took up residence in a four-story brick-and-stucco cliffhanger named the Casa Kimberly, after its owner, in the "Gringo Gulch" section of Puerta Vallarta. Michael Wilding arranged for the rental of the Mediterranean-style villa (which the Burtons eventually bought for about $40,000). A massive black wrought-iron gate led into a large courtyard complete with papaya, banana trees, and cocoanut palms. The house consisted of six bedrooms and six baths and all white-tiled floors. Elizabeth and Burton took the penthouse floor, a full suite complete with kitchen. Liza, Burton's secretary James Benton, two maids, gardeners, two dogs, and a cat were the other inhabitants. An armed guard was added after a drunken tourist shinnied up the wall because "I must speak to Miss Taylor" and Jim Benton threw him out.

What was termed the "lavish Mexican decor" contained no glass windows, only shutters to keep out occasional tropical downpours. Hence a can of spray stood ready in each room to fight the insects and mosquito netting was a necessity in the bedrooms. Elizabeth wasn't complaining. The isolation of Puerta Vallarta was paradise after the public pressures of the recent past.

The only way in was via Mexican Airlines from Los Angeles or Guadalajara, "not counting the bus, which looks as if it carried school kids in Bratislava in 1912," groaned one traveler. There were neither telephones nor television; a telegraph line was the only link with civilization. "That was the wonderful part of Puerta Vallarta," Elizabeth subsequently told a press conference. "No telephones. Some days you don't get a newspaper. I sympathize with you. I sympathize with your job. But some of the things are pretty repellent in the papers."

Most of *Iguana* was filmed in Mismaloya, twenty-five miles to the south. Elizabeth frequently visited quietly on the set when she wasn't teaching Liza how to read from primers sent from New York. Her sons were in school and with their father in Los Angeles, and Maria was in the care of Sara and Francis in England, undergoing further treatment on her hip. Elizabeth and Burton went on frequent sails on their rented cabin cruiser, the *Taffy*, and on horseback rides into the interior. "I can barely stay seated on a horse," Burton noted wryly, "while Elizabeth, who has known horses since she was in *National Velvet*, rides like a dream. She can bring a hack from a start to a trot to a canter and then a dead stop in ten seconds. It's discouraging."

As often as not the couple relaxed in the bar of Puerta Vallarta's Oceana Hotel at the end of a day's shooting. There the press pursued the pair and the final bits of *le scandale* were played out—to Elizabeth's intense annoyance. Eddie Fisher had completed six weeks' residence in Nevada and told the press he was waiting to hear from Elizabeth in the matter of a quickie divorce. Informed of this, Elizabeth countered, "Why doesn't Mr. Fisher get in touch with me if he wants to say something like that? Why does he use the press as an intermediary in such matters?" Again a reporter conveyed a personal message from Eddie that he would do as she wished. Elizabeth was exasperated, knowing full well the behind-the-scenes impasse which was blocking the settlement of their joint financial affairs. "I wish he would tell that to his lawyer instead of to me."

In December, Sybil Burton finally yielded to the inevitable and won a Mexican divorce *in absentia* charging "abandonment and cruel and inhuman treatment," noting that her husband was "in the constant company of another woman." *Newsweek* called that "the throwaway line of the decade." Sybil made her exit with the same civilized control she had exhibited publicly throughout the affair. "It hurts more than I can tell you," she told reporters upon leaving the New York courtroom. "I never expected it would come to this, never. I want it to end quietly.

I don't want acrimony or calumny to rear its head. I couldn't stand it that way."

Acrimony and calumny were only waiting for Sybil to leave the scene before coming onstage at full throttle. Upon news of Sybil's decree, Burton spoke for himself and Elizabeth: "We're very happy now but we'll be happier when we're married—just as soon as possible and the sooner the better." Speculating on a quickie divorce at Juárez to expedite matters, Eddie Fisher commented, "I would like to be out of this thing—whatever it is—as soon as possible." Elizabeth vetoed the idea: "I want this marriage to be thoroughly legal." Then, stung by reports that his demands for a larger cut of the *Cleopatra* grosses were holding up the works, Eddie Fisher finally lost his public cool.

"I wouldn't stand in the way of this earth-shattering, world-shaking romance for anything in the world," he declared sarcastically. "I tried for months to get Elizabeth on the phone to say let's get it over with. She wouldn't talk to me. Now all of a sudden I'm supposed to be standing in the way of the marriage of this lovely young couple who have been going together for so long. Legal matters take time and the great lovers will just have to bear up a few more days or maybe weeks. They stamp their feet, and if they don't get what they want, the world must stop. They're acting like a couple of kids in a playpen. They've been in their playpen long enough. They can wait a few days. I don't condemn them for anything except trying to put the blame on me now. I'm just as anxious as Sir Richard the Lion-hearted Burton to get this thing over with." To which he later added, "I pray that nothing will hold up anything that will keep this thing from coming to an immediate conclusion, as all fairy tales, mystery stories, or bad novels should—even comedies. I don't know what category it falls under as a story but it's getting kind of stale."

Time reported most of the above in a little Christmas present for Elizabeth entitled "A Funny Thing Happened on the Way to Decorum." There were snide references to Burton becoming "the fifth Mr. Taylor," Elizabeth's "forever proud and beaming mother and father (whose usual expression is uncertainty)," etc. When it came to Elizabeth, *Time* was still in there slugging at the same old stand, that is, north of the knees and south of the belt. A better Christmas present—one of the best ever—was Elizabeth's when Sara and Francis flew in for the holidays and Maria walked down the ramp without a trace of a limp. After which the child fell ill, her temperature soared to 104, and the isolation of Puerta Vallarta temporarily lost all its charm as Elizabeth had a terrible time getting a doctor in to treat her.

Elizabeth's final action in Mexico in January 1964 was to sue Eddie Fisher for divorce on grounds of abandonment. After which she and Burton flew in to Los Angeles en route to Toronto, for the first tryout engagement of Burton as *Hamlet* under Gielgud's direction. Elizabeth had radioed ahead agreeing to a news conference but the by-now standard mob of photographers, reporters, and fans changed her mind. There was a swaying, stumbling twenty-minute fight to the limousine which would take them to the Presidential Suite of the Beverly Wilshire Hotel. Photographers banged into garbage cans, one fell into a dog cage, others tripped and stumbled over luggage. The L.A. *Times* called it "an event of nearly riotous character. Teenagers squealed. One father held up a small boy to see the famous couple. The boy was crying. Police whistles split the air. The scene was turned to daylight by floodlights. The queen was home."

Before leaving Mexico, Burton had declared Eddie's settlement demands to be "in the realm of the fantastic and quite intolerable. Fisher must now decide whether to live up to his public image and do what he calls the 'gentlemanly thing.'" Eddie Fisher fielded that one and hurled it back with sizzling force.

"I have just read Mr. Burton's latest pronouncement on the behavior of a gentleman and I am convinced now more than ever before that he deserves an Oscar for sheer gall. I have never advised one way or the other on Mr. Burton's treatment of *his* wife and I would thank him to refrain from commenting about my actions concerning *my* wife. To set the record straight, I have not nor would I ever demand any money from Elizabeth. But on the other hand, I have no intention of surrendering to her and Mr. Burton the property which I own, especially in light of Elizabeth's preposterous divorce complaint that I 'abandoned' her. Mr. Burton is a fine actor but it would seem to me wise for him to keep his Shakespearean posturings to the stage. I hardly think Mr. Burton is the one to lecture on morals, integrity, and honesty—to me or anyone else. I have no fantastic deals to make. I just want to get the whole thing over with as soon as possible."

Elizabeth's lawyers challenged the statement by asserting that Eddie was demanding $1 million and that Elizabeth "refuses to pay for a divorce."

From Eddie: "Fantasy! How do you answer fantasy with logic?"

From Elizabeth: "Then why doesn't he sign the papers?"

A press conference was then held for eighty photographers and newsmen at the Beverly Wilshire. "I'm always afraid somebody's going to throw acid," Burton muttered nervously. "I hope as many people come to see *Hamlet*. If the critics don't like us I'll be unemployed. So I hope as many people come to see *Hamlet* as are here today." Regarding Elizabeth's impending divorce, Burton refused to tilt publicly with Eddie Fisher, contenting himself instead with a few terse observations made through tightly clenched teeth. "No one better be lying. I'm not saying anyone is lying. I hope someone will not behave badly. I hope things will not go wrong. I hope there is no viciousness. I don't want anybody to get unpleasant."

Typical of the stratagems employed to prevent public demonstrations, Elizabeth and Burton announced they would be taking the *Super Chief* to Chicago and would travel from there to Toronto. Instead they flew direct from Los Angeles traveling as "Walter Rule" and "Miss Rosamund Sutherland," and beat press and public by having Jim Benton leave two hours later with the luggage. In Toronto they took the three-bedroom Royal Suite on the eighth floor of the King Edward Hotel. Armed guards stood at the door around the clock. Outside *le scandale* swirled with undiminished force.

"What are young people to think when they see those people put on a pedestal?" publicly deplored the Reverend Robert Kerr of Trinity Presbyterian Church. "I think it is a crying shame of our society when this thing happens." Was he referring to Elizabeth? "I don't even want to use her name," he demurred piously. "They are doing publicly what a lot of people do privately," a Unitarian minister shot back. "They are being honest and courageous. Society is critical of people like them because we want to claim that sin brings its consequences. We are content to join the wolf pack and hound this couple for something we would like to do ourselves." The U. S. Congress got back on the horn as Representative Michael A. Feighan (Democrat of Ohio) requested the State Department to revoke Burton's visa because his behavior "was detrimental to America's morals." Finally an ad hoc committee of University of Toronto students placed pickets outside the King Edward with signs reading "Victorian Crusade Against Cleo" to spoof the uproar.

Elizabeth attended the musical then playing at the O'Keefe Center, and young women oohed and aahed audibly while middle-aged women voiced obscenities, equally audibly. As usual she gave no sign that she heard any of it. This was as nothing compared to what happened February 26 on the night of *Hamlet*'s dress rehearsal preview. Elizabeth was driven directly to the stage door and entered the theater quietly. At the end of the first act ushers ran down the aisle to clear her way to spend intermission in the director's suite. The cat was out of the bag. At the next intermission the entire house was on its feet craning for a look as ushers vainly entreated the audience to sit down so that the third act could start.

"Elizabeth's presence put twenty-eight minutes on the play," Burton noted at the time. "Ladies would come right down to her seat and stare at her through lorgnettes, and talk about her, saying, 'Her eyes are blue, not violet.' She doesn't hear what people say, even to her face. I'll ask her, 'What did the sons of bitches say the other night?' She doesn't know. There's a case she gets inside of. She has a genuine fear of crowds, of being made ridiculous. She withdraws, becomes monosyllabic. She projects a kind of frozen image." Elizabeth is all too dismally aware of it because, against her will, she is transformed on public occasions into something she isn't. To a basic shyness among crowds is added a very legitimate fear, from past experience, of being physically mauled and insulted at close quarters in several different languages. So the mask goes on—icy, defensive, remote—regrettable but necessary.

The worst period of her life, when she had found the public mask a constant necessity, was now almost at an end. On March 6 her divorce was granted in Puerta Vallarta since Eddie Fisher had not contested it within a twenty-one-day time limit. She shared champagne with Burton in his dressing room that night, and then they went out to a small party in the Franz Josef Room at Toronto's Walker House, where Burton celebrated with a steak and Elizabeth settled for a hot dog. The President of the Mexican Academy of Legal Procedure got some publicity by asserting that the Puerta Vallarta judge "usurped jurisdiction" and that, in his opinion, the divorce was "null and void." The Provincial Premier of Ontario grabbed a headline by proclaiming that "our laws are extremely stiff and complex" and that their request for permission to wed in Toronto "may be turned down." He needn't have worried. "They will marry and it probably will happen so quietly that not even I will know," declared their public relations man, John Springer. "The last thing they want is publicity." He proved an apt prophet.

On March 15 a chartered Viscount flew Elizabeth, Richard Burton, and eleven guests from Toronto to Montreal. There the party repaired to the eighth-floor bridal suite of Montreal's

Ritz-Carlton. Elizabeth was attired in a yellow chiffon daffodil-
styled Empire creation, moderately low at the neck. Irene Sharaff designed it remembering that Elizabeth had been wearing that
color and style in Rome when Richard Burton fell in love with
her. For jewelry Elizabeth wore only an emerald-and-diamond
clip, and that too went back to those early days in Rome. It
was the first gem Burton gave her for a collection that has since
become world-famous. He had summoned Bulgari of Rome, who
came to the dressing room at Cinecittà bearing a tray of emeralds,
diamonds, and rubies. Burton's eye lit on a certain pigeon ruby
but Elizabeth favored the emerald. Francis Taylor was of the
opinion that the latter was more elegant and that decided it.
Burton handed it to her and then asked Bulgari the price. He
replied, "Ninety-three thousand dollars." The miner's son from
Wales spoke straight from shock. "I never bought anything so
expensive in my life." As she pinned it on, Elizabeth replied,
"And this is the most expensive piece I've ever owned." On this
day of days it was fitting that she wear it in solitary splendor.

Burton's Best Man was his black friend, Bob Wilson, who had
originally served him as his dresser on *Camelot*. Elizabeth was
unattended and walked unescorted from one room of the suite
into another where Burton awaited her. The nuptial pair gave
their respective religions as Presbyterian and Jewish, after which
the Unitarian minister began the ceremony by declaring, "You
have gone through great travail in your love for each other."

As a definitive explanation of the word "understatement" that
one could successfully challenge any other. For love of this
woman, this man had done the previously unthinkable—gone
out from the safe family haven that had been his rock through
all the changing fortunes of his professional life and various
personal involvements outside of that haven—gone out from it
to cast his lot with a woman whose prior marital record was not
promising for their future—suffered the torment of separation
from his children and constant criticism and derision because
life commanded him to go forward to his completion—and he
would not avoid it. For love of this man, this woman had
challenged and stunned the world. Once she had been through
the fire and had seemingly lost everything, only to win it back
with interest when she came within moments of dying and the
world graciously forgave her. Now she had the mind-boggling
effrontery to make it known that if that arrangement did not
include this man, then all of that was worthless trash. She placed
her personal and professional fortunes right on the line to live
proudly and defiantly with him in what legal jargon termed

"open and notorious association." Accordingly the mighty organs of press and pulpit all over the world roared and thundered at her in a deafening fortissimo for two long years. The union of this man and this woman would be a disgrace, a shame, an abomination. In the end, their love, and the courage and determination born of it, prevailed. On March 15, 1964, that which could not be, finally came to pass.

"Elizabeth Burton and I are very, very happy," Richard Burton proclaimed after the ceremony. To which Elizabeth added, "I'm so happy you can't believe it." The groom further confessed that "I have been so nervous about this and having to play *Hamlet* eight times a week that I've lost twelve pounds. Now I just feel terribly relieved." They spent their wedding night in the Ritz-Carlton and, according to Elizabeth, "we sat and talked and giggled and cried until seven in the morning"— reveling in the joy and wonder that what they had so long wanted was finally theirs. Then it was back to Toronto for a lavish buffet-and-bar reception set up in the Green Room of the O'Keefe and hosted by the Hume Cronyns. The *Hamlet* cast chipped in with various homey gifts like rolling pins, mousetraps, a tiny coffee pot, and a first-aid book from Alfred Drake inscribed: "Statistics show most domestic mishaps occur in the kitchen, bathroom, and law courts. Hoping this is of help in the first two."

At the March 16 performance of *Hamlet*, after several curtain calls, Richard Burton stepped forward: "I would just like to quote from the play—Act Three, Scene One. 'We will have no more marriages.'" The house roared its approval. And in the roar of that approval, *le scandale* came to an end.

PART IV

MRS.
RICHARD BURTON
1964-

Maybe we have loved each other too much . . .
  —*Elizabeth Taylor*

Unless you love someone, nothing makes any sense.
  —*Richard Burton*

Their marriage in Montreal was the legal milestone in the continuation of a close-knit personal and professional relationship without peer in the history of motion pictures—twelve films together (counting Elizabeth's unbilled bit in *Anne of the Thousand Days*) in almost a dozen years. Of the depth of their love for each other there was never any doubt. Each showered the other with lavish public expressions of affection. Thus Burton at the beginning:

"I fell in love at once. She was like a mirage of beauty of the ages, irresistible, like the pull of gravity. She has everything I want in a woman. She is quite unlike any woman I have ever known. She makes me not want to know any other woman, believe me sincerely. I think of her morning, noon, and night. I dream of her. She will be my greatest happiness—forever, of course."

Sometimes the outrageous tease in him would get the upper hand:

"She is an extremely beautiful woman, lavishly endowed by nature with but a few flaws in the masterpiece: she has an insipid double chin, her legs are too short, and she has a slight pot-belly. She has a wonderful bosom, though."

Once he ripped off thumbnail descriptions of Elizabeth's former husbands. Nicky Hilton, "a complete mistake"; Michael Wilding, "handicapped by an enormous difference in ages"; Mike Todd, "perfect but dead"; Eddie Fisher, "deplorable." Which led him into a comment about critics of Elizabeth's private life. "You'd be surprised at the morals of many women stars who are regarded by the public as 'Goody Two-shoes.' They leap into bed with any male within grabbing distance. That's what makes me mad when I read stuff hinting that Elizabeth is a scarlet woman because she's been married five times. She's only had five men in her life, whereas those 'Goody Two-shoes' have lost count."

Then it was back to "my nagging, scheming, seductive, honest wife," as he called her. "She often tells me off in front of people when I upset her. She is also very jealous and doesn't fancy my taking two looks at the same pretty girl. She gives me hard kicks under the table, but I go on looking because it does her good to feel a little uncertain at times." As for anyone making a pass at Elizabeth, "If a man were so much as to touch Elizabeth, I would kick him right in the face."

In 1968 Burton vetoed the idea of another pregnancy for his wife as too risky.

"I cannot see life without Elizabeth. She is my everything— my breath, my blood, my mind, and my imagination. If anything happened to her I would die." Subsequently he observed, "Elizabeth is an incomparable woman in many ways. She matches me in intelligence, which is important, but not intellectually, which is perhaps more important. She is pulchritudinous beyond one's imagination. She is very passionate by nature. She's like a mother, like a daughter, like a lover. She is a fairly complete wife."

At the end of their first decade together, he was asked, "What sustains this highly entertaining relationship of yours?" Burton replied, "We have genuine adoration and love for each other." A publicity photo was released showing Elizabeth running toward the camera in *X, Y & Zee* and Burton provided his own caption for it.

"Sometimes, unexpectedly, in the early morning, I will imagine an extraordinary woman—lush and lavish and lovely—and I will reach out with my hand and find the reality of the dream woman. She exists and, lo and behold, she is alive. She is warm. She responds. She murmurs. She weeps. She is wild. She is dangerous. But sometimes, like this photograph, she will come running at me with all the beauty of the unmistakable tide coming in on the rough shore. And I lie there like a rock."

Of his marriage, "I think it will last as long as the lungs keep functioning and the heart keeps beating." Elizabeth had earlier observed, "It gets better every day."

"My God, I was on a merry-go-round for so long," she noted in her memoir. "Now I've stopped spinning. I'm not afraid of myself. I'm no longer afraid of what I will do. I have absolute faith in our future. Richard has given me all this."

Her memoir contains pages of her feeling for her husband, of which the following is a fair sample:

"I am so proud of Richard. He's so total, so complete. I love not being Elizabeth Taylor, but being Richard's wife. I would be quite content to be his shadow and live through him. He has such fun, it's contagious. His relish, his energy—it's like knowing a whirlwind that sparkles and shoots off and people catch the sparkle. He has this mercurial, retentive, darting brain—there's something wild, rather like a running deer, about his thinking."

In various interviews Elizabeth isolated different appealing facets of Burton's personality:

"Richard has such a softness, but not sentimentality, about him. He has a generosity of being, a softness of the soul, a caring for people. He absorbs and retains and cares. He remembers almost everything ever said to him." There were other aspects of her marriage important to her. "Just reaching out in the middle of the night and touching . . . saying 'I love you' for no reason. Knowing that he is aware that I am there even when I am silent. *And that I matter.*" As with Mike Todd, a feeling of equality was indispensable to her. "I like a man to be the dominating figure in my life, but I also want to be his equal," she told an interviewer. "I don't want someone telling me what to do just for the sake of telling me what to do." With Richard Burton, she had again found her ideal.

"I think Richard and I have give-and-take, yes, an equal relationship that is for me ideal. He's strong, but needs cuddling sometimes. I hope I'm the same. I am liberated. I don't understand women whose importance to themselves depends on their husband's job or his importance. It wouldn't matter to me what Richard did and I don't think it would matter to Richard what I did. Equality in our house is absolute. There's no professional jealousy."

"I love more than anything else being married to Richard," Elizabeth affirmed early in 1973. "I am married to one man and I plan on staying married to that man." Despite what the future holds for them, and whatever trials may lie ahead, these mutual expressions of devotion down through the years express the basic truth of their relationship, and he who says otherwise, lies. Along with the love went a mutual professional respect that was total.

"Working with Richard is working with the absolute pro," Elizabeth declared. "He gives you the feeling of antennae—a quivering, positive contact. He can turn emotion on and off in seconds, having it under complete control, yet you sense the latent power all the time like a volcano about to erupt. Nerves are the nemesis of all actors and Richard will do anything at his own expense to put other actors at their ease, even to fluffing his own line or knocking something over—anything so the cut in the film will be his fault." Furthermore, "I know of no other film actor who knows the whole script, everybody's lines, the day before he starts working." Finally, "I think he's one of the greatest actors, without question, who has ever worked on the screen or in the theater. He's wonderful to work with because he gives so much. Unlike so many actors, he's not a stone wall. He has electricity. He speaks verse like prose, and his prose sounds like poetry. It all really sounds like someone thinking aloud."

Richard Burton fully returned the compliments.

"Elizabeth is one of the most remarkably talented actresses I've ever worked with. She surprises the devil out of you. If you don't know her, and you watch her rehearse, you say, 'Oh, dear, here comes nothing.' She goes through rehearsals sort of like a sleepwalker. 'Is this the way I should walk? Is that the way you want me to walk?' But when that camera starts whirring, she turns it on, the magic, and you can't believe your eyes. She has great power and an uncanny instinct for the right thing."

The Burtons once discussed his initial impression of her technique on a TV interview, and it went as follows:

BURTON: "I thought, 'She can't do it. She's not doing anything.'"

ELIZABETH: "A lot of people have said that, sweetheart. For a long time."

BURTON: "Yeah, but they're all dead."

"I suppose the major change in my film acting technique has been effected by Elizabeth," Burton declared, after their relationship had vaulted him to a new cinematic high, both critically and financially. "She's the consummate cinematic technician. I learn a great deal from her."

Along with the expressions of personal devotion and professional respect went a long, well-publicized string of material gifts—from Elizabeth to Richard, seven-hundred-odd books in the Everyman Library, beautifully bound in calf's leather; also, a $500,000 French-made Alouette Helicopter. From Richard to Elizabeth, a $1 million Hawker-Siddeley twin-jet aircraft christened *Elizabeth* which seated ten, slept two, with a built-in movie projector. And, of course, a fabulous collection of jewels worth several million dollars, crowned by the Cartier-Burton diamond, the Krupp diamond, and La Peregrina pearl. More important than the public expression and the possessions was the vibrant life they found in each other's presence.

"Her spirit bubbles with an inner force like life itself," Burton declared. "She's a very funny girl with a rearing sense of humor that tends toward the ironic and satirical." She provided him with "continuous excitement, this wonderful creature called Elizabeth who fills me with spiritual and physical joy every time I see her." Elizabeth responded in kind. "Richard is just like a well: there's no plumbing the depths. You can't describe a volcano erupting. You can't describe the sound of the wind in the trees when there is no wind. He's indefinable because he's on so many levels, intellectually and emotionally. He can be an absolutely idiot clown, or he can be your Professor Higgins. A great raconteur. A great lover."

Their friends paid admiring tribute to the qualities of their life together.

"The amazing thing about the Burtons is that they never seem to bore each other," one noted. "It's almost unnatural. They're like children, in a wonderful way. I envy them this. Not their fame." To which another added, "They're not like other movie or theater people at all. They're intelligent. Those others can see only as far as their next performance. And their emptiness is like the Grand Canyon. The Burtons have something inside them."

The very real difference in their basic personalities was half the fun. One writer shrewdly noted that had both of them been born animals, Elizabeth would have been a cat and Burton a dog—she independent, diffident, selective, secretive, aristocratic; he open, gregarious, eager to charm, dependent, democratic. He marveled at her fantastic popularity and ability to command, seemingly without lifting a finger—the world came to her, not she to it. She, naturally shy, admired his hold over audiences wherever they went, all of them sitting raptly as he spun stories endlessly.

In terms of the psychology of Jung, Burton operates largely on the levels of thinking and sensation, while Elizabeth works from feeling and intuition. Naturally this made for different modes of expression and articulation. Like Shakespeare's Casca, Richard Burton was "quick mettle when he went to school," but unlike Casca, Burton stayed that way. He is capable of tearing off a dazzling burst of opinions, judgments, pronouncements, and what not with the speed and precision of a machine gun. This is not Elizabeth's way, unless she happens to be deeply moved by something at gut level, for example, her fury at people who trashed her son Michael for his "hippie" appearance, her bitter scorn at anti-Semites who make fawning "exceptions" for her as a Jew. Then she uncorks her feeling and it erupts wild, uncontrolled, without regard to verbs parsed or prepositions dangled, without regard to what kind of impression she is making, without regard to who or what is being interrupted. Bystanders are advised to stand well clear. Such a display may not hit all the points of grammar or etiquette but it is absolutely real. Otherwise, in public, she prefers to let her ideas and impressions work slowly below the surface, saying little. For interview purposes, she once characterized herself as "monosyllabic."

This combination of Burton's rat-a-tat articulation with Elizabeth's subterranean gradualism made for some volatile combustion between them before they had grasped the mechanism of what was happening and could laugh at it. A subject would arise, Burton would have covered all possible bases (in his own mind) in a fast thirty seconds and be on to something else, while Elizabeth was still struggling to the surface with fragments of what she intended to assemble in her own good time. To shortcut that process, Burton would snatch the fragments, do some rearranging, and then tell her what she meant to say or what she *should* have meant to say. That kind of thing made for some amusing fireworks. Since both of them firmly believed in a good fight now and again to clear the air, the fireworks were frequent.

Early on they laid down certain rules, for example, no swearing, since the proceedings could degenerate into ugliness. Also, points of real vulnerability were to be avoided, for example, pockmarks and double chins. Otherwise it was no-holds-barred on a wide range of things. What Elizabeth regarded as the pompous condescension of some theater people toward the movies versus Burton's essential view of films as inferior to the stage was always good for a few rounds. So was Burton's tendency to tank up and then get loquacious with the press. So was Elizabeth's perennial tardiness. "Isn't that wife of mine here *yet?* I swear to you she'd be late for the Last Bloody Judgment!" was heard so often Burton should have taped it for suitable occasions, of which there were many.

"We nag each other a bit," he revealed. "As a housewife, Elizabeth is highly naggable and limited. She's a good cook and makes marvelous breakfasts but she cannot brush a floor, for instance. I doubt if she can make a bed. When she cooks for an hour, it takes me four hours to clean up afterwards. I'm always cleaning up after her. I'm fantastically neat and tidy." Burton's objection that Elizabeth's habit of casual swearing was the sign of a limited vocabulary was countered by her accusation that he was being just plain stuffy. They eventually compromised: Elizabeth would swear quietly. In Welsh. The resolution of this issue was announced to the press in a classic little put-on.

ELIZABETH: "You know, I don't use four-letter words any more. Richard has broken me of the habit."

BURTON: "That's right. I've cured Elizabeth of that unfortunate tendency."

ELIZABETH: "You bet your ass!"

BURTON (hastily): "That's a three-letter word."

As a put-on artist and wicked tease, Richard Burton is right up there with the best of them. There was the time he took part in a charity auction and was auctioned off by Leonard Bernstein to Elsa Maxwell for $1,200. "At the dinner which followed, I was seated next to a prominent socialite," he recalled. "After a time, she whispered to me, 'Is it true that all actors are homosexual?' I responded, 'Yes, every one of them.' She answered, 'Everyone? You too?' And I assured her, 'Of course.' I've often wondered just how she looked at Fonda and Wayne and Clint Eastwood after that," he concluded gleefully.

The Burton Pekes, E'en So and O Fie, were so named for Burton's rummage through Shakespeare for Chinese-sounding phrases. In an interview with a Hollywood columnist, who sounded somewhat overwhelmed by the honor, Burton told her that E'en So was "named for a Shakespearean character misunderstood," and the columnist printed it as gospel. After all, how much Elizabethan English could the poor dear have absorbed under the hair dryer at beauty school?

Elizabeth was well aware of her husband's perverse propensities but getting taken in was half the fun and Burton developed a fine feeling for how to get her going. Nothing was sacred, not even Elizabeth's Judaism, with its tender roots in her life with Mike Todd.

"I'm more Jewish than she is, you know," Burton informed a reporter. "My great-grandfather was a Polish Jew named Jan Ysar—and that was the family name until they changed it to Jenkins. It's true. I'm one-eighth Jewish. Elizabeth doesn't have a drop of Jewish blood in her! I've told her so. Makes her furious." That would lead to something like the following:

BURTON (tauntingly with feeling): "You don't become a Jew by going to a hospital and having a little piece of something cut off! You have to be born Jewish! You have to feel Jewish blood in your veins! You're not Jewish at all! If there's any Jew in the family, it's ME! *I'm* the only Jew in this family!"

ELIZABETH (turning white with rage): "I'm JEWISH! And you can _____ OFF!" (Which was an exception to the no-swear rule but understandable under the circumstances.)

The important thing about all of these examples, and any number like them, was that they were simply exercises, a way of "Walking our wits," as Burton called it. Occasionally their two tempers would detonate over something fundamental, at which point everyone else would, as Bob Wilson phrased it, "head for the hills." The moments passed, even their celebrated public fracas in 1970 at Bumbles, the discothèque in Los Angeles. This one provided everyone with a delightful exercise in multiple choice.

Depending upon which version you heard or read, (A) Elizabeth exclaimed, "That's it! I can't take any more!" rose, and fled to spend the night with old pal Edith Goetz or (B) she did all of the foregoing but punched Burton in the nose on the way out or (C) she merely left, went to Edith Goetz's, but returned to the Beverly Hills where they made up or (D) she did all of "C" but punched Burton at the Beverly Hills, not Bumbles. Who really cared? Whatever it was, it was all over in a matter of hours.

As for the rest of what they brought to each other: His relationship with Elizabeth finally made Richard Burton a viable film personality and enriched his acting for the screen beyond measure. Four Academy Award nominations and numerous citations and trophies in the 1960s attest to it. Back in the dark period of the '50s, *Prince of Players* director Philip Dunne had observed, "Something Burton had right there before you on a sound stage, something exciting, vivid, and flawless, did not register at all on the finished film." When he left Hollywood his work was stamped "cold," "flat," "ineffective." All that was a thing of the past, particularly when he was involved with his material (about which much more anon), so much so that one could wonder if those comments had been made about the same person.

For his part Burton encouraged Elizabeth to stretch, to widen the range of her possibilities, to try, to dare, to succeed. Somehow the theory got about that the Welsh wizard from the Old Vic had totally transformed the Hollywood star, beautiful but dumb, as, of course, all of them were. A little bit of that went a long way with Elizabeth.

"I know, I know," she impatiently interrupted one interviewer who was trying that tack. "What you're trying to say is that most people thought I was the village idiot before he got me in tow. Well, he hasn't been my Svengali, but he has widened my scope. He insists I be self-sufficient and independent. He introduced me to poetry, for instance, though I'd always been scared of it. I didn't think I could 'say' poetry and he said that was silly since I understood it."

Burton agreed with that assessment. "Elizabeth is extremely intelligent though she lacks in formal education—how can you possibly be educated at MGM? I tried her out with IQ tests and she is well above the average. The only thing I can credit myself with is in increasing her awareness of the world."

So there they were—two people whose love for each other was unfeigned, deep and intense, public, bawdy, lavish, vibrant, joyous, and clear beyond question to anyone who was ever in the same room with it. Professionally they held each other in the greatest mutual respect, had enriched each other, had triumphed together. Paradoxically, it was the particular nature of their love, and the ultimate development of their professional association, which brought them to the danger point in July 1973 and threatened the continuation of either.

"The way to get along with Elizabeth is to act with a certain casualness and a certain friendliness," Dick Hanley once instructed an interviewer. "Most people are in awe of her. Pomp and circumstance don't sit well with Elizabeth." Such tips were necessary since most people *were* in awe of her, as witness this impression from an interviewer on the set of *The Sandpiper:*

"She was breathtakingly implausible in the flesh. A cloud of long black hair, the ultra violet eyes, the famous face—and she was quite petite—much slighter than screen size. She startles at first, being the overfamiliar embodiment of all those dark hours American dreamers have spent in motion picture houses watching her grow from the little girl in *National Velvet* into the current roles where many find it so hard to extricate her film performances from the flood of publicity about her private life."

Additional testimony came from an interview on the set of *The Comedians:*

"The first thing that strikes you about her is not her body but her eyes. They rivet on you when she talks and they reflect her moods like a kaleidoscope (within seconds they can switch from anger to anguish, from boredom to absorption, from gaiety to sadness)." They could also frost at ten paces anyone who presumed to press too closely into her private life, or glaze with indifference at a flood of inane questions she had answered at least a dozen times previously, or flicker with scorn at a questioner whose banalities hid the inquiries he was dying to make and dared not. Anyway you looked at it, it could be an unsettling experience.

"I want to be known as an actress," she told the New York *Times* in 1964. "I'm not royalty." Technically, no, but if movie stars are indeed America's uncrowned royalty, and there are still a few around to wear the crowns of kings and queens, then Elizabeth is reigning empress. That is indisputable. Richard Burton was her consort, not her emperor. Only two male stars in film history have ever commanded the particular degree and quality of public passion which envelops Elizabeth, and both are gone: Rudolph Valentino and Clark Gable. That she would need a court to insulate and protect her from insatiable public demands which could have destroyed her was obvious, and already in 1964 the walls were beginning to go up.

"There isn't much that the press can do either to or for Miss Taylor, but she has become a tricky, touchy woman," *Esquire* observed in November. "Press-bruised, press-pressed, probably indifferent by now to personal criticism or notoriety, she is nevertheless almost impossible to interview. She will on the rarest of occasions, grant an audience, but then only to a few proven journalists she has reason to believe she can trust, and even then only after they have proved themselves by working up through the complicated chain of command that starts with John Springer and goes through Hanley and leads through Burton on the way to Taylor."

"I don't think of myself as Taylor any more. I much prefer being Burton. It more than keeps me busy. It's a full-time occupation," she said at the time. "I'm totally and completely different in ways too subtle and too close to talk about. Otherwise they wouldn't be close. Anyone who knows me knows there's a difference. I certainly know. I don't find any problem being Mrs. Richard Burton. I think it would be marvelous to walk in the streets and go into stores and have nobody pay any attention to me at all. I would take the children. I would go to the park. I would go to the zoo."

That such activities were impossible was proved the fine sunny Sunday morning the Burtons left the Regency Hotel to stroll up to Central Park to enjoy it. "Fans always seem to know where we are," Burton once muttered, "as if there were an underground spy system, flashing messages." The mob scene which ensued on this particular morning forced them to return to the hotel after ten minutes. Of the money they were making and the need for it, Burton commented, "People are awfully catty about our getting nearly three million a film between us. But in fact all this money is fairy wealth—it doesn't really exist. Seventy-five per cent goes before we see it. We need so many people to help us who have to be paid. For example, we need at least four guards to watch the villa or someone will try crawling over the wall to photograph us in the lavatory."

By 1967, on the set of *Boom!* in Sardinia, the inner circle had multiplied mightily and the New York *Times* found the general aura redolent of Versailles pre-1789.

"The Burtons are insulated by a gaggle of retainers—managers, press secretaries, secretaries with their own secretaries, makeup men, hairdressers and dressers, even a boy to retouch any still photographs taken of them. Every journalist or photographer allowed anywhere near is approved beforehand. Some journalists are barred because they have misbehaved in print in the past. All photographs taken are inspected and approved before publication. Interviews, you are told when you arrive, can probably be obtained sooner or later, although you gather that such favors are treasures indeed. You might even get lucky and be allowed to carry one of the Burtons' Pekingese. The Court of Louis XIV must have been a little like this. The reality of meeting, thank God, is a little different."

By 1971, on the set of *X, Y & Zee*, an eyewitness listed the following entourage which surrounded Elizabeth more or less constantly: her husband (over on frequent visits from the set of *Villain*), her son Michael, her son Christopher, her makeup man, Ron Berkeley, her personal photographer Gianni Bozzachi, her chauffeur Gaston Sanz, her personal hairdresser Claudia Bozzachi, a wardrobe woman, Burton's executive assistant Bob Wilson, and Burton's personal secretary Jim Benton. By now Elizabeth had enveloped herself in a golden cocoon every bit as removed and unreal as the one she had complained of and fought her way out of after seventeen years in Culver City. In a combination of choice and necessity, her husband was part of it from the beginning.

Burton noted then, "Elizabeth and I wouldn't have been ready for all this ten years ago. We met then and carefully avoided each other. Now we find we share the same sense of comedy and the ridiculous. That's why we love each other. We feel exactly the same way about things." This statement, with its exclusive overtone, evidenced the traditional two-becoming-one view of the marital state. If additionally it smacked faintly of a "we-two-against-the-world" approach to their love, that was understandable, given the mountain they had moved to get it on in the first place.

"We feel particularly unsure of ourselves when we are in front of lots of people at a party because no one really wants to know us," Burton explained. "They simply stare at us as if we are prize animals. What we do when we go to parties is drink to kill the feeling of icy isolation and wait for the attacks to begin." Since neither had any desire whatever to go on making public appearances as the World's Most Famous Freaks, they would withdraw for the most part into a world of their own making, living for each other, surrounded by those whom they loved, and those who served as the buffers which would make such a world possible. This decision led naturally to the physical and professional togetherness which became intrinsic to their relationship.

"Well, if I'm away from Richard I feel like half a pair of scissors," Elizabeth commented in a phrase of Benjamin Franklin's she had first used when married to Mike Todd. "Really, if we are only separated for a few hours I go crazy. It has only happened twice that we have been separated—when my father was sick and I had to fly to California from Ireland, and when my chauffeur's son died and I went to the funeral. So we are only apart when it is a matter of life and death. It's certainly nothing I planned. It's something we can't help—a marvelous accident of the heart to feel this way."

Burton joked about it when he was on location in Mexico for *Raid on Rommel* and kept in frequent touch with Elizabeth in Los Angeles via telephone.

"There is her sweet, dulcet voice saying, 'Richard, it's absolutely extraordinary when you are away. I wandered round the bedroom last night and found a pair of your socks the dogs had been chewing. And I mooned over them.' I was very flattered. I told everyone that Elizabeth goes to bed with my socks when she is on her own."

The depth of his feeling about possible separation was revealed in the strenuous session they went through over whether Elizabeth would or would not attend the Academy Award Ceremonies in 1967 (the year she won for *Virginia Woolf*). They were then filming *The Comedians* in Nice, and though Burton was still at work, Elizabeth's part was finished. She had promised Jack Warner she would attend. Burton was initially outraged that she would even think of going without him and forbade it. His attitude confronted her with the loathsome prospect of either defying her husband or breaking her pledged word. Frost had begun to form on the walls.

"Richard had a nightmare," Elizabeth explained. "He dreamt the plane I was flying back to California in crashed—and he saw me dead. We've never been separated. Now he doesn't want me to go. He's my husband and I'm not going." Five minutes later she was walking around with the problem again. "I was up all night but there's nothing else I can do. We've almost never been separated. He gets into a terrible state when I'm away, especially when he gets tanked up. And he's my *husband*. How can I leave him if he wants me to stay! The only trouble is that I told them I'd go. Now what am I supposed to tell them? 'I can't come to your Academy Award Dinner because my husband had a nightmare?'"

Subsequently she informed Jack Warner and a cable came back with a pointed piece of advice, "Do not burn the bridges you have built." "There's no guarantee she'll win," Burton observed. "She could fly all that way and lose." Which was possible but, since Elizabeth already had the National Board of Review and New York Film Critics Circle awards in her pocket, highly improbable. "They'll never nominate me for an Award again," Elizabeth wailed at one point. Then, in an example of the mutual accommodation which characterized their relationship, Burton thought he might rearrange his schedule and frantically tried to get the time off. In the end he couldn't and that decided it. Elizabeth did not go and took some fierce static for her absence in the Hollywood press.

"I'm like a bloke with a pimple," Burton explained. "He can't let it alone and I can't let *her* alone. I have to know she's somewhere around the house." Additionally they both had legitimate fears of the trouble certain people and the press could make if their work kept them apart. So, because the business of actors is acting, and because they did not wish to be separated, they would either act together or in films shot simultaneously in the same location. "Acting is a kind of showing off and the best person to show off to is your wife," Burton announced. "I find it very embarrassing to work with any other actress after Elizabeth—as gifted as I think other actresses are." Occasionally he doubted the professional wisdom of this position. "Look, baby," he once told his wife, "if we do any more films together they'll think we're Laurel and Hardy." To which Elizabeth retorted smartly, "So what's wrong with Laurel and Hardy?" As to who would have the chief say in the choice of their material there was never any doubt. "It's the little lady who calls the shots," Bob Wilson once revealed, and in Burton's mind that was as it should be.

"Elizabeth is the only absolutely real star in the world. She is the only star whose films make money regardless—from *Lassie* to *The Sandpiper*," he said in 1965. "She has an unerring eye for what is going to make a fortune. She chooses very carefully. When I was asked to do *Becket*, I said to Elizabeth, 'It's a marvelous piece of writing but it won't make a penny.' She said 'It will make a fortune.' It will make twenty million. Look at *The Sandpiper*. It is making a fortune."

Five years later, after these judgments had passed under an ominous cloud, Burton was still discussing his selection of films in the same terms.

"At one time I had no choice. I was under contract to Fox for fourteen years. That ended about ten years ago. But you did whatever they chucked at you. Still, I am under contract to Elizabeth Taylor now. I am dominated a good deal by her judgment, and she has been about seventy-five per cent right, which is a remarkably good record."

The nature of their particular life together, insulated and isolated, was bound to become claustrophobic at times. What no one foresaw was the depressing effect a long stretch of professional embarrassment would produce. But, then, who could have predicted such a thing for those two? Weren't they the two stars most in demand in the entire galaxy of world cinema? Could they not have any script of their choice merely for the asking? How could such a thing have happened?

They met professionally on *Cleopatra*, and no matter what else could be said about *The V.I.P.'s* and *The Sandpiper*, they made big money. *Who's Afraid of Virginia Woolf?* and *The Taming of the Shrew* would bring them artistic and financial triumph in full measure. From then on, with one exception, it would be all downhill in a dismaying bag of promising properties which fizzled, potboilers, artistic sacrifices, and flat-out disasters—*The Comedians, Doctor Faustus, Boom!, Hammersmith Is Out, Under Milk Wood*, and *Divorce His; Divorce Hers* (theirs); *Reflections in a Golden Eye, Secret Ceremony, The Only Game in Town, X, Y & Zee* (hers); *Candy, Where Eagles Dare, Staircase, Raid on Rommel, Villain, Assassination of Trotsky, Bluebeard* (his).

The one exception in this dismal parade was *Anne of the Thousand Days* which was at least a moderate critical and financial success and which, ironically, was first offered to both Burtons by Producer Hal Wallis in 1964. By 1969 Elizabeth would have really appreciated a triumph in that title role. His work as Henry VIII enabled Richard Burton to go up in his sixth try for an Academy Award, only to be gunned down by John Wayne in the finals.

Other than that, the news was all bad, increasingly compounded by press sniping at the regal trappings of the Burtons' private life. The public was fed a steady diet of trivia about new baubles and trinkets, yachts, homes in Mexico and Switzerland, property in Ireland and the Canary Islands, a birthday blowout in Budapest, and could only contrast this with the drivel that was going up on the screen. The question was plain. What on earth—to use a fine British phrase—was all this in aid of? *Candy? Boom!? Hammersmith? Divorce His; Divorce Hers?* Was somebody kidding?

A 1971 Los Angeles *Times* piece entitled "Living on Love," viciously slanted when not factually in error, nevertheless posed some urgent questions which could not be begged much longer. "Was there something about the two of them together, offscreen and on—artistic, behavioral, psychological, whatever—that was poisonous to their potential, lethal to their careers?" Again: "So what does it matter if they are out of touch with reality? That they have become an anachronistic king and queen whose domain has shrunk to the dimensions of two deferment contracts? Why should they care if, increasingly, their efforts turn into bombs rather than Roman candles?"

This view was complemented by a *Cosmopolitan* observation in the July 1973 issue: "Probably Elizabeth herself no longer recognizes the unreality of her charmed existence, enclosed as she is within a magic circle, guarded by hotel major domos, chauffeurs, lawyers, bodyguards, servants, studio protectors, press agents, secretaries, and assorted adoring 'tweenies.'"

The views were wrong on both counts. Elizabeth *did* care and she *was* aware. "Elizabeth isn't an intellectual but she has a basic sound intelligence that is very rare," Richard Burton once commented. "She absolutely can't be fooled. This is very likely because she doesn't fool herself. She keeps a very sharp eye on reality."

On July 3, 1973, with that issue of *Cosmopolitan* still on the newsstands, John Springer summoned newsmen to the Regency Hotel in New York City and distributed a statement which stunned newspaper readers around the world. Elizabeth was depressingly aware of the personal and professional rut into which they had fallen, and her prescription for the Burtons was drastic. Their love for each other was not at issue. The salvation of their future together was all. In a life packed with crises and filled with decisions, it may well have been one of the healthiest moves she had ever made, and she had made it for both of them.

"I am convinced it would be a good and constructive idea if Richard and I are separated for a while," Elizabeth declared. "Maybe we have loved each other too much (not that I ever believed such a thing was possible) but we have been in each other's pockets constantly, never being apart except for matters of life and death and I believe it has caused a temporary breakdown in communication. I believe with all my heart that this separation will ultimately bring us back to where we should be—and that is together. Wish us well during this most difficult and unhappy time."

At first Richard Burton denied the split.

"I don't consider Elizabeth and I are actually separated. It's just that our private and professional interests are keeping us apart." Later he confessed, "I can't imagine life without her. But if Elizabeth wants a separation—so be it."

Explosive evidence of the necessity for the circumstances which had brought them to this point was furnished exactly one week after they first were wed in Montreal.

❀ 27 ❀

Any notion held by either Elizabeth or Richard Burton that the act of matrimony would magically make mob scenes a thing of the past was soon dispelled. The most violent one yet awaited them in Boston, to which they flew for the next leg of the *Hamlet* tryout. One thousand fans greeted their arrival in the lobby of the Sheraton-Plaza Hotel and turned it into a screaming, clawing riot.

LIZ NEARLY KILLED BY MOB OF FANS! shrieked the headline and it was no lie. The Burtons got separated in the frenzy as two parts of the throng bore Elizabeth triumphantly away, each in possession of one arm and each tugging in opposite directions. The rest of the mass kept surging against her, finally slamming her into a wall where hair was torn from her head for souvenirs. As Elizabeth best remembered it, that happened when a piercing male voice screamed, "See if she's got her wig on!" His confederate grabbed a hunk and snapped her head back and forth and, sure enough, it was no wig. "Grab some for a souvenir," came the next command and, while this was happening, her shoulder was sprained as two groups fought to see which one could twist her around for the better look at her face.

"She was being pulled in opposite directions at the same time," a witness stated. "People were tugging at each arm and even crushed her face against the wall when she attempted to free herself. They yanked on her arms and pulled her hair and there was nothing she could do because she was pinned against that wall."

Burton finally fought his way through to her and grabbed one arm, tugging her toward the safety of the elevator. Not to be done out of its prize, the mob kept pulling violently in the other direction. For a moment Elizabeth was mortally certain that, after all they'd been through to get to the altar, her new groom was finally going to wind up with literally half a bride. Finally they all slid into a half-horizontal pile in the elevator.

Elizabeth was put to bed, treated for the shoulder, strain in the neck, numerous contusions and abrasions of the scalp, and then sedated. "I have encountered mobs all over the world," she later commented, "but never anything to this extent—never anything that affected me so physically." Burton was livid with rage. "My wife was almost killed. I never saw anything like this before. It is outrageous. We had crowds like this in Toronto but the police gave us adequate protection." He threatened to lodge a formal complaint with the Boston Police Commissioner. On *Hamlet*'s opening night Elizabeth was properly wary of the fresh hordes gathered at both the Sheraton-Plaza and the Shubert Theater. She arrived after the first act and slipped in unnoticed. The play got six curtain calls and mixed notices. After a two-week run it was on to New York and solid triumph.

The seventeen-week run for the Burton *Hamlet* shattered all records for the play since Shakespeare first conceived it in 1600, and, thanks to the Electronovision film version made from it, was financially the most successful as well. Some carped at the style—rehearsal clothes on a bare stage. (At the opposite extreme, the Old Vic had most recently sent over a *Hamlet* done in post-bellum General Grant Era style, in which the "gentle nymph" Ophelia waddled around in yards of crinoline and several of the bearded gentry looked like nothing so much as the Smith Bros. in the cough drop ads.) Those who prefer their Dane melancholy and introspective found plenty to quibble about in Burton's energetic *Hamlet* but they could not fairly fault the high intelligence, breadth of conception, and consistency which stamped the characterization.

An elegant opening night soiree was held in the Rainbow Room of Rockefeller Plaza for six hundred guests. There were four uniformed police among a total security force of one hundred and forty. The tables groaned with champagne, lobster, steak, and stuffed tomatoes. At one point John Gielgud was seen gliding smoothly over the dance floor with Lillian Gish. When the Burtons finally arrived, flashbulbs lit up the scene like the aurora borealis. "Mr. Taylor! Mr. Taylor!" cried one excited lensman. "Mr. Burton!" was the firm rejoinder, after which her husband steered Elizabeth away muttering, "Let's get away from this rubbish." The pair then table-hopped, talking animatedly, and ultimately fled early through the kitchen to escape the cameras. "Ten thousand dollars! It cost me ten thousand dollars," moaned *Hamlet* producer Alexander Cohen to nearby detectives, "and you let those photographers drive them out!"

This was a small sample of what was to become a unique occurrence in a city which has seen more than its share of distinctive sights. "I learned in New York," Elizabeth wrote, "that there is no deodorant like success." Not only were numbers of old acquaintances all suddenly becoming eagerly available again, but the nightly ritual at the Lunt-Fontanne was a genuine mindblower.

The word had got out that Elizabeth customarily came to pick up her husband at least three times a week promptly at eleven o'clock. As the crowds began to swell, Burton grew nervous and asked her not to come. A few nights of that and the crowds had grown larger than ever. At which point Elizabeth returned to the nightly ritual, six mounted police were assigned to guard her limousine, and sixteen policemen manned the barriers at Broadway and Forty-sixth Street.

"She is wearing yellow or lavender or green or rose or some other color, never anything she has worn before or will again," reported one onlooker. "The audience—approximately a thousand nightly—surges forward. She crosses the sidewalk in seven steps or three seconds. A dazzling smile and into the limousine." This mass spontaneous public tribute went on for seventeen weeks. "You're the one they're coming to see. You're the Frank Sinatra of Shakespeare," Elizabeth quipped to her husband, to which Burton replied, "Oh, come now, get hold of yourself, luv." There was some truth to it, though. When he was out two performances with an abscessed tonsil, almost half of each audience demanded its money back. They would have Richard Burton or no one.

Burton had had his fill of the great roles in Britain at the Vic in the '50s and had lost all desire to return to them. It was Elizabeth who finally persuaded him to get together with Gielgud on *Hamlet* and get it on. Now, in an early example of the give-and-take and mutual growth that characterized their relationship since it began, Burton returned the favor. His foster-father, Philip Burton, was on the faculty of the American Musical and Dramatic Academy, and they were discussing fund-raising ideas for the school. At length they hit on the idea of a poetry reading, and Richard Burton suggested that Elizabeth be included as well. Philip Burton approached her convinced she would turn down the idea, and was amazed when she said yes.

"I was beyond measure delighted and I marveled at her courage," he recollected. "She had never appeared in a public performance before." Which, discounting that 1935 ballet recital, was technically true, although her debut appearance had been made three months earlier in Toronto. It was *Hamlet*'s closing night and after several curtain calls, Richard Burton thanked everyone for coming and then made the following announcement: "Some of you have come to see Alfred Drake, some have come to see Eileen Herlie, some have come to see Hume Cronyn, and some have even come to see Elizabeth Taylor. For the first time on any stage, Elizabeth Taylor will be here to see you." The crew then literally pushed her out from the wings and there at the O'Keefe, flustered and blushing, she took a bow and made her formal stage debut as the house rocked with applause. One impromptu bow, however, was a universe away from what was being asked of her now.

She lacked confidence in her ability to "say" poetry. Burton retorted that that was nonsense; she loved poetry and she understood it. What made her think she couldn't "say" it? Besides, they had worked together on the excerpts of *Elizabeth Taylor in London* and that had gone well. Yes, but that had been on film, and this would be live, and *that* was the sticking point to which, as Lady Macbeth puts it, she would have to "screw her courage and not fail."

"She is highly intelligent, deeply sensitive, and abrasively honest," Philip Burton wrote. "She knew that many in the audience would come for the ghoulish joy of watching a high-wire artist working without a safety net."

Elizabeth worked tirelessly with Philip Burton every night for six weeks on the program, entitled *World Enough and Time,*

eclectic excerpts culled chiefly from Shakespeare, D. H. Lawrence, Edwin Markham, and the Beatles' John Lennon. Burton
shrewdly worked to lessen her reliance on any technical equipment. "Now pretend that I'm at the back of the theater and
project your voice to me," he would call to her. "But, Phil, we're
going to have a microphone," the child of the camera replied,
eagerly looking forward to *something* to cling to on the dread
night. "Never mind—you must stand back from it and not rely
on it."

On June 23 a capacity audience filed expectantly into the Lunt-
Fontanne, having paid $35 per seat. Only on the previous evening
had Richard and Philip and Elizabeth put it all together, with
the elder Burton to serve as moderator. Now Elizabeth appeared on stage, stunning in an Irene Sharaff-designed off-the-
shoulder silk jersey gown of iridescent midnight blue, her hair
piled high in Greco-Roman fashion, her only accessories diamond pendant earrings. She got an ovation as she stood for her
first bit of poetry. "Now she'll make a mess of it," mumbled
her helpful (and nervous) husband. She saw dark blotches on her
beautiful gown and realized that sweat was squirting from her
hands. Her eyes were riveted to the pages of script and she
fumbled a line from a somber seventeenth-century elegy about
pestilential death. "I'll begin again," she announced. "I got it
screwed up." Giggles. "It's getting funnier than *Hamlet*," Burton added. He was so nervous for her that, in their first joint
selection, he kept reading her lines, which cracked them both up
to the point where they finally turned their backs and found
the stage backdrop terribly interesting for a few necessary moments.

Then Elizabeth felt the adrenalin surge through her, and with
it came assurance, and the ability to get her eyes up off the page,
and to confront that audience, and to roll out the poetry
with the sensitivity and precision she had worked for for six
weeks. "I didn't know she was going to be this good," her
honestly delighted husband exclaimed. At which point, shrewdly
sensing the mood of most of that particular audience, Beatrice
Lillie turned to her neighbor and whispered wickedly, "If she
doesn't get worse soon, they'll be leaving."

Afterward Richard Burton shouted, "Wasn't the old lady
marvelous?" to all who rushed backstage. "She has a modest
stage manner, an evident desire to please, and undeniable charm,"
reported *Variety*. "Considering her lack of stage experience,
she did remarkably well." The event raised over $30,000 for
Philip Burton's school and the Burtons were flooded with over

half-a-million dollars' worth of offers for more of the same. "I'm not terribly proud of much that I've done as an actress," Elizabeth wrote, "but I was proud of myself at that poetry reading"— as well she should have been. She had looked two fears full in the face—of a live audience and of reading poetry—had worked hard and had mastered them. She did not know it but it was just the springboard for a great leap forward into a little something by Edward Albee and, right after that, a little something else by William Shakespeare. First, however, there would be five steps backward into something called *The Sandpiper*.

Anyone who suffers through this ponderous mess today is bound to wonder how two people of proven talent and intelligence ever got involved in it. It happened for at least a couple of reasons. "There was a time after the scandal when we couldn't get a job," Burton told an interviewer. "*Hamlet* was the breakthrough. Yes, luv, we had some dark days." As always he was being protective and chivalrous toward his wife. Richard Burton has not wanted for a day's work of his choice since he returned to films in *Cleopatra*. At this point he had just done *Becket* and *Iguana* back-to-back, made a film of his *Hamlet*, and *The Spy Who Came in From the Cold* awaited him.

It was Elizabeth who, by virtue of the continuing hassle over *Cleopatra* had suddenly apparently become both uninsurable and unemployable. She sweated out the situation for several anxious months. Finally *The Sandpiper* offered to meet her million-dollar price, and even though they had no finished shooting script, director William Wyler was the prize bait and Elizabeth snapped it up. Fourteen times performers had won Oscars under this master's hand, among them Bette Davis, Greer Garson, Olivia de Havilland, Audrey Hepburn, Charlton Heston, and Barbra Streisand. Elizabeth eagerly looked forward to working with him at last. Then Wyler pulled out and everyone lost all the way around. *The Sound of Music*, which he had postponed, had now passed to Robert Wise (who won his second Oscar for it), and Wyler instead went on to nightmare labors on *The Collector*. Elizabeth maneuvered *The Sandpiper* package from Columbia over to MGM and selected Vincente Minnelli for her director. Burt Lancaster had also backed away from the male lead, but Elizabeth had her candidate for that as well.

"She is a great charmer, cajoling, flattering, and crafty," Burton once said of his wife. "There is no guile or hideous scheme known to woman that she is unable to employ." Elizabeth must have pulled out all the stops on this job. Burton had always been wary of signing a contract before reading a script, but the *Cleo-*

patra experience had turned wariness into phobia. The emerging pattern of their professional togetherness finally overcame it. Out went the announcement; the Burtons would start on *The Sandpiper* in California in the fall.

In August at *Hamlet*'s closing night party, Michael Jr. surprised and delighted Burton by doing a cutting from *Twelfth Night*, having been carefully coached for the surprise by Elizabeth and Philip Burton. Then the Burtons took the train to Chicago, where Elizabeth placed a single rose on the grave of Mike Todd, and took the *Super Chief* from there to Los Angeles. The cross-country train trip is noteworthy because Elizabeth took along her usual pile of reading material and got so absorbed in one specimen that she "didn't sleep all night after," as she put it. It was the script of Edward Albee's new sensation, *Who's Afraid of Virginia Woolf?* What Elizabeth experienced that night is analogous to a situation which occurred in London in 1936.

Gone With the Wind had scaled the bestseller lists and relatively unknown stage actress Vivien Leigh read it and couldn't get the character of Scarlett O'Hara out of her mind. Director Victor Saville even phoned her to observe mischievously, "I've just read a novel called *Gone With the Wind*. The heroine is a perfect bitch, Vivien, and you'd be just right for it." She subsequently bravely informed co-workers that she would one day go to Hollywood and play that part and, as she afterward remembered, "was laughed to scorn on the subject."

Similarly Elizabeth's fierce desire to play the role of Martha took instant root, countered by the enormity of what she was contemplating. The age thing was wrong by at least ten years. She had never done character work. She had no experience whatever with Albee's brand of vitriolic comedy. Nor had she ever attempted a characterization which, on the surface, was so far from her real self. Not all she had done in over twenty years of films put together could come up to half the demands of this script. A nice feel for young passion in *A Place in the Sun*, the monologue in *Raintree*, some flashy work in *Cat*, the final scene in *Suddenly Last Summer*—these were the highpoints, and they looked puny compared to what would be demanded in *Virginia Woolf*. Nor did anyone call Elizabeth up to tell her she'd be "just right" for Martha. Still—it was a role in a thousand, the kind she had eyed enviously when the commercial demands of the Iron Lung made that kind of role impossible for her. And as Charles Laughton once counseled Bette Davis, "Once you stop trying to hang yourself, artistically, you're dead."

The object of Elizabeth's avid interest first opened at the Billy Rose Theater in New York on October 13, 1962, with Alan Schneider directing and Uta Hagen and Arthur Hill in the leads as Martha and George. It was a sensation with the unmistakable aura of high creative endeavor, that is, a rich surface and resounding depths. Audiences could gorge themselves just on the main action alone, while those so-minded could bivouac behind the lines and find any number of puzzles to play with. What did George and Martha's "child" really stand for? And George and Martha who? Washington? If so, might Albee be saying something about the United States? And what about the theory that George and Martha were surrogates for two self-destructive, narcissistic homosexuals? What did *that* imply about contemporary relationships? And just when a viewer might think he had it all neatly sorted out, Albee tantalized his audience with several cryptic exchanges, like the one toward the end in which Nick murmurs dazedly, "Oh, my God, I think I understand this," and George replies evenly, "Do you?" Thus confronted with the incredible complexity of any "truth" *per se*, a viewer might go back to check his premises and start off in different directions. It was, among other things, an examination of the ages-old dilemma of distinguishing between truth and illusion, reality and fantasy, the very materials with which Tenneessee Williams began to stun audiences in *The Glass Menagerie*.

Theater lovers unable to undergo all this agitation in person could at least buy the original cast album and have a go at it with the hi-fi, the central question generally resolving itself into—did or did not married couples and/or people generally behave like this? The play took the New York Drama Critics Circle Award, five Tony awards, and prompted two members of the Pulitzer Committee to resign in a fury when it wasn't voted the Pulitzer Prize for Drama as well. George and Martha thus triumphantly joined the select company of such as Romeo and Juliet, Lord and Lady Macbeth, Don Quixote and Sancho Panza, Soames and Irene Forsyte, Billie Dawn and Harry Brock, Natasha and Pierre, Rhett and Scarlett, Blanche and Stanley, Willy and Linda Loman, and others whose reality transcends that of most mere mortals.

Having finally stormed the commercial heights after the limited success of Off-Broadway, Albee was adamantly opposed to surrendering the film rights to his opus without retaining a generous measure of artistic control. Possibly he recalled the hassle Vivien Leigh, Elia Kazan, and Tennessee Williams had undergone to bring *A Streetcar Named Desire* to the screen. Of crucial importance to Blanche's behavioral motivation was the fact that she had taunted her young husband for his homosexuality and felt enormous guilt and responsibility for his subsequent suicide. When *Streetcar* went into the Hollywood wash, all of that unpleasantness was neatly laundered out.

If George and Martha were going to any Hollywood party, as far as Albee was concerned, they would come as they were or not at all. George and Martha were a gamy pair (pun intended) and the frankness of the dialogue alone made this prospect almost a fantasy. Several tempting offers were made but Albee stood firm for over two years. Then, weary of the haggling and undoubtedly fearing the worst, he finally sold the rights to Jack Warner for the not-inconsiderable sum of $500,000 in March 1964, the same month in which Elizabeth married Richard Burton.

In April, Warner announced that Ernest Lehman would script and produce the film, and that Fred Zinnemann would direct it. Everyone began to voice an opinion about the casting. "How about Cary Grant and Ingrid Bergman for the older couple?" suggested the Los Angeles *Times*. Grant was always being put forward for something or other (Hitchcock once semi-seriously considered doing *Hamlet* with him), and a classic story concerned the occasion when Jack Warner offered him Henry Higgins in *My Fair Lady*, and Grant allegedly retorted, "Not only will I not do it, but if you don't get Rex Harrison, I won't even go see it!" James Mason and Bette Davis were prominently mentioned for George and Martha. Rosalind Russell was also a chief contender for Martha, but by August the favorite in the columns was Patricia Neal.

As for George, had Henry Fonda's agents not incredibly rejected the original playscript without even showing it to him, a Broadway success in the part would probably have cinched the film for him. Albee must have thought so; he had personally sent him that script. With the casting of the film still open, Fonda was again a strong possibility, in probable conjunction with Bette Davis. The spectacle of Miss Davis making her entrance croaking drunkenly about ". . . some goddamn Bette Davis picture . . . some goddamn Warner Brothers epic . . ." might have produced a scene of camp so high it could literally have been out of sight. But it was not to be. Ernest Lehman had caught Nancy Kelly and Shepperd Strudwick in the Los Angeles presentation, had flown to London to see Uta Hagen and Arthur Hill do it there, and had evolved some unorthodox casting ideas of his own. Somewhere along the line, his willingness to take a chance, coupled with a shrewd eye on the box office, connected with Elizabeth's intense interest in the possibilities.

When Elizabeth first told Burton of the offer, he remarked, "Baby, you're fifteen years too young." Her passionate desire to have the role plus her belief in her ability to bring it off finally brought him round to the opinion that "you've got to do it to prevent anyone else from doing it." As for himself, he did not remotely envision himself as George—a burnt-out, harassed, wife-racked college professor, and an American to boot. With Elizabeth up front for the money, he thought the role would probably go to Arthur Hill, who had been brilliant in it, or to someone else who was right for it. Elizabeth thought so too. Which made the following information from Sheilah Graham all the more puzzling. Never one to leave a stone unthrown where Elizabeth was concerned, Sheilah speculated that Burton would also sign for the film and opined, "I can see Richard in the role. But Liz will have to convince me." Lehman finally flew over to the Paris location of *The Sandpiper* and signed them both—not, however, before the Burtons had checked it out with a perfectly satisfied Edward Albee.

The betting odds on eventual success, not to mention eventual triumph, were anything but favorable. *Who's Afraid of Virginia Woolf?* was now slated to be written and produced by a man whose last script had been *The Sound of Music* and who had never produced a film in his life. Lumpy brown material was already hitting the fan at the very idea of Elizabeth as Martha. Burton's doubts were varied and vocal. "I'm worried about doing the American accent. I don't know—the man is so weak, so overrun by that woman." He further confided, "I've had nightmares about this picture. I wake up shaking. I told Elizabeth, 'No matter how intelligent one is, the part rubs off. It's going to be a rough ride for us.'" He had ample grounds for his fears judging from letters and telegrams which were arriving with the dire warning: "Virginia Woolf today, divorce tomorrow!"

If Lehman were a risky choice for producer, and if his casting ideas were offbeat, the Burtons' choice of a director was really far out—Mike Nichols, the brilliant satirist-turned-Broadway director, then the wearer of a triple crown for three successive hit comedies all running simultaneously: *Barefoot in the Park*, *Luv*, and *The Odd Couple*. Very nice—but how Neil Simon prepared one for Edward Albee was debatable. And just to keep the four legs of this enterprise all equally wobbly, Mike Nichols had naturally never directed a film. Ironically, the choice of Nichols freed Fred Zinnemann, who, after the disappointment of *Behold a Pale Horse* and two fruitless years spent on *Hawaii*, would go on to recoup with *A Man for All Seasons*, the film which would successfully challenge *Virginia Woolf* for the top awards of 1966.

Word of his selection reached Mike Nichols while he was vacationing in Jamaica. The Burtons, *Virginia Woolf*, and a $250,000 fee for his first film notwithstanding, Nichols returned to the States with apprehensions about having to battle against wide-screen and color, among other things, and with the problems of the script looming largest of all. He was promptly peppered with a barrage of casting critiques, the general tenor of which ran: "Elizabeth Taylor? That's the goddamnedest thing I ever heard of! They must be out of their minds!" Nichols retorted with some heat, "I say, wait and see. Everyone is going to be surprised. Personally, I consider her one of the greatest cinema actresses the screen has ever produced. I've seen *A Place in the Sun* eighteen times, and I don't know anyone in the business who could've done what she did in *Suddenly Last Summer*." That was *his* opinion, but in the fall of 1964, the not-so-silent majority waited to be convinced.

Meanwhile Elizabeth and Richard Burton had done a month's location work on *Sandpiper* up in Carmel, California, and then gone on to Paris for the interiors. Going abroad was a necessity since, had Burton remained in the States any longer, the tax bite would have been gigantic. But filming it in Paris or Hollywood or London or Shangri-la would have made no difference to the agony of this particular experience. Not since *Butterfield 8* had Elizabeth had something like this to struggle with. Burton had come to it directly from seventeen weeks in what is arguably the greatest play by the greatest playwright who ever lived. The adjustment was bound to be severe but this was ludicrous. The producer could loftily refer to the plotline as a passionate encounter between "the Galsworthy Minister and the Thoreauvian Painter" but anyway you sliced this script, soap bubbles rose *en masse*. After a lengthy hassle with Minnelli over the sheer impossibility of one of the scenes, Burton snapped, "For the money we will dance!" It was good money: $1 million to Elizabeth and $500,000 to himself. Fiscal joy was considerably dimmed by daily proofs of the old adage that "money isn't everything."

"On *The Sandpiper* the words were torture," Burton later reminisced. "The dialogue was so awful that you'd die a little each day from sheer embarrassment. We only got into the picture because Elizabeth wanted to work with William Wyler and we didn't read the script first. We'll never make that mistake again. I had this kind of experience when I was under contract to Fox and Warners. The roles were so awful that I just walked through them like a zombie. You'd accept a film just to fulfill your contractual number and get out."

Off-camera, Vincente Minnelli talked about the woman he'd known since she first came to Metro as a child of ten. "She was eighteen when I first worked with her in *Father of the Bride*. We talked often of working together after that but our times never jibed. Now she is astonishing because she has so much to give. She has electricity and radiance. She can turn on enormous dynamic power." To which Irene Sharaff added, "I think, from someone who was a slightly provincial girl of Hollywood, she has become a true woman of the world. Nobody fools her; she is very perceptive and astute. I believe, for the first time, she is realizing what she was born with." But not all of Elizabeth's professional pizzazz or growing personal assurance doubled in spades could have turned this sudsy hooey into anything real. When Metro released *The Sandpiper* in July 1965 the critics murdered it.

"Truly contemptible," "turgid, overlong, and dull," "mess of windy platitudes and stale stereotypes," "interminable $5.3 million sleeping pill" were sample opinions. "A huge, soggy, wooly, maundering, bumbling, expensive movie," declared *The New Yorker*. "Well, it does end—I'll say that for it—and on such a note of heartbreak, uplift, and sense of financial expectation for the producer that I can barely bring myself to think about it." He was so right. Strictly in tribute to the stars' charisma, *The Sandpiper* grossed about $14 million world-wide, and set three records at Radio City Music Hall: Biggest Opening Day, Biggest Non-Holiday Friday and Saturday, and new all-time Four Day record.

To give the film its due, Milton Krasner's color cinematography of California's Big Sur country is truly breath-taking to behold. Again, given this lemon, Krasner was passed over for an Oscar nomination, though to be fair, 1965 provided a strong nominations card for Color Cinematography (*The Agony and the Ecstasy, Doctor Zhivago* the winner, *The Great Race, The Greatest Story Ever Told*, and *The Sound of Music*). Not any amount of shortcomings in the script or elsewhere, however, could alter the fact that Johnny Mandel and Paul Francis Webster had contributed one of the most beautiful songs ever composed for a motion picture and "The Shadow of Your Smile" took the Oscar as 1965's Best Song. Unfortunately it crowns the sound track of a film that feels as if it were marinated in marzipan and spliced with molasses. In one of her satiric thrusts Elizabeth noted, "We never thought it would be an artistic masterpiece." Right on!

Directly after they finished it the Burtons went on holiday vacation in Switzerland, where Elizabeth put another notch on her accident record by getting a black eye playing in the snow. They returned to London where Burton was scheduled to begin *The Spy Who Came in From the Cold* and promptly ran into the great citizenship flap, which agitated newspaper readers for a week.

LIZ GIVING UP U.S. CITIZENSHIP blared the headlines. "Star to Become British Subject With Burton." As the possessor of dual citizenship since birth, Elizabeth had quietly decided to renounce the American half of it in Paris in October. Too quietly, as it turned out. She had deliberately signed the papers in her hotel suite to avoid publicity, but U.S. law prescribed that she do it in person at the embassy. Furthermore her personal deletion of the phrase, "abjure all allegiance and loyalty to the United States," was unacceptable to the State Department. Elizabeth tried explaining all this to newsmen in London.

"It's not true that I love America less but I love my husband more. It is true that I am trying to give up my American citizenship and become completely British. I want to become British more than anything else. I like the British best of all."

Possibly sensing an international incident in the making, Burton hustled her into a car, muttering, "Don't say anything. Don't say anything about it at all." Next day he remarked diplomatically, "I could not care less whether she remains an American citizen. It is entirely up to her. I adore the Americans and I love the British." At week's end the U. S. Embassy in London quietly returned the American passport Elizabeth had surrendered in Paris in October. Thus ended the reading of that particular lesson.*

The Burtons had returned to London to be greeted by an old friend. Burton had come on alone from Switzerland via Paris, utilizing various stratagems to avoid the press. He even took the service elevator to his Dorchester Hotel suite, and was just congratulating himself for having brought it off successfully when ten press cameras flashed in his face, and a properly respectful

---

* Elizabeth ultimately became solely a British subject in 1966, a fact only recently revealed by the U. S. Internal Revenue Service.

voice boomed, "Welcome to London, Your Majesty!" There stood a grinning Peter O'Toole, and the salute was a jesting tribute to Burton's new eminence in the film world.

The *Motion Picture Herald* had just listed his box office position as No. 10 (Mrs. Burton was No. 11). Furthermore, the organization which keeps tabs on such things reported that Richard Burton rated more newspaper space in 1964 than any other actor (Mrs. Burton was No. 2). A recording he had made of something called "Married Man" was, as the recording industry puts it, "getting hot on the charts." He had come cresting into 1965 on the strength of three excellent performances, in *Becket*, *The Night of the Iguana*, and *Hamlet*. *Hamlet* was ineligible for Academy Award consideration because it had been given only two days of special showings in the Los Angeles area (instead of seven days within the calendar year which Academy rules require). But he was certain to be Oscar-nominated for either *Becket* or *Iguana* and Elizabeth told him she feared he would be nominated for both and thus "kill himself off." As it happened, his next three screen performances were to take him to a new level, and to remain the high-water mark of his film work to date.

While Burton went to work on *Spy*, Elizabeth occupied herself with planning for the challenge of Martha, and signed with Seven Arts to costar, for the fourth time, with Montgomery Clift in the film version of Carson McCullers' *Reflections in a Golden Eye*, to begin filming on Southern U.S. locations in November, after *Virginia Woolf* was expected to be finished. Burton found the time to do the narration for a ten-minute short on World War I poet Wilfred Owen, *The Days of Wilfred Owen*.

The Burtons also agreed to help actor Clifford Evans establish a National Theatre of Wales in Cardiff, under control of the St. David's Theatre Trust, to which they subscribed $28,000 apiece. After which the *Spy* company moved on to Dublin, Ireland, and the Burtons experienced unpleasant evidence of the lingering aftermath of *le scandale*. Good friend Cyril Cusack had arranged for them to do a poetry reading at the Abbey Theater, proceeds to go to the Medical Mission of Mary, which is especially active in missionary work in Africa. The Archbishop of Dublin put his disapproving foot down on the idea and that was that.

March was the kind of month which was bad news from one end to the other. For openers, Elizabeth's hotel suite in Dublin was burglarized of $50,000 worth of jewels. Then her chauffeur's sixteen-year-old son was killed in a shooting accident in France, and Elizabeth accompanied the bereaved father across the Channel to bury him. Promptly upon their return, they were riding through Dublin when the chauffeur struck down and killed a woman. A week later, Eddie Fisher sued to get partial custody of Liza. And one day after *that*, Francis Taylor, then sixty-five, was stricken with a cerebral hemorrhage at six in the evening at his Bel Air home and rushed to Cedars of Lebanon. Elizabeth flew to Los Angeles, was cleared by Customs on the plane, and taken via helicopter to the hospital. "What comment can I make?" she told assembled newsmen. "I can only pray." After an anxious week, marked by fluctuations and diagnostic surgery, Francis was pronounced out of danger, and Elizabeth returned to Dublin. "He is much better," she reported. "I wouldn't have left Los Angeles unless I was happy with his condition. He is still seriously ill but thank goodness he is off the critical list."

April brought better news. *The Spy Who Came in From the Cold* finished shooting, thus enabling Richard Burton to take the first extended vacation he had had in some fifteen months. Elizabeth's chauffeur was cleared of criminal charges and Francis Taylor went home from Cedars of Lebanon. It was also in April that Academy Awards were bestowed for 1964 achievements.

Burton was spared the risk of knocking himself out with simultaneous nominations. Instead, both he and Peter O'Toole were nominated for *Becket*, that classic cinema confrontation of the irresistible force (O'Toole as Henry II) with the immovable object (Burton as Becket). Together they gave two of the most complementary, perfectly matched performances ever seen in one film, thus killing each other off. On Oscar night, Rex Harrison, holding the New York Critics Award for Henry Higgins, and Anthony Quinn, armed with the Award of the National Board for Zorba, squared off for the big one. As expected, Harrison went home the winner.

In May, Elizabeth underwent minor surgery of an undisclosed nature at a London hospital. On June 25, their vacation behind them, the Burtons sailed into New York harbor aboard the S.S. *Michelangelo* en route to Hollywood. Earlier in the month, Sybil Burton had wed Jordan Christopher and the press, with their usual finesse, badgered Burton for comments. He replied smoothly, "I always thought she had very good taste—except for me."

A few days later they were en route to Los Angeles via train. Why a train? "I just love trains," Elizabeth said. "If we had the

time, that's the way we'd always travel." They took the pre-
caution of getting off at Pomona, but a small contingent of press
were tipped off and waiting. "We got off here to avoid you
people," Burton greeted them genially. Were Richard Burton
and Elizabeth Taylor as George and Martha to be construed as
typecasting? "No. My own marriage seems to be working out all
right—at least from my half." This with a glance at Elizabeth,
who was again trying to explain the great citizenship flap. "I
wanted to do it for my husband. But they wanted me to sign
something abjuring all my loyalty to America. I couldn't sign
that. I have a great loyalty to America. A great gratitude. I have
always loved America." After which they got into the studio
limousine and were whisked off to Los Angeles—initially to
settle into a rented $4,000-per-month Bel Air manse with two
pools that were to get scant use for social purposes.

For the Burtons, the crucial testing time was at hand. Their
celebrity had secured them the dramatic sensation of the decade.
Now the public awaited the proof that their talents could do it
justice.

❁ 28 ❁

At Warner Bros., Mike Nichols and Ernest Lehman had been
doggedly at work for over six months and gone through multiple
revisions of the script of *Virginia Woolf*, attempting to adapt
the language to the requirements of the Production Code.
Finally they quit trying.

"Disguising profanity with clean but suggestive phrases is
really dirtier," Nichols announced. "It reminds me of an old
Gary Cooper movie when somebody said, 'He's so poor he hasn't
got a pot to put flowers in.' "

They did change a number of "Jesus Christs!" to "Oh my
Gods!" when they thought they would be equally effective.
Other than that they were prepared to go with a script of uncompromising power. *Life* magazine later counted eleven "god-
damns," seven "bastards," five "sons of bitches," and such assorted graphic phrases as "screw you," "up yours," and "hump
the hostess." Missing from the *Life* tally were such endearments
as "monkey-nipples" and "angel-boobs," also hardly the common

coin of the silver screen. Were they at all apprehensive about taking a trip so far out into uncharted waters?

"Sure we were scared," Lehman admitted. "But we felt the artistic intent of the film would be so clear it would overcome any objections." In that judgment they had the hearty concurrence of none other than Jack Warner.

Warner had been the butt of many a story, like the time he visited Bette Davis on the first day's shooting of *Dark Victory*, which was to be probably her greatest popular success. "Who's going to want to see a picture about a girl who dies?" he reportedly asked her. But he allowed it to be made. Again, when the *Treasure of Sierra Madre* company was deep in the wilds of Mexico and going way over buget, Warner muttered "I know whose gold they're going after. Mine!" But the picture was made.

Jack and the Brothers had originally taken the biggest gamble of all with *The Jazz Singer* and, for better or worse, given Hollywood a voice. Nor was it commercial consideration alone that cast George Arliss as Disraeli, or Paul Muni as Zola, and Joseph Schildkraut as Dreyfus. When MGM was busy pushing Ma Hardy's apple pie, and the Fox lot resounded to the musical tinkle of Shirley Temple and Alice Faye, Warner Bros. turned out a creditable number of films dealing with matters of social conscience: *I Am a Fugitive From a Chain Gang, Cabin in the Cotton, Wild Boys of the Road, Black Fury, Black Legion, The Story of Louis Pasteur, They Won't Forget, The Life of Emile Zola, Confessions of a Nazi Spy, Juarez,* and *Dr. Ehrlich's Magic Bullet.* Now Jack Warner was about to deliver his valedictory. Having originally taught the screen to talk, he was finally going to make it talk like an adult.

On July 6 the Burtons, Nichols, Lehman, and George Segal and Sandy Dennis (in the parts of Nick and Honey) met on Stage Eight at Warners for the start of three weeks of intensive rehearsals prior to shooting. By prearranged plan, given the nature of the venture and the celebrity of the principals, the work was to go forward in an atmosphere of absolute secrecy, a policy which shrewdly increased public interest to crescendo proportions by the time the film premiered a year later.

With doors barred and armed guards enforcing the policy, Stage Eight was closed absolutely tight to everyone but Jack Warner and Frank Sinatra (a Warner stockholder and executive). Lehman remarked that his secretary, who had then been with Warners twenty-eight years, couldn't even get on the set. "I realize we sound like an atom-bomb project," he admitted, "but otherwise it would be a circus." To which Burton added, "Edward Albee is well known, Mike is well known, and Elizabeth and I are *fairly* well known. If we belch, they photograph it. So we're all for the present policy." Then, with a glance at the guards, "It's just that I think they may be carrying it to ridiculous extremes."

At Warners, cast and director were investigating the nuances of a screenplay reportedly "guarded like the Holy Grail—George Segal hadn't seen it until he reported for work." The crew were meanwhile going about their assorted businesses with various instructions from Mike Nichols, like the following to the prop men: "The glasses at the bar should be jelly glasses and things that once held pimento cheese. And get me some of those terrible green mugs with no saucers from the dime store." Irene Sharaff was encouraged to "look at unknown people around real universities" to lend authenticity to the costumes. Nichols was characteristically careful not to let the pressures crack his easy-going surface.

"That's all I'm really doing out here," he quipped, "giving the little girl her first big chance." But he knew exactly what he was after and would brook no compromise with it. His cinematographer was the brilliant Harry Stradling, who two months previously had taken home an Oscar for his stunning work on *My Fair Lady*. While viewing some *Virginia Woolf* test footage together, Nichols inquired, "What are those ravishing shadows on Elizabeth's throat?" To which Stradling replied, "Well, we don't want to emphasize the double chin." Exit Harry Stradling; enter Haskell Wexler.

Meanwhile life at the Warner Publicity Department was anything but cheery, hemmed in as they were by the unusual restrictions. In July they sent out a release concerning a direct order to a star not ordinarily amenable to such a procedure. "Oh, boy!" Elizabeth later sighed. "That was one of the nicest orders I've ever been given."

"Upon the express orders of the director and producer," the release read, "Miss Taylor has been making every effort to gain weight for her role in the picture. She has been observing a special pound-adding diet to help give her the heavier appearance of a middle-aged woman."

By August they were down to a trickle of trivia, in one item of which Elizabeth supposedly spotted Forrest Tucker's golf cart (a unique custom-job) on the Warner lot and offered to trade him a Rolls for it. He courteously refused.

On Stage Eight and off the order of the day was work that

approached the obsessive. "We all got possessed by the picture," Nichols recalled. "The Burtons told me they talked about nothing else when they got home." That wasn't the half of it.

Elizabeth tackled the job of creating Martha from several angles. She, Nichols, and Lehman mutually agreed that Martha was about forty-five, and she went through eight different makeups before they selected the one they could all agree on. It was while making wardrobe tests that she hit upon Martha's particular walk, a moment Helen Hayes used to pray for in rehearsals because it usually meant that everything else would fall into place as well. Elizabeth dropped her voice well down to give Martha her basic, boozy, guttural tones, and a bawdy, vulgar cackle was an additional vocal touch.

Somehow it all began to work together and Elizabeth experienced an exhilarating freedom she had never known in a role before. The deeper into it she got, the more secure she felt, and the freer she felt to cut loose and try different things without fear. As a novice at this kind of thing, she was initially worried that she would be unable to get back into Martha fresh each morning so she naturally took her home with her. "For Christ's sake! What the hell are you talking about?" would come crackling into the middle of one of Burton's sentences, stopping him cold. Fortunately, Burton was not only flattening his vowels as a concession to his American character, but he too took George home with him, the better to get a grasp on what made the man tick. So, for about a month, George and Martha played more or less continuously on and off the lot. This total commitment left the Burtons little time for anything else, as the task of transferring *Who's Afraid of Virginia Woolf?* to the screen took top priority.

"Basically she's a lazy girl," Joe Mankiewicz once observed of Elizabeth, "but a real professional in front of the camera. She brings to a role the kind of emotional intensity you can use. You have to dig for it but it's there." Mike Nichols dug, working intensively with Elizabeth and the rest of the cast to bring them to their individual creative peaks. Occasionally he used unorthodox methods to do it. One night, for example, everyone worked till dawn. As Nichols explained, "It's easy to say you're tired, and you've been drinking a lot, and it's five-thirty in the morning, but how do you *really* feel? We wanted to do it and we found some things we hadn't thought about."

If the company were unwilling to divulge any secrets about *Virginia Woolf*, they were perfectly amenable to talking about each other. Thus Burton on Nichols:

"He is a perverse and brilliant genius. His mind is an enchantment. We asked him to direct this picture and there was the natural opposition from the diehards. I said that everyone has to direct his first film sometime." Furthermore: "Mike's a very disturbing man. You cannot charm him—he sees right through you. He's among the most intelligent men I've ever known and I've known most of them. I dislike him intensely—he's cleverer than I am. But, alas, I tolerate him." Finally and more seriously: "He is the best possible audience. Also he has the one thing that no other director and very few actors have—timing of a line. He knows how to hit the operative word. This is inevitably a tragic comedy—you must get the laugh, even to the death. And it *must* be timed perfectly."

As for Elizabeth: "I *adore* Mike. He is so inventive and has this peculiar, bizarre mind that sees only things that he can see. He's a hinting director, which makes you get all excited and start inventing and participating in his inventions. That's where he's so wise. He gives you freedom. But at the same time he's the only director I know who has memorized the entire script and quietly feeds you your lines if you dry up. He's one of the most brilliant and nicest people I've ever known."

Nichols had earlier paid tribute to the Elizabeth he knew in the following terms:

"Every time you pick up a magazine you read all the wrong things—about her tragic loves, her tragic life, her tragic future. It's all bunk. She's one of the happiest people in the world, and a great campy girl. I like her because she knows how to handle success and still have fun. Most of the new kids who are becoming big stars don't have any fun with their lives or their successes."

To which he now added: "The main thing is, I am just constantly surprised at how good Elizabeth and Richard are. Their flexibility and talent and cooperativeness is overwhelming. I can't think of one disagreeable thing. I've had more trouble with little people you've never heard of—temper tantrums, upstaging, girls' sobbing—than with the so-called legendary Burtons. The Burtons are on time, they know their lines, and if I make suggestions, Elizabeth can keep in her mind fourteen dialogue changes, twelve floor marks, and ten pauses—so the cutter can get the shears in and still keep the reality."

In November with *Virginia Woolf* already running over schedule and over budget, the Burtons paid a Sunday visit to Elizabeth's brother Howard's home in Del Mar. There, her nephew Leyton, then four and a half, was demonstrating his popgun toy and proceeded to pop her in the right eye with a pellet. Elizabeth was rushed to St. Joseph's Hospital in Burbank, treated and released. The gods were doubtless having their little grim joke by decreeing that Elizabeth end the year with a black eye, having begun it with one. The eye was badly bruised and discolored and necessitated further production delay. Jack Warner said nary a word. His knowledge of film was too acute not to have told him what he was on the verge of achieving.

On December 13, shooting finished on *Who's Afraid of Virginia Woolf?* The following evening the Burtons rented an orchestra and hosted a post-production party at the Bel Air manse. Upcoming were twin confrontations with Christopher Marlowe and William Shakespeare. Of immediate note was the fact that the Burtons were currently featured not only on the movie pages but in the literary reviews as well.

Harper & Row had published *Elizabeth Taylor* by Elizabeth Taylor, "and one might suggest they add: 'And *for* Elizabeth Taylor,'" reviewer Jim Bishop noted sourly. He found it "thin, superficial, and prattling." The L.A. *Times* agreed: "If we are to judge her by this book, we can only find her guilty of shallowness, poor taste, poor writing, and vanity." Elizabeth shrugged off the press pans. "Well, it was taken as a literary work, which, of course, it wasn't meant to be. It was just a series of tape-recorded conversations. A lot of people must have felt gypped because I didn't tell *all*. You know—it wasn't 'The Confessions of Elizabeth Taylor.'" A lot of people *did* feel gypped and the publisher took a bath.

Though the book observed a rough chronology, it grievously lacked the carefully noted factual data which might have given it needed heft. Some stars live surrounded by voluminous scrapbooks and can cite chapter and verse at the press of a tape-recorder button. Elizabeth is not one of them. "She's never saved a clipping in her life, that girl," Dick Hanley once noted. "She doesn't have one to her name, not even to show the kids." Hiring a ghost to punch it up was out of the question.

"I am disgusted by the amount of myth that now is accepted as fact," she declared forthrightly. "The public me, the one named Elizabeth Taylor, has become a lot of hokum and fabrication—a bunch of drivel—and I find her slightly revolting." She would tell her story in her own words and in her own way. As an indication of the things she found important as she looked back, and for the exact flavor of how she thought and phrased at the time, it was interesting and valuable. Fine writing, careful research, and/or an exposé it wasn't.

Richard Burton had also landed on the book pages with a little something called *Meeting Mrs. Jenkins,* an incisive paean to Elizabeth in twenty-four brief pages, including pictures. Reading time was about twenty minutes, as originally measured when it first appeared in *Vogue* under the title "Burton Writes of Taylor." The price of $2.95 was an outrage long before the era of Nixonomics and Phases One through Four. The painstaking, inventive quality of his prose, however, was a further indication that should Burton ever actually give up acting (as he continually threatens to), a writing career would be his if he truly wanted it. Every human is said to have one great secret fear. Franklin D. Roosevelt's, for example, was of a fire in the middle of the night, because once he had been put to bed, he was totally helpless. Burton's is of blindness. "As long as I can read, I'll be all right," he has often said. He'll be all right as long as he can write, too.

Before the Burtons could meet their next commitments in 1966, *Cleopatra* was upon them again. The $50 million Fox lawsuit was approaching its day in court. Oral depositions began January 5 in the Beverly Hills Hotel. After twelve days, fifty hours, and fifteen hundred transcribed pages of oral deposition, Elizabeth pleaded for an end to it, stressing the upcoming commitment for herself and Burton at Oxford in February. The matter was argued out in Federal Court.

"She has already undergone twelve days of boring and tedious questioning," her lawyer told the court. He accused Fox of deliberately annoying and harassing her. "The very idea that we are out here to annoy and harass Miss Taylor is so preposterous as to be beyond belief," thundered Fox's lawyer in response. "The essence of this complaint is that these two by their irresponsibility and illicit conduct directly or indirectly caused expense of more than $1 million to 20th Century-Fox because of the absences of Miss Taylor, which she said was related to her emotional and distraught condition. On one occasion these two people sneaked away from Rome to a hideaway over the Easter weekend. As a result of being there, Miss Taylor came back with a black eye and a cut nose, causing her to be unphotographable for two weeks"—at $50,000 per week, he said, which was a far cry from the "between $150,000 and $175,000 a day" Fox had talked about in 1964.

The judge gave Fox one more week to take oral depositions. On the last day of it Elizabeth was sick—"oppressed, annoyed, and unnerved by boring and tedious questions during fourteen days of oral examination." The judge then ruled that Fox could send her written questions up to sixty days, and Elizabeth would have an additional sixty days to answer them. At that point, over 2,500 pages of legal transcript had been taken. There the matter faded into the limbo of dissolution or out-of-court settlement where most good little (or whopping) movie lawsuits eventually go.

Over at Oxford, Neville Coghill, Merton Professor of English Literature, had been directing for the Oxford University Dramatic Society since 1934. In 1944 he had directed a young Richard Burton as Angelo in *Measure for Measure*. It was Coghill's dream to build an Oxford University Theatre Centre. To help his old mentor, Richard Burton, with Elizabeth, came to Oxford to appear for five nights in Marlowe's *Doctor Faustus*, with Elizabeth doing a four-minute silent walk-on as Helen of Troy. Neither took any salary for the engagement, which raised some 17,000 pounds (almost $41,000) for the Centre. On opening night Burton met the press and told them that in a few years, he'd like to try *Lear* "when I have more weight." Elizabeth leaned over and whispered in his ear. "Elizabeth says she'll give me some of hers," he announced.

The review split pro and con. "The seven deadly sins are paraded before Faustus. Boredom was not mentioned. It should have been, for it had pride of place," decided the *Daily Mirror*. On the other hand, the Manchester *Guardian* found the evening "rich and successful—the final scene makes a tremendous effect." As for Elizabeth as Helen: "Without a word to say she decorated the stage as no woman ever has or ever will." Commented Elizabeth, "All I had to do was kiss Richard and I know I do that well."

Before they left England they dined with John Gielgud. As they were leaving, with what was upcoming very much on her mind, Elizabeth asked Sir John if he might find the time to teach her how to speak Shakespeare. "Yes, my dear," he replied smoothly, "if you will teach me how to speak Tennessee Williams." From this it was off to a short stay in Switzerland, and in late March the Burtons drove over the border into Italy in an Oldsmobile, with a Rolls-Royce bringing up the rear as a luggage cart for thirty suitcases. "The Rolls holds bags better," Elizabeth explained. "Richard thinks the Olds rides better."

The Taming of the Shrew was to be the first film of director Franco Zeffirelli, as yet unfettered by a dismaying preference for acting tyros which would hamper his second film and cripple his third. *The Shrew* is the most filmed of Shakespeare's plays, having come to the screen six times previously: in 1908 (D. W.

Griffith), 1911 (British film of a Stratford production), 1929 (Mary Pickford and Douglas Fairbanks), 1933 (British), 1942 (Italian), and 1953 (in the musical *Kiss Me, Kate*). Zeffirelli was noted in his theatrical productions for crowding the stage and packing every inch of a scene with movement and business. Additionally he once did a *Hamlet* in which the hero came out to startle the audience by intoning, "To be or not to be/What the hell!" *His* version of *The Shrew* promised to be at least lively and unconventional. He had originally wanted Marcello Mastroianni and Sophia Loren but seeing Burton in *Hamlet* in New York changed his mind. The salary hurdle was jumped when the Burtons agreed to co-produce (for an investment variously reported at from $1.4 to $3 million) and to defer their salaries.

A press conference was scheduled to mark the first time they had worked in Rome since *Cleopatra* and Burton told the assembled newsmen, "Gentlemen, now that we are respectable, I hope you will give us the same attention as you did when we were unrespectable." After which he went directly before the cameras and, a month later, quaking like jelly, Elizabeth followed him.

"I was so scared," she later recalled. "It was the first time I'd tried to do Shakespeare. And my beloved was no help at all. 'You do it on your own,' he said. The first couple of days I was so frightened I couldn't even say 'hello.' So they had to redo them. Richard *did* advise me, 'Don't think of it as verse—don't pronounce it to a metronome as you were taught in school.' And gradually I began to have fun with it."

The greatest fun for the audience, if not the actors, was the famed wooing scene, in which Petruchio informs Katharina, "Now, Kate, thou must be married to no man but me," all the while attempting to bend her will to that end. For her part, Elizabeth had to smack Burton with a mandolin, beat on him with her fists, hurl wooden barrels at him with gusto and accuracy, throw a broken stairway railing at him, sit on a trapdoor and load it with heavy sacks (as he attempted to come up through it), and flail at him with a long pole (as he swung at her on a trapeze). Burton had to spank her, chase her up a flight of stairs, break through a wall to get at her, lift the loaded trapdoor, and swing back and forth on the trapeze. ("That's enough of that bloody Tarzan act," he decided after three takes of it. "Let's get on to something else.") Together they went into a delicate balancing act on a tile roof, whereupon the roof gave way and the two hurtled into a pile of sheep's wool below, where the whole matter was wrestled through to final resolution. The entire sequence lasts seven minutes on film and took eight days to shoot.

"Here I am with six inches of my spine fused and they expect me to toss Richard over my shoulder," Elizabeth groaned during the shooting of the wrestling sequence. As Katharina, Elizabeth was to be "pummeled, pounded, kicked, slapped, spanked, and generally knocked about" from one end of the film to the other. She had run her weight up to 143 pounds for *Virginia Woolf* but *The Shrew* knocked her down to 120 pounds, most of them a welter of bumps, bruises, and black-and-blue marks. The one thing she would not do for Zeffirelli, even though she was playing one of the most truculently self-proclaimed virgins of all time, was take off her wedding ring. A pearl was sewn over it for each day's shooting.

Another issue she felt strongly about was the matter of billing —not hers but Shakespeare's. In the first ads the screenplay was credited solely to Paul Dehn, Suso Cecchi D'Amico, and Franco Zeffirelli. The name of William Shakespeare was conspicuously absent. Said Columbia: "Advertisements are a combination of selling points and contractual billing obligations"—meaning that Shakespeare was poor box office and had no agent. Elizabeth worried that the credit to the three screenwriters alone would get more laughs than the immortal credit on the Pickford-Fairbanks *Shrew* which read: "Play by William Shakespeare/ Additional Dialogue by Sam Taylor." Ultimately the credit to the three writers was followed by "With Acknowledgements to William Shakespeare, Without Whom They Would Have Been at a Loss for Words."

Burton teased that what was really bothering Elizabeth was his top billing, which he got in the original ads. On one of them he scribbled: "Dear Snapshot: I couldn't help it. Honest. They just insisted that the money should come first. Your ever loving leading man, Richard (First Billing) Burton." A string of XXXXX's was followed by a P.S. "It had to happen sooner or later. What a shame it should happen when you're only 43." (She was 34.) Elizabeth then had her own ad printed up, which proclaimed triumphantly: ELIZABETH TAYLOR, ACADEMY AWARD WINNING ACTRESS, IN THE TAMING OF THE SHREW. And underneath, in the finest of print: "And Introducing Richard Burton." (Elizabeth eventually got top billing.)

In the midst of all this horseplay, physical mayhem, and hard work, the word came that Warner Bros. was finally ready to unveil *Who's Afraid of Virginia Woolf?* "Tell Jack Warner we're sick about not being able to make the *Virginia Woolf* opening in New York," Elizabeth told a friend. "It's the only premiere I've ever really wanted to attend."

After a lifetime of being dismissed by the serious critics as a movie star whose greatest performances had been given in newspaper headlines, Elizabeth's hour as an actress had finally come. Not unnaturally she wanted to be there for the plaudits, the glory, the acclaim. She was on the verge of her greatest artistic triumph to date, and she knew it.

※ 29 ※

Back in January, Mike Nichols felt assured enough about *Virginia Woolf* to declare, "Our own excitement tells us nothing, and we don't fool ourselves about that. But as I sit here in the cutting room and look at the film again, I am excited and satisfied." Which puts one in mind of David Selznick's agonized comments when he was hip-deep in all the celluloid yardage of *Gone With the Wind:* "At noon I think it's the greatest picture ever made, and at midnight I think it's lousy. But I'll be content if it's just a good picture." For *Virginia Woolf* the verdict was six months away.

Meanwhile first publicity photos went out to every major newspaper in the United States, Canada, and Europe. The Hollywood *Reporter* called this "the largest single exposure of still photographs in Hollywood history." Feature stories with cover art began to break in all of the big magazines—*Life, Look, Saturday Evening Post*, etc.—to further whet the public appetite. One further obstacle remained before the public sat down to dine, and that was the two-headed ogre of film censorship, represented by the National Catholic Office for Motion Pictures (formerly The Legion of Decency) and the Motion Picture Producers Association (which gave the Code Seal of Approval). There they sat, like the legendary Scylla and Charybdis, and somehow *Virginia Woolf*, plowing up the saltiest spray of any Hollywood film in history, would have to be steered through them and brought safely to shore.

What was manifestly impossible, on the face of it, became reality largely due to a strategy decreed by Jack Warner. *Vir-*

ginia Woolf had come in at a cost of $7.5 million, making it the most expensive black-and-white nonspectacle ever made (the spectacular *Longest Day* cost $10 million). Furthermore, in an unprecedented act of artistic faith, *Virginia Woolf* had been shot minus any alternative "clean" covering scenes, the usual hedge against censorship. The fact that Edward Albee had been flown to Los Angeles to see it—the only outsider who had, at this point—and had been obviously deeply moved by what he saw, only strengthened its makers' resolve to fight the battle through to the finish. Warner paved the way with the following remarks:

"The play was undoubtedly a play for adults and we have gone ahead to make *Virginia Woolf* a film for adults. I don't believe a controversial, mature subject should be watered down so that it is palatable for children. When that is done, you get a picture which is not palatable for children or for anyone else."

He then unveiled Warners' strict rental terms. No one under eighteen to be admitted unless accompanied by an adult, said terms to be written into the distributor-exhibitor contract, with a threat to yank the film should the terms not be strictly complied with. Warner called this "a firm demonstration of responsibility to the American moviegoing public by a company which underestimates neither the influence of the film medium nor the intelligence and taste of our vast audience." Having fired the opening gun, Warner awaited the verdicts of the censors, privately remarking to an associate, "We've opened a can of peas but I believe I've done the right thing," that is, given the industry a strong shove in the direction of classification of films.

In April eighty-one Catholic raters viewed the film at Warners and the majority voted to approve the film. Though they disapproved of much of the material in the film *per se*, their general feeling was that the ingredients were not sensationalized but were vital to the artistic life of the film. Reported Monsignor Thomas Little:

"We have judged *Virginia Woolf* in its totality. It dramatizes man's need to face the challenge of reality in order, by achieving self-knowledge, to build a capacity for love. In the context of this film, the elements have a dramatic vitality. It is all right to use erotic elements when everything jells in artistic integrity." Rating—A-4: "Morally unobjectionable for adults, with reservations."

Over at the Producers Association, Geoffrey Shurlock struggled futilely to thrash out the problem to everyone's satisfaction. On the one hand, he had a code book of strict rules, and on the other, a film of inadmissible boldness which all of his artistic sense told him was creative work of the highest order. On June 6, with the premiere fifteen days away, Shurlock handed down his verdict: no Code Seal. "Right now it is the one to beat for the Academy Award; anyone who thinks otherwise would be an idiot," he declared. "But I cannot give it the seal with that language. It clearly violates the code."

Warner promptly appealed the decision to the Code Review Board, asking for an exemption, that is, the classification of *Virginia Woolf* as "an exception—approval of material in a specific, important film which would not be approved for a film of lesser quality or a film designed to exploit language for language's sake." On June 13 the Board granted the exemption after two deletions: "friggin'" (said by someone with his back to the camera and thus not missed) and "screw you" (even though "screw" shows up in two other places on the sound track). With the observation that *Virginia Woolf* was "not designed to be prurient" and that it "reflects the tragic realism of life," the Board finally granted the Code Seal of Approval.

A vigorous dissent was voiced in the *Motion Picture Herald* by editor Martin Quigley, Jr., under the title "The Code Is Dead." Having reviewed the long, sad story of the Code's obstinate refusal to come to terms with reality, Quigley observed, "While the causes of the Code's long sicknesses are many, the cause of death is one. The Code died because of *Virginia Woolf*." Furthermore, "There is no such thing as 'good taste' in blasphemy, profanity, or obscenity. The English language is rich with several million words. Hence there is no justification for a torrent of blasphemy, profanity, and obscenity on the screen."

The worth of *Virginia Woolf* notwithstanding, the root concern of the dissenters was that now, with the precedent set, the floodgates would be opened to an ocean of smut. Put another way, *Virginia Woolf* had acted as elegant stalking horse for a collection of mangy nags fit only for the glue factory, and certainly not for public exhibition. The eventual controversial Classification System (G-PG-R-X) was foreseen by Warner when he opened his "can of peas." But a sizable body of public opinion had long asserted that there never should have been a lid on the can in the first place.

All of that was in the future as public excitement intensified just prior to the black-tie world premiere of *Who's Afraid of Virginia Woolf?* on June 21, 1966, at the Pantages Theater in Hollywood. The famous ad line had already appeared in the local press: "You are cordially invited to George and Martha's for an evening of fun and games . . ." but the veil of secrecy still hid the finished product. *"Who's Afraid of Virginia Woolf? Who can be?"* moaned a Hollywood trade paper, with the trade screenings not scheduled till the day before the premiere.

On the big night, searchlights swept the heavens, three thousand fans jammed the bleachers set up on Hollywood Boulevard, and harassed studio officials realized they could have packed the 1,512-seat Pantages twice over. ("When Rock Hudson asks for tickets and you haven't got them, you're in some kind of trouble.") Jack Warner escorted Merle Oberon and left *his* tickets in the car. He and Mike Nichols and Ernest Lehman were present, but the Burtons were still in Italy working on *The Shrew* and Sandy Dennis and George Segal were likewise absent. When it was over, the stunned looks on the faces of Julie Andrews, Pat Boone, Jonathan Winters, and others of the star-studded audience were eloquent witness to a triumph of towering proportions.

The excitement begins right at the first frame. Far away a group of people are leaving a house late at night, and as two of them move in the direction of the camera, the titles begin—tantalizing titles because we are anxious to see the famous pair, and particularly Elizabeth as Martha, but the angles make it impossible. Only when all the titles have passed off the screen and the couple enter their house do we get the first full shot of her.

There she stands, blinking angrily into the harsh light: stout, gross, thick-figured, her tousled salt-and-pepper hair a wild tangle, with double chin, bags under eyes, bulging belly, and squat legs. She surveys the scene with weary disgust and in a contemptuous contralto declares, "What a dump!" In any history of great entrances of the screen, this one has to be right up there with the best of them.

Her manner is querulous, demanding, overpowering. Her walk is a sort of squat trudge, stolid and graceless. The state of the kitchen tells us she is anything but fastidious. She reaches into the jumble in the refrigerator, pulls out a chicken leg, gnaws away, meanwhile following up a superb Bette Davis imitation with random movie-plot details. She is badgering George about *Beyond the Forest,* a campy 1949 melodrama which abruptly terminated Bette Davis' long association with Warner Bros.

Burton has meanwhile come on as George: tired, timid, henpecked, weary, and seemingly resigned to it all. The measure of Burton's achievement is how he builds this character from

"Georgie-Porgie-Put-Upon-Pie" to the real strength and the dominant figure in the relationship at the end. At first we watch him hectored by Martha, verbally in the kitchen, and physically up in the bedroom, as she rides him and pounds him. Then a clue drops when he ever-so-quietly rejects her sexually, and we realize this harridan isn't quite the ruler of the roost she appears because we move in close on Martha, and her sexual frustration is apparent. Her badgering now becomes vicious, springing from her seeming inability to command him into the sack. This seems to be the one thing she cannot do, and his quiet refusal is the subtle measure of just who, ultimately, is in command.

"I'm loud and I'm vulgar," she tells him at one point, "and I wear the pants in this house because somebody's got to!" Only she doesn't. The pants she has in mind are Daddy's. George has his own—as she will eventually learn.

When the guests arrive, George reacts to Nick with that peevish intellectual antagonism so marked in academic types when threatened by young male animal bravado and all of the sweats and sounds which exist beyond the kingdom of books. But Burton's George is composed of more than mere castration and physical intimidation. He badgers Nick into open hostility, then charmingly overrides his protests and remains fully in command. The smoldering Martha then brings on the whole arsenal: vulgarity, profanity, the sexual approaches to Nick, various humiliations of George (ordering him to the door, to make drinks, etc.), culminating in her venomous recitation of George's pitiful performance in the History Department. George then regains control via the brilliant stunt with the trick shotgun that fires a parasol.

An interlude follows in the garden, a set piece for George, superbly crafted by Burton in closeup: George telling the story of his childhood and the death of his parents. In return, he gets information on Nick's marriage to Honey ("shotgun" via hysterical pregnancy; also, Daddy had money). Honey becomes sick from too much brandy, and on the way to being taken home, Nick inadvertently reveals George's confession in the garden. Stopping off for dancing at a roadhouse, Martha makes a blatant attempt to sexually arouse Nick on the dance floor. She then reveals that George actually put all of that confession into a novel, which her father forbade him to publish on pain of dismissal from his job. This, coupled with the earlier leak about their "child," drives George to strangle Martha, stopped by Nick.

George then takes over. They've played a good game of

Humiliate the Host. Now what will it be? Hump the Hostess or Get the Guests? Actually it will be both. Get the Guests is accomplished when Honey learns that Nick has revealed the circumstances of their marriage. Martha, fearing that the games are getting out of hand, tries a last stand out in the parking lot. George protests that he can stand no more. "You can stand it!" she flings at him. "You married me for it!" He demurs, but after their mutual declaration of total war, followed by her solo departure, a lingering shot of his face mingles love and admiration in an unspoken declaration that she is right.

The first attempt to Hump the Hostess—by Nick, up in the bedroom—is a flop. The second attempt is a bull's-eye: George's announcement that their "son" is dead. Martha protests in vain but submits, dawn breaks, the guests leave, and George is the quietly commanding figure of the two as the film ends.

Mike Nichols' primary task was to film a brilliant theatrical talkathon in fluid cinematic terms. Claustrophobia is removed at the outset by starting George and Martha at Daddy's door and walking them back to their house behind the titles, rather than starting right off in the house. The action then moves from the kitchen, upstairs to the bedroom, back down to the living room, is varied by George's trip to the closet to get the gun, by Honey's quick trip to the bathroom, by George and Nick out on the lawn, by the trip to the roadhouse and the scene inside, by the confrontation in the parking lot, by a longshot of Martha wandering outside trying to find everyone else, by George and Honey on the front porch, and by Martha and Nick in the kitchen. Ultimately, everyone moves back into the living room for the climax.

Within the living room, where most of the action passes, the shots are varied and interesting: full shots, two-shots, huge closeups, quick reaction shots to Nick and Honey. Nichols has a fine ear for the superb rhythms of the dialogue and effects lightning transitions to keep it moving. The tempo is well served with jump cuts to George's appearance with the gun, and again, to the speeding car, and again, from the slamming on of brakes to an overhead shot of Honey whirling drunkenly on the dance floor in the roadhouse.

The development and progressive revelation in the film are masterful. The sets also play a major role in the total effect. Nichols personally crammed the refrigerator full of half-opened what nots and odorous remnants to help Elizabeth with the quality of Martha's domestic propensities (or lack of them). The kitchen is cluttered, the bedroom reveals an unmade bed and scattered clothing (all to be hidden under the hastily assembled bedclothes), George's desk area and the living-room mantel are fussy with gloomy-looking objects right down to an antique map of Martha's Vineyard Island. Haskell Wexler's cameras capture all of this with needle-sharp accuracy. The leaves in the opening shot are so crisply defined they give off the effect of 3-D.

With his supporting players, Nichols probably had the greater luck with Sandy Dennis. "Before Mike," she told an interviewer, "I never worked with a good director in my life." From her point of view that must have been the truth. Early on she apparently reached the conclusion that not only must her work possess emotional truth, but that her truth would have to be commercial, that is, people must want to pay to see it, and furthermore, that she would have to get it all together without any help from anybody. To that end, she had accumulated one of the most amazing collections of facial tics, starts-and-stammers, stops-and-go's or what-have-you to be seen this side of psychosis. Nichols patiently pared off the excess and helped her integrate the mannerisms into the character of a mousy little creature who dives into the brandy bottle and never comes out. The drunkenness works with the mannerisms into a performance with some affecting moments, none more so than in the roadhouse where, like a mouse petrified by a large cat, she is hanging fascinatedly onto George's revelations about her private life, afraid to hear more but compelled to learn just how much Nick has told.

As Nick, George Segal worked hard and well with only limited success, for possibly two reasons. As conceived and written, his role is essentially the weakest of the four. And though he may be someone's idea of a cornfed Mr. America from the Midwest, his frame of reference is East Coast cosmopolis, and everything he is and says and does proclaims it. Not all of his professional finesse can disguise the fact that he is temperamentally incapable of truth in such a role. He does the best he can under the circumstances, but they are not truly those of the character. (Frank Sinatra's struggles with Nathan Detroit in *Guys and Dolls,* and Bette Davis' labors in *The Catered Affair* come most readily to mind in this regard.) Despite the initial misgivings by some people, generally, and by Burton, in particular, no such considerations are at all applicable to the work by the principals.

Watching Elizabeth grand-slamming her way through the role of Martha is watching somebody who has finally been allowed to come fully to life. She serves up a sizzling, snarling, stunning, sumptuous smörgåsbord of bitchery, crudity, lechery, rage, frustration, misery, satire, and compassion, and sends it spewing across the screen with all the eruptive force of white-hot lava. Wiped out in one masterful stroke are all those Technicolor-tinted, glamorously clothed, frostily beautiful, petulant, and empty Girls Who Had Everything. She joyously submits to messy makeup, harsh lighting, and unflattering camera angles and squeezes every opportunity to shed all of the previous paraphernalia of Elizabeth Taylor/Movie Goddess. At one point, she pours herself into a pantsuit, which makes her the ludicrous picture of an aging, voracious female on the trail of fresh, young meat. And if Mike Nichols had done nothing else, he would have won Elizabeth's eternal gratitude for finally allowing her satiric-sardonic sense of humor to flow uninhibitedly on the screen—in the Bette Davis imitation, as she trills "just a gigolo" to Nick, in her wild recitation in the roadhouse of George's attempt at a novel, etc. Her finest moments, perhaps, are in the kitchen scene with Nick wherein, in that beautiful speech shot through the screen door, she lays bare her understanding of her relationship with George—"whom I will not forgive for having come to rest; for having seen me and having said: yes; this will do; who has made the hideous, the hurting, the insulting mistake of loving me and must be punished for it. George and Martha: sad, sad, sad." Other highpoints: her first humiliation of George before the guests, her roadhouse recitation, her reaction to the news that their "son" is dead.

Richard Burton's performance is of a brilliance so absolute as to amply repay countless viewings of it. He is completely in control of every nuance and shade of the performance from first to last, yet remains vibrantly alive moment to moment. Forgotten are the old accusations of coldness on the screen. Burton's George radiates awareness and humanity at every turn. He goes about his business slowly, surely, and with marvelous subtlety. The growth in audience awareness from what they originally thought he was to what he really is testifies to artistry of the highest order.

Curiously enough, the roles caused the Burtons to work in reverse, and therein lay the full measure of their achievement. When *Cleopatra* was finally finished, Richard Burton spoke of what has always been Elizabeth's strongest card as a film actress:

"Elizabeth is terribly like Marlon Brando, who, I think, is the best actor America has ever had. She has the same qualities I would use to describe Marlon: slow-moving, quiet, with a suggestion of infinite power. Both of them never move directly toward an object. An actor like myself lunges at it. Instead they circumlocute the object, sort of meander around it. They are evasive and you can't quite catch them. That's why they are such remarkable stars."

So that Elizabeth, who long ago learned to dominate the screen by a quiet suggestion of enormous power, had now, as Martha, to literally explode all over it. And Burton, who had always admired her supreme quality as a film actress, had, as George, to make it his own.

"I suppose the major change in my film acting technique has been effected by Elizabeth," Burton had said. "She's the consummate cinematic technician. I learn a great deal from her." In *Virginia Woolf* he proved it beyond doubt. Afterward he was to be questioned about his greatest film acting challenges to date, and his reply was unhesitating:

"Playing those roles in *Spy* and *Woolf*. Before, I would never have dreamed of portraying such thin, seedy, famished men. You know I have always acted in the bravo or panache tradition. In those two parts, logically speaking, I was supremely miscast. Not that I didn't like it. I did. It was immensely challenging but it was such agony. Playing everything down, down, holding myself in all the time. The tiniest gesture, the slightest word was crucial in characterizing them. I had to watch myself constantly. I really felt like a very tensed-up labyrinth. Really, would you ever think of me as a harassed, has-been of a college professor? A couple of stars turned the role down because they felt they just couldn't get away with it. If I had played the man as being afraid of that crazed, wonderful woman, the whole thing would have been a disaster."

The day after the triumphant premiere, Warners had five Pinkerton cops on duty at the Pantages (two for the matinee trade, three for the evening) to police ticket-buyers. Forty-six juveniles were pulled out of line on opening day to show that the restricted-admissions policy would be enforced. Jack Warner later pronounced the policy a complete success.

On June 23, *Who's Afraid of Virginia Woolf?* had its New York premiere, a joint benefit for the Richard Burton Hemophilia Fund of the National Hemophilia Foundation and the American Musical and Dramatic Academy. The premiere raised $75,000.

By July 1, *Virginia Woolf* had opened in forty key cities across the United States and Canada to record-breaking grosses (as of January 1, 1970, the film had realized $14,200,000 on domestic rentals alone, aside from the world profit and Warner's subsequent deal for prime-time showing with CBS-TV). The only serious censorship challenge occurred in Nashville, Tennessee, where a minor flap occurred at the Crescent Theater. A policeman barged into the projection room, seized a reel of the film, and stopped the showing, on his personal reading of a Nashville obscenity ordinance which actually applied only to live performances. The theater manager slapped him with a $50,000 damage suit, the police complaint was dismissed, the reel was returned, and the show resumed the following day.

The mass openings of *Virginia Woolf* were followed by generally ecstatic critical reactions. In the New York *Times*, Stanley Kauffmann hailed it as "one of the most scathingly honest American films ever made." Of Elizabeth as Martha: "She does the best work of her career, sustained and urgent . . . She gets vocal variety, never relapses out of the role, and she charges it with the utmost of her powers—which is an achievement for any actress, great or little." Other reviewers joined the chorus of high praise:

"An honest, corrosive film of great power and final poignancy. Elizabeth Taylor is a revelation. Burton's acting is the best of his film career." (*Life*)

"The screen has never held a more shattering and ravaging and indelible drama . . . a motion picture masterpiece . . . an instant film classic . . . Elizabeth Taylor reaches the fullest of her powers as Martha. The actress' beauty and the richness of her personal life have repeatedly obscured the fact that she can be, when she cares to be, an actress of extraordinary power. Miss Taylor is a prime reason the film seems so very seldom a drama, and almost always a violation of privacy, captured with hidden cameras and microphones." (Hollywood *Reporter*)

Next came laurels and various awards. The Triple Crown of Film Acting (Academy Award, New York Film Critics Circle Award, National Board of Review Award) rarely sits on the same actor and actress in any one year. Even when Patricia Neal turned the trick in 1963 for *Hud*, the male laurels split three ways: Academy Award to Sidney Poitier (*Lilies of the Field*), New York Film Critics Circle Award to Albert Finney (*Tom Jones*), National Board of Review Award to Rex Harrison (*Cleopatra*). Only once before had both actor and actress been triple winners in any one year. That happened in 1955, when Ernest Borgnine (*Marty*) and Anna Magnani (*The Rose Tattoo*) were the honored pair. The second time was 1966.*

* It has since happened a third time, in 1970, with George C. Scott (*Patton*) and Glenda Jackson (*Women in Love*).

Elizabeth took the Awards of the National Board of Review, the New York Film Critics Circle (in a tie with Lynn Redgrave), and at the annual Oscar ceremonies, in her fifth time at bat, she triumphed over Anouk Aimee (*A Man and a Woman*), Ida Kaminska (*The Shop on Main Street*), Lynn Redgrave (*Georgy Girl*), and Vanessa Redgrave (*Morgan*) to win her second Academy Award.

The knowledge that this one had been fully earned, minus the mitigating sentiment which had surrounded her first victory, was enormously satisfying. But her earnest hopes that her male consort as triple winner was to be Richard Burton were doomed to disappointment. Three times *Who's Afraid of Virginia Woolf?*, Richard Burton, and Mike Nichols went up against the combined onslaught of *A Man for All Seasons*, Paul Scofield, and Fred Zinnemann, and three times they went down to defeat.

When news of the Oscar win reached her in Cannes, where she was working on *The Comedians*, Elizabeth angrily refused to see newsmen or make any comment whatever. The anger masked a hurt at Burton's loss that went too deep to permit her the luxury of smiling graciously and airily pretending that it didn't matter. Her sense of reality was built, in part, on an uncompromising refusal to play "let's pretend" about the things which really mattered to her. Characteristically, she did no crying about it in public. But she'd be damned if she'd sing about it, either.

For the New Year, 1970, columnist Joyce Haber polled the film industry for their personal picks for the outstanding achievements of the '60s. For the decade's Best Performance by an Actor, Richard Burton's George easily outpointed Paul Scofield's Sir Thomas More and every other male Oscar-winner from Burt Lancaster to John Wayne. Elizabeth might well have asked the voters, "Where were you all in 1967?"

In addition to the Oscar for Elizabeth, *Virginia Woolf* also brought Academy Awards to Sandy Dennis, Richard Sylbert and George James Hopkins (for Art Direction and Set Decoration), Haskell Wexler (Cinematography), and Irene Sharaff (Costumes). It swept *Film Daily*'s 1966 Poll, bringing laurels to its four stars, director, cameraman, and to Ernest Lehman in both his producing and writing capacities. The British Film Critics Guild chose *Who's Afraid of Virginia Woolf?* Best American Film of 1966, as did the Foreign Press Association, which bestowed additional awards on Elizabeth and on Mike Nichols. Together the Burtons were recipients of the Silver Masks of Italy as the year's Best Foreign Film Actors, and Richard

Burton also picked up the Award of the British Film Academy as well. And the indispensable ingredient of all this success?

"Guts!" So said Ernest Lehman when *Who's Afraid of Virginia Woolf?* first went into production. "Jack L. Warner had guts to buy the play and make it a film. Elizabeth Taylor and Richard Burton have guts to lay themselves on the line and take such an artistic chance."

Their next artistic gamble, *The Taming of the Shrew*, had its world premiere, a Royal Command Performance, at the Odeon in London in February 1967. Princess Margaret attended amid strong rumors that her marriage was in deep trouble, and the following exchange took place:

BURTON: "I hope you are not as nervous tonight, M'am, as I am."

PRINCESS MARGARET: "Would you like to bet?"

BURTON: "I wouldn't like to bet. I've got some of my money in the film."

As to why they had taken such a gamble, Burton commented wittily, "We made *The Taming of the Shrew* because I wanted to act a rough role as far away as possible from those Rex Harrison parts with nice suits and freshly laundered shirts, and my wife because she wanted to talk English for a change. In *Shrew* she shows definite Shakespearean feeling, the only difficulties being some of the Bard's words that are alien to her. For instance, 'how durst thou' is not common talk in California."

Earlier Burton had speculated that "with its vital and earthy characteristics, I think it may possibly turn out to be—and here let us touch every possible piece of wood in sight—the first Shakespearean film ever to become a commercial success immediately." Its world-wide gross of over $7 million on its initial release proved him right. The gamble that one of Shakespeare's lesser efforts could be taken and shaken into a film that would win mass audience favor had paid off handsomely.

Lines, speeches, whole passages had been cut, deleted, relocated, altered, at times even invented—all for the purpose of translating the play into fluid filmic terms, for example, visualizing onscreen the church marriage of Petruchio to Kate, a gem of pure farce (highlighted by Burton's lunge for the sacramental wine), and then their stormy journey (through snow, yet!) to Petruchio's country house.

Burton and Zeffirelli had produced possibly the most Italian-in-feeling *Shrew* ever done, certainly ever filmed. The gorgeous photography is warm, sunny, sensual, hot-blooded. Cinematographer Oswald Morris pre-exposed the film stock to amber light

to produce the lush Renaissance effect. The proceedings themselves are lusty, brawling, noisy, and bawdy—a continuous, delicious air of high spirits, of what the Elizabethans called "capital
foolery" is a constant throughout. The supporting cast all work
energetically in the spirit of this romp, with special mention to
the Baptista of Michael Hordern and the Hortensio of Victor
Spinetti.

It was the general opinion that Elizabeth's best moments as
Katharina come during her transformation (including the journey through rain and snow and a dunk from off the back of an
ass into a pond on the way to her wedding night) right up to
her climactic two-and-a-half-minute monologue ("Fie, fie! un-
knit that threatening unkind brow . . ."), so well delivered that
the cast gave her an ovation when she filmed it. Critical opinion
of Elizabeth and the film ran the gamut.

"A pox on ye widescreen!" declaimed Wilfred Sheed in *Esquire*. As for Elizabeth: "Of Miss Taylor there is little to say.
She will never really be adequate to any classical role. Her acting
was fixated at the age of twelve in *National Velvet* and has not
moved an inch forward or back since then. She is, as she should
be, a cinematic professional. But when it comes to brewing up a
real emotion, such as shrewish rage, she can only flutter her
surface and hope for the best."

The *Saturday Review*'s Hollis Alpert could not have agreed
less on either score. He found *The Shrew* "a quite literally
gorgeous piece of film-making . . . a quintessential rendering of
the play . . . the virtues of this production are so many, the
achievement so splendid, that not much more is required of the
critic than a listing of what is available for the price of admission."
As for Elizabeth: "There was never very much doubt about the
abilities of Burton; there was more question about Miss Taylor,
originally a product of MGM's star system, and star-crossed in
her love and marital life. Her movie performances during the
past ten years have ranged from mediocre to very good and I, for
one, found her splendid in *Who's Afraid of Virginia Woolf?*—the
equal of some of our more prestigious stage actresses and
equipped as well with the kind of camera sensitivity that only
laborious experience can bring. But Shakespeare is another kind
of peak to climb, and the challenge to Miss Taylor must have
been a big one. She had to contend with her husband at his absolute best in a role for which he is extremely well-suited, and
she was up against other gifted actors . . . Well, not only has
she managed it; she has come through the ordeal with honor. She
has held nothing back in attacking the role with blazing fury,

and in her final moments, when she is at last the tamed wife—adjusted to her situation, so to speak—she is magnificent. I don't know exactly why I felt proud of her, but I did."

If there were differences of opinion about the merits of Elizabeth and the film, Burton's notices as Petruchio were all solid gold. It was widely expected that he would follow *Spy* and *Virginia Woolf* with another Oscar nomination for the third year in a row. Like 1958, however, 1967 yielded another embarrassment of riches, this time among actors. Richard Burton for *The Taming of the Shrew*, Sidney Poitier for *In the Heat of the Night*, Dirk Bogarde for *Accident*, Peter Finch for *Far From the Madding Crowd*, and Robert Blake and Scott Wilson as the murderers in *In Cold Blood* all gave award-caliber performances, but none was Oscar-nominated, not even Finch, who won the National Board of Review Award. The final five were Spencer Tracy (posthumously, for *Guess Who's Coming to Dinner*), Paul Newman (*Cool Hand Luke*), Warren Beatty (*Bonnie and Clyde*), Dustin Hoffman (*The Graduate*), and Rod Steiger (the winner, for *In the Heat of the Night*).

A special United Nations Cultural Awards Plaque went to the Burtons for *The Taming of the Shrew*, and both picked up Italy's David di Donatello Awards as Best Foreign Actor and Actress of the year as well (Burton put his with the one he had won in the previous year for *Spy*).

With unqualified triumph in *Virginia Woolf*, and high marks for Shakespeare, Elizabeth now possessed the one thing lacking back in 1961 at the previous summit of her professional achievement: recognition as a serious actress. As to future use of her new-found prestige there were to be two views. The repeated announcements that she would soon be essaying such challenges as Lady Macbeth on the screen and Sartre's *The Devil and the Good Lord* on the stage were admirable. The reality of what she was actually doing was something else.

❀ 30 ❀

Elizabeth's stay among the Top Ten Box Office Stars (as measured by the *Motion Picture Herald*'s Annual Exhibitor Poll) lasted for a decade. She was No. 2 in 1958, absent in 1959, No. 4 in

1960, No. 1 in 1961, No. 6 in 1962 and 1963, had slipped to No. 11 in 1964, was No. 9 in 1965, No. 3 in 1966, No. 6 in 1967, No. 10 in 1968, and vanished thereafter and has yet to reappear.

"Elizabeth Taylor Had a Three-Flop Year." So noted *Variety* in January 1969, looking back at box office performance in 1968. "It was a rough stretch for Elizabeth Taylor, with or without Richard Burton. The year that counted her *The Comedians*, *Reflections in a Golden Eye*, and *Boom!* had to subject this $1,000,000-a-film star to some discount as box office insurance."

Actually it was a *five*-flop year. Within roughly a twelve-month period, *Reflections*, *Comedians*, *Doctor Faustus*, *Boom!* and *Secret Ceremony* briefly brightened theater marquees and were gone—bombs all. After another such, *The Only Game in Town*, withheld for release for almost a year, a disturbed Elizabeth withdrew totally from filmmaking for two years. The new industry conditions for packaging, financing, and distributing a film were bewildering and exasperating enough. But what had happened to her vaunted ability to pick moneymaking scripts? Most dismaying of all, *Virginia Woolf* had brought her work to a new level which she had sustained admirably. Whether as army officer's wife, ambassador's wife, rich bitch, prostitute, or Vegas showgirl, there was a careful attention to detail and sharpening in characterization previously unknown. And none of it seemed to work.

Doctor Faustus led off this twit parade. "Probably one of the most desperately noncommercial enterprises in motion picture history," *Variety* called it, "a curio unlikely to recover its negative cost." Elizabeth and Richard Burton made it in Rome right after they finished with *The Shrew*, and Burton additionally co-directed and co-produced. Financing was difficult "because," as Burton noted tartly, "most of the people who have money in this world never heard of it." The Burtons took no salary, and the forty-eight Oxford students got the union minimum of eighteen pounds per week. Director Burton did everything possible to put these nervous students at ease in their film debuts.

"You may think that I am always calm when acting," he told them one day. "But though I appear impassive, I wear out three pairs of socks a day by involuntarily wriggling my toes. When my brother Ivor first saw me at the Old Vic, I thought he'd congratulate me on my calm professionalism. Instead, he said, 'Man, you never keep your toes still.' Since then I've never worn sandals while acting."

Elizabeth did box office duty sans dialogue as a walking fleshpot in a total of nine appearances as the personification of Lust.

We first see her strolling toward the camera dressed in white, then in ropes of pearls, then decked out in diamonds, in a red wig as a diseased whore, in a long blond wig, sprayed in silver paint as the paramour of Alexander the Great, as Helen of Troy, in a love scene with Faustus, and finally in green flesh and a huge wig accompanying him in a cackling descent into hell. Her cackle is her only audible function. She has her own theme which is heard every time she appears and sounds identical to the opening notes of Gloria's Theme from *Butterfield 8*.

Elizabeth did this chore with the best will in the world, to help sell tickets to the film version of a literary classic which needed all the help it could get. Asking movie audiences to accept Elizabeth Taylor as either an abstract concept or a subsidiary attraction, however, was asking the impossible. (She would later do *Under Milk Wood* with the same motives and the same results.) The critics were unusually free with the vitriol.

"Her makeup varies from Greek statuesque to a head-to-toe spray job of aluminum paint," reported *Time*. "When she welcomes Burton to an eternity of damnation, her eyeballs and teeth are dripping pink in what seems to be a hellish combination of conjunctivitis and trenchmouth."

Giving Richard Burton's performance high praise, and discounting the eternal (not to say, infernal) "busy-ness" of the production—cluttered sets, a plethora of effects, etc.—the chief problem, unfortunately, is Christopher Marlowe. "Rigorously medieval in viewpoint," one critic noted of *Faustus*, "it has little to say to modern man." The entrenched hosts of academe will now rise up in righteous wrath to smite such heresy, but anyone who thinks that the seven deadly sins, the flames of hell, and melodramatic posturings about sin and damnation are anything more than vintage curiosities in this day and age has obviously been shut up in the library too long. There was no way a faithful rendering of this antique could have been made comprehensible to the modern mass audience and it wasn't.

Elizabeth went directly from *Faustus* into *Reflections in a Golden Eye*, also filmed in Italy. It was based on the 1941 novella by Carson McCullers, whose slight corpus of work in the Southern Gothic genre had gained her a fanatic following among the intelligentsia. Many high-powered talents had cast envious eyes on this property at one time or another—the production team of Hecht-Lancaster, directors Tony Richardson and Peter Glenville, and writers Francis Ford Coppola and Truman Capote, to name five. Richard Burton had even been part of one proposed production.

On July 23, in the midst of filming *The Shrew*, Elizabeth had received a piece of news that staggered her. Montgomery Clift was found dead of a heart attack in his New York apartment at the age of forty-five. Of immediate importance was the fact that the male lead in *Reflections* would have to be recast. But the personal loss went well beyond such momentary matters.

Monty Clift—whom she had first met when they did *A Place in the Sun* together—who had encouraged her professional ambitions for herself when her employers still regarded her as little more than a valuable Technicolor trifle—Monty the brilliant, tormented, self-destructive, fun-loving, kind and unkind, spartan and hedonistic, and any of dozens of other adjectives you cared to apply to a man who was his own rich, contradictory universe —Montgomery Clift was gone. Through three films together and fifteen years, their lives were interwoven in a bond of mutual love and affection permanently untouched by any transient crisis or what the world happened to be saying about either of them at any particular moment. And now the bond was cut.

"I've told him everything," Elizabeth once said, "even the things I'm ashamed of." Nonconformist though he might be in his life-style, like all her true friends he conformed to the *sine qua non* of real friendship with Elizabeth: he kept his mouth shut. And took his share of their personal memories with him.

Two weeks before shooting on *Reflections* began, Producer Ray Stark scored a real coup: Marlon Brando was persuaded to take the vacated role. Here was the consummation devoutly to be wished: Marlon Brando and Elizabeth Taylor, two of the greatest stars and cinematic professionals, together at last for what promised to be extraordinary celluloid combustion. Rounding out the star quartet would be the fine talents of Brian Keith and Julie Harris. The director would be John Huston, whose creative light had burned brilliantly in the '40s, flickered fitfully in the '50s, and had all but sunk from sight in the '60s. Still, there was always the hope that a top cast and script might rekindle the fires of yore.

What emerged from all of this heady expectation was an exasperating, repulsive mishmash—an appalling example of how the mass movie audience was lost, and not only lost, but deliberately alienated. The film was shot in Technicolor and then washed out or "desaturated" in the printing, which produced a sepia monotone with occasional flashes of pink. Explained Ray Stark, "The picture is a mood picture and we don't want the audience disturbed by loud colors." Color would have been absolutely the least disturbing factor in this enterprise, as a brief rundown on the six central characters should make clear.

On a U. S. Army post circa 1948, a major who is an impotent, latent homosexual is married to an infantile birdbrain who never misses an opportunity to ridicule his masculine failings. He displaces his hostility by brutally flogging her horse and she retaliates by humiliating him before a houseful of guests, repeatedly slashing him across the face with her riding crop. She is also committing adultery with the officer next door, whose wife cut off her nipples with garden shears when she first heard about it. This poor creature has sought solace in the ministrations of her houseboy, who can only be characterized, with sincere apologies to Gay Lib, as a flaming faggot. Eventually the mutilated wife will be carted off to a sanitarium where she will promptly die of a heart attack. The sixth character is a darkly handsome noncom, a voyeur and lingerie-fondler, given to nightly appearances as a peeping tom in the birdbrain's bedroom and daily sessions of running around in the middle of the woods stark naked. He is coveted by the major, who will ultimately murder him. "As unsavory a half-dozen characters as have ever been put on the screen," decided the *Motion Picture Herald* between gasps.

Now neurosis and psychosis are certainly nothing new to films. Bette Davis and Barbara Stanwyck, to name two, built a large part of their distinguished careers out of such material. Though often criticized for an excessive preoccupation with the abnormal, there is definitely a method to the madness one encounters in Southern Gothic. Generally it attempts to create an atmosphere of brooding and unknown terror. Tennessee Williams has further defined it as "a sense, an intuition, of an underlying dreadfulness in modern life." The surrounding *mise en scène* is to be interpreted symbolically and not literally or as the only truth at work. But if the events are too sensational, too far off the beaten track, the average spectator is too busy gagging on what's in front of him to even think about what's behind it, or even to care. Which was a pity in this case because the acting is absolutely first-rate all along the line.

Brando's latent homosexual is full of pain, fear, self-pity, and self-loathing, and he fleshes him out with a multitude of brilliant touches. When we first see him, he is lifting weights and is superbly inept at it. As he is at horseback riding, where he suffers the ultimate humiliation of falling off his horse before his wife and her lover, and even his falling off has a peculiar quality of klutzy clumsiness. His failure to fulfill his masculine image of himself sends him into impotent rages and a crackup while lecturing his class. He talks to himself in mirrors, tries on cold cream, gobbles sleeping pills, and hides his secret life in a box in his desk. The final touch, and a memorable one, is when he sees the noncom sneaking into the house and, thinking he is finally coming for him, Brando primps a bit and then sits down expectantly on the edge of the bed, primly, like a nice girl waiting to be picked up for her first date.

Elizabeth matches her costar, in that most exacting of acting assignments: the creation of a character of limited personality and imagination, working strictly from that character's limited resources, so that what emerges is more creation than performance. Watching Elizabeth's lips move as she laboriously scrawls her party invitations, all the while devastated about the correct spelling of "cordially," is watching the real thing—lightweight, pulchritudinous, and ding-y. So is watching her trip off into erotic transports as she describes all the food and refreshments she plans to serve at her party. Her fourteen dresses—flamboyant, low-cut thin silks with gauche patterns of vibrant violet-blues and purples—are also a big help with the character.

Brian Keith and Julie Harris as the couple next door, Robert Forster as the noncom and Zorro David as the houseboy likewise fill their roles admirably. The setting is faithful right down to 1948 license plates, 78-rpm records, and Oxydol boxes. Unfortunately all goes for naught as the characters merely plunk around in Panavision, ankle-deep in 108 minutes of psychic sewage totally unredeemed by any point of view or shaping of this dismal material whatever. A persuasive argument can be advanced that the much-vaunted *auteur* theory of film, that is, that a movie is the sole creation of the director (something like Athena springing full-blown from the brow of Zeus), is ruinous nonsense, academic twaddle, or propaganda for the Directors Guild. If there is any truth to it at all, and it encompasses blame as well as praise, then *Reflections in a Golden Eye* is Exhibit A.

"Director John Huston spills the novel's poetry on the way to the screen, leaving only its gothic husk and a gallery of grotesques," pronounced *Time*. The Motion Picture Producers Association gave it a Code Seal with the tag, "Suggested for Mature Audiences," but the Legion of Decency castigated it as "ludicrous" and "morbid" and slammed it with a Condemned rating. "It's dirty!" gleefully announced the ads, "a combination of lust, impotency, vulgarity, nudity, neurosis, brutality, voyeurism, hatred, and insanity that culminates in murder." Warner Bros.–Seven Arts had lifted that from a review, but accusations of poor taste induced them to drop it in favor of the single ad line,

"Leave the Children at Home." At that point audiences had gotten the word and most of the adults stayed home too.

Elizabeth next went into another costarring stint with Burton in which, for the first and only time, he got top billing and more money ($750,000 to her $500,000). This unusual state of affairs prevailed because Elizabeth's role was distinctly secondary and she was not originally supposed to be on board but, as with *The V.I.P.'s*, first-choice Sophia Loren again got bumped. It was the film version of *The Comedians* by Graham Greene, and when director Peter Glenville came to Rome to get Burton's name on the contract, Elizabeth inquired about the femme lead. "Elizabeth, I'd love you to do it," Glenville told her, "if you don't mind supporting your husband, for it's only a small role." To which Elizabeth replied, "There's no one I'd rather support." The Burtons later explained what happened:

BURTON: "I was against her doing it, particularly as she's only on screen for twenty minutes. But a certain amount of persuasion was used."

ELIZABETH: "They conned me. I was told that Sophia Loren was dying to do the role—'and you wouldn't want anyone else to do those kissing scenes with Richard, would you?' They got me for half pay on the strength of that argument."

BURTON: "I couldn't have done them with any other actress. It never mattered to me before, but now it does. I just don't enjoy kissing other ladies anymore."

As things turned out, Elizabeth would have been better off out of this one. With the exception of Alec Guinness in drag and the sight of stouthearted Lillian Gish beating off big bad Raymond St. Jacques, most of the excitement took place offscreen. Graham Greene titled his book *The Comedians* to indicate all the role-playing and the parts people elect to play in life. Assuredly there was nothing funny about this damning indictment of Haiti, then in the longtime grip of dictator François "Papa Doc" Duvalier and his black terror squad known as "Tonton Macoutes."

Glenville read the book in galleys and not only got the film rights but persuaded Greene to do the script. Greene insisted, however, that Glenville visit Haiti to get the true feel of the place. "But you've got to get to Haiti before the book comes out or you'll be killed," he added helpfully. Glenville took his art director with him on the pretext of researching a prospective film about Haiti's legendary King Henri Christophe. Duvalier even extended an invitation to the presidential palace but Glenville dodged it. He was due to leave Haiti the day before *The Comedians* was published, but the American publisher jumped the gun and Glenville spent a few nervous hours at the airport before he got safely out of there.

Filming in Haiti was obviously impossible so MGM chose Dahomey in West Africa for the major location work, with final work in Paris and Nice. The Haitian Ambassador to Dahomey left the country in a huff, and the company spent six weeks filming there amid persistent rumors that Tonton Macoutes were being smuggled in to assassinate them all. Only one Haitian dared appear in the film—others refused for fear of reprisal to relatives. Actually Dahomey was about as lively as a graveyard, though at the height of the film's voodoo ceremony, the voodoo priest bit the head off a live chicken, whereupon the still photographer threw up. For once the Burtons could go about in public with no commotion whatever. At night in the local bar, Burton spun his endless tales and Elizabeth chimed in hourly with her standard request, "Don't you think it's time we went home, Richard?" When he was involved in two weeks of night shooting, Elizabeth had midnight supper ready on the hot plate she kept in her dressing room. During the three weeks of filming in Paris, *Comedians* cast members showed up at a cocktail party and a batch of Haitian diplomats exited in a fury.

"Ours is the only major movie ever made that overtly attacks another existing regime in a time of peace," Glenville boasted proudly, as Haiti filed an official protest with the U. S. Government. Duvalier himself taped a ninety-minute rebuttal with an American radio commentator, and the Haitian Ambassador insisted that Haiti is "a land of smiling, singing, dancing, happy people with a joy of living." Not in *The Comedians*.

The atmosphere of menace, terror, backwardness, and the law of the jungle is established at the outset. Security forces are omnipresent. The airport crawls with beggars and a taxi is a dilapidated piece of junk. A bribe to the Minister of Social Welfare makes the point that anyone is for sale. That there is no respect for anyone, living or dead, becomes joltingly apparent when a corpse is literally stolen at a funeral. "Duvalierville," supposedly a showplace for the regime, turns out to be a typhoon-stripped junkyard.

With the background thus carefully established, the film falls heavily, and for a numbing 156 minutes, between the two stools of political indictment and anguished love story. The latter is for the Burtons, he as anti-hero, she as German wife to ambassador Peter Ustinov. For this role, Elizabeth studied audio tapes of German actresses who had conquered their accents so that she might acquire just that vestigial accent remaining in the most cultured voices. Unfortunately, if *Reflections in a Golden Eye* was an audience-alienating exercise, *Comedians* is yet another choice exhibit in how to keep the cash customers away. As the central character, give them someone who cares about nothing or nobody. This anti-hero is a burnt-out case full of apathy and self-loathing and Burton etches him with a skillful display of that sensitive self-disgust that was becoming his stock-in-trade. It is really difficult for an audience to feel anything for anyone who feels nothing for himself, however, and that's what did *The Comedians* in at the box office. As an additional irritant, every time the political action heats up (with brutal murder, Tonton raids, political espionage), this love story which is obviously going nowhere keeps cluttering up the screen. Still there is Alec Guinness as a political agent forced to take refuge in blackface drag, undulating to safety with a huge bundle on his head, quite the most fetching-looking calypso domestic since Flora Robson in *Saratoga Trunk*.

The Hollywood *Reporter* called *The Comedians* "tasteful, intelligent, well-produced, and provocative" in one breath, and "restrained, overlong, overcivilized, and cluttered" in the next. *Variety* was blunter, calling it "plodding, low-key, tedious, routine, and seemingly interminable." With such reviews from the trades, the notices in magazines and big-city papers are best passed over in a merciful silence. However, there was yet another sample of the type of critical acid which inferred a combination of genuine disappointment that the Burtons were settling for inferior material coupled with the irresistible urge to throw rocks at two such outsized celebrities. Earlier Pauline Kael greeted *Doctor Faustus* with the judgment that "Faustus and Helen of Troy are not characters from Marlowe or actors playing them; they are Liz and Dick, Dick and Liz—the King and Queen of a porny comic strip." This time it was *Newsweek*'s turn:

"You can tell that Elizabeth Taylor is playing a German in *The Comedians* by her accent, and if you mistake the accent for catarrh, you can tell by her Mercedes . . . He is what he is in every picture he makes these days, The Man Who Has Lost Faith."

Their next dabble in red ink resulted in total immersion—a calamity so humiliating that they did not reunite onscreen for four years thereafter. This was *Boom!*, the film version of Tennessee Williams' *The Milk Train Doesn't Stop Here Anymore*, a far-out, plot-slim shuttle which never left the station in two Broadway attempts. Hermione Baddeley and Paul Roebling got

69 performances out of it in 1963. In 1964, with David Merrick producing, Tony Richardson directed the dazzling duo of Tallulah Bankhead and Tab Hunter into a five-performance flop.

Tennessee Williams apparently never gives up and seemingly never throws anything away. One factor sorely lacking in his genius is objectivity about his own work (he would later publicly call *Boom!* "a beautiful picture, the best ever made of one of my plays"). For years he attended faithfully to his writing each morning, seated at a workbench piled high with odds and ends, bits and pieces of new material, short stories being transformed into plays, prior failures being reworked.

Then there is the cop-out for certain of Tennessee Williams' minor efforts—*Camino Real* being the most conspicuous example—which goes: "Everyone *knows* its a masterpiece, my dear. Too bad it never had a production worthy of it." Possibly the Burtons allowed themselves to be seduced by this kind of snake oil, and Elizabeth may further have reflected that *Cat on a Hot Tin Roof* and *Suddenly Last Summer* had given her two of her greatest triumphs. The third time, however, was to be no charm.

What plot there is gives us Elizabeth as Flora Goforth, The World's Richest Woman, dying by hard-fought inches on her Mediterranean island. In attendance are a recently widowed secretary (Joanna Shimkus) and a totalitarian grotesque (Michael Dunn) who presides over the cream of the K-9 Corps, that is, the hungriest ones. Noel Coward also drops by briefly, a gay senior citizen from Capri, lonely and pathetic, gloating over Flora's approaching demise with ill-concealed malice.

Into this vortex of fear, pain, torment, cruelty, eye-popping wealth, anguished reminiscenses, and vehement profanity—all weapons in Flora's unrelenting battle against the fact of her mortality—comes Burton, an aging drifter whose thing is playing Angel of Death to wealthy women about to kick off, preparing them to meet their maker and/or reconciling them to the brief, meaningless facts of human existence (your choice). So much for plot.

On the location in Sardinia, Production Designer Richard MacDonald conceived a $200,000 stunner: a glistening white, sculptured, clifftop villa constructed on the edge of a two-hundred-foot drop to a stormy Mediterranean cove below. The villa was designed to blend into the cliff from one linear curve to another so that nowhere is there a straight line. "Oh, how beautiful. How baroque," exulted Tennessee on first sight of it. "Just what I had in mind." The elaborately carved doors were copied from originals by Botticelli. Outside there were five fifteen-foot monoliths set up to represent each of Flora's former husbands.

During the eleven weeks in Sardinia a storm did severe damage to the set, which, incidentally, could well have been the last thing Elizabeth saw on this earth. One day, minutes after she'd stepped out of it, her $28,000 dressing-room trailer plunged over the cliff and into the sea. It slipped its brakes and safety blocks and narrowly missed six crew members as it careened off the edge. "Accidents, fires, floods, dogs, disease," director Joseph Losey was heard to mutter at one point. "We've had them all on this picture." Given Losey's expert eye for total effect, the general decor—color schemes, furnishings, costumes—is ravishing and the color is exquisite. If only there'd been a decent script.

"Williams' dialogue is very difficult to learn," Elizabeth commented on the set. "There's something about the changing rhythms that throws you. I found Shakespeare and *The Shrew* much easier. So was Albee. But the only thing that matters about any writing is 'Are the words good?'" Audiences could make their own judgment from among the following random samples.

Elizabeth (after a glimpse of Burton swimming in the raw): "I can't take the beach today. You got more things going for you than your teeth, baby." After which it's back to dictating her memoirs into a loudspeaker system which pipes the sound all over the villa. Everyone thus drops everything to listen respectfully to the news that Flora had a sixth husband "who fell to his death from a mountaintop." He was "a wildly beautiful, beautifully wild young poet." A bit later: "Sooner or later a person is obligated to face *The Meaning of Life!*" Also: "The Boss may be dying under the unsympathetic, insincere sympathy of the faraway stars."

Amid this depressingly steady flow of trivial, banal, pretentious, and empty dialogue, there are several production matters worthy of note. *Boom!* marks the first and only film appearance of Elizabeth's brother Howard. He is the bearded skipper who brings Burton to Flora's island and then throws him out of the boat to swim ashore. Howard, Mara, and their five children were visiting on the location. When the actor set for the role failed to arrive on schedule, Elizabeth prevailed upon Howard to fill in.

Boom! also marked the next to last of the brilliant Noel Coward's eleven film appearances—sadly, in this case, as an aging homosexual in a real rinky-dink role. He is arch, precious, and embarrassing. His sorry plight may be explained by the fact that the role, the Witch of Capri, was originally conceived for Patricia Neal, and then underwent a hasty sex change. Somewhere in the script, Elizabeth was to tell Burton, "My bedroom is full of treasures—including myself," at which point she was expected to strip for a complete inventory. Uh-uh; out went *that* scene. "I think nude scenes in films are utterly absurd," Elizabeth has stated flatly. "What is more, I also happen to think it quite strange the way women, even respectable women, will strip for magazines."

Her film record bears her out. In that opening scene in *Butterfield 8*, she rises from the bed demurely wrapped in a sheet. There is the famous back massage in *Cleopatra*, in deference to history and partially obscured by a clutch of handmaidens. In *The Sandpiper*, the better to shock her clergyman-lover, she faces him nude to the waist, but Elizabeth's hands and arms are strategically in place where needed. They had to talk long and hard to convince her that even this was necessary to the scene. Nor were there any cheap thrills for the production crew. "I had somebody standing in front of me with a towel while I covered myself with my hands," she noted. "I turned puce from head to foot." She derides Brando's impotence in *Reflections* by tauntingly strolling to her bedroom stark naked. The nude backside you see moving up the stairs belongs to Italian actress Paola Rosi. A similar nude backside shot in *Faustus* is likewise doubled. Finally, the body being dragged from that suicidal tub in *X, Y & Zee* belongs to British actress Yvonne Paul. That's about it.

In *Boom!* Richard Burton is somewhat awkwardly cast at the receiving end of Elizabeth's brilliantly bitchy pyrotechnics. As an imperious she-dragon, Elizabeth is alternately earthy, bored, cynical, pain-racked, horny, and penurious, and Burton takes the brunt of all of it. His mission is to bring final comfort and he suffers all the slings and arrows of Flora's outrageous fortune in the calm and assured confidence that she cannot evade him in the end. At one point, he is wandering around famished, decked out in a flowing samurai robe complete with ceremonial sword, all but perishing for something to eat. The final scene between the Burtons has power and shape and holds interest—what interest can be recaptured, that is, from whatever portion of the audience is still there.

The critics took one look at *Boom!* and lowered their own. Under the title "Dick and Liz Dare Us to Stay Away," *Life* fired the now-standard broadside at the Burtons, this one the most damning to date:

"Ordinarily one would discreetly avert one's eyes from something as humiliating as this, but *Boom!* represents a kind of perverse challenge. When people reach a certain status in show biz—

have plenty of 'clout' as they like to say—a kind of arrogance seems to set in. They get to thinking, perhaps unconsciously, that they can dare us to reject anything they feel like shoveling out. The Burtons are particularly afflicted with this malaise. Suitably stimulated, as they apparently were by *Virginia Woolf*, the Burtons can still be effective. But there is a tired, slack quality in most of their work that is, by now, a form of insult. They don't so much act as deign to appear before us and there is neither discipline nor dignity in what they do. She is fat and will do nothing about her most glaring defect, an unpleasant voice which she cannot adequately control. He, conversely, acts with nothing but his voice, rolling out his lines with much elegance but with no feeling at all. Perhaps the Burtons are doing the very best they can, laden as they are by their celebrity. But if they are not cynics, overestimating their charisma and underestimating our intelligence, then they are guilty of a lack of esthetic and self-awareness that is just as disheartening."

After that one, the Burtons decided to retire from joint target practice for a good long stretch. Burton went off to waste himself in a highly profitable piece of World War II rubbish entitled *Where Eagles Dare*. His children had complained that the Adults Only tag barred them from some of his films, and furthermore, he was dying at the end of too many, for example, *Cleopatra*, *Becket*, *Spy*, and *Faustus*. That did it. "Get me a film in which I kill a great many people," he told the producers, "but do not get killed in the end. It must be a picture which can be seen by children." Later Burton reflected, "It is the only film that I have been in that I have seen and thoroughly enjoyed. I didn't believe a word of it."

Concurrently Elizabeth and costar Mia Farrow expended skillful labor on an esoteric whatsit called *Secret Ceremony*. Elizabeth had to carefully steer her character in and out of role-play, to maneuver between fantasy and reality, and she negotiated all the turns admirably. Mia exhibited a comprehension of derangement that was uncanny. Alas, the enterprise was a loser and the good work went for naught. Robert Mitchum was the third star, and if he was unhappy with his role in *Two for the Seesaw* (and he was), the unresolved mystery of who he was and what he was doing in this one could have unhinged an actor who was a less-stalwart survivor than Mitchum.

The plot of *Secret Ceremony* is simple. In London, an orphaned heiress (Mia) encounters an aging hooker (Elizabeth) on a bus and takes her home, setting her up as "mum." The prostitute, who secretly grieves for her lost child, consents to the masquerade. Along the way two of Mia's rapacious aunts (Peggy Ashcroft and Pamela Brown) come to the house to loot. A mysterious character, allegedly Mia's dead mother's lover (Mitchum) also shows up, and the conflict between Elizabeth and Mitchum for control of Mia results in tragedy. This slight story was all but smothered in director Joseph Losey's well-known obsession with inanimate objects and surfaces to establish nuance and mood. The result delighted the few and dismayed the many.

The Hollywood *Reporter* spoke for the few, calling *Secret Ceremony* "a richly atmospheric, respectable and flawed study of submerged lust and guilt. Losey's film deals with the more pernicious and symbiotic of human relationships, role reversals, exorcisms of guilt, in a manner ellipsoidal rather than explicit, spare of action and dialogue, subjective in approach, heavy with mood and symbol, more often coldly intellectual, too often humorless." Eschewing such detailed analysis, most critics threw up their hands and rejected the film in toto.

Newsweek found it "ineffably silly," and *The New Yorker* proclaimed it "truly terrible," adding, "I know that some people are going to love it. Sometimes it seems that the nuttier a picture is, the more eager some people are to get caught up in it." What happened when *Secret Ceremony* was sold to TV was ruinous, in terms of what was done to the picture, and ominous for the fate of future theatrical films turned over to the tender mercies of the tube.

NBC apparently felt that—notwithstanding the audience bait of Taylor, Farrow, and Mitchum—the story needed a little something extra. Accordingly, fourteen minutes were chopped out of the film and replaced by a scene specifically filmed for TV in which a lawyer and a psychiatrist "explain" the characters. All profanity was excised and Elizabeth's occupation underwent a surprising change. Her character was referred to as a "dikey prostitute" in the film publicity. "She now works in a shop selling wigs," primly noted an NBC press release. (Pieces of film were intercut showing Elizabeth indeed dickering with a wig.) "Wigmaker?!" Elizabeth exploded angrily when she heard about this. "That's the first time I've ever heard a prostitute called a wigmaker. How can I be removed physically from that picture? What recourse do I as an actress have?"

None, obviously, though Losey angrily demanded that his name be removed from the TV print, and small wonder. Not only is there the opening fourteen minutes of tripe but voice-over dialogue between lawyer and psychiatrist continues on the sound track, explaining the obvious, filling every pause with hokey banality, crashing in with a flat-footed literalness that is nothing short of stupefying, totally at odds with Losey's approach, as explicit as he is oblique. That a flop on the screen was made disastrous on the tube is of small moment. Questions of merit aside, *Secret Ceremony* will be remembered as the first film over which was superimposed on the small screen the unsettling warning, "Revised and Edited for Television." Producer John Heyman quite properly sounded the alarm: "It's a dangerous precedent. It means that a film can reach television in an unrecognizable state but still have the benefit of the title and other values of its theater exploitation."

The last snowfall in this particular winter of Elizabeth's professional discontent was called *The Only Game in Town*. She did it in Paris at the end of 1968, a year in which the Burtons made news of one sort or another in every single month. It was not a triumphant year for either of them, but they were at the floodtide of their celebrity and the public appetite for news of their various activities was apparently insatiable.

"For some reason I feel kind of apologetic about costing somebody a million dollars for a picture," Elizabeth revealed in January. "It is still like a dream—I still can't believe it, especially when I never see it, and especially when people would be flabbergasted to know how little of my pay ever becomes mine." A large hunk of it went into trusts for the children and, in any event, this was the last year she would be feeling apologetic on this particular score.

In February the Burtons attended the Paris opening of the fashion boutique in which they had become partners in the previous October. The managers were former Parsons School students Vicki Tiel and Mia Fonssagrives. For the opening Elizabeth contributed a wedding gown of her own design: a white bodystocking worn under a diaphanous floor-length veil embroidered in flowers. In person Elizabeth stopped traffic in a tunic and tights of "hyperkinetic geometric pattern." Explained Mia Fonssagrives: "She's not supposed to be chic. Her career requires that she be stupefying." During the fashion show, a whole parade of luscious models flounced by the Burtons' table, all of them under specific instructions to "shake your bum at Burton."

February also brought the news that *Around the World in 80 Days* was about to be reissued prior to its sale to TV. Forty-per-cent owner Elizabeth found the time to tape her segment of reminiscences, along with those of Gypsy Rose Lee and others, for a TV tribute to the film's producer called *Around the World of Mike Todd.* It was shown on CBS the following September, and it marked Elizabeth's third time on the tube, the first being *Elizabeth Taylor in London,* and the second a guest stint with Burton (for a joint fee of $50,000) on *The Sammy Davis Show,* in which they all warbled a chorus of "What Do the Simple Folks Do?" from *Camelot.*

In March a 120-foot, $500,000 yacht called *The Beatriz of Bolivia* sailed up the Thames and tied up at the Tower of London pier, thus continuing a saga begun the previous June in Monaco. There the Burtons had rented a 279-ton, 110-foot yacht called *The Odysseia* for a cruise around the Mediterranean. Elizabeth promptly took a tumble on deck, aggravating her chronically obstreperous left knee. For a while she was on crutches and in and out of Princess Grace Hospital in Monte Carlo, but she didn't blame the yacht. The Burtons eventually bought it for around $192,000 and renamed it the *Kalizma,* in honor of daughters Kate, Liza, and Maria. It was then left in drydock in Marseille in the winter of 1968 for general overhaul, refitting, and redecoration (lots of canary yellow, Elizabeth's favorite color; two Chippendale replica mirrors in the master bedroom; luxurious carpeting on which E'en So and O Fie could work their unhousebroken will, etc.).

While this $240,000 refurbishing was in progress, the Burtons rented the *Beatriz* (at $2,400 per month) to take them to England for their respective film commitments. Then it developed that quarantine regulations forbade the Burtons to bring their dogs into the kingdom. So, with a bobby posted on guard at the Tower of London pier, a crew of ten on the *Beatriz* attended to the various wants and needs of Georgia, Cuthburt, O Fie, and E'en So. According to Burton, the chief reason for this floating kennel was E'en So. Elizabeth had acquired O Fie when she made *Shrew* in Rome, just the latest participant in Elizabeth's lifelong love affair with the animal kingdom. Burton's nose was getting out of joint about it all. "Animals love Elizabeth; even cheetahs go up and lick her. Then came this ugly Peke. She walked into the room, stuck her nose up at Elizabeth and came over to me. My own dog! I thought it would never happen." To the vast amusement of everyone but the authorities, the *Beatriz* became a well-publicized adjunct to the Tower of London guided tour, and Elizabeth and Burton trekked down from the Dorchester on frequent visits.

In April, Elizabeth and Frank Sinatra signed to do *The Only*

Game in Town, to begin shooting in September. For this one, Fox paid $500,000 prior to its Broadway opening, the highest price ever in a preproduction deal. With Tammy Grimes and Barry Nelson in the leads, the final curtain fell after only sixteen performances. It was a bad omen since, unlike the successful two-character *Two for the Seesaw,* Fox had laid out a bundle and now there would be no presold title magic to help the film. The director would be Elizabeth's old *Place in the Sun–Giant* mentor, George Stevens. She and Stevens had almost reunited in 1965 on *The Greatest Story Ever Told.* Elizabeth would have done Mary Magdalene, but they couldn't agree on terms and it went to somebody else. At last these two, whose prior collaborations had been milestones for both, would be together again at a time when Elizabeth's career badly needed a boost.

In May the Port of London authorities, fed up with jokes about going into the kennel business, commandeered the pier space and ordered the *Beatriz* to anchor out in the Thames. "We're pretty broad-minded but enough's enough." Any inconvenience was mitigated by the news of the *Kalizma*'s imminent arrival from Marseille, and by the present Burton bought for Elizabeth from New York's Parke-Bernet Galleries two days later. He laid out $305,000 for an emerald-cut, 33.19-carat diamond, nicknamed the "Krupp," because it came from the estate of Vera Krupp, ex-wife of the German munitions tycoon. On June 1 it was disclosed that Burton had parted with an additional $200,000, this time to buy two seats on the Board of Harlech TV, which beams to Wales and the West of England. This was accompanied by a spate of exciting speculation about further Burton involvement and participation in programming. And on June 17, in the wake of the Robert F. Kennedy assassination, a full-page ad appeared in the New York *Times* in which over four hundred celebrities pleaded for more stringent gun controls. Elizabeth initiated that ad and paid for it.

In July financial news gave way to items that were disturbingly personal. Early in the month Elizabeth had given voice to various female complaints, and she was ordered into London's Fitzroy Nuffield Nursing Home. LIZ HAS MYSTERY OPERATION read the headline on July 19. Anesthesiologist J. Middleton Price was again on hand, almost as a good-luck charm for Elizabeth. "We never reveal the nature of operations here," a matron stiffly told reporters. It was apparently an exploratory operation because the major surgery took place four days later. It was described as "just this side of a hysterectomy," that is, her uterus was removed but not her ovaries. "It was not a comfortable operation but she is progressing satisfactorily," Dick Hanley told the press, adding that there was, thankfully, no sign of cancer. The surgery and subsequent convalescence would put the start-date of *Only Game* off to October, and upon news of that, Frank Sinatra, who was already booked for a November opening at Caesar's Palace, pulled out of the film.

A day after Elizabeth's operation, Richard Burton was fired by director Tony Richardson after two weeks' work on *Laughter in the Dark*. The cause given was "consistent lateness," and how much of the trouble was due to anxiety over Elizabeth's condition is an imponderable. (Nicol Williamson took over the role and the film was subsequently whisked in and out of theaters to thunderous public indifference.) Amid charges, countercharges, and the threat of a suit for libel and slander, Burton then suffered a family tragedy that hit him like a sledgehammer. In a freak accident in Switzerland, his beloved brother Ivor was completely and hopelessly paralyzed.

Against this doleful background Elizabeth and Richard Burton came to Paris in October for the humiliating finale to the inflationary spiral of fiscal lunacy that had begun for both of them with *Cleopatra*. She had maintained her million-dollar price throughout the decade and now, with *Only Game*, surpassed it by another quarter of a million. "Am I surprised producers pay me $1,250,000 per picture?" she reflected rhetorically. "They must be out of their tiny Chinese minds!" They were, but if they were willing to part with that kind of money, she would certainly take it. Who wouldn't? Even more amazing, Burton was pulling in $1,250,000 at the same time for costarring with Rex Harrison as two aging homosexual lovers in the film version of *Staircase*.

So Fox had shelled out $2.5 million to get the Burtons. Fine. But since *Staircase* took place in London, and *Only Game* in Las Vegas, what were they all doing in Paris? (A) Paris would provide a tax break for both Burtons, and (B) Since the Burtons would only work if they could work simultaneously in the same place, Paris it had to be. On one set, there was a London barbershop, and surrounding environs; on the other, a re-creation of Las Vegas—skyline, casino, crap tables, slots and all. "Power is being able to do what you want to do," Elizabeth remarked to an interviewer. Put another way, it was simply charging all the traffic would bear, and the traffic ultimately found the end results simply unbearable.

Burton and Harrison had earlier shared a giggle about being the only two actors whose well-known private preferences could enable them to play those two characters in *Staircase* and get away with it. From the time they arrived in Paris, however, they wondered why in hell they had ever signed to do it. Both were ragged unmercifully. "Mr. Burton tells us that you are a very nice girl," a reporter informed Elizabeth at a foreign press reception. "I'm glad he decided that," she riposted. "Considering the part he's playing now in *Staircase*, he's a very nice girl too."

Additionally Burton was told that after five unsuccessful tries for an Academy Award, this time he could go up for the Best Actress Oscar and that would undoubtedly "turn the trick." He and Harrison actually worked together skillfully and well, but what did them in was the fact that they were playing two of the dullest queens since Catherine of Aragon and Catherine Parr (the first and the last of Henry VIII's harem). In a career that now spans thirty-nine films in forty-five years, *Staircase* rests in Rex Harrison's memory as absolutely the worst of the lot.

"Burton and I agreed to do it on the strength of the play," he said later. "I'd seen Paul Scofield in it and loved it. But I was terribly upset by the script. Donen (the director) had dirtied it up. I tried everything to get out of it. Fox said they'd sue for a million dollars, and I wish now I'd given them the million and never done it."

Over on the *Only Game* set, Elizabeth had gone from post-operative convalescence straight into intermittently excruciating back pain. One of the reconstructed spinal discs from the 1957 operation was degenerating. "I wake up in the morning and there is this beautiful lady beside me—no makeup, but fresh as the dawn, absolutely glowing," commented Burton. "She gets out of bed and she takes the tiny little steps that come of a hurting back and she is an old lady." Frequent requests for a "Jack-on-the-rocks" (Jack Daniel's over ice) helped her over the worst moments. What later proved to be the inspired choice of Warren Beatty to replace Frank Sinatra in the film was likewise a big help in getting through it. Once he came over to her on the set between takes, looked at her, and burst out laughing. Elizabeth demanded to know what was so funny. "I laughed," he finally told her, "because nobody can be that beautiful." (Roddy McDowall has done the same thing over the years and for the same reason.) Elizabeth's spirits were further buoyed by her continual delight in her new diamond. "I never stop looking at it, admiring it, not getting over the fact that it's really mine"—this while turning it in the light to give off myriad reflections. "Is that the famous diamond?" a reporter inquired. "Yes, it is. Mr. Burton gave it to me," Elizabeth replied. "It came from the Krupp people . . . KRUPP . . . as in German munitions. I think it's rather nice that a little Jewish girl has it now."

A month after shooting began, physical pain was compounded by family sorrow. On November 20 the sad word came from Los Angeles that Francis Taylor had died in his sleep in the early morning hours. This handsome patrician had sired a daughter who had grown up to become the most famous woman in the world. "If you want to talk about Women's Lib, in terms of being self-supporting, then I've been Women's Lib ever since I was a baby," Elizabeth once said. True enough, and Francis Taylor had not originally wanted this for his child. Fate decreed otherwise. When she left their home on the occasion of her first marriage, he had to hope that the precepts and values he and her mother had passed on to her would help her through whatever would be her portion in life. In every major crisis he had come to her side, and—here a fact that shames praise, given the circumstances and the ample opportunities to do otherwise—anything he ever had to say to her about any of it was said only to her. He had survived two strokes, in 1965 and 1967, and now he was gone. Elizabeth and Richard Burton flew in to Los Angeles for the simple services conducted by a Christian Science Reader at Westwood Village Mortuary. Francis Taylor was then laid to rest in Westwood Memorial Park.

After another production delay, when Elizabeth's back made it impossible for her to work at all, the *Only Game* company moved to Las Vegas for ten days, and George Stevens wrapped the film in February 1969. What he had achieved is a finely crafted tale of two losers: she, a chorus girl unhappily involved with a married man; he, a cocktail pianist with gambling fever for whom Las Vegas is truly, as the local sick joke has it, Lost Wages. They meet and ultimately decide to commit themselves to winning together.

Fox took a look at this and hadn't a clue as to what to do with it. It didn't have Jon Voight being done in the balcony of a Forty-second Street grindhouse, or Gig Young ditto by Jane Fonda in his office in the middle of a dance marathon. It wasn't Dennis Hopper spaced out on a motorcycle. Nor Natalie Wood having a go at mate-swapping. What in this brave new world of kinky sex, dope, and fashionable alienation did you do with something like this? With a minor change in the bedroom scene Joan Crawford and Clark Gable could have done it in the '30s. "It's just a simple love story between two people," Stevens remarked to his friend, screenwriter-historian De Witt Bodeen. "I don't think the public is ready for it yet." Fox's solution was to sit on it for the rest of the year, and then dump it out the following January, the traditional dog days of distribution (because anything thought remotely worth a tub thump is rushed out in December for Oscar consideration).

The public dismissed *Only Game* fairly quickly (it did a meager $1.5 million domestically, five-sixths of which was swallowed up in Elizabeth's salary) but the critics were generally fond of it. Anyone who has allowed Warren Beatty's good looks and/or his amatory escapades and/or his bad press to obscure what a really outstanding film talent he is should make it a point to watch him in this film. He and Elizabeth vibrate genuine costarring chemistry and both were highly praised. One critic probably best expressed the varying feelings about the film when he called it "old-fashioned, farfetched, trivial, melodramatic, ponderous in parts, and strained in others. Surprisingly it is also the sweetest, gentlest, and saddest film in some time. I loved it." Television can only enhance it since this kind of careful, closeup character study always looks good on the small screen.

That would be small consolation to 20th Century-Fox. They had paid $2.5 million for the Burtons, met their terms, and come up empty with both hands. *Staircase* was likewise a bust, just the latest addition to a dismal string for Richard Burton: *Faustus*, *Candy*, *Boom!*, the *Laughter in the Dark* fiasco, and now this one. Fortunately he was heading into the film version of the play in which pal Rex Harrison had first electrified Broadway audiences twenty years earlier: *Anne of the Thousand Days*.

With the gold plate still gleaming on her second Oscar, it had taken six films in just three years to run Elizabeth's newly won prestige right into the ground. Her box office was shot and her million-dollar days were done. Curiously enough it had taken just six films to do in the first double-Oscar winner, Luise Rainer. Miss Rainer chose to retire, and it looked for a while as if Elizabeth might follow her example. Could she really quit permanently? "Like a shot. I'll do it someday. I won't make a big deal out of it. I'll just quietly lope off one morning and be gone." Later she announced, "I am seriously considering retiring from the screen. I may never work again. Unless something comes along that absolutely captivates me, the life of leisure—if you can call being married to Richard Burton and the mother of four, leisure—is for me."

The life of leisure would last for two years. And the stability in her marriage for just two more.

❁ 31 ❁

The first item to be attended to in Elizabeth's new life of leisure was her back. She had worn a back brace throughout *Only Game* filming, and now, again in severe pain, she went into Cedars of Lebanon in March 1969 for tests and X rays on that degenerating disc. Rex Kennamer attempted to squelch then-rampant cancer rumors by announcing that "nothing showed up on the X rays and there is absolutely no truth to the rumors that Elizabeth is suffering cancer of the spine." That didn't prevent a Hollywood columnist from breathlessly affirming that she had actually "seen the fatal X rays." Elizabeth's comment was succinct: "How could that silly bitch have read my X rays? She can't even read PERIOD!"

After a long rest in Puerta Vallarta, the Burtons returned to England in May for the filming of *Anne of the Thousand Days*. For luck, Elizabeth did a day's work unbilled. She donned Elizabethan costume, put on her La Peregrina pearl, and slipped into a court dancing scene in which, as one of the revelers, she enters while clapping a mask over her face. In October, La Peregrina was permanently eclipsed by the world's costliest single piece of jewelry ever offered at auction. It was a perfect 69.42-carat white diamond the size of a peach pit. Elizabeth bid $1 million for it but Cartier's outbid her by $50,000. Burton then got together with Cartier's and bought it for an undisclosed sum.

Elizabeth first wore it the following month to Princess Grace's Scorpio Party, in honor of Grace's fortieth birthday ("the last birthday I'll ever admit to"). At the ball, it dangled at the end of a diamond necklace. At brunch on Sunday, it was mounted on a ring worn on her left hand. Two cars full of police, one before and one behind, accompanied her to the Monte Carlo Casino, and Monaco's Prefect of Police hovered nervously at her elbow throughout the ball and the brunch.

The Cartier-Burton Diamond (as it came to be called) was the crown of a collection which has become the eye-popping wonder of women around the world. Elizabeth's personal fortune was once loosely estimated at some $23.5 million, and whatever it actually is, a respectable portion of it reposes in this collection. It is a natural magnet for jewel thieves and in August 1970, knowing that the Burtons were in residence, three bandits burst into New York's Regency Hotel, handcuffed fifteen employees, and wailed away at various strongboxes with gusto. They came away empty. Such of Elizabeth's ice as was traveling with her was stashed in an unusual deep-freeze.

"It was under the couch," Aaron Frosch later revealed, "but I won't tell you who was sitting on the couch." He further noted that the Burtons were guarded at all times by a security force varying in number and identity from day to day and place to place. "Sometimes there are guards that even Elizabeth and Richard don't know about." Lest anyone think that such caution reeked of paranoia squared, a rundown on the collection might prove helpful.

First, the Cartier-Burton diamond—69.42 carats—$1 million-plus.

Then, the Krupp diamond—33.19 carats—$305,000. Elizabeth has always gotten great joy out of letting others wear it or try it on. Dick Hanley's friend and associate, John Lee, used to dangle it on his pinkie finger, and probably every chambermaid at the Dorchester has had it on at one time or another. Elizabeth agrees with those who gush over it in unabashed admiration: "It's not exactly chopped chicken liver." Shortly after she acquired it, Elizabeth reportedly ran into Princess Margaret and showed it off to her.

MARGARET (loftily): "That's the most vulgar thing I've ever seen."

ELIZABETH (generously): "Want to try it on?"

A pause while Margaret admired it on her own finger.

ELIZABETH (sweetly): "See—it's not so vulgar now."

La Peregrina pearl—a shimmering milky-white pendant for $37,000. Balboa apparently stumbled on it in 1520, the year after he stumbled into the Pacific Ocean. He sent it back to his king, and Philip II of Spain subsequently bestowed it on his bride, Mary Tudor of England. The name means "The Wanderer" and it has lived up to it on at least three occasions. The week after Burton bought it, he and Elizabeth went for the *Only Game* location shooting to Las Vegas, a city Richard Burton genuinely loathes. He was utilizing various stratagems to keep from going bananas, including sending room service on a frenzied hunt for jellied eels. Then, as the last straw, La Peregrina disappeared. Just as they'd about given up hope, one of the Pekes spotted what she thought was a new bone in the corner and began chewing away. Her teeth marks are still on it.

Enamel cameo bracelet—supposedly once the possession of the Empress Josephine or of Napoleon's sister, Élise (possibly both). This one came to Elizabeth when *Shrew* director Zeffirelli admired the diamond earrings with which Mike Nichols had gifted her at the close of *Virginia Woolf*. "*They* were a present from a director," Elizabeth noted. "It was *his* first film too," she added helpfully. "But I think it will be very difficult to find something that will top those earrings," replied Zeffirelli, backing off nervously. The next day he gave her the bracelet. (At the finish of *Shrew*, Elizabeth gifted Zeffirelli with a superb cigarette case of heavy gold decorated with a large sapphire and inscribed: *Caro Franco—From the Shrew and Her Tamer.*)

Ping-Pong diamond—.042 carats—150 francs (about $38). This one was a prize of war. "Richard is really almost professional at ping-pong. He told me, 'If you can win a game—if you can even take ten points—I'll give you a perfect gem.' I got him sloshed, and I not only took the ten points, I beat him!"

Other gems of the collection in no particular order of value:

> Platinum wedding ring from Richard Burton
> A $93,000 emerald clip from Burton which Elizabeth called her engagement present
> A 27-carat diamond engagement ring from Mike Todd
> Approximately $160,000 worth of rubies set with diamonds
> Diamond-and-pearl necklace and matching earrings from Mike Todd
> Diamond-encrusted emerald necklace and matching teardrop earrings
> A 40-carat, $65,000 blue sapphire broach, one inch long, surrounded by diamonds in a Tiffany mounting
> A belt of real diamonds
> Assorted earrings, bracelets, and pins of precious stones
> French Military Medal (Burton has one too)—a gold medallion the size of two U.S. silver dollars, outlined in diamonds to be worn on a chain. Given to Elizabeth for her services on behalf of French war orphans
> Twelve gold bangles hung with collector's-item British coins from Victoria's time up through the rare commem-

orative medal for Edward VIII, plus ancient Greek and
Roman coins, and doubloons rescued from sunken treasure ships
A $20 gold piece, surrounded by rubies—Burton's gift
on their tenth wedding anniversary

A much-publicized addition to the collection was presented
by Richard Burton to Elizabeth on her fortieth birthday. It
was a heart-shaped diamond pendant first given by Taj Mahal-
builder Emperor Shah Jehan to his beloved young wife in 1621.
The diamond is set in a heart-shaped gold mounting, ringed by
rubies and emeralds, and hangs on a diamond-studded gold
chain executed by Cartier's. Engraved in the gold mounting is
the message, "Eternal love 'til Death." Burton refused to divulge
either the number of carats or the cost, estimated between
$50,000 and $100,000.

On the subject of the collection, Burton commented, "It *is*
pleasant to buy for Elizabeth, she is so mad for gems. She loves
wearing her things. I remember once at a party, the room was
full of rich, middle-aged women who all knew she'd be wearing
the Krupp. So they came with no jewels at all. It made me feel
good—power, I guess. A feeling of power." Then, on a more
practical note, "I have had two wives. The first one hated
jewelry and the second lusts after it. I buy it to please her and
because it is a great investment. You can buy small artifices,
exquisite things from Webb and Schlumberger, but they haven't
the resale value. So I prefer the great whoppers. I know they can
be split up and resold if you need them. As you see, I still have
one foot in the working man's world. To me, of course, the
greatest diamond in the world is still a lump of coal."

If a sizable chunk of Elizabeth's fortune rests in her jewel
box, another chunk hangs on the walls. Thanks to the advice
and/or gifts of Francis Taylor, her uncle Howard Young, Mike
Todd, plus her own expert art sense, Elizabeth owns a nice
collection of French Impressionist and twentieth-century mas-
ters. Her father started her off with a wedding present in 1950,
and Elizabeth now possesses valuable works by Degas, Hals,
Cassatt, Pissarro, Monet, Modigliani, Renoir, Rouault, Utrillo, and
Van Gogh ("Van Gogh always makes me cry," she once said).

The news in 1970 that Elizabeth had acquired another luxurious
possession received usual reportage and some vehement reader
reaction. *Look* magazine revealed that Burton had paid $125,000
for a mink coat made of forty-two Kojah pelts. The magazine
had been one of the few publications Elizabeth trusted and she

had given them several interviews over the years. *Look* subsequently went out of business, which, from the point of view of future Elizabeth Taylor interviews, was just as well. With this one, they not only blotted their copybook, they drowned it.

Under the title "How Do I Love Thee? Let Me Count the Ways," *Look* informed readers that "42 Kojah pelts were just dying to be the world's costliest fur coat for a fading movie queen who has much and wants more." Burton was identified as "Big Giver"; "Big Getter" was Elizabeth. "In my particular case, and with my particular wife, she's just as excited if you give her something that costs $3.75 as if you give her a million-dollar diamond—both of which I've done," said Burton. To which an irritated Elizabeth added, "Anyway, who the hell's business is it?"

Any article about Elizabeth since the mid-1950s has been guaranteed to produce the whole sizzling spectrum of human emotion. For example, Walter Wanger's *Cleopatra* article in a 1963 *Saturday Evening Post* produced a cataract, of which the following is a small trickle:

"Your June 1 issue with its indecent pictures and disgusting article landed in our family garbage tin. My husband and I are trying to raise good, clean-living, well-adjusted sons and daughters." Furthermore: "The original Cleo/Rest and keep her/Would have worked/A whole lot cheaper." Finally: "In some things I'm undecided/But one thing is certain/I've had enough/Of Elizabeth and Burton." (So why write about it?)

A year later the *Life* excerpts of Elizabeth's memoir sent the letter writers into another frenzy:

"Cheer, cheer, cheer for Elizabeth Taylor that she has brought it all off: that she continues beautiful, that she has cheated death, that she got the man she wanted, that her children flourish, and that she has the guts to say 'the public be damned.'" On the other hand: "Did you feel the need to provide her with a platform from which she could scream her defiance to the American public?"

On the occasion of a lovely 1964 mother-and-daughter essay called "Elizabeth and Liza":

"I must confess that, almost against my will, my heart went out to this tremendously complex woman, so warm and compelling was this essay of love. How easy to see why she is called the greatest star who ever lived."

Phooey: "Liz Taylor's immorality is exceeded only by her ignorance."

And that ain't all: "Quite clearly you can tell from her daughter's expression that she doesn't like her mother."

Then, the prize with regard to Elizabeth's expression of mother love:

"It is impossible for me to believe that the quotes provided in 'Elizabeth and Liza' could actually have been made by Miss Taylor without a great deal of coaching."

The present instance of "Big Giver," "Big Getter," and the 42 Kojah pelts brought forth the usual:

"Your article was insulting, tasteless, and irrelevant. Too bad 'Big Giver' didn't give *your* reporter a little something—a fat lip, for a start."

But to be fair: "Have they ever done anything worth while with their millions? Have they any sense of stewardship? If so, you owe it to them to tell that story too."

That story has never been fully told because Elizabeth would not have it so. Quite rightly she regards her personal charities and acts of kindness as her own private business. Enough notice of them has surfaced over the years, however, to indicate that with all the diamonds and gems, million-dollar fees, yachts, planes, paintings, minks, and what not on one side of the scale, the other side has gone far from empty.

Her 1959 purchase of $100,000 in Israeli bonds was the most public of several contributions to Israeli causes. $70,000 donated to build a theater in Tel Aviv was another. These have cost her more than just the money. She has suffered a long-term boycott of her films throughout the Arab world. Besides the money, she is charged with "participating in films glorifying Israel." In what? *Jane Eyre? Little Women? Under Milk Wood?* If portraying a persecuted twelfth-century English Jewess over twenty years ago (in *Ivanhoe*) is the reason, then one can give the boycotters the line *Ivanhoe*-costar George Sanders gave to Marilyn Monroe in *All About Eve:* "You have a point. An idiotic one, but a point." Additionally Elizabeth has become a prime target of Arab terrorist organizations. When their murderous frenzy erupted at the 1972 Olympics in Munich, Elizabeth was filming there at the time, and sound-stage security was necessarily severe.

Her 1961 testimony at the Mt. Sinai–Cedars of Lebanon Medical Center fund-raiser helped produce over $7 million in pledges.

As to other causes: There was the gun-control ad after Robert Kennedy's death. Also that medal from the French Government honoring her work for war orphans. In 1966 Elizabeth established a heart disease research foundation in memory of Montgomery Clift and endowed it with $1 million. Britain's National Society for Mentally Handicapped Children is dear to her heart. All the profits on her Harlech TV stock go to this society, and in 1969 Elizabeth presented a check to Lord Segal, its chairman, for $243,000. The money had been raised from varied sources over a three-year period. In 1970 Jane Fonda got $3,000 apiece from Burton and Elizabeth to defray lawyer costs for Black Panthers then in jail, not because Elizabeth necessarily sympathized with Panther aims and methods but because it was her understanding that, under American justice, anyone accused of crime is entitled to his full constitutional rights. Elizabeth received a $10,000 fee for her work on the 1970 *Here's Lucy* TV show. She donated it to the Oxford University Theatre Centre, and followed that in 1972 with a further gift (in conjunction with Burton) of $260,000. Later that year she made good on a promise, and presented the United Nations Children's Fund with a check for $45,000. Elizabeth had pledged that whatever was the ultimate cost of her fortieth birthday celebration in Budapest, she would match it with a gift to UNICEF. In early 1973, when professional commitments made it impossible for the Burtons to appear at a London medical fund-raiser headed by Princess Margaret, Her Royal Highness received a joint check for 100,000 pounds ($225,000) to cover their absence. Finally Elizabeth lent her prestige and support to the cause of endangered wild life. In 1970 she formally pledged "not to buy, use, or promote the use of wild animals for the sake of fashion." (This, incidentally, does not include mink, since mink are bred specifically to be worn.)

As to acts of personal kindness: At Christmas, 1963, $500 worth of toys were distributed to the children of Puerta Vallarta, just one of several such occasions. A little boy found suffering a cataract in Puerta Vallarta was sent to Guadalajara for eye surgery. Jack Richardson was Burton's chauffeur on *The V.I.P.'s.* Burton confessed to a liking for good roast pork. Said Jack, "If you want to taste real roast pork, you should taste my wife's." Over to the Richardsons went the Burtons, and Elizabeth liked it so much, she took pork pieces and crackling back to the Dorchester in a newspaper. Jack and Beryl Richardson were then invited to the *Iguana* location in Mexico for three months, all expenses paid.

It was revealed in July 1963 that Elizabeth had secretly paid for two years' worth of lessons at the Royal Ballet School for Anita Desmarais, a thirteen-year-old whose family couldn't afford them, and whose talents Elizabeth learned about from Margot Fonteyn. The disclosure came about because the night Anita danced with the visiting Bolshoi in the Covent Garden performance of *Cinderella,* her mother came to the Dorchester to personally thank Elizabeth, who thereupon lent her a black velvet lynx-lined coat to wear to the ballet that evening. Finally, in 1969, twenty-one-year-old David Ryder, a polio victim, hobbled on crutches 856 miles from the northern tip of Scotland to the southern tip of England to raise money for charity. Elizabeth greeted him at journey's end, offered to pay his expenses and further help publicize the event.

As aforestated, all of the above is an incomplete listing and takes no account of the myriad charity premieres, benefit performances, visits to hospitals and other like activities which thread through Elizabeth's career. If it helps even partially to answer that question about "a sense of stewardship," then the purpose is served.

Looking back on her leisure period, Elizabeth recalled, "The two years that I didn't work I was Richard's camp follower. It didn't bother me, not working or being the center of attention." After Burton finished *Anne of the Thousand Days,* and with the children all away at their various schools, the way was clear, both in Gstaad and Puerta Vallarta, for the times Elizabeth liked best.

"Just being together, very quiet and alone, absolutely alone—that's our idea of complete bliss. Just pottering around, going for a walk together, taking the dogs out. Just sitting around and reading a book, occasionally looking up and talking about what we've just read. An ideal day for us is Sunday. We sleep until around nine-thirty or ten, get up, preferably without any servants around, read the newspapers, and discuss whatever's going on."

At her wedding reception in 1964, Elizabeth had been gifted with a tiny coffee pot. "I don't know how to make coffee, except instant," she confessed joyfully, "but I can learn." And so she did, in her own inimitable, free-style fashion. "I've become a good cook," she later proclaimed proudly. "I do dishes I've tasted. I'll either ask for the recipe or remember it by my taste buds. I try to remember what the seasoning was and try to fiddle it. I don't know how to read a cookbook or anything like that. When it says 'fold in' and 'flap over' and all those other cooking terms, I don't know what they're talking about." (The immediate image is of Katharine Hepburn intimidated by all that burgeoning waffle batter in *Woman of the Year.*) Her husband was no competition at all. "He's a hopeless cook. He can't boil an egg."

As Burton told it, "She loves cooking but she's rather erratic. She can't leave well enough alone. She discovers some splendid new dish but the second time, she starts 'improving' on it. It's still pretty good but it's not the same dish as before. At our house in Switzerland," he added, "we don't have any help at all. Elizabeth does all the cooking and I do all the cleaning. I rather enjoy it. It's the touch of the feminine in my nature, I suppose. I like washing dishes and stuff like that. All those scourers and detergents. But I must be left alone." Here was a perfect match: a wife cheerfully laying out a great gooey profusion of pans, mixing bowls, spoons, spatulas, and what not in her culinary laboratory, and a husband who was perfectly happy to eat the results and then come in and clean up after her.

"We don't bother about clothes," Burton continued. "Elizabeth slops about in jeans until she suddenly decides to dress up. Then even if we stay in she'll put on something exotic—sometimes erotic! Generally speaking, if we are alone, we don't eat out much." Occasionally they might go out to a local pub for a meal, and during the evening, might tap each other lightly under the table to the opening bars of Beethoven's Fifth Symphony. "We worked it out," Elizabeth revealed. "I tap 'I love you' to the rhythm and Richard squeezes back 'me too'—but don't print that. It's our private thing." Then she burst out laughing. "I guess it's okay. We won't have a secret left."

From time to time Burton would come up with a surprise, the offshoot of his genuine aversion to giving gifts on set occasions like birthdays and anniversaries. "He never does do that, as a rule," Elizabeth revealed. "He'll just bring me something absolutely wonderful because it's a Wednesday. But my birthday? Forget it—not a thing usually. I've gotten used to it. But I love it when he surprises me with a bunch of flowers or any kind of present, no matter what it is. Sometimes they are big, sometimes they are tiny, sometimes it's a bunch of flowers that he has picked on the heath."

And their very favorite time of all?

"We sit around in the middle of the night wherever we are and dream of places we have been to or know," Burton revealed. "My wife is a bad sleeper and worries about spiders and mosquitoes, and the middle of the night is sometimes an open forum on where would you like to be now?" Actually, it was an open forum on anything, period, and for Elizabeth it always has been. It is the one time, with the world off her back and securely removed beyond the confines of the bedroom, that she can totally relax and lay out all her thoughts, dreams, and reflections about people and things in a random stream of consciousness that can last for hours. "I think our favorite time together is when all the lights are off and he smokes the last cigarette in bed," she noted. "Sometimes we chat for three hours, talking about everything. Especially when we don't have to get up the next day."

Ordinarily, on nonworking occasions, Elizabeth will rarely make it downstairs before noon. Anyone watching her retire the previous midnight might be pardoned for wondering at this unusual need for sleep, but going to bed and going to sleep have always meant two different things. Reading and talking in bed were varied by another cherished pastime, and this one usually solo. ("There are two real bones of contention between myself and Elizabeth," Burton once noted. "She is never on time and she loves films.") If there were something good on the Late Show, Elizabeth would get herself all set with a midnight snack, and then settle into the film, and the sadder the better. For a woman who would go to the Cross before she gave way to public displays of emotion, Elizabeth is unashamedly fond of a good weepie. As she once recollected, the night she watched *Make Way for Tomorrow*, Leo McCarey's classic 1937 tearjerker in which Victor Moore and Beulah Bondi are shunted off to the old folks' home by ungrateful offspring, the sheets got saturated.

As the world turned the corner into 1970, and Richard Burton was assured of an Oscar nomination as Henry VIII, Elizabeth prepared to interrupt this idyllic existence. She has been called the last, and possibly the greatest, of that long line of Hollywood's Great Stars: Gable, Wayne, Dietrich, Cooper, Bogart, Tracy, Hepburn, Davis, Crawford, Cagney, Hayworth, Turner, Gardner. Their individual differences notwithstanding, all of them intuitively understood that constant exposure on television could only devalue their professional image. Why, they reasoned, should people pay to see on the screen what they could get free on the tube? They either appeared very seldom on TV or avoided it altogether. In twenty years of commercial television, Elizabeth had graced the tube just three times. Now she was about to appear three times in one month and for the best of motives: she was going all out to help her husband win that Academy Award. "I want Richard to win the Oscar," she said jokingly but nonetheless sincerely, "because then we could mate ours and have little babies."

The first joint Burton appearance was on a segment of CBS's *Sixty Minutes* and the host was their Puerta Vallarta neighbor,

Charles Collingswood. Elizabeth stopped him cold right at the outset. "Well," Collingswood began expansively, "your wedding anniversary is coming up. You've been together—what, now—six years?" Elizabeth smiled sweetly and interjected smoothly, "What do you mean? Legally?" While the CBS Standards and Practices people were still recovering from such unaccustomed candor, the interview moved on to safer ground, for example, diamonds, and Burton's Oscar chances.

The David Frost interview a week later provided a delightful example of how the Burtons loved to send each other up. Burton was on for the first hour solo, with film clips and reminiscences, and then Elizabeth appeared to tremendous applause, without makeup, for what was supposed to be "a lightning, surprise appearance." As the minutes ticked by, she laughingly complained, "I thought you just got me out here to say 'Hello'!" Then she launched into a story and, noticing a strange amount of audience tittering, stopped right in the middle of it and turned to her husband. "Are you making faces?" she asked him. "Not many," he replied. She took a slow pause and then purred sweetly, "You're not *on* anymore, are you?" The audience roared. "You'll notice, ladies and gentlemen," Burton declared, "that the only quarrels we have are public."

The third and final appearance was at the Academy Award Ceremonies. Elizabeth had agreed to present the Oscar for Best Picture. The 1969 Best Actor card was a strong one: Richard Burton, Dustin Hoffman and Jon Voight (*Midnight Cowboy*), Peter O'Toole (*Goodbye, Mr. Chips*), and John Wayne (*True Grit*). Voight already had the New York Film Critics Circle Award, Hoffman the British Film Academy Award, and O'Toole the Award of the National Board. In the Oscar sweepstakes, Voight and Hoffman could be counted on to kill each other off, and O'Toole was disadvantaged by having done excellent work in what the industry is pleased to call a dog. It was between Burton and Wayne, and Richard Burton put it this way:

"The Oscars this year are in the generation gap. To presume that either the Duke or I is Establishment is ridiculous. But there it is. It amuses me. It's the old guys against the young guys, and I'll tell you what: the old guys are going to win." Burton was right, but it was the other "old guy" who won. Shortly after that occurred, Elizabeth appeared, concealing her disappointment like the proud professional she is, radiant in an Edith Head creation with the great diamond a dazzling sunburst at her bosom. This most resplendent survivor of the Old Hollywood then presented the Best Picture Oscar to that ultimate cinematic creation of the New Hollywood: *Midnight Cowboy*.

If their stay in Hollywood did not produce the Oscar for Burton, it nevertheless led to something delightful and totally unexpected. It began at the huge bash the British Consul threw for David Frost. With Elizabeth at his side, Burton was holding forth to concentric rings of admirers when, through the crush, he spotted Lucille Ball and producer-husband Gary Morton. "I think your show is absolutely marvelous. I'd like to be on it sometime," Burton shouted at Lucy over the din. "Thanks," the surprised Lucy shouted back, "but how would we ever get you?" Burton said he was available and Elizabeth then chimed in, "He must play a diamond merchant and I'll come in at the end of the show. Come over to the Beverly Hills after this and we'll talk." Lucy did just that and walked into a party. "I found myself mixing drinks and fixing sandwiches. Not once did the subject of the show come up. Gary and I went home believing it was just one of those things."

The next day Burton called his agent. "Please call Lucille Ball for me. I told her last night that we want to do her show and I don't think she believed me." Ten days later Lucy trotted back to the Beverly Hills, script in hand. "I was absolute spaghetti—the worst case of nerves since I auditioned for Scarlett O'Hara." The Burtons heard the script, liked it, and agreed to do it. Elizabeth asked for Edith Head for wardrobe, Sidney Guilaroff for her hair, and, additionally, she asked that real Dom Pérignon 1961 be used in the party scene (instead of the customary tea). The Burtons were early on set throughout the filming at Paramount, and there was only one moment of anything approaching tension.

With that superb comic sense that the years of experience have refined into a science, Lucy had counted on fifteen solid laughs in the opening scene. Right up through dress rehearsal they weren't there. The World's Queen of Comedy was nervous. "'Who am I to tell Richard Burton how to read a line?" she thought to herself. Before the show her professional concern overcame her nerves: "Richard, I hope you won't mind my making a suggestion, but some of the laughs aren't coming in the hotel-room scene. Perhaps the audience can't hear them." To which he replied defensively, "Well, luv, perhaps they aren't funny to begin with." Lucy dropped it. Came performance time and Burton punched them out one after another. Later he whispered to her, "You were right, luv. I clocked fifteen laughs." The show was the *Here's Lucy* September 1970 season opener and earned one of her highest ratings for a lady who has had enough of them to paper her walls.

The wacky plot has the Burtons in town awaiting a press reception in the evening at which Elizabeth will exhibit her famous ring. Since fans are as thick as flies in their hotel, Burton poses as a plumber to make it through the lobby incognito. Lucy nabs him there to come and fix her leaky faucet. After he has allowed himself to be dragooned into doing this, Burton drops the mask:

BURTON: "I might as well tell you the truth. I am Richard Burton."

LUCY: "Oh, sure—and I'm Elizabeth Taylor!" (Big laugh)

BURTON (after a measured pause): "Believe me—you're not!" (Bigger laugh)

Burton convinces her and goes on his way, inadvertently leaving "the ring" in the pocket of his discarded plumber's outfit. Lucy finds it, tries it on, can't get it off. Burton returns to reclaim the ring and winds up dragging Lucy to his hotel suite where a horrified Elizabeth works to no avail to get "the ring" off Lucy's finger. At one point they try champagne. "Champagne is good for everything," Elizabeth remarks brightly. "I wash my hair in it!" Throughout these amusing calisthenics Lucy keeps dropping into a curtsy, addressing Elizabeth as "Your Highness" and "Your Majesty," thus neatly spoofing Elizabeth's legendary status in the public mind.

Eventually the press reception finds Elizabeth backed up against a curtain, behind which Lucy stands, her arm thrust through to simulate Elizabeth's (which is hidden). Lucy's hand is dead-white to make a hilarious contrast with Elizabeth's well-sunburned appearance. Then, as various members of the press come up to view "the ring," Lucy's hand takes on a hysterical life all its own. The whole thing is pure farce, played at a good clip, and excellently done by all hands.

Immediately after she finished it Elizabeth went into Cedars of Lebanon for what was termed "minor gynecologic surgery," and in June followed it up with more of the same at Desert Hospital in Palm Springs. After which she rested for the summer, mainly in Los Angeles, and Burton went down to Mexico to waste himself in an unprofitable potboiler called *Raid on Rommel*. He followed it with yet another forgettable, this one called *Villain*, in which he portrayed a Cockney homosexual ganglord. It began filming in London in mid-autumn and Elizabeth was there as well, for she was about to end her life of leisure and go before the cameras.

Before that occurred, on October 6, Michael Wilding, Jr., then seventeen, married Beth Clutter of Portland, Oregon, at the Caxton Hall Registry in London, where his mother and father had wed almost twenty years before. His mother and stepfather witnessed the ceremony and gave the newly-wed Wildings a new Jaguar and a $70,000 townhouse adjacent to their own in the Hampstead Heath section of London.

In November, Elizabeth went back before the cameras with that low-key, no-big-thing approach on the set which has always been her style. "The unfortunate thing is I enjoy acting, but I'm slothful," she said. "I'm so bloody lazy. I think I should retire. I should quit and raise cats." The second day they handed her a big scene and she hit the panic button. "I was afraid my memory had gone." At home that night Burton told her that in no case should she look at the script because it would only make it worse. He was right. The next day she went back and ripped right through it. "I knew those words very well. It was all psychosomatic."

Nor had she come back to filmmaking for any million dollars. "Now you have to be realistic," she commented in a nod to current film industry economics. "I'm taking a percentage and expenses. We all sink or swim together. It makes everyone work harder to bring the picture in. If you win, it's like winning on the red. If you lose, well, it's roulette—but not Russian roulette."

The film was *X, Y & Zee*, in which hubby Michael Caine has found greener grass in the pale and placid pastures of Susannah York. Gaudy, bawdy wife Elizabeth will use any means to hang on to hubby, and they eventually include attempted suicide and Lesbian seduction. At the end, she stands triumphantly in the doorway and throws out the film's last line: "Maybe we'll all get together for dinner one night, talk about old times—old loves." Then, to her late-arriving husband: "Well, come on, daddy, baby needs something to eat. It's been a hell of a day." The day they shot the scene Elizabeth took Susannah to lunch and the menu included a goodly portion of Elizabeth's favorite Dom Pérignon. Then they went back to the scene. Susannah's previous experience in *The Killing of Sister George* hadn't made participation in these goings-on any easier, but she got through her part of the scene in one perfect take. Caine and director Brian Hutton came over and congratulated her. "Oh, thank you," she sighed. "It must have been Elizabeth's champagne."

X, Y & Zee ultimately turned out to be splashy, trashy, and far less than the sum of its often highly entertaining parts. There's a lot of talk—much of it bright, amusing, "effective"—but it doesn't really tell you anything, particularly about basic motivations and prior background. The only real development is in plot manipulation and this makes for lack of urgency and involvement. Under those circumstances the careful acting of Michael Caine and Susannah York gives off a curiously constipated air, as if they weren't sure about how seriously they were supposed to be taking all this. There is absolutely no doubt in Elizabeth's mind. If her vehicle has problems, she will get through it no matter what, and she rides it with all the determined power and fury of Gable driving that rickety wagon through the fires of Atlanta.

Author Edna O'Brien described the character of Zee thus: "Her aura is crimson, her body beautiful but barren, her manner a trifle raucous, her face masked with mechanical joy, her wardrobe of clothes vast; her energy, ruthlessness, and will power are prodigious. Perhaps she is a monster. Zee is a ruthless survivor." As to wardrobe, Elizabeth wears a dazzling mod array including caftans, poncho tops, mauve hot-pants, a blue-green suede trouser suit, a multicolored orange and red organza maxi-gown, and a black velvet trouser suit from Dior topped by a dramatic cavalier plumed hat. As she barges dynamically from scene to scene, she sometimes looks like a great animated psychedelic tent. Does that bother her? Hell, no! "I just *love* eating between meals," she squeals at one point, in an echo of an earlier outburst in *Secret Ceremony* ("God, I'm getting so *fat!*"). Elizabeth's spectacular tour-de-force bitchery reaches a comic highpoint after a bedroom argument in which she has successfully worked Michael Caine into a furious lather. "Quite frankly, Scarlett," she flings at him in conclusion, "I don't give a shit!"

X, Y & Zee brought Elizabeth Italy's David di Donatello as 1972's Best Actress, and a whole brace of excellent personal notices. "Her jangling performance is what gives this movie its energy," proclaimed Pauline Kael. "The ageing beauty has discovered in herself a gutsy, unrestrained spirit that knocks two very fine performers right off the screen—and, for the first time that I can recall, she appears to be having a roaring good time on camera. Like everyone else, I adored the child Elizabeth Taylor, but I have never liked her as much since as in this bizarre exhibition. I don't think she's ever been as strong a star personality." No critic, however, had much use for the film as a whole, and there was some pained dissent as to the uses to which Elizabeth had put her flamboyant talents.

A drastic rerouting of her talent might have occurred had Elizabeth at long last attempted Lady Macbeth with her husband producing (and possibly costarring) and Roman Polanski directing. The deal fell through. Polanski went on to direct it, with *Playboy*'s Hugh Hefner producing, and on the one hand, their film won the National Board Award as the Best Film of 1971, and on the other, disappeared so quickly that there is legitimate doubt that it ever existed. This would not have surprised English actors of the old school, to whom *Macbeth* is Friday the thirteenth, black cats, and whistling in the dressing room all rolled into one baleful package. A deal for a film version of Charles Collingswood's *The Defector*, with Gregory Peck as a CIA agent and Elizabeth as a shady lady called La Bomba, likewise came to nothing.

What Elizabeth actually did after *X, Y & Zee* was to join Peter O'Toole in contributing her services for expenses only in a cameo part supporting Richard Burton in the visually stunning ear-ravishing film version of *Under Milk Wood*, fellow Welshman Dylan Thomas' radio-drama originally written for Burton. "Presumably Elizabeth Taylor was part of the deal that included Burton," noted Stanley Kauffmann. "Cosmetized and fineried, she looks less like a small-town Welsh whore than like part of the deal that included Burton." Then it was off to Cuernavaca, Mexico, in May 1971, for the filming of *Hammersmith Is Out*, a modern variation on the Faust legend directed by and costarring the Burtons' good friend Peter Ustinov. The film was independently financed by trailer-maker J. Cornelius Crean and the Burtons again took expenses only, deferring to a percentage of the gross. The fourth star spot, originally intended for Clint Eastwood, went to Beau Bridges.

In this bizarre black comedy, which managed to convulse one half of an audience while enraging the other, the world is a loony bin presided over by Jehovah Ustinov. Satan, in the person of Hammersmith as Burton, is safely under wraps there until his repeated promises of worldly power and dominion seduce attendant Billy Breedlove (Bridges) into letting him out. Billy persuades Hammersmith to let him take hashhouse waitress Jimmie Jean Jackson (Elizabeth) along on their trip to glory. After several weird and wacky adventures, Burton decides that it would suit his purposes to permanently paralyze Billy, the better to work his will on Elizabeth. Jehovah has meanwhile left the asylum and is hot on the trail of his Fallen Angel. In the end, Ustinov catches up with Burton and loads him into a helicopter for the return trip. Elizabeth is left carrying Rosemary's Baby— as it turns out, a girl, which apparently is what repeatedly happens everytime Hammersmith gets out and tries to sire a son. The last shot has Burton back in his strait jacket impassively droning, "Let me out!" waiting for the next impressionable attendant to come along.

Depending upon your point of view, several bits and pieces in *Hammersmith* will seem either inspired or outrageous. The first shot of Ustinov finds him chuckling uproariously and, on closer inspection, the book he's reading turns out to be *Studies in Anal Retention*. At the diner Beau manages to maneuver Elizabeth into a back room for some quick sex. While the camera discreetly looks away, there are the sounds of uncertain grappling and then what must be the world's loudest female climax overwhelms the sound track. Before he leaves the asylum, Beau turns around and whips off a good loud fart right in Ustinov's face. "Oh, anyone can do that," remarks Ustinov, unimpressed.

The strange trio of Hammersmith, Billy, and Jimmie Jean progress to a drive-in, for the beginning of a superb sendup of *Cleopatra*. We hear the sounds of an ancient spectacular on the screen, some moaning of "Oh, Caesar! Caesar!" and then after much ado about there being enough asses' milk for the bath, a sepulchral feminine voice intones, "Let all the asses of Egypt be put to death at the foot of our passion!" While these lofty sentiments are sounding, Billy is busy picking his nose (an unbreakable habit) and getting ready to fornicate with Jimmie Jean right there between cars.

The spoof of *Cleo* continues as Burton enters a steam parlor called Caesar's Couch. Finally the trio enter a discothèque where the topless entertainers are a go-go group called, forthrightly, "The Tits." As one of them wraps a viper around herself, Burton remarks slyly, "One of the first things I remember is a lady with a snake."

Billy makes his fortune with a pill company which "cured diseases and caused more." One of those he climbs over in his rise is gangster George Raft, whom we last see sailing out of a fourteenth-floor men's room window. Another is Henry Joe, a winsome cretin who has Texas oil millions and looks like a county-fair prize porker. At one point he is making love to Elizabeth:

HENRY JOE (pleadingly): "Say something terrible dirty!"

ELIZABETH (fervently, after much thought): "Pee-pee!"

Henry Joe gets his, along with the whole oil corporation, at the hands of Hammersmith, as Ustinov narrates solemnly, "Henry Joe was the last to go—and he went as if indeed the eyes of Texas were upon him. He was reciting the Twenty-third Psalm and remembering the Alamo." Billy eventually buys a U.S. President "for $40 million," is appointed an ambassador-at-

large, foments a war, and then retires to a castle in Spain. Jimmie
Jean has long since ceased to please him. "That's the dumbest
bitch I ever saw!" he announces, in a classic pot-and-kettle parlay. He orders Hammersmith to permanently stifle Jimmie Jean.
Instead, Hammersmith ruins Billy in a water-skiing accident and
then impregnates Jimmie Jean. With Billy a hopeless cripple,
Jimmie Jean taunts him with endearments like "Monkey Dick"
and "Peanut Balls," and then exults in Hammersmith's prowess
as a lover. "You should have seen him in the bedroom. He was a
bull!"

Obviously this bawdy bitter brew was not everyone's cup of
tea, and people who didn't like it really got angry at it. *Hammersmith* was slammed as "a tasteless and tedious little atrocity"
by one critic, echoed by another who thought it "possibly the
most inept, certainly the most tasteless, and probably the most
self-blinded movie to hit the screen in years. Its black comedy
theme is totally mishandled." On the other hand, it was called
"poorly written, long-winded, and often ludicrous, but just as
often entertaining," and "among the sickest—and the funniest—
of the current crop."

The more violent reactions baffled Elizabeth. "We had fun
doing it and came in a month under schedule. Did it on a shoe-
string. Maybe it's a mistake to have fun from the way the critics
acted." They had absolutely no quarrel with her. It was the
general consensus that her hash-slinging ding-a-ling transformed
into jet-set beauty contained some of her best work, helped
enormously by the fact that not since the banquet scene on Cleopatra's barge had she been in such superb physical shape. Her
weight had been a problem through the decade. Rex Reed had
even ungallantly asserted that in *Only Game* she looked like "a
Goodyear blimp pumped full of Chasen's chili." Not on this one.
For the first time since *Suddenly Last Summer* a dozen years
before, she displayed herself in a bathing suit and the sight was
spectacular.

"One look at her goes a long way to explain two decades of
hyperbole," wrote a witness who was on the set with her. "Forty
next year, she is in better shape than at any time within recent
memory. Even a cheap, crazy-mop, blond-streaked wig and an
ordinary waitress uniform can't conceal that. In the snug-fitting,
hash-slinger's outfit, her overpublicized frontal appendages seem
like the prows of a catamaran about to loose themselves from a
veil of giftwrap. Below the somewhat tanky, too-short torso, her
legs are still supremely shapely. Her eyes will never be anything

but the radioactive cobalt blue that an alchemist might dream of concocting; her face, as ever, is exquisite."

Elizabeth won the Silver Bear Award as Best Actress at the 1972 Berlin Film Festival, helped mightily by Beau Bridges, playing that mangy, brainless, nose-picking lout to perfection. For Richard Burton, unhappily, there were no awards; only brickbats. He had elected to play his infernal character—haughty, fastidious, icy and implacable—as a creature who never blinks. "*I* thought Richard was wonderful," Elizabeth asserted loyally, "—that terrible mad stare!" She was in a tiny minority.

"Burton goes through the film with a single bored expression," reported *Variety*. The following critical comment was disturbing evidence of what a lot of people were beginning to think: "It's getting uncomfortably difficult to watch Richard Burton now without thinking of John Barrymore in his last days, parading the bleary remnants of a considerable talent through material at once third-rate and self-parodying." Here was the man once called "one of the half-dozen great actors in the English-speaking world." In five years, nine flops—whether financial, artistic, or both—had filled his cup brimful with professional humiliation. Incredibly, the worst was still to come, as Elizabeth Taylor and Richard Burton headed into the most explosive act of their life together.

❀ 32 ❀

The curtain rose on a very bizarre scene indeed. After they finished with *Hammersmith*, the Burtons returned to Puerta Vallarta, and one night went to visit a circus playing locally. The spotlight fell on knife-thrower Alejandro Fuentes. "He said something in Spanish and I thought he wanted to announce Elizabeth and introduce her to the crowd," remembered Burton. "The next thing I knew he was throwing daggers at her."

"What we didn't know," continued Elizabeth, "was that the knife-thrower was saying, 'Is anyone brave enough to take a chance with my daggers?' He mentioned my name and I went into the ring all smiles, thinking he was just going to introduce me. Those knives really thumped around. Richard suddenly jumped into the ring from over the barrier. I shouted to him to stop. I don't know what he thought he could do."

Burton didn't stop to think twice. "I sprinted into the ring. After all, I didn't know he was good with his knives." He found out. Having got Elizabeth safely out of there, he bravely agreed to hold one balloon between his teeth and another between his fingers, and the knife-thrower then promptly (and safely) burst both.

After this it was off to England and a long, leisurely cruise on the yacht. When the *Kalizma* was somewhere in the middle of the Mediterranean, Marlene Dietrich finally rid herself of a title she had never wanted. The new World's Most Glamorous Grandmother flew into London to see the new addition to her family: a six-pound, two-ounce girl born three months prematurely to Michael and Beth Wilding, and named Leyla. "You ask me if she is a star," Elizabeth replied to a reporter's question. "She is a planet, a constellation. She is her own being, her very own piece of this world. I hope it's a better one when she is grown up."

While Burton went on to successive impersonations of Yugoslavia's Marshal Tito (in *Sujetska*) and Russia's Leon Trotsky (in *The Assassination of Trotsky*), Elizabeth luxuriated in another hiatus from filmmaking which eventually stretched out to a year. Burton was busy enough for both of them. After his chores in the two historicals, he took on the title role of *Bluebeard*, supported by such luscious victims as Raquel Welch, Virna Lisi, and Joey Heatherton. The film was shot in Budapest and it was there, in February 1972, that Elizabeth celebrated her fortieth birthday—"the big four-oh," as she called it.

LIZ TAYLOR IS 40! trumpeted the cover of *Life* in affectionate salute, but there were some jarring notes in what was expected to be a triumphant occasion. David Frost came over to tape a two-part interview, and, unlike their first encounter, this one was a real bummer. Frost exuded an air of unctuous idolatry, almost as if someone had crossed Uriah Heep with that mudlark who finally got in to see Queen Victoria. Though she got off some good stories, Elizabeth seemed curiously spaced-out through it all, too often lapsing into one of those incredible Ginger Rogers impersonations of swank.

Burton originally thought of chartering France's Concorde SST, and conducting a celestial birthday party while streaking across the heavens at twice the speed of sound. When that came to nothing, he'd do it on a jumbo jet which would fly around the world, picking up revelers at all the best watering places. Maybe a private train traveling from Paris to Budapest was the right setting. Ultimately it came down to a festive blowout in Budapest. Even though she matched the $45,000 cost with that donation to UNICEF, there was some press flak about the splurge and Elizabeth was irked. The canals of Venice could light up from time to time with three-day, jet-set orgies with scarcely a ripple in the press. Let the Burtons throw their first shindig in ten years together and all the critics came out to carp. Well, to hell with them. "Our love is so deep that I don't give a goddamn what people think or say about us," she fired back.

Behind the bravado the worries were multiplying. Disquieting rumors were abroad about Burton's relationship with Nathalie Delon and supposed dalliance with certain *Bluebeard* costars. The movie business Elizabeth loved had seemingly gone from bad to worse. "I'm terribly worried about our industry because it seems so bloody disorganized," she said. "For my next picture (*Night Watch*), the money's being put up by a perfume maker. For my last, it came from a manufacturer of trailers." And Burton's intermittent rumbles about the agonies of acting were approaching crescendo pitch.

He has always been of several minds about this, almost as if he had put himself where he didn't truly belong and were somehow forever on the outside looking in. His well-known aversion to seeing himself on film is as if the original Richie Jenkins from Wales were deep down inside, disapproving of all this superstar rigmarole and obstinately refusing to confront it. Burton did suffer through a viewing of his first film, *The Woman of Dolwyn,* walked out midway through the second, and the pattern was set. He saw *Becket* because Elizabeth finally ran it on the yacht, and *Anne of the Thousand Days* he checked out because he had two daughters in it. He lasted twenty minutes in *Look Back in Anger,* and then ran off on a gigantic toot. Ten minutes were all he could take of *The Spy Who Came in From the Cold,* and there is no public evidence that he has ever seen *Who's Afraid of Virginia Woolf?*

This "I-can't-bear-to-watch-myself-on-film" routine accords well with those phony-baloney notions of modesty and lack of self-love with which various religions have oppressed mankind for far too long. There is another standard reason for not seeing one's self on film and Burton once gave it. "It's too frustrating. I see a gesture or I hear a line I'd like to improve and there is nothing I can do about it. So now I stay away." As Laurence Olivier and Fredric March (to name two) could tell him, that won't quite float.

Among actors who have regularly played both stage and

screen, Olivier and March are generally accorded the eminence of having achieved the greatest measure of success, in England and America respectively. They learned early on that there were far more cogent reasons for watching one's screen work than just to have a love-feast with yourself in the dark. The only instrument an actor has is himself. As objectively as possible, you checked yourself out physically, watched how you were relating and reacting, and were particularly on the lookout for distracting mannerisms, whether of body or voice, which had somehow crept into your work without your realizing it. Then you could prune where necessary, and particularly for when you went back to work on the stage. For Richard Burton, this last possibility had dwindled almost to nothingness. It would require a concentrated discipline which, for him, was fast becoming a dim memory. His views of acting and why he was doing it ran the gamut.

"There is nothing quite like acting, regardless of how much fun they make of us," he said in the mid-'60s. "There is nothing quite so powerful and fascinating as acting. I think people attack actors because we are so famous and command so much money. I'm used to this but I still hate to be insulted in the newspapers." Occasionally he would joke about his profession. "I don't have to do this for a living. As a long-time employee of MGM, Elizabeth gets a pension. Did you know? That's why I married her really—for the pension." As the string of bombs lengthened ominously, a new reason was added: "I'm simply not happy when I'm not working. The acting bug, once it bites, bites very deep." As the 1970s dawned, the easy banter took on a bitter edge:

"Acting is really nonsense. I really don't know what it is, except that basically it's a matter of personality. Some have it and some don't. The fact that I have it is only important because it was a way out of the coal mines for me. If you want to know the truth, I really don't care a damn about acting at all. It bores me." A year later lethargy seemed to have given way to loathing: "I hate acting. I can't bear it. After the initial excitement it becomes tedious."

So why go on doing it?

"They have an enormous overhead," Bob Wilson remarked. "All those houses and cars, all the people on the payroll, the yacht—it's a matter of economics." To which Elizabeth once added defensively, "He doesn't do films cynically but he worries a bit more about money than I do. He was raised in extreme poverty." If economics were the reason, what kind of strange new math resulted from deferring salaries and taking percentages on films which increasingly made no money?

Possible boredom was another reason. "I wouldn't know what to do if I weren't working. I *have* to work." But why at acting? On good mornings Burton was in his studio at seven pounding away at the typewriter. "I write about two thousand words or so every morning," he told an interviewer. "I give it to Elizabeth. No one else reads it. It's not very good, you see. It's only interesting, valuable personally, because Elizabeth sometimes wakes me up in the middle of the night and asks, 'Where were we in September, 1961?' And I can just flip through my journal and find out."

Enough of his pieces have been published—on boxing, rugby, Elizabeth, travels, and Christmas in Wales—to reveal a fine writing talent. "Maybe that's what I'll do," he has said from time to time. These pronouncements can be stacked next to a similar batch about going off to teach part-time at Oxford, made with such monotonous regularity that Oxford, almost in self-defense, finally announced that it only remained for him to name the time.

Actually, Richard Burton probably gave the whole game away when he once casually remarked, "I can only think of two people who gave up acting and continued to be anybody—Garbo and Sir Johnston Forbes-Robertson." Richie Jenkins had come up from Wales with dreams of international fame and fortune, and that part of him which learned to know London like the back of his hand when he walked all over it for want of a farthing to do anything else, remembered those dreams. Even though they were turning to ashes, they were hard to renounce.

"Make up your mind, dear heart," Olivier had counseled him in that famous cablegram. "Do you wish to be a household word or a great actor?" Burton had replied jauntily, "Both!" In going for the impossible, he had achieved the best of neither. Alfred Lunt, Olivier, Ralph Richardson, Gielgud, Paul Scofield, Guinness—these were enrolled in the pantheon of great actors as a matter of their absolute, unwavering choice, with all the discipline, sacrifice, and dedication which that choice demanded. Richard Burton no longer aspired to that company, partly because he refused to continue the level of work which would have assured him a place, possibly because he never really wanted to be there badly enough.

As for being a household word—of the above, Laurence Olivier could probably have had this at the time he and Vivien Leigh were at the height of their passion and in the first flush of their film fame—he as Heathcliff, she as Scarlett. Both of them resolutely rejected it despite everything the press could do to have it otherwise (Sample: "Their love is really like a beautiful fairy tale."). Richard Burton had become a household word, all right, but in the eyes of the world that word now stood, fairly or unfairly, for an unappetizing display of personal hedonism and professional mediocrity. Increasing mortification drove him back to the hard drinking he had successfully renounced for over a year. The dark moods came more frequently and lasted longer.

"We all go through periods of indecision in which we cannot channel ourselves," Laurence Harvey would later say. "Richard doesn't know what he wants to do. He doesn't want to act. He doesn't know." At the onset of this period Elizabeth had again forsworn work, the better to help him as he sorted it all out. "Her life revolves around the man," *Life* remarked. "Theirs is obviously not only a good marriage, but a great one. It is, however, one wrapped in isolation. The Burtons move from hotel suite to hotel suite across the world, rarely doing or seeing or feeling things the rest of us do."

An illuminating example of the above occurred when Elizabeth and Warren Beatty played a scene in a Las Vegas supermarket on location for *Only Game*. After the take, Elizabeth got a chance to do something which millions do daily but which was unique for her. She got the chance to actually go shopping in a supermarket without causing a small riot. She was going along exclaiming happily at this and that until the price of pork chops at the meat counter stopped her cold. "My God!" she blurted at the butcher. "How can the poor people in this country afford to eat!" How indeed.

On location in Yugoslavia for *Sujetska*, Burton took his lumps from several local actors, who complained that he remained aloof and had a butler on hand somewhere in the wilds of Bosnia to serve drinks. Military helicopter ferried him back and forth from the location to the *Kalizma*, anchored in the Adriatic. Several of Burton's old friends had long since given up trying to get through the entourage and were busy bad-mouthing him. That gave Stanley Baker, still a loyal friend, plenty to do in rebuttal. Another friend, actor Michael Hordern, publicly defended the Burtons' ivory-tower existence. "They are practically like royalty. They have to build a wall around themselves in self-defense." On *Divorce His; Divorce Hers*, the last film of the Burtons, the usual preparations for a state of siege prevailed. "They have a building to themselves: endless rooms *en suite* with a security guard downstairs to check your badge." Burton's recent biographers found all of this very fitting, in a passage reeking with outraged *lèse majesté* which might have been hilarious under other circumstances.

In London in 1970 a double bill of *Virginia Woolf* and *Boom!* had a special intermission feature. The Burtons would appear *in person* for "their first-ever open public discussion of their work." (Small pause for the enormity of such an occasion to register properly.) Security forces apparently hovered in a profusion generous enough to put even Charles de Gaulle's ample nose out of joint. Then—*O tempora! O mores!*—the fans asked questions which were "impertinent," "too familiar," "totally improper." In opposition to Burton's distaste for nudity on film, several of the audience purportedly threatened to strip right on the spot. Well! "The evening left behind a nasty taste," the writers tut-tutted in conclusion. "It was a timely reminder of how necessary it had become for the Burtons to keep themselves aloof and inaccessible."

Now how—in the sacred name of Thespis—had two performers permitted themselves to be painted into such a position? What kind of super-celebrity imposed the obligation to, in effect, abdicate from the human race? "You'd think it would make us free," muttered Burton. "But it doesn't, of course. It's just another bar on the window." The bars on that window had multiplied dangerously, and the amounts of light and oxygen behind it were diminishing rapidly.

The one thing that Elizabeth bridled at was the repeated assertion that she was living an artificial, jet-set existence. "Jet-set" conjured up frivolous images of bleach-blond gooney birds flitting aimlessly from fittings to parties to an occasional roost at Venice or St. Tropez. Elizabeth didn't see herself in that picture at all. "I haven't lived in a vacuum," she firmly declared. "We don't live in the jet set at all. We go to two or three parties a year. That's how jet-set we are!" Maybe so. But if flashing your new diamond in Monaco accompanied by two cars full of police—or appearing at Guy de Rothschild's Ball of the Century looking like a Christmas tree with $3 million worth of decorations —or having a little *tête-à-tête* with Ari at Rome's Hostaria Dell'Orso (where Onassis spritzed away a horde of paparazzi with champagne as Elizabeth dived under the table)—if all that wasn't a little jet-setty around the edges, then newspaper readers could be forgiven their confusion.

Whatever it was, shortly after his mother's fortieth birthday, Michael Wilding, Jr., dropped out of it, publicly and emphatically. He had served a stint in the entourage as assistant to Gianni Bozzachi, his mother's personal photographer, and was through with that. Elizabeth reportedly offered him her support to get started in whatever line of endeavor he next chose, but she balked at supporting the commune of street people which Michael wanted to maintain in the townhouse. Michael then split, taking his wife and daughter to a communal setup headquartered in a Victorian farmhouse in the west of Wales.

LIZ'S DROPOUT SON: MICHAEL WILDING JR. LIVES THE HIPPIE LIFE TO GET AWAY FROM ALL THOSE DIAMONDS, headlined London's tabloid *Daily Mirror*. "Mother's life seems just as fantastic to me as it must appear to everyone else," he was quoted as saying. "I just don't dig all those diamonds and things. I suppose I've always rebelled against it. I really don't want any part of it." Coming as it did during an already-unsettled time in his mother's life, it was unfortunate, to say the least.

In keeping with her firm belief that family business is private, and that her children must eventually be free to find their own way, Elizabeth said nothing. Nor had she anything to say the following September when the Wildings separated, and her daughter-in-law took her granddaughter and went to live with Howard Taylor and his family on Kauai.

Richard Burton had always enjoyed an excellent relationship with the children. For example, the boys went to see *Easy Rider* so many times it probably played in their dreams. Their stepfather thought it a fair travelogue but he loyally mustered what enthusiasm he could. As for what he valued the most in their relationship, "The chief thing is honesty. They don't cheat on me or their mother. If they do something that we generation-gap people consider to be reprehensible, they will actually tell us what they've done. And I value that almost more than anything."

In deference to Elizabeth, the gregarious Burton was carefully circumspect in whatever he had to say about the children in public. But Michael's latest action, and the cruel irony that he would actually choose a life of poverty in Wales, really bit deep. "I know. It sounds corny, but there it is: I made it up and the boy's trying to make it down, and I try not to interfere, but I still get goddamned mad. When I think what it took to climb *out!*"

In the summer of 1972 Burton returned to Yugoslavia for more work as Tito, and Elizabeth went before the cameras in London in *Night Watch*, a thriller from the play by Lucille Fletcher, author of the classic *Sorry, Wrong Number*. The Burtons also signed to do their first movies for television, to begin shooting in Rome in August. Elizabeth eventually got into a severe time-bind because the *Night Watch* company began to believe that a jinx was on it and wondered if they'd ever get the film into the can.

Before shooting even began the production manager fell ill and had to be replaced. Then Elizabeth backed off a set platform, and in attempting to cushion the fall, fractured her left index finger. ("My thirtieth operation," she noted breezily, referring to the subsequent operation to reset it properly. The excision of a facial sebaceous cyst and Swiss surgery on a severed artery were also referred to as "my thirtieth operation," because Elizabeth— along with everybody else—long ago lost count of her physical mishaps.) Director Brian Hutton contracted severe bronchitis, causing a week's delay, and then Laurence Harvey had to have emergency abdominal surgery and that closed down *Night Watch* for a month.

During this hiatus Elizabeth flew over to Yugoslavia to see how Burton was doing. Not well. During the shooting of a scene in which Tito and his Partisans ford a river under German bomber attack, an explosion in the water slammed him up against a rock and injured his leg. The grand finale occurred when Elizabeth slipped on some swimming pool steps, fell on a piece of tile, and laid open her left inner forearm, severing an artery and a bunch of muscles and nerves. After emergency stitching, she was rushed to Switzerland where the whole thing was reopened, cleaned out, and restitched.

In this sad shape, she returned to London to finish *Night Watch*. "You can't touch her," Laurence Harvey joked to an interviewer. "You can't pick her up. There's no place to get a grip on this woman, this sex symbol. This isn't a particularly sexy film, but occasionally we do touch, and when I come near her, she screams. Yesterday she said, 'There's no place you can lift me except under this left armpit.'"

Elizabeth eventually finished *Night Watch* and rushed to Rome to join Burton, already at work on *Divorce His; Divorce Hers*. The idea was to do a pair of back-to-back films examining a divorce from the separate perspectives of husband and wife. Originally the scripts were of reasonably modest proportions involving an ordinary British couple who could have lived in Tunbridge Wells. That was before the Burtons got into the picture— "these stars who are now so big that they are more important than any script, however good or bad," as the New York *Times* had it. Suddenly the couple became wealthy Americans resident in Rome, he involved in some sort of multimillion-dollar conglomerate. Director John Frankenheimer withdrew, ostensibly because of a schedule conflict, and was replaced by BBC-TV veteran Waris Hussein. The company did exterior location work in Rome and then moved on to Munich in September for the interiors.

The Burton shooting sets had usually been known for an easygoing lack of pressure. In order to break the tension during the murder scene in *The Assassination of Trotsky*, Burton quipped to Alain Delon, who was playing the killer, "You'd better be careful how you handle that ax. There are plenty of French actors around, but if you kill me, there goes one-sixth of all the Welsh actors in the world." Recently their sets had also become known for what one witness called "campy carrying on, overt hedonism, and blatant exhibitionism"—so much so that one could wish, for the sake of entertainment, they had burned the scripts and then filmed the on-set activity. Which they might have if they thought they could ever get some of it past the censors.

One day on the set of *X, Y & Zee*, for example, Elizabeth asked director Brian Hutton if she could go home at five-twenty, and it went as follows:

HUTTON (in mock despair): "Five-twenty! Half the time you're not even *here* by five-twenty. Why do you want to leave at five-twenty today?"

ELIZABETH: "Richard says if you let me go at five-twenty, and I'm home before he is, he will _____ me."

HUTTON: "Tell Richard that if I let you go at five-twenty, Columbia will _____ *me!*"

During a dressing-room interlude on *Night Watch*, Elizabeth goaded old pal Laurence Harvey into displaying the scar of his recent surgery to an interviewer. "Go on, Larry," she coaxed him. "Show her your scar. Go on." Harvey did so, letting everything hang out in the process. "My scar is great and has a long nose at the end of it," he explained gleefully. "Oh, Larry!" Elizabeth cried out in mock disapproval. "Why don't you wear shorts?"

The relaxed doings on *Divorce His; Divorce Hers* went the absolute limit. Actress Carrie Nye played the Other Woman in this enterprise, and gave the most convincing impersonation of a zombie to be seen since the salad days of Lon Chaney, Jr. Ms. Nye later recollected her strange experience for *Time* magazine, and aside from a moment's wonder at why on earth an actress would actually advertise her presence in such a complete catastrophe, the piece is as enjoyably wicked and witty a report on filmmaking as has been seen in some time.

After a deep curtsy to Burton's inebriated condition, Nye noted that "it became apparent that Mr. Burton did not do an awful lot of work after lunch, and Mrs. Taylor-Burton, whom I had yet to clap eyes on, did not generally arrive until about a quarter of three in the afternoon." Then, "After a while we began to be invited to luncheon *chez* Burton. What was actually eaten, if anything, at these cozy impromptus for twelve (most of whom are in the Burtons' permanent employ, as opposed to us temporary help) is lost to memory. What was imbibed will be permanently inscribed on my liver for the rest of my days. There was a goodly amount of joshing about who drank the most Jack Daniel's, or tequila, or Jack Daniel's with tequila, or vodka and champagne, or Sterno and Scotch, and in just which European capital, South American port, or Balkan satellite these epic cases of alcohol poisoning took place. All this good fun would be punctuated by phone calls from the anguished director to inquire when, if ever, work could be resumed. Mr. Burton could generally be relied upon to knock off work early, usually with a magnificent display of temper, foot stamping, and a few exit lines delivered in the finest St. Crispin's Day style. My favorite was 'I am old and gray and incredibly gifted!' "

Divorce His; Divorce Hers was basically a good idea and was being made, as a co-production of America's ABC-TV and Britain's Harlech TV, with the best of motives. After exciting hints for four years about Burton participation in Harlech—during which he watched the Board veto all his suggestions while his stock continued to make money—the Burtons were actually making one for Harlech. The plan was eventually to cut both films into one feature and play it off world-wide (exclusive of Britain and North America). Why hadn't they done this before? "The things they wanted us to do were trash," Burton remarked. "The present scripts are fine."

That last could really have come back to haunt him if, on another occasion at roughly the same time, he had not given full voice to his basic frustration. "We cannot just go on playing ourselves. I don't want to be known as just a voice. I'm tired of being disembodied. I want a good script!" As to why he and Elizabeth had made such a string of losers, Burton confessed, "We're in such bloody demand and we're so bloody weak at saying no." In all the ten years since *Cleopatra*, if ever there were one crucial time when they should have said no, this was it. "We've been in and out of favor several times," Burton once said. "Whatever happens, we are used to it and can take it." Not this time.

Divorce His; Divorce Hers was televised in the United States on February 6 and 7, 1973, and was universally deplored—

which was putting it mildly. (ABC-TV actually had the shameless effrontery to give these two duds repeat showings later in the season.) "A matched pair of thudding disasters," thought *Time*. "A boring, tedious study of the crumbling marriage of two shallow people," echoed the Hollywood *Reporter*. "Holds all the joy of standing by at an autopsy," declared *Variety*.

Almost nothing works from start to finish. The dialogue is banal, the situations are unbelievable, the people are unlikable, and—worst of all—the script not only fails to move us at the thought of the divorce, it sets us to actively wondering why these two people ever got married in the first place.

"We had something special," Elizabeth tells Burton. "We had something more than most." Not that we ever get to see. Where —in the fundamental name of Scriptwriting 1.A—are the flashback scenes with the joy and some of the great moments that would have backed up that line? And, more important, make us care that the couple stay together. Burton is so repressed, so mechanical in feeling, that one wonders how Elizabeth could ever have loved him. Was he ever more alive, vital, likable?

Into this ocean of hifalutin' torpor and fashionable ennui comes Carrie Nye, apparently a member of the Walking Dead. "How could *anyone* have an affair with you?" Elizabeth flings at her. "You're not even beautiful!" Presumably she could be had with a pillow case over her face, if it came to that. The real put-off— to anyone but a necrophiliac, that is—is the idea of copulating with a cadaver.

The second part (*Divorce Hers*) is far more interesting, partly because we now know all the people involved, and partly because Elizabeth is the focus and, unlike her costar, some rigorous experience at MGM taught her how to get through even the most unpromising of situations. As Director Hussein said, "Elizabeth knows exactly what to do. She's an incredible performer. Nothing that can happen will faze her." In this instance it meant putting a maximum of presence and believability into a soapy, mis-scripted situation, and this she does.

For Burton, in a career with some great highs and some spectacular lows, this was the absolute nadir. His Shakespearean days long gone, he had survived a long stretch of junk on the remnants of his prestige, seeming at times to be working with only the left hand, in a contemptuous demonstration that he could still get by in even this limited fashion. Now the left hand had become palsied from so much misuse and he had simply ceased to function at all. He seems to be playing (when he is actually playing anything) a combination of stuffed-shirt and burnt-out case and as his son says in the script, "He's not very interesting." Every so often he goes off to business conferences, which are specious, unconvincing, and lack a shred of believability. His rare spurts of anger—pale, puny things—come out of the script, never from him. "I remember everything!" he tells Elizabeth—"and show nothing," he might well have added. He is abysmally, horrifyingly, shockingly boring.

Later it would be said that the universal condemnation of this effort had sent Richard Burton into deep depression. It had taken more than this and had been building far longer. And over and above what anyone else thought was the salient fact that he was now face-to-face, finally and irrevocably, with the hard place to which he had brought himself. His obsession with the Faust legend—that tale of the man who sold his soul for power and riches—had already resulted in two debacles on the screen. Now the ironic parallel with the debacle in his own life could not have escaped a man of his sensitivity and intelligence. So that what was to happen five months hence should not have been all that surprising when one looks back. The wonder and the pity is that if it had to happen—and it did—it didn't happen a whole lot sooner.

Before it happened, the Burtons went to Cortina d'Ampezzo where, from March to June, Elizabeth made *Ash Wednesday* with Henry Fonda and Helmut Berger. And, incidentally, suffered through a five-day quarantine with German measles. The way was then cleared for the climax, which began in New York City in June.

"If I could age like my mother, I'd be very, very happy, but I doubt whether I will grow old gracefully," Elizabeth said early in 1973. "The thing is, I've led such a very rushed and hectic life—and my mother doesn't drink or smoke. The poor thing is very sick for the first time in her life, but she looks absolutely remarkable for her age."

Sara Taylor had indeed been ailing since emergency surgery in Los Angeles in 1972. The Burtons had upcoming film commitments in Rome—Elizabeth on *The Driver's Seat*, Burton on *The Voyage*—to be preceded by a journey to the Moscow Film Festival in the company of Carlo Ponti and Sophia Loren. Nevertheless, they decided to make a quick trip to the United States to visit Elizabeth's mother. Initially they planned to stay at Aaron Frosch's home out in Quogue, Long Island. With Maria coming on later from Europe, it was apparently decided that Elizabeth would go on to Los Angeles first, and Burton would meet Maria and join her later.

Out in Los Angeles, Elizabeth checked into the Beverly Hills, where, coincidentally, Eddie Fisher was also in residence. Reportedly, Eddie, who filed for bankruptcy in 1970, asked Elizabeth for a little financial help, mainly on his back taxes, and she agreed to help him. On the first night, old friend Peter Lawford took Elizabeth to see Sara, and on the next night, Lawford and his eldest son, Christopher, accompanied Elizabeth to Laurence Harvey's home for a private screening of *Night Watch*. Roddy McDowall and Rex Kennamer were also among those in attendance. According to Lawford, "She was all fun—the greatest girl. She laughed a lot and we talked about old times."

The fun and the laughs vanished the next day with a telephone command from Burton. According to a Hollywood columnist, it was blunt and to the point: "Get your ass back here or you won't have an ass to sit on." What was expected to be a two-week stay terminated abruptly. Burton met his wife at Kennedy Airport, and the fireworks began, continuing on the drive out to Long Island. By the time they had reached the Frosch residence they were at an impasse. Elizabeth ordered her bags put back into the car and returned to the Regency Hotel solo.

The knowledge that the Burtons could be under separate roofs while in the same vicinity was bound to arouse curiosity. On July 2 a reporter called Elizabeth to check out the rift rumors. "Ha, ha—funny fella," she replied. "I'm here on business. It's not true." The rumors were fueled by the most curious statement publicist John Springer ever issued on behalf of Elizabeth. "The only thing I can say is that nobody else is involved if there is a split temporary or otherwise and I'm not admitting there is." After giving it some careful thought, Elizabeth put an end to the speculation on July 3, ironically on the eve of Independence Day:

"I am convinced it would be a good and constructive idea if Richard and I are separated for a while," began the statement, carefully hand-lettered in block capitals on Regency Hotel stationery. In conclusion: "I shall return to California where I have my mother and many good and true friends. Wish us well during this difficult time."

On July 5, pursued and surrounded by an army of newsmen and photographers, Elizabeth shielded Maria under her arm and struggled through the Regency Hotel lobby and out to the limousine that would take them to the airport. "I said all I can," Elizabeth replied to repeated questions from reporters. Fabergé chief George Barrie had thoughtfully provided her with his private twin-engine Grumman G-2 jet for the flight to California. At the airport in Los Angeles, Elizabeth and Maria sat on the plane for thirty minutes to avoid newsmen until the limousine arrived to whisk them away—supposedly to the home of Edith Goetz, but actually to Casa Ladera, the Mexican-style villa of Edith Head and her husband, two-time Oscar-winning Art Director and architect Wiard Ihnen.

Upon Elizabeth's arrival, Peter Lawford, complaining that he found himself "enveloped in this murky cloud of media dust," decided to say something before things got out of hand. When Lawford, fifty, wed Mary Rowan, twenty-two, in 1972, the father of the bride (Dan Rowan) had pointedly managed to contain his enthusiasm. The marriage came apart after eight months, and after a short separation, Mary Rowan had recently filed for a divorce. Still in the midst of trying to patch it up, Lawford was apparently being accused of breaking up somebody else's.

"I am forced to say that my own marital problems take priority at this time. I happen to be in love with my wife Mary. My prime wish is that our situation may be resolved before the specter of finality becomes tangible." Reports that Elizabeth had become infatuated with what the press was pleased to call his "exceptionally handsome twenty-four-year-old son, Christopher," amazed him. "It's hysterical. Christopher isn't even twenty-four. He's only eighteen." A bit of checking and some elementary math could have prevented this press gaffe since this was 1973, and Peter Lawford married Patricia Kennedy (Christopher's mother) in 1954. By this time no one was doing any careful checking about anything as speculators worked overtime to try to figure out the reason for the split.

Was it Burton's drinking? Back in New York he had initially denied the separation. "I even have Elizabeth's passport in my possession," he said plaintively. "Does that sound as if she's left me?" Then he acknowledged it, in an interview with a London *Daily Mail* correspondent, who noted that Burton "paused to pour a large 10 A.M. vodka and orange juice." By the time the reporter was gone so was all the vodka. "She's an all-day-long eater and I'm the kind of drinker who, when a bottle is opened, has to finish it," Burton once confessed. Subsequently he reportedly had some sessions with New York internist Dr. William Hitzig and went back on the wagon with such a vengeance "that he now looks at a lemonade with suspicion," according to a friend.

A Hollywood columnist pooh-poohed all that and declared that if a reconciliation "hinges on Richard's drinking, then I think the whole thing is preposterous." TAYLOR, BURTON TROUBLES —NON-ALCOHOLIC, blared the headline on his column, an amazing display of that infantile Hemingway-Peckinpah version of *machismo* in which jolly-green-giant-size quantities of booze, brawls, and broads are the true measure of a man. "Once down in Puerta Vallarta, I saw Richard consume twenty-three shots of tequila and walk upright to his jeep." Further chuckles were provided by items about drinking matches and the vision of Peter O'Toole falling dead-drunk flat on his face. This same columnist once lovingly quoted Burton's boast that he had consumed a quart of brandy during a *Hamlet* performance "and was shrieking gaily at the end." If these kind of tales really turn him on, he should stop by any meeting of the Hollywood Chapter of Alcoholics Anonymous. He can get an evening's worth of jollies from a roomful of unhappy people who used to do this sort of thing and it won't cost him a dime.

Burton's drinking was only one item being swirled in the rumor pot. As possible suitors for Elizabeth there were Peter Lawford, Warren Beatty, Helmut Berger, and Roger Vadim, sexy French ex-husband of Brigitte Bardot and Jane Fonda. One report had it that tale-bearing in the Burton entourage had caused the trouble. In another, Burton had supposedly written an intimate, wounding letter to his wife and then taken it from her and destroyed it. Two West German publications pitched in some garbage about flagrant infidelities and physical violence. As always, Elizabeth's closest friends loyally refused to discuss the details of her private life. "I've had call after call," Roddy McDowall reported. "I really deeply feel that these things are the business of the people involved. I really don't know a thing. If I did, I wouldn't say." As to the primary reason for the separation, Peter Ustinov probably put it best. "They have been driven apart by the pressure of being the Burtons." In a comment overlooked at the time, Edith Goetz revealed that she had the inside track on the eventual outcome. "I'm very, very sad about this because there's a kind of finality about it."

In Hollywood, Elizabeth varied the picnics and barbecues at the Casa Ladera with a descent onto Disneyland in a party of over twenty which filled four helicopters. She also went out with Peter Lawford to the Candy Store, a Beverly Hills discothèque, where she met millionaire Los Angeles businessman Henry Wynberg, who later pursued her to Rome. Burton had meanwhile returned to Europe, and it was announced that, after his trip to Moscow with Carlo Ponti, he and Elizabeth would meet each other in Rome. The entire separation had been punctuated by a spate of optimistic pronouncements from officials in the Burton empire. "I certainly hope they will get back together," declared John Springer, echoed by Aaron Frosch. "There is a serious aspect to this situation that shall be over-come." He did not elaborate. Burton allowed as how he had been on the telephone with Elizabeth "as many as three times a day."

On July 20, at Rome's Fiumicino Airport, an obviously nerv-ous Elizabeth, in jeans and matching jean jacket, came down the ramp and was hustled through the cluster of paparazzi and reporters over to the green Rolls-Royce in which her husband awaited her. She slid into the back seat, Burton clutched her to him, they kissed, and the Rolls sped off to the Carlo Ponti villa outside Rome, pursued by a motorcade of press cars. "Every-thing is fine now," John Springer told the press.

It was almost as if it had never been, and a large segment of the public continued to believe that it never really *had* been. The Burtons might squabble from time to time—that was part of what made them interesting—but really serious trouble? Hardly. And divorce? Unthinkable; they were an institution. Possibly the nonbelievers were influenced by the garbled rendering of a remark Burton made in Moscow. He had been asked about a report of imminent divorce and had dismissed it as "a journalistic joke." Some sources then printed that the whole separation had been a journalistic joke, and the following letter to the L.A. *Times* expressed a common view that it had never been any-thing else:

"I am bored with the stories of the so-called separation of Elizabeth Taylor and Richard Burton. The whole episode is nothing less than an attempt to get publicity which, after their lengthy series of flops, they need. Now that Liz has returned to Rome and announced that all is well again, won't that bring joy to the world?"

No, it wouldn't, and it brought no lasting joy to Elizabeth Taylor and Richard Burton, either. What had begun in Rome eleven years before had ended there. On July 31, Elizabeth moved into Rome's Grand Hotel and instructed Aaron Frosch to take the final step. The divorce was to be filed on her behalf in Switzerland, the country of her legal residence.

"The grounds will probably be incompatibility or some such moderate grounds," Frosch told the press. "In other words it won't be adultery. They are very amiable, and no third party exists in either case. Also there are no financial issues to be settled. There is no hysteria, no name calling and no vilification. There are no issues, no problems, no squabbles. Now you're going to ask me why they're getting divorced. All I can answer you is that I'm a lawyer, not a psychiatrist." Later he told a questioner, "I am now planning for a divorce. If they get back together again, I'll be very happy but you ask me if I'm optimistic about it—the answer is no."

They had been unhappy for some time with their professional life together. Increasingly the suffocating nature of their personal life had also brought unhappiness. Finally they had become unhappy with each other. After a public command performance that had lasted over a decade, the Royal Couple of Romance had apparently decided to abdicate for good.

* * *

"It takes one day to die—another to be born."

So Elizabeth responded to producer Franco Rossellini's effort to console her as she took up work on *The Driver's Seat*. After the racking period of her divorce from Nicky Hilton, Michael Wilding had said of Elizabeth, "People forget she has been through a very trying year. She wants to be married to someone who will love and protect her." Now, in an uncanny echo twenty years later, Henry Wynberg came to Rome and told newsmen, "What she needs is comfort and lots of it."

Sitting in lonely solitude in her dressing-room trailer, another line from her past might have occurred to her, this one from *Cat on a Hot Tin Roof:* "I guess things never turn out the way you dream they are going to turn out." No indeed. "I genuinely do not believe in divorce," she once wrote. Now she was facing her fourth. Like many another couple, the Burtons had pushed each other to the brink before but had always drawn back. This time they went over it.

Down in Naples on *The Voyage* location, Richard Burton kept a low profile, numbed by the stunning fact that, as he later put it, "I threw Elizabeth out, told her to get out—and to my surprise she went. I couldn't believe it." A passage from Shakespeare continually tormented him. It is Othello's anguished realization of what he has done in killing Desdemona:

> ". . . Then must you speak
> Of one that loved not wisely but too well;
> Of one not easily jealous, but, being wrought,
> Perplex'd in the extreme; of one whose hand,
> Like the base Indian, threw a pearl away
> Richer than all his tribe . . ."

In Rome, Elizabeth bravely determined not to yield to the impulse to withdraw into painful isolation, but events continually conspired against her. Her unpunctual personal appearance at Spain's San Sebastian Film Festival (to promote *Night Watch*) was greeted with ferocious jeers and catcalls. *Night Watch* itself turned out to be a gimmicky thriller which did absolutely nothing for her. Her costar and old friend Laurence Harvey was now in the final stage of terminal cancer, and a saddened Elizabeth did her best to cheer him with personal visits. An October meeting in Rome with her husband failed to resolve their impasse. In November "severe stomach cramps" sent her into the Scripps Institute in La Jolla for a week. This was merely prelude to a two-and-a-half-hour surgery at the U.C.L.A. Medical Center in which her right ovary was removed and an intestinal abnormality corrected. At month's end Paramount released *Ash Wednesday*, a beautiful but static travelogue in which the promising topic of cosmetic surgery aborted in ineptitude nothing short of infuriating. There had been five months of personal and professional doldrums. They were about to lift, but only temporarily.

On December 8 Richard Burton came from Italy to his wife's bedside at U.C.L.A. He left it only for a quick jaunt to a Beverly Hills jeweler. On December 10 a radiant Elizabeth made yet another of those wheelchair-bound hospital exits, a smiling husband at her side. A new heart-shaped diamond pendant proclaimed the fact of reconciliation, which was handled by both with a reserve both pleasing and sensible. "We have no statement because it is statement enough that we are together," Burton told onlookers. To which Elizabeth later added, "We are here together. Doesn't that say everything?" On to Naples, where *The Voyage* company worked until the beginning of the holiday hiatus on December 22. On that date the Burtons flew to their home in Gstaad for as joyous a Christmas as any they had spent in their ten years of married life. Four months later the marriage again shuddered to a stop. "This time it is for good," a close friend remarked. "Elizabeth has had it. And I think Richard has too."

Along with the personal sadness came professional good news which could only happen to Elizabeth. It was absolutely and uniquely hers. On the one hand, *Box Office* magazine released its 1973 listing of the twenty-five Top Moneymakers and Elizabeth's name was nowhere to be found. Granted that women have been getting the short end recently in terms of good parts, eight actresses still managed to make the list—Barbra Streisand, Liza Minnelli, Diana Ross, Ali MacGraw, Dyan Cannon, Jane Fonda, Glenda Jackson, and Goldie Hawn. But not Elizabeth. On the other hand, the 1973 Photoplay Gold Medal Award went to Elizabeth as Favorite Actress, and at the 1974 Golden Globe Awards she was crowned World Film Femme Favorite. So large segments of her public might avoid some of her films, but the love and loyalty remain undiminished. This was just the latest paradox in a life that has been full of them.

The father who had initial misgivings about an acting career for his daughter was himself the unwitting agent of her entry into films. Without an acting lesson of any kind she went on to win every top award bestowed for performing excellence in the cinema arts. During two major scandals which could have destroyed almost anyone else, the press did its worst and large segments of the public vilified her. Then they jammed the theaters, thus assuring her survival. For her was created the longest and most expensive motion picture in film history—which then turned out to be the most humiliating experience of her professional career. In London, one illness almost killed her, while in Los Angeles, another saved her life. As a woman who holds some firm Victorian convictions about sexual love and marital fidelity, she must have been privately mortified to suddenly find herself with a reputation that would have given pause to Polly Adler. "I still believe I have a right to privacy," she defiantly declared. The world then rewarded these sentiments by making her the most relentlessly publicized personality in the history of show business.

How she appears in the eyes of the world has never concerned her unduly but she used to be more uncertain about it than she is now. At the height of *le scandale*, she declared, "You know, one's public image doesn't necessarily correspond to the real person. To tell you the truth I haven't kept track of my so-called 'public image.' I know that, in the American press, I must get *shtichlech*, which is a good Jewish word for 'needles,' right below the heart. But my secretary tries to keep the clippings and the letters I call scorchers away from me. He loves me too much to let them hurt me. Why get a heart attack over them? I suppose they rather regard me as a scarlet woman. I guess I seem so scarlet I'm almost purple."

Recently she restated a position which she has adamantly maintained through all the years of triumph and turmoil.

"The public has a preconceived idea of me, of what I am, and I'm not about to justify myself. I don't give a damn about what people think about me. I live my life the way I want to live my life. I'm responsible to and for people that I love. I'm my own being. I'm my own person. In that sense I will not be shoved around."

In her memoir she sounded a note of regret:

"I know that I will never be able to be really and truly digni-fied in the eyes of the public. I shall not be allowed to be. It is very difficult once you have become public domain to be taken seriously. Part of me is sorry that I became a public utility." There were certain other regrets, mainly to do with not being able to provide her children with as much stability as she would have liked. Given her particular personality, her celebrity, and the circumstances, she had done the best she could.

Elizabeth wastes so little time living in the past that she some-times has difficulty recalling parts of it. "It's very difficult for me to remember what it was like to be married to Michael Wil-ding," she once wrote. "In fact sometimes it is very difficult to believe that we were *ever* married." She wasn't the only one who had this problem. After a nod to the fact that Wilding had finally found marital happiness with Margaret Leighton, John Gielgud one day unthinkingly remarked, "Michael is all right, you know. It's just those dreadful women he married." The stunning silence was broken by Elizabeth: "Well, who the hell do you think I was? Daisy Mae?" The next day an expensive Shih Tzu puppy arrived, a present from Sir John. Elizabeth named her Daisy Mae. (Daisy Mae later produced a litter of five —not in Dogpatch, but in Budapest, in April 1972.)

As to questions of public image, and who she was and who she is, Elizabeth nailed that down on the occasion of her fortieth birthday. "I don't entirely approve of some of the things I have done, or am, or have been. But I'm me. God knows I'm me."

How could the World's Most Beautiful Woman (a title she has always steadfastly refused to acknowledge)—a talented creature seemingly gifted with everything that nature has to offer—have led such a crisis-filled existence?

Part of that answer lies in her own nature and she knows it. "I'm unpredictable. What could be more boring than to be mar-ried to someone who is always the same? Or, even worse, to be predictable yourself?" Richard Burton once confirmed that: "She has an amazing facility for being raucous one moment and then almost shyly little-girl the next. I never quite know what to ex-pect."

So she is unpredictable. Also basically shy, still apt to be un-punctual, and a far better handler of criticism than compliments. "You said some great things in your life," David Frost once told her, to which Elizabeth immediately riposted, "I must have been drunk!" Another interviewer who laid the "world's most beautiful woman" tag on her was told, "I am not. I AM NOT. I'm an old bag." She is also possessive and demanding, fiercely loyal, physically courageous, a firm respecter of the pledged word (hers and yours), great fun when she's in a happy mood, stubborn in her beliefs, protective of her privacy, generous and compassionate, forthright and candid (sometimes brutally so), and a lot of other things, knowable and unknowable, which all go together to make up the Elizabeth Taylor who has now been in the public eye for almost a third of a century.

Fortunately for Elizabeth, a whole generation is coming up for whom Hilton nuptials and Mike Todd and Eddie and Debbie and scandal in Rome will mean nothing. She will be increasingly free to live the more open life she craves, finally out from under the fierce publicity and pressure and demands which have been her constant companions for twenty years. We who grew up with her—who love, admire, and appreciate her (and we are legion)—can only be glad for that. For us, she will always have a special place, uniquely hers and uniquely personal, for she has been a part of us for all of our lives. Some voice the fervent wish that she now utilize all those years of professional expertise to secure better films for herself in the future. The basic, universal wish is what it has always been. Whatever she chooses to do, personally and professionally, may it bring her fulfillment and happiness as a return for the gift of that shimmering presence which has enriched and infuriated and delighted and amused and amazed so many people for so many years.

"I'm Mother Courage," she once declared. "I'll be dragging my sable coat behind me into old age." So she will. And when her race is run, her epitaph will be ready. She has already written it:

HERE LIES ELIZABETH TAYLOR.
THANK YOU FOR EVERY MOMENT, GOOD AND BAD.
I'VE ENJOYED IT ALL!

Appendix

The Films of Elizabeth Taylor

1. There's One Born Every Minute (Universal, 1942)

Director: Harold Young. Associate Producer: Ken Goldsmith. Screenplay: Robert B. Hunt, Brenda Weisberg. Original Story: Robert B. Hunt. Cinematography: John Boyle. Art Director: Jack Otterson. Costumes: Vera West. Sound: Bernard B. Brown and Charles Carroll. Editor: Maurice Wright. Assistant Director: Seward Webb. 59 Minutes.

Lemuel	Hugh Herbert
Helen	Peggy Moran
Jimmy	Tom Brown
Cadwalader	Guy Kibbee
Minerva	Catherine Doucet
Moe Carson	Edgar Kennedy
Lester	Scott Jordan
Quisenberry	Gus Schilling
Gloria	Elizabeth Taylor
Trumbull	Charles Halton
Miss Phipps	Renie Riano
Junior	Alfalfa Switzer

2. Lassie Come Home (MGM, 1943)

Producer: Sam Marx. Director: Fred Wilcox. Assistant Director: Al Raboch. Technicolor Cinematography: Leonard Smith. Screenplay: Hugo Butler. From the Novel by Eric Knight. Art Direction: Cedric Gibbons, Paul Groesse. Set Decoration: Edwin B. Willis, Mildred Griffiths. Music: Daniele Amfitheatrof. Special Effects: Warren Newcombe. Editor: Ben Lewis. 90 Minutes.

Joe Carraclough	Roddy McDowall
Sam Carraclough	Donald Crisp
Rowlie	Edmund Gwenn
Dolly	Dame May Whitty
Duke of Rudling	Nigel Bruce
Mrs. Carraclough	Elsa Lanchester
Priscilla	Elizabeth Taylor
Hynes	J. Patrick O'Malley
Dan'l. Fadden	Ben Webster

APPENDIX

Snickers	Alec Craig
Buckles	John Rogers
Jock	Arthur Shields
	and Lassie

3. *Jane Eyre* (20th Century-Fox, 1944)

Executive Producer: William Goetz. Director: Robert Stevenson. Screenplay: Aldous Huxley, Robert Stevenson, and John Houseman. Cinematography: George Barnes. Production Design: William Pereira. Art Direction: James Basevi, Wiard B. Ihnen. Set Decoration: Thomas Little, Ross Dowd. Costumes: Rene Hubert. Music: Bernard Herrmann. Scenario Assistant: Barbara Keon. Research: De Witt Bodeen. Sound: W. D. Flick, Roger Heman. Special Effects: Fred Sersen. Editing: Walter Thompson. 95 Minutes.

Edward Rochester	Orson Welles
Jane Eyre	Joan Fontaine
Adele Varens	Margaret O'Brien
Jane (as a child)	Peggy Ann Garner
Dr. Rivers	John Sutton
Bessie	Sara Allgood
Brocklehurst	Henry Daniell
Mrs. Reed	Agnes Moorehead
Colonel Dent	Aubrey Mather
Mrs. Fairfax	Edith Barrett
Lady Ingram	Barbara Everest
Blanche Ingram	Hilary Brooke
Grace Poole	Ethel Griffies
Leah	Mae Marsh
Miss Scatcherd	Eily Malyon
Mrs. Eshton	Mary Forbes
Sir George Lynn	Thomas London
Mason	John Abbott
John	Ronald Harris
Auctioneer	Charles Irwin
and (credit omitted)	
Helen Burns	Elizabeth Taylor

4. *The White Cliffs of Dover* (MGM, 1944)

Producer: Sidney Franklin. Director: Clarence Brown. Screenplay: Claudine West, Jan Lustig, and George Froeschel. Based on the Poem, "The White Cliffs of Dover," by Alice Duer Miller. Additional Poetry by Robert Nathan. Cinematography: George Folsey. Art Direction: Cedric Gibbons, Randall Duell. Set Decoration: Edwin B. Willis, Jacques Mesereau. Music: Herbert Stothart. Costumes: Irene. Special

Effects: Arnold Gillespie, Warren Newcombe. Editing: Robert J. Kern. 125 Minutes.

Susan Ashwood	Irene Dunne
Sir John Ashwood III	Alan Marshall
Hiram Dunn	Frank Morgan
Nanny	Dame May Whitty
Colonel	C. Aubrey Smith
Lady Jean Ashwood	Gladys Cooper
Mrs. Bancroft	Isobel Elsom
Betsy (age 10)	Elizabeth Taylor
John Ashwood III (as a boy)	Roddy McDowall
John Ashwood III (age 24)	Peter Lawford
Sam Bennett	Van Johnson
Reggie	John Warburton
Rosamund	Jill Esmond
Gwennie	Brenda Forbes
Mrs. Bland	Norma Varden
Betsy (age 18)	June Lockhart

5. *National Velvet* (MGM, 1945)

Producer: Pandro S. Berman. Director: Clarence Brown. Screen-play: Theodore Reeves and Helen Deutsch. Based on the Novel by Enid Bagnold. Technicolor Cinematography: Leonard Smith. Art Direction: Cedric Gibbons, Urie McCleary. Set Decoration: Edwin B. Willis, Mildred Griffiths. Special Effects: Warren Newcombe. Music: Herbert Stothart. Costumes: Irene. Editing: Robert J. Kern. 123 Minutes.

Mi Taylor	Mickey Rooney
Mr. Brown	Donald Crisp
Velvet Brown	Elizabeth Taylor
Mrs. Brown	Anne Revere
Edwina Brown	Angela Lansbury
Malvolia Brown	Juanita Quigley
Donald Brown	Jack Jenkins
Farmer Ede	Reginald Owen
Ted	Terry Kilburn
Tim	Alec Craig
Mr. Taski	Eugene Loring
Miss Sims	Norma Varden
Mr. Hellam	Arthur Shields
Mr. Greenford	Dennis Hoey
Entry Official	Aubrey Mather
Stewart	Frederick Warlock
Man with Umbrella	Arthur Treacher

6. *Courage of Lassie* (MGM, 1946)

Producer: Robert Sisk. Director: Fred Wilcox. Screenplay: Lionel Houser. Technicolor Cinematography: Leonard Smith. Co-Director of Animal Sequences: Basil Wrangel. Art Direction: Cedric Gibbons, Paul Youngblood. Set Decoration: Edwin B. Willis, Paul Huldschinsky. Costumes: Irene. Music: Scott Bradley, Bronislau Kaper. Editing: Scott A. Nervig. 94 Minutes.

Kathie Merrick	Elizabeth Taylor
Harry MacBain	Frank Morgan
Sgt. Smitty	Tom Drake
Mrs. Merrick	Selena Royle
Judge Payson	Harry Davenport
Old Man	George Cleveland
Alice Merrick	Catherine McLeod
Farmer Crews	Morris Ankrum
Freddie Crews	Arthur Walsh
Farmer Elson	Mitchell Lewis
Mrs. Elson	Jane Green
Pete Merrick	David Holt
Sergeant	William Lewin
Sheriff Grayson	Minor Watson
Youth	Windy Cook
Charlie	Donald Curtis
Casey	Clancy Cooper

and Lassie as "Bill"

7. *Cynthia* (MGM, 1947)

Producer: Edwin H. Knopf. Director: Robert Z. Leonard. Screenplay: Harold Buchman and Charles Kaufman. Based on the Play, *The Rich Full Life,* by Viña Delmar. Cinematography: Charles Schoenbaum. Art Direction: Cedric Gibbons, Edward Carfagno. Set Decoration: Edwin B. Willis, Paul G. Chamberlain. Music: Bronislau Kaper. Musical Numbers: Johnny Green. Costumes: Irene. Editing: Irvine Warburton. 97 Minutes.

Cynthia Bishop	Elizabeth Taylor
Larry Bishop	George Murphy
Prof. Rosenkranz	S. Z. Sakall
Louise Bishop	Mary Astor
Dr. Fred I. Jannings	Gene Lockhart
Carrie Jannings	Spring Byington
Ricky Latham	James Lydon
Will Parker	Scotty Beckett
Fredonia Jannings	Carol Brannan

Miss Brady	Anna Q. Nilsson
Mr. Phillips	Morris Ankrum
McQuillan	Kathleen Howard
Stella Regan	Shirley Johns
Alice	Barbara Challis
J. M. Dingle	Harlan Briggs
Gus Wood	Will Wright

8. *Life With Father* (Warners Bros., 1947)

Producer: Robert Buckner. Director: Michael Curtiz. Screenplay: Donald Ogden Stewart. From the Play by Howard Lindsay and Russell Crouse. Technicolor Cinematography: Peverell Marley and William V. Skall. Art Direction: Robert Haas. Set Decoration: George James Hopkins. Music: Max Steiner. Costumes: Milo Anderson. Editing: George Amy. Sound: C. A. Riggs. Assistant Director: Robert Vreeland. Technical Adviser: Mrs. Clarence Day. 118 Minutes.

Father	William Powell
Vinnie	Irene Dunne
Mary	Elizabeth Taylor
Rev. Dr. Lloyd	Edmund Gwenn
Cora	Zasu Pitts
Clarence	Jimmy Lydon
Margaret	Emma Dunn
Dr. Humphries	Moroni Olsen
Mrs. Whitehead	Elizabeth Risdon
Harlan	Derek Scott
Whitney	Johnny Calkins
John	Martin Milner
Annie	Heather Wilde
Policeman	Monte Blue
Nora	Mary Field
Maggie	Queenie Leonard
Mrs. Wiggins	Clara Blandick
Dr. Somers	Frank Elliott

9. *A Date With Judy* (MGM, 1948)

Producer: Joe Pasternak. Director: Richard Thorpe. Screenplay: Dorothy Cooper and Dorothy Kingsley. Based on the Characters Created by Aleen Leslie. Technicolor Cinematography: Robert Surtees. Art Direction: Cedric Gibbons, Paul Groesse. Set Decoration: Edwin B. Willis, Richard A. Pefferle. Musical Direction: Georgie Stoll. Music Arrangements: Leo Arnaud, Albert Sondrey, Robert Franklin. Songs: "It's a Most Unusual Day" (McHugh-Adamson), "Judaline" (Raye-de Paul), "I'm Strictly on the Corny Side" (Unger-Templeton), "I've Got a Date with Judy" and "I'm Gonna Meet

My Mary" (Katz-Jackson). Dance Direction: Stanley Donen. Costumes: Helen Rose. Sound: Douglas Shearer. Editing: Harold F. Kress. 113 Minutes.

Melvin R. Foster	Wallace Beery
Judy Foster	Jane Powell
Carol Pringle	Elizabeth Taylor
Rosita Conchellas	Carmen Miranda
Cugat	Xavier Cugat
Stephen Andrews	Robert Stack
Lucien T. Pringle	Leon Ames
Mrs. Foster	Selena Royle
"Oogie" Pringle	Scotty Beckett
Gramps	George Cleveland
Pop Scully	Lloyd Corrigan
Jameson	Clinton Sundberg
Mitzie	Jean McLaren

10. *Julia Misbehaves* (MGM, 1948)

Producer: Everett Riskin. Director: Jack Conway. Screenplay: William Ludwig, Harry Ruskin and Arthur Wimperis. Adaptation: Gina Kaus and Monckton Hoffe. Based on the Novel, *The Nutmeg Tree*, by Margery Sharp. Cinematography: Joseph Ruttenberg. Art Direction: Cedric Gibbons, Daniel B. Cathcart. Set Decoration: Edwin B. Willis, Jack D. Moore. Music: Adolph Deutsch. Special Effects: Warren Newcombe. Editing: John Dunning. 100 Minutes.

Julia Packett	Greer Garson
William Packett	Walter Pidgeon
Ritchie Lorgan	Peter Lawford
Susan Packett	Elizabeth Taylor
Fred Ghenoccio	Cesar Romero
Mrs. Packett	Lucile Watson
Col. Willowbrook	Nigel Bruce
Ma Ghenoccio	Mary Boland
Benjamin Hawkins	Reginald Owen
Lord Pennystone	Henry Stephenson
Vicar	Aubrey Mather
Hobson	Ian Wolfe
Pepite	Fritz Feld
Daisy	Phyllis Morris
Louise	Veda Ann Borg

11. *Little Women* (MGM, 1949)

Producer-Director: Mervyn LeRoy. Screenplay: Andrew Solt, Sarah Y. Mason, Victor Heerman. Based on the Novel by Louisa May Alcott. Technicolor Cinematography: Robert Planck, Charles Schoenbaum. Art Direction: Cedric Gibbons, Paul Groesse. Set Decoration: Edwin B. Willis, Jack D. Moore. Music: Adolph Deutsch. Costumes: Walter Plunkett. Special Effects: Warren Newcombe. Editing: Ralph Winters. 122 Minutes.

Jo	June Allyson
Laurie	Peter Lawford
Beth	Margaret O'Brien
Amy	Elizabeth Taylor
Meg	Janet Leigh
Prof. Bhaer	Rossano Brazzi
Marmee	Mary Astor
Aunt March	Lucile Watson
Mr. Lawrence	Sir C. Aubrey Smith
Hannah	Elizabeth Patterson
Mr. March	Leon Ames
Dr. Barnes	Harry Davenport
John Brooke	Richard Stapley
Mrs. Kirke	Connie Gilchrist
Sophie	Ellen Corby

12. Conspirator (MGM, 1950)

Producer: Arthur Hornblow Jr. Director: Victor Saville. Screenplay: Sally Benson. Adaptation: Sally Benson, Gerard Fairlie. Based on the Novel by Humphrey Slater. Cinematography: F. A. Young. Art Direction: Alfred Junge. Music: John Wooldridge. Sound: A. W. Watkins. Editing: Frank Clarke. 95 Minutes.

Major Michael Curragh	Robert Taylor
Melinda Croyton	Elizabeth Taylor
Capt. Hugh Ladholme	Robert Fleming
Col. Hammerbrook	Harold Warrender
Joyce Penistone	Honor Blackman
Aunt Jessica	Marjorie Fielding
Broaders	Thora Hird
Lord Penistone	Wilfred Hyde-White
Lady Penistone	Marie Noy
Henry Raglan	Jack Allen
Mrs. Hammerbrook	Cicely Paget-Bowman
Mark Radek	Karl Stepanek
Alek	Nicholas Bruce
Inspector Weldon	Cyril Smith

13. The Big Hangover (MGM, 1950)

Production-Direction-Screenplay: Norman Krasna. Cinematography: George Folsey. Art Direction: Cedric Gibbons, Paul Groesse. Set Decoration: Edwin B. Willis, Henry W. Grace. Costumes: Helen

Rose. Music: Adolph Deutsch. Special Effects: Warren Newcombe. Editing: Fredrick Y. Smith. 82 Minutes.

David Maldon	Van Johnson
Mary Belney	Elizabeth Taylor
John Belney	Percy Waram
Martha Belney	Fay Holden
Uncle Fred Mahoney	Edgar Buchanan
Kate Mahoney	Selena Royle
Charles Packford	Gene Lockhart
Carl Bellcap	Leon Ames
Claire Bellcap	Rosemary DeCamp
Doctor Lee	Philip Ahn
Samuel C. Lang	Pierre Watkin
Steve Hughes	Russell Hicks
Williams	Gordon Richards
Mrs. Packford	Kathleen Lockhart

14. Father of the Bride (MGM, 1950)

Producer: Pandro S. Berman. Director: Vincente Minnelli. Screenplay: Frances Goodrich and Albert Hackett. Based on the Novel by Edward Streeter. Cinematography: John Alton. Art Direction: Cedric Gibbons, Leonid Vasian. Set Decoration: Edwin B. Willis, Keogh Gleason. Music: Adolph Deutsch. Costumes: Helen Rose, Walter Plunkett. Makeup: Jack Dawn. Hair Styles: Sidney Guilaroff. Editing: Ferris Webster. 92 Minutes.

Stanley T. Banks	Spencer Tracy
Ellie Banks	Joan Bennett
Kay Banks	Elizabeth Taylor
Buckley Dunstan	Don Taylor
Mrs. Doris Dunstan	Billie Burke
Mr. Massoula	Leo G. Carroll
Herbert Dunstan	Moroni Olsen
Mr. Tringle	Melville Cooper
Warner	Taylor Holmes
Rev. Galsworthy	Paul Harvey
Joe	Frank Orth
Tommy Banks	Rusty Tamblyn
Ben Banks	Tom Irish
Delilah	Marietta Canty
Dixon	Willard Waterman
Fliss	Nancy Valentine
Effie	Mary Jane Smith
Peg	Jacqueline Duval
Miss Bellamy	Fay Baker
Duffy	Frank Hyers

15. *Father's Little Dividend* (MGM, 1951)

Producer: Pandro S. Berman. Director: Vincente Minnelli. Screenplay: Albert Hackett and Frances Goodrich. Based on Characters Created by Edward Streeter in His Book, *Father of the Bride.* Cinematography: John Alton. Art Direction: Cedric Gibbons, Leonid Vasian. Set Decoration: Edwin B. Willis, Keogh Gleason. Costumes: Helen Rose. Music: Albert Sendrey. Editing: Ferris Webster. 82 Minutes.

Stanley Banks	Spencer Tracy
Ellie Banks	Joan Bennett
Kay Dunstan	Elizabeth Taylor
Buckley Dunstan	Don Taylor
Doris Dunstan	Billie Burke
Herbert Dunstan	Moroni Olsen
Police Sergeant	Richard Rober
Delilah	Marletta Canty
Tommy Banks	Rusty Tamblyn
Ben Banks	Tom Irish
Dr. Andrew Nordell	Hayden Rorke
Rev. Galsworthy	Paul Harvey

16. *Quo Vadis* (MGM, 1951)

Elizabeth is one of hundreds of Christian martyrs fleeing from hungry lions in the Colosseum. No billing.

17. *A Place in the Sun* (Paramount, 1951)

Producer-Director: George Stevens. Screenplay: Michael Wilson and Harry Brown. Based on the Novel, *An American Tragedy,* by Theodore Dreiser, and the Patrick Kearney Play Adapted from the Novel. Cinematography: William C. Mellor. Special Photographic Effects: Gordon Jennings. Process Photography: Farciot Edouart and Loyal Griggs. Art Direction: Hans Dreier and Walter Tyler. Set Decoration: Emile Kuri. Costumes: Edith Head. Music: Franz Waxman. Associate Producer: Ivan Moffat. Associate Director: Fred Guiol. Editing: William Hornbeck. Sound: Gene Merrett and Gene Garvin. 122 Minutes.

George Eastman	Montgomery Clift
Angela Vickers	Elizabeth Taylor
Alice Tripp	Shelley Winters
Hannah Eastman	Anne Revere
Earl Eastman	Keefe Brasselle
Bellows	Fred Clark
Marlowe	Raymond Burr
Charles Eastman	Herbert Heyes

Anthony Vickers	Shepperd Strudwick
Mrs. Vickers	Frieda Inescort
Mrs. Louise Eastman	Kathryn Givney
Jansen	Walter Sande
Judge	Ted de Corsia
Coroner	John Ridgely
Marsha	Lois Chartrand
Mr. Whiting	Wm. B. Murphy
Boatkeeper	Douglas Spencer
Kelly	Charles Dayton
Morrison	Paul Frees

18. Callaway Went Thataway (MGM, 1951)

Elizabeth guest-starred as herself in a Hollywood nightclub sequence.

19. Love Is Better Than Ever (MGM, 1952)

Producer: William H. Wright. Director: Stanley Donen. Screenplay: Ruth Brooks Flippen. Cinematography: Harold Rosson. Art Direction: Cedric Gibbons, Gabriel Scognamillo. Music: Lennie Hayton. Editing: George Boemler. 81 Minutes.

Jud Parker	Larry Parks
Anastacia Macaboy	Elizabeth Taylor
Mrs. Macaboy	Josephine Hutchinson
Mr. Macaboy	Tom Tully
Mrs. Levoy	Ann Doran
Pattie Marie Levoy	Elinor Donahue
Mrs. Kahrney	Kathleen Freeman
Albertina	Doreen McCann
Hamlet	Alex Gerry
Smittie	Dick Wessel

20. Ivanhoe (MGM, 1952)

Producer: Pandro S. Berman. Director: Richard Thorpe. Screenplay: Noel Langley. Adaptation: Aeneas MacKenzie. From the Novel by Sir Walter Scott. Technicolor Cinematography: F. A. Young. Technicolor Consultant: Joan Bridge. Art Direction: Alfred Junge. Photographic Effects: Tom Howard. Music: Miklos Rozsa. Costumes: Roger Furse. Sound: A. W. Watkins. Editing: Frank Clarke. 107 Minutes.

Ivanhoe	Robert Taylor
Rebecca	Elizabeth Taylor
Rowena	Joan Fontaine
DeBois-Guilbert	George Sanders
Wamba	Emlyn Williams
Prince John	Guy Rolfe

Sir Hugh de Bracy	Robert Douglas
Cedric	Finlay Currie
Isaac	Felix Aylmer
Austrian Monk	Carl Jaffe
King Richard	Norman Wooland
Waldemar Fitzurse	Basil Sydney
Locksley	Harold Warrender
Philip de Malvoisin	Patrick Holt
Ralph de Vipont	Roderick Lovell
Clerk of Copmanhurst	Sebastian Cabot
Hundebert	John Ruddock
Baldwin	Michael Brennan
Norman Guard	Valentine Dyall
Roger of Bermondsley	Lionel Harris

21. *The Girl Who Had Everything* (MGM, 1953)

Producer: Armand Deutsch. Director: Richard Thorpe. Screenplay: Art Cohn. Based on *A Free Soul* by Adela Rogers St. Johns. Cinematography: Paul Vogel. Art Direction: Cedric Gibbons, Randall Duell. Music: Andre Previn. Costumes: Helen Rose. Editing: Ben Lewis. 69 Minutes.

Jean Latimer	Elizabeth Taylor
Victor Y. Ramondi	Fernando Lamas
Steve Latimer	William Powell
Vance Court	Gig Young
"Chico" Menlow	James Whitmore
John Ashmond	Robert Burton
Julian	William Walker

22. *Elephant Walk* (Paramount, 1954)

Producer: Irving Asher. Director: William Dieterle. Screenplay: John Lee Mahin. Based on the Novel by Robert Standish. Technicolor Cinematography: Loyal Griggs. Technicolor Consultant: Richard Mueller. Special Photographic Effects: John P. Fulton, Paul Lerpae. Process Photography: Farciot Edouart, Wallace Kelley. Art Direction: Hal Pereira, Joseph McMillan Johnson. Music: Franz Waxman. Costumes: Edith Head. Sound: Gene Merritt, John Cope. Editing: George Tomasini. Assistant Director: Francisco Day. Choreography: Ram Gopal. 102 Minutes.

Ruth Wiley	Elizabeth Taylor
Dick Carver	Dana Andrews
John Wiley	Peter Finch
Appuhamy	Abraham Sofaer
Dr. Pereira	Abner Biberman
Planter (Atkinson)	Noel Drayton

Mrs. Lakin	Rosalind Ivan
Planter (Strawson)	Barry Bernard
Planter (Ralph)	Philip Tonge
Planter (Gregory)	Edward Ashley
Planter (Chisholm)	Leo Britt
Rayna	Mylee Haulani

and

The Madhyma Lanka Mandala Dancers

23. Rhapsody (MGM, 1954)

Producer: Lawrence Weingarten. Director: Charles Vidor. Screenplay: Fay and Michael Kanin. Adaptation: Ruth and Augustus Goetz. Based on the Novel, *Maurice Guest,* by Henry Handel Richardson. Technicolor Cinematography: Robert Planck. Art Direction: Cedric Gibbons, Paul Groesse. Set Decoration: Edwin B. Willis, Hugh Hunt. Musical Score and Adaptation of the Tchaikovsky Violin Concerto and the Rachmaninoff Second Piano Concerto by Bronislau Kaper. Music Conducted by Johnny Green. Piano Solos: Claudio Arrau. Violin Solos: Michael Rabin. Costumes: Helen Rose. Special Effects: A. Arnold Gillespie, Warren Newcombe. Montage: Peter Ball Busch. Editing: John Dunning. Assistant Director: Ridgeway Callow. 115 Minutes.

Louise Durant	Elizabeth Taylor
Paul Bronte	Vittorio Gassman
James Guest	John Ericson
Nicholas Durant	Louis Calhern
Prof. Schuman	Michael Chekhov
Effie Cahill	Barbara Bates
Bruno Furst	Richard Hageman
Otto Krafft	Richard Lupino
Frau Sigerist	Celia Lovsky
Dove	Stuart Whitman
Mrs. Cahill	Madge Blake
Edmund Stroller	Jack Raine
Madeleine	Birgit Nielsen
Yvonne	Jacqueline Duval
Student-Pianist	Norma Nevens

24. Beau Brummel (MGM, 1954)

Producer: Sam Zimbalist. Director: Curtis Bernhardt. Screenplay: Karl Tunberg. Based on the Play Written for Richard Mansfield by Clyde Fitch. Eastman Color Cinematography: Oswald Morris. Print by Technicolor. Photographic Effects: Tom Howard. Art Direction: Alfred Junge. Mr. Granger's Costumes: Walter Plunkett. Miss Taylor's Costumes: B. J. Simmons. Other Costumes: Elizabeth Haffenden. Music: Richard Addinsell. Editing: Frank Clarke. 111 Minutes.

Beau Brummel	Stewart Granger
Lady Patricia	Elizabeth Taylor
Prince of Wales	Peter Ustinov
King George III	Robert Morley
Lord Edwin Mercer	James Donald
Mortimer	James Hayter
Mrs. Fitzherbert	Rosemary Harris
William Pitt	Paul Rogers
Lord Byron	Noel Willman
Midger	Peter Dyneley
Sir Geoffrey Baker	Charles Carson
Doctor Warren	Ernest Clark
Mr. Fox	Peter Bull
Mr. Burke	Mark Dignam
Colonel	Desmond Roberts
Thurlow	David Horne
Sir Ralph Sidley	Ralph Truman
Mr. Tupp	Elwyn Brook-Jones
Dr. Dubois	George De Warfaz
Dr. Willis	Henry Oscar
Mayor	Harold Kasket

25. *The Last Time I Saw Paris* (MGM, 1954)

Producer: Jack Cummings. Director: Richard Brooks. Screenplay: Julius J. and Philip G. Epstein, and Richard Brooks. Based on a Story by F. Scott Fitzgerald. Technicolor Cinematography: Joseph Ruttenberg. Art Direction: Cedric Gibbons, Randall Duell. Set Decoration: Edwin B. Willis, Jack D. Moore. Costumes: Helen Rose. Music: Conrad Salinger. Song: "The Last Time I Saw Paris" (Kern-Hammerstein). Special Effects: A. Arnold Gillespie. Assistant Director: William Shanks. Editing: John Dunning. 116 Minutes.

Helen Ellswirth	Elizabeth Taylor
Charles Wills	Van Johnson
James Ellswirth	Walter Pidgeon
Marion Ellswirth	Donna Reed
Lorraine Quarl	Eva Gabor
Maurice	Kurt Kaszner
Claude Martine	George Dolenz
Paul	Roger Moore
Vicki	Sandy Descher
Mama	Celia Lovsky
Barney	Peter Leeds
Campbell	John Doucette
Singer	Odette

26. *Giant* (Warner Bros. 1956)

Producers: George Stevens and Henry Ginsberg. Director: George Stevens. Screenplay: Fred Guiol and Ivan Moffat. From the Novel by Edna Ferber. WarnerColor Cinematography by William C. Mellor. Second Unit Cinematography: Edwin DuPar. Production Design: Boris Leven. Set Decoration: Ralph Hurst. Music: Dimitri Tiomkin. Costumes: Marjorie Best and Moss Mabry. Editing: William Hornbeck. Sound: Earl Crain Sr. 198 Minutes.

Leslie Benedict	Elizabeth Taylor
Bick Benedict	Rock Hudson
Jett Rink	James Dean
Luz Benedict II	Carroll Baker
Vashti Snythe	Jane Withers
Uncle Bawley	Chill Wills
Luz Benedict	Mercedes McCambridge
Angel Obregon III	Sal Mineo
Jordan Benedict III	Dennis Hopper
Mrs. Horace Lynnton	Judith Evelyn
Dr. Horace Lynnton	Paul Fix
Sir David Karfrey	Rodney Taylor
Bob Dace	Earl Holliman
Pinky Snythe	Robert Nichols
Old Polo	Alexander Scourby
Judy Benedict	Fran Bennett
Whiteside	Charles Watts
Juana	Elsa Cardenas
Lacey Lynnton	Carolyn Craig
Bale Clinch	Monte Hall

27. *Raintree County* (MGM, 1957)

Producer: David Lewis. Director: Edward Dmytryk. Screenplay: Millard Kaufman. Based on the Novel by Ross Lockridge Jr. Technicolor Cinematography: Robert Surtees. Art Direction: William A. Horning, Urie McCleary. Set Decoration: Edwin B. Willis, Hugh Hunt. Music: Johnny Green. Special Effects: Warren Newcombe. Costumes: Walter Plunkett. Editing: John Dunning. Sound: Dr. Wesley C. Miller. Makeup: William Tuttle. Hair Styles: Sidney Guilaroff. Assistant Director: Ridgeway Callow. Songs by Johnny Green and Paul Francis Webster: "Never Till Now" and "Song of the Raintree" (sung by Nat King Cole). Filmed in the MGM Camera 65 Process. 168 Minutes.

John Shawnessy	Montgomery Clift
Susanna Drake	Elizabeth Taylor
Nell Gaither	Eva Marie Saint

Jerusalem Stiles	Nigel Patrick
"Flash" Perkins	Lee Marvin
Garwood B. Jones	Rod Taylor
Ellen Shawnessy	Agnes Moorehead
T. D. Shawnessy	Walter Abel
Barbara Drake	Jarma Lewis
Bobby Drake	Tom Drake
Ezra Gray	Rhys Williams
Niles Foster	Russell Collins
Southern Officer	DeForrest Kelley

28. Cat on a Hot Tin Roof (MGM, 1958)

Producer: Lawrence Weingarten. Director: Richard Brooks. Screenplay: Richard Brooks and James Poe. Based on the Play by Tennessee Williams. Metrocolor Cinematography: William Daniels. Art Direction: William A. Horning, Urie McCleary. Set Decoration: Henry Grace, Robert Priestley. Special Effects: Lee LeBlanc. Editing: Ferris Webster. Costumes: Helen Rose. Hair Styles: Sidney Guilaroff. Makeup: William Tuttle. An Avon Production. 108 Minutes.

Maggie	Elizabeth Taylor
Brick	Paul Newman
Big Daddy	Burl Ives
Gooper	Jack Carson
Big Mama	Judith Anderson
Mae	Madeleine Sherwood
Dr. Baugh	Larry Gates
Deacon Davis	Vaughn Taylor
Dixie	Patty Ann Gerrity
Sonny	Rusty Stevens
Buster	Hugh Corcoran
Trixie	Deborah Miller
Boy	Brian Corcoran
Lacey	Vince Townsend Jr.
Brightie	Zelda Cleaver

29. Suddenly Last Summer (Columbia, 1959)

Producer: Sam Spiegel. Director: Joseph L. Mankiewicz. Screenplay: Gore Vidal and Tennessee Williams. Adapted from the Play by Tennessee Williams. Cinematography: Jack Hildyard. Production Design: Oliver Messel. Art Direction: William Kellner. Set Decoration: Scot Slimon. Photographic Effects: Tom Howard. Associate Costume Designer: Joan Ellacott. Music: Buxton Orr and Malcolm Arnold. Sound: A. G. Ambler, John Cox. Editing: Thomas G. Stanford. Filmed at Shepperton Studios, England, and on the Costa Brava, Spain. 112 Minutes.

Catherine Holly	Elizabeth Taylor
Mrs. Venable	Katharine Hepburn
Dr. Cukrowicz	Montgomery Clift
Dr. Hockstader	Albert Dekker
Mrs. Holly	Mercedes McCambridge
George Holly	Gary Raymond
Miss Foxhill	Mavis Villiers
Nurse Benson	Patricia Marmont
Sister Felicity	Joan Young
Lucy	Marie Britneva
Medical Secretary	Sheila Robbins
Young Blond Intern	David Cameron

30. Scent of Mystery (Michael Todd Jr., 1960)

In "the only movie that ever smelled on purpose," Elizabeth is the mystery heroine (in disguise until the finale) being pursued all over Spain for her $3,000,000 inheritance. Later released, minus Glorious Smell-o-Vision, as *Holiday in Spain.*

31. Butterfield 8 (MGM, 1960)

Producer: Pandro S. Berman. Director: Daniel Mann. Screenplay: Charles Schnee and John Michael Hayes. Based on the Novel by John O'Hara. Metrocolor Cinematography: Joseph Ruttenberg, Charles Harten. Art Direction: George W. Davis, Urie McCleary. Set Decoration: Gene Callahan, J. C. Delaney. Music: Bronislau Kaper. Costumes: Helen Rose. Associate Producer: Kathryn Hereford. Assistant Directors: Hank Moonjean, John Clarke Bowman. Sound: Franklin Milton. Editing: Ralph E. Winters. An Avon-Lindbrook Production. CinemaScope. 109 Minutes.

Gloria Wandrous	Elizabeth Taylor
Weston Liggett	Laurence Harvey
Steve Carpenter	Eddie Fisher
Emily Liggett	Dina Merrill
Mrs. Wandrous	Mildred Dunnock
Mrs. Thurber	Betty Field
Bingham Smith	Jeffrey Lynn
Happy	Kay Medford
Norma	Susan Oliver
Dr. Tredman	George Voskovec
Clerk	Virginia Downing
Mrs. Jescott	Carmen Matthews
Anderson	Whitfield Connor

32. *Cleopatra* (20th Century-Fox, 1963)

Producer: Walter Wanger. Director: Joseph L. Mankiewicz. Screenplay: Joseph L. Mankiewicz, Ranald MacDougall, Sidney Buchman. Based upon Histories by Plutarch, Suetonius, Appian, Other Ancient Sources, and *The Life and Times of Cleopatra* by C. M. Franzero. De Luxe Color Cinematography: Leon Shamroy. Art Direction: John De Cuir, Jack Martin Smith, Hilyard Brown, Herman Blumenthal, Elven Webb, Maurice Pelling, Boris Juraga. Set Decoration: Walter M. Scott, Paul S. Fox, Ray Moyer. Music: Alex North. Costumes: Irene Sharaff, Vittorio Nino Novarese, Renie. Special Effects: L. B. Abbott, Emil Kosa Jr. Editing: Dorothy Spencer. Todd-AO. 243 Minutes.

Cleopatra	Elizabeth Taylor
Mark Antony	Richard Burton
Julius Caesar	Rex Harrison
High Priestess	Pamela Brown
Flavius	George Cole
Sosigenes	Hume Cronyn
Apollodorus	Cesare Danova
Brutus	Kenneth Haigh
Agrippa	Andrew Keir
Rufio	Martin Landau
Octavius	Roddy McDowall
Germanicus	Robert Stephens
Eiras	Francesca Annis
Pothinus	Gregoire Aslan
Ramos	Martin Benson
Theodotus	Herbert Berghof
Phoebus	John Cairney
Lotus	Jacqui Chan
Charmian	Isabelle Cooley
Achilles	John Doucette
Canidius	Andrew Faulds
Metullus Cimber	Michael Gwynne
Cicero	Michael Hordern
Cassius	John Hoyt
Euphranor	Marne Maitland
Casca	Carroll O'Connor
Ptolemy	Richard O'Sullivan
Calpurnia	Gwen Watford
Decimus	Douglas Wilmor
Titus	Finlay Currie
Queen at Tarsus	Marina Berti
High Priest	John Carlson
Caesarion (4)	Loris Loddy

Caesarion (7)	Del Russell
Caesarion (12)	Kenneth Nash
Octavia	Jean Marsh
Marcellus	Gin Mart
Mithridates	Furio Meniconi
Vallus	John Valva
Archesilaus	Laurence Naismith
1st Officer	John Alderson
2nd Officer	Peter Forster

33. *The V.I.P.'s* (MGM, 1963)

Producer: Anatole de Grunwald. Director: Anthony Asquith. Screenplay: Terence Rattigan. Metrocolor Cinematography: Jack Hildyard. Art Direction: William Kellner. Set Decoration: Pamela Cornell. Wardrobe Supervisor: Felix Evans. Miss Taylor's Wardrobe: Givenchy, Paris. Music: Miklos Rozsa. Editing: Frank Clarke. Sound: Bill Creed. Associate Producer: Roy Parkinson. Production Adviser: Margaret Booth. Assistant Director: Kip Gowans. Panavision. 119 Minutes.

Frances Andros	Elizabeth Taylor
Paul Andros	Richard Burton
Marc Champselle	Louis Jourdan
Gloria Gritti	Elsa Martinelli
Duchess of Brighton	Margaret Rutherford
Miss Mead	Maggie Smith
Les Mangrum	Rod Taylor
Max Buda	Orson Welles
Miriam	Linda Christian
Commander Millbank	Dennis Price
Sanders	Richard Wattis
Reporter	David Frost
Joslin	Ronald Fraser
John Coburn	Robert Coote
Airport Director	Michael Hordern
Schwutzbacher	Martin Miller
BOAC Official	Lance Percival
Miss Potter	Joan Benham
Doctor	Peter Sallis
Hotel Waiter	Stringer Davis
Jamaican Passenger	Clifton Jones
Air Hostess	Moyra Fraser

34. *The Sandpiper* (MGM, 1965)

Producer: Martin Ransohoff. Director: Vincente Minnelli. Screenplay: Dalton Trumbo and Michael Wilson. Adaptation: Irene and

Louis Kamp. Story: Martin Ransohoff. Metrocolor Cinematography: Milton Krasner. Art Direction: George W. Davis. Urie McCleary. Set Decoration: Henry Grace, Keogh Gleason. Costumes: Irene Sharaff. Music: Johnny Mandel. Song: "The Shadow of Your Smile" (Mandel-Webster). Sound: Franklin Milton. Editing: David Bretherton. Associate Producer: John Calley. Panavision. 117 Minutes.

Laura Reynolds	Elizabeth Taylor
Dr. Edward Hewitt	Richard Burton
Claire Hewitt	Eva Marie Saint
Cos Erickson	Charles Bronson
Ward Hendricks	Robert Webber
Larry Brant	James Edwards
Judge Thompson	Torin Thatcher
Walter Robinson	Tom Drake
Phil Sutcliff	Doug Henderson
Danny Reynolds	Morgan Mason

35. Who's Afraid of Virginia Woolf? (Warner Bros., 1966)

Producer: Ernest Lehman. Director: Mike Nichols. Screenplay: Ernest Lehman. From the Play by Edward Albee. Cinematography: Haskell Wexler. Production Design: Richard Sylbert. Set Decoration: George James Hopkins. Music: Alex North. Costumes: Irene Sharaff. Sound: M. A. Merrick. Editing: Sam O'Steen. Assistant Director: Bud Grace. 129 Minutes.

Martha	Elizabeth Taylor
George	Richard Burton
Nick	George Segal
Honey	Sandy Dennis

36. The Taming of the Shrew (Columbia, 1967)

A Burton-Zeffirelli Production. Director: Franco Zeffirelli. Executive Producer: Richard McWhorter. Screenplay: Paul Dehn, Suso Cecchi D'Amico, Franco Zeffirelli (With Acknowledgments to William Shakespeare, Without Whom They Would Have Been at a Loss for Words). Technicolor Cinematography: Oswald Morris. Production Supervisor: Guy Luongo. Art Direction: Elven Webb, Giuseppe Mariani. Set Decoration: Dairo Simoni, Luigi Gervasi. Production Design: Renzo Mongiardino, John De Cuir. Music: Nino Rota. Costumes: Irene Sharaff, Danilo Donati. Editing: Peter Taylor. Assistant Directors: Carlo Lastricati, Rinaldo Ricci, Albino Cocco. A Royal Films International-F.A.I. Production. Panavision. 122 Minutes.

Katharina	Elizabeth Taylor
Petruchio	Richard Burton
Grumio	Cyril Cusack

Baptista	Michael Hordern
Tranio	Alfred Lynch
Gremio	Alan Webb
Hortensio	Victor Spinetti
Biondello	Roy Holder
Vincentio	Mark Dignam
The Widow	Bice Valeri
Bianca	Natasha Pyne
Lucentio	Michael York
The Priest	Giancarlo Gobelli
Pedant	Vernon Dobtcheff
Tailor	Ken Parry
Haberdasher	Anthony Gardner

37. *Reflections in a Golden Eye* (Warner Bros.-Seven Arts, 1967)

Producer: Ray Stark. Director: John Huston. Screenplay: Chapman Mortimer and Gladys Hill. Based on the Novel by Carson McCullers. Technicolor Cinematography: Aldo Tonti. Production Designer: Stephen Grimes. Art Direction: Bruno Avesani. Set Decoration: William Kiernan. Costumes: Dorothy Jeakins. Music: Toshire Mayuzumi. Editing: Russell Lloyd. Sound: Basil Fenton-Smith, John Cox. Assistant Director: Vana Caruso. Panavision. 108 Minutes.

Leonora Penderton	Elizabeth Taylor
Maj. Weldon Penderton	Marlon Brando
Lt. Col. Morris Langdon	Brian Keith
Alison Langdon	Julie Harris
Private Williams	Robert Forster
Anacleto	Zorro David
Stables Sgt.	Gordon Mitchell
Capt. Weincheck	Irvin Dugan
Susie	Fay Sparks

38. *The Comedians* (MGM, 1967)

Producer-Director: Peter Glenville. Screenplay (From His Novel): Graham Greene. Metrocolor Cinematography: Henri Decae. Art Direction: Francois de Lamophe. Set Decoration: Robert Christides. Music: Laurence Rosenthal. Sound: Cyril Swern. Editing: Francoise Javet. Assistant Director: Jean-Michel Lacore. Panavision. 156 Minutes.

Brown	Richard Burton
Martha	Elizabeth Taylor
Jones	Alec Guinness
Ambassador	Peter Ustinov
Smith	Paul Ford

Mrs. Smith	Lillian Gish
Henri Philipot	George Stanford Brown
Pierre	Roscoe Lee Browne
Mrs. Philipot	Gloria Foster
Dr. Mapot	James Earl Jones
Michel	Zakes Mokae
Joseph	Donta Seck
Concasseur	Raymond St. Jacques

39. Doctor Faustus (Columbia, 1968)

Producers: Richard Burton and Richard McWhorter. Directors: Richard Burton and Neville Coghill. Screenplay: Neville Coghill, adapted from *The Tragical History of Doctor Faustus* by Christopher Marlowe. Technicolor Cinematography: Gabor Pogany. Production Design: John De Cuir. Art Direction: Boris Juraga. Set Decoration: Dario Simoni. Music: Mario Nascimbene. Costumes: Peter Hall. Editing: John Shirley. Sound: David Hildyard, John Aldred. Assistant Director: Gus Agosti. 92 Minutes.

Starring Richard Burton as Doctor Faustus—Introducing the Oxford University Dramatic Society—Also Starring Elizabeth Taylor as Helen of Troy.

40. Boom! (Universal, 1968)

Producers: John Heyman and Norman Priggen. Director: Joseph Losey. Screenplay: Tennessee Williams, Based on His Play, *The Milk Train Doesn't Stop Here Anymore*. Technicolor Cinematography: Douglas Slocombe. Production Design: Richard MacDonald. Music: John Barry. Editing: Reginald Beck. Sound: Leslie Hammon, Gerry Humphreys. Assistant Director: Carlo Lastricati. Panavision. 115 Minutes.

Flora Goforth	Elizabeth Taylor
Chris Flanders	Richard Burton
Witch of Capri	Noel Coward
Blackie	Joanna Shimkus
Rudy	Michael Dunn
Doctor	Romolo Valli
Servants	Fernando Piazza, Veronica Wells

41. Secret Ceremony (Universal, 1968)

Producers: John Heyman and Norman Priggen. Director: Joseph Losey. Screenplay: George Tabori. Based on a Short Story by Marco Denevi. Technicolor Cinematography: Gerald Fisher. Production Design: Richard MacDonald. Art Direction: John Clark. Set Decoration: Jill Oxley. Music: Richard Rodney Bennett. Costumes: Marc Bohan. Editing: Reginald Beck. Sound: Leslie Hammond. Assistant Director: Richard Dalton. Filmed on London locations and at Associated British Studios, Elstree. 109 Minutes.

Leonora	Elizabeth Taylor
Cenci	Mia Farrow
Albert	Robert Mitchum
Hannah	Peggy Ashcroft
Hilda	Pamela Brown

42. *Anne of the Thousand Days* (Universal, 1969)

In a court dancing scene, Elizabeth is one of the revelers who enters while clapping a mask over her face. No billing.

43. *The Only Game in Town* (20th Century-Fox, 1970)

Producer: Fred Kohlmar. Director: George Stevens. Screenplay: Frank D. Gilroy (Based on His Play). De Luxe Color Cinematography: Henri Decae. Art Direction: Herman Blumenthal, Auguste Capelier. Set Decoration: Walter M. Scott, Jerry Wunderlich. Special Photographic Effects: L. B. Abbott, Art Cruckshank. Music: Maurice Jarre. Costumes: Mia Fonssagrives, Vicki Tiel. Sound: Joe de Bretagne, David Deckendorf. Editing: John W. Holmes, William Sands, Pat Shade. 113 Minutes.

Fran Walker	Elizabeth Taylor
Joe Grady	Warren Beatty
Lockwood	Charles Brasswell
Tony	Hank Henry

44. *X, Y & Zee* (Columbia, 1972)

A Kastner-Ladd-Kanter Production. Director: Brian Hutton. Screenplay: Edna O'Brien. Technicolor Cinematography: Billy Williams. Art Direction: Peter Mullins. Set Decoration: Arthur Takson. Costumes: Beatrice Dawson. Editing: Jim Clark. Sound: Cyril Swern and Bob Jones. 110 Minutes.

Zee	Elizabeth Taylor
Robert	Michael Caine
Stella	Susannah York
Gladys	Margaret Leighton
Gordon	John Standing
Rita	Mary Larkin
Gavin	Michael Cashman
Headwaiter	Gino Melvazzi
Oscar	Julian West
Shaun	Hilary West

45. *Hammersmith Is Out* (J. Cornelius Crean Films, 1972)

Producer: Alex Lucas. Director: Peter Ustinov. Screenplay: Stanford Whitmore. Technicolor Cinematography: Richard H. Kline. Costumes: Edith Head. Editing: David Blewitt. Sound: Neil Brummenkant, Jim Bullock, Norman Suffern. 108 Minutes.

Jimmie Jean Jackson	Elizabeth Taylor
Hammersmith	Richard Burton
Doctor	Peter Ustinov
Billy Breedlove	Beau Bridges
Gen. Sam Penbroke	Leon Ames
Dr. Krodt	Leon Akin
Henry Joe	John Schuck
Cleopatra	Carl Doun
Guido Scartucci	George Raft
Princess	Marjorie Eaton
Kiddo	Lisa Jak
Miss Quinn	Linda Gaye Scott
Fat Man	Mel Berger
Oldham	Anthony Holland
Pete Rutter	Brook Williams
Duke	Jose Espinoza

46. *Under Milk Wood* (Altura Films International, 1972)

Executive Producers: Jules Buck and Hugh French. Associate Producer: John Comfort. Written and Directed by Andrew Sinclair from the Verse Drama by Dylan Thomas. Technicolor Cinematography: Bob Huke. Art Direction: Geoffrey Tozer. Editing: Willy Kemplen. Sound: Cyril Collick. 90 Minutes.

Cast: Richard Burton, Elizabeth Taylor, Peter O'Toole, Glynis Johns, Vivien Merchant, Sian Phillips, Victor Spinetti, Ryan Davies, and others.

47. *Divorce, His; Divorce, Hers* (ABC-TV, 1973)

Executive Producer: John Heyman. Producers: Terence Baker and Gareth Wigan. Director: Waris Hussein. Teleplay: John Hopkins. Camera: Ernst Wild and Gabor Pogany. Costumes: Edith Head. Music: Stanley Myers. Editing: John Bloom. Filmed by General Continental Productions in association with Harlech TV at Bavaria Studios, Munich, and on location in Rome, for ABC-TV. 180 Minutes.

Cast: Elizabeth Taylor and Richard Burton with Carrie Nye, Gabriele Ferzetti, Barry Foster, Daniela Surina, Thomas Baptiste, Ronald

Radd, Rudolph Walker, Mark Colleano, Rosalyn Landor, Eva Griffith, Marietta Schupp, and Denis Burgess.

48. Night Watch (Avco Embassy, 1973)

Producers: Martin Poll, George W. George, Bernard Strauss. Director: Brian Hutton. Screenplay: Tony Williamson. Additional Dialogue: Evan Jones. Based upon the Play by Lucille Fletcher. Technicolor Cinematography: Billy Williams. Art Direction: Peter Murton. Costumes: Valentino. Music: John Cameron. Song: "The Night Has Many Eyes" (Barrie-Cahn). Editing: John Jympson. Sound: Jonathan Bates. A Joseph E. Levine and Burt Productions Presentation. 105 Minutes.

Ellen Wheeler	Elizabeth Taylor
John Wheeler	Laurence Harvey
Sarah Cooke	Billie Whitelaw
Appleby	Robert Lang
Tony	Tony Britton
Inspector Walker	Bill Dean
Sergeant Norris	Michael D. Walker
Dolores	Rosario Serrano
Secretary	Pauline Jameson
Girl in Car	Linda Hayden
Carl	Kevin Colson
Florist	Laon Maybanke

49. Ash Wednesday (Paramount, 1973)

Producer: Dominick Dunne. Director: Larry Peerce. Screenplay: Jean-Claude Tramont. Technicolor Cinematography: Ennie Guarnieri. Art Direction: Phil Abramson. Costumes: Edith Head. Wardrobe Supervisor: Annalisa Nasalli Rocca. Editing: Marion Rothman. Sound: Basil Fenton-Smith. Associate Producer: Jean-Claude Tramont. Assistant Directors: Steve Barnett, Tony Brandt. A Sagittarius Production. Filmed in Widescreen in Cortina d'Ampezzo and Lake Como, Italy. 93 Minutes.

Barbara	Elizabeth Taylor
Mark	Henry Fonda
Erich	Helmut Berger
David	Keith Baxter
Dr. Lambert	Maurice Taynac
Kate	Margaret Blye
Mario	Dino Mele
Paolo	Carlo Puri
Simone	Jill Pratt
Count D'Arnoud	Andrea Esterhazy
Silvana	Irina Wassilchikoff

Tony Gutierrez	Jose de Vega
Nurse Ilse	Dina Sasseli
Viet Hartung	Max Windes-Graetz
Helga	Nadia Stancioff
Gregory de Rive	Raymond Vignale
American Producer	Jack Repp
Hotel Director	Piero Baccante
Concierge	Gianni Rossi
Mandy	Kathy Heinsieck

50. *The Driver's Seat* (1974)

Producer: Franco Rossellini. Director: Giuseppe Patroni-Griffi. Screenplay: Muriel Spark (from Her Novel).

Cast: Elizabeth Taylor, Ian Bannon, Guido Mannari, Luigi Squarzina.

INDEX

INDEX

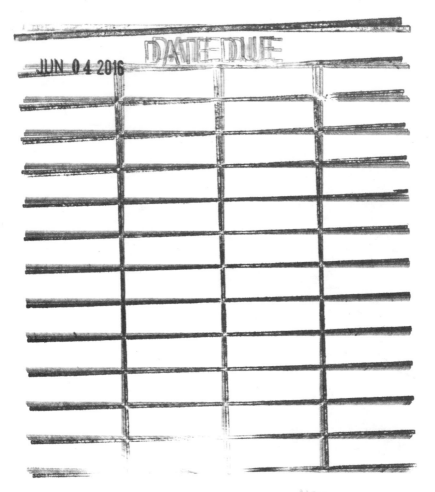